ART HISTORY

Volume 2

Marilyn Stokstad

Custom Edition for New York University

Taken from:
Art History, Third Edition
by Marilyn Stokstad

Custom Publishing

New York   Boston   San Francisco
London   Toronto   Sydney   Tokyo   Singapore   Madrid
Mexico City   Munich   Paris   Cape Town   Hong Kong   Montreal

Cover photograph courtesy of Robert Newcombe / The Nelson-Atkins Museum of Art, Kansas City, Missouri.

Taken from:

Art History, Third Edition
by Marilyn Stokstad
Copyright © 2008, 2005 by Pearson Education, Inc.
Published by Prentice Hall
Upper Saddle River, New Jersey 07458

This special edition published in cooperation with Pearson Custom Publishing.

Printed in the United States of America

10 9 8 7 6 5 4 3

2009120004

CA/KL

**Pearson
Custom Publishing**
is a division of

PEARSON

www.pearsonhighered.com

ISBN 10: 0-558-31753-7
ISBN 13: 978-0-558-31753-9

BRIEF CONTENTS

CONTENTS

I4−I | CHI RHO IOTA PAGE FROM THE BOOK OF KELLS Matt. 1:18. Probably made at Iona, Scotland. Late 8th or early 9th century. Oxgall inks and pigments on vellum, 12¾ × 9½" (325 × 24 cm). The Board of Trinity College, Dublin.

MS 58, fol. 34r.

CHAPTER FOURTEEN

EARLY MEDIEVAL ART IN EUROPE

According to legend, the Irish prince Colum Cille (c. 521–97), scholar, scribe, and churchman, who was canonized as Saint Columba, caused a war by secretly copying a psalter (psalm book). After King Finnian, the owner of the original, found out and petitioned for possession of the copy, and even after the king ruled, "To every cow its calf, to every book its copy," Colum Cille still refused to relinquish it. Instead he incited his kinsmen to fight for the precious book. Whether fleeing from his enemies or to atone for his actions (the legend is unclear), Colum Cille left Ireland forever in self-imposed exile in 563. He established a monastery on Iona, an island off the western coast of Scotland.

As described by the eighth-century Anglo-Saxon historian Bede, such remote monasteries stood "among craggy and distant mountains, which looked more like lurking places for robbers and retreats for wild beasts than habitation for men." Nevertheless, they became centers of Celtic Christendom—their monks as famous for writing and copying books as for their missionary fervor. But, wealthy, isolated, and undefended, they fell victim to Viking attacks beginning at the end of the eighth century. Only the stormy seas could save the treasures of the monasteries. As one monk wrote:

Bitter is the wind tonight,
It tosses the ocean's white hair:
Tonight I fear not the fierce warriors of Norway
Coursing on the Irish Sea.

(translated by Kuno Meyer, *Selections from Ancient Irish Poetry.* London: Constable, 1959 [1911])

In 806, the monks, fleeing Viking raids on Iona, established a refuge at Kells on the Irish mainland. They may have brought with them the Gospel book now known as the **BOOK OF KELLS** (FIG. 14–1). To produce this illustrated version of the Gospels entailed a lavish expenditure: Four scribes and three major illuminators worked on it (modern scribes take about a month to complete a page comparable to the one illustrated here), 185 calves were slaughtered to make the vellum, and the colors for the paintings came from as far away as Afghanistan.

Throughout the Middle Ages monasteries were the centers of art and learning. While religious services remained their primary responsibility, some talented monks and nuns also spent many hours as painters, jewelers, carvers, weavers, and embroiderers. These arts, used in the creation of illustrated books and liturgical equipment, are often called the "cloister crafts." Few cloisters could claim a work of art like the *Book of Kells.*

The twelfth century priest Gerald of Wales aptly described just such a Gospel book when he wrote:

Fine craftsmanship is all about you, but you might not notice it. Look more keenly at it, and you will penetrate to the very shrine of art. You will make out intricacies, so delicate and subtle, so exact and compact, so full of knots and links, with colors so fresh and vivid, that you might say that all this was the work of an angel, and not of a man.

(cited in Henderson, page 195)

441

THE EARLY MIDDLE AGES

As the Roman Empire declined in the fourth century and came to an end in the fifth, its authority was supplanted by "barbarians," people from outside the empire who could only "barble" Greek or Latin.

At this point we have seen these "barbarians" only through Greek and Roman eyes—as the defeated Gauls at Pergamon (FIG. 5–63), on the Gemma Augustea (FIG. 6–24), or on the Ludovisi Sarcophagus (FIG. 6–69). Trajan's Column (FIG. 6–50) shows only Roman triumphs in the barbarians' homeland beyond the Danube River. Hadrian's Wall (FIG. 6–57), built to defend the northern frontier in Britain, marks the extent of the empire. But by the fourth century many Germanic tribes were allies of Rome. In fact, most of Constantine's troops in the decisive battle with Maxentius (page 226) were Germans.

A century later the situation was entirely different. In 410 the Visigoths under Alaric besieged and captured Rome. The adventures of the Byzantine princess Galla Placidia, whom we have met as a patron of the arts (FIG. 7–19), bring the situation vividly to life. She had the misfortune to be in Rome when Alaric and the Visigoths sacked the city (the emperor and pope were living safely in Ravenna). Carried off as a prize of war by the Goths, Galla Placidia had to join their migrations through France and Spain and eventually married the Gothic king, who was soon murdered. Back in Italy, married and widowed yet again, Galla Placidia ruled the Western Empire as regent for her son from 425 to 437/8. She died in 450, before having to endure yet another sack of Rome, this time by the Vandals, in 455. The fall of Rome shocked the Christian world, although the wounds were more psychological than physical. Saint Augustine was inspired to write *The City of God,* a cornerstone of Christian philosophy, as an answer to people who claimed that the Goths represented the vengeance of the pagan gods on people who had abandoned them for Christianity.

Who were these people living outside the Mediterranean orbit? Their wooden architecture is lost to fire and decay, but their metalwork and use of animal and geometric ornament is well established. The people were hunters and fishermen, shepherds and farmers living in villages with a social organization based on extended families and tribal loyalties. They engaged in the essential crafts—pottery, weaving, woodwork—and they fashioned metals into weapons, tools, and jewelry. We saw examples of Bronze and Iron Age (Celtic) art in Chapter 1.

The Celts controlled most of Europe, and the Germanic people—Goths and others—lived around the Baltic Sea. Increasing population evidently forced the Goths to begin to move south, into better lands and climate around the Mediterranean and Black Seas, but the Romans had extended the borders of their empire across the Rhine and Danube rivers. Seeking the relative security and higher standard of living they saw in the Roman Empire, the Germanic people crossed the borders and settled within the empire.

The tempo of migration speeded up in the fifth century when the Huns from central Asia swept down on western Europe. Only the death of their leader Attila in 453 saved Europe. The Arian Ostrogoths (Eastern Goths) moved into Italy, and in 476 they deposed the last Roman emperor. They made Ravenna their capital until they were in turn defeated by the Byzantines. The Visigoths (Western Goths) ended their wanderings in Spain. The Burgundians settled in Switzerland and eastern France; the Franks in Germany, France, and Belgium. Meanwhile the Vandals moved through France and Spain, crossed over into Africa, making Carthage their headquarters, and then returned back to Italy, sacking Rome in 455.

At first Christianity was not a unifying force. As early as 345 the Goths adopted Arian Christianity, beliefs considered heretical by the Church in Rome. Not until 589 did they accept Roman Christianity. In contrast to the Arian Goths, the Franks under Clovis (ruled 481–511), influenced by his Burgundian wife Clotilda, converted to Roman Christianity in 496, beginning a fruitful alliance between French rulers and the popes.

Bewildering as the period seems, the Europe we know today was beginning to take shape. Relationships of patronage and dependence between powerful men and their retainers remained important, ultimately giving rise to a political and economic system based on family and clan ties, on

MAP I4–I | **EUROPE OF THE EARLY MIDDLE AGES**

On this map, modern names have been used for medieval regions in northern and western Europe to make sites of artworks easier to locate.

personal loyalty and mutual support, and on the exchange of personal service and labor for protection. This system became formalized as *feudalism*.

Mutual support also developed between secular and religious leaders. Kings and nobles defended the claims of the Roman Church, and the pope, in turn, validated their authority. As its wealth and influence increased throughout Europe, the Church emerged as the principal patron of the arts to fulfill growing needs for buildings and liturgical equipment, including altars, altar vessels, crosses, candlesticks, containers for the remains of saints **(reliquaries),** vestments (ritual garments), images of Christian figures and stories, and copies of sacred texts such as the Gospels.

The Art of People Associated with the Roman Empire

As Christianity spread north beyond the borders of what had been the Western Roman Empire, northern artistic traditions similarly worked their way south. Out of a tangled web of themes and styles originating from inside and out of the empire, from pagan and Christian beliefs, from urban and rural settlements, brilliant new artistic styles were born.

THE VISIGOTHS. Among the many people who had lived outside the Roman Empire and then moved within its borders, the Visigoths migrated across southern France and by the sixth century had settled in Spain, where they became an elite group ruling the indigenous population. They adopted Latin for writing, and in 589 they accepted Roman Christianity. Saint Isidore, patron saint of historians (including art historians), was a Visigothic bishop.

Following the same late–Roman-Germanic tradition they shared with other Gothic peoples, the Visigoths were superior metalworkers and created magnificent colorful jewelry. In the eagle brooch (FIG. 14–2), the artist rendered the bird in flight with outspread wings and tail, profile head with curved beak, and large round eye. This brooch displays a rich assortment of gems. Besides the red garnets interspersed with blue and green stones, the circle that represents the eagle's body has a *cabochon* (polished but unfaceted) crystal at the

The roughly 1,000 years of European history between the collapse of the Western Roman Empire in the fifth century and the Italian Renaissance in the fifteenth are known as the Middle Ages, or the medieval period. These terms reflect the view of Renaissance humanists who regarded the period that preceded theirs as a "dark age" of ignorance, decline, and barbarism, standing in the *middle* and separating their own "golden age" from the golden ages of ancient Greece and Rome. Although we now recognize the Middle Ages as a period of great richness, complexity, and innovation, the term has endured.

Art historians commonly divide the Middle Ages into three periods: Early Medieval (ending in the early eleventh century), Romanesque (eleventh and twelfth centuries), and Gothic (extending from the mid-twelfth into the fifteenth century). We shall look at only a few of the many cultures that make up the Early Medieval period. For convenience, we will use modern geographical names (MAP 14–1)—in fact, the nations we know today did not yet exist.

14–2 | EAGLE BROOCH
One of a pair. Spain. 6th century. Gilt, bronze, crystal, garnets, and other gems. Height 5⅝" (14.3 cm). The Walters Art Museum, Baltimore.

center. Round amethyst in a white meerschaum frame forms the eyes. Pendant jewels originally hung from the birds' tail. The eagle remained one of the most popular motifs in Western art, owing in part to its continuing significance—first as an ancient sun symbol, then as a symbol of imperial Rome, and later as the emblem of Saint John the Evangelist.

THE LOMBARDS. Among those who established kingdoms in the heart of what had been the Roman Empire in Italy were the Lombards. The Lombards had moved from their northern homeland into the Hungarian plain and then traveled west into Italy, where they became a constant threat to Rome. Like other migrating people, the Lombards excelled in fine metalwork. The huge jeweled cross in Brescia (east of Milan) shows their skillful use of precious metals and spectacular jewels (FIG. 14–3). The cross has a Byzantine form—equal arms widening at the ends joined by a central disc with a relief figure of Christ enthroned in a jeweled mandorla, indicating divine light emanating from the figure. More than 200 jewels, engraved gems, antique **cameos,** and glass pseudo-cameos adorn the cross. At the bottom of the cross is a gold glass Roman portrait medallion (SEE FIG. 6–68). According to tradition, the last Lombard king, Desiderius (ruled 757–74), gave the cross to the Church of Santa Giulia in Brescia. Scholars cannot agree on its date; they place the cross somewhere between the late seventh and early ninth centuries.

The patron who gathered this rich collection of jewels and ordered the cross to be made intended it to glorify God with glowing color and was evidently not concerned that nearly all the engraved gems and cameos have pagan subjects. The cross typifies this turbulent period in the Western European history of art. Made for a Western Christian church but having the form associated with the Byzantine East and using engraved jewels and cameos from the ancient world (even when they had to fake some in glass), the makers of the cross achieve an effect of extraordinary splendor.

The Art of People Outside the Roman Sphere of Influence

In Scandinavia (present-day Denmark, Norway, and Sweden), which was never part of the Roman Empire, people spoke variants of the Norse language and shared a rich mythology with other Germanic peoples. In the British Isles, where the Romans had built Hadrian's Wall to mark the boundaries between civilization and the wilds of Scotland, the ancient Celtic culture flourished.

14–3 CROSS
Church of Saint Giulia, Brescia, Italy. Late 7th–early 9th century. Gilded silver, wood, jewels, glass, cameos, and gold-glass medallion of the third century, 50 × 39" (126 × 99 cm). Museo di Santa Giulia, Brescia.

At the beginning of the fifth century the Roman army abandoned Britain. The economy faltered, and large towns lost their commercial function and declined as Romanized British leaders vied for dominance with the help of Germanic mercenary soldiers from the Continent.

THE NORSE. Scandinavian artists had exhibited a fondness for abstract patterning from early prehistoric times. During the first millennium BCE, trade, warfare, and migration had brought a variety of jewelry, coins, textiles, and other portable objects into northern Europe. The artists incorporated the solar disks and stylized animals on these objects into their already rich artistic vocabulary (SEE FIG. 1–20).

By the fifth century CE, the so-called **animal style** dominated the arts, displaying an impressive array of serpents, four-legged beasts, and squat human figures, as can be seen in

their metalwork. The **GUMMERSMARK BROOCH** (FIG. 14–4), for example, is a large silver gilt pin dating from the sixth century CE in Denmark. This elegant ornament consists of a large, rectangular panel and a medallionlike plate covering the safety pin's catch connected by an arched bow. The surface of the pin seethes with human, animal, and geometric forms. An eye-and-beak motif frames the rectangular panel; a man is compressed between dragons just below the bow; and a pair of monster heads and crouching dogs with spiraling tongues frame the covering of the catch.

Certain underlying principles govern works with animal style design: The compositions are generally symmetrical, and artists depict animals in their entirety either in profile or from above. Ribs and spinal columns are exposed as if they had been x-rayed; hip and shoulder joints are pear-shaped; tongues and jaws extend and curl, and legs end in large claws.

14–4 GUMMERSMARK BROOCH
Denmark. 6th century. Silver gilt, height 5¾" (14.6 cm).
Nationalmuseet, Copenhagen.

The northern jewelers carefully crafted their molds to produce a glittering surface on the cast metal, turning a process intended to speed production into an art form of great refinement.

THE CELTS AND ANGLO-SAXONS. After the Romans departed, Angles and Saxons from Germany and the Low Lands and Jutes from Denmark crossed the sea to occupy southeastern Britain. Gradually they extended their control northwest across the island. Over the next 200 years, the arts made a brilliant recovery as the fusion of Celtic, Romanized British, Germanic, and Norse cultures generated a new culture and style of art, known as Hiberno-Saxon (from the Roman name for Ireland, *Hibernia*). Anglo-Saxon literature is filled with references to splendid and costly jewelry and weapons made of or decorated with gold and silver.

The Anglo-Saxon epic *Beowulf*, composed perhaps as early as the seventh century, describes its hero's burial with a hoard of treasure in a grave mound near the sea. Such a burial site was discovered near the North Sea coast in Suffolk at a site called Sutton Hoo (*hoo* means "hill" or "headland"). The

grave's occupant had been buried in a ship whose traces in the earth were recovered by the careful excavators. The wood—and the hero's body—had disintegrated, and no inscriptions record his name. He has sometimes been identified with the ruler Redwald, who died about 625. The treasures buried with him confirm that he was, in any case, a wealthy and powerful man.

The burial ship at Sutton Hoo was 90 feet long and designed for rowing, not sailing. In it were weapons, armor, other equipment to provide for the ruler's afterlife, and many luxury items, including Byzantine silver bowls. Also found was a large purse filled with coins. Although the leather of the pouch and the bone or ivory of its lid have disintegrated, the gold and garnet fittings survive (**FIG. 14–5**). The artist, using the **cloisonné** technique (cells formed from gold wire to hold shaped pieces of garnet or glass), frequently seen in Byzantine enamels, created figures of gold, garnets, and blue-checkered glass (known as *millefiore glass*). Polygons decorated with purely geometric patterns flank a central plaque of four animals with long interlacing legs and jaws. Below, large hawks attack ducks, and men are spread-eagled between two rampant beasts.

Themes, techniques, and styles from many places are represented on the purse cover. The motif of a human being flanked by a pair of animals is widespread in ancient Near Eastern art and in the Roman world (as is the motif of the predator vanquishing the prey). The hawks with rectangular eyebrows and curving beaks, twisted wings and square tails are Norse in style, and the interlacing four-legged, long-jawed animals characterize the Germanic animal style. The use of bright color—especially red and gold—reflects an Eastern European tradition. All in all, the purse displays the rich blend of motifs that marks the complex Hiberno-Saxon style that flourished in Britain and Ireland during the seventh and eighth centuries.

The Coming of Christianity to the British Isles

Although the Anglo-Saxons who settled in Britain had their own gods and myths, Christianity survived the pagan onslaught. Monasteries flourished in the Celtic north and west, and Christians from Ireland founded influential missions in Scotland and northern England. Cut off from Rome, these Celtic Christians developed their own liturgical practices, church calendar, and distinctive artistic traditions. Then, in 597, Pope Gregory the Great (ruled 590–604) dispatched missionaries from Rome to the Anglo-Saxon king Ethelbert of Kent, whose Christian wife Bertha was sympathetic to their cause. The head of this successful mission, the monk Augustine (Saint Augustine, d. 604), became the archbishop of Canterbury in 601. The Roman Christian authorities and the Irish monasteries, although allied in the effort to Christianize the British Isles, came into conflict over their divergent practices. The Roman Church eventually triumphed and brought British Christians under its authority. Local traditions, however, continued to influence their art.

14–5 | PURSE COVER, FROM THE SUTTON HOO BURIAL SHIP
Suffolk, England. First half of 7th century. Cloisonné plaques of gold, garnet, and checked millefiore glass, length 8″ (20.3 cm). The British Museum, London.

Only the decorations on this purse cover are original. The lid itself, of a light tan ivory or bone, deteriorated and disappeared centuries ago, and the white backing is a modern replacement. The purse was designed to hang at the waist. The leather pouch held thirty-seven coins, struck in France, the latest dated in the early 630s.

ILLUSTRATED BOOKS. Among the richest surviving artworks of the period were the beautifully written, illustrated, and bound manuscripts, especially the Gospel books. Gospel books were essential for the missionary activities of the Church throughout the early Middle Ages, not only for the information they contained—the "good news" of Christianity—but also as instruments to glorify the Word of God. Often bound in gold and jeweled covers, they were placed on the altars of churches and carried in processions. Thought to protect parishioners from enemies, predators, diseases, and all kinds of misfortune, these books were produced by monks in local monastic workshops called *scriptoria* (see "The Medieval Scriptorium," page 448).

One of the many elaborately decorated Gospels of the period is the **GOSPEL BOOK OF DURROW**, dating to the second half of the seventh century (FIG. 14–6). The format and text of the book reflect Roman Christian models, but its paintings are an encyclopedia of contemporary design. Each of the four Gospels is introduced by a page with the symbol of its evangelist author, followed by a page of pure ornament and finally the decorated letters of the first words of the text *(the incipit).*

14–6 | PAGE WITH MAN, GOSPEL BOOK OF DURROW
Gospel of Saint Matthew. Probably made at Iona, Scotland, or northern England, second half of 7th century. Ink and tempera on parchment, 9⅜ × 6⅛″ (24.4 × 15.5 cm). The Board of Trinity College, Dublin.
MS 57 fol, 21v.

THE MEDIEVAL *SCRIPTORIUM*

Today books are made with the aid of computer software that can lay out pages, set type, and insert and prepare illustrations. Modern presses can produce hundreds of thousands of identical copies in full color. In Europe in the Middle Ages, however, before the invention there of printing from movable type in the mid-1400s, books were made by hand, one at a time, with ink, pen, brush, and paint. Each one was an important, time-consuming, and expensive undertaking. Medieval books were usually made by monks and nuns in a workshop called a *scriptorium* (plural *scriptoria*) within the monastery. As the demand for books increased, lay professionals joined the work, and great rulers set up palace workshops supervised by well-known scholars. Books were written on animal skin—either **vellum,** which was fine and soft, or **parchment,** which was heavier and shinier. (Paper did not come into common use in Europe until the early 1400s.) Skins for vellum were cleaned, stripped of hair, and scraped to create a smooth surface for the ink and water-based paints, which themselves required time and experience to prepare. Many pigments—particularly blues and greens—had to be imported and were as costly as semiprecious stones. In very rich books, artists also used gold leaf or gold paint.

Sometimes work on a book was divided between a scribe, who copied the text, and one or more artists, who did the illustrations, large initials, and other decorations. Although most books were produced anonymously, scribes and illustrators signed and dated their work on the last page, called the **colophon** (SEE FIG. 14–9). One scribe even took the opportunity to warn the reader: "O reader, turn the leaves gently, and keep your fingers away from the letters, for, as the hailstorm ruins the harvest of the land, so does the injurious reader destroy the book and the writing" (cited in Dodwell, page 247).

In the *Gospel Book of Durrow* the Gospel of Matthew is preceded by his symbol, the man, but a man such as to be seen only in jeweled images made by an Irish or Scandinavian metalworker. A colorful checkered pattern resembling the millefiore glass inlays of Sutton Hoo forms the rectangular, armless body. Had the artist seen Byzantine figures wearing colorful brocades, or was he thinking of gold-framed jewels? In Saint Matthew's symbol a startling unshaven face stares glumly from rounded shoulders. The hair framing the man's high forehead follows the tonsure (the ceremonial hairstyle that distinguishes monks from laymen) of the early Celtic church. The figure seems to float with dangling feet against a neutral ground, which is surrounded by a wide border filled with a curling interlacing ribbon. Although the ribbon is continuous, its color changes from segment to segment, establishing yet another pattern. On other pages the ribbons turn into serpents.

The Gospel book known as the *Book of Kells* is one of the most beautiful, original, and inventive of the surviving Hiberno-Saxon Gospel books. A close look at its most celebrated page—the page introducing Matthew (1:18–25) that begins the account of Jesus's birth (SEE FIG. 14–1)—seems at first glance a tangle of colors and lines. But for those who would "look more keenly," there is so much more—human and animal forms—in the dense thicket of spiral and interlace patterns derived from metalwork.

The *Kells* style is especially brilliant in the monogram page with which we opened this chapter (FIG. 14–1). The artists reaffirm their Celtic heritage with the spirals and trumpet shapes that they combine with Germanic animal interlaces to embellish the monogram of Christ (the three Greek letters XPI, *chi rho iota*) and the words *Christi autem generatio* ("now this is how the birth of Jesus Christ came about" [Matt. 1:18]). A giant *chi* establishes the basic composition of the page. The word *autem* appears as a Latin abbreviation resembling an *h;* and *generatio* is spelled out.

The illuminators outlined each letter, and then they subdivided the letters into panels filled with interlaced animals and snakes, as well as extraordinary spiral and knot motifs. The spaces between the letters form an equally complex ornamental field, dominated by spirals. In the midst of these abstractions, the painters inserted numerous pictorial and symbolic references to Christ—including his initials, a fish (the Greek word for "fish," *ichthus,* comprises in its spelling the first letters of *Jesus Christ, Son of God, Savior),* moths (symbols of rebirth), the cross-inscribed wafer of the Eucharist, numerous chalices and goblets, and possibly in two human faces, one at the top of the page and one at the end of the Greek letter *P* (*rho*). Three angels along the left edge of the stem of the Greek letter *X* (*chi*) are reminders that angels surrounded the Holy Family at the time of the Nativity, thus introducing Matthew's story while supporting the monogram of Christ.

In a particularly intriguing image, to the right of the Greek letter *chi's* tail, two cats pounce on a pair of mice nibbling the Eucharistic wafer, and two more mice torment the vigilant cats (FIG. 14–7). As well as being a metaphor for the struggle between good (cats) and evil (mice), the image may also remark upon the perennial problem of keeping the monks' food and the sacred Host safe from rodents.

14–7 ┆ **CATS AND MICE WITH HOST, DETAIL OF FIG. 14–1**
Chi Rho Iota page, Book of Kells, Matt.1:18. Probably made at Iona, Scotland. Late 8th or early 9th century. Oxgall inks and pigments on vellum. 12¾ × 9½" (325 × 24 cm). The Board of Trinity College, Dublin.
MS 58, fol. 34r.

14–8 ┆ **SOUTH CROSS, AHENNY**
County Tipperary, Ireland. 8th century. Stone.

IRISH HIGH CROSSES. Metalwork's influence is seen not only in manuscripts, but also in the monumental stone crosses erected in Ireland during the eighth century. In Irish high crosses, so called because of their size, a circle encloses the arms of the cross. This Celtic ring has been interpreted as a halo or a glory (a ring of heavenly light) or as a purely practical support for the arms of the cross. The **SOUTH CROSS OF AHENNY**, in County Tipperary, is an especially well-preserved example of this type (**FIG. 14–8**). It seems to have been modeled on metal ceremonial or reliquary crosses, that is, cross-shaped containers for holy relics. It is outlined with ropelike, convex moldings and covered with spirals and interlace. The large **bosses** (broochlike projections), which form a cross within the cross, resemble the jewels that were similarly placed on metal crosses.

THE MUSLIM CHALLENGE IN SPAIN

In 711, Islamic invaders conquered Spain, ending Visigothic rule. The invaders brought a new art as well as a new religion and government into Spain (see Chapter 8). Muslim armies swept over the Iberian Peninsula. Bypassing a small Christian kingdom on the north coast, Asturias, they crossed the Pyrenees Mountains into France, but in 732 Charles Martel and the Frankish army stopped them before they reached Paris. The Muslims retreated back across the mountains, and the Christians, led by the Asturians, slowly drove them southward. Even so, the Moors, as they were known in Spain, remained for nearly 800 years, until the fall of the last Moorish kingdom, Granada, to the Christians in 1492.

Mozarabic Art

With some exceptions, Christians and Jews who acknowledged the authority of the new rulers and paid the taxes required of non-Muslims were left free to follow their own religious practices. The Iberian Peninsula became a melting pot of cultures in which Muslims, Christians, and Jews lived and worked together, all the while officially and firmly separated. Christians in the Muslim territories were called Mozarabs (from the Arabic *mustarib*, meaning "would-be Arab").

The conquest resulted in a rich exchange of artistic influences between the Islamic and Christian communities. Christian artists adapted many features of Islamic art, creating a unique, colorful new style known as *Mozarabic*. When the Mozarabic communities migrated to northern Spain, which returned to Christian rule not long after the initial Islamic invasion, they took this Mozarabic style with them.

BEATUS MANUSCRIPTS. One of the most influential books of the eighth century was the *Commentary on the Apocalypse*, compiled by Beatus, abbot of the Monastery of San Martín at Liébana in the northern kingdom of Asturias. Beatus described the end of the world and the Last Judgment of the Apocalypse,

14–9 | Emeterius and Senior **COLOPHON PAGE, COMMENTARY ON THE APOCALYPSE BY BEATUS AND COMMENTARY ON DANIEL BY JEROME**
Made for the Monastery of San Salvador at Tábara, León, Spain. Completed July 27, 970. Tempera on parchment, 14¼ × 10⅛″ (36.2 × 25.8 cm).
Archivo Histórico Nacional, Madrid.
MS 1079B f. 167.v.

The colophon provides specific information about the production of a book. In addition to identifying himself and Senior on this colophon, Emeterius praised his teacher, "Magius, priest and monk, the worthy master painter," who had begun the manuscript prior to his death in 968. Emeterius also took the opportunity to comment on the profession of bookmaking: "Thou lofty tower of Tábara made of stone! There, over thy first roof, Emeterius sat for three months bowed down and racked in every limb by the copying. He finished the book on July 27th in the year 1008 [970, by modern dating] at the eighth hour" (cited in Dodwell, page 247).

as first depicted in the Revelation to John in the New Testament, which vividly describes Christ's final, fiery triumph.

In 970, the monk Emeterius and a scribe-painter named Senior completed a copy of Beatus's **COMMENTARY** (FIG. 14–9). They worked in the *scriptorium* of the Monastery of San Salvador at Tábara in the Kingdom of León. Unlike most monastic scribes at this time, Mozarabic scribes usually signed their work and occasionally offered the reader their own comments and asides (see "The

Medieval *Scriptorium*," page 448). On the **colophon** (the page at the end of a book with information about its production) is a picture of the five-story tower of the Tábara monastery and the two-story *scriptorium* attached to it, the earliest known depiction of a medieval *scriptorium* and an unusual representation of a bell tower.

The tower and the workshop have been rendered in a cross section that reveals the interior and exterior of the buildings simultaneously. In the *scriptorium,* Emeterius on the right and Senior on the left, identified by inscriptions over their heads, work at a small table. A helper in the next room cuts sheets of **parchment** or **vellum** for book pages. A monk standing at the ground floor of the tower pulls the ropes attached to the bell in the turret while three other men climb ladders between the floors, apparently on their way to the balconies on the top level. Brightly glazed tiles in geometric patterns and horseshoe-arched openings are a common feature of Islamic architecture.

Another copy of Beatus's *Commentary* was produced five years later for Abbot Dominicus. The colophon identifies Senior as the scribe for this project. Emeterius and a woman named Ende (or simply En), who signed herself "painter and servant of God," shared the task of illustration. For the first time in the West, a women artist is identified by name with a specific surviving work of art. Using abstract shapes and brilliant colors recalling Visigothic jewel work, Emeterius and En illustrate a metaphorical description of the triumph of Christ over Satan (FIG. 14–10).

In the illustration, a peacock grasps a red and orange snake in its beak. The text tells us that a bird with a powerful beak and beautiful plumage (Christ) covers itself with mud to trick the snake (Satan). Just when the snake decides the bird is harmless, the bird swiftly attacks and kills the snake. "So Christ in his Incarnation clothed himself in the impurity of our [human] flesh that through a pious trick he might fool the evil deceiver. . . . [W]ith the word of his mouth [he] slew the venomous killer, the devil" (from the Beatus *Commentary,* cited in Williams, page 95). The Church often used such symbolic stories, or allegories, to convey ideals in combinations of recognizable images, making their implications accessible to people at any level of education. Elements of Mozarabic art lasted well into the twelfth century.

THE CAROLINGIAN EMPIRE

During the second half of the eighth century, while Christians and Muslims were creating a rich multicultural art in Spain, a new force emerged in Continental Europe. Charlemagne, or Charles the Great (*Carolus Magnus* is Latin for "Charles the Great"), established a dynasty and an empire known today as "Carolingian." The Carolingians were Franks, a Germanic people who had settled in northern Gaul (parts of present-day France and Germany) by the end of the fifth century. Under Charlemagne (ruled 768–814), the

14–10 Emeterius and Ende, with the scribe Senior
BATTLE OF THE BIRD AND THE SERPENT, COMMENTARY ON THE APOCALYPSE BY BEATUS AND COMMENTARY ON DANIEL BY JEROME, (DETAIL)
Made for Abbot Dominicus, probably at the Monastery of San Salvador at Tábara, León, Spain. Completed July 6, 975. Tempera on parchment, 15¾ × 10¼" (40 × 26 cm). Cathedral Library, Gerona, Spain.
MS 7[11], fol. 18v.

Carolingian realm reached its greatest extent, encompassing western Germany, France, the Lombard kingdom in Italy, and the Low Countries (present-day Belgium and Holland). Charlemagne imposed Christianity throughout this territory. In 800, Pope Leo III (papacy 795–816) crowned Charlemagne emperor in a ceremony in Saint Peter's Basilica in Rome, declaring him the rightful successor to Constantine, the first Christian emperor. This endorsement reinforced Charlemagne's authority and strengthened the bonds between the papacy and secular government in the West.

Charlemagne sought to restore the Western Empire as a Christian state and to revive the arts and learning. As inscribed on his official seal, Charlemagne's ambition was "the Renewal of the Roman Empire." To lead this revival, Charlemagne turned to the Benedictine monks and nuns. By the early Middle Ages, monastic communities had spread across Europe. In the early sixth century, Benedict of Nursia (c. 480–547) wrote his *Rule for Monasteries*, a set of guidelines for monastic life that became the model for monastic orders. Benedictine monasticism soon displaced earlier forms, including the Celtic monasticism in the British Isles.

Both the Benedictines and Charlemagne emphasized education, and the Benedictine monks soon became Charlemagne's "cultural army." The court at Aachen, Germany, became one of the leading intellectual centers of Western Europe. Charlemagne's architects, painters, and sculptors looked to Rome and Ravenna for inspiration, but what they created was a new, northern version of the Imperial Christian style.

Carolingian Architecture

Functional plans inspired by Roman and Early Christian architecture were widely adopted by the Carolingian builders. Charlemagne's palace complex at Aachen provides an example of the Carolingian synthesis of Roman, Early Christian, and northern styles. Charlemagne, who enjoyed hunting and swimming, built a headquarters and palace complex amid the forests and natural hot springs of Aachen in the northern part of his empire and installed his court there about 794. The palace complex included a large audience hall and a chapel facing each other across a large square (as seen in a Roman forum), a monumental gateway supporting a hall of judgment, other administrative buildings, a palace school, homes for his circle of advisers and his large family, and workshops supplying all the needs of church and state.

THE PALACE CHAPEL AT AACHEN. Directly across from the royal audience hall on the north-south axis of the complex stood the **PALACE CHAPEL** (FIGS. 14–11, 14–12). This structure functioned as Charlemagne's private chapel, the church of his imperial court, a place for precious relics, and, after the emperor's death, the imperial mausoleum. To satisfy all these needs, the emperor's architects created a large, central-plan building similar to the Church of San Vitale in Ravenna (FIG. 7–28), which they reinterpreted in the distinctive Carolingian style.

The westwork—church entrances traditionally faced west—is a combined narthex (vestibule) and chapel joined by tall, cylindrical stair towers. The ground-level entrance accommodated the public. On the second level, a throne room opened onto the chapel rotunda, allowing the emperor to participate in the Mass from his private throne room. (The throne is visible through the arch.) At Aachen, this throne room could be reached from the palace audience hall and hall of justice by way of a gallery. The room also opened outside into a large walled forecourt where the emperor could make public appearances and speak to the assembled crowd. Relics were housed above the throne room on the third level. Spiral stairs in the twin towers joined the three levels. Originally designed to answer practical requirements

14–11 | **PALACE CHAPEL OF CHARLE-MAGNE**
Interior view, Aachen (Aix-la-Chapelle), Germany. 792–805.

Extensive renovations took place in the nineteenth century, when the chapel was reconsecrated as the Cathedral of Aachen, and in the twentieth century, after it was damaged in World War II.

14–12 | **RECONSTRUCTION DRAWING OF THE PALACE CHAPEL OF CHARLEMAGNE,** Aachen (Aix-la-Chapelle), Germany. 792–805.

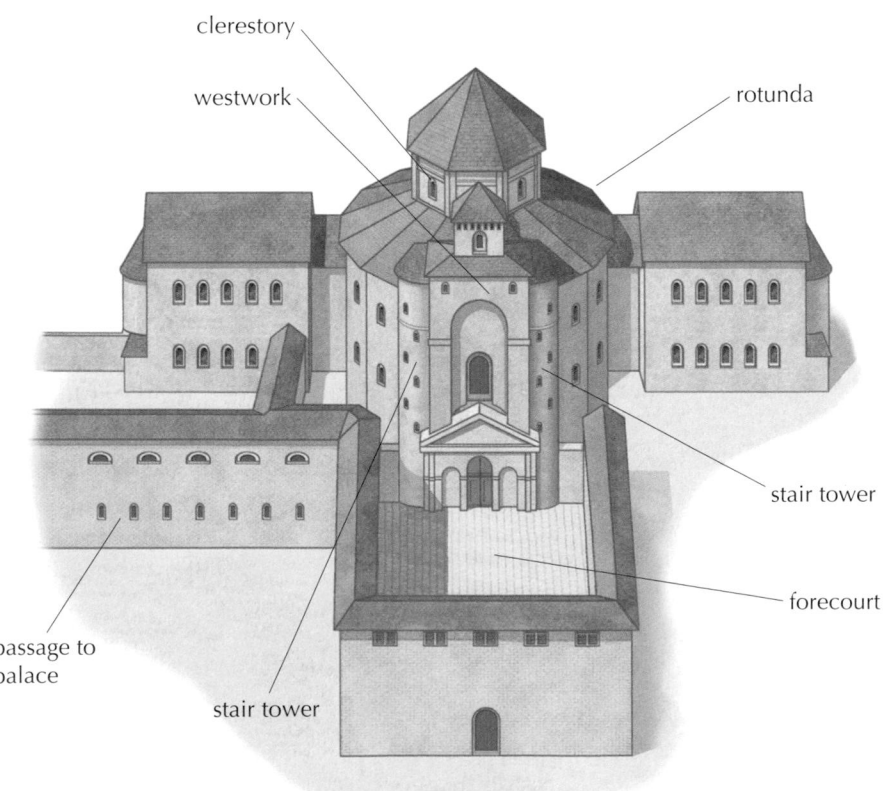

clerestory

westwork

rotunda

stair tower

forecourt

passage to palace

stair tower

of protection and display, the soaring multitowered west-work came to function symbolically as the outward and very visible sign of an imperial building.

At Aachen, the core of the chapel is an octagon surrounded by an ambulatory and gallery in alternating square and triangular bays that produce a sixteen-sided outer wall. The central octagon rises to a clerestory above the gallery level and culminates in eight curving triangular segments that form an octagonal dome. In contrast, at the Byzantine Church of San Vitale, the central octagon was covered by a round dome and supported by half domes over the eight exedras (SEE FIG. 7–28). The chapel at Aachen has sharply defined spaces created by flat walls and angled piers. Byzantine Ravenna has curving surfaces and flowing spaces. In the gallery at Aachen, two tiers of Corinthian columns in the tall arched openings and bronze grills at floor level create a fictive wall that enhances the clarity and geometric quality of the design. The chapel's interior space is defined by eight panels that create a powerful upward movement from the floor of the central area to the top of the vault. Rich materials, some imported from Italy, and mosaics cover the walls. (The mosaic in the vault depicting the twenty-four Elders of the Apocalypse has been replaced with a modern interpretation.) This use of rich materials over every surface was inspired by Byzantine art, but the emphasis on verticality and the clear division of larger forms into separate parts are hallmarks of the new Carolingian style.

THE CHURCH OF SAINT RIQUIER.
The Palace Chapel was a special building. Most Carolingian churches followed the basilican plan, often with the addition of a transept inspired by Old Saint Peter's in Rome. Charlemagne's biographer, Einhard, reported that the ruler, "beyond all sacred and venerable places . . . loved the church of the holy apostle Peter at Rome." Charlemagne's churches, however, were not simply imitations of Roman and Early Christian structures.

The Abbey Church of Saint Riquier, in the monastery at Centula in northern France, illustrates the Carolingian reinterpretation of the Early Christian basilica. Built by Angilbert, a lay abbot (781–814) and Frankish scholar at the court, the church was finished about 799. Destroyed by Viking raids in the ninth century, it is known today from archaeological evidence and a seventeenth-century engraving of a lost eleventh-century drawing (FIG. 14–13). For the abbey's more than 300 monks, the enclosure between the church and two freestanding chapels evidently served as a cloister—cloisters are arcaded courtyards linking the church and the living and working areas of the monastery. Three kinds of church buildings are represented. Simplest is the small, barnlike chapel (at the right in the print) dedicated to Saint Benedict. The more elaborate structure, a basilica with a rotunda ringed with chapels (lower left), was dedicated to the Virgin Mary and the Twelve Apostles. The interior probably had an altar to the Vir-

gin in the center, an ambulatory, and chapels with altars for each of the apostles against the outside walls.

The principal church, dedicated to Saint Riquier, displays a Carolingian variation of the basilica plan. The nave has side aisles and clerestory windows, and recent excavations have revealed a much longer nave than is indicated in the print. Giving equal weight to both ends of the nave are a multistory westwork including paired towers, a transept, and a crossing tower (at the left in the print), and, at the east end of the church (on the right), a crossing tower, which rises over the transept, and an extended sanctuary and apse.

The westwork served almost as a separate church. The main altar was dedicated to Christ the Savior and used for important church services. The boys' choir sang from its galleries, filling the church with "angelic music," and its ground floor had additional altars with important relics. Later the altar of the Savior was moved to the main body of the church, and the westwork was rededicated to the archangel Michael, whose chapel was usually located in a tower or other high place.

Saint Riquier's many towers would have been the building's most striking feature. The two tall towers at the crossing of the transepts soared upward from cylindrical bases through

14–13 | ABBEY CHURCH OF SAINT RIQUIER, MONASTERY OF CENTULA
France. Dedicated 799. Engraving dated 1612, after an 11th-century drawing. Bibliothèque Nationale, Paris.

three arcaded levels to cross-topped spires. They served a practical function as bell towers and played a symbolic role, designating an important building. Meant to be seen from afar, towers visually dominated the countryside. The vertical emphasis created by integrating towers into the basilican design was a northern contribution to Christian church architecture.

THE SAINT GALL PLAN. Monastic communities had special needs. The life of monks revolved around prayer and service in the church and work for the community. In the early ninth century, Abbot Haito of Reichenau developed an ideal plan for the construction of monasteries for his colleague Abbot Gozbert of Saint Gall near Lake Constance in Switzerland (**FIG.14–14**). Abbot Haito laid out the plan on a square grid, as with an ancient Roman army camp, and indicated the size and position of the buildings and their uses.

Since Benedictine monks celebrate Mass as well as the eight "canonical" hours every day, they needed a church building with ample space for many altars, indicated in the plan as standing in the nave and aisles as well as chapels. In the Saint Gall plan, the church had large apses at both the east and west ends of the nave. North of the church were public buildings such as the abbot's house, the school, and guest-house. The south side was private—the cloister and the complex of monastic buildings surrounding it. The dormitory was built on the east side of the cloister, and for night services the monks entered the church directly from their dormitory. The refectory (dining hall) stood on the south of the cloister, with the kitchen, brewery, and bakery attached. A huge cellar (indicated on the plan by giant barrels) was on the west side. The Saint Gall plan indicates beds for seventy-seven monks in the dormitory and space for thirty-three more elsewhere. Practical considerations for group living include latrines attached to every unit—dormitory, guesthouse, and abbot's house. (The ratio of latrine holes to beds exceeds the standards of the U.S. Army today.) Six beds and places in the refectory were reserved for visiting monks. In the surrounding buildings, monks pursued their individual tasks. Scribes and painters, for example, spent much of their day in the *scrip-*

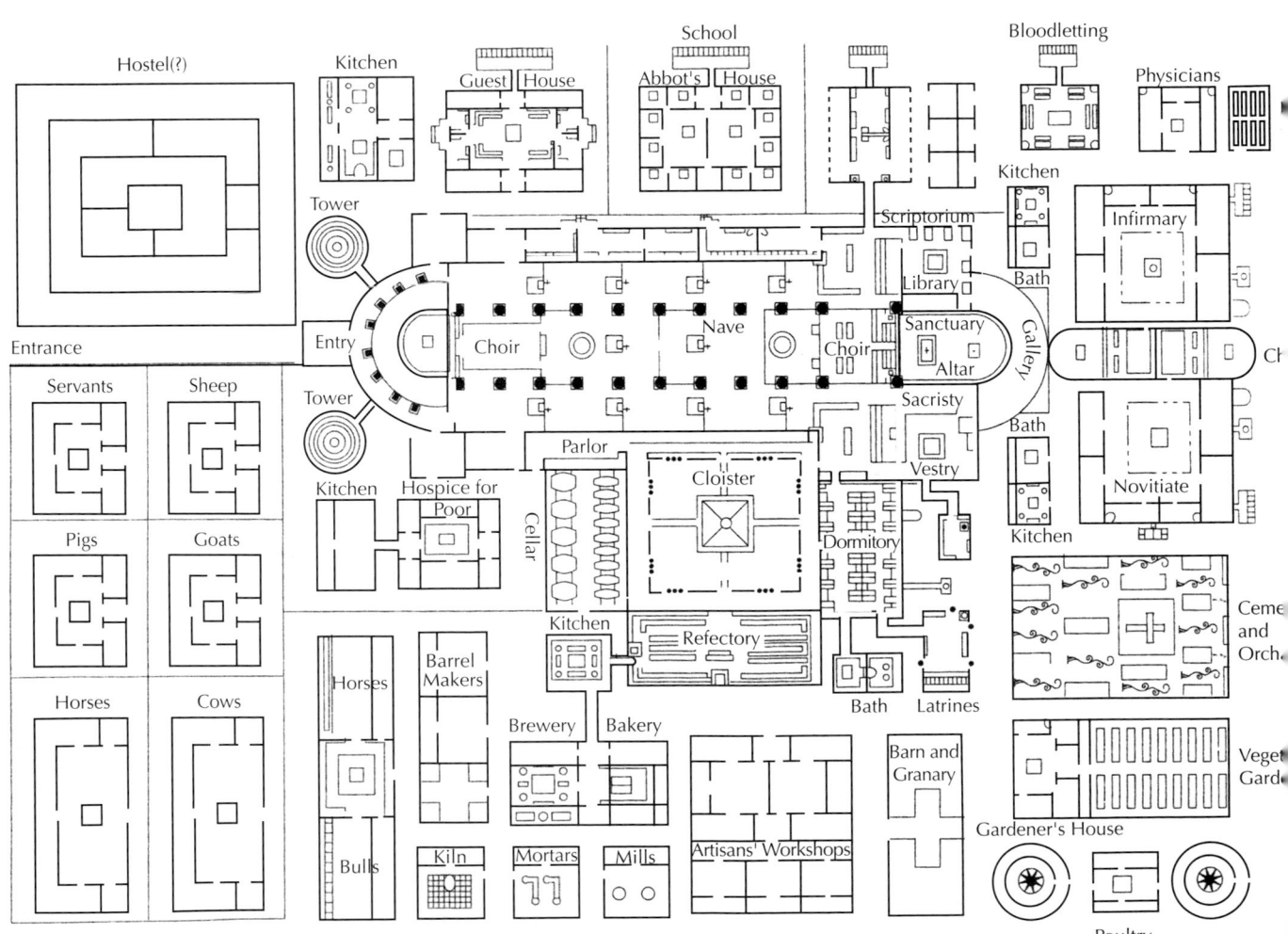

I4–I4 PLAN OF THE ABBEY OF SAINT GALL (REDRAWN)
c. 817. Original in red ink on parchment, 28 × 44⅛" (71.1 × 112.1 cm). Stiftsbibliothek, St. Gallen, Switzerland.
Cod. Sang. 1092.

torium studying and copying books, and teachers staffed the monastery's schools and library. Saint Benedict had directed that monks extend hospitality to all visitors, and the large building in the upper left of the plan may indicate the guesthouse. The plan also included a hospice for the poor and an infirmary. Around this central core were the workshops, farm buildings, and housing for the lay community. Essentially self-supporting, the community needed barns for livestock, kitchen gardens (grain fields and vineyards lay outside the walls), and, of course, a cemetery. The monastery was often larger than the local villages.

The Scriptorium and Illustrated Books

Books played a central role in the efforts of Carolingian rulers to promote learning, propagate Christianity, and standardize Church law and practice. One of the main tasks of the imperial workshops was to produce authoritative copies of key religious texts, free of the errors introduced by tired, distracted, or confused scribes. The scrupulously edited versions of ancient and biblical texts that emerged are among the lasting achievements of the Carolingian period. The Anglo-Saxon scholar Alcuin of York, whom Charlemagne called to his court, spent the last eight years of his life producing a corrected copy of the Latin Vulgate Bible. His revision served as the standard text of the Bible for the remainder of the medieval period and is still in use.

Generations of copying had led to a shocking decline in penmanship. To create a simple, legible Latin script, the scribes and scholars developed uniform letters. Capitals (*majuscules*) based on ancient Roman inscriptions were used for very formal writing, titles and headings, and the finest manuscripts. *Minuscules* (now called *lower-case letters,* a modern printers' term) were used for more rapid writing and ordinary texts. The Caroline script is comparatively easy to read, although the scribes did not use punctuation marks or spaces between words.

Like the builders who transformed inherited classical types such as the basilican church into the new and different Carolingian monastic church, the scribes and illuminators revived and revitalized the Christian manuscript tradition. The human figure, which was absent or barely recognizable in early medieval books, returned to a central position.

Every monastic *scriptorium* developed its own distinctive forms in harmony with local artistic traditions and the books available as models in the library or treasury. The evangelist portraits (a man seated at a desk writing) in the three Gospel Books discussed here—the **GODESCALC GOSPEL LECTIONARY,** the **CORONATION GOSPELS,** and the **EBBO GOSPELS**—demonstrate the range and variety of Carolingian styles. Although the scribes intended to make exact copies of the texts and illustrations, they brought their own distinctive training to the work and so transformed the images into something new and different.

14–15 | **PAGE WITH MARK THE EVANGELIST, GODESCALC GOSPEL LECTIONARY**
Gospel of Mark. 781–83. Ink, gold, and colors on vellum, 12½ × 8½″ (32.1 × 21.8 cm). Bibliothèque Nationale, Paris. MS lat. 1203, fol. 16.

THE GODESCALC GOSPEL LECTIONARY. One of the earliest surviving manuscripts in the new script produced at Charlemagne's court was the **GODESCALC GOSPEL LECTIONARY (FIG. 14–15),** a collection of selections from the Gospels to be read at Mass. Commissioned by Charlemagne and his wife Hildegard, perhaps to commemorate the baptism of their sons in Rome in 781, the *Godescalc Gospels* provided a model for later luxuriously decorated Gospel books.

The colophon indicates that the book was finished before the death of Hildegard in 783 and was made by the Frankish scribe Godescalc. This richly illustrated and sumptuously made book, with gold and silver letters on purple-dyed vellum, has a full-page portrait of the evangelist at the beginning of each Gospel. The style of these illustrations suggests that Charlemagne's artists were familiar with the author portraits of imperial Rome, as they had been preserved in Byzantine manuscripts.

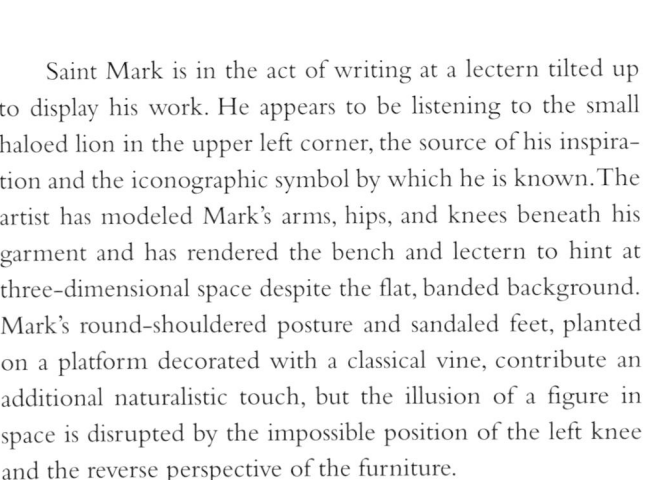

14–16 | **PAGE WITH SAINT MATTHEW THE EVANGELIST, CORONATION GOSPELS**
Gospel of Matthew. Early 9th century. 12¾ × 9⅞″ (36.3 × 25 cm). Kunsthistorische Museum, Vienna.

14–17 | **PAGE WITH MATTHEW THE EVANGELIST, EBBO GOSPELS**
Gospel of Matthew. Second quarter of 9th century. Ink, gold, and colors on vellum, 10¼ × 8¾″ (26 × 22.2 cm). Bibliothèque Municipale, Épernay, France.
MS 1, fol. 18v.

Saint Mark is in the act of writing at a lectern tilted up to display his work. He appears to be listening to the small haloed lion in the upper left corner, the source of his inspiration and the iconographic symbol by which he is known. The artist has modeled Mark's arms, hips, and knees beneath his garment and has rendered the bench and lectern to hint at three-dimensional space despite the flat, banded background. Mark's round-shouldered posture and sandaled feet, planted on a platform decorated with a classical vine, contribute an additional naturalistic touch, but the illusion of a figure in space is disrupted by the impossible position of the left knee and the reverse perspective of the furniture.

THE GOSPELS OF CHARLEMAGNE, KNOWN AS THE *CORONATION GOSPELS*. Classical Early Christian and Byzantine art seem very close to the style of the **CORONATION GOSPELS** (FIG. **14–16**), in which the Carolingian painters seem to have rediscovered Roman realistic painting. Ways of creating the illusion of figures in space may have been suggested by Byzantine manuscripts in the library, or an artist from Byzantium may have actually worked at the Carolingian court. (Charlemagne had hopes of marrying the Byzantine Empress

Irene. She turned him down—in her eyes he was a barbarian.) Tradition says that the book was placed in the tomb of Charlemagne and that in the year 1000 Emperor Otto III removed it (see page 464). It was used in the coronation of later German emperors. The evangelist portraits in this book show full-bodied, white-robed figures represented in brilliant light and shade and seated in a freely depicted naturalistic landscape. The frame enhances the classical effect of a view through a window.

THE GOSPELS OF ARCHBISHOP EBBO OF REIMS. Patronage of scribes and painters continued under Louis the Pious, Charlemagne's son and successor (ruled 814–840). Louis appointed his childhood friend Ebbo to be archbishop of Reims (ruled 816–35, 840–45). Ebbo was an important patron of the arts. A portrait of Matthew from a Gospel book made for the archbishop, either in Reims or a nearby *scriptorium*, illustrates the unique style associated with Reims (FIG. **14–17**). The artist interprets the author's portrait with a frenetic intensity that turns the face, drapery, and landscape into swirling expressive colored lines. The author and his angelic inspiration (the tiny figure in the upper right corner) seem to

14–18 | PAGE WITH PSALM 23, UTRECHT PSALTER.
Second quarter of 9th century. Ink on vellum or parchment, 13 × 9⅞" (33 × 25 cm). Universiteitsbibliotheek, Utrecht, Holland. MS 32, fol. 13r.

hover over a landscape so vibrant that both threaten to run off the page. Even the golden acanthus leaves in the frame seem windblown.

The artist uses the brush like a pen, focusing attention less on the evangelist's physical appearance than on his inner, spiritual excitement as he transcribes the Word of God coming to him from the distant angel, Matthew's symbol. Saint Matthew's head and neck jut out of hunched shoulders, and he grasps his pen and inkhorn. His twisted brow and prominent eyebrows lend his gaze an intense, theatrical quality. Swept up in Matthew's turbulent emotions, the saint's desk, bench, and footstool tilt every which way, as the top of the desk seems about to detach itself from the pedestal. Gold highlights the evangelist's hair and robe, the furniture, and the landscape. The accompanying text is written in magnificent golden capitals.

THE UTRECHT PSALTER. The most famous Carolingian manuscript, the **UTRECHT PSALTER,** or Old Testament Book of Psalms, is illustrated with ink drawings that have the same linear vitality as the paintings in Archbishop Ebbo's Gospel book. Psalms do not tell a straightforward story and so are exceptionally difficult to illustrate. The *Utrecht Psalter* artists solved this problem by interpreting individual words and images literally. Their technique can be likened to a game of charades in which each word must be acted out.

The words of the well-known Twenty-third Psalm are illustrated literally **(FIG. 14–18).** "The Lord is my shepherd; I shall not want" (verse 1): The psalmist (traditionally King David) sits in front of a table laden with food; he holds a cup (verse 5). He is also portrayed as a shepherd in a pasture filled with sheep, goats, and cattle, "beside the still water" (verse 2). Perhaps the stream flows through "the valley of the shadow of death" (verse 4). An angel supports the psalmist with a "rod and staff" and anoints his head with oil (verses 4 and 5). "Thou prepares a table before me in the presence of mine enemies" (verse 5): The enemies gather at the lower right and shoot arrows, but the psalmist and angel ignore them and focus on the table and the House of the Lord. The basilica curtains are drawn back to reveal an altar and hanging votive crown: "I will dwell in the house of the Lord forever" (verse 6). Illustrations like this convey the characteristically close association between text and illustration in Carolingian art.

Carolingian Goldsmith Work

The magnificent illustrated manuscripts of the medieval period represented an enormous investment in time, talent, and materials, so it is not surprising that they were often protected with equally magnificent covers. But because these covers were themselves made of valuable materials—ivory, enamelwork, precious metals, and jewels—they were frequently reused or stolen. The elaborate book cover of gold

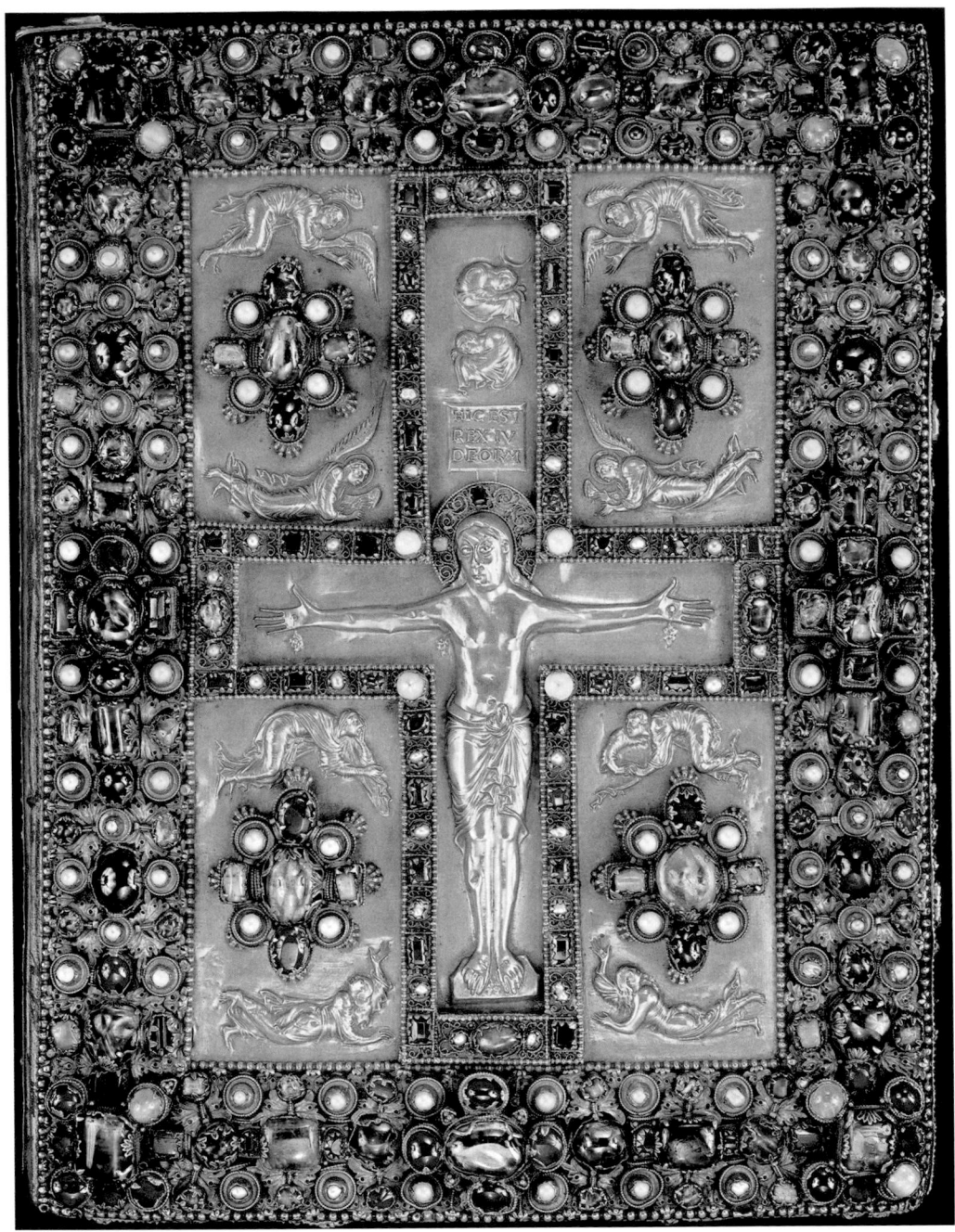

14–19 · CRUCIFIXION WITH ANGELS AND MOURNING FIGURES, LINDAU GOSPELS.
Outer cover. c. 870–80. Gold, pearls, sapphires, garnets, and emeralds, 13¾ × 10⅜"
(36.9 × 26.7 cm). The Pierpont Morgan Library, New York.
MS 1

and jewels, now the cover of the Carolingian manuscript known as the **LINDAU GOSPELS** (FIG. 14–19), was probably made between 870 and 880 at one of the monastic workshops of Charlemagne's grandson, Charles the Bald (ruled 840–77). Charles inherited the portion of Charlemagne's empire that corresponds roughly to modern France after the death of his father, Louis the Pious. It is not known what book the cover was made for, but sometime before the sixteenth century it became the cover of the *Lindau Gospels,* prepared at the Monastery of Saint Gall in the late ninth century.

The Cross and the Crucifixion were common themes for medieval book covers. The Crucifixion scene on the front cover of the *Lindau Gospels* is made of gold with figures in *repoussé* (low relief produced by pounding out the back of the panel to produce a raised front) surrounded by heavily jeweled frames. The jewels are raised on miniature arcades. By raising the jewels from the gold ground, the artist allowed reflected light to enter the gemstones from beneath, imparting a lustrous glow. Such luxurious gems are meant to recall the jeweled walls of the Heavenly Jerusalem.

Angels hover above the arms of the cross. Over Jesus's head, hiding their faces, are figures representing the sun and moon. The graceful, expressive poses of the mourners—Mary, John, Mary Magdalene, and Mary Cleophas—who seem to float around the jewels below the arms of the cross, reflect the expressive style of the *Utrecht Psalter* illustrations. Jesus, on the other hand, has been modeled in a rounded, naturalistic style suggesting the influence of classical sculpture. His erect posture and simplified drapery counter the emotional expressiveness of the other figures. Standing upright and wide-eyed with outstretched arms, he announces his triumph over death and welcomes believers into the faith.

In 843, the Carolingian empire was divided into three parts, ruled by three grandsons of Charlemagne. Although a few monasteries and secular courts continued to patronize the arts, intellectual and artistic activity slowed. Torn by internal strife and ravaged by Viking invaders, the Carolingian empire came to a bloody and inglorious end in the ninth century.

THE VIKING ERA

In the eighth century seafaring bands of Norse seamen known as Vikings (*Viken*, "people from the coves") descended on the rest of Europe. Setting off in flotillas of as many as 350 ships, they explored, plundered, traded with, and colonized a vast area during the ninth and tenth centuries. Frequently, their targets were wealthy isolated Christian monasteries. The earliest recorded Viking incursions were two devastating attacks: one in 793, on the religious community on Lindisfarne, an island off the northeast coast of England, and

another in 795, at Iona, off Scotland's west coast. In France they besieged Paris in 845 and later destroyed Centula as they harried the northern and western coasts of Europe.

Norwegian and Danish Vikings raided and settled a vast territory stretching from Iceland and Greenland, where they settled in 870 and 985, respectively, to Ireland, England, Scotland, and France. The Viking Leif Eriksson reached North America in 1000. In good weather a Viking ship could sail 200 miles in a day. In the early tenth century, the rulers of France bought off Scandinavian raiders (the Normans, or North men) with a large grant of land that became the duchy of Normandy. Swedish Vikings turned eastward and traveled down the Russian rivers to the Black Sea and Constantinople, where the Byzantine emperor recruited them to form an elite personal guard. Others, known as Rus, established settlements around Novgorod, one of the earliest cities in what would become Russia. They settled in Kiev in the tenth century and by 988 had become became Orthodox Christians (see Chapter 7).

The Oseberg Ship

Since prehistoric times Northerners had represented their ships as sleek sea serpents, and as we saw at Sutton Hoo they used them for burials as well as sea journeys. The ship of a dead warrior symbolized his passage to Valhalla, and Viking chiefs were sometimes cremated in a ship in the belief that this hastened their journey. Women as well as men were honored by ship burials. A 75-foot-long ship discovered in Oseberg, Norway, and dated 815–20 served as the vessel for two women on their journey to eternity in 834 (**FIG. 14–20**). Although the burial chamber was long ago looted of jewelry

14–20 | **QUEEN'S SHIP**
Oseberg, Norway. c. 815-20; burial 834. Wood, length 75'6" (23 m). Vikingskiphuset, Universitets Oldsaksamling, Oslo, Norway.

creatures with bulging eyes, short muzzles, snarling mouths, and large teeth. Their bodies are encrusted with geometric ornament. Images of these strange beasts adorned all sorts of Viking belongings—jewelry, houses, tent poles, beds, wagons, and sleds. Traces of color—black, white, red, brown, and yellow—indicate that the carved wood was painted.

All women, including the most elite, worked in the fiber arts. The Oseberg queen had her spindles, a frame for sprang (braiding), tablets for tablet weaving, as well as two upright looms. Her cabin walls had been hung with tapestries, fragments of which survive. Women not only produced clothing and embroidered garments and wall hangings, but they also wove the huge sails of waterproof unwashed wool that gave the ships a long-distance capability. The entire community—men and women—worked to create the ships, which represent the Viking's most important contribution to world architecture.

Picture Stones at Jelling

Both at home and abroad, the Vikings erected large memorial stones. Those covered mostly with inscriptions are called **rune stones**; those with figural decoration are called **picture stones**. Runes are twiglike letters of an early Germanic alphabet. Traces of pigments suggest that the memorial stones were originally painted in bright colors.

About 980 the Danish king Harald Bluetooth (c. 940–987) ordered a picture stone to be placed near the family burial mounds at Jelling (**FIG. 14–22**). Carved in runes on a boulder 8 feet high is the inscription, "King Harald had this memorial made for Gorm his father and Thyra his mother: that Harald who won for himself all Denmark and Norway and made the Danes Christians." (The prominent place of women in Viking society is noteworthy.) Harald and the Danes had accepted Christianity in c. 960, but Norway did not become Christian until 1015.

During the tenth century, a new style emerged in Scandinavia and the British Isles, one that combined simple foliage elements and coarse ribbon interlaces with animals that are more recognizable than the gripping beasts of the Oseberg ship. On one face of the Jelling Stone the sculptor carved the image of Christ robed in the Byzantine manner, with arms outstretched as if crucified. He is entangled in a double-ribbon interlace instead of a cross. A second side holds the runic inscriptions, and a third, a striding creature resembling a lion fighting a snake. The coarse, loosely twisting double-ribbon interlace covering the surface of the stone could have been inspired by Hiberno-Saxon art. New to the north, however, are bits of foliage that spring illogically from the animal—the Great Beast's tail, for example, is a rudimentary leaf. The Great Beast symbolizes the Lion of Judah, an Old Testament prefiguration of the militant Christ, and thus is wholly appropriate for a royal monument commemorating the conversion of the Danes and Harald's victorious dynasty.

14–21 | **GRIPPING BEASTS, DETAIL OF OSEBERG SHIP**
c. 815-20. Wood. Vikingskiphuset, Universitets Oldsaksamling, Oslo, Norway.

and precious objects, the ship itself and its equipment attest to the wealth and prominence of the ship's owner.

This vessel, propelled by both sail and oars, was designed for travel in the relatively calm waters of fjords (narrow coastal inlets), not for voyages in the open sea. The burial chamber held the bodies of two women—a queen and her companion or servant. At least twelve horses, several dogs, and an ox had been sacrificed to accompany the women on their last journey. A cart and four sleds, all made of wood with beautifully carved decorations, were also stored on board. The cabin contained empty chests that no doubt once held precious goods.

The prow and stern of the Oseberg ship rise and coil, the spiraling prow ending in a tiny serpent's head. Bands of interlaced animals carved in low relief run along the ship's bow and stern. Viking beasts are broad-bodied creatures that clutch each other with sharp claws; in fact, these animals are known as "gripping beasts" (**FIG. 14–21**). They are grotesque catlike

I4–22 | ROYAL RUNE STONES
Left: Raised by Gorm the Old to honor his wife Thyra. Right: Raised by Harald Bluetooth to honor his parents Gorm and Thyra and to commemorate the conversion of the Danes to Christianity. Jelling, Denmark 960-985, granite, height of Harald's stone about 8' (2.44 m). The stone church in the background dates c. 1100 and replaces a series of wooden churches on the site.

THE URNES CHURCH PORTAL. The penchant for carved relief decorations seen on the Oseberg ship endured in the decoration of Scandinavia's great halls and later churches. The façades of these structures often teem with intricate animal interlace. A church at Urnes, Norway, although entirely rebuilt in the twelfth century, preserved its original eleventh century doorway (FIG. 14–23), carved with an interlace of serpentine creatures snapping at each other like the vicious little gripping beasts of Oseberg. New in the Urnes style, however, is the satin-smooth carving of rounded surfaces, the contrast of thick and very thin elements, and the organization of the interlace into harmoniously balanced patterns, which have the effect of aesthetic elegance and technical control rather than the wild disarray of earlier carving.

The images on the Urnes doorway panels suggest the persistence of Scandinavia's mythological tradition even as Christianity spread through the country. The Great Beast standing at the left of the door, fighting serpents and dragons, continued to be associated with the Lion of Judah (as at Jelling) and with Christ, who fought Satan and the powers of darkness and paganism (like the peacock and snake image in Mozarabic art). With Christianity, the Great Beast became a positive, protective force.

Timber Architecture

In Scandinavia vast forests provided the materials for timber buildings of all kinds (FIG. 14–24). Two forms of timber construction evolved: one that stacked horizontal logs, notched at the ends, to form a rectangular building (the still popular log cabin); and the other that stood the wood on end to form a palisade or vertical plank wall, with timbers set directly in the ground or into a sill (a horizontal beam).

14—23 | **PORTAL, SET INTO WALL OF LATER STAVE CHURCH**
Urnes, Norway. 11th century.

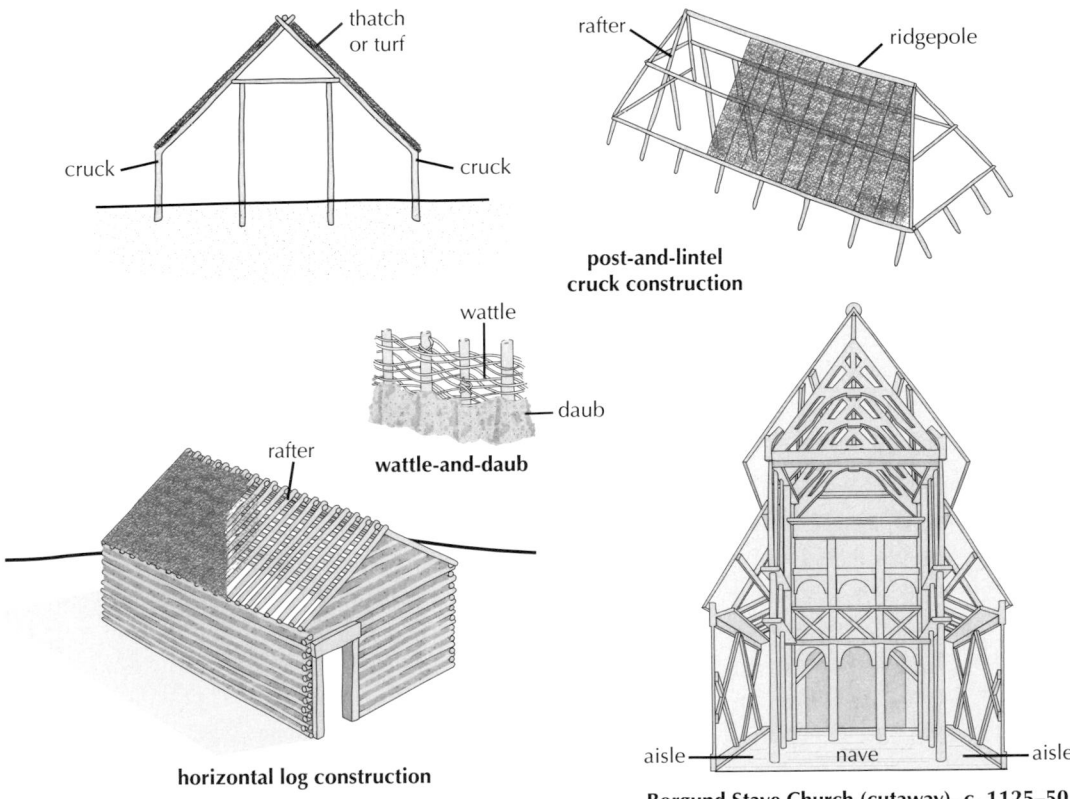

thatch or turf

cruck

cruck

rafter

ridgepole

post-and-lintel cruck construction

wattle

daub

wattle-and-daub

rafter

horizontal log construction

aisle

nave

aisle

Borgund Stave Church (cutaway), c. 1125–50

14—24 | **DIAGRAMS OF WOOD BUILDINGS IN NORTHERN EUROPE**
Horizontal log construction; wattle and daub used to plaster between timbers; stave church is a
highly crafted version of plank wall construction.

I4–25 | STAVE CHURCH, BORGUND, NORWAY
c. 1125–50.

More modest buildings consisted of wooden frames filled with wattle-and-daub (woven branches covered with mud or other substances). Typical buildings had a turf or thatched roof supported on interior posts. The same basic structure was used for almost all building types—feasting and assembly halls, family homes (which were usually shared with domestic animals), workshops, barns, and sheds. The great hall had a central open hearth (smoke escaped through a louver in the roof) and an off-center door designed to reduce drafts. People secured their residences and trading centers by building massive circular earthworks topped with wooden palisades.

THE BORGUND STAVE CHURCH.   Subject to decay and fire, early timber buildings have largely disappeared, leaving only post-holes and other traces in the soil; however, a few timber churches survive in rural Norway. They are called stave churches, from the four huge timbers (staves) that form their structural core. Borgund Church, from about 1125–50 (**FIG. I4–25**), has four corner staves supporting the central roof, with additional interior posts that create the effect of a nave and side aisles, narthex, and choir. A rounded apse covered with a timber tower is attached to the choir. Upright planks slotted into the sills form the walls. A steep-roofed gallery rings the entire building, and steeply pitched roofs covered with wooden shingles protect the walls from the rain and snow. Openwork timber stages set on the roof ridge create a tower and give the church a steep pyramidal shape. On all the gables are both crosses and dragons to protect the church and its congregation from trolls and demons.

14–26 | **OTTO I PRESENTING MAGDEBURG CATHEDRAL TO CHRIST**
One of a series of seventeen ivory plaques known as the *Magdeburg Ivories*, possibly carved in Milan c. 962-68. Ivory, 5 × 4½″ (12.7 × 11.4 cm). The Metropolitan Museum of Art, New York.
Bequest of George Blumenthal, 1941 (41.100.157)

The End of the Viking Era

The Vikings were not always victorious. Their colonies in Iceland and the Faeroe Islands survived, but in North America—in Canada—their trading posts eventually had to be abandoned. In Europe, south of the Baltic Sea, a new German dynasty challenged and then defeated the Vikings. During the eleventh century the Viking era came to an end.

OTTONIAN EUROPE

When Charlemagne's grandsons divided the empire in 843, Louis the German took the eastern portion. His family died out at the beginning of the tenth century, and a new Saxon dynasty came to power in lands corresponding roughly to present-day Germany and Austria. This dynasty was called Ottonian after its three principal rulers—Otto I (ruled 936–73), Otto II (ruled 973–83), and Otto III (ruled 994–1002; queens Adelaide and Theophanu had ruled as regents for him, 983–94). The Ottonian armies secured the territory by defeating the Vikings in the north and the Magyars (Hungarians) on the eastern frontier. Relative peace permitted increased trade and the growth of towns, making the tenth century a period of economic recovery. Then, in 951, Otto I gained control of northern Italy by marrying the wid-

owed Lombard Queen Adelaide. He was crowned emperor by the pope in 962, and so reestablished Charlemagne's Christian Roman Empire. The Ottonians and their successors so dominated the papacy and appointments to other high Church offices that in the twelfth century this union of Germany and Italy under a German ruler came to be known as the Holy Roman Empire. The empire survived in modified form as the Habsburg Empire into the twentieth century.

The Ottonian Empire was of necessity a military state. Aware of the threat of the pagan Slavs, in the 960s Otto established a buffer zone on the border with its headquarters in Magdeburg, the site of a frontier monastery. In 968 the pope made Magdeburg his administrative center in the region as well. Otto brought the relics of Saint Maurice from Burgundy, in France, to Magdeburg in 960. Saint Maurice, an African Christian commander in third century Gaul, was executed with all his troops for refusing to sacrifice to pagan Roman gods (as commander of the Theban Legion, Maurice was often represented as an African, SEE FIG. 16–37). The warrior saint became the patron of the Ottonian Empire.

THE MAGDEBURG IVORIES. The unity of church and state is represented on an ivory plaque, one of several that may once have been part of the decoration of an altar or pulpit presented to the cathedral at the time of its dedication in 968. Saint Maurice wraps his arm protectively around Otto I, who with solemn dignity presents a model of the cathedral to Christ and Saint Peter (**FIG. 14–26**). Hieratic scale demands that the mighty emperor be represented as a tiny, doll-like figure, and that the saints and angels, in turn, be taller than Otto but smaller than Christ. The cathedral Otto holds is a basilica with prominent clerestory windows and rounded apse that are intended to recall the churches of Rome.

Ottonian Architecture

The Ottonian rulers, in keeping with their imperial status, sought to replicate the splendors of the Christian architecture of Rome. German officials knew the basilicas well, since the German court in Rome was located near the Early Christian Church of Santa Sabina. The buildings of Byzantium were another important influence, especially after Otto II married a Byzantine princess, cementing a tie with the East. But while Ottonian patrons saw, envied, and ordered buildings to rival the sophisticated architecture of imperial Rome and Byzantium, the locally trained masons and carpenters could only struggle to comply. They built large timber-roofed basilicas that were terribly vulnerable to fire. Magdeburg Cathedral burned in 1008, only forty years after its dedication; it was rebuilt in 1049, burned in 1207, and rebuilt yet again. In 1009, the Cathedral of Mainz burned down on the day of its consecration. The Church of Saint Michael at Hildesheim was destroyed in World War II. Luckily the convent Church of Saint Cyriakus at Gernrode, Germany, still survives.

14–27 CHURCH OF SAINT CYRIAKUS
Gernrode, Germany. Begun 961; consecrated 973.

The apse seen here replaced the original portal of the westwork in the late twelfth century.

Sequencing Events
THE TENTH CENTURY—THE STATE OF CHRISTIANITY IN EUROPE

910	William, Duke of Aquitaine, and his wife, Ingelborga, seeking reform in Western monasticism, give the Benedictine Order the town and manor of Cluny
911	The Viking Rolf accepts Christianity and becomes Rollo, Duke of Normandy
912–61	Muslim ruler Abd-al-Rahman, Caliph of Cordoba, pushes back Christians in northern Spain
960	Harald Bluetooth, king of Denmark and Norway, accepts Christianity
962	Supremacy of church over state proclaimed when Christian king Otto I of Germany is crowned emperor by the pope in Rome
988	Grand Prince Vladimir in Kiev, Ukraine, accepts Orthodox Christianity

THE CHURCH OF SAINT CYRIAKUS, GERNRODE. During the Ottonian Empire, aristocratic women often held positions of authority, especially as the leaders of religious communities. When in 961 the provincial military governor Gero founded the convent and church of Saint Cyriakus, he made his widowed daughter-in-law the convent's first abbess. The church was designed as a basilica with a westwork, an architectural feature that took on greater importance with the increasing elaboration of the liturgy (FIG. 14–27). At Gernrode, the exterior appearance of the westwork was changed in the late twelfth century by the addition of an apse, although the two tall cylindrical towers continue to dominate the skyline. At the eastern end of the church a transept with chapels led to a choir with an apse built over a crypt. This development at both the east and west ends of the nave gave the building the "double-ended" look characteristic of major Ottonian churches. The nuns entered the church from the convent through modest side doors. Pilasters, joined by arches attached to the wall, form blind arcades, and windows also break the severity of the church's exterior.

The interior of Saint Cyriakus (FIG. 14–28) has three levels: an arcade separating the nave from the side aisles, a gallery with groups of six arched openings, and a clerestory. The flat ceiling is made of wood and must have been painted. Galleries over aisles were used in Byzantine architecture but rarely in the West, and their function in Ottonian architecture is uncertain.

14–28 NAVE, CHURCH OF SAINT CYRIAKUS

THE ⦿BJECT SPEAKS

THE DOORS OF BISHOP BERNWARD

The design of the magnificent doors at Bishop Bernward's abbey church in Hildesheim, Germany, anticipated by centuries the great sculptural programs that would decorate the exteriors of European churches in the Romanesque period. The awesome monumentality of the towering doors—nearly triple a person's height—is matched by the intellectual content of their iconography. The doors spoke eloquently to the viewers of the day and still speak to us through a combination of straightforward narrative history and subtle interrelationships, in which Old Testament themes, on the left, illuminate New Testament events, on the right. Bernward must have designed the iconographical program himself, for only a scholar thoroughly familiar with Christian theology could have conceived it.

The Old Testament history begins in the upper left-hand panel with the Creation and continues downward to depict Adam and Eve's Expulsion from Paradise, their difficult and sorrowful life on earth, and, in the bottom panel, the tragic fratricidal story of their sons, Cain and Abel. The New Testament follows, beginning with the Annunciation at the lower right and reading upward through the early life of Jesus and his mother, Mary, through the Crucifixion to the Resurrection, symbolized by the three Marys at the tomb.

The way the Old Testament prefigured the New in scenes paired across the doors is well illustrated, for example, by the third set of panels, counting down from the top. On the left, we see the Temptation and Fall of Adam and Eve in the Garden of Eden, believed to be the source of human sin, suffering, and death. This panel is paired on the right with the Crucifixion of Jesus, whose suffering and sacrifice redeemed humankind, atoned for Adam and Eve's Original Sin, and brought the promise of eternal life. Another example is the recurring pairing of the "two Eves": Eve, who caused humanity's Fall and Expulsion from Paradise and whose son Cain committed the first murder; and Mary, the "new Eve," through whose son, Jesus, salvation will be granted. In one of the clearest juxtapositions, in the sixth pair down, Eve and Mary are almost identical figures, each holding her first-born son; thus, Cain and Jesus (evil and goodness) are also paired.

DOORS OF BISHOP BERNWARD   Made for the Abbey Church of Saint Michael, Hildesheim, Germany. 1015. Bronze, height 16′6″ (5 m).

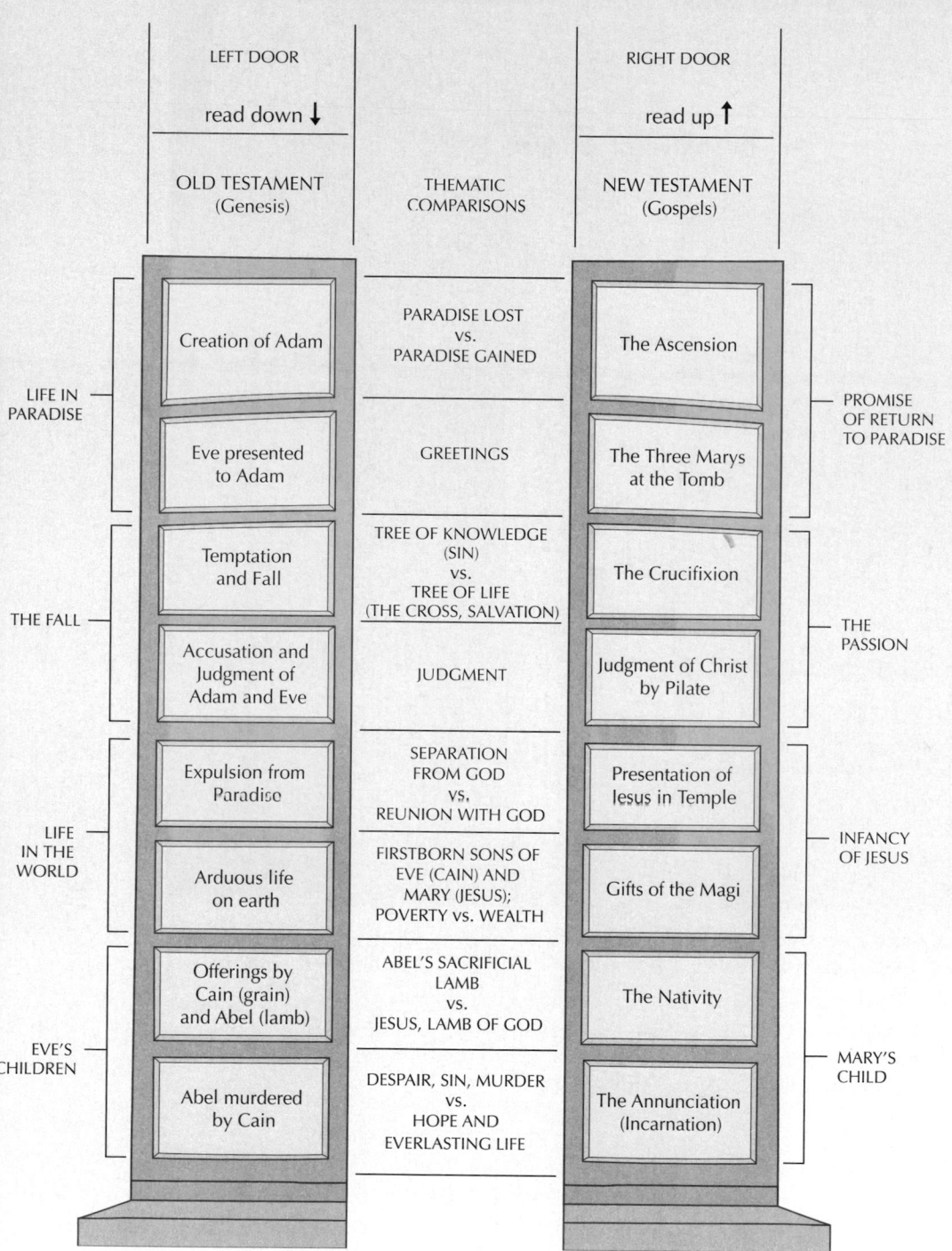

LEFT DOOR		RIGHT DOOR
read down ↓		read up ↑
OLD TESTAMENT (Genesis)	THEMATIC COMPARISONS	NEW TESTAMENT (Gospels)

LIFE IN PARADISE

Creation of Adam — PARADISE LOST vs. PARADISE GAINED — The Ascension

Eve presented to Adam — GREETINGS — The Three Marys at the Tomb

PROMISE OF RETURN TO PARADISE

THE FALL

Temptation and Fall — TREE OF KNOWLEDGE (SIN) vs. TREE OF LIFE (THE CROSS, SALVATION) — The Crucifixion

Accusation and Judgment of Adam and Eve — JUDGMENT — Judgment of Christ by Pilate

THE PASSION

LIFE IN THE WORLD

Expulsion from Paradise — SEPARATION FROM GOD vs. REUNION WITH GOD — Presentation of Jesus in Temple

Arduous life on earth — FIRSTBORN SONS OF EVE (CAIN) AND MARY (JESUS); POVERTY vs. WEALTH — Gifts of the Magi

INFANCY OF JESUS

EVE'S CHILDREN

Offerings by Cain (grain) and Abel (lamb) — ABEL'S SACRIFICIAL LAMB vs. JESUS, LAMB OF GOD — The Nativity

Abel murdered by Cain — DESPAIR, SIN, MURDER vs. HOPE AND EVERLASTING LIFE — The Annunciation (Incarnation)

MARY'S CHILD

SCHEMATIC DIAGRAM OF THE MESSAGE OF THE DOORS OF BISHOP BERNWARD OF HILDESHEIM

14–29 | GERO CRUCIFIX
Cologne Cathedral, Germany. c. 970. Painted and gilded wood, height of figure 6′2″ (1.88 m).

This life-size sculpture is both a crucifix to be suspended over an altar and a special kind of reliquary. A cavity in the back of the head was made to hold a piece of the Host, or communion bread, already consecrated by the priest. Consequently, the figure not only represents the body of the dying Jesus but also contains within it the body of Christ obtained through the Eucharist.

They may have provided space for choirs as music became more elaborate in the tenth century. They may have held additional altars. They may have been simply a mark of status.

The alternation of columns and rectangular piers in Saint Cyriakus creates a rhythmic effect more interesting than that of the uniform colonnades of the Early Christian churches. Saint Cyriakus is also marked by vertical shifts in visual rhythm, with two arches on the nave level surmounted by six arches on the gallery level, surmounted in turn by three windows in the clerestory. This seemingly simple archi-

tectural aesthetic, with its rhythmic alternation of heavy and light supports, its balance of rectangular and round forms, and its combination of horizontal and vertical movement found full expression later in the Romanesque period.

Ottonian Sculpture

Ottonian artists worked in ivory, bronze, wood, and other materials rather than stone. Like their Early Christian and Byzantine predecessors, they and their patrons focused on church furnishings and portable art rather than architectural sculpture. Drawing on Roman, Early Christian, Byzantine, and Carolingian models, they created large sculpture in wood and bronze that would have a significant influence on later medieval art.

THE GERO CRUCIFIX. The **GERO CRUCIFIX** is one of the few large works of carved wood to survive from the early Middle Ages (FIG. 14–29). Archbishop Gero of Cologne (ruled 969–76) commissioned the sculpture for his cathedral about 970. The figure of Christ is more than 6 feet tall and is made of painted and gilded oak. The focus here, following Byzantine models, is on Jesus's suffering. He is shown as a tortured martyr, not as the triumphant hero of the *Lindau Gospels* cover (SEE FIG. 14–19). Jesus's broken body sags on the cross and his head falls forward, eyes closed. The straight, linear fall of his golden drapery heightens the impact of his drawn face, emaciated arms and legs, sagging torso, and limp, bloodied hands. In this image of distilled anguish, the miracle and triumph of the Resurrection seem distant indeed.

THE HILDESHEIM BRONZES. Under the last of the Ottonian rulers, Henry II and Queen Kunigunde (ruled 1002–24), an important artist and patron was Bishop Bernward of Hildesheim. His biographer, the monk Thangmar, described Bernward as a skillful goldsmith who closely supervised the artisans working for him. Bronze doors made under his direction for the Abbey Church of Saint Michael in Hildesheim represented the most ambitious and complex bronze-casting project undertaken since antiquity (see "The Doors of Bishop Bernward," page 466). As tutor for Otto III, the bishop had lived in Rome, where he would have seen the carved wooden doors of the fifth-century Church of Santa Sabina, located near Otto's palace.

The doors' rectangular panels recall not only Santa Sabina (SEE FIG. 7–14) but also resemble the framed miniatures in Carolingian Gospel books. The style of the sculpture is reminiscent of illustrations in manuscripts such as the *Utrecht Psalter*. Animated small figures populate spacious backgrounds. Architectural elements and features of the landscape are depicted in very low relief, forming little more than a shadowy stage for the actors in each scene. The figures stand out prominently, in varying degrees of relief, with their heads fully modeled in three dimensions. The result is lively, visually stimulating, and remarkably spontaneous for so monumental an undertaking.

Illustrated Books

Book illustration in the Ottonian period is not as varied as it is in Carolingian manuscripts, although artists continued to work in widely scattered centers, using different models or sources of inspiration. The **LIUTHAR** (or **AACHEN**) **GOSPELS** (named for the scribe or patron) were made for Otto III around 996 in a monastic *scriptorium* near Reichenau. The dedication page (FIG. 14–30) is a work of imperial propa-

14–30 | **PAGE WITH OTTO III ENTHRONED, LIUTHAR GOSPELS (AACHEN GOSPELS)**
c. 996. Ink, gold, and colors on vellum, 10⅞ × 8½″ (27.9 × 21.8 cm). Cathedral Treasury, Aachen.

ganda meant to establish the divine underpinnings of Otto's authority and depicts him as a near-divine being himself. He is shown enthroned in heaven, surrounded by a mandorla and symbols of the evangelists. The hand of God descends from above to place a crown on his head, and Otto holds the Orb of the World surmounted by a cross in his right hand. His throne, in a symbol of his worldly dominion, rests on the crouching Tellus, the personification of earth. In what may be a reference to the dedication on the facing page—"With this book, Otto Augustus, may God invest thy heart"—the evangelists represented by their symbols hold a white banner across the emperor's breast. On each side of Otto, male figures bow their crowned heads as subordinate rulers acknowledging his sovereignty. The bannered lances they hold may allude to the Ottonians' most precious relic, the Holy Lance, believed to be the one with which the Roman soldier Longinus pierced Jesus's side. In the lower register, two warriors face two bishops, symbolizing the union of secular and religious power under the emperor.

A second Gospel book made for Otto III in the same *scriptorium* illustrates the painters' narrative skill. In an episode

14–31 | **PAGE WITH CHRIST WASHING THE FEET OF HIS DISCIPLES, AACHEN GOSPELS OF OTTO III.**
c. 1000. Ink, gold, and colors on vellum, approx. 8 × 6″ (20.5 × 14.5 cm). Staatsbibliothek, Munich.
Nr. 15131, Clm 4453, fol 237r.

recounted in Chapter 13 of the Gospel according to John, Jesus, on the night before his Crucifixion, gathered his disciples together to wash their feet (FIG. 14–31). Peter, who felt unworthy, at first protested. The painting shows a towering Jesus in the center extending an elongated arm and hand in blessing toward the elderly apostle. Peter, his foot in a basin of water, reaches toward Jesus with similarly elongated arms. The two figures fix each other with wide-eyed stares. Gesture and gaze carry the meaning in Ottonian painting: A disciple on the far right unbinds his sandals, and another, next to him, carries a basin of water while the other disciples look on. The light behind Jesus has turned to gold, which is set off by buildings suggesting the Heavenly Jerusalem. The painter conveys a sense of spirituality and contained but deeply felt emotion, as well as the austere grandeur of the Ottonian court.

These manuscript paintings summarize the high intellectual and artistic qualities of Ottonian art. Ottonian artists drew inspiration from the past to create a monumental style for a Christian, German-Roman empire. From the groundwork laid during the early medieval period emerged the arts of the Romanesque and Gothic periods in Western Europe.

IN PERSPECTIVE

People living outside the Roman Empire had a heritage of both imaginative abstract art and well-observed animal images. They also had an exceptionally high level of technical skill in the crafts, especially metalwork, and in wooden architecture and sculpture. The Celts, Norse, Goths, and Saxons sought to capture the essence of forms in dynamic, colorful, linear art. From astonishingly complex geometric patterns and interlaces they created imaginary creatures. They loved light and color in the form of gold and jewels. As exchanges of intellectual and artistic influences took place among the diverse groups that populated Europe, an extraordinary amalgam of ancient classical forms and Celtic and Germanic styles took place. The new narrative and figurative art that emerged was also richly decorative and expressive.

As the Western Roman Empire disintegrated, the Christian Church assumed an ever greater social as well as spiritual role. Although the Roman Empire itself was no longer a vital entity, the idea of imperial Rome—both as a secular empire and as the headquarters of the Christian Church—remained strong in people's minds. Twice, charismatic leaders gathered disparate factions together into short-lived but powerful empires—the Carolingians at the end of the eighth and beginning of the ninth centuries, and the Ottonians in the tenth century. The pope in Rome emerged as the supreme leader of the Church, and the Germanic rulers reinforced their power by supporting Rome.

Carolingian artists following ancient models brought together the classical perception of human forms, of weight and mass, with the highly developed decorative sensibility and impeccable craftsmanship of Hiberno-Saxon artisans. The arts provided a splendid and symbolic setting for the Carolingian monarchs and served to advance their imperial ambitions. This flowering of art and scholarship as well as the Christian mission came to a halt during the devastating raids of Viking adventurers. The Vikings had their own cultural and artistic traditions, dating back to their Norse ancestors. Theirs was an animal art very different from the imperial and humanistic Mediterranean arts.

Otto the Great defeated the Vikings and created a new Germanic empire in Germany and Italy. Artists served both the empire and the revitalized Church where spiritual values were considered to be superior to the material world. They created a monumental art, with images of overwhelming solemnity. Their work has a directness that often hides complex meanings. Conservative in their reference to Early Christian, Byzantine, and Carolingian art and innovative in their subordination of earlier northern styles to the new imperial ideal, Ottonian artists reaffirmed the value of art and architecture to carry powerful secular and religious messages. As they brought monumentality, dignity, and grandeur to the art of the West, they paved the way for the mature Christian art in Western Europe.

GUMMERSMARK BROOCH
6TH CENTURY

GOSPEL BOOK OF DURROW,
PAGE WITH MAN
SECOND HALF 7TH CENTURY

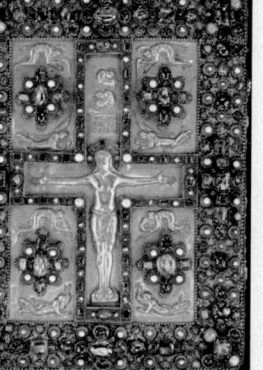

LINDAU GOSPEL COVER
C. 870–80

EMERITUS AND ENDE.
BATTLE OF BIRD AND SERPENT,
BEATUS'S COMMENTARY
975

ROYAL RUNE STONE,
JELLING
C. 980

500

600

700

800

900

1000

1100

EARLY MEDIEVAL ART IN EUROPE

◀ **Rule of St. Benedict** c. 530 CE

◀ **Lombards in Italy** c. 568–774 CE
◀ **Visigoths in Spain Adopt Western Christianity** c. 589 CE
◀ **St. Augustine in England** 597 CE

◀ **Muslims Conquer Spain** 711 CE

◀ **Carolingian Empire** c. 768–887 CE
◀ **Viking Raids Begin** 793 CE
◀ **Charlemagne Crowned Emperor by the Pope in Rome** 800 CE

◀ **Cluny Founded** 910 CE
◀ **Ottonian Empire** c. 919–1024 CE

◀ **Viking Settlement in North America** 1000 CE

15–1 | **CHRIST AND DISCIPLES ON THE ROAD TO EMMAUS**   Cloister of the Abbey of Santo Domingo, Silos,
Castile, Spain. Pier relief, figures nearly life-size. c. 1100.

CHAPTER FIFTEEN

ROMANESQUE ART

15

Three men, together under an arch supported by slender columns, seem to glide forward on tiptoe (FIG. 15–1). The leader turns back, reversing their forward movement. The men's bodies seem almost boneless, their legs cross in slow curves rather than vigorous strides; their shoulders, elbows, and finger joints seem to melt; draperies are reduced to delicate curving lines. Framed by haloes, three bearded faces—foreheads covered by locks of hair—stare out with large wide eyes under strong arched brows. The figures interrelate and interlock without exceeding the limits of the controlling architecture.

Captivated by tranquility, the viewer only gradually realizes that this panel is more than mere decoration. The leader is identified as Christ by his large size and cruciform halo. He wears a ribbed cap and carries a satchel and a short staff. The scene depicts Christ and two disciples on the road from Jerusalem to the village of Emmaus (Luke 24: 13–35). Christ has the distinctive attributes of a pilgrim—a hat, a satchel, and a walking stick. A final surprise rewards a close examination—a scallop shell on Christ's satchel. The scallop shell is the badge worn by the pilgrims to the shrine of Saint James in Santiago de Compostela, Spain. Early pilgrims reaching this destination in the far northwestern corner of the Iberian Peninsula continued to the coast to pick up a shell as evidence of their journey. Soon shells were gathered (or made from metal as brooches) and sold to the pilgrims by authorized persons—a lucrative business for both the sellers and the church. On the return home the shell became the pilgrim's passport.

The *Road to Emmaus* was carved on a corner pier in the cloister of the monastery of Santo Domingo de Silos, south of the pilgrimage road across Spain (see "The Pilgrim's Journey," page 480). Santo Domingo was the eleventh century abbot of Silos. The monastery had a flourishing *scriptorium* and metal smithing shops where artists as well as sculptors worked in a Mozarabic style.

The sculpture at Silos is filled with the spirit of the Romanesque. The art is essentially figurative, narrative, and didactic; it is based on Christian story and belief. It develops out of a combination of styles, not only ancient Roman art as the name might suggest. The sculpture is shaped by a new awakening. Pilgrimages to visit the scenes of Christ's life and the tombs of martyrs (those who died for their faith) inspired not only architecture and the arts. The conflict between Christians and Muslims—and the ensuing Christian Crusades to win back conquered territories and gain access to sacred places like Jerusalem—taught more than military tactics. Travel as a Crusader or a pilgrim opened the mind to a world beyond the familiar towns and agricultural villages of home. The distinctive style of the Romanesque signifies a new era in the social and economic life of Europe, an awakening of intellectual exploration.

EUROPE IN THE ROMANESQUE PERIOD

At the beginning of the eleventh century, Europe was still divided into many small political and economic units ruled by powerful families, such as the Ottonians in Germany (Chapter 14). The nations we know today did not exist, although for convenience we will use present-day names of countries. The king of France ruled only a small area around Paris known as the Ile-de-France. The southern part of modern France had close linguistic and cultural ties to northern Spain; in the north the Duke of Normandy (heir of the Vikings) and in the east the Duke of Burgundy paid the French king only token homage.

When in 1066 Duke William II of Normandy (ruled 1035–87) invaded England and, as William the Conqueror, became that country's new king, Norman nobles replaced the Anglo-Saxon nobility there, and England became politically and culturally allied with Normandy in France. As astute and skillful administrators, the Normans formed a close alliance with the Church, supporting it with grants of land and gaining in return the allegiance of abbots and bishops. Normandy became one of Europe's most powerful feudal domains.

In the eleventh century, the Holy Roman Empire (formerly the Ottonian empire), which encompassed much of Germany and northern Italy (Lombardy), became embroiled in a conflict with the papacy. In 1075, Pope Gregory VII (papacy 1073–85) declared that only the pope could appoint bishops and abbots; the emperor demanded the right for himself. Not only nobles, but cities took sides. In the power struggle between the Holy Roman emperor and the pope, the pope emerged victorious. The conflict persisted in the wars between the great German families, the Welfs of Saxony (known in Italy as the Guelfs), who supported the pope, and the Hohenstaufens of Swabia (or, in Italy, the Ghibellines), who backed the emperor.

Meanwhile, the Iberian Peninsula remained divided between Muslim rulers in the south and Christian rulers in the north. The power of the Christian rulers grew as they joined forces through marriage and inheritance and fought to extend their territory southward. By 1085, Alfonso VI of Castile and León (ruled 1065–1109) had conquered the Muslim stronghold of Toledo, a center of Islamic and Jewish culture in the kingdom of Castile. By this victory he acquired treasures, vast territories, and a skilled work force of Christians, Muslims, and Jews. Catalunya (Catalonia) emerged as a power along the Mediterranean coast.

By the end of the twelfth century, however, a few exceptionally intelligent and aggressive rulers began to create national states. The Capetians in France and the Plantagenets in England were especially successful. In Germany and northern Italy the power of local rulers and towns prevailed, and Germany and Italy remained politically fragmented until the nineteenth century.

Political and Economic Life

Although towns and cities with artisans and merchants gained importance, Europe remained an agricultural society, with land the primary source of wealth and power for a hereditary aristocracy. *Feudalism,* a system of mutual obligation and exchange of land for services that had developed in the early Middle Ages, governed social and political relations, especially in France and England. A landowning lord granted property and protection to a subordinate, called a vassal. In return, the vassal pledged allegiance and military service to the lord.

The economic foundation for this political structure was the manor, a self-sufficient agricultural estate where peasants worked the land in exchange for a place to live, military protection, and other services from the lord. Economic and political power depended on a network of largely inherited but constantly shifting allegiances and obligations among lords, vassals, and peasants.

THE WORCESTER CHRONICLE. The social and economic classes become vividly clear in the **WORCESTER CHRONICLE**, which depicts the three classes of medieval society: the king and nobles, the churchmen, and the peasant farmers (FIG. 15–2). The book is the earliest known illustrated record of contemporary events in England and was written by John, a monk of Worcester. He described the nightmares of King

MAP 15–1 | EUROPE IN THE ROMANESQUE PERIOD

Although a few large political entities began to emerge in places like England and Normandy, Burgundy, and Leon-Castle, Europe remained a land of small economic entities. Pilgrimages and crusades acted as unifying international forces. Modern names of countries have been added for convenience.

Henry I (ruled 1100–35) in 1130 in which the people demanded tax relief. On the first night, angry farmers, still carrying their shovels, forks, and scythes, hold up their list of grievances; in the second dream, armed knights confront the king; and then on the third night, monks, abbots, and bishops challenge the sleeping king, who is observed by the royal physician Grimbald. Finally, the king is caught in a storm at sea and saves himself by promising to lower taxes for a period of seven years. Speech is indicated by pointing a finger; sleep, by propping the head on a hand or arm; and royal status, by the crown worn by the sleeping king. Since the goal of the artist was to communicate clearly, not to decorate the text, the illustrations give an excellent idea of the appearance of the people.

The Church

In the early Middle Ages, church and state had forged an often fruitful alliance. Christian rulers helped insure the spread of Christianity throughout Europe and supported monastic communities with grants of land. Bishops and abbots were often their relatives, younger brothers and cousins, who pro-

vided rulers with crucial social and spiritual support and supplied them with educated administrators. As a result, secular and religious authority became tightly intertwined.

PILGRIMAGES. Reinforcing the importance of religion were two phenomena of the period: pilgrimages and the Crusades. Pilgrimages to the holy places of Christendom—Jerusalem, Rome, and Santiago de Compostela—increased, despite the great financial and physical hardships they entailed (see "The Pilgrim's Journey," page 480). As difficult and dangerous as these journeys were, rewards awaited courageous travelers along the routes. Pilgrims could stop to venerate the relics of local saints and visit the places where miracles were believed to have taken place. They also learned about people and places far removed from their isolated village life.

CRUSADES. In the eleventh and twelfth centuries, Christian Europe, previously on the defensive against the expanding forces of Islam, became the aggressor. In Spain, Christian armies of the north were increasingly successful against the

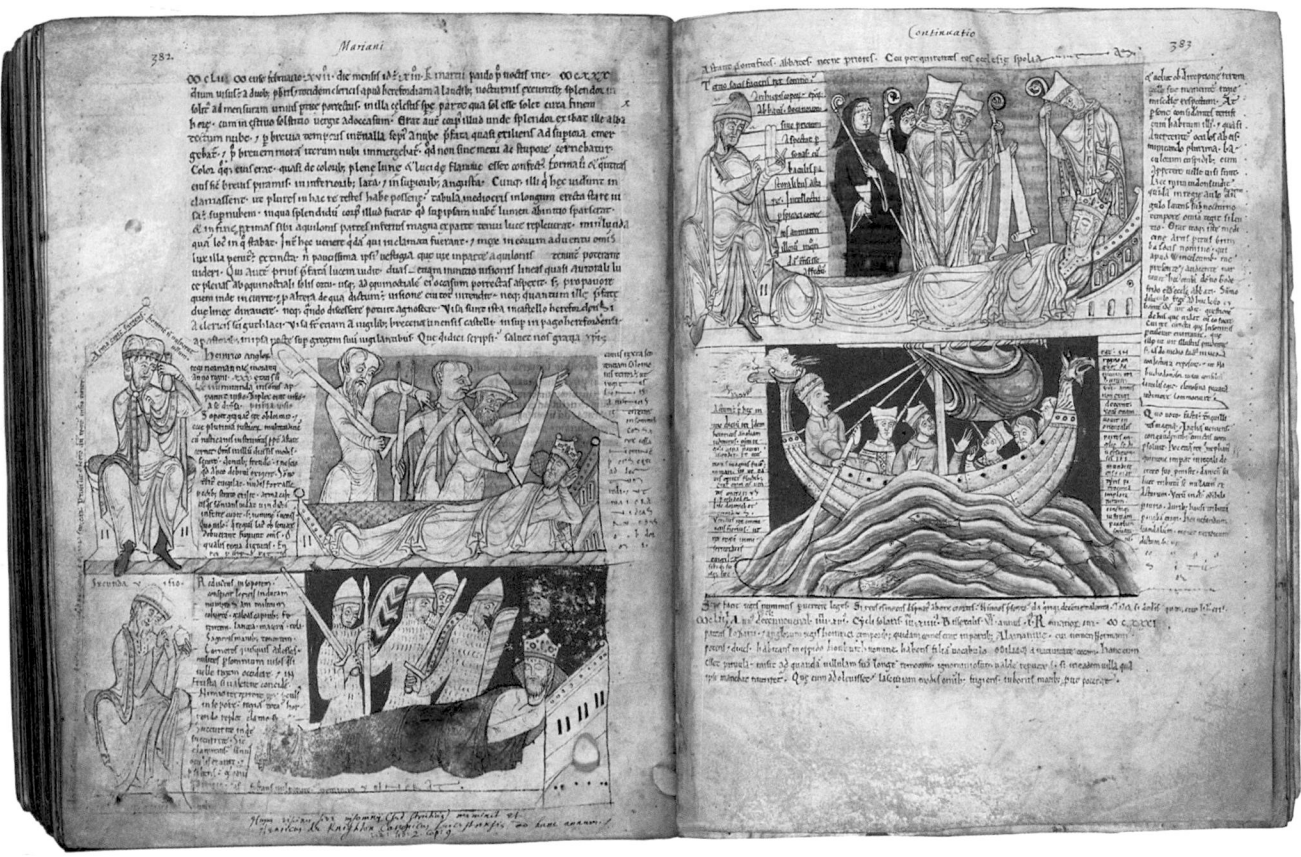

15–2 | John of Worcester **THOSE WHO WORK; THOSE WHO FIGHT; THOSE WHO PRAY—THE DREAM OF HENRY I, WORCESTER CHRONICLE WORCESTER**
England. c. 1140. Ink and tempera on vellum, each page 12¾ × 9⅜" (32.5 × 23.7 cm). Corpus Christi College, Oxford.
CCC MS 157, pages 382–83

Islamic south. At the same time, despite the schism within the Church (SEE Chapter 7), the Byzantine emperor asked the pope for help in his war with the Muslims. The Western Church responded in 1095 by launching a series of military expeditions against Islamic powers known as the Crusades. The word *crusade* (from "crux") refers to the cross worn by Crusaders and pilgrims.

This First Crusade was preached by Pope Urban II (a Cluniac monk and pope from 1088 to 1099) and supported by the lesser nobility of France, who had economic and political as well as spiritual goals. The Crusaders captured Jerusalem in 1099 and established a short-lived kingdom. The Second Crusade in 1147, preached by Saint Bernard and led by France and Germany, accomplished nothing. The Muslim leader Saladin united the Muslim forces and captured Jerusalem in 1187, inspiring the Third Crusade, led by German, French, and English kings. (This is the period of Richard Lionheart and Robin Hood.) The Christians recaptured some territory, but not Jerusalem, and in 1192 they concluded a truce with the Muslims, permitting the Christians access to the shrines in Jerusalem. Crusades continued to be mounted against non-Christians and foes of the papacy. Today the word *crusade* still implies zealous devotion to a cause.

The crusading movement had far-reaching cultural and economic consequences. The Westerners' direct encounters with the more sophisticated material culture of the Islamic world and the Byzantine Empire created a demand for goods from the East. This in turn helped stimulate trade and with it an increasingly urban society during the eleventh and twelfth centuries.

Intellectual Life

The eleventh and twelfth centuries were a time of intellectual ferment as Western scholars rediscovered the classical Greek and Roman texts that had been preserved in Islamic Spain and the eastern Mediterranean. The first universities were established in the growing cities—Bologna (eleventh century) and Paris, Oxford, and Cambridge (twelfth century). Monastic communities continued to play a major role in the intellectual life of Romanesque Europe. Monks and nuns also provided valuable social services, including caring for the sick and destitute, housing travelers, and educating the people. Because monasteries were major landholders, abbots and priors were part of the feudal power structure. The children of aristocratic families who joined religious orders also helped forge links between monastic communi-

Art and Its Context

SAINT BERNARD AND THEOPHILUS: OPPOSING VIEWS ON THE ART OF THEIR TIME

I n a letter to William of Saint-Thierry, Bernard of Clairvaux wrote,

But in the cloister, under the eyes of the Brethren who read there, what profit is there in those ridiculous monsters, in that marvellous and deformed comeliness, that comely deformity? To what purpose are those unclean apes, those fierce lions, those monstrous centaurs, those half-men, those striped tigers, those fighting knights, those hunters winding their horns? Many bodies are there seen under one head, or again many heads to a single body. Here is a four-footed beast with a serpent's tail; there, a fish with a beast's head. Here again the forepart of a horse trails half a goat behind it, or a horned beast bears the hinder quarters of a horse. In short, so many and so marvellous are the varieties of divers shapes on every hand, that we are more tempted to read in the marble than in our books, and to spend the whole day in wondering at these things rather than in meditating the law of God. For God's sake, if men are not ashamed of these follies, why at least do they not shrink from the expense?

(from Caecilia Davis-Weyer. *Early Medieval Art 300–1150: Sources and Documents.* New Jersey: Prentice-Hall, 1971, p. 170.)

"Theophilus" is the pseudonym used by a monk who wrote an artist's handbook, *On Divers Arts*, about 1100. The book gives detailed instructions for painting, glassmaking, and goldsmithing. In contrast to the stern warnings of Abbot Bernard, "Theophilus" assured artists that "God delights in embellishments" and that artists worked "under the direction and authority of the Holy Spirit."

He wrote

most beloved son, you should not doubt but should believe in full faith that the Spirit of God has filled your heart when you have embellished His house with such great beauty and variety of workmanship . . . Set a limit with pious consideration on what the work is to be, and for whom, as well as on the time, the amount, and the quality of work, and, lest the vice of greed or cupidity should steal in, on the amount of the recompense.

(Theophilus, page 43).

---

ties and the ruling elite. The dominant order had been the Benedictines, but as life in Benedictine communities grew increasingly comfortable, reform movements arose. Reformers claimed to return to the original austerity and spirituality of earlier times. The most important for the arts was the congregation of Cluny founded in the tenth century in Burgundy (in eastern-central France) and the Cistercians in the eleventh century.

ROMANESQUE ART

The word *Romanesque* means "in the Roman manner," and the term applies specifically to eleventh- and twelfth-century European architecture and art. The word was coined in the early nineteenth century to describe European church architecture, which often displayed the solid masonry walls and the rounded arches and vaults characteristic of imperial Roman buildings. Soon the term was applied to all the arts of the period from roughly the mid-eleventh to the late-twelfth century, even though the art reflects influences from many sources, including Byzantine, Islamic, and early medieval European art.

The eleventh and twelfth centuries were a period of great building activity in Europe. Castles, manor houses, churches, and monasteries arose everywhere. As one eleventh-century monk noted, "Each people of Christendom rivaled with the other, to see which should worship in the finest buildings. The world shook herself, clothed everywhere in a white garment of churches" (Radulphus Glaber, cited in Holt, *A Documentary History of Art*, vol. I, page 18). Increased prosperity in spite of frequent domestic warfare made the resources available to build monumental stone architecture. The desire to glorify the house of the Lord and his saints (whose earthly remains in the form of relics kept their presence alive in the minds of the people) increased throughout Christendom.

Both inside the church and outside, especially around the entrance, sculpture and paintings illustrated important religious themes; they served to instruct as well as fascinate the faithful. These awe-inspiring works of art and architecture had a Christian message and purpose. One monk wrote that by decorating the church "well and gracefully" the artist showed "the beholders something of the likeness of the paradise of God" (Theophilus, page 79). (See "Bernard and Theophilus," above.)

15–3 | INTERIOR, CHURCH OF
SANT VINCENC, CARDONA
1020s–30s.

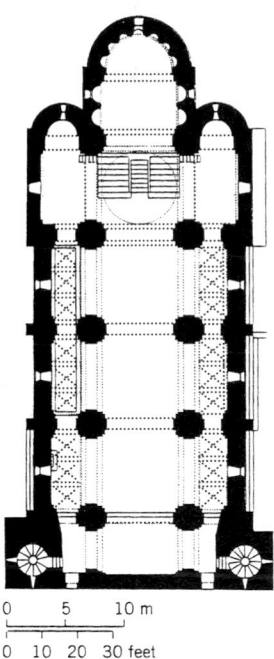

0 5 10 m
0 10 20 30 feet

15–4 | PLAN OF CHURCH
OF SANT VINCENC,
CARDONA
1020s–30s.

ARCHITECTURE

Romanesque architecture and art are regional phenomena. Romanesque churches were the result of master builders solving the problems associated with each individual project with the resources at hand: its site, its purpose, the building materials, the work force available, the builders' own knowledge and experience, and the wishes of the patrons who provided the funding. The process of building could be slow, often requiring several different masters and teams of masons over the years.

In general, the basic form of the Romanesque church, like that of Carolingian churches, follows the plan arrived at by the builders of the early Christian basilicas; however, Romanesque builders made several key changes. They added apses or wide projecting transepts, creating complex sanctuaries. A variety of arrangements of ambulatories (walkways) and chapels accommodated the many altars and the crowds of worshipers. Although wooden roofs were still in widespread use, many builders adopted the stone masonry developed by Lombard and Catalan builders. Masonry vaults enhanced the acoustical properties of the building and the effect of the Gregorian chant (plainsong, named after Pope Gregory, papacy 590–604). Masonry also provided some protection against fire, a constant danger from candlelit altars and torchlight processions.

Tall towers marked the church as the most important building in the community. The two-towered west façade, derived in part from traditional fortified gateways, became not only the entrance into the church but also, by extension, the gateway to Paradise.

The Early Romanesque Style: The "First Romanesque"

By the year 1000—by which time the pope had crowned Otto III (page 464) and Radulphus Glaber commented on the rise of church building across the land—patrons and builders in Catalunya (Catalonia) in northeast Spain, southern France, and northern Italy were constructing masonry churches. Based on methods used by late Roman (SEE FIG. 6–71, Trier) and Early Christian (SEE FIG. 7–29, Ravenna) builders, the Catalan and Lombard masons developed a distinctive early Romanesque style. Many buildings still survive in Catalunya where the authorities had introduced the Benedictine Order into their territory.

THE CHURCH OF SANT VINCENC, CARDONA. One of the finest examples of these masonry buildings is the church of Sant Vincenc (Saint Vincent) in the castle of Cardona on the Catalan side of the Pyrenees Mountains (FIGS. 15–3, 15–4). Begun in the 1020s, it was consecrated in 1040. Castle residents entered the church through a two-story narthex into a nave with low narrow side aisles that permitted windows in the nave wall. The transept had two apses and a low crossing tower that emphasized the importance of the choir, large apse, and altar. The sanctuary was raised dramatically over an aisled crypt. The different sizes of the apses, caused by the difference in the widths of the nave and the narrower side aisles, created a stepped outline that came to be called the **Benedictine plan**. The masons hoped to build practical, sturdy, fireproof walls and vaults. Catalan and Lombard masons used local materials—small split stones, bricks, even river pebbles, and very strong mortar—to raise plain walls and round barrel vaults or groin vaults. Today we can admire their skillful stone work both inside and out, but the builders originally covered their masonry with stucco.

To strengthen the walls and vaults the masons added bands of masonry (called strip buttresses) joined by arches and additional courses of masonry (arched corbel tables) to counter the outward thrust of the vault and to enliven the wall. Late Roman and Early Christian builders had used these techniques, but the eleventh century masons went further. They turned strip buttresses and arched corbel tables into a regular decorative system. On the interior they added masonry strips to the piers and continued these bands across the vault (a transverse arch). They added bands on the underside of the arches of the nave arcade as well. The result was a simple compound pier. The compound piers and transverse

15–5 | TRANSEPT, CATHEDRAL OF SAINT JAMES, SANTIAGO DE COMPOSTELA
Galicia, Spain. View toward the crossing, 1078–1122.

arches dividing the nave into a series of bays that clarify and define the space became an essential element in Romanesque architecture.

The "Pilgrimage Church"

The growth of a cult of relics and the desire to visit shrines such as Saint Peter's in Rome or Saint James in Spain inspired people to travel on pilgrimages (see "The Pilgrim's Journey," page 480). Christian victories against Muslims also opened roads and encouraged travel. To accommodate the faithful and instruct them in Church doctrine, many monasteries on the major pilgrimage routes built large new churches and filled them with sumptuous altars and reliquaries.

THE CATHEDRAL OF SAINT JAMES IN SANTIAGO DE COMPOSTELA. One major goal of pilgrimage was the Cathedral of Saint James in Santiago de Compostela (FIG. 15–5), which held the body of Saint James, the apostle to the Iberian Peninsula. Builders of the Cathedral of St. James and other major churches along the roads leading through France to the shrine developed a distinctive church plan designed to accommodate the crowds of pilgrims and give them easy access to the relics (see "Relics and Reliquaries," page 484).

THE PILGRIM'S JOURNEY

Western Europe in the eleventh and twelfth centuries saw an explosive growth in the popularity of religious pilgrimages. The rough roads that led to the most popular destinations—the tomb of Saint Peter and the Constantinian churches of Rome, the Church of the Holy Sepulchre in Jerusalem, and the Cathedral of Saint James in Santiago de Compostela in the northwest corner of Spain—were often crowded with pilgrims. Their journeys could last a year or more; church officials going to Compostela were given sixteen weeks' leave of absence. Along the way the pilgrims had to contend with bad food and poisoned water, as well as bandits and dishonest innkeepers and merchants.

The stars of the Milky Way, it was said, marked the road to Santiago de Compostela (SEE FIGS. 15–5, 15–6). Still, a guidebook helped, and in the twelfth century the priest Aymery Picaud wrote one for pilgrims on their way to the great shrine through what is now France. Like travel guides today, Picaud's book provided advice on local customs, comments on food and the safety of drinking water, and a list of useful words in the Basque language. In Picaud's time, four main pilgrimage routes crossed France, merging into a single road in Spain at Puente la Reina and leading on from there through Burgos and León to Compostela. Conveniently spaced monasteries and churches offered food and lodging. Roads and bridges were maintained by a guild of bridge builders and guarded by the Knights of Santiago.

Picaud described the best-traveled routes and most important shrines to visit along the way. Chartres, for example, housed the tunic that the Virgin was said to have worn when she gave birth to Jesus. The monks of Vézelay had the bones of Saint Mary Magdalene, and at Conques, the skull of Sainte Foy was to be found. Churches associated with miraculous cures—Autun, for example, which claimed to house the relics of Lazarus, raised by Jesus from the dead—were filled with the sick and injured praying to be healed.

The great pilgrimage churches in Compostela, Toulouse, Limoges, and Conques became models of functional planning and traffic control. To the aisled nave the builders added aisled transepts with chapels leading to an ambulatory with additional radiating chapels around the apse (FIGS. 15–6, 15–7). This system of continuous aisles and ambulatory allowed worshipers to move around the church, visiting all the chapels and saying their own prayers, without disrupting services at the high altar. An octagonal windowed lantern tower over the crossing flooded the sanctuary with daylight, drawing the people forward to the shrines.

Building usually proceeded from east to west. Individual elements produce a series of simple geometric forms that express the internal arrangements of the church—chapels are attached to aisles and ambulatory; the ambulatory then circles the apse and choir, which in turn lead to the wide transept marked by a tall crossing tower. The nave culminates in western towers, an entrance porch, or a narthex. Each element of the building has a distinct geometric form; added together, they produce the powerful impression and solidity characteristic of Romanesque architecture.

15–6 | RECONSTRUCTION DRAWING (AFTER CONANT) OF CATHEDRAL OF SAINT JAMES, SANTIAGO DE COMPOSTELA
1078–1122, western portions later.

Pilgrims usually entered the church through the large double doors at the ends of the transepts rather than through the western portal, which served ceremonial processions. Pilgrims from France entered the north transept portal; the approach from the town was through the south portal. They found themselves in a transept in which the design exactly mirrored the nave in size and structure. The nave and transept have two stories—an arcade and a gallery. Compound piers with attached half columns on all four sides support the immense ribbed barrel vault. The vaulted gallery over the aisles buttresses the nave vault for its entire length (FIG. 15–8). Quadrant vaults, each with an arc of one-quarter of a circle, strengthen the building by carrying the outward thrust of the high barrel vault to the outer walls and buttresses. The compound piers and transverse ribs give sculptural form to the interior as they mark off individual vaulted bays in which the sequence is as clear and regular as the ambulatory chapels of the choir. Three different kinds of vaults are used: ribbed

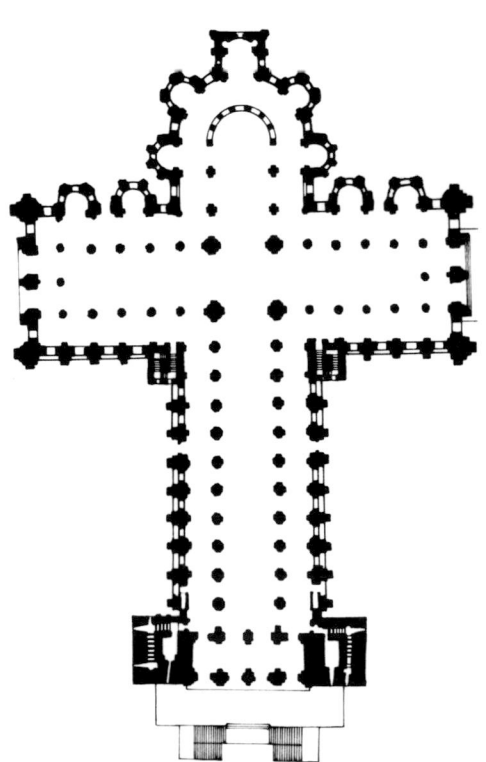

15–7 | PLAN OF CATHEDRAL OF SAINT JAMES, SANTIAGO DE COMPOSTELA

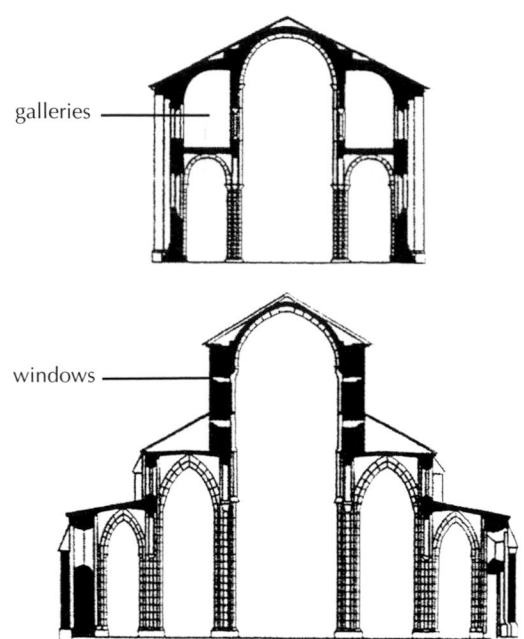

galleries

windows

15–8 | CROSS SECTION OF THE CATHEDRAL OF SAINT JAMES, SANTIAGO DE COMPOSTELA (DRAWING AFTER CONANT)

barrel vaults cover the nave; groin vaults span the side aisles; and half-barrel or quadrant vaults cover the galleries. Without a clerestory, light enters the nave only indirectly, through windows in the outer walls of the aisles and upper-level galleries that overlook the nave.

The building is made of local granite that has weathered to a golden brownish-gray color. In its own time, the cathedral was admired for the excellence of its construction—"not a single crack is to be found," according to the twelfth-century pilgrims' guide—"admirable and beautiful in execution . . . large, spacious, well-lighted, of fitting size, harmonious in width, length, and height . . ."

Pilgrims arrived at Santiago de Compostela weary after weeks of difficult travel through dense woods and mountains. Grateful to Saint James for his protection along the way, they entered a church that welcomed them with open portals. The cathedral had no doors to close—it was open day and night. Its portals displayed didactic sculpture, a notable feature of Romanesque churches. Santiago de Compostela was more than a pilgrimage center; it was a cathedral, the seat of a bishop and later an archbishop and consequently the administrative headquarters of the church in the northwest of the Iberian Peninsula.

The Monastery of Cluny in Burgundy

In 909 the Duke of Burgundy gave land for a monastery to Benedictine monks intent on strict adherence to the original rules of Saint Benedict. They established the reformed congregation of Cluny. From its foundation, Cluny had a special

independent status; its abbot answered directly to the pope in Rome rather than to the local bishop or feudal lord. This unique freedom, jealously safeguarded by a series of long-lived and astute abbots, enabled Cluny to keep the profits from extensive gifts of land and treasure. Independent, wealthy, and a center of learning, Cluny and its affiliates became important patrons of the arts.

Cluny was a city unto itself. By the second half of the eleventh century, there were some 200 monks at Cluny and troops of laymen on whom they depended for material support. As we have seen in the Carolingian Saint Gall plan for monasteries (SEE FIG. 14–14), the cloister lay at the center of the community, joining the church with the domestic buildings and workshops (FIG. 15–9). In wealthy monasteries the arcaded galleries of the cloister had elaborate carved capitals as well as relief sculpture on piers (SEE FIG. 15–1). The capitals may even have served as memory devices to direct the monks' thoughts and prayers.

Benedictine monks and nuns observed the eight Hours of the Divine Office (including prayers, scripture readings, psalms, and hymns) and the Mass, which was celebrated after the third hour (terce). Cluny's services were especially elaborate. During the height of its power, the plainsong (or Gregorian chant) filled the church with music twenty-four hours a day. When the monks were not in the choir, they dedicated themselves to study and the cloister crafts, including manuscript production.

The hallmark of Cluny—and Cluniac churches—was their functional design that combined the needs of the monks with the desire of pilgrims to visit shrines and relics, their fine stone masonry with rich sculptured and painted decoration, and their use of elements from Roman and Early Christian art, such as fluted pilasters and Corinthian capitals. Individual Cluniac monasteries were free to follow regional traditions and styles; consequently, Cluny III was widely influential, though not copied exactly.

THE ABBEY CHURCH OF SAINT PETER. The original church, a small barnlike building, was soon replaced by a basilica with two towers and narthex at the west and a choir with tower and chapels at the east. Hugh de Semur, abbot of Cluny for sixty years (1049–1109), began rebuilding for the third time at Cluny in 1088 (FIG. 15–10). Money paid in tribute by Muslims to victorious Christians in Spain financed the building. When King Alfonso VI of León and Castile captured Toledo in 1085, he sent 10,000 pieces of gold to Cluny. The church (known to art historians as Cluny III because it was the third building at the site) was the largest church in Europe when it was completed in 1130. Huge in size—550 feet long—with five aisles like Constantine's churches in Rome, built with superb masonry, and richly carved, painted, and furnished, Cluny III was a worthy home for the relics of Saint Peter and Saint Paul, which the monks acquired from Saint Paul's Outside the Walls in Rome.

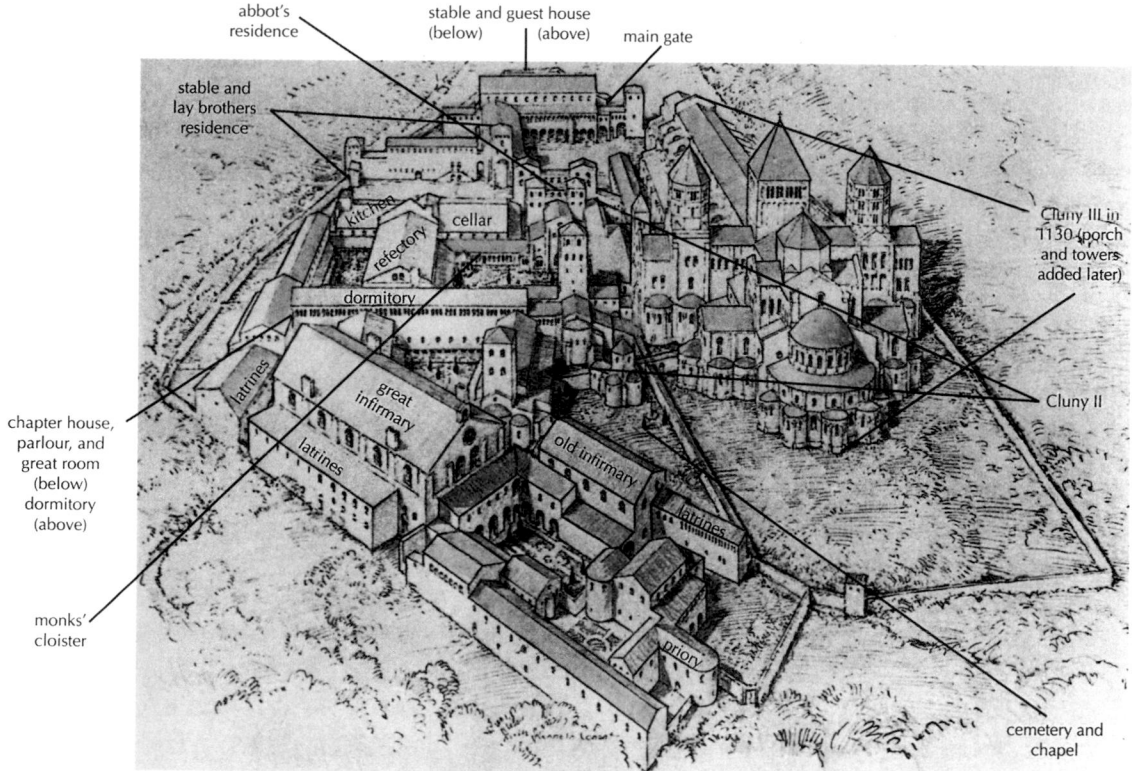

15–9 | **RECONSTRUCTION DRAWING OF THE ABBEY AT CLUNY**
Burgundy, France. 1088–1130. View from the east.

The monastery of Cluny expanded to accommodate its increasing responsibilities and number of monks. In this reconstruction, Cluny III, the abbey church (on the right), dominates the complex. Other buildings are loosely organized
around cloisters and courtyards. The cloisters link buildings and provide private space for the monks; the two principal
cloisters—for choir monks and for novices—lie to the south of the church.

In simple terms, the church was a basilica with five aisles,
double transepts with chapels, and an ambulatory and radiating chapels around the high altar. The large number of altars
was required by the monks who celebrated Mass daily.
Octagonal towers over the two crossings and additional towers over the transept arms created a dramatic pyramidal
design at the east end. Pope Urban II, while in Burgundy in
1095 to preach the First Crusade, consecrated the high altar.

The nave of Cluny III had a three-part elevation like
Saint Peter's in Rome. In the nave arcade tall compound piers
with pilasters and engaged columns supported pointed
arches. At the next level a blind arcade and pilasters created a
triforium that resembled a classical Roman triumphal arch,
and finally triple clerestory windows let sunlight directly into
the church. A ribbed vault, which rose to the daring height of
98 feet with a span of about 40 feet, was made possible by
giving the vaults a steep profile (rather than being round as at
Santiago de Compostela) and slightly decreasing the width of
the nave at the top of the wall.

15–10 | **THE CHURCH CHOIR FROM THE TRANSEPT AT
CLUNY (DRAWING AFTER CONANT)**

RELICS AND RELIQUARIES

hristians turned to the heroes of the Church, the martyrs who had died for their faith, to answer their prayers and to intercede with Christ on their behalf at the Last Judgment. In the Byzantine church people venerated icons, that is, pictures of the saints, but Western Christians wanted to be close to the actual earthly remains of the saints. Scholars in the church assured the people that the veneration of icons or relics was not idol worship. Bodies of saints, parts of bodies, things associated with the Holy Family or the saints were kept in richly decorated containers called reliquaries. Reliquaries could be simple boxes, but they might also be given the shape of the relic—the head of Saint John the Baptist, the rib of Saint Peter, the sandal of Saint Andrew.

Churches were built in cemeteries, over and around the martyrs' tombs. By the eleventh century, many different arrangements of crypts, chapels, and passageways gave people access to the relics. When the Church decided that every altar required a relic, the saints' bodies and possessions were subdivided. Ingenious churchmen came up with the idea of the *brandea*, a strip of linen that took on the powers of the relic by touching it. In this way relics were multiplied; for example, hundreds of churches held relics of the true cross.

Owning and displaying these relics so enhanced the prestige and wealth of a community that people went to great lengths to acquire relics, not only by purchase but also by theft. In the ninth century, for example, the monks of Conques stole the relics of the child martyr Sainte Foy (Saint Faith) from her shrine at Agent. Such a theft was called "holy robbery," for the new owners insisted that the saint had encouraged them because she wanted to move. In the late ninth or tenth century the monks of Conques encased their relic—the skull of Sainte Foy—in a jewel-bedecked and gilt statue whose head was made from a Roman statue. Over the centuries, added jewels, cameos, and other gifts from pilgrims enhanced the splendor of the statue.

RELIQUARY STATUE OF SAINTE FOY (SAINT FAITH)
Abbey Church of Conques, Conques, France. Late 9th or 10th century with later additions. Silver gilt over a wood core, with added gems and cameos of various dates. Height 33″ (85 cm). Church Treasury, Conques, France.

The Church was consecrated in 1130, but building continued at Cluny. A narthex, added at the west end of the nave, was finished at the end of the twelfth century in early Gothic style. The monastery suffered during the French Revolution, and the church was sold and used as a stone quarry. Today the site is an archeological park.

The Cistercians

New religious orders devoted to an austere spirituality arose in the late eleventh and early twelfth centuries. Among these were the Cistercians, who spurned Cluny's elaborate liturgical practices and emphasis on the arts. The Cistercian reform began in 1098 with the founding of the Abbey of Cîteaux (*Cistercium* in Latin, hence the order's

name). Led in the twelfth century by the commanding figure of Abbot Bernard of Clairvaux, the Cistercians advocated strict mental and physical discipline and a life devoted to prayer and intellectual pursuits combined with shared manual labor, although like the Cluniacs, they depended on the work of laypersons. To provide for their minimal physical needs, the Cistercians settled and reclaimed swamps and forests in the wilderness, where they then farmed and raised sheep. In time, their monasteries could be found from Russia to Ireland.

THE ABBEY AND CHURCH OF NOTRE-DAME AT FONTENAY. Cistercian architecture reflects the ideals of the order—simplicity and austerity—in their building. Always practical, the

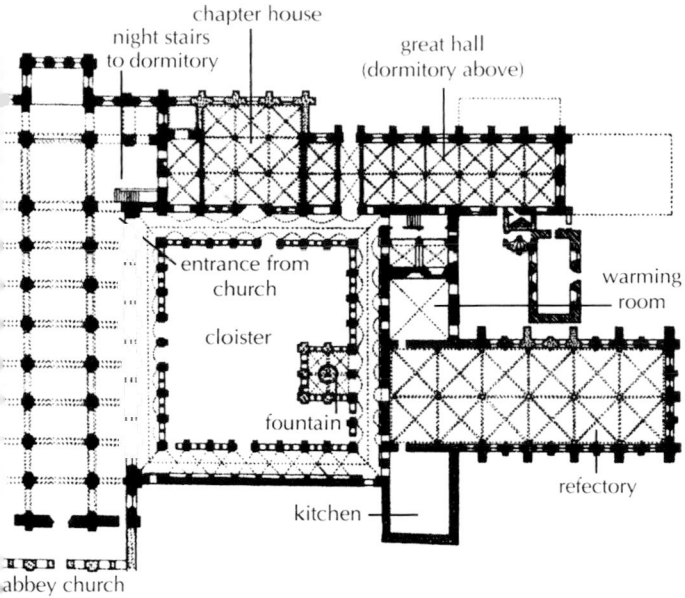

15–11 | **PLAN OF THE ABBEY OF NOTRE-DAME, FONTENAY**
Burgundy, France. 1139-47.

15–12 | **NAVE, ABBEY CHURCH OF NOTRE-DAME, FONTENAY** 1139–47.

Cistercians made a significant change to the already very efficient monastery plan. They placed key buildings such as the refectory at right angles to the cloister walk so that the building could easily be extended should the community grow. The cloister fountain was relocated from the center of the cloister to the side, conveniently in front of the refectory. The monks entered the church from the cloister into the south transept or from the dormitory by way of the "night stairs."

The Cistercians dedicated all their churches to Mary, to Notre Dame ("Our Lady"). The Abbey Church of Notre-Dame at Fontenay was begun in 1139. It has a simple geometric plan (FIG. 15–11): a long nave with rectangular chapels off the square-ended transept arms and a shallow choir with a straight east wall.

A feature of Fontenay often found in Cistercian architecture is the use of pointed ribbed barrel vaults over the nave and pointed arches in the nave arcade and side-aisle bays (FIG. 15–12). The pointed arch and vault may have derived from Islamic architecture. Pointed arches are structurally more stable than round ones, directing more weight down into the floor instead of outward to the walls. Consequently, they can span greater distances at greater heights without collapsing. Pointed arches have a special aesthetic effect, for they narrow the eye's focus and draw the eye upward, an effect intended to direct thoughts toward heaven.

The Cistercians relied on harmonious proportions and fine stonework, not elaborately carved and painted decoration, to achieve beauty in their architecture. Church furnishings included little else than altars with crosses and candles. The large windows in the end wall, rather than a clerestory, provided light. The sets of triple windows reminded the monks of the Trinity. Situated far from the distractions of the secular world, the building made few concessions to the popular taste for architectural adornment, either outside or inside. In other ways, however, Fontenay and other Cistercian monasteries fully reflect the architectural developments of their time in their masonry, vaulting, and proportions.

This simple architecture spread from the Cistercian homeland in Burgundy to become an international style. From Scotland and Germany to Spain and Italy, Cistercian designs and building techniques varied only slightly. The masonry vaults and harmonious proportions influenced the development of the Gothic style in the years leading to the twelfth century (Chapter 16).

Regional Styles in Romanesque Architecture

The Cathedral of Santiago de Compostela and the Abbey church at Cluny reflect the international aspirations of the pope and the impact of the Crusades and pilgrimages, but Europe remained a land divided by competing kingdoms, regions, and factions. Romanesque architecture reflects this regionalism in the wide variety of its styles and building techniques, only a few of which will be noted here.

15–13 | **CATHEDRAL COMPLEX, PISA**
Tuscany, Italy. Cathedral, begun 1063; Baptistry, begun 1153; Campanile, begun 1174; Campo Santo, 13th century.

When finished in 1350, the Leaning Tower of Pisa stood 179 feet high. The campanile had begun to tilt while still under construction, and today it leans about 13 feet off the perpendicular. In the latest effort to keep it from toppling, engineers filled the base with tons of lead.

EARLY CHRISTIAN INSPIRATION IN PISA. Throughout Italy artists looked to the still-standing remains of imperial Rome. The influence remained especially strong in Pisa, on the west coast of Tuscany. Pisa became a maritime power, competing with Barcelona and Genoa as well as the Muslims for control of trade in the western Mediterranean. In 1063, after a decisive victory over the Muslims, the jubilant Pisans began an imposing new cathedral dedicated to the Virgin Mary (FIG. 15–13). The cathedral complex eventually included the cathedral building itself, a campanile (a freestanding bell tower—now known for obvious reasons as "the Leaning Tower of Pisa"), a baptistry, and the later Gothic Campo Santo, a walled burial ground. The cathedral was designed by the master builder Busketos, who adopted the plan of a cruciform basilica. A long nave with double side aisles (the five-aisle building always pays homage to Rome) is crossed by projecting transepts, designed like basilicas with aisles and apses. The builders added galleries above the side aisles, and a dome covers the crossing.

Unlike Early Christian basilicas, the exteriors of Tuscan churches were richly decorated with marble—either panels of green and white marble or with arcades. At Pisa, pilasters, blind arcades, and narrow galleries in white marble adorn the five-story façade. A trophy captured from the Muslims, a bronze griffin, stood atop the building until 1828 (SEE FIG. 8–19).

Other buildings in the complex soon followed the cathedral. The baptistry, begun in 1153, has arcading and galleries on the lower levels of its exterior that match those on the cathedral (the baptistry's present exterior dome and ornate upper levels were built later). The campanile (bell tower) was begun in 1174 by the Master Bonanno. Built on inadequate foundations, it began to lean almost immediately. The cylindrical tower is encased in tier upon tier of marble columns. This creative reuse of the ancient, classical theme of the colonnade, turning it into a decorative arcade, is characteristic of Tuscan Romanesque art; artists and architects in Italy seem always to have been conscious of their Roman past.

MONTE CASSINO AND ROME; THE CHURCH OF SAN CLEMENTE, ROME. From 1058 to 1086 Abbot Desiderius ruled Monte Cassino, the mother house of the Benedictine order. At the end of his life he was elected pope, taking the name Victor III. He rebuilt the abbey church at Saint Benedict's monastery of Monte Cassino using Saint Peter's basilica in Rome as his model—with important modifications. Since a monastic church did not have to accommodate crowds of pilgrims, single aisles and a short transept provided sufficient space. A chapel off the transept, facing each aisle, produced a distinctive stepped, triple-apse plan. The eastern portion of the church was raised above the level of the nave to accommodate an open, partially underground crypt. The church, consecrated in 1071, set the pattern for Benedictine churches thereafter.

In the late eleventh century the Benedictines turned to Desiderius's church for technical assistance and inspiration to rebuild the Church of San Clemente in Rome. The new church, consecrated in 1128, was built on top of the previous

I5-I4 | NAVE, CHURCH OF SAN CLEMENTE, ROME Consecrated 1128.

San Clemente contains one of the finest surviving collections of early church furniture: choir stalls, pulpit, lectern, candlestick, and also the twelfth-century inlaid floor pavement. Ninth-century choir screens were reused from the earlier church on the site. The upper wall and ceiling decoration are eighteenth century.

church (which had been built over a Roman sanctuary of Mithras). Although the architecture and decoration reflect a conscious effort to reclaim the artistic and spiritual legacy of the early church (FIG. 15-14), a number of features mark San Clemente as a twelfth-century building. Early Christian basilicas, for example, have parallel rows of identical columns, which create a strong, regular horizontal movement down the nave to the sanctuary. In the new church of San Clemente, however, rectangular piers interrupt the line of Ionic columns and divide the nave into bays. (As with the columns of Santa Sabina (SEE FIG. 7–13), the columns in San Clemente are *spolia;* that is, they were taken from ancient Roman buildings.) The church had a timber roof now disguised by an ornate ceiling. The construction of timber-roofed buildings continued throughout the Middle Ages. Its advantage of being slightly easier and cheaper to build was offset by its vulnerability to fire.

The nave and aisles at San Clemente end in semicircular apses. The central apse was too small to accommodate the increased number of participants in the twelfth-century liturgy. As a result, the choir was extended into the nave and defined by a low barrier made up of ninth-century relief panels saved from the earlier church. In early Christian basilicas, the area in front of the altar had been enclosed by a screen wall (SEE FIG. 7–13, Santa Sabina), and the later builders may have wanted to revive what they considered a glorious early Christian tradition. A **baldachin** (*baldacchino* or *ciborium*), symbolizing the Holy Sepulchre, covers the main altar in the apse.

THE BARREL VAULTED CHURCH OF SAINT-SAVIN-SUR-GARTEMPE. At the Benedictine abbey church in Saint-Savin-sur-Gartempe in western France, a tunnel-like barrel vault runs the length of the nave and choir (FIG. 15–15). Supported directly by tall columns and consequently without galleries or clerestory windows, the nave at Saint Savin approaches the form of a "hall church," where the nave and aisles rise to an equal height. At Saint Savin the vault is unbroken. The continuous vault is ideally suited for paintings (see page 502 FIG. 15–31).

More often in Romanesque churches, transverse arches divide the space into bays, as at the Cathedral of Santigo de Compostela (SEE FIG. 15–5). These transverse arches provide little extra support for the vault once it is in place, but they allow the vault to be constructed in segments. They also enhance the rhythmic and "additive" aesthetic quality of the building.

FOUR-PART RIBBED VAULTS AT SANT'AMBROGIO, MILAN. About 1080, at the height of the struggles between the pope and the emperor, construction began in the city of Milan in Lombardy on a new Church of Sant'Ambrogio. The church had been founded by the city's first bishop, Saint Ambrose (d. 397), one of the Fathers of the Christian Church. This new church replaced a ninth-century building. Then, following an earthquake in 1117, masons had to rebuild the church again. This time they used a technically advanced system of four-part rib vaulting (FIG. 15–16). With a nave wider than that of Cluny III, but, at 60 feet, only a little more than half as high, the vault presented a challenge.

Massive compound piers support three huge ribbed groin vaults over the square bays of the nave. The Romans had used groin vaults, and the Romanesque Lombard builders added diagonal and transverse ribs that had supported scaffolds during construction and now also helped to stabilize the vault. Smaller intermediate piers support the small groin vaults over the side-aisle bays, and vaulted galleries buttress the walls and vaults. Since the builders used round arches throughout the construction, in each bay the diagonal ribs had a greater diameter and therefore greater

15–15 | CHURCH OF SAINT-SAVIN-SUR-GARTEMPE, POITOU
France. Choir c.1060-75; nave c. 1095-1115.

height than the transverse and lateral ribs, and each bay rises up into a domical form, emphatically defining each bay. The builders did not risk weakening the structure with window openings, so there is no clerestory. The dimly lit nave makes the light streaming down in front of the altar from the lantern tower all the more dramatic.

THE IMPERIAL CATHEDRAL OF SPEYER. Ties between northern Italy and Germany established by the Carolingian and Ottonian rulers remained strong, and the architecture of Switzerland, southern Germany, and especially the Rhine Valley is closely related to that of Lombardy. The Imperial Cathedral at Speyer in the Rhine River valley was a colossal structure rivalled only by Cluny III. The Ottonian wooden-roofed church built between 1030 and 1060 was given a masonry vault c. 1080–1106 (FIG. 15–17). Massive compound piers mark each nave bay and support the transverse ribs of a vault that rises to a height of over 100 feet. These compound piers alternate with smaller piers that support the vaults of the aisle bays. This rhythmic pattern of heavy and light elements, first suggested for aesthetic reasons in Ottonian wooden-roofed architecture (SEE FIG. 14–27, Gernrode), became an important design element in Speyer. Since groin vaults concentrate the weight and thrust of the vault on the four corners of the bay, they relieve the stress on the side walls of the building. Windows can be safely inserted in each bay (something the builders of Sant'Ambrogio dared not do). The result is a building flooded with light.

The exterior of Speyer Cathedral emphasizes its Ottonian (and even Carolingian) qualities. Soaring towers and wide transepts mark both ends of the building, although a narthex, not an apse, stands at the west. Like the arrangement of the east end first seen at Saint Riquier (SEE FIG. 14–13), a large apse housing the high altar abuts the flat wall of the choir; transept arms project at each side; a large octagonal tower rises over the crossing; and a pair of tall slender towers flanks the choir (FIG. 15–18). A horizontal arcade forms an exterior gallery at the top of the apse and transept wall. Stepped niches follow the line of the choir roof, and arched corbel

15–16 | **NAVE, CHURCH OF SANT'AMBROGIO, MILAN**
Lombardy, Italy. Begun 1080; vaulted after an earthquake in 1117.

15–17 | **INTERIOR, SPEYER CATHEDRAL**
Speyer, Germany. As remodeled c. 1080–1106.

15–18 | **EXTERIOR, SPEYER CATHEDRAL**
c. 1080–1106 and second half of the 12th century.

tables also define the roof line and the stages of the towers. This decorative scheme has been adapted from the Lombard-Catalan builders. (The startling green copper roofs seen in the photograph are modern.)

EXPERIMENTAL VAULTS IN DURHAM. In Durham, a military outpost near the Scottish border, builders were experimenting with masonry vaults. When the British turned from timber architecture to stone and brick, they associated masonry buildings—whether church, feasting hall, or castle—with the power and glory of ancient Rome and to some extent with Charlemagne and the Continental powers. As a practical matter, they also appreciated the greater strength and resistance to fire of masonry walls, although they often continued to use wooden roofs.

In Durham, one man, a count-bishop, had both secular and religious authority. For his headquarters he chose a natural defensive site where the oxbow of the River Wear formed a natural moat. Durham grew into a powerful fortified complex including a castle, a monastery, and a cathedral. The great tower of the castle defended against attack from the land, and an open space between buildings served as the bailey of the castle and the cathedral green.

Durham Cathedral, begun in 1087 and vaulted beginning in 1093, is an impressive Norman church, but like most buildings that have been in continuous use, it has been altered several times (FIG. 15–19). The nave retains its Norman character, but the huge circular window lighting the choir is a later Gothic addition. The cathedral's size and decor are ambitious. Enormous compound piers alternating with robust columns form the nave arcade. The alternating circular and clustered piers establish the typical alternating rhythm. The columns are carved with chevrons, spiral fluting, and diamond patterns, and some have scalloped, cushion-shaped capitals. The arcades have multiple round moldings and chevron ornaments. All this carved ornamentation was originally painted.

Above the cathedral's massive piers and walls rise a new system of ribbed vaults and buttresses. Masons in Santiago de Compostela, Cluny, Milan, Speyer, and Durham were all experimenting with vaults—and reaching different conclusions. Unlike the masons at Sant' Ambrogio, the designers in Durham wanted a unified, well-lit space. In the vault, the Durham builders divided each bay with two pairs of diagonal crisscrossing ribs and so kept the crowns of the vaults close in height to the keystones of the transverse arches (FIG. 15–20).

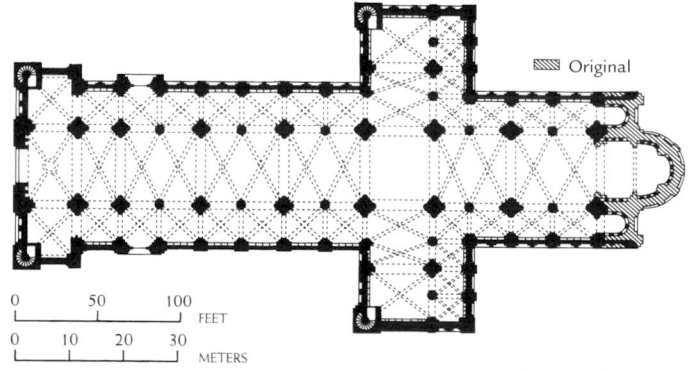

15–19 | NAVE, DURHAM CATHEDRAL
England. 1087–1133. Original east end replaced by a Gothic choir, 1242–c. 1280. Vault height about 73′ (22.2 m).

15–20 | PLAN OF DURHAM CATHEDRAL
Showing original east end.

15–21 | NAVE, CHURCH OF SAINT-ÉTIENNE, CAEN
Normandy, France c. 1060-77; vaulted c. 1130.

run unbroken the full height of the nave, emphasizing its height. The walls seem designed for a masonry vault, but in fact supported a timber roof.

Sometime after 1120—perhaps as late as 1130–35—Saint-Étienne's original timber roof was replaced by a masonry vault. The masons joined two bays to form square bays defined by the heavy piers (that is, the piers with the pilaster-backed columns) and by six-part vaults. The six-part vault combines two systems—transverse ribs crossing the space at every pier and ribbed groin vaults springing from the heavy piers. To accommodate the lower masonry vault under the timber roof, the triple arches of the clerestory were reduced to two.

Soaring height was a Norman architectural goal, and the façade towers continue the tradition of church towers begun by Carolingian builders. This preference for verticality is seen in the west façade of Saint-Étienne, which was designed at the end of the eleventh century, probably about 1096–1100 (FIG. 15–23). Wall buttresses divide the façade into three vertical sections corresponding to the nave and side aisles. Narrow **stringcourses** (unbroken horizontal moldings) at each window level suggest the three stories of the building's nave elevation. This concept of reflecting the plan and elevation of the church in the design of the façade was later adopted by Gothic builders. Norman builders, with their brilliant techni-

The eye runs smoothly down the length of the vault. In the transept, the builders divided the square bays in two to produce four-part ribbed vaults over rectangular bays. They also experimented with buttresses that resembled later Gothic systems (see Chapter 16). Although the buttresses were not a success, the germ of the idea was there.

THE CHURCH OF SAINT-ÉTIENNE, CAEN. The Benedictine abbey church of Saint-Étienne (FIG. 15–21) in Caen was originally built as a wooden-roofed basilica nearly a generation before Durham Cathedral. William the Conqueror, while still only Duke of Normandy, had founded the monastery and had begun the construction of its church before 1066. He dedicated the church in 1077 and was buried there in 1087. His wife, Queen Matilda, established an abbey for women and built a church dedicated to the Trinity.

William's original church provides the core of the building we see today (FIG. 15–22). The nave wall has a three-part elevation (nave arcade, gallery, and clerestory) with exceptionally wide arches both in the nave arcade and the gallery. At the clerestory level, an arcade of three small arches on colonettes runs in front of the windows, creating a passageway within the thickness of the wall. On each pier, engaged columns alternate with columns backed by pilasters. They

15–22 | COMPOSITE DIAGRAM OF CHURCH OF SAINT-ÉTIENNE, CAEN
Showing original 11th-century timber roof and later 12th-century six-part vault inserted under the roof.

15–23 | **CHURCH OF SAINT-ÉTIENNE, CAEN**
Normandy, France. c. 1060–77; façade c.
1096–1100; spires 13th century.

cal innovations and sophisticated designs, prepared the way for the architectural feats accomplished by Gothic architects in the twelfth and thirteenth centuries. The elegant spires topping the tall towers are examples of the Norman Gothic style.

Secular Architecture: Dover Castle, England

The need to provide for personal security in a period of constant local warfare and political upheaval, as well as the desire to glorify the house of the lord and his saints, meant that communities used much of their resources for churches and castles. Fully garrisoned, castles were sometimes as large as cities. In the twelfth century, Dover Castle, safeguarding the coast of England from invasion, was a magnificent demonstration of military power (FIG. 15–24). It illustrates the way in which a key defensive position developed over the centuries. The Romans had built a lighthouse on the point where the English Channel separating England and France narrows. The Anglo-Saxons added a church (both lighthouse and church can be seen behind the tower, surrounded by the remains of earthen walls). In the early Middle Ages, earthworks topped by wooden walls provided a measure of security, and a wooden tower signified an important administrative building and residence. The advantage of fire-resistant walls was obvious, and in the twelfth and thirteenth centuries, military engineers replaced the timber tower and palisades with stone walls. They added the massive stone towers we see today.

The **Great Tower**, as it was called in the Middle Ages (but later known as a **keep** in England, and **donjon** in France), stood in a courtyard (called the **bailey**) surrounded by additional walls. Ditches outside the walls added to the height of the walls. In some castles, ditches were filled with water to form **moats**. A gatehouse—perhaps with a drawbridge—controlled the entrance. In all castles the bailey was filled with buildings, the most important of which was the lord's hall, which was used for a court and for feasts and ceremonial occasions. Timber buildings housed troops, servants, and animals. Barns and workshops, ovens and wells were also needed since the castle had to be self-sufficient.

If enemies broke through the outer walls, the castle's defenders retreated to the Great Tower. The landwalls of Constantinople (SEE FIG. 7–24) had demonstrated the value of defense in depth. In the thirteenth century, the builders at Dover doubled the walls and strengthened them with towers, even though the castle's position on cliffs overlooking the sea made scaling the walls nearly impossible. The garrison could be forced to surrender only by starving its occupants.

During Dover Castle's heyday improving agricultural methods and growing prosperity provided the resources for increased building activity in Europe. Churches, castles, halls, houses, barns, and monasteries proliferated. The buildings that still stand—despite the ravages of weather, vandalism, neglect, and war—testify to the technical skills of the builders and the power, local pride, and faith of the patrons.

15–24 | **DOVER CASTLE**
Dover, England

Air view overlooking the harbor and the English Channel. Center distance: Roman lighthouse tower, rebuilt Anglo-Saxon church, earthworks. Center: Norman Great Tower, surrounding earthworks and wall, twelfth century. Outerwalls, thirteenth century. Modern buildings have red tile roofs. The castle was used in World War II and is now a museum.

THE DECORATION OF BUILDINGS

Like Cluny and unlike the severe churches of the Cistercians, many Romanesque churches have a remarkable variety of painting and sculpture. Christ Enthroned in Majesty in heaven may be carved over the entrance or painted in the half-dome of the apse. Stories of Jesus among the people or images of the lives and the miracles of the saints cover the walls; the art also reflects the increasing importance accorded to the Virgin Mary. Depictions of the prophets, kings, and queens of the Old Testament symbolically foretell people and events in the New Testament, but also represented are contemporary bishops, abbots, other noble patrons, and even

ordinary folk. A profusion of monsters, animals, plants, geometric ornament, allegorical figures such as Lust and Greed, and depictions of real and imagined buildings surround the major works of sculpture. The elect rejoice in heaven with the angels; the damned suffer in hell, tormented by demons; biblical and historical tales come alive, along with scenes of everyday life. All these events seem to take place in a contemporary medieval setting.

Inside the building paintings covered walls, vaults, and even piers and columns with complex imagery that combined biblical narratives and Christian symbolism with legends, folklore, and history.

Architectural Sculpture

Architecture dominated the arts in the Romanesque period—not only because it required the material and human resources of an entire community but because, by providing the physical context for sculpture and painting, it also established the size and shape of images. Sculptured façades and large and richly carved portals with symbolic and didactic images are a significant innovation in Romanesque art.

The most important imagery is usually in the semicircular tympanum directly over the door. **Archivolts**—curved moldings composed of the wedge-shaped stone voussoirs of the arch—frame the tympanum. On both sides of the doors, the jambs and often a central pier (called the **trumeau**), which support the lintel and archivolts, may have figures or columns. The jambs form a shallow porch.

WILIGELMUS AT THE CATHEDRAL OF MODENA. The spirit of ancient Rome pervades the sculpture of Romanesque Italy. The sculptor Wiligelmus may have been inspired by ancient sarcophagi still visible in cemeteries when he carved the horizontal reliefs with heavy-set figures across the west façade of Modena Cathedral, c. 1099. Wiligelmus's work is some of the earliest narrative sculpture in Italy. He took his subjects from Genesis, beginning with the Creation and the Fall of Adam and Eve (FIG. 15–25). On the far left, God, in a mandorla supported by angels, appears in two persons as both the creator and Christ, identified by a cruciform halo. He brings Adam to life, then brings forth Eve from Adam's side. On the right, Adam and Eve cover their genitals in shame as they greedily eat the fruit of the forbidden tree, around which the serpent twists.

Wiligelmus's deft carving gives these low-relief figures a strong three-dimensionality. Adding to their tangibility is Wiligelmus's use of a miniature arcade to establish a stagelike setting. The rocks on which Adam lies, or the fatal tree of Paradise, seem like stage props for the figures. Adam and Eve stand awkwardly, with pot bellies and skinny arms and legs, but they exude a sense of life and personality that gives an emotional depth to the narrative. Bright paint, now almost all lost, increased the impact of the sculpture. An inscription reads: "Among sculptors, your work shines forth, Wiligelmus." This self-confidence turned out to be justified. Wiligelmus's influence can be traced throughout Italy and as far away as the Cathedral of Lincoln in England.

15–25 | Wiligelmus **CREATION AND FALL, WEST FAÇADE, MODENA CATHEDRAL**
Modena, Emilia, Italy. Building begun 1099; sculpture c. 1099. Height approx. 3′ (92 cm).

THE PRIORY CHURCH OF SAINT-PIERRE, MOISSAC. The Cluniac priory of Saint-Pierre at Moissac was a major pilgrimage stop and Cluniac administrative center on the route to Santiago de Compostela. The original shrine at the site was reputed to have existed in the Carolingian period. After joining the congregation of Cluny in 1047, the monastery prospered from the donations of pilgrims and the local nobility, as well as from its control of shipping on the nearby Garonne River. Moissac's monks launched an ambitious building campaign, and much of the sculpture from the cloister (c. 1100) and the church portal and porch (1100–30) has survived. Abbot Ansquetil (ruled 1085–1115) built the cloister and portal, which must have been finished by his death in 1115, and Abbot Roger (c. 1115–31) added a porch with sculpture. The sculpture of the portal represents a genuine departure from earlier works in both the quantity and the quality of the carving.

The image of Christ in Majesty dominates the huge tympanum (FIG. 15–26). The scene combines the description of the Second Coming of Christ in Chapters 4 and 5 of the Book of Revelation with Old Testament prophecies. A

15–27 | **TRUMEAU, SOUTH PORTAL, PRIORY CHURCH OF SAINT-PIERRE, MOISSAC**
Tarn-et-Garonne, France. c. 1115.

15–26 | **SOUTH PORTAL AND PORCH, PRIORY CHURCH OF SAINT-PIERRE, MOISSAC**
Tarn-et-Garonne, France. c. 1115.

gigantic Christ, like an awe-inspiring Byzantine Pantokrator, stares down at the viewer as he blesses. He is enclosed by a mandorla, and a cruciform halo rings his head. Four winged creatures symbolizing the evangelists—Matthew the Man (upper left), Mark the Lion (lower left), Luke the Ox (lower right), and John the Eagle (upper right)—frame Christ on either side, each holding a scroll or book representing his Gospel. Two elongated seraphim (angels) stand one on either side of the central group, each holding a scroll. Rippling bands represent the waves of the "sea of glass like crystal" (Revelation 4:6), defining three registers in which twenty-four elders with "gold crowns on their heads" are seated holding either a harp or a gold bowl of incense (Revelation 4:4 and 5:8). According to the medieval view, the elders were the kings and prophets of the Old Testament and, by extension, the ancestors and precursors of Christ.

The figures in the tympanum relief reflect a hierarchy of scale and location. Christ, the largest figure, sits at the top center, the spiritual heart of the scene. The evangelists and angels are smaller, and the elders, farthest from Christ, are roughly one-third his size. Despite this formality and the limitations forced on them by the architecture, the sculptors achieve variety by turning and twisting the gesturing figures, shifting their poses off-center, and avoiding rigid symmetry or mirror images. Foliate and geometric ornament covers every surface. Monstrous heads in the lower corners of the tympanum spew ribbon scrolls, and other creatures appear at each end of the lintel, their tongues growing into ropes encircling acanthus rosettes.

Two side jambs and a central trumeau support the weight of the lintel and tympanum. These elements have scalloped profiles (a motif inspired by Islamic art) that control the design of the sculpture. Saint Peter (holding his attribute, the key to the gates of heaven) and the prophet Isaiah are carved on the jambs. Peter, a tall, thin saint, steps away from the door but twists back to look through it. His shoulder, knees, and feet reflect the pointed cusps of the scalloped jamb; the vertical folds of his cloak repeat the framing colonettes. The trumeau depicts crisscrossing pairs of lions. A tall, thin figure of Saint Paul is on the left, and an Old Testament prophet, usually identified as Jeremiah, twists toward the viewer, with his legs crossed in the walking pose seen at Silos (FIG. 15–27). The sculptors placed him skillfully within the constraints of the scalloped trumeau; his head, pelvis, knees, and feet fall on the pointed cusps. This decorative scalloping as well as the rosettes, lions, and ribbons reveal a knowledge of Islamic art. Moissac was on the road to Compostella. Furthermore, it was being built shortly after the First Crusade when many Europeans first encountered the Islamic art and architecture of the Holy Land. People from the region around Moissac participated in the Crusade and presumably brought Eastern objects and ideas home with them.

GISLEBERTUS AND THE LAST JUDGMENT AT AUTUN. A different pictorial style is seen in the Last Judgment at Autun on the main portal of the Cathedral of Saint-Lazare (FIG. 15–28).

15–28 | Gislebertus **LAST JUDGMENT, TYMPANUM ON WEST PORTAL, CATHEDRAL (ORIGINALLY ABBEY CHURCH) OF SAINT-LAZARE, AUTUN**
Burgundy, France. c. 1120–30 or 1130-45.

15–29 | CAPITAL: SUICIDE OF JUDAS. CATHEDRAL OF SAINT-LAZARE, AUTUN Burgundy, France. c. 1125.

Christ has returned to judge the cowering, naked human souls at his feet. The damned writhe in torment, while the saved enjoy serene bliss. The inscribed message reads: "May this terror frighten those who are bound by worldly error. It will be true just as the horror of these images indicates" (translated by Petzold). A lengthy inscription identifies the Autun tympanum as the work of Gislebertus, who oversaw the sculpture and probably did much of the work himself.

The overall effect of the tympanum is less consciously balanced than the pattern-filled composition at Moissac. Christ dominates the composition, but the surrounding figures are arranged in less regular compartmentalized tiers than seen at Moissac. Thinner and taller, stretched out and bent at sharp angles, the stylized figures are powerfully expressive. They convey the terrifying urgency of the moment as they swarm around the magisterially detached Christ. Delicate weblike engraving on the robes seems inspired by metalwork or manuscript illumination. The scene is filled with human interest. Some angels trumpet the call to the Day of Judgment; others help the souls rise from their tombs and line up to await judgment. In the bottom register, two pilgrims—one to Jerusalem and one to Santiago de Compostela—can be identified by the cross and scallop-shell badges on their satchels. But, ominously, a pair of giant, pincerlike hands

scoops up a soul at the far right of the lintel. Above these hands, the archangel Michael competes with devils for souls being weighed on the scale. Michael shelters some souls in the folds of his robe and seems to be jiggling the scales. Another angel boosts a saved soul into heaven, bypassing the gate and Saint Peter. By far the most riveting players in the drama are the grotesquely decomposed, screaming demons grabbing at terrified souls and trying to cheat by pushing down souls and yanking the scales to favor damnation.

HISTORIATED CAPITALS. An important Romanesque contribution to architectural decoration was the ingenious compression of instructive narrative scenes into the geometric confines of column capitals, a feature known as the **historiated capital**. Gislebertus developed this idea into a series of personalized narratives, such as **THE SUICIDE OF JUDAS** (FIG. 15–29), illustrating the Bible and the lives of the saints.

Corinthian capitals (see Introduction, Fig. 3) from among the ruins of Roman cities inspired the design of Romanesque capitals, on which spiky acanthus leaves and ribbonlike volutes surround an inverted bell shape and support a wide abacus. The Romanesque sculptors such as Gislebertus, however, turned the capital into an educational or symbolic narrative.

THE ROLE OF WOMEN IN THE INTELLECTUAL AND SPIRITUAL LIFE OF THE TWELFTH CENTURY

One would expect women to have a subordinate position in this hierarchical, military society. On the contrary, aristocratic women took responsibility for managing estates in their male relatives' frequent absences during wars or while attending to duties at court. Among peasants and artisans, women and men worked side by side.

Women also achieved positions of authority and influence as the heads of religious communities. Convents of educated women lived under the direction of abbesses such as Hildegard of Bingen and Herrad of Landsberg, abbess of Hohenburg in Alsace. The original illuminated manuscripts containing their writings did not survive the wars of the nineteenth and twentieth centuries, but copies exist.

The *Liber Scivias* by Hildegard of Bingen (1098–1179) opened with a portrait of the author at work. Born into an aristocratic German family, Hildegard transcended the barriers that limited most medieval women. She began serving as leader of her convent in 1136, and about 1147 she founded a new convent near Bingen. With the assistance of the monk Volmar, she began to record her visions in a book, *Scivias* (from the Latin *scite vias lucis*, "know the ways of the light"). The opening page of this copy shows Hildegard receiving a flash of divine insight, represented by the tongues of flame encircling her head. She wrote, "a fiery light, flashing intensely, came from the open vault of heaven and poured through my whole brain." She records her visions on tablets, while Volmar, her scribe, writes to her dictation. Hildegard also wrote on medicine and natural science. A major figure in the intellectual life of her time, she corresponded with emperors, popes, and the Cistercian abbot Bernard of Clairvaux.

Herrad (1130–96), the Abbess of Hohenburg, wrote an encyclopaedia—*Hortus Deliciarum (The Garden of Delights)*—in which she combined a history of the world from its creation to the Last Judgment with a compendium of all human knowledge, using almost 1200 quotations from scholars as well as sermons and poems. For example, when she told the story of the Magi following the star to Bethlehem she added a discussion of astronomy and astrology. She also devised a complex scheme of illustrations as part of her educational program. She explained her intentions: "Like a small active bee, I have extracted the sugar of the flowers of divine and philosophical literature. . ." for "my sisters in Jesus." Today, such books guide scholars who try to decode the meaning of medieval artworks.

HILDEGARD AND VOLMAR, LIBER SCIVIAS
1165–75. Facsimile frontispiece.

In the *Suicide of Judas* from Autun, flat split-leaf acanthus fronds curl up to form volutes and establish the architectural frame. Two demons string up Judas's limp ugly corpse. The strange noose they use has been identified as the bag of money Judas accepted for his betrayal of Christ or as a wrestler's belt, the symbol of useless worldly physical strength. The screaming demons with contorted faces, vicious teeth, and flaming hair embody evil. With scrawny limbs, bloated bodies, and upswept wings they reinforce the shape of the capital. The sculptors achieve a crispness and clarity by slightly undercutting the forms so that the edges are sharpened by shadows. This clarity was important when the capitals had to be seen at a distance.

Mosaics and Murals

Church interiors were not the bare expanses of stone we see today. Throughout Europe colorful murals glowed in flickering candlelight amid clouds of incense. Wall painting was subject to the same influences as the other visual arts; that is, the painters were inspired by illuminated manuscripts, or ivories, or enamels in their treasuries or libraries. Some must have seen examples of Byzantine art; others had Carolingian or even Early Christian models. During the Romanesque period, painted decoration largely replaced mosaics on the walls of churches. This change occurred at least partly because the growing demand by the greater number of churches led to the use of less expensive materials and techniques.

15–30 | **CHRIST IN MAJESTY**
Detail of apse, Church of San Climent, Taull, Catalunya, Spain.
1123. Museu Nacional d'Art de Catalunya, Barcelona.

THE MOSAICS OF SAN CLEMENTE, ROME. The apse of San Clemente, richly decorated with colored marbles and a gold mosaic in the semidome, recalls the lost mosaics of the church at Monte Cassino, south of Rome. Abbot Desiderius built a new headquarters Church for the Benedictine Order that he intended should rival the churches of Constantinople. He brought artists from Byzantium to create mosaics and to teach the technique to his most talented monks. In Rome, where Desiderius ruled briefly as Pope Victor III, mosaics were added to a few chapels and churches in spite of the difficulty getting the expensive materials and specialized artists. In the church of San Clemente (SEE FIG. 15–14), the mosaics seem to recapture the past, with the trees and rivers of Paradise, a vine scroll inhabited by figures surrounding the crucified Christ. Mary and Saint John stand below, and twelve doves on the cross and twelve sheep represent the apostles. Stags (symbols of resurrection) drink from streams flowing from the cross, the tree of life in Paradise.

Although the iconography of the mosaic is Early Christian, the style and technique are clearly Romanesque. The artists made no attempt to create an illusion of the natural world. The hard dark outlines and bright flat colors turn the figures into ornamental patterns typical of the twelfth century. The doves on the cross, the repeated circular vine scrolls ending in bunches of leaves and flowers, even the animals, birds, and humans among the leaves are reduced to elements in a formal design. When compared with Early Christian and Byzantine mosaics (see Chapter 7), the mosaic seems evidence of a decline in standards of craftsmanship. However, the irregular setting of tesserai in visibly rough plaster is intentional and actually heightens the color and increases the glitter of the gold. Light reflects off the irregular surface of the apse, causing the mosaic to sparkle.

These rich surfaces continue through the choir and across the pavement in San Clemente. As in other Italian churches of the period, inlaid geometric patterns in marble embellish the floors in an ornamental style known as Cosmati work, after the family who perfected the technique.

MURALS IN TAULL (TAHULL), CATALUNYA, SPAIN. Artists in Catalunya brilliantly combined the Byzantine style with their own Mozarabic and classical heritage. In the Church of San Climent in Taull (Tahull), consecrated in 1123, a magnificently expressive **CHRIST IN MAJESTY** fills the curve of the half-dome of the apse (FIG. 15–30). Christ's powerful presence recalls the Byzantine depiction of Christ Pantokrator, ruler and judge of the world. The iconography is traditional: Christ sits within a mandorla; the Greek letters alpha and omega hang from strings beside his head. He holds the open Gospel inscribed "*Ego sum lux mundi*" ("I am the light of the world," John 8:12). Four lively angels, each grasping an evangelist's symbol, appear beside him. In the arcade at Christ's feet are six apostles and the Virgin Mary.

The columns with stylized capitals have wavy lines of paint indicating marble shafts.

The San Climent artist was one of the finest Spanish painters of the Romanesque period, but where he came from and where he learned his art is unknown. His use of elongated oval faces, large staring eyes, and long noses, as well as the placement of figures against flat bands of color and his use of heavy outlines, reflect the Mozarabic style (Chapter 14). At the same time his work shows the prevailing influence of Byzantine art, although he simplified the style. His painting technique—modeling from light to dark—is Byzantine, accomplished through repeated colored lines of varying width in three shades—dark, medium, and light. But instead of blending the colors, he delights in the striped effect. Details of faces, hair, hands, and muscles also become elegant patterns. The intensity of the colors was created by building up many thin coats of paint, a technique called **glazing**.

MURALS IN THE CHURCH OF SAINT-SAVIN-SUR-GARTEMPE, FRANCE. The paintings in the Church of Saint-Savin (SEE FIG. 15–15) have survived almost intact. The nave vault has scenes from the Old and New Testaments, and the lives of two local saints, Savin and Cyprian, provide imagery for the crypt. The narthex was also painted, as were the columns.

The nave was built c. 1095–1115, and the painters seem to have followed the masons immediately in order to use the same scaffolding. Perhaps this intimate involvement with the building process accounts for the vividness with which they portrayed the biblical story of the **TOWER OF BABEL** (FIG. 15–31).

According to the account in Genesis (11:1–9), God punished the prideful people who tried to build a tower to heaven by scattering them and making their languages mutually unintelligible. The tower in the painting is a medieval structure, reflecting the practice of depicting distant or legendary events in contemporary settings. Workers haul heavy stone blocks to the tower, lifting them to masons on the top with a hoist. The giant Nimrod, on the far right, simply hands over the blocks. The paintings recall the energy and narrative drama of early medieval art. God confronts the people. He steps away from them even as he turns back to chastise them. The scene's dramatic action, large figures, strong outlines, broad areas of color, and simplified modeling all help make it intelligible to a viewer looking up at it in the dim light from far below. The painters did not use the wet-plaster fresco technique favored in Italy for its long-lasting colors, but they did moisten the walls before painting, which allowed some absorption of pigments into the plaster, making them more permanent than paint applied to a dry surface. Several artists, or teams of artists, worked on the church.

15–31 | **TOWER OF BABEL**
Detail of painting in nave vault, Abbey Church of Saint-Savin-sur-Gartempe, Poitou, France. c. 1115.

THE CLOISTER CRAFTS

Monastic *scriptoria* and other workshops continued to dominate the production of works of art, although more and more secular artists could be found producing high-quality pieces in the towns and in workshops attached to courts. The cloister crafts include a wide range of media from illuminated manuscripts to goldsmithing, ivory carving, and embroidery; and the designation "cloister crafts" replaces the term "decorative arts," which suggests less important work. In the Middle Ages small precious objects, as well as works in readily available material like wood, often carried profound meaning. Neither the *Mayestat Batlló* nor the *Mary as the Throne of Wisdom* can be categorized as "decorative."

Portable Sculpture

Painted wood was commonly used when abbey and local parish churches of limited means commissioned statues. Wood was not only cheap, it was lightweight, a consideration since these devotional images were frequently carried in processions.

15–32 | **CRUCIFIX (MAJESTAT BATLLÓ)**
Catalunya, Spain. Mid-12th century. Polychromed wood, height approx. 37¾″ (96 cm). Museu Nacional d'Art de Catalunya, Barcelona.

The cross was hung near the entrance or the altar and might be carried in processions.

15–33 | **VIRGIN AND CHILD**
Auvergne region, France. Late 12th century.
Oak with polychromy, height 31"
(78.7 cm).
The Metropolitan Museum of Art,
New York.

Gift of J. Pierpont Morgan, 1916 (16.32.194)

CHRIST ON THE CROSS (*MAJESTAT BATLLÓ*). Sculptors—image makers—found sources and inspiration in Byzantine art. The image of Jesus in a mid–twelfth-century crucifix from Catalunya, known as the **MAJESTAT BATLLÓ (FIG. 15–32)**, recalls the Volto Santo (Holy Face) of Lucca, thought to have been brought from Palestine to Italy in the eighth century. Legend had it that the sculpture had been carved by Nicodemus, who helped Joseph of Arimathea remove the body of Christ from the cross.

The Byzantine robed Christ, rather than the nude, tortured Jesus of Byzantine Daphni (SEE FIG. 7–43) or the Ottonian Gero Crucifix (SEE FIG. 14–29), inspired the Catalan sculptor. Christ wears royal robes that emphasize his kingship (SEE THE *Rabbula Gospels*, FIG. 7–36), although Jesus's bowed head, downturned mouth, and heavy-lidded eyes con-

vey a sense of deep sadness or contemplation. His long, medallion-patterned tunic has pseudo-kufic inscriptions—designs meant to resemble Arabic script—on the hem, a reminder that silks from Islamic Spain were highly prized in Europe at this time. Islamic textiles were widely used as cloths of honor hung behind thrones and around altars to designate royal and sacred places. They were used to wrap relics and to cover altars with apparently no concern for their Muslim source.

MARY AS THE THRONE OF WISDOM. Any image of Mary seated on a throne and holding the Christ Child on her lap is known as "The Throne of Wisdom." In a well-preserved example in painted wood dating from the second half of the twelfth century (FIG. 15–33), Mother and Child are frontally

THE BAYEUX TAPESTRY

Rarely has art spoken more vividly than in **THE BAYEUX TAPESTRY**, a strip of embroidered linen that tells the history of the Norman conquest of England. On October 14, 1066, William, Duke of Normandy, after a hard day of fighting, became William the Conqueror, king of England. The story told in embroidery is a straightforward justification of the action, told with the intensity of an eyewitness account: The Anglo-Saxon nobleman Harold initially swears his feudal allegiance to William, Duke of Normandy, but later betraying his feudal vows, he accepts the crown of England for himself. Unworthy to be king, he dies in battle at the hands of William and the Normans.

At the beginning of the Bayeux story, Harold is a heroic figure. Then events overtake him. After his coronation, cheering crowds celebrate—until a flaming star crosses the sky. (We now know that it was Halley's Comet, which appeared shortly after Harold's coronation and evidently reached astonishing brightness.) The Anglo-Saxons see the comet as a portent of disaster; the crowd cringes and gestures at this ball of fire with a flaming tail, and a man rushes to inform the new king. Harold slumps on his throne in the Palace of Westminster. He foresees what

MESSENGERS SIGNAL THE APPEARANCE OF A COMET (HALLEY'S COMET), THE BAYEUX TAPESTRY   Norman–Anglo-Saxon embroidery from Canterbury, Kent, England, or Bayeux, Normandy, France. c. 1066–82. Linen with wool, height 20″ (50.8 cm). Centre Guillaume le Conquérant, Bayeux, France.

is to come: Below his feet is his vision of a ghostly fleet of Norman ships already riding the waves. William, Duke of Normandy, has assembled the last great Viking flotilla on the Normandy coast.

The designer was a skillful storyteller who used a staggering number of images. In the fifty surviving scenes are more than 600 human figures; 700 horses, dogs, and other creatures; and 2,000 inch-high letters. Perhaps he or she was assisted by William's half-brother, Bishop Odo, who had fought beside William. As a man of God, he used a club, not a sword, to avoid spilling blood.

BISHOP ODO BLESSING THE FEAST, THE BAYEUX TAPESTRY
Norman–Anglo-Saxon embroidery from Canterbury, Kent, England, or Bayeux, Normandy, France. c. 1066–82. Linen with wool, height 20″ (50.8 cm). Centre Guillaume le Conquérant, Bayeux, France.

Odo and William are feasting before the battle. Attendants bring in roasted birds on skewers, placing them on a makeshift table made of the knights' shields set on trestles. The diners, summoned by the blowing of a horn, gather at a curved table laden with food and drink. Bishop Odo—seated at the center, head and shoulders above William to his right—blesses the meal while others eat. The kneeling servant in the middle proffers a basin and towel so that the diners may wash their hands. The man on Odo's left points impatiently to the next event, a council of war between William (now the central and tallest figure), Odo, and a third man labeled "Rotbert," probably Robert of Mortain, another of William's half-brothers.

Translation of text: ". . . and here the servants (*ministra*) perform their duty. /Here they prepare the meal (*prandium*) /and here the bishop blesses the food and drink (*cibu et potu*). Bishop Odo. William. Robert."

The tragic drama has spoken to audiences over the centuries. It is the story of a good man who, like Shakespeare's *Macbeth*, is overcome by his lust for power and so betrays his king. The images of this Norman invasion also spoke to people during the darkest days of World War II. When the Allies invaded Nazi-occupied Europe in June 1944, they took the same route in reverse from England to beaches on the coast of Normandy. The *Bayeux Tapestry* still speaks to us of the folly of human greed and ambition and of two battles that changed the course of history.

EMBROIDERY

The *Bayeux Tapestry* is really embroidery, not tapestry. In tapestry, colored threads are woven to form the image or pattern; embroidery consists of stitches applied to a woven ground. The embroiderers, probably Anglo-Saxon women, worked in tightly twisted wool that was dyed in eight colors. They used only two stitches: the quick, overlapping stem stitch that produced a slightly jagged line or outline, and the time-consuming laid-and-couched work used to form blocks of color. The embroiderer first "laid" a series of long, parallel covering threads; then anchored them with a second layer of regularly spaced crosswise stitches; and finally tacked all the strands down with tiny "couching" stitches. Some of the laid-and-couched work was done in contrasting colors to achieve particular effects. Some of the coloring was fanciful; for example, some horses have legs in four different colors. Skin and other light-toned areas were represented by the bare linen cloth that formed the ground of the work. The embroiderers of the *Bayeux Tapestry* probably followed drawings provided by a Norman, who may have been an eyewitness to some of the events depicted.

DETAIL, BISHOP ODO BLESSING FEAST, THE BAYEUX TAPESTRY
Norman–Anglo-Saxon embroidery from Canterbury, Kent, England, or Bayeux, Normandy, France. c. 1066–82. Linen with wool, embroidery, height 20″ (50.8 cm). Centre Guillaume le Conquérant, Bayeux, France.

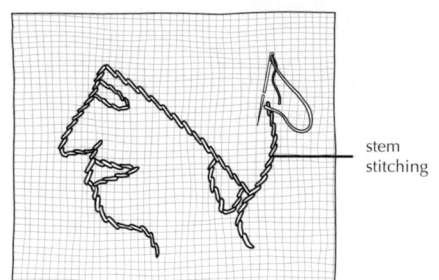

stem stitching

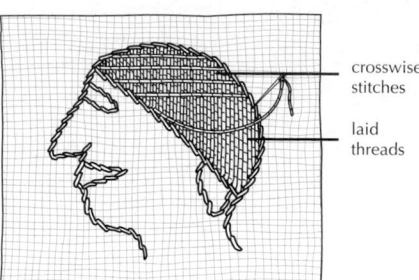

crosswise stitches

laid threads

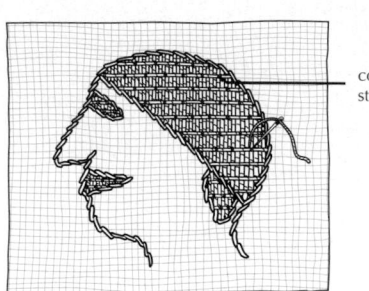

couching stitches

erect, as rigid as they are regal. Mary's thronelike bench symbolized the lion-throne of Solomon, the Old Testament king who represented earthly wisdom in the Middle Ages. Mary, as Mother and "God-bearer" (the Byzantine Theotokos), gave Jesus his human nature. She forms a throne on which he sits in majesty. She also represents the Church. Although the Child's hands are missing, we can assume that the small but adult Jesus held a book—the Word of God—in his left hand and raised his right hand in blessing.

A statue of the Virgin and Child, like the sculpture here, could have played a role in the liturgical dramas being added to church services at that time. At the Feast of the Epiphany, which in the Western Church celebrates the arrival of the Magi to pay homage to the baby Jesus, participants representing the Magi acted out their journey by searching through the church for the newborn king. The roles of Mary and Jesus were "acted" by the sculpture, which the Magi discovered on the altar. In such simple ways theater and the performing arts returned to the West.

Metalwork

Three geographical areas—the Rhineland, the Meuse River valley, and German Saxony—continued to supply the best metalwork for aristocratic and ecclesiastical patrons. Metalworkers in these areas drew on a variety of stylistic sources, including the work of contemporary Byzantine and Italian artists, as well as classical precedents as reinterpreted by their Carolingian and Ottonian forebears.

TOMB OF RUDOLF OF SWABIA. In the late eleventh century, Saxon metalworkers, already known for their large-scale bronze casting, began making bronze tomb effigies (portraits of the deceased). The oldest known bronze tomb effigy is that of **KING RUDOLF OF SWABIA** (**FIG. 15–34**), who died in battle in 1080, having sided with the pope against the emperor during the Investiture Controversy. The spurs on his oversized feet identify him as a heroic warrior, and he holds a scepter and cross-surmounted orb, emblems of Christian kingship. Although the tomb is in the Cathedral of Merseburg, in Saxony, the effigy has been attributed to an artist originally from the Rhine Valley. Nearly life-size, it has fine linear detailing in **niello,** an incised design filled with a black alloy. The king's head has been modeled in high relief and stands out from his body like a detached shield.

REINER OF HUY. Renier of Huy (Huy is near Liège in present-day Belgium) worked in the Mosan region under the profound influence of ancient art as interpreted by Carolingian and Byzantine forebears. He was also influenced by the humanistic learning of Church scholars. Liege was called the "Athens of the North." Artists like Renier created a style that seems classical in its depiction of human figures with dignity, simplicity, and harmony (**FIG. 15–35**). Between 1107 and 1118 he cast a

15–34 | **TOMB COVER WITH EFFIGY OF RUDOLF OF SWABIA**
Saxony, Germany. c. 1080. Bronze with niello, approx. 6′5½ × 2′2½″ (1.97 × 0.68 m). Cathedral of Merseburg, Germany.

15–35 | Renier de Huy **BAPTISMAL FONT, NOTRE-DAME-AUX-FONTES**

Liege, France. 1107–18. Bronze, Height, 23⅝" (60 cm); diameter, 31¼" (79 cm). Now in the Church of St. Barthelemy, Liège.

bronze baptismal font for Notre-Dame-aux-Fonts in Liège (now in the Church of Saint Barthelemy) that was inspired by the basin carried by twelve oxen in Solomon's Temple in Jerusalem (I Kings 7:23–24). Christian philosophers identified the twelve oxen as the twelve apostles and the basin as the baptismal font. On the sides of the font, Renier placed images of Saint John the Baptist, preaching and baptizing Christ, Saint Peter baptizing Cornelius, and Saint John the Evangelist baptizing the philosopher Crato. Renier constructs sturdy idealized bodies—nude or with clinging drapery—that move and gesture with convincing reality. His intuitive understanding of anatomy required close observation of the people around him. These figures also convey a sense of space, however shallow, where landscape is reduced to rippling ground lines, a few miniature trees used to separate the scenes, and waves of water rising (in Byzantine fashion) to discreetly cover nude figures. Renier's bronze sculptures demonstrate the survival of a classical and humanistic art in northern Europe.

Illustrated Books

Illustrated books played a key role in the transmission of artistic styles and other cultural information from one region to another. The output of books increased dramatically in the twelfth century, despite the labor and materials involved. Monastic and convent *scriptoria* continued to be the centers of production. The *scriptoria* sometimes also employed lay scribes and artists who traveled from place to place. In addition to the books needed for the church services, scribes produced scholarly commentaries, lives of saints, collections of letters, and even histories (SEE FIG. 15–2). Liturgical works were often large and lavish; other works were more modest, their embellishment confined to initial letters.

SAINT MATTHEW IN THE CODEX COLBERTINUS. The portrait of Saint Matthew from the **CODEX COLBERTINUS**, in contrast to the Hiberno-Saxon and Carolingian author portraits, is an entirely Romanesque conception. Like the sculptured pier figures of Silos (SEE FIG. 15–1), he stands within an architectural frame that controls his size and form (FIG. 15–36). A compact figure, he blesses and holds his book—rather than writing it. His dangling feet bear no weight. Blocks of color fill in outlines without giving the figure any three-dimensional quality. The evangelist is almost part of the text—the opening lines *Liber Generationes*.

The L of *Liber* (Book) is formed of plants and animals and is called a historiated initial. The L established the size and shape of the figurative panel, just as the architectural elements controlled the figures and composition in historiated capitals. The geometric underpinnings are filled with acanthus leaves and interlacing vines. Dogs or catlike animals and long-necked birds twist, claw, and bite each other and themselves while, in the center, two humans—one dressed and one nude—clamber up the letter. This manuscript was made in the region of Moissac at about the same time that sculptors were working on the abbey church.

THE HELLMOUTH IN THE WINCHESTER PSALTER. Religious texts dominated the work of the *scriptorium*. The **WINCHESTER PSALTER,** commissioned by the English king's brother, Henry of Blois, the Bishop of Winchester, contains a dramatic image of hell (FIG. 15–38). The page depicts the gaping jaws of hell, a monstrous head with dragons sprouting from its mane. Hell is filled with a tangled mass of sinners, among whom are kings and queens with golden crowns and monks with shaved heads, a daring reminder to powerful rulers and the clergy of the vulnerability of their own souls. Hairy, horned demons torment the lost souls, who tumble around in a dark void. An impassive and very elongated angel locks the door.

This vigorous narrative style had its roots in the Carolingian art of the *Utrecht Psalter* (SEE FIG. 14–18), a manuscript which was then in an English monastic library. Here, by comparison, the free pen work of the *Utrecht Psalter* has become controlled and hard. The composition of the intricate interlocking forms is carefully worked out using strong framing devices. For all its vicious energy, the page seems dominated by the ornamental frame.

15–36 | **ST. MATTHEW, FROM THE CODEX COLBERTINUS**
c. 1100. Tempera on vellum, 7½ × 4″ (19 × 10.16 cm).
Bibliothèque National Paris.

15–37 | **The Nun Guda** **BOOK OF HOMILIES**
West, Germany. Early 12th century. Ink on parchment.
Stadtund Universitäts-Bibliothek, Frankfurt, Germany.
MS. Barth. 42, folio 110v

THE GERMAN NUN GUDA. In another historiated initial, this one from Westphalia in Germany, the nun Guda has a more modest role. In a book of homilies (sermons), she inserted her self-portrait into the letter D and signed it as scribe and painter, "Guda, the sinful woman, wrote and illuminated this book" (FIG. 15–37). A simple drawing with a little color in the background, Guda's self-portrait is certainly not a major work of art. Its importance lies in its demonstration that women were far from anonymous workers in German *scriptoria* in the Romanesque period. Guda's image is the earliest signed self-portrait by a woman in Western Europe. Throughout the Middle Ages, women were involved in the production of books as authors, scribes, painters, and patrons.

ICI EST ENFERS ELIANGELS RI ENFEROOS LOS PORTES:

15–38 | THE MOUTH OF HELL,
WINCHESTER PSALTER
Winchester, England. c. 1150. Ink
and tempera on vellum, 12¾ × 9⅛″
(32.5 × 23 cm). The British
Library, London.

The inscription reads: "Here is hell and
the angels who are locking the doors."

There are fascinating parallels between the images of the mouth of Hell and the liturgical dramas—known in English as "mystery plays"—that were performed throughout Europe from the tenth through the sixteenth century. On stage, voracious Hellmouth props featured prominently, to the delight of audiences. Carpenters made the infernal beast's head out of wood, papier-mâché, fabric, and glitter and placed it over a trapdoor onstage. The wide jaws of the most ambitious Hellmouths, operated by winches and cables, opened and closed on the actors while emitting smoke, flames, foul smells, and loud noises. Hell scenes, with their often scatological humor, were by far the most popular parts of the plays.

CISTERCIAN DEVOTION TO MARY, THE TREE OF JESSE. The Cistercians were particularly devoted to the Virgin and are also credited with popularizing themes such as the Tree of Jesse as a device for showing her position as the last link in the genealogy connecting Jesus Christ to King David. (Jesse, the father of King David, was an ancestor of Mary and, through her, of Jesus.) Saint Jerome's **COMMENTARY ON ISA- IAH**, a manuscript made in the *scriptorium* of the Cistercian mother house at Cîteaux about 1125, contains an image known as the **TREE OF JESSE** (FIG. 15–39).

A monumental Mary, standing on the forking branches of the tree, dwarfs the sleeping patriarch, Jesse, a small tree trunk grows from his body. The Christ Child sits on her veiled right arm. The elongated but still human figure of Mary, emphasized by the vertical lines and V-shaped folds of the drapery and the soft colors, suggests a new sense of humanity. The artist has drawn, rather than painted, with colors, the subtle tints creating an image in keeping with Cistercian restraint. Following late Byzantine and Romanesque convention, Christ is portrayed as a miniature adult with his right hand raised in blessing. His cheek presses against Mary's, a display of affection similar to that shown in Byzantine icons of the time, like the *Virgin of Vladimir* (SEE FIG. 7–39). Mary holds a flowering sprig from the tree— another symbol for Christ.

The building held by the angel on the left equates Mary with the Church, and the crown held by the angel on the right is hers as Queen of Heaven. The dove above her halo represents the Holy Spirit. The jeweled hems of Mary's robes reflect her elevated status as Queen of Heaven. In the early decades of the twelfth century, Church doctrine came increasingly to stress the role of the Virgin Mary and the saints as intercessors who could plead for mercy on behalf of repentant sinners, and devotional images of Mary became increasingly popular during the later Romanesque period.

ataın lı
omelıe
ſ appella
ıcam ex
ıt dıdım̄
ıptum ē
otes. lod
decem
ꝛꝛ ſuo ſic
puncꝰ
15 . gꝛan
ntarıoꝛ
quo anım
rı quoꝛ
prurıs
ectantur.
ıas. xıı.
urr maıoꝛ
uco diſpu
ſımılıa ſt.
. Nolıu
ınſımplı
ı ıam ꝓ

15–39 | **PAGE WITH THE TREE OF JESSE,** *EXPLANATIO IN ISAIAM* **(SAINT JEROME'S COMMENTARY ON ISAIAH)**
Abbey of Cîteaux, Burgundy, France. c. 1125. Ink and tempera on vellum, 15 × 4¾" (38 × 12 cm). Bibliothèque Municipale, Dijon, France.
MS 129, fol. 4v

IN PERSPECTIVE

Wiligelmus, Roger, Gislebertus, Guda, and many anonymous women and men of the eleventh and twelfth centuries created a new art that—although based on the Bible and the lives of the saints—focused on human beings, their stories, and their beliefs. The artists worked on a monumental scale in painting, sculpture, and even embroidery, and their art moved from the cloister to the public walls of churches.

The sheer size of churches, the austere majesty of their towers, their interior spaces often covered with masonry vaults, their marvelously functional plans and elevations reflect a culture that saw the church as not only the Heavenly Jerusalem but as a bulwark against the ever-present demonic forces of evil. Equally mighty castle walls stood against actual earthly enemies. A source of local and even regional pride, the cathedral, monastic church, or castle required the most creative and highest quality work, and rulers and communities contributed material resources and labor.

Many Romanesque churches have a remarkable variety of painting and sculpture. Christ enthroned in majesty may be carved over the entrance or painted in the half-dome of the apse. Scenes from the life of Christ or images of the lives and the miracles of the saints cover the walls. Romanesque art also reflects the increasing importance accorded to the Virgin Mary. The elect rejoice in heaven; the damned suffer in hell. A profusion of monsters, animals, plants, geometric ornament, and depictions of real and imagined buildings fill the spaces. While the artists emphasized the spiritual and intellectual concerns of the Christian Church, they also began to observe and record what they saw around them. In so doing they laid the groundwork for the art of the Gothic period.

CATHEDRAL COMPLEX,
PISA
CATHEDRAL BEGUN 1063

DURHAM CATHEDRAL,
NAVE
1087–1133

TRUMEAU SOUTH PORTAL,
MOISSAC
c. 1115

CRUCIFIX (MAJESTAT BATLLÓ)
MID 12TH CENTURY

THE MOUTH OF HELL,
WINCHESTER PSLATER
c. 1150

1050

1100

1120

1140

1150

ROMANESQUE ART

◄ **Henry IV Rules Germany and Holy Roman Empire** 1056–1106

◄ **William of Normandy Invades England** c. 1066

◄ **Investiture Controversy** c. 1075

◄ **First Crusade** 1095–99
◄ **Cistercian Order Founded** 1098

◄ **Eleonor of Aquitaine Queen of France with Louis VII** 1137–52

◄ **Hildegard of Bingen Writes** *Scivias* c. 1141–1151

◄ **Second Crusade** 1147–49

◄ **Eleanor of Aquitaine Queen of England with Henry II** 1154–1189

16–1 | **INTERIOR, ABBEY CHURCH OF SAINT-DENIS, CHOIR** France. 1140–44; 1231–81.

CHAPTER SIXTEEN

GOTHIC ART OF THE TWELFTH AND THIRTEENTH CENTURIES

The twelfth-century Abbot Suger of Saint-Denis (1081–1151) was, according to his biographer Willelmus, "small of body and family, constrained by twofold smallness, [but] he refused, in his smallness, to be a small man" (cited in Panofsky, page 33). Educated at the monastery of Saint-Denis, near Paris, he became a powerful and trusted adviser to kings Louis VI and Louis VII. Suger governed France as regent when Louis VII and Eleanor of Aquitaine were absent from France during the Second Crusade (1147–49). He also built what many consider the first Gothic church in Europe.

After Suger was elected abbot of Saint-Denis, he was determined to build a new church to replace the old Carolingian one. He waged a successful campaign to gain both royal and popular support for his rebuilding plans. The old building, he pointed out, had become inadequate. With a touch of exaggeration, he claimed that the crowds of worshipers had become so great that women were being crushed and monks sometimes had to flee with their relics by jumping through windows.

The abbot had traveled widely—in France, the Rhineland, and Italy, including four trips to Rome—and so he was familiar with the latest architecture and sculpture of Romanesque Europe. As he began planning the new church,

he also turned for inspiration to books in the monastery's library, including the writings of a late fifth-century Greek philosopher known as the Pseudo-Dionysius, who had identified radiant light with divinity (see "Abbot Suger on the Value of Art," page 516). Seeing the name "Dionysius," Suger thought he was reading the work of Saint Denis, also known as Dionysius the Aeropagite, the first-century convert of Saint Paul (Acts 17:34). Not unreasonably, he adapted the concept of divine luminosity into the redesign of the church dedicated to Saint Denis. In the choir of the new church, he created "a circular string of chapels by virtue of which the whole [church] would shine with the wonderful and uninterrupted light of most luminous windows, pervading the interior beauty" (cited in Panofsky, page 101).

Although Abbot Suger died before he was able to finish rebuilding Saint-Denis, his presence remained: The cleric had himself portrayed in a sculpture at Christ's feet in the central portal and in a stained-glass window in the apse. Suger is remembered not for these portraits, however, but for his inspired departure from traditional architecture in order to achieve a flowing interior space and an all-pervasive, colored interior light. His innovation led to the widespread use of large stained-glass windows that bathed the inside walls of French churches with sublime washes of color (FIG. 16–1).

THE EMERGENCE OF THE GOTHIC STYLE

In the middle of the twelfth century, a distinctive new architecture known today as Gothic emerged in the Île-de-France, the French king's domain around Paris (MAP 16–1). The appearance there of a new style and building technique coincided with the emergence of the monarchy as a powerful centralizing force in France. Soon, the Gothic style spread throughout Western Europe, gradually displacing Romanesque forms while taking on regional characteristics inspired by those forms. The term *Gothic* was first used by Italians in the fifteenth and the sixteenth centuries when they disparagingly attributed the style to the Goths, the Germanic invaders who had destroyed the classical civilization of the Roman Empire that they so admired. In its own day the Gothic style was simply called the "modern" style or the "French" style.

Gothic architecture sought to express the aspiration for divinity through a quest for height and luminosity. Its soaring stonework and elegance of line, and the light, colors, and sense of transparency produced by its great expanses of glass—all became more pronounced over time. The style was adapted to all types of structures—including town halls, meeting houses, market buildings, residences, synagogues, and palaces—and its influence extended beyond architecture and architectural sculpture to painting and other mediums.

The Rise of Urban Life

The Gothic period was an era of both communal achievement and social change. Although Europe remained rural, towns gained increasing prominence. Some cities were freed from obligations to local feudal lords, and, as protected centers of commerce, became sources of wealth and power for the king. Intellectual life was also stimulated by the interaction of so many people living side by side. Universities in Bologna, Padua, Paris, Cambridge, and Oxford supplanted rural monastic schools as centers of learning. Brilliant teachers like Peter Abelard (1079–1142) drew crowds of students, and in the thirteenth century a Dominican professor from Italy, the theologian Thomas Aquinas (1225–74), made Paris

the intellectual center of Europe. This period saw the flowering of poetry and music as well as philosophy and theology.

As towns grew, they became increasingly important centers of artistic patronage. The production and sale of goods in many towns was controlled by **guilds.** Merchants and artisans of all types, from bakers to painters, formed these associations to advance their professional interests. Medieval guilds also played an important social role, safeguarding members' political interests, organizing religious celebrations, and looking after members and their families in times of trouble.

A town's walls enclosed streets, wells, market squares, shops, churches, and schools. Homes ranged from humble wood-and-thatch structures to imposing town houses of stone. Although wooden dwellings crowded together made fire an ever-present danger and although hygiene was rudimentary at best, towns fostered an energetic civic life. This strong communal identity was reinforced by public projects and ceremonies.

The Age of Cathedrals

Urban cathedrals, the seats of the ruling bishops, superseded rural monasteries as centers of religious patronage. So many of these churches were rebuilt between 1150 and 1400—often after fires—that the period has been called the "Age of Cathedrals." Cathedral precincts functioned almost as towns within towns. The great churches dominated their surroundings and were central fixtures of urban life (SEE FIG. 16–8). Their grandeur inspired admiration; their great expense and the intrusive power of their bishops inspired resentment. In the twelfth century, the laity experienced a decisive growth in religious involvement. In the early thirteenth century members of two new religious orders, the Franciscans and the Dominicans, known as mendicants (beggars) because they were meant to be free of wordly goods, went out into the world to preach and to minister to those in need, rather than secluding themselves in monasteries. (see "The Mendicant Orders: Franciscans and Dominicans" page 524).

Scholasticism and the Arts

The Crusades—which continued throughout the thirteenth century—and the trade that followed these military ventures

MAP 16–1 | **EUROPE IN THE GOTHIC ERA**

The Gothic period witnessed the emergence of England, France, Portugal, and Spain (Castile) as nations, while the pope wielded political as well as religious power throughout the West. The residents of cities rose to challenge the power of landed nobility.

brought Western Europeans into contact with the Byzantine and Islamic worlds, where—unlike in the West—literary works of classical antiquity had been preserved. The "rediscovery" of these works, particularly the philosophy of Aristotle, posed a challenge to Christian theology because they promoted rational inquiry rather than faith as the path to truth, and their conclusions did not always suit Church doctrine.

A system of reasoned analysis known as Scholasticism emerged to reconcile Christian theology with classical philosophy. Scholastic thinkers used a question-and-answer method of argument and arranged their ideas into logical outlines. Thomas Aquinas, the foremost Scholastic, applied Aristotelian logic to comprehend religion's supernatural aspects. His great philosophical work, the *Summa Theologica,* which attempted to reconcile rationalism with religious faith, has endured as a basis of Catholic thought to this day. Scholastic thinkers applied reasoned analysis to a vast range of subjects. Vincent de Beauvais, a thirteenth-century Parisian Dominican, organized his eighty-volume encyclopedia, the *Speculum Maius (Greater Mirror),* in which he intended to

encompass all human knowledge, into four categories: the Natural World, Doctrine, History, and Morality.

This all-pervasive intellectual approach had a profound influence on the arts. Like the philosophers, master builders saw divine order in geometric relationships and used these relationships as the underpinnings of architectural and sculptural programs. Sculptors and painters created naturalistic forms that reflected the combined idealism and analysis of Scholastic thought. Gothic religious imagery expanded to incorporate a wide range of subjects from the natural world, and like Romanesque imagery its purpose was to instruct and convince the viewer. In the Gothic cathedral, Scholastic logic intermingles with the mysticism of light and color to create for the worshiper the direct, emotional, ecstatic experience of the church as the embodiment of God's house, filled with divine light.

GOTHIC ART IN FRANCE

The initial flowering of the Gothic style took place in France against the backdrop of the growing power of the French Capetian monarchy. Louis VII (ruled 1137–80) and Philip

ABBOT SUGER ON THE VALUE OF ART

From *De administratione*, Ch. XXVII, Of the Cast and Gilded Doors:

Bronze casters having been summoned and sculptors chosen, we set up the main doors on which are represented the Passion of the Saviour and His Resurrection, or rather Ascension, with great cost and much expenditure for their gilding as was fitting for the noble porch. . . .

The verses on the door are these:

Whoever thou art, if thou seekest to extol the glory of these doors,
Marvel not at the gold and the expense but at the craftsmanship of the work,

Bright is the noble work; but being nobly bright, the work
Should lighten the minds, so that they may travel, through the true lights,
To the True Light where Christ is the true door,
In what manner it be inherent in this world the golden door defines:
The dull mind rises to truth through that which is material
And, in seeing this light, is resurrected from its former subversion.

Panofsky, Erwin. *Abbot Suger on the Abbey Church of St.-Denis and its Art Treasures*. 2nd ed. By Gerda Panofsky-Soergel. Princeton, NJ: Princeton University Press, 1979, pp. 47; 49.

Augustus (ruled 1180–1223) consolidated royal authority in the Île-de-France and began to exert control over powerful nobles in other regions. Before succeeding to the throne, Louis VII had married Eleanor of Aquitaine (heiress to all southwestern France). When the marriage was annulled, Eleanor took her lands and married Henry Plantagenet—count of Anjou, Duke of Normandy—who became King Henry II of England. The resulting tangle of conflicting claims kept France and England at odds for centuries. Through all the turmoil, the French kings continued to consolidate royal authority and to increase their domains and privileges at the expense of their vassals and the Church.

Early Gothic Architecture

The political events of the twelfth and thirteenth centuries were accompanied by energetic church building, often made necessary by the fires that constantly swept through towns. It has been estimated that during the Middle Ages several million tons of stone were quarried to build some eighty cathedrals, 500 large churches, and tens of thousands of parish churches and that within a hundred years some 2,700 churches were built in the Île-de-France region alone. This explosion of building began at a historic abbey church on the outskirts of Paris.

THE ABBEY CHURCH OF SAINT-DENIS. The Benedictine monastery of Saint-Denis, a few miles north of central Paris, had great symbolic significance for the French monarchy (SEE FIG. 16–1). It housed the tombs of the kings of France and their courts, regalia of the French Crown, and the relics of Saint Denis, the patron saint of France, who, according to tradition, had been the first bishop of Paris. In the 1130s, under the direction of Abbot Suger, construction began on a new abbey church (FIG. 16–2).

Suger described his administration of the abbey and the building of the Abbey Church of Saint-Denis in three books (see "Abbot Suger on the Value of Art," above). Suger prized magnificence. Having traveled widely, he combined design ideas from many sources. Suger invited masons and sculptors from other regions, making his abbey a center of artistic exchange. (Unfortunately, Suger did not record the names of the masters he employed, nor did he give information about them.) For the rebuilding, he received substantial annual revenues from the town's inhabitants, and he established free housing on abbey estates to attract peasant workers. For additional funds, he turned to the royal coffers and fellow clerics.

Suger began the rebuilding in 1135, with a new west façade and narthex (SEE FIG. 16–2). The design combined a Norman tripartite façade design, as seen in the abbey church in Caen (SEE FIG. 15–23), with sculptured portals like those at Autun (SEE FIG. 15–28). Two towers, a round window, and narrative sculpture over not one but three portals completed the magnificent composition. Within the narthex Suger's masons built highly experimental ribbed groin vaults over both square and rectangular bays (see "Rib Vaulting," page 521). (Much of the sculpture was destroyed or damaged in the eighteenth century, and the north tower had to be removed after it was struck by lightning in the nineteenth century.)

Suger's renovation of the choir at the east end of the church represented an equally momentous departure from the Romanesque style (SEE FIG. 16–1). Completed in three years and three months (1140–44), timing that the abbot found auspicious, the choir resembled a pilgrimage church, with a semicircular sanctuary surrounded by an ambulatory and seven radiating chapels (FIG. 16–3). Its large stained-glass windows, however, were new. While all the architectural elements of the choir—ribbed groin vaults springing from

Louis VII and Eleanor of Aquitaine attended the consecration of the new choir on June 14, 1144. Shortly thereafter the Second Crusade became the primary recipient of royal resources, leaving Suger without funds to replace the old nave and transept at Saint-Denis. After Suger died in 1151, his church remained unfinished for another century (see page 536).

The Abbey Church of Saint-Denis became the prototype for a new architecture of space and light based on a highly adaptable skeletal framework constructed from buttressed perimeter walls and pointed arch interior vaulting with masonry ribs. It initiated a period of competitive experimentation in France that resulted in ever larger churches, enclosing increasingly taller interior spaces, walled with ever greater expanses of colored glass. These great churches, with their unabashed decorative richness, were part of Abbot Suger's legacy to France.

AN EARLY GOTHIC CATHEDRAL: NOTRE DAME OF PARIS.
The Cathedral of Paris, known simply as Notre Dame ("Our Lady," the Virgin Mary), bridges the period between Abbot Suger's rebuilding of his abbey church and the High Gothic

16–2 | WEST FAÇADE, ABBEY CHURCH OF SAINT-DENIS
France. 1135–44, engraving made before 1837.

round piers, pointed arches, wall buttresses to relieve stress on the walls, and adequate window openings—had already appeared in Romanesque buildings, the achievement of Suger's master mason was to combine these into a fully integrated architectural whole. Sanctuary, ambulatory, and chapels open into one another to create a feeling of open, flowing space. Walls of stained glass replace masonry, permitting colored light to permeate the interior. These effects rely on the masterful use of vaulting techniques, the culmination of half a century of experiment and innovation.

The choir of Saint-Denis represented a new architectural aesthetic based on open spaces rather than massive walls. Suger considered light and color to be a means of illuminating the soul and uniting it with God. For him, the colored lights of stained-glass windows, like the glint of gems and gold in the chalice he gave to his church transfixed the world with the splendor of Paradise

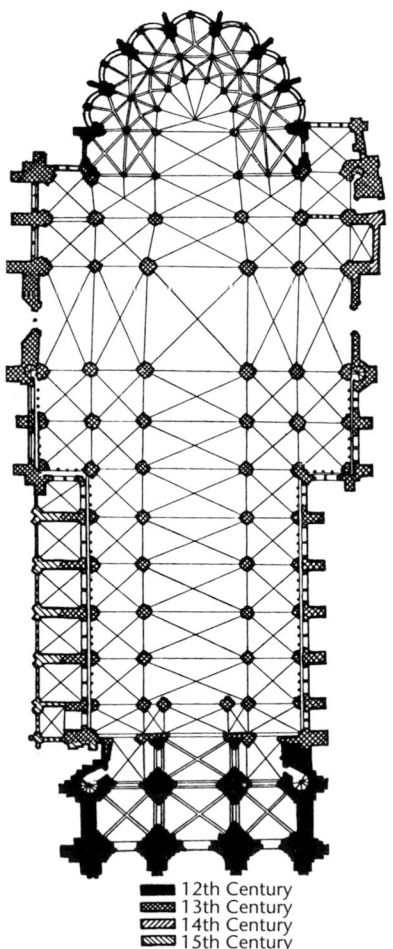

■ 12th Century
▨ 13th Century
▧ 14th Century
▨ 15th Century

16–3 | ABBEY CHURCH OF SAINT-DENIS, PLAN
West façade 1135–40; choir 1140–44; nave 1231–81.

16–4 | **CATHEDRAL OF NOTRE-DAME, PARIS**
Begun 1163; choir chapels, 1270s; crossing spire, 19th-century replacement. View from the south.

cathedrals of the thirteenth century (FIG. 16–4). As the city and royal court grew, Paris needed a larger cathedral. According to tradition, in 1163, Pope Alexander II laid the cornerstone of a new church.

The nave, with its massive walls and buttresses and six-part vaults adopted from Norman Romanesque architecture (SEE FIG. 15–19), dates to 1180–1200. The nave had four stories: an arcade surmounted by a gallery and two levels of rather small windows, including both lancets and round "bull's eye" windows (SEE FIG. 16–12). To increase the window size and secure the vault, the builders built the first true flying buttresses. The *flying buttress,* a gracefully arched, skeletal exterior support, counters the outward thrust of the nave vault by carrying the weight over the side aisles to the ground (see "Rib Vaulting," page 521). Although the nave was huge, it must have seemed very old fashioned by the thirteenth century. After 1225, new masters modernized the building by reworking the two upper levels into the large clerestory windows we see today. The huge flying buttresses rising dramatically to support the 115-foot high vault at Notre Dame are the result of later remodeling. (The 290-foot spire over the crossing is the work of the nineteenth-century architect Eugène-Emmanuel Viollet-le-Duc.)

From Early to High Gothic: Chartres Cathedral

The structural techniques and new conception of space applied at Saint-Denis and Notre Dame in Paris were taken one step further at Chartres Cathedral. It is here that the transition from Early to High Gothic is most eloquently

expressed. The great Cathedral of Notre-Dame in Chartres dominates this town southwest of Paris (SEE FIG. 16–8 and "The Gothic Church," page 522). For many people, Chartres Cathedral is a near-perfect embodiment of the Gothic spirit in stone and glass. Constructed in several stages beginning in the mid-twelfth century and extending into the mid-thirteenth, with additions such as the north spire as late as the sixteenth century, the cathedral reflects the transition from an experimental twelfth-century architecture to a mature thirteenth-century style.

FOUR HUNDRED YEARS AT CHARTRES. Chartres was the site of a pre-Christian virgin-goddess cult, and later, dedicated to the Virgin Mary, it became one of the oldest and most important Christian shrines in France. Its main treasure was a piece of linen believed to have been worn by Mary when she gave birth to Jesus. The so-called Tunic of the Virgin was a gift from the Byzantine Empress Irene to Charlemagne, whose grandson, Charles the Bald, donated it to the church in 876. The relic was kept below the high altar in a huge basement crypt. The healing powers attributed to the cloth made Chartres a major pilgrimage destination, especially as the cult of the Virgin grew in popularity in the twelfth and thirteenth centuries.

The theologians of Chartres tried to present all of Christian history in the sculpture and stained glass of their cathedral. On the west, in the Royal Portal, the sculpture is dedicated to Christ (FIG. 16–5). The north transept portal and the stained glass above it depict the world before Christ, with Saint Anne and the Virgin Mary. On the south transept, the

16–5 | **WEST FAÇADE, CHARTRES CATHEDRAL (THE CATHEDRAL OF NOTRE-DAME)**
Chartres, France. West façade begun c. 1134; cathedral rebuilt after a fire in 1194; building continued to 1260; north spire 1507–13.

viewers learn of later events in Christian history, including the lives of the saints and the Last Judgment.

Chartres' decoration also encompasses number symbolism. The number three represents the spiritual world of the Trinity, while the number four represents the material world (the four winds, the four seasons, the four rivers of Paradise). Combined, they form the perfect and all-inclusive number seven, expressed in the seven gifts of the Holy Spirit. References to three, four, and seven recur throughout the cathedral imagery. On the west façade, for example, the seven liberal arts surround the image of Mary and Jesus.

THE ROYAL PORTAL. From a distance, the most striking features of the west façade, constructed after a fire in 1134, are its prominent rose window—a huge circle of stained glass—and two towers with their spires. But up close, the western façade's three doorways—the so-called Royal Portal, inspired by the portal of the Church of Saint-Denis—capture the attention with their sculpture.

In the center of the west façade, on the central tympanum, Christ is enthroned in royal majesty with the four evangelists (FIG. 16–6). He appears imposing but more benign than at Autun. The apostles, organized into four groups of

16–6 | ROYAL PORTAL, WEST FAÇADE, CHARTRES CATHEDRAL
c. 1145-55.

Right—Tympanum: Mary enthroned with Christ Child (Throne of Wisdom); Lintels: Annunciation, Visitation, Nativity and Shepherds, Presentation; Archivolts: The Liberal Arts. Center—Tympanum: The Second Coming, Christ and the Four Apostles; Lintels: Apostles; Archivolts: The Twenty-Four Elders. Left—Tympanum: Ascension; Lintels: Angels and Apostles; Archivolts: Zodiac and Labors of the Months; Capitals: Life of Christ; Statue Columns: Old Testament Kings and Queens.

three, fill the lintel, and the twenty-four elders of the Apocalypse line the archivolts. The portal on Christ's left (the viewer's right) is dedicated to Mary and the early life of Christ, from the Annunciation to the Presentation in the Temple. On the left portal, Christ ascends heavenward in a cloud, supported by angels. Running across all three portals, storied capitals depict his earthly activities.

Flanking the doorways are monumental jamb figures (FIG. 16–7) depicting Old Testament kings and queens, the precursors of Christ. These figures convey an important message—just as the Old Testament supports and leads to the New Testament, so too these biblical kings and queens support Mary and Christ in the tympana above. They also lead the worshiper into the House of the Lord. The depiction of Old Testament kings and queens reminded people of the close ties between the Church and the French royal house. During the French Revolution, sculptures of kings and queens were removed from churches and destroyed. The Chartres figures are among the few that survived.

16–7 | ROYAL PORTAL, WEST FAÇADE, CHARTRES CATHEDRAL
Detail: Prophets and Ancestors of Christ (Kings and Queens of Judea). Right side, Central Portal, c. 1145-55.

Jamb figures became standard elements of Gothic church portals. They developed from shaftlike reliefs to fully three-dimensional figures that appear to interact. Earlier sculptors had achieved dramatic effects by compressing, elongating, and bending figures to fit an architectural framework. At Chartres, the sculptors sought to pose their figures naturally and comfortably in their architectural settings. The erect, frontal column statues, with their slender proportions and vertical drapery, echo the cylindrical shafts from which they seem to emerge. Their heads are finely rendered with idealized features. Calm and order prevails in all the elements of the portal, in contrast to the crowded imagery of the Romanesque churches.

REBUILDING CHARTRES. A fire in 1194 destroyed most of the church at Chartres but spared the Royal Portal and its windows and the crypt with its precious relics. A papal representative convinced reluctant local church officials to rebuild. He argued that the Virgin permitted the fire because she wanted a new and more beautiful church to be built in her honor. Between 1194 and about 1260, the chapter and people built a new cathedral (FIG. 16–8).

To erect such an enormous building required vast resources—money, raw materials, and skilled labor. A contemporary painting shows a building site with the masons at work (FIG. 16–9). Carpenters have built scaffolds, platforms, and a lifting machine. Master stone cutters measure and cut the stones, and in many cases sign their work with a "mason's mark." Workmen carry and hoist the blocks by hand or with a lifting wheel. Thousands of stones had to be accurately cut and placed. In the illustration a laborer carries mortar up a ladder to men working on the top of the wall, where the lifting wheel delivers cut stones.

The highly skilled men who carved capitals and portal sculpture were members of the masons' guild. Skilled stone cutters earned more than simple workmen, and the master usually earned at least twice what his men received (see "Master Builders," page 525).

An important innovation of Romanesque and Gothic builders was **rib vaulting**. Rib vaults are a form of **groin vault** (SEE "arch, vault, and dome," PAGE 172), in which the ridges (groins) formed by the intersecting vaults may rest on and be covered by curved moldings called ribs. After the walls and piers of the building reached the desired height, timber scaffolding to support the masonry ribs was constructed. After the ribs were set, the web of the vault was then laid on forms built on the ribs. After all the temporary forms were removed, the ribs provided strength at the intersections of the webbing to channel the vaults' thrust outward and downward to the foundations. In short, ribs formed the "skeleton" of the vault; the webbing, a lighter masonry "skin." In late Gothic buildings additional, decorative ribs give vaults a lacelike appearance.

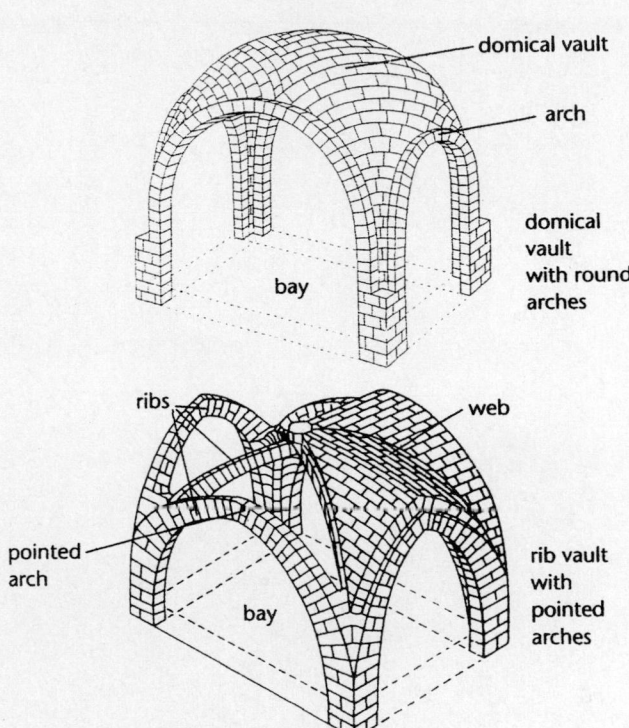

domical vault

arch

domical vault with round arches

bay

ribs

web

pointed arch

bay

rib vault with pointed arches

Elements *of* Architecture
THE GOTHIC CHURCH

ELEMENTS OF THE GOTHIC CHURCH

1 Portals
2 Jambs
3 Rose window
4 Gables
5 Pinnacles and finials
6 Lancets
7 Stringcourse
8 Buttress piers
9 Flying Buttress
10 Tracery
11 Nave

12 Side aisles
13 Compound pier with
   engaged colonettes
14 Triforium
15 Clerestory
16 Rib vaults
17 Crossing
18 Transept
19 Choir
20 Apse
21 Apsidal Chapels

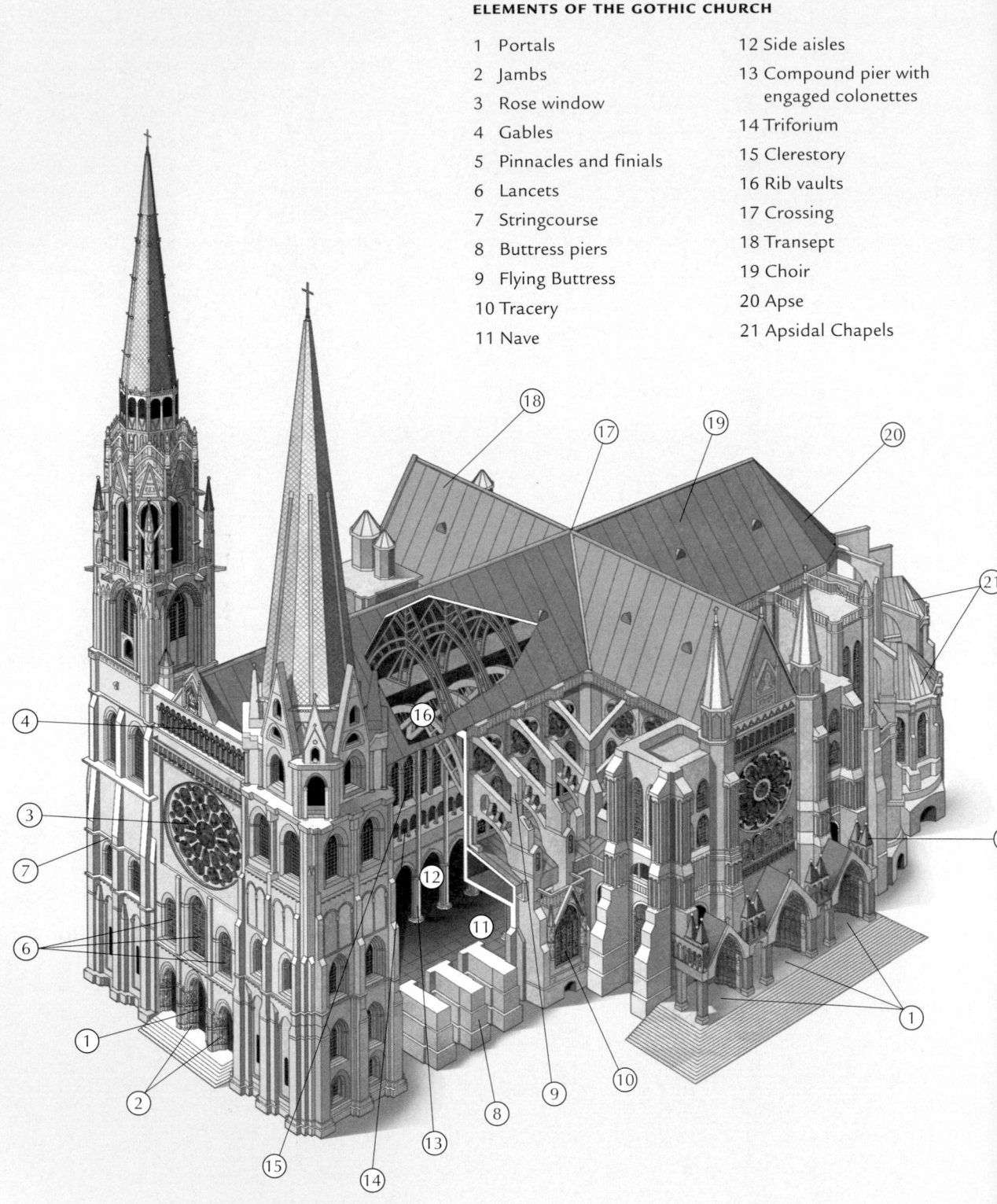

16–8 | **CHARTRES CATHEDRAL, AIR VIEW FROM SOUTHEAST**

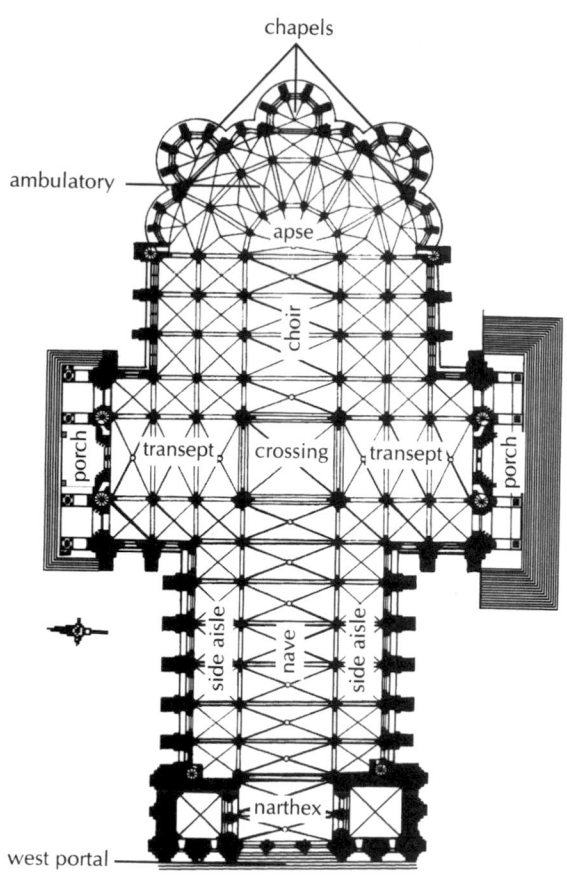

16–10 | **CHARTRES CATHEDRAL, PLAN**
c. 1194–1220.

16–11 | **NAVE, CHARTRES CATHEDRAL**
c. 1194–1220.

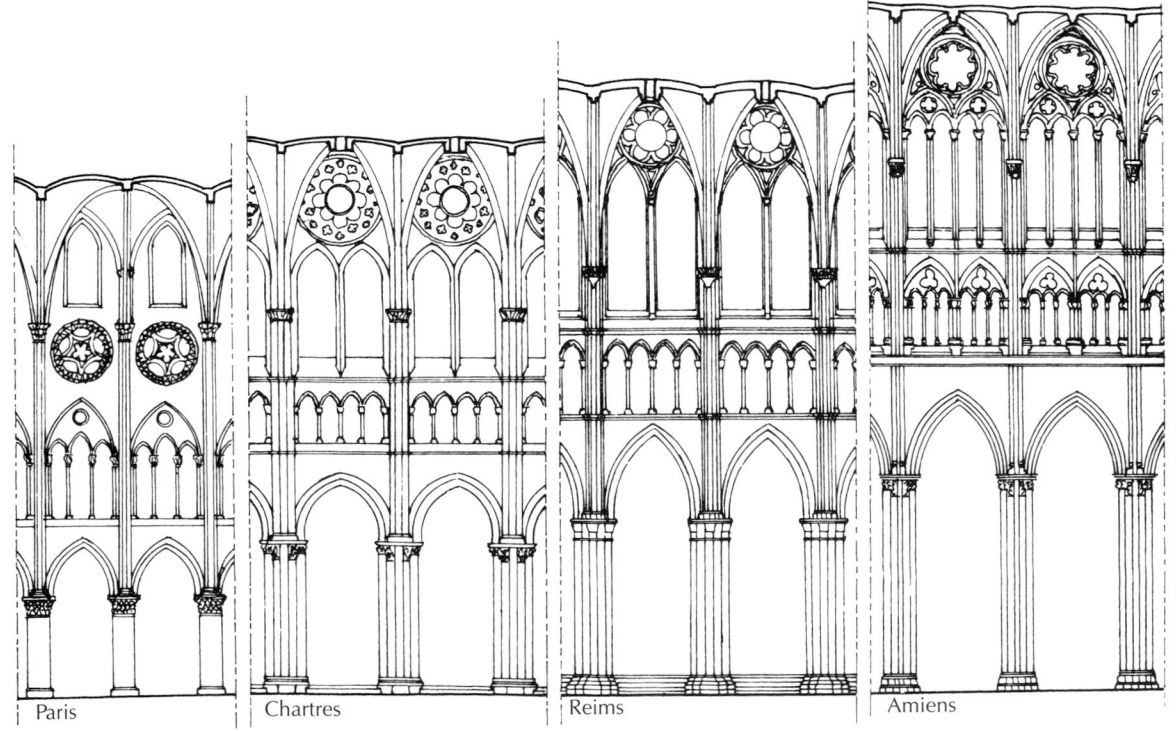

Paris   Chartres   Reims   Amiens

16–12 | **COMPARATIVE CATHEDRAL NAVE ELEVATIONS**
From Louis Grodecki, *Gothic Architecture*, New York, 1985. Paris, h. 115′ (35 m), w. 40′ (12 m); Chartres, h. 120′ (37 m), w. 45′ 6″ (17 m); Reims h. 125′ (38 m), w. 46′ (14 m); Amiens, h. 144′ (44 m), w. 48′ (15 m).

HIGH GOTHIC ARCHITECTURE AT CHARTRES, 1194 TO 1260.
Building on the concept pioneered at Saint-Denis of an elegant masonry shell enclosing a large open space, the masons at Chartres erected a church over 45 feet wide with vaults that soar approximately 120 feet above the floor. In the plan, the enlarged sanctuary with its ambulatory and chapels, a feature inspired by the church at Saint-Denis, occupied one-third of the building (FIG. 16–10). The actual cross section of the nave is an equilateral triangle measured from the outer line of buttresses to the keystone of the vault. The worshiper's gaze is drawn forward toward the choir where the high altar was situated behind a choir screen and at the same time upward to the clerestory windows and the soaring vaults (FIG. 16–11).

By making the open nave arcade and glowing clerestory nearly equal in height, the architect creates a harmonious elevation (FIG. 16–12). Relatively little interior architectural decoration interrupts the visual rhythm of compound piers with their engaged shafts supporting pointed arches. Four-part vaulting has replaced more complex systems found in churches such as Durham or Caen (SEE FIG. 15–21). The alternating heavy and light piers typical of Romanesque naves such as that at Speyer Cathedral (SEE FIG. 15–17) become a subtle alternation of round and octagonal compound piers. The gallery, now a narrow arcaded triforium passage, forms a horizontal band running the length of the nave. The large and luminous clerestory is formed by windows whose paired **lancets** are surmounted by small circular windows, or **oculi** (bull's-eye windows). The technique used is known as **plate tracery**; that is, holes are cut in the stone of the wall and filled with stained glass. Glass fills nearly half the wall surface. This lightening of the structure is made possible by the ingenious system of flying buttresses on the exterior.

THE GLORY OF STAINED GLASS. Chartres is unique among French Gothic buildings in that most of its stained-glass windows have survived. Stained glass is an expensive and difficult medium, but its effect on the senses and emotions makes the effort worthwhile. The light streaming in through these windows changes with the time of day, the seasons, and the movement of clouds.

Chartres was famous for its glassmaking workshops, which by 1260 had installed about 22,000 square feet of stained glass in 176 windows (see "Stained-Glass Windows," page 528). Most of the glass dates between about 1210 and 1250, but a few earlier windows, from around 1150 to 1170, survived the fire of 1194.

Among the twelfth-century works of stained glass in the west wall of the cathedral is the **TREE OF JESSE** window (FIG. 16–13). The treatment of this subject, much more complex than its depiction in an early twelfth-century Cistercian manuscript (SEE FIG. 15–39), was apparently inspired by a similar window at Saint-Denis. Jesse, the father of King David and an ancestor of Mary, lies at the base of the tree whose trunk grows out of his body, as described by the prophet Isaiah

16–13 | **TREE OF JESSE, WEST FAÇADE, CHARTRES CATHEDRAL**
c. 1150–70. Stained and painted glass.

Technique
STAINED-GLASS WINDOWS

The basic technique for making colored glass has been known since ancient Egypt. It involves the addition of metallic oxides—cobalt for blue, manganese for red and purple—to a basic formula of sand and ash or lime that is fused at high temperature. Such "stained" glass was used on a small scale in church windows during the Early Christian period and in Carolingian and Ottonian churches. Colored glass sometimes adorned Romanesque churches, but the art form reached a pinnacle of sophistication and popularity in the cathedrals and churches of the Gothic era.

Making a stained-glass image was a complex and costly process. A designer first drew a composition on a wood panel the same size as the opening of the window to be filled, noting the colors of each of the elements in it. Glassblowers produced sheets of colored glass, and artisans cut individual pieces from these large sheets and laid them out on the wood template. Painters added details with enamel emulsion, and the glass was reheated to fuse the enamel to it. Finally, the pieces were joined together with narrow lead strips, called **cames.** The assembled pieces were set into iron frames that had been made to fit the stonework of the window opening.

The colors of twelfth-century glass—mainly reds and blues with touches of dark green, brown, and orange-yellow—were so dark as to be nearly opaque, and early uncolored glass was full of impurities. But the demand for stained-glass windows stimulated technical experimentation to achieve new colors and greater purity and transparency. The Cistercians adorned their churches with *grisaille* windows, painting foliage and crosses onto a gray glass, and Gothic artisans developed a clearer material onto which elaborate narrative scenes could be drawn.

By the thirteenth century, many new colors were discovered, some accidentally, such as a sunny yellow produced by the addition of silver oxide. *Flashing*, in which a layer of one color was fused to a layer of another color, produced an almost infinite range of hues. Blue and yellow, for example, could be combined to make green. In the same way, clear glass could be fused to layers of colored glass in varying thicknesses to produce a range of hues from light to dark. The deep colors of early Gothic stained-glass windows give them a saturated and mysterious brilliance. The richness of some of these colors, particularly blue, has never been surpassed. Pale colors and large areas of *grisaille* glass became increasingly popular from the mid-thirteenth century on, making the windows of later Gothic churches bright and clear by comparison.

(11:1–3). The family tree literally connects Jesus with the house of David (Matthew 1:1–17). In the branches above him appear four kings of Judea (Christ's royal ancestors), then the Virgin Mary, and finally Christ himself. Seven doves, symbolizing the seven gifts of the Holy Spirit, encircle Christ, and fourteen prophets stand in the semicircles flanking the tree. The glass in the *Tree of Jesse* window is set within an iron framework visible as a rectilinear pattern of black lines.

Twelfth-century windows are remarkable for their simple geometric compositions—usually squares and circles and the intensity of the color of the glass. In the color symbolism of the time, blue signified heaven and fidelity; red, the Passion; white, purity; green, fertility and springtime. Yellow as a substitute for gold could represent the presence of God, the sun, or truth; but plain yellow could also mean deceit and cowardice. Stained-glass windows changed the color and quality of light to inspire devotion and contemplations. Their painted narratives also educated the viewers.

Most of the windows in the new church were glazed between 1210 and 1250. In the aisles and chapels where the windows were low enough to be easily seen, there were elaborate narratives using many small figures. Tracery—geometric decorative patterns in stone or wood that filled window openings—became increasingly intricate. In the clerestory windows, glaziers used single figures that could be seen at a distance because of their size, simple drawing, and strong colors. In the north transept, five lancets and a rose window (over 42 feet in diameter) fill the upper wall (FIG. 16–14).

The North transept windows may have been a royal commission, a gift from Queen Blanche of Castile (mother of Louis IX, regent, 1226–34), whose heraldic castles symbolizing the country of Castile (Spain) join the golden lilies of France in the spandrels. In the lancets, Saint Anne and the infant Mary have the place of honor. Saint Anne is flanked by Old Testament figures: the priests Mechizedek and Aaron and the kings David and Solomon. In the center of the rose window, Mary is enthroned with the Christ Child. Radiating from the holy pair are lattice-filled panels displaying four doves (the Gospels) and eight angels, the prophets, and the Old Testament ancestors of Christ.

High Gothic: Amiens and Reims Cathedrals

New cathedrals in other rich commercial cities of northern France reflected both the piety and civic pride of the citizens. The cathedrals of Chartres, Amiens, and Reims were being built at the same time, and the master masons at each site borrowed ideas from one another. Amiens was an important trading and textile-manufacturing center north of Paris. The cathedral housed relics of Saint John the Baptist. When Amiens burned in 1218, church officials devoted their resources to making its replacement as splendid as possible.

16–14 ❘ **CHARTRES CATHEDRAL, NORTH TRANSEPT, ROSE WINDOW AND LANCETS, KNOWN AS THE "ROSE OF FRANCE"**
North transept, Chartres Cathedral. c. 1220, stained and painted glass.

16–15 | **NAVE, AMIENS CATHEDRAL**
France. 1220–88; upper choir reworked after 1258.

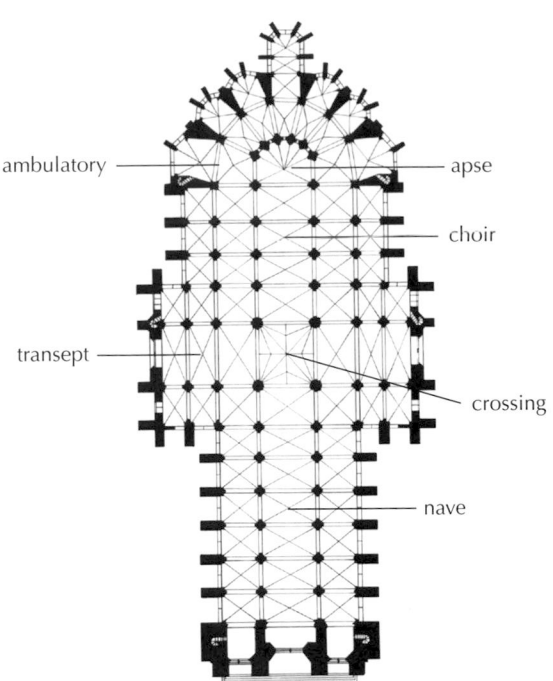

16–16 | Robert de Luzarches, Thomas de Cormont, and Renaud de Cormont **PLAN OF CATHEDRAL OF NOTRE-DAME, AMIENS**
1220–88.

Their funding came mainly from the cathedral's agricultural estates and from the city's important trade fairs. Construction on the new church began in 1220. The lower parts date from about 1220–36, with major work continuing until 1288. Robert de Luzarches (d. 1236) was the builder who established the overall design. He was succeeded by Thomas de Cormont, who was followed by his son Renaud.

NAVE AND CHOIR: AMIENS CATHEDRAL. The church at Amiens became the archetypical Gothic cathedral (FIG. 16–15). Robert de Luzarches made critical adjustments that simplified, clarified, and unified the plan of Amiens Cathedral as compared with Chartres Cathedral. He eliminated the narthex and expanded the transept and sanctuary (comprising the apse, ambulatory chapels, and choir), thus shortening the nave and creating a plan that seems to balance east and west around the crossing (FIG. 16–16). In the choir, chapels of the same size and shape enhance the clarity of the design. The nave elevation is also balanced and compact. Uniform and evenly spaced compound piers, with engaged half columns topped by foliage capitals, support the arcades. Tracery and colonnettes (small columns) unite the triforium and the clerestory, and together they equal the height of the nave arcade. An ornate floral molding below the triforium runs uninterrupted across the wall surfaces and the colonnettes, providing a horizontal counterpoint to the soaring verticality of the design. This sculptural detail adds an elegant note to the severe architecture.

16–17 | **VAULTS, SANCTUARY, AMIENS CATHEDRAL**
France. Upper choir after 1258; vaulted by 1288.

Amiens is a supreme architectural statement of the Gothic desire for both actual and perceived height (FIG. 16–17). The nave, only 48 feet wide, soars upward 144 feet; consequently, not only is the nave in fact exceptionally tall, its narrow proportions (3:1, height to width) create an exaggerated sense of

16–18 | **WEST FAÇADE, CATHEDRAL OF NOTRE-DAME, REIMS**

France. Rebuilding begun 1211; façade begun c. 1225; to the height of rose window by 1260; finished for the coronation of Philip the Fair in 1286; towers left unfinished in 1311; additional work 1406–28.

The cathedral was restored in the sixteenth century and again in the nineteenth and twentieth centuries. During World War I it withstood bombardment by some 3,000 shells, an eloquent testimony to the skills of its builders.

height. A comparison of Louis Grodecki's nave elevations of the cathedrals of Paris, Chartres, Reims, and Amiens—drawn to the same scale—demonstrates the change in height and design of cathedrals over time (SEE FIG. 16–12).

The lower portions of the church were substantially finished by about 1240. The vault and the light-filled choir date to the second phase of construction, directed by Thomas de Cormont, perhaps after a fire in 1258 (FIG. 16–17). The choir is illuminated by large windows subdivided by **bar tracery** (in bar tracery, thin stone strips, called **mullions,** form a lacy matrix for the glass). In the Amiens choir, the tracery divides the windows into slender lancets crowned by **trefoils** (three-lobed designs) and circular windows.

THE WEST FAÇADE AT REIMS CATHEDRAL.
In the Church hierarchy, the bishop of Amiens was subordinate to the archbishop of Reims. Reims, northeast of Paris, was the coronation church of the kings of France and, like Saint-Denis, had been a cultural and educational center since Carolingian times. When in 1210 fire destroyed this vital building, the community at Reims began to erect a new structure. The cornerstone was laid in 1211, and work on the cathedral continued throughout the century. The expense of the project sparked such local opposition that twice in the 1230s revolts drove the archbishop and canons into exile. At Reims five masters directed the work on the cathedral over the course of a century—Jean d'Orbais, Jean le Loup, Gaucher de Reims, Bernard de Soissons, and Robert de Coucy. If Amiens Cathedral has the ideal Gothic nave and choir, Reims Cathedral's west front takes pride of place among Gothic façades. The major portion of this magnificent structure must have been finished in time for the coronation of Philip the Fair in 1286 (FIG. 16–18). Its tall gabled portals form a broad horizontal base and project forward to display an expanse of sculpture. Their soaring peaks, the middle one reaching to the center of the rose window, unify the façade vertically. Large windows fill the tympana, instead of the sculpture usually found there. The deep porches are encrusted with sculpture that lacks the unity seen at Amiens, reflecting instead 100 years of changes in plan, iconography, and workshops.

16–19 | **NAVE, REIMS CATHEDRAL**
Looking west. Begun 1211; nave c. 1220.

In a departure from tradition, Mary rather than Christ dominates the central portal, a reflection of the popularity of her cult. Christ crowns her as Queen of Heaven in the central gable. The enormous rose window is the focal point of the façade. The towers were later additions, as was the row of carved figures that runs from the base of one tower to the other above the rose window. This "gallery of kings" is the only strictly horizontal element of the façade.

Inside the church, remarkable sculpture and stained glass fill the west wall (**FIG. 16–19**), which visually "dissolves" in colored light. The great rose window fills the clerestory level; a row of lancets illuminate the triforium; and a smaller rose window replaces the stone of the tympanum of the portal. This expanse of glass was made possible by bar tracery, a technique invented or at least perfected at Reims. The circles of the two rose windows are anchored visually by a masonry grid of tracery and sculpture covering the inner wall of the façade.

Here ranks of carved Old Testament prophets and Christ's royal ancestors serve as moral guides for the newly crowned monarchs who faced them after the coronation ceremonies.

High Gothic Sculpture

Like Greek sculpture, Gothic sculpture evolved from static forms to moving figures, from formal geometric abstraction though an idealized phase, to a surface realism that could be highly expressive. As in ancient art, Gothic sculpture was originally painted and sometimes gilded. The stone surfaces were not entirely covered but subtly colored and decorated to enhance the realism of the figures. Recent cleaning at Amiens and Reims has revealed remarkable amounts of color—borders of garments painted to indicate rich embroidery, gilded angel wings, colored foliage, and chevron-patterned colonettes.

AMIENS. The worshipers approaching the main entrance—the west portals—of Amiens Cathedral encountered an overwhelming array of images. Figures of apostles and saints line the door **jambs** and cover the projecting buttresses (**FIG. 16–20**). Most of them were produced by a large workshop in only twenty years, between about 1220 and perhaps 1236/40, making the façade stylistically more coherent than those of many other cathedrals. In the mid-thirteenth century, Amiens-trained sculptors traveled across Europe and carried their style into places like Spain and Italy.

The Amiens central portal is dedicated to Christ and the Apostles, with the Last Judgment in the tympanum above, surrounded by angels and saints in the voussoirs. At the right is Mary's portal, where she is depicted as Queen of Heaven. The left portal is dedicated to local saints with Saint Firmin, the first bishop of Amiens, in the **trumeau.** At Amiens the master designer introduced a new feature: At eye-level, on the base below the jamb figures, are **quatrefoils** (four-lobed medallions) containing lively illustrations of good (Virtues) and evil (Vices) in daily life, the seasons and labors of the months, the lives of the saints, and biblical stories (**FIG. 16–21**). At last the natural world enters the ideal Christian vision.

All this imagery revolves around Christ standing in front of the trumeau of the central portal. Known as the **BEAU DIEU,** meaning "Noble (or Beautiful) God," Christ as the teacher-priest bestows his blessing on the faithful (**FIG. 16–22**). This exceptionally fine sculpture may well be the work of the master of the Amiens workshop himself. The figure establishes an ideal for Gothic figures. The broad contours of the heavy drapery wrapped around Christ's right hip and bunched over his left arm lead the eye up to the Gospel book he holds and, following his right hand, raised in blessing, to his face, which is that of a young king. He stands on a lion and a dragonlike creature called a *basilisk,* symbolizing his kingship and his triumph over evil and death (Psalm 91:13).

16–20 | **WEST FAÇADE, AMIENS CATHEDRAL**
c. 1220–36/40 and continued through the 15th century.

With its clear, solid forms, elegantly cascading robes, and interplay of close observation with idealization, the *Beau Dieu* embodies the Amiens style and the Gothic spirit.

REIMS. At Reims, sculptors from major workshops, such as Chartres and Amiens, as well as local sculptors worked together for decades. Most of the sculpture was done in a twenty-year period between 1230 and 1250, although sculpture in the upper regions of the façade may be as late as 1285.

Complicating the study of the sculpture at Reims is the fact that many figures have been moved from their original locations. On the right jamb of the central portal of the western façade, a group of four figures—depicting the *Annunciation* and the *Visitation*—illustrates three of the characteristic

16–21 | **WEST FAÇADE, CENTRAL AND NORTH PORTALS. AMIENS CATHEDRAL.**
c. 1220–1236/40. Central portal: tympanum: Last Judgement; trumeau: Christ (Beau Dieu); jambs: Apostles. Height of figures, 7-8′.

Reims styles (FIG. 16–23). Art historians have given names to the styles: the Classical Master (or the Master of Antique Figures), the Amiens Master, and the Master of the Smiling Angels. The pair on the right, the *Visitation,* is the work of the Classical Shop, which was active as early as the 1220s and 1230s. Mary (left), pregnant with Jesus, visits her older cousin Elizabeth (right), who is pregnant with John the Baptist.

The sculptors drew on classical sources—either directly from Roman sculpture (Reims had been an important center under ancient Rome) or indirectly through Mosan metalwork (SEE FIG. 16–35). The heavy figures have a solidity seen in Roman sculpture, and Mary's full face, gently waving hair, and heavy mantle recall imperial portrait statuary. The contrast between the features of the young Mary and the older

Elizabeth recall ancient Roman sculpture (compare the portrait of the Flavian woman in FIG. 6–45). The Classical Master of Reims used deftly modeled drapery not only to provide volume, but also to create a stance in which the apparent shift in weight of one bent knee allows the figures to seem to turn toward each other. The new freedom, movement, and sense of implied interaction inspired later Gothic artists toward ever greater realism.

In the *Annunciation* two other masters were at work, one probably from Amiens and the other a new artist whose antecedents are still unknown. The Amiens Master's Mary is a quiet, graceful figure, with a slender body and restrained gestures—a striking contrast to the bold tangibility of the Classical Master's Mary. The broad planes of simple drapery suggest

16–22 | **CHRIST: BEAU DIEU**
Trumeau, central portal, west façade, Amiens
Cathedral. France. c. 1220–36/40.

16–23 | **WEST FAÇADE, CENTRAL PORTAL, RIGHT SIDE, REIMS CATHEDRAL**
Annunciation (left pair: Mary [right] c. 1245, angel [left] c. 1255) and *Visitation* (right pair: Mary [left] and Elizabeth [right] c. 1230).

the Amiens shop, but her pinched features are the sculptor's personal style. The sculptor here was one of a large team that made most of the other sculptures of the west entrance.

The figure of the angel Gabriel is the work of the Master of the Smiling Angels. This artist created tall, gracefully swaying figures that in body type, features, pose, and gestures suggest the fashionable refinement associated with the Parisian court at mid-century. The angel Gabriel is typical. His small, almost triangular head with a broad brow and pointed chin is framed by wavy hair; his puffy, almond-shaped eyes are set under arching brows; he has a well-shaped nose and thin lips curving into a slight smile. The cocked head, hint of a smile, and mannered gestures as he draws his voluminous drapery into elegant folds suggest aristocratic,

courtly elegance. Later in the century (and during the fourteenth century), artists from Paris to Prague imitated this style, as grace and refinement became a guiding ideal in sculpture and painting (see Chapter 17).

The Rayonnant Style

In the second half of the thirteenth century artists fell under the spell of the Master of the Smiling Angels of Reims as well as the luminous west façade of Reims and choir of Amiens. They created a new variation of the Gothic style of architecture, known today as the Rayonnant (Radiant) or Court Style (referring to the Parisian court). Using this style, they finished older buildings, such as the abbey church of Saint-Denis, and added transepts and chapels to Notre Dame in Paris.

16–24 | UPPER CHAPEL, SAINTE-CHAPELLE
Paris. 1243–48.

At Saint-Denis (SEE FIG. 16–1), work began in 1231 to complete Abbot Suger's church. The new nave, transept, and upper part of the choir attach seamlessly to the twelfth-century narthex and lower part of the choir (SEE FIG. 16–3). Its glazed triforium and tall clerestory windows filled with bar tracery and stained glass are visually united by the continuous shafts rising from the base of clustered columns to the rib vault. The builders achieved the effects of spatial unity and an interior filled with the jewel-like colored space dreamed of by Suger.

The remodeling and construction of the transepts at Paris, the choir at Amiens, and the façade at Reims all reflect a courtly style characterized by interlocking and overlapping forms, linear patterns, and above all, spatial unity and luminosity. The Rayonnant style continued through the fourteenth and into the fifteenth centuries and influenced the Gothic art of Germany, Italy, and Spain.

THE SAINTE-CHAPELLE IN PARIS. The masterpiece of Rayonnant style is the palace chapel in Paris—the Sainte-Chapelle, or Holy Chapel—ordered by Louis IX (FIG. 16–24). Louis IX (ruled 1226–70) avidly collected relics of Christ's Passion sold to him by his cousin, who was ruling Constantinople after the Fourth Crusade. In 1239 Louis acquired the crown of thorns and in 1241 other relics,

including a bit of the metal lance tip that pierced Christ's side, the vinegar-soaked sponge offered to wet Christ's lips, a nail used in the Crucifixion, and a fragment of the True Cross (or so people believed). He kept these treasures in the palace while he built a chapel to house them. Construction moved rapidly. The building may have been finished in 1246, and it was consecrated in 1248.

The Sainte-Chapelle resembles a giant reliquary, one made of stone and glass instead of gold and gems. Built in two stories, the ground-level chapel is accessible from a courtyard, and a private upper chapel is entered from the royal residence. The ground-level chapel has a nave and narrow side aisles, but the upper level is a single room with a western porch and a rounded east wall. The design of the exterior, with gables and wall buttresses framing huge windows, inspired the artist who created a psalter for the king (discussed on the facing page).

16–25 | QUEEN BLANCHE OF CASTILE AND LOUIS IX, MORALIZED BIBLE
Paris. 1226–34. Ink, tempera, and gold leaf on vellum, 15 × 10½″ (38 × 26.6 cm). The Pierpont Morgan Library, New York.
MS. M. 240, f. 8

This page was placed at the end of the manuscript as a colophon (comparable to a title page in a modern book). Thin sheets of gold leaf were painstakingly attached to the vellum and then polished to a high sheen with a tool called a burnisher. Gold was applied to paintings before pigments.

16–26 | **ABRAHAM, SARAH, AND THE THREE STRANGERS FROM THE PSALTER OF SAINT LOUIS**
Paris. 1253–70. Ink, tempera, and gold leaf on vellum, 5 × 3½" (13.6 × 8.7 cm). Bibliothèque Nationale, Paris.

of books. The Court Style had enormous influence throughout northern Europe, spread by artists, especially manuscript illuminators, who flocked to Paris from other regions. There they joined workshops affiliated with the Confrérie de Saint-Jean (Guild of Saint John), supervised by university officials who controlled the production and distribution of books. These works ranged from practical manuals to elaborate devotional works illustrated with exquisite miniatures. Women played an important role in book production. Widows continued their husband's businesses; they even took oaths as commercial book producers.

LOUIS IX AND BLANCHE OF CASTILE. Paris was a major center of book production in the Gothic period, and the royal library in Paris was especially renowned. Not only the king, but his mother, Blanche of Castile, commissioned and collected books (FIG. 16–25). Blanche and the young king appear here seated on ornate thrones against a gold background. Colorful Gothic architecture suggests the royal palace, where the manuscript may actually have been made. Below, a scholar-monk dictates, and the scribe works on a page with a column of circles that will hold the illustrations. This compositional format derives from stained-glass lancets organized as columns of images in medallions. The illuminators show their debt to stained glass in their use of glowing red and blue colors and reflective gold surfaces.

THE PSALTER OF SAINT LOUIS. In the opulence, number, and style of its illustrations, the **PSALTER OF SAINT LOUIS** defines the Court style in manuscript illumination just as Louis' chapel does the architecture (FIG. 16–26). The book, containing seventy-eight full-page illuminations, was created for the king's private devotions, probably after his return from the Fourth Crusade in 1254. The illustrations fall at the back of the book, preceded by Psalms and other readings. Intricate scrolled borders frame the narratives, and figures are rendered in a style that reflects the sculpture of the Master of the Smiling Angels of Reims.

Whether entering the upper level, walking through the palace halls, or climbing up the narrow spiral stairs from the lower level, the visitor emerges into a kaleidoscopic jewel box. The walls have been reduced to clusters of slender colonnettes framing tall windows filled with shimmering glass. Bar tracery in the windows is echoed in the blind arcading and tracery decorating the lower walls. The stone surfaces are painted and gilded—red, blue, and gold—so that stone and glass seem to merge in the multicolored light. Painted statues of the twelve apostles stand between window sections, linking the walls and the stained glass. The windows contain narrative and symbolic scenes. Those in the curve of the sanctuary behind the altar and relics, for example, illustrate the Nativity and Passion of Christ, the Tree of Jesse, and the life of Saint John the Baptist. The story of Louis' acquisition of his relics is told, and the Last Judgment appeared in the original rose window on the west.

Illuminated Manuscripts

France gained renown in the thirteenth century not only for its new architecture and sculpture but also for the production

Depicted here is the Old Testament story of Abraham and Sarah's hospitality to three strangers, that is, God in the three persons (compare the later Byzantine icon, FIG. 7–51). Sarah watches from the entryway of their tent, while the strangers—angels representing God—tell the elderly couple that Sarah will bear a child, Isaac. The story is yet another instance of the Old Testament prefiguring the New. To the medieval reader, the three strangers were symbols of the Trinity, and God's promise to Sarah foreshadowed the angel's annunciation of the Christ Child's birth to Mary.

The architectural frame, depicting gables, pinnacles, and windows modeled on the Sainte-Chapelle, establishes a narrow stage on which the story unfolds. Wavy clouds floating within the arches under the gables indicate an outdoor setting. The oak tree, representing the biblical oaks of Mamre (Genesis 18:1), has stylized but recognizable oak leaves and acorns. The oak establishes the specific location of the story. At the same time, the angel's blessing gesture and Sarah's pres-ence indicate a specific moment. This new awareness of time and place, as well as the oak leaves and acorns, reflect a tentative move toward the representation of the natural world that will gain momentum in the following centuries.

GOTHIC ART IN ENGLAND

Plantagenet kings ruled England from the time of Henry II and Eleanor of Aquitaine until 1485. Many of the kings, especially Henry III (ruled 1216–72), were great patrons of the arts. During this period, London grew into a large city, but most people continued to live in rural villages and bustling market towns. Textile production dominated manufacture and trade, and fine embroidery continued to be an English specialty. The French Gothic style influenced English architecture and manuscript illumination. However, these influences were tempered by local materials, methods, and artistic traditions such as an expressive use of line and an interest in surface decoration.

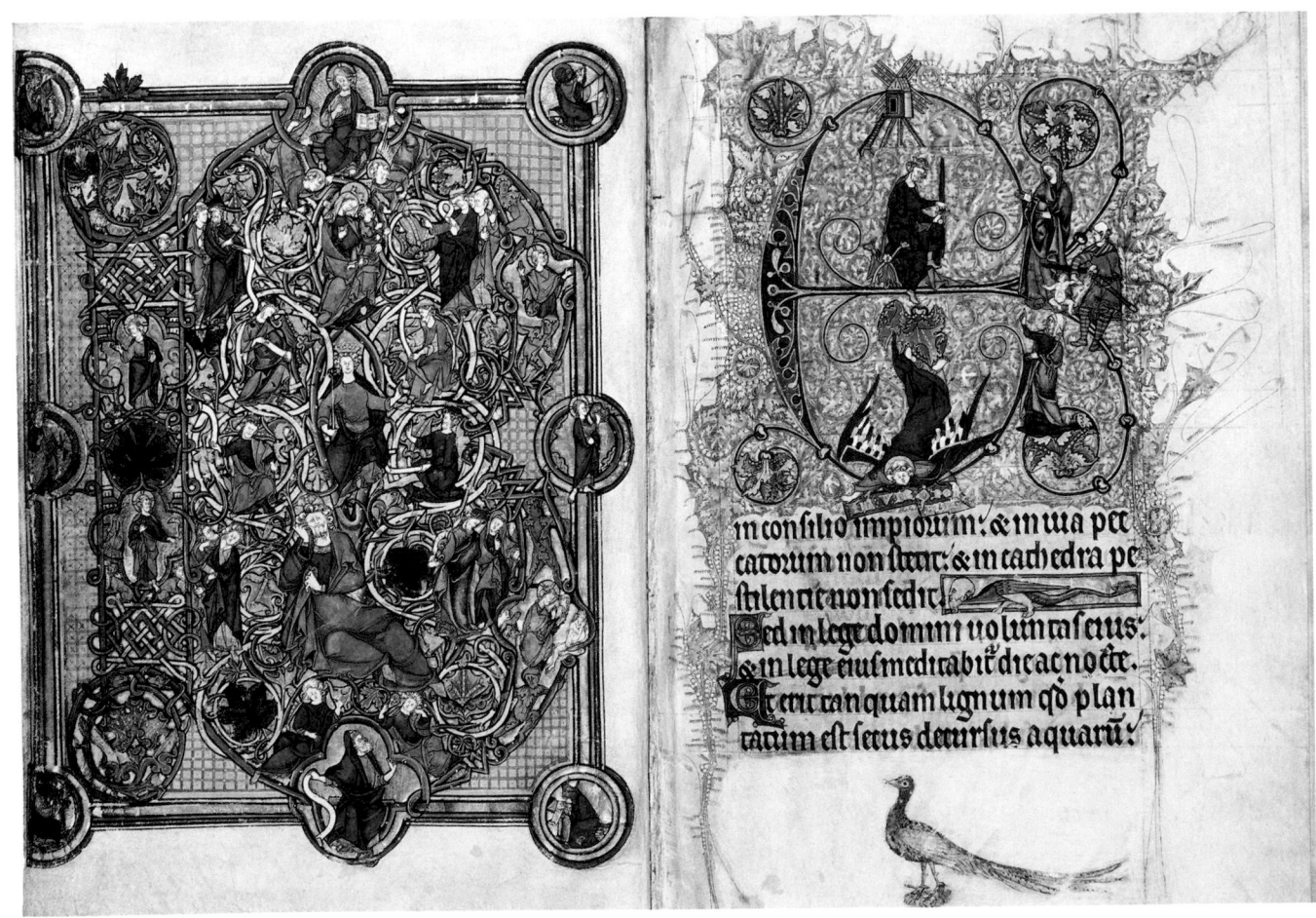

16–27 | **PSALM 1 (BEATUS VIR) FROM THE WINDMILL PSALTER**
London. c. 1270–80. Ink, pigments, and gold on vellum, each page 12¾ × 8¾" (32.3 × 22.2 cm). The Pierpont Morgan Library, New York.
M. 102, f. lv-2

Manuscript Illumination

The universities of Oxford and Cambridge dominated intellectual life, but monasteries continued to house active *scriptoria,* in contrast to France, where book production became centralized in the professional workshops of Paris. By the end of the thirteenth century, secular workshops became increasingly active in England, reflecting a demand for books from newly literate landowners, townspeople, and students. These people read books for entertainment and general knowledge as well as for religious enlightenment.

The dazzling artistry and delight in ambiguities that had marked early medieval manuscripts in the British Isles reappear in the **WINDMILL PSALTER** (FIG. 16–27). The elegance of French Gothic visible in the elongated proportions and dainty heads of the figures is combined with the English tradition of draftsmanship visible in the interlaced tendrils and stylized drapery folds.

Psalm 1 begins with the words *"Beatus vir qui non abiit"* ("Blessed is the man who does not follow [the counsel of the wicked]," Psalm 1:1). The letter *B,* the first letter of the Psalm, fills the left-hand page, and an *E* occupies the top at the right. The rest of the opening words appear on a banner carried by an angel at the bottom of the *E.* The *B* outlines a densely interlaced Tree of Jesse. The *E* is formed from large tendrils that escape from delicate background vegetation to support characters in the story of the Judgment of Solomon (I Kings 3:16–27). The story, seen as a prefiguration of the Last Judgment and an illustration to the phrase "his delight is in the law of the Lord" (Psalm 1:2), relates how two women (at the right) claiming the same baby came before King Solomon (on the crossbar) to settle their dispute. The king ordered his knight to slice the baby in half and give each woman her share. This trick revealed the real mother, who hastened to give up her claim in order to save the child's life.

Realistic and surprising images appear everywhere—note how the knight hooks his toe under the cross bar of the *E* to maintain his balance. Visual puns on the text abound. The meaning of the pheasant at the bottom of the page remains a mystery, but the windmill at the top of the letter *E* (which gives the name to the *Windmill Psalter*) is typical of this new realism. It illustrates the verse that tells how wicked people would not survive the Judgment but would be "like chaff driven away by the wind" (Psalm 1:4). The imagery thus encouraged further thought on the text's familiar messages.

Architecture

The Gothic style in architecture appeared early in England under the influence of local Cistercian and Norman builders and by traveling master builders. A typical thirteenth-century English cathedral seems to hug the earth more like a Cistercian monastery (see Fontenay in Burgundy, FIG. 15–12)

than compact and vertical French cathedrals like Chartres (SEE FIG. 16–8). English builders also favored a screenlike façade that does not usually reflect the interior distribution of space, a characteristic that is at odds with the architectural logic of French Gothic.

SALISBURY CATHEDRAL. The thirteenth-century cathedral in Salisbury is an excellent example of English interpretation of the Gothic style. It had an unusual origin. The first Salisbury Cathedral had been built within the castle complex of the local lord. In 1217, Bishop Richard Poore petitioned the pope to relocate the church, claiming the wind on the hilltop howled so loudly that the clergy could not hear themselves sing the Mass. A more pressing concern was probably his desire to escape the lord's control. As soon as he moved, the bishop established a new town, called Salisbury. Material from the old church carted down the hill was used in the new cathedral, along with dark, fossil-filled Purbeck stone from quarries in southern England and limestone imported from Caen. Building began in 1220, and most of the cathedral was finished by 1258, an unusually short period for such an undertaking (FIG. 16–28).

A general comparison between the major features of French High Gothic cathedrals and Salisbury is instructive, for the builders took very different means to achieve their goal of creating the Heavenly Jerusalem on earth. In contrast to French cathedral façades, whose mighty towers flanking deep portals suggest monumental gateways to Paradise, English façades have a horizontal emphasis suggesting the jeweled walls of the celestial city.

At Salisbury, the west façade was completed by 1265. The small flanking towers of the west front project beyond the side walls and buttresses, giving the façade an increased width, underscored by tier upon tier of blind tracery and arcaded niches. Instead of a western rose window floating over triple portals (as seen in France), the English masters placed tall lancet windows above rather insignificant doorways. A mighty crossing tower (the French preferred a slender spire) became the focal point of the building. (The huge crossing tower and its 400-foot spire are a fourteenth-century addition at Salisbury, as are the flying buttresses, which were added to stabilize the tower.) The slightly later cloister and chapter house provided for the cathedral's clergy.

Salisbury has an equally distinctive plan, with wide projecting double transepts, a square east end with a single chapel, and a spacious sanctuary—like a monastic church (FIG. 16–29). The nave interior reflects the Norman building tradition of heavy walls and a tall nave arcade surmounted by a gallery and a clerestory with simple lancet windows (FIG. 16–30). The walls alone are enough to buttress the four-part ribbed vault. The emphasis on the horizontal movement of the arcades, unbroken by colonnettes, directs worshipers' attention forward toward the altar behind the choir screen, rather than upward into the vaults, as preferred in France (SEE FIG. 16–15). The use of color in the stonework is reminiscent of Romanesque interiors: The shafts supporting the four-part rib vaults are made of dark Purbeck stone that contrasts with the lighter limestone of the rest of the interior. The stonework was originally painted and gilded.

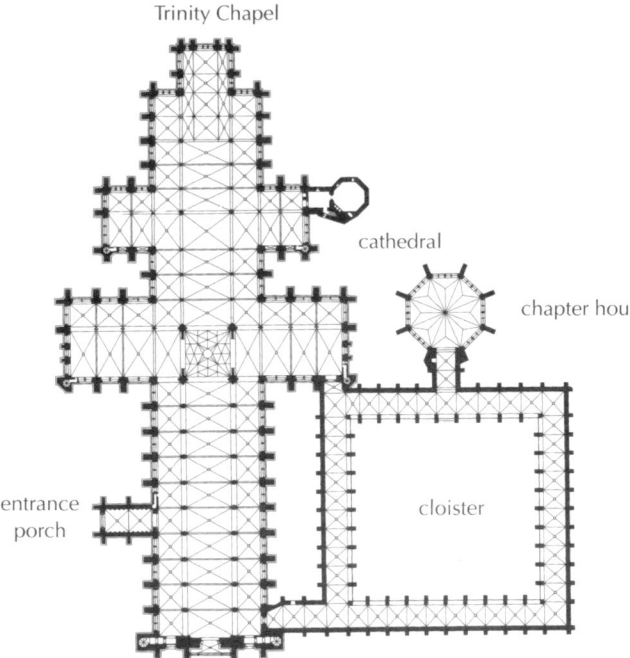

16–29 | **SALISBURY CATHEDRAL, PLAN**

16–28 | **SALISBURY CATHEDRAL**
Salisbury, England. 1220–58; west façade finished 1265; spire c. 1320–30; cloister and chapter house 1263–84.

16–30 | **NAVE, SALISBURY CATHEDRAL**

In the eighteenth century, the English architect James Wyatt subjected the building to radical renovations, during which the remaining stained glass and figure sculpture were removed or rearranged. Similar campaigns to refurbish medieval churches were common at the time. The motives of the restorers were complex and their results far from our notions of historical authenticity today.

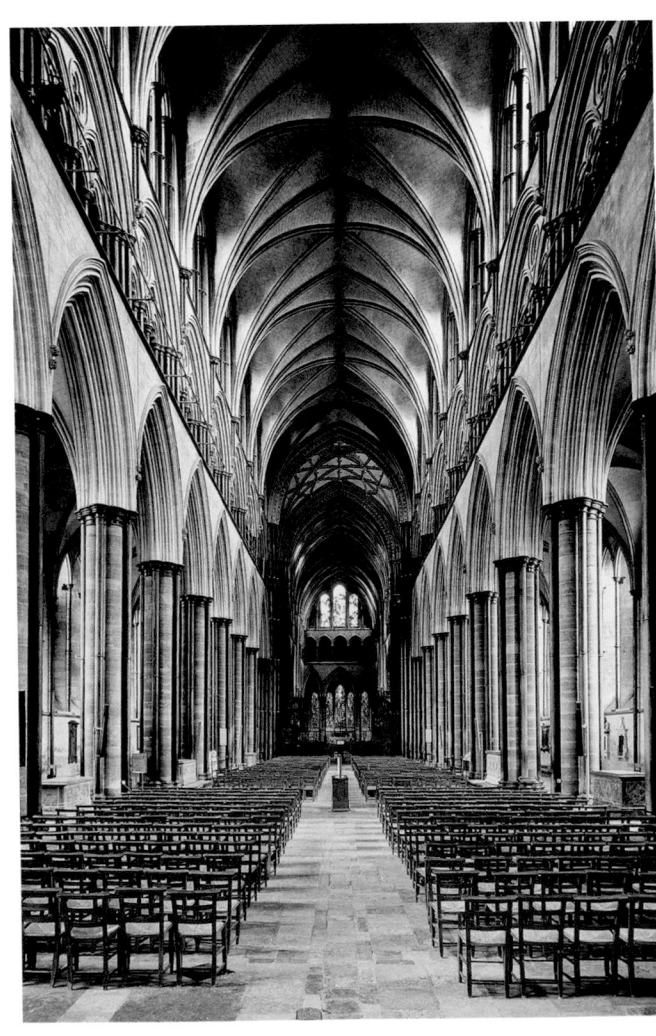

MILITARY AND DOMESTIC ARCHITECTURE. Cathedrals were not the only structures that underwent development during the Early and High Gothic periods. Western European knights who traveled east during the Crusades were inspired by the architectural forms they saw employed in Muslim castles and the mighty defensive land walls of Constantinople (SEE FIG. 7–24). When they returned home, Europeans built their own versions of these fortifications. Castle gateways now became complex, nearly independent fortifications often guarded by twin towers rather than just one. New D-shaped and round towers eliminated the corners that had made earlier square towers vulnerable to battering rams; and crenellations (notches) were added to tower tops in order to provide stone shields for more effective defense. The outer, enclosing walls of the castles were strengthened. The open, interior space was enlarged and filled with more comfortable living quarters for the lord and wooden buildings to house the garrison and the staff necessary to repair armor and other equipment. Barns and stables for animals, including the extremely valuable war horses, were also erected within the enclosure (SEE FIG. 15–24).

STOKESAY CASTLE. Military structures were not the only secular buildings outfitted for defense. In uncertain times, the manor (a landed estate), which continued to be an important economic basis in the thirteenth century, also had to fortify its buildings. A country house that was equipped with a tower and crenellated rooflines became a status symbol as well as a necessity. Stokesay Castle, a remarkable fortified manor house, survives in England near the Welsh border. In 1291 a wool merchant, Lawrence of Ludlow, acquired the property of Stokesay and secured permission from King Edward I to fortify his dwelling—officially known as a "license to crenellate" (FIG. 16–31). He built two towers, including a massive crenellated south tower and a great hall. The defense walls of Stokesay are gone, but the two towers and the great hall survive.

Life in the Middle Ages revolved around the hall. Windows on each side of Stokesay's hall open both toward the courtyard and out across a moat toward the countryside. By the thirteenth century people began to expect some privacy as well as security; therefore at both ends of the hall are two-story additions that provided retiring rooms for the family and workrooms for women to spin and weave. Rooms on the north end could be reached from the hall, but the upper chamber at the south was accessible only by means of an exterior stairway. A tiny window—a peephole—let women and members of the household observe the often rowdy activities in the hall below.

Furnishings defined and dignified the rooms. Of prime importance were textiles in the form of wall hangings, cushions, and coverlets (see *Christine de Pizan and the Queen of France* for an example of a furnished room, Introduction, Fig. 21). In both layout and décor, there was essentially no

16–31 | **EXTERIOR OF THE TOWER AND GREAT HALL, STOKESAY CASTLE**
Late 13th century. Royal permission to build granted in 1291.

difference between this manor far from the London court and the mansions built by the nobility in the city. A palace followed the same pattern of hall and retiring rooms; it was simply larger than a manor. The great hall was also the characteristic domestic architectural feature on the Continent.

GOTHIC ART IN GERMANY AND THE HOLY ROMAN EMPIRE

The Holy Roman Empire, weakened by internal strife and a prolonged struggle with the papacy, ceased to be a significant power in the thirteenth century. England and France were becoming strong nation-states, and the empire's hold on southern Italy and Sicily ended at midcentury with the death of Emperor Frederick II, who was also king of Sicily. The emperors—who were elected—had only nominal authority over a loose union of Germanic states. After Frederick, German lands increasingly became a conglomeration of independent principalities, bishoprics, and free cities. As in England, the French Gothic style, avidly embraced in the western Germanic territories, shows regional adaptations and innovations.

Architecture

In the thirteenth century, the increasing importance of the sermon in church services led architects in Germany to further develop the **hall church**, a type of open, light-filled interior space that appeared in Europe in the early Middle Ages but was particularly popular in Germany. The hall church is characterized by a nave and side aisles whose vaults all reach the same height. Large windows in the outer walls create a well-lit interior. The spacious and open design of the hall church provided accommodation for the large crowds drawn by charismatic preachers.

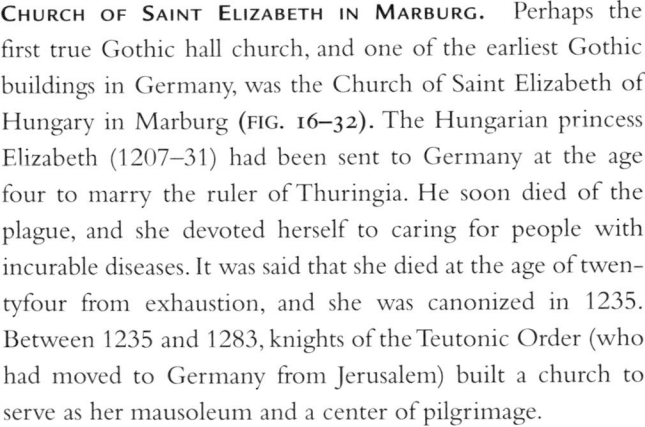

16–32 | EXTERIOR, CHURCH OF SAINT ELIZABETH
Marburg, Germany. 1235–83.

16–33 | INTERIOR, CHURCH OF SAINT ELIZABETH
Marburg, Germany. 1235–83.

CHURCH OF SAINT ELIZABETH IN MARBURG.   Perhaps the first true Gothic hall church, and one of the earliest Gothic buildings in Germany, was the Church of Saint Elizabeth of Hungary in Marburg (FIG. 16–32). The Hungarian princess Elizabeth (1207–31) had been sent to Germany at the age four to marry the ruler of Thuringia. He soon died of the plague, and she devoted herself to caring for people with incurable diseases. It was said that she died at the age of twenty-four from exhaustion, and she was canonized in 1235. Between 1235 and 1283, knights of the Teutonic Order (who had moved to Germany from Jerusalem) built a church to serve as her mausoleum and a center of pilgrimage.

The plan of the church is an early German form, a trefoil with choir and transepts of equal size. The elevation of the building, however, is new—the nave and aisles are of equal height. On the exterior wall, buttresses run the full height of the building and emphasize its verticality. The two rows of windows suggest a two-story building, which is not the case. Inside, the closely spaced piers of the nave support the ribbed vault and, as with the buttresses, give the building a vertical, linear quality (FIG. 16–33). Light from the two stories of tall windows fills the interior, unimpeded by walls, galleries, or triforia. Both the circular piers with slender engaged columns and the window tracery resemble those of the cathedral of Reims. The hall church design was adopted widely for civic and residential buildings in Germanic lands and also for Jewish architecture.

THE ALTNEUSCHUL.   Built in the third quarter of the thirteenth century, Prague's Altneuschul ("Old-New Synagogue") is the oldest functioning synagogue in Europe and one of two principal synagogues serving the Jews of Prague (FIG. 16–34). The Altneuschul demonstrates the adaptability of the Gothic hall-church design for non-Christian use. Like a hall church, the vaults of the synagogue are all the same height. Unlike a basilican church, with its division into nave and side aisles, the Altneuschul has only two aisles, each with three bays. The six bays are supported by the walls and two octagonal piers. The bays have Gothic four-part ribbed vaulting to which a nonfunctional fifth rib has been added. Some say that this fifth rib was added to remove the cross form made by the ribs.

The medieval synagogue was both a place of prayer and a communal center of learning and inspiration where men gathered to read and discuss the Torah. The synagogue had two focal points, the *aron,* or shrine for the Torah scrolls, and a raised reading platform called the *bimah.* The congregation faced the *aron,* which was located on the east wall, in the direction of Jerusalem. The *bimah* stood in the center of the hall, straddling the two center bays, and in Prague it was surrounded by a fifteenth-century ironwork open screen. The single entrance was placed off-center in a corner bay at the west end. Men worshiped and studied in the principal space; women had to worship in annexes on the north and west sides.

16–34 | **INTERIOR, ALTNEUSCHUL**
Prague, Bohemia (Czech Republic). c. late 13th century; *bimah* after 1483.

Sculpture

Germanic lands had a distinguished tradition of sculpture and metalwork. One of the creative centers of Europe since the eleventh century had been the Rhine River valley and the region known as the Mosan (from the Meuse River, in present-day Belgium), with centers in Liège and Verdun. Ancient Romans built their camps and cities in this area, and classical influence lingered on through the Middle Ages. Nicholas of Verdun was a pivotal figure in the development of Gothic sculpture. He and his fellow goldsmiths inspired a new classicizing style in the arts. Masters of the Classical Shop at Reims, for example, must have known his work.

SHRINE OF THE THREE KINGS. For the archbishop of Cologne, Nicholas created a magnificent reliquary to hold what were believed to be relics of the Three Magi (c. 1190–1205/10). Called the **SHRINE OF THE THREE KINGS**, the reliquary has the shape of a basilican church (**FIG. 16–35**). It is made of gilded bronze and silver, set with gemstones and dark blue enamel plaques that accentuate its architectural

16–35 | Nicholas of Verdun and workshop   **SHRINE OF THE THREE KINGS**
Cologne (Köln) Cathedral, Germany c. 1190–c. 1205/10. Silver and gilded bronze with enamel and gemstones,
5′8″ × 6′ × 3′8″ (1.73 × 1.83 × 1.12 m).

details. Nicholas and other Mosan artists were inspired by ancient Roman art still found in the region. Their figures are fully and naturalistically modeled and swathed in voluminous but revealing drapery. The three Magi and the Virgin fill the front gable end, and prophets and apostles sit in the niches in the two levels of arcading on the sides. The work combines robust, expressively mobile sculptural forms with a jeweler's exquisite ornamental detailing to create an opulent, monumental setting for its precious contents.

STRASBOURG CATHEDRAL. At the cathedral in Strasbourg (a border city variously claimed by France and Germany over the centuries), sculpture in the south transept portal reflects the Mosan style as interpreted by Reims masters. A relief (c. 1240) depicting the death and Assumption of Mary fills the tympanum (FIG. 16–36). While Mary lies on her deathbed surrounded by distraught apostles, Christ has received her soul (the doll-like figure in his arms) and will carry her directly to heaven. The theme is Byzantine, where the subject is known as the Dormition (Sleep) of the Virgin. The apostles are dynamically expressive figures with large heads, their grief vividly rendered. Their short bodies are clothed in fluid drap-

16–36 | **DORMITION OF THE VIRGIN**
South transept portal tympanum, Strasbourg Cathedral, Strasbourg, France. c. 1240.

ery. Deeply undercut, each stands out dramatically in the crowded scene. Strasbourg sculpture has an emotional expressiveness unknown earlier, and this depiction of intense emotion became characteristic of German medieval sculpture.

16–37 | **SAINT MAURICE**
Magdeburg Cathedral, Magdeburg, Germany. c. 1240-50.
Dark sandstone with traces of polychromy.

16–38 | **EKKEHARD AND UTA**
West chapel, Naumburg Cathedral, Naumburg, Germany.
c. 1245-60. Stone, originally polychromed, approx. 6'2"
(1.88 m).

SAINT MAURICE. In addition to emotional expressionism, a powerful current of realism runs through German Gothic sculpture. Some works suggest a living model, among them a statue of Saint Maurice in Magdeburg Cathedral, where his relics were preserved. Carved about 1240–50 (FIG. 16–37), Maurice, the commander of Egyptian Christian troops in the Roman army, was martyred together with his men in 286. As patron saint of Magdeburg, he was revered by Ottonian emperors and became a favorite saint of military aristocrats. Because he came from Egypt, Saint Maurice was commonly portrayed with black African features. Dressed in a full suit of chain mail covered by a sleeveless coat of leather, he represents a distinctly different military ideal (SEE FIG. 14–26).

NAUMBURG. As portraitlike as medieval figure sculpture sometimes seems, the figures represented ideal types, not actual individuals. Such is the case in the portrayal of the ancestors of the bishop of Wettin, Dietrich II. About 1245 he ordered sculptures for the family funeral chapel, built at the west end of Naumburg Cathedral. Bishop Dietrich had life-size statues of twelve of his ancestors, who had been patrons of the church, placed on pedestals around the chapel.

In the representations of Margrave Ekkehard of Meissen and his Polish-born wife, Uta (FIG. 16–38), the sculptor created extraordinarily lifelike and individualized figures and faces. The Margrave seems to be a proud warrior and no-nonsense administrator (a *margrave*—count of the march or border—was a territorial governor whose duty it was to

THE ◉BJECT SPEAKS

THE CHURCH OF ST. FRANCIS AT ASSISI

Shortly after Saint Francis's death, the church in his birthplace, Assisi, was begun (1228). It was nearly finished in 1239 but was not dedicated until 1253. Unusually elaborate in its design with upper and lower sections in two stories and a crypt, it is set into the hillside. Both upper and lower churches have a single nave of four square vaulted bays, and both end in a transept and a single apse. The lower church has massive walls and a narrow nave flanked by side chapels. The upper church is a spacious, well-lit hall designed to accommodate crowds. People went there to listen to the friars preach as well as to participate in church rituals, so Franciscan churches had to provide lots of space and excellent visibility and acoustics. The friars' educational mission utilized visual as well as spoken messages, so their churches had expanses of unbroken wall space suitable for educational and inspirational paintings.

Wall painting became a preeminent art form in Italy. The growing demand for painting reflected the educational mission of the mendicant orders—the Franciscans and the Dominicans—as well as the new sources of patronage created by Italy's burgeoning economy and urban society. Art proclaimed a patron's status as much as it did his or her piety.

The Church of Saint Francis is much more richly decorated than most Franciscan churches, although the architecture itself is simple. Typical Franciscan churches were barnlike structures with wooden roofs, but in the Church of Saint Francis the nave is divided by slender clustered, engaged columns that rise unbroken to Gothic ribbed vaults. At the window level, the walls are set back to make walkways down the nave. Single two-light windows pierce the upper walls of each bay. Painting covers every surface, even the vaults where large figures float against a bright blue heaven. The amount of decoration is surprising in the mother church of a monastic order dedicated to poverty and service.

On the morning of September 27, 1997, tragedy struck. An earthquake convulsed the small town of Assisi. It shook the Church of Saint Francis, causing great damage to the architecture and paintings. The vault collapsed in two places, causing priceless frescoes to shatter and plunge to the floor. The photographer Ghigo Roli had just finished recording every painted surface of the interior when the sound of the first earthquake was heard in the basilica. As the building shook, the paintings on the vaults fell. "I wanted to cry," Ghigo Roli later wrote.

When such a disaster happens, the whole world seems to respond. Volunteers immediately established organizations to raise money to restore the frescoes, with the hope and intention of paying the costs of repairing and strengthening the basilica, reassembling the paintings from millions of tiny pieces, and finally reinstalling the restored treasures. So successful was the effort that visitors today would not guess that an earthquake had brought down the vaults only a decade ago.

Church of Saint Francis, Assisi, Italy during the 1997 earthquake. (Above)

Church of Saint Francis, Assisi, Italy restored. (Right)
1228–53.

Caught by a television camera during the quake, some of the vaults and archivolts in the upper church plunged to the floor, killing four people. The camera operator eventually emerged, covered with the fine dust of the shattered brickwork and plaster, as a "white, dumbfounded phantom."

defend the frontier). Uta, coolly elegant and courtly, seems to draw her cloak artfully to her cheek. Traces of color indicate that painting added to the realistic impact of the figures. Such realism became characteristic of German Gothic art and ultimately had a profound impact on later art, both within Germany and beyond.

GOTHIC ART IN ITALY

The thirteenth century was a period of political division and economic expansion for the Italian peninsula. Part of southern Italy and Sicily was controlled by Frederick II von Hohenstaufen (1194–1250), king of Sicily from 1197 and Holy Roman emperor from 1220. Called by his contemporaries "the wonder of the world," Frederick was a politically unsettling force. He fought with a league of north Italian cities and briefly controlled the Papal States. On his death, Germany and the Holy Roman Empire ceased to be an important factor in Italian politics and culture. Instead, France and Spain began to vie for control of parts of the peninsula and the island of Sicily.

In northern Italy, in particular, organizations of successful merchants created communal governments in their prosperous and independent city-states and struggled against powerful families for control of them. Growing individual power and wealth inspired patronage of the arts. Artisans began to emerge as artists in the modern sense, both in their own eyes and the minds of their patrons. They joined together in urban guilds and independently contracted with wealthy clients and with civic and religious groups.

Sculpture: The Pisano Family

During his lifetime, the culturally enlightened Holy Roman emperor Frederick II had fostered a classical revival. He was a talented poet, artist, and naturalist, and an active patron of the arts and sciences. In the Romanesque period, artists in southern Italy had sometimes relied on ancient sculpture for inspiration. But Frederick, mindful of his imperial status as Holy Roman emperor, commissioned artists who turned to ancient Roman sculpture to help communicate a message of power. He also encouraged artists to look anew at the natural world around them. Nicola Pisano (active in Tuscany c. 1258–78), who came from the southern region of Apulia, one of the territories where imperial patronage under Frederick had flourished, became the leading exponent of the style that had developed in southern Italy.

NICOLA PISANO'S PULPIT AT PISA.   An inscription identifies the marble pulpit in the Pisa Baptistry as Nicola's work (FIG. 16–39). Clearly proud of his skill, he wrote: "In the year 1260 Nicola Pisano carved this noble work. May so gifted a hand be praised as it deserves." Columns topped with leafy Corinthian capitals support standing figures and Gothic

16–39 │ Nicola Pisano   PULPIT, BAPTISTRY, PISA
1260. Marble; height approx. 15′ (4.6 m).

trefoil arches, which in turn provide a base for the six-sided pulpit. The columns rest on high bases carved with crouching figures, domestic animals, and shaggy-maned lions. The panels illustrate New Testament subjects, each framed as an independent composition.

Panels illustrate several scenes in a continuous narrative—the Annunciation, Nativity, and Adoration of the Shepherds. The Virgin reclines in the middle of the composition (FIG. 16–40). The upper left-hand corner holds the Annunciation, and the scene in the upper right combines the annunciation to the shepherds with their adoration of the Child. In the foreground, midwives wash the infant Jesus as Joseph looks on. The viewer's attention moves from group to group within the shallow space, always returning to the regally detached Mother of God. The format, style, and technique of Roman sarcophagus reliefs—readily accessible in the burial ground near the Baptistry (SEE FIG. 15–13)—may have provided models for carving. The sculptural treatment of the deeply cut, full-bodied forms is classically inspired, as are their

16–40 | Nicola Pisano **NATIVITY**
Detail of pulpit, Baptistry, Pisa, Italy. 1260. Marble,
33½ × 44½" (85 × 113 cm).

16–41 | Giovanni Pisano **NATIVITY**
Detail of pulpit, Pisa Cathedral, Pisa. 1302–10. Marble,
34⅜ × 43" (87.2 × 109.2 cm).

heavy, placid faces. The closely packed composition recalls the Ludovisi Battle Sarcophagus (FIG. 6–69), although the shifts in scale are typically Gothic.

GIOVANNI PISANO'S PULPIT AT PISA. Nicola's son Giovanni (active c. 1265–1314) both assisted his father and learned from him, and he may also have worked or studied in France. By the end of the thirteenth century Giovanni emerged as a versatile artist in his own right. Between 1302 and 1310, he and his shop carved a huge pulpit for Pisa Cathedral that is similar to his father's in conception but significantly different in style and execution. In his **NATIVITY** panel Giovanni places graceful, animated figures in an uptilted, deeply carved landscape (FIG. 16–41). He replaces Nicola's impassive Roman matron with a slender young Mary who, sheltered by a shell-like cave, gazes delightedly at her baby. Below her, the

16–42 | **SIENA CATHEDRAL**
Siena, Italy. Lower west façade, 1284–99.

16–43 | Coppo di Marcovaldo **CRUCIFIX**
Tuscany, Italy. c. 1250-70. Tempera and gold on wood panel, 9'7⅛" × 8'1¼"
(2.93 × 2.47 m). Pinacoteca, San Gimignano, Italy.

midwife who doubted the virgin birth has her withered hand restored by the baby's bath water. Sheep, shepherds, and angels spiral up through the trees at the right and more angelic onlookers replace the Annunciation. Giovanni's sculpture is as dynamic as Nicola's is static.

THE CATHEDRAL FAÇADE AT SIENA. Between 1284 and 1299 Giovanni Pisano worked as architect, designer, and sculptor of the façade of the Cathedral of Our Lady in the central Italian city of Siena (FIG. 16–42). He incorporated elements of the French Style, such as Gothic gables with classical columns and moldings, to produce a richly ornamented screen independent of the building behind. High on the façade he placed figural sculptures, including dramatically gesturing and expressive prophets and sibyls. (The sculpture is now in the museum and has been replaced by copies.) Rather than the complex narrative sculptural programs typical of French Gothic façades, in Italy there was often an emphasis on architectural detailing of lintels and on narrative

door panels, as well as on figural sculpture placed across the façade. Inside, the focus was on furnishings such as pulpits, tomb monuments, baptismal fonts, and on paintings (see "The Church of Saint Francis at Assisi," page 546).

Painting

The capture of Constantinople by Crusaders in 1204 that brought relics to France also resulted in an influx of Byzantine art and artists to Italy. The imported style of painting, the *maniera greca* ("in the Greek manner"), influenced thirteenth- and fourteenth-century Italian painting in style and technique and introduced a new emphasis on pathos and emotion.

A "HISTORIATED CRUCIFIX." One example, the large wooden crucifix attributed to the thirteenth-century Florentine painter Coppo di Marcovaldo (FIG. 16–43), represents the *Christus patiens,* or suffering Christ: a Byzantine type with closed eyes and bleeding, slumped body that emphasized emotional realism (SEE FIGS. 7–43, 14–29). The cross is also a "historiated

16–44 | **LIFE OF SAINT FRANCIS, MIRACLE OF THE CRIB AT GRECCIO**
Church of Saint Francis, Assisi, Italy. Fresco, late 13th century?

crucifix," with scenes at each side that tell the Passion story. Such crosses were mounted on the choir screen that separated the clergy in the sanctuary from the lay people in the nave (one can be seen with its wooden bracing in FIG. 16–44).

MURAL PAINTING AT ASSISI.   Colorful, educational paintings covered the walls of Italian churches. The *Life of Saint Francis,* a series of narratives depicting the saint's life in the upper church of Saint Francis in Assisi, provides a vivid example of Gothic mural painting. Scholars differ on whether the murals were painted as early as 1290. Many have adopted the neutral designation of the artist as the "Saint Francis Master." **THE MIRACLE OF THE CRIB AT GRECCIO (FIG. 16–44)** portrays Saint Francis making the first Christmas manger scene in the church at Greccio and also vividly documents the appearance

of an Italian Gothic church. A large wooden crucifix, similar to the one by Coppo di Marcovaldo, has been suspended from a stand on top of a screen separating the sanctuary from the nave. The cross has been reinforced on the back and tilted forward to hover over people in the nave, whom we see through an open door in the choir screen. A pulpit, with stairs leading up to its entrance and candlesticks at its corners, rises above the screen at the left. An elaborate carved *baldacchino* (canopy) surmounts the altar at the right, and an adjustable wooden lectern stands in front of the altar.

Other small but telling touches include a seasonal liturgical calendar posted on the lectern, foliage swags decorating the *baldacchino,* and an embroidered altar cloth. Candles in tall candlesticks stand on the top of the screen and on wire frames above the lectern and altar. Saint Francis, in the foreground, reverently holds the Holy Infant above a plain, box-like crib next to representations of various animals that might have been present at the Nativity. The scene depicts the astonishing moment when, it was said, the Christ Child appeared in the manger. The tableau is recreated at Christmas by many families and communities today.

IN PERSPECTIVE

From its beginnings in France, Gothic art spread throughout Europe. In media as diverse as tiny book illustrations and enormous stained-glass windows, Gothic artists proclaimed the Christian message. These works were both educational and decorative. Inspired by biblical accounts of the jeweled walls of heaven and the golden gates of Paradise, Christian patrons and builders labored to erect glorious dwelling places for God and the saints on Earth. In order to intensify the effects of light and color, they constructed ever-larger buildings with higher vaults and thinner walls that permitted the insertion of huge windows. The glowing, back-lit colors of stained glass and the soft sheen of mural paintings dissolved the solid forms of masonry, while within the church the reflection of gold, enamels, and gems on altars and gospel book covers, on crosses and candlesticks, captured the splendor of Paradise on Earth. Subtle light and dazzling color created a mystical visual pathway to heaven as artists gave tangible form to the unseen and unknowable.

ABBEY CHURCH OF ST. DENIS
1140–44; 1231–81

CHARTRES.
**◀ TRANSEPT, ROSE WINDOW
AND LANCETS**
ABOUT 1220

PSALM1 (BEATUS VIR).
WINDMILL PLASTER
C. 1270–80

NICHOLAS OF VERDUN AND
WORKSHOP.
SHRINE OF THE THREE KINGS
C. 1190–1205/10

COPPO DI MARCOVALDO.
CRUCIFIX
C. 1250–1270

GIOVANNI PISANO.
NATIVITY, DETAIL OF PULPIT
1302–10

GOTHIC ART OF THE TWELFTH AND THIRTEENTH CENTURIES

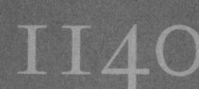

◀ **Second Crusade** 1147–49

◀ **Plantagenet Dynasty Ruled England**
1154–1485

◀ **Third Crusade** 1188–92

◀ **Fourth Crusade Takes Constantinople**
1204

◀ **Franciscan Order Founded** 1209

◀ **Western Control of Constantinople
Ends** 1261

◀ **Thomas Aquinas Begins Writing**
Summa Theologica 1266

1140

1200

1250

1300

17–1   Andrea Orcagna **TABERNACLE**   Orsanmichele, Florence, Probably begun 1355, completed 1359.
Marble, mosaic, gold, lapis lazuli.
Bernardo Daddi   **MADONNA AND CHILD**   1346–7. Tempera and gold on wood panel.

CHAPTER SEVENTEEN

FOURTEENTH-CENTURY ART
IN EUROPE

17

One of the many surprises greeting the modern visitor to Florence is a curious blocky building with statue-filled niches. Originally a **loggia** (a covered, open-air gallery), today its dark interior is dominated by a huge and ornate tabernacle built to house the important **MADONNA AND CHILD** (**FIG. 17–1**) by Bernardo Daddi. Daddi was commissioned to create this painting in 1346/47, just before the Black Death swept through the city in the summer of 1348.

Daddi's painting was the second replacement of a late thirteenth-century miracle-working image of the Madonna and Child. The original image had occupied a simple shrine in the central grain market, known as *Orsanmichele* (Saint Michael in the Garden). The original painting may have been irreparably damaged in the fire of 1304 that also destroyed the first market loggia, built at the end of the thirteenth century. A second painting, also lost, was made sometime later, but it was believed that the healing power of the image passed from painting to painting with continued potency.

Florence grew rapidly in the late Middle Ages. By the fourteenth century two-thirds of the city's grain supply had to be imported. The central grain market and warehouse established at Orsanmichele, as insurance against famine, made that site the economic center of the city. The Confraternity (charitable society) of Orsanmichele was created to honor the image of the Madonna and Child and to collect and distribute alms to needy citizens. In 1337 a new loggia

was built to protect the miracle-working image, and two upper stories were added to the loggia to store the city's grain reserves.

Orsanmichele remained Florence's central grain market for about ten years after Daddi painted the newest miracle-working *Madonna and Child* in 1346/47. As a reflection of its wealth and piety, the Confraternity of Orsanmichele commissioned Andrea di Cione, better known as Orcagna (active c. 1343–68), to create a new and rich tabernacle for Daddi's painting. A member of the stone- and woodworkers guild, Orcagna was in charge of building and decorating projects at Orsanmichele. To protect and glorify the *Madonna and Child*, he created a tour-de-force of architectural sculpture in marble, encrusted with gold and glass mosaics. In Orcagna's shrine, Daddi's *Madonna and Child* seems to be revealed by a flock of angels drawing back carved curtains. Sculpted saints stand on the pedestals against the piers, and reliefs depicting the life of the Madonna occupy the structure's base. The tabernacle was completed in 1359, and a protective railing was added in 1366.

Orsanmichele answered practical economic and social needs (granary and distribution point for alms), as well as religious and spiritual concerns (a shrine to the Virgin Mary), all of which characterized the complex society of the fourteenth century. In addition, Orsanmichele was a civic rallying point for the city's guilds. The significance of the guilds in the life of cities in the later Middle Ages cannot be overestimated. In

Florence, guild members were not simple artisans; the major guilds, composed of rich and powerful merchants and entrepreneurs, dominated the government and were key patrons of the arts. For example, the silk guild oversaw the construction of Orsanmichele. In 1380, the arches of the loggia were walled up. At that time, fourteen of the most important Florentine guilds were each assigned an exterior niche on the ground level in which to erect an image of their patron saint.

The cathedral, the Palazzo della Signoria, and Orsanmichele, three great buildings in the city center, have come to symbolize power and patronage in the Florentine Republic. But of the three, the miraculous Madonna in her shrine at Orsanmichele witnessed the greatest surge of interest in the years following the Black Death. Pilgrims flocked to Orsanmichele, and those who had died during the plague left their estates in their wills to the shrine's confraternity. On August 13, 1365, the Florentine government gathered the people together to proclaim the Virgin of Orsanmichele the special protectress of the city.

CHAPTER-AT-A-GLANCE

EUROPE IN THE FOURTEENTH CENTURY

By the middle of the fourteenth century, much of Europe was in crisis. Earlier prosperity had fostered population growth, which by about 1300 had begun to exceed food production. A series of bad harvests then meant that famines became increasingly common. To make matters worse, a prolonged conflict known as the Hundred Years' War (1337–1453) erupted between France and England. Then, in the middle of the fourteenth century, a lethal plague known as the Black Death swept across Europe, wiping out as much as 40 percent of the population (see "The Triumph of Death," page 556). By depleting the labor force, however, the plague gave surviving peasants increased leverage over their landlords and increased the wages of artisans.

The papacy had emerged from its conflict with the Holy Roman Empire as a significant international force. But its temporal success weakened its spiritual authority and brought it into conflict with growing secular powers. In 1309, after the election of a French pope, the papal court moved from Rome to Avignon, in southern France. Italians disagreed, and during the Great Schism from 1378 to 1417, there were two popes, one in Rome and one in Avignon, each claiming legitimacy. The Church provided some solace but little leadership, as rival popes in Rome and Avignon excommunicated each other's followers. Secular rulers took sides: France, Scotland, Aragon, Castile, Navarre, and Sicily supported the pope in Avignon; England, Flanders, Scandinavia, Hungary, and Poland supported the pope in Rome. Meanwhile, the Church experienced great strain from challenges from reformers like John Hus (c. 1370–1415) in Bohemia. The cities and states that composed present-day Germany and the Italian Peninsula were divided among different factions.

The literary figures Dante, Petrarch, and Boccaccio (see "A New Spirit in Fourteenth-Century Literature," page 561) and the artists Cimabue, Duccio, and Giotto fueled a cultural explosion in fourteenth-century Italy. In literature, Petrarch (Francesco Petrarca, 1304–74) was a towering figure of change, a poet whose love lyrics were written not in Latin but in Italian, marking its first use as a literary language. A similar role was played in painting by the Florentine Giotto di Bondone (c. 1277–1337). In deeply moving mural paintings, Giotto not only observed the people around him, he ennobled the human form by using a weighty, monumental style, and he displayed a new sense of dignity in his figures' gestures and emotions

This new orientation toward humanity, combined with a revived interest in classical learning and literature, we now designate as *humanism*. Humanism embodied a worldview that focused on human beings; an education that perfected individuals through the study of past models of civic and personal virtue; a value system that emphasized personal effort and responsibility; and a physically active life that was directed toward the common good as well as individual

MAP 17–1 | Europe in the Fourteenth Century

Avignon in Southern France, Prague in Bohemia, and Exeter in Southern England joined Paris, Florence, and Siena as centers of art patronage in the late Gothic period.

nobility. For Petrarch and his contemporaries an appreciation of Greek and Roman writers became the defining element of the age. Humanists mastered the Greek and Latin languages so that they could study the classical literature—including newly rediscovered works of history, biography, poetry, letters, and orations.

In architecture, sculpture, and painting, the Gothic style—with its soaring vaults, light, colorful glass, and linear qualities—persisted in the fourteenth century, with regional variations. Toward the end of the century, devastation from the Hundred Years' War and the Black Death meant that large-scale construction gradually ceased, ending the great age of cathedral building. The Gothic style continued to develop, however, in smaller churches, municipal and commercial buildings, and private residences. Many churches were modernized or completed in this late Gothic period.

From the growing middle class of artisans and merchants, talented and aggressive leaders assumed economic and in some places political control. The artisan guilds—organized by occupation—exerted quality control among members and supervised education through an apprenticeship sys-

tem. Admission to the guild came after examination and the creation of a "masterpiece"—literally, a piece fine enough to achieve master's status. The major guilds included cloth finishers, wool merchants, and silk manufacturers, as well as pharmacists and doctors. Painters belonged to the pharmacy guild, perhaps because they used mortars and pestles to grind their colors. Their patron saint, Luke, who was believed to have painted the first image of the Virgin Mary (see Chapter 7, page 266), was also a physician—or so they thought. Sculptors who worked in wood and stone had their own guild, while those who worked in metals belonged to another guild. Guilds provided social services for their members, including care of the sick and funerals for the deceased. Each guild had its patron saint and maintained a chapel and participated in religious and civic festivals.

Complementing the economic power of the guilds was the continuing influence of the Dominican and Franciscan religious orders (see Chapter 16), whose monks espoused an ideal of poverty, charity, and love and dedicated themselves to teaching and preaching. The new awareness of societal needs manifested itself in the

THE ⊙BJECT SPEAKS

THE TRIUMPH OF DEATH

The Four Horsemen of the Apocalypse—Plague, War, Famine, and Death—stalked the people of Europe during the fourteenth century. France, England, and Germany pursued their seemingly endless wars, and roving bands of soldiers and brigands looted and murdered unprotected peasants and villagers. Natural disasters—fires, droughts, floods, and wild storms—took their toll. Disease spread rapidly through a population already weakened by famine and physical abuse.

Then a deadly plague, known as the Black Death, spread by land and sea from Asia. The plague soon swept from Italy and France across the British Isles, Germany, Poland, and Scandinavia. Half the urban population of Florence and Siena—some say 80 percent—died in the summer of 1348. To people of the time the Black Death seemed to be an act of divine wrath against sinful humans.

In their panic, some people turned to escapist pleasures; others to religious fanaticism. Andrea Pisano and Ambrogio Lorenzetti were probably among the many victims of the Black Death. But the artists who survived had work to do—chapels and hospitals, altarpieces and votive statues. The sufferings of Christ, the sorrows as well as the joys of the Virgin, the miracles of the saints, and new themes—"The Art of Dying Well," and "The Triumph of Death"—all carried the message "Remember, you too will die." An unknown artist, whom we call the Master of the Triumph of Death, painted such a theme in the cemetery of Pisa (Camposanto).

The horror and terror of impending death are vividly depicted in the huge mural, THE TRIUMPH OF DEATH. In the center of the wall dead people lie in a heap while devils and angels carry their souls to hell or heaven. Only the hermits living in the wilderness escape the holocaust. At the right, wealthy young people listen to music under the orange trees, unaware of Death flying toward them with a scythe. At the left of the painting, a group on horseback who have ridden out into the wilderness discover three open coffins. A woman recoils at the sight of her dead counterpart. A courtier covers his nose, gagging at the smell, while his wild-eyed horse is terrified by the bloated, worm-riddled body in the coffin. The rotting corpses remind them of their fate, a medieval theme known as "The Three Living and the Three Dead."

Perhaps the most memorable and touching images in the huge painting are the crippled beggars who beg Death to free them from their earthly miseries. Their words appear on the scroll: "Since prosperity has completely deserted us, O Death, you who are the medicine for all pain, come to give us our last supper!"* The painting speaks to the viewer, delivering its message in words and images. Neither youth nor beauty, wealth nor power, but only piety like that of the hermits provides protection from the wrath of God.

Strong forces for change were at work in Europe. For all the devastation caused by the Four Horsemen, those who survived found increased personal freedom and economic opportunity.

* Translated by John Paoletti and Gary Radke, *Art in Renaissance Italy*, 3rd ed. Upper Saddle River, New Jersey. Pearson Prentice Hall, 2005. p. 154.

Master of the Triumph of Death (Buffalmacco?)   **THE TRIUMPH OF DEATH**
Camposanto, Pisa. 1330s. Fresco, 18'6" × 49'2" (5.6 × 15 m).

Reproduced here in black and white, photo taken before the fresco was damaged by American shells during World War II.

17–2 | **PIAZZA DELLA SIGNORIA WITH PALAZZO DELLA SIGNORIA (TOWN HALL)**
1299–1310 and **LOGGIA DEI LANZI (LOGGIA OF THE LANCERS)**
Florence. 1376–82. Speakers' platform and since the sixteenth century a guard station and sculpture gallery.

architecture of churches designed for preaching as well as liturgy, and in new religious themes that addressed personal or sentimental devotion.

ITALY

Great wealth and a growing individualism promoted art patronage in northern Italy. Artisans began to emerge as artists in the modern sense, both in their own eyes and in the eyes of patrons. Although their methods and working conditions remained largely unchanged, artisans in Italy contracted freely with wealthy townspeople and nobles and with civic and religious bodies. Their ambition and self-confidence reflect their economic and social freedom.

Florentine Architecture and Sculpture

The typical medieval Italian city was a walled citadel on a hilltop. Houses clustered around the church and an open city square. Powerful families added towers to their houses both for defense and out of family pride. In Florence, by contrast, the

ancient Roman city—with its rectangular plan, major north–south and east–west streets, and city squares—remained the foundation for civic layout. The cathedral stood northeast of the ancient forum. The north–south street joining the cathedral and the Piazza della Signoria followed the Roman line.

THE PALAZZO DELLA SIGNORIA. The governing body of the city (the Signoria) met in the **PALAZZO DELLA SIGNORIA,** a massive fortified building with a tall bell tower 300 feet (91 m) high (**FIG. 17–2**). The building faces a large square, or piazza, which became the true civic center. Town houses often had seats along their walls to provide convenient public seating. In 1376 (finished in 1381/82), a huge loggia was built at one side to provide a covered space for ceremonies and speeches. After it became a sculpture gallery and guard station in the sixteenth century, the loggia became known as the **LOGGIA OF THE LANCERS.** The master builders were Berici di Cione and Simone Talenti. Michelangelo's *David* (SEE FIG. 20–10) once stood in front of the Palazzo della Signoria facing the loggia (it is replaced today by a modern copy).

THE CATHEDRAL. In Florence, the cathedral (*duomo*) (FIGS. 17–3, 17–4) has a long and complex history. The original plan, by Arnolfo di Cambio (c. 1245–1302), was approved in 1294, but political unrest in the 1330s brought construction to a halt until 1357. Several modifications of the design were made, and the cathedral we see today was built between 1357 and 1378. (The façade was given its veneer of white and green marble in the nineteenth century to coordinate it with the rest of the building and the nearby Baptistry of San Giovanni.)

Sculptors and painters rather than masons were often responsible for designing Italian architecture, and as the Florence Cathedral reflects, they tended to be more concerned with pure design than with engineering. The long, square-bayed nave ends in an octagonal domed crossing, as wide as the nave and side aisles. Three polygonal apses, each with five radiating chapels, surround the central space. This symbolic Dome of Heaven, where the main altar is located, stands apart from the worldly realm of the congregation in the nave. But the great ribbed dome, so fundamental to the planners' conception, was not begun until 1420, when the architect Filippo Brunelleschi (1377–1446) solved the engineering problems involved in its construction (see Chapter 19).

THE BAPTISTRY DOORS. In 1330, Andrea Pisano (c.1290–1348) was awarded the prestigious commission for a pair of gilded bronze doors for the Florentine Baptistry of San Giovanni. (Although his name means "from Pisa," Andrea was not related to Nicola and Giovanni Pisano.) The Baptistry doors were completed within six years and display

I7–3 FLORENCE CATHEDRAL (DUOMO)
Plan 1294, costruction begun 1296, redisegned 1357 and 1366, drum and dome 1420-36.
Illustration by Philipe Biard in Guide Gallimard Florence © Gallimard Loisirs.

17–4 | Arnolfo di Cambio, Francesco Talenti, Andrea Orcagna, and others **FLORENCE CATHEDRAL (DUOMO)**
1296-1378; drum and dome by **Brunelleschi**, 1420-36; bell tower (Campanile) by **Giotto, Andrea Pisano**, and
Francesco Talenti, c. 1334–50.

The Romanesque Baptistry of San Giovanni stands in front of the *Duomo*.

twenty scenes from the life of John the Baptist (San Giovanni) set above eight personifications of the Virtues (FIG. 17–5). The reliefs are framed by quatrefoils, the four-lobed decorative frames introduced at the Cathedral of Amiens in France (SEE FIG. 16–21). The figures within the quatrefoils are in the monumental, classicizing style inspired by Giotto then current in Florentine painting, but they also reveal the soft curves of northern Gothic forms in their gestures and draperies, and a quiet dignity of pose particular to Andrea. The individual scenes are elegantly natural. The figures' placement, on shelflike stages, and their modeling create a remarkable illusion of three-dimensionality, but the overall effect created by the repeated barbed quatrefoils is two-

dimensional and decorative, and emphasizes the solidity of the doors. The bronze vine scrolls filled with flowers, fruits, and birds on the lintel and jambs framing the door were added in the mid-fifteenth century.

Florentine Painting

Florence and Siena, rivals in so many ways, each supported a flourishing school of painting in the fourteenth century. Both grew out of the Italo-Byzantine style of the thirteenth century, modified by local traditions and by the presence of individual artists of genius. The Byzantine influence, also referred to as the *maniera greca* ("Greek manner"), was characterized by dramatic pathos and complex iconography and showed

17–5 | Andrea Pisano LIFE OF JOHN THE BAPTIST
South doors, Baptistry of San Giovanni, Florence. 1330–36. Gilded bronze, each panel 19¼ × 17" (48 × 43 cm).
Frame, Ghiberti workshop, mid-15th century.

itself in such elements as elongated figures, often exaggerated, iconic gestures, stylized features including the use of gold for drapery folds, and striking contrasts of highlights and shadows in the modeling of individual forms. By the end of the fourteenth century, the painter and commentator Cennino Cennini (see "Cennino Cennini [c. 1370–1440] on Painting," page 564) would be struck by the accessibility and modernity of Giotto's art, which, though it retained traces of the "Greek manner," was moving toward the depiction of a humanized world anchored in three-dimensional form.

CIMABUE. In Florence, the transformation of the Italo-Byzantine style began a little earlier than in Siena. About 1280, a painter named Cenni di Pepi (active c. 1272–1302), better known by his nickname "Cimabue," painted the VIRGIN AND CHILD ENTHRONED (FIG. 17–6), perhaps for the main altar of the Church of Santa Trinita in Florence. At almost 12 feet tall, this enormous panel painting set a new precedent for monumental altarpieces. Cimabue uses the traditional Byzantine iconography of the "Virgin Pointing the Way," in which Mary holds the infant Jesus in her lap and points to him as the path to salvation. Mother and child are surrounded by saints, angels, and Old Testament prophets.

A comparison with a Byzantine icon (SEE FIG. 7–51) shows that Cimabue employed Byzantine formulas in determining the proportions of his figures, the placement of their schematic features, and even the tilt of their haloed heads. Mary's huge throne, painted to resemble gilded bronze with inset enamels and gems, provides an architectural framework for the figures. To render her drapery and that of the infant Jesus, Cimabue used the Italo-Byzantine technique of highlighting drapery with thin lines of gold to indicate divinity. The viewer seems suspended in space in front of the image, simultaneously looking down on the projecting elements of the throne and Mary's lap, while looking straight ahead at the prophets at the base of the throne and the angels at each side. These spatial ambiguities, the subtle asymmetries within the centralized composition, the Virgin's thoughtful gaze, and the individually conceived faces of the old men enliven the picture with their departure from Byzantine tradition. Cimabue's concern for spatial volumes, solid forms delicately modeled in light and shade, and warmly naturalistic human figures contributed to the course of later Italian painting.

GIOTTO DI BONDONE. Compared to Cimabue's *Virgin and Child Enthroned,* Giotto's painting of the same subject (FIG. 17–7), done about 1310 for the Church of the Ognissanti (All Saints) in Florence, exhibits a groundbreaking spatial consistency and sculptural solidity while retaining some of Cimabue's conventions. The central and overtly symmetrical composition and the position of the figures reflect Cimabue's influence. Gone, however, are Mary's modestly inclined head and the delicate gold folds in her drapery. Instead, her face is

Art and Its Context

A NEW SPIRIT IN FOURTEENTH-CENTURY LITERATURE

For Petrarch and his contemporaries—Boccaccio, Chaucer, Christine de Pizan—the essential qualifications for a writer were an appreciation of Greek and Roman authors and an ability to observe and appreciate people from every station in life. Although fluent in Latin, they chose to write in the language of their own daily life—Italian, English, French. Leading the way was Dante Alighieri (1265–1321), who wrote *The Divine Comedy,* his great summation of human virtue and vice, and ultimately human destiny, in Italian. Dante established the Italian language as worthy of great themes in literature.

Francesco Petrarca, called simply Petrarch (1304–74), raised the status of secular literature with his sonnets (love lyrics) to his unobtainable, beloved Laura; his histories and biographies; and his discovery of the ancient Roman writings on the joys of country life. Petrarch's imaginative updating of classical themes in a work called *The Triumphs*—which examines the themes of Chastity triumphant over Love, Death over Chastity, Fame over Death, Time over Fame, and Eternity over Time—provided later Renaissance poets and painters with a wealth of allegorical subject matter.

More earthy, Giovanni Boccaccio (1313–75) perfected the art of the short story in *The Decameron,* a collection of amusing and moralizing tales told by a group of young Florentines who moved to the countryside to escape the Black Death. With wit and sympathy, Boccaccio presents the full spectrum of daily life in Italy. Such secular literature, including the discovery and translation of ancient authors (for some of the tales had a long lineage), written in Italian as it was then spoken in Tuscany, provided a foundation for the Renaissance of the fifteenth century.

In England, Geoffrey Chaucer (c. 1342–1400) was inspired by Boccaccio to write his own series of short stories, *The Canterbury Tales,* told by pilgrims traveling to the shrine of Saint Thomas à Becket (1118?–1170) in Canterbury. Observant and witty, Chaucer depicted the pretensions and foibles, as well as the virtues, of humanity.

Christine de Pizan (1364–c. 1431), born in Venice but living and writing at the French court, became an author out of necessity when she was left a widow with three young children and an aged mother to support. Among her many works are a poem in praise of Joan of Arc and a history of famous women—including artists—from antiquity to her own time. In *The Book of the City of Ladies* she defended women's abilities and argued for women's rights and status. These writers, as surely as Giotto, Duccio, Peter Parler, and Master Theodoric, led the way into a new era.

individualized, and her action—holding her child's leg instead of merely pointing to him—seems entirely natural. This colossal Mary seems too large for the slender Gothic tabernacle, where figures peer through the openings and haloes overlap the faces. In spite of the formal, enthroned image and flat, gold background, Giotto renders the play of light and shadow across these substantial figures to create a sense that they are fully three-dimensional beings inhabiting real space. Details of the Virgin's solid torso can be glimpsed under her thin tunic, and Giotto's angels, unlike those of Cimabue, have ample wings that fold over in a resting position.

According to the sixteenth-century chronicler Vasari, "Giotto obscured the fame of Cimabue, as a great light out-shines a lesser." Vasari also credited Giotto with "setting art upon the path that may be called the true one [for he] learned to draw accurately from life and thus put an end to the crude Greek [i.e., Italo-Byzantine] manner" (translated by J. C. and P. Bondanella).

Giotto may have collaborated on murals at the prestigious Church of Saint Francis in Assisi (see "The Church of Saint Francis at Assisi," page 546). Certainly he worked for the Franciscans in Florence and reacted to their teaching. Saint Francis's message of simple, humble devotion, direct experience of God, and love for all creatures was gaining followers throughout Western Europe, and it had a powerful impact on thirteenth- and fourteenth-century Italian literature and art.

17–6 | Cimabue VIRGIN AND CHILD ENTHRONED
Most likely painted for the high altar of the Church of Santa Trinita, Florence. c. 1280. Tempera and gold on wood panel, 12′17″ × 7′ 4″ (3.53 × 2.2 m). Galleria degli Uffizi, Florence.

Early in the fourteenth century Giotto traveled to northern Italy. While working at the Church of Saint Anthony in Padua, he was approached by a local banker, Enrico Scrovegni, to decorate a new family chapel. He agreed, and the **SCROVEGNI CHAPEL** was dedicated in 1305 to the Virgin of Charity and the Virgin of the Annunciation. (The chapel is also called the "Arena Chapel" because it and the family palace were built on and in the ruins of an ancient Roman arena.) The building is a simple, barrel-vaulted room (**FIG. 17–8**). As viewers look toward the altar, they see the story of Mary and Jesus unfolding before them in a series of rectangular panels. On the entrance wall Giotto painted the Last Judgment.

17–7 | Giotto di Bondone **VIRGIN AND CHILD ENTHRONED**
Most likely painted for the high altar of the Church of the Ognissanti (All Saints), Florence. 1305–10. Tempera and gold on wood panel, 10′8″ × 6′ 8¼″ (3.53 × 2.05 m). Galleria degli Uffizi, Florence.

Technique
CENNINO CENNINI
(c. 1370–1440) ON PAINTING

Cennino Cennini's *Il Libro dell' Arte (The Book of Art)* is a handbook of Florentine and north Italian painting techniques from about 1400. Cennini includes a description of the artist's life as well as step-by-step painting instructions.

"You, therefore, who with lofty spirit are fired with this ambition, and are about to enter the profession, begin by decking yourselves with this attire: Enthusiasm, Reverence, Obedience, and Constancy. And begin to submit yourself to the direction of a master for instruction as early as you can, and do not leave the master until you have to" (Chapter III).*

The first step in preparing a panel for painting is to cover its surface with clean white linen strips soaked in a **gesso** made from gypsum. Gesso provides a ground, or surface, on which to paint. Cennini specified that at least nine layers of gesso should be applied. The gessoed surface should then be burnished until it resembles ivory. The artist can now sketch the composition of the work with charcoal. At this point, advised Cennini, "When you have finished drawing your figure, especially if it is in a very valuable [altarpiece], so that you are counting on profit and reputation from it, leave it alone for a few days, going back to it now and then to look it over and improve it wherever it still needs something . . . (and bear in mind that you may copy and examine things done by other good masters; that it is no shame to you). The final version of the design should be inked in with a

fine squirrel-hair brush, and the charcoal brushed off with a feather. Gold leaf should be affixed on a humid day, the tissue-thin sheets carefully glued down with a mixture of fine powdered clay and egg white, on the reddish clay ground (called bole). Then the gold is burnished with a gemstone or the tooth of a carnivorous animal. Punched and incised patterning should be added to the gold leaf later."*

Italian painters at this time worked in **tempera** paint, powdered pigments mixed most often with egg yolk, a little water, and an occasional touch of glue.

Cennini specified a detailed and highly formulaic painting process. Faces, for example, were always to be done last, with flesh tones applied over two coats of a light greenish pigment and highlighted with touches of red and white. The finished painting was to be given a layer of varnish to protect it and enhance its colors. An elaborate frame, which included the panel or panels on which the painting would be executed, would have been produced by a specialist according to the painter's specifications and brought fully assembled to the studio.

Cennini claimed that panel painting was a gentleman's job, but given its laborious complexity, that was wishful thinking. The claim does, however, reflect the rising social status of painters.

* Cennino Cennini, *The Craftsman's Handbook (Il Libro dell' Arte)*. Trans. by Daniel V. Thompson. New York: Dover, 1960. pp. 3, 16, 75.

A base of faux marble and allegorical *grisaille* (gray monochrome) paintings of the Virtues and Vices support vertical bands painted to resemble marble inlay and carved relief and containing quatrefoil portrait medallions. The central band of medallions spans the vault, crossing a brilliant, lapis blue, star-spangled sky in which large portrait disks float like glowing moons. Set into this framework are the rectangular narrative scenes juxtaposing the life of the Virgin with that of Jesus (FIG. 17–9).

Both the individual scenes and the overall program display Giotto's genius for distilling a complex narrative into a coherent visual experience. The life of the Virgin Mary begins the series and fills the upper band of images. Following in historical sequence, events in the life and ministry of Jesus circle the chapel in the middle band, while scenes of the Passion (the arrest, trial, and Crucifixion of Jesus) fill the lowest band. Read vertically, however, each set of three scenes foreshadows or comments on the others.

The first miracle, when Jesus changes water to wine during the wedding feast at Cana, recalls that his blood will become the wine of the Eucharist, or Communion. The raising of Lazarus becomes a reference to Jesus's Resurrection. Below, the Lamentation over the body of Jesus by those closest

to him leads to the Resurrection, indicated by angels at the empty tomb and his appearance to Mary Magdalen in the *Noli Me Tangere* ("Do not touch me"). The juxtaposition of dead and live trees in the two scenes also becomes a telling detail of death and resurrection. Giotto used only a few large figures and essential props in settings that never distract the viewer by their intricate detail. The scenes are reminiscent of *tableaux vivants* ("living pictures"), in which people dressed in costume re-created poses from familiar works of art—scenes that were played out in the city square in front of the chapel in Padua.

Among Giotto's achievements was his ability to model form with color. He rendered his bulky figures as pure color masses, painting the deepest shadows with the most intense hues and highlighting shapes with lighter shades mixed with white. These sculpturally modeled figures enabled Giotto to convey a sense of depth in landscape settings without relying on the traditional convention of an architectural framework.

In one of the most moving works, **LAMENTATION** (FIG. 17–10), in the lowest **register** (horizontal band) of the Arena Chapel, Giotto focused the composition off center for maximum emotional effect, concentrating on the faces of Mary and the dead Jesus. A great downward-swooping ridge—its barrenness emphasized by a single dry tree, a medieval

17–8 | Giotto di Bondone **SCROVEGNI (ARENA) CHAPEL,**
Frescoes, Padua. 1305–6. View toward east wall.

17–9 | Giotto di Bondone
**MARRIAGE AT CANA,
RAISING OF LAZARUS,
RESURRECTION,** and **NOLI ME
TANGERE** and **LAMENTATION**
Frescoes on north wall of
Scrovegni (Arena) Chapel,
Padua. 1305–6. Each scene
approx. 6′5″ × 6′ (2 × 1.85 m).

17–10 | Giotto di
Bondone **LAMENTATIO**
Fresco in the Scrovegni
(Arena) Chapel, Padua.
1305–6. Approx.
6′5″ × 6′ (2 x 1.85 m).

symbol of death—carries the psychological weight of the scene to its expressive core. Mourning angels hovering overhead mirror the anguish of Jesus's followers. The stricken Virgin communes with her dead son with mute intensity, while John the Evangelist flings his arms back in convulsive despair and other figures hunch over the corpse. Instead of symbolic sorrow, more typical of art from the early Middle Ages, Giotto conveys real human suffering, drawing the viewer into the circle of personal grief. The direct, emotional appeal of his art, as well as its deliberate plainness, seems to embody Franciscan values.

BERNARDO DADDI. Giotto dominated Florentine painting in the first half of the fourteenth century. His combination of humanism and realism was so memorable that other artists' work paled beside his. The artists who worked in his studio picked up the mannerisms but not the essence of his style. Bernardo Daddi (active c. 1312–48), who painted the *Madonna and Child* in Orsanmichele (SEE FIG. 17–1), typifies the group with his personal reworking of Giotto's powerful figures. Daddi's talent lay in the creation of sensitive, lyrical images rather than the majestic realistic figures. He may have

been inspired by courtly French art, which he would have known from luxury goods, such as imported ivory carvings. The artists of the school of Giotto were responsible for hundreds of panel paintings. They also frescoed the walls of chapels and halls (see "Buon Fresco," page 569).

Sienese Painting

Like their Florentine rivals, the Sienese painters at first worked in a strongly Byzantine style. Sienese painting continued to emphasize abstract decorative qualities and a love of applied gold and brilliant colors. Consequently, Sienese art often seems slightly conservative.

DUCCIO DI BUONINSEGNA. Siena's foremost painter in the later Gothic period was Duccio di Buoninsegna (active 1278–1318). Duccio knew thirteenth-century Byzantine art, with its elongated figures, stacks of angels, patterned textiles, and lavish use of gold. Between 1308 and 1311, Duccio painted a huge altarpiece for the high altar of Siena Cathedral. The **MAESTÀ (MAJESTY)** was dedicated, like the town itself, to the Virgin (FIGS. 17–11, 17–12).

17–11 | Duccio di Buoninsegna **VIRGIN AND CHILD IN MAJESTY,** Central Panel from Maestà Altarpiece
Siena Cathedral. 1308–11. Tempera and gold on wood panel, 7′ × 13′6″ (2.13 × 3.96 m).
Museo dell'Opera del Duomo, Siena.

"On the day that it was carried to the [cathedral] the shops were shut, and the bishop conducted a great and devout company of priests and friars in solemn procession, accompanied by . . . all the officers of the commune, and all the people, and one after another the worthiest with lighted candles in their hands took places near the picture, and behind came the women and children with great devotion. And they accompanied the said picture up to the [cathedral], making the procession around the Campo [square], as is the custom, all the bells ringing joyously, out of reverence for so noble a picture as is this" (Holt, page 69).

17–12 | **PLAN OF FRONT AND BACK OF THE MAESTÀ ALTARPIECE**

Creating this altarpiece was an arduous undertaking. The central panel alone was 7 by 13 ½ feet, and it had to be painted on both front and back, because it was meant to be seen from both sides. The main altar for which it was designed stood beneath the dome in the center of the sanctuary. Inscribed on Mary's throne are the words, "Holy Mother of God be thou the cause of peace for Siena and, because he painted thee thus, of life for Duccio" (cited in Hartt and Wilkins 4.2, page 104).

Mary and Christ, adored by angels and the four patron saints of Siena—Ansanus, Savinus, Crescentius, and Victor—kneeling in front, fill the large central panel. This *Virgin and Child in Majesty* represents both the Church and its specific embodiment, Siena Cathedral. Narrative scenes from the early life of the Virgin and the infancy of the Christ Child appear below the central image. The **predella** (the lower zone of the altarpiece) was entirely painted with the events in the childhood of Jesus. The back of this immense work was dedicated to scenes of his adult life and the miracles. The entire composition was topped by pinnacles—on the front, angels and the later life of the Virgin, and on the back, events after the Passion.

Duccio created a personal style that combines a softened Italo-Byzantine figure style with the linear grace and the easy relationship between figures and their settings characteristic of French Gothic. This subtle blending of northern and southern elements can be seen in the haloed ranks of angels around Mary's architectonic throne. The central, most holy figures retain a solemnity and immobility with some realistic touches, such as the weighty figure of the child; the adoring saints reflect a more naturalistic, courtly Gothic style that became the hallmark of the Sienese school for years to come. The brilliant palette, which mingles pastels with primary hues, the delicately patterned textiles that shimmer with gold, and the ornate **punchwork**—tooled designs in gold leaf on the haloes—are characteristically Sienese.

In 1771 the altarpiece was broken up, and individual panels were sold. One panel—the **NATIVITY WITH PROPHETS ISAIAH AND EZEKIEL**—is now in Washington, D.C. Duccio represented the Nativity in the tradition of Byzantine icons. Mary lies on a fat mattress within a cave hollowed out of a jagged, stylized mountain (**FIG. 17–13**). Jesus appears twice: first lying in the manger and then with the midwife below. However, Duccio followed Western tradition by placing the scene in a shed. Rejoicing angels fill the sky, and the shepherds and sheep add a realistic touch in the lower right corner. The light, intense colors, the calligraphic linear quality, even the meticulously rendered details recall Gothic manuscripts (see Chapter 16). The tentative move toward a defined space in the shed as well as the subtle modeling of the figures point the way toward future development in representing people and their world. Duccio's graceful, courtly art contrasts with Giotto's austere monumentality.

Technique
BUON FRESCO

The two techniques used in mural painting are **buon** ("true") **fresco** ("fresh"), in which paint is applied with water-based paints on wet plaster, and **fresco secco** ("dry"), in which paint is applied to a dry plastered wall. The two methods can be used on the same wall painting.

The advantage of *buon fresco* is its durability. A chemical reaction occurs as the painted plaster dries, which bonds the pigments into the wall surface. In *fresco secco*, by contrast, the color does not become part of the wall and tends to flake off over time. The chief disadvantage of *buon fresco* is that it must be done quickly without mistakes. The painter plasters and paints only as much as can be completed in a day. In Italy, each section is called a **giornata**, or day's work. The size of a *giornata* varies according to the complexity of the painting within it. A face, for instance, can occupy an entire day, whereas large areas of sky can be painted quite rapidly.

In medieval and Renaissance Italy, a wall to be frescoed was first prepared with a rough, thick undercoat of plaster. When this was dry, assistants copied the master painter's composition onto it with charcoal. The artist made any necessary adjustments. These drawings, known as **sinopia**, have an immediacy and freshness lost in the finished painting. Work proceeded in irregularly shaped sections conforming to the contours of major figures and objects. Assistants covered one section at a time with a fresh, thin coat of very fine plaster over the *sinopia*, and when this was "set" but not dry, the artist worked with pigments mixed with water. Painters worked from the top down so that drips fell on unfinished portions. Some areas requiring pigments such as ultramarine blue (which was unstable in *buon fresco*), as well as areas requiring gilding, would be added after the wall was dry using the *fresco secco* method.

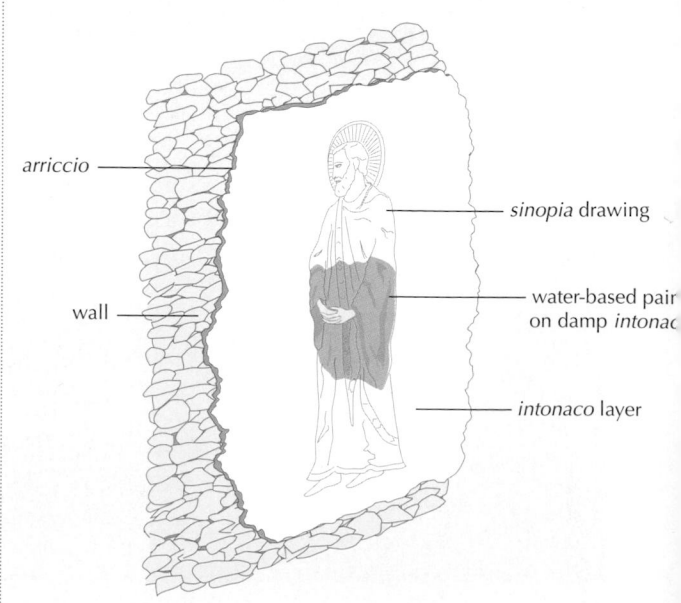

arriccio

wall

sinopia drawing

water-based paint on damp intonaco

intonaco layer

17–13 Duccio di Buoninsegna **NATIVITY WITH PROPHETS ISAIAH AND EZEKIEL**
Predella of the Maestà Altarpiece, 17 × 17½" (44 × 45 cm); Prophets, 17¼" × 6½" (44 × 16.5 cm).
National Gallery, Washington, D.C.

17–14 Ambrogio Lorenzetti **FRESCO SERIES OF THE SALA DELLA PACE, PALAZZO PUBBLICO**
Siena city hall, Siena, Italy. 1338–40. Length of long wall about 46′ (14 m).

AMBROGIO LORENZETTI. In Siena, a strain of seemingly native realism also began to emerge. In 1338, the Siena city council commissioned Ambrogio Lorenzetti to paint in fresco the council room of the Palazzo Pubblico (city hall) known as the **SALA DELLA PACE (CHAMBER OF PEACE)** (FIG. 17–14). The murals were to depict the results of good and bad government. On the short wall Ambrogio painted a figure symbolizing the Commune of Siena, enthroned like an emperor holding an orb and scepter and surrounded by the Virtues. Justice, assisted by Wisdom and Concord, oversees the local magistrates. Peace lounges on a bench against a pile of armor, having defeated War. The figure is based on a fragment of a Roman sarcophagus still in Siena.

Ambrogio painted the results of both good and bad government on the two long walls. For the **ALLEGORY OF GOOD GOVERNMENT,** and in tribute to his patrons, Ambrogio created an idealized but recognizable portrait of the city of Siena and its immediate environs (FIG. 17–15). The cathedral dome and the distinctive striped campanile (see Chapter 16) are visible in the upper left-hand corner; the streets are filled with productive citizens. The Porta Romana, Siena's gateway leading to Rome, divides the city from the country. Over the portal

17–15 | Ambrogio Lorenzetti **ALLEGORY OF GOOD GOVERNMENT IN THE CITY AND IN THE COUNTRY**
Sala della Pace, Palazzo Pubblico, Siena, Italy. 1338–40. Fresco, total length about 46′ (14 m).

stands the statue of the wolf suckling Romulus and Remus, the legendary founders of Rome. Representations of these twin boys were popular in Siena because of the legend that Remus's son Senus founded Siena. Hovering above outside the gate is a woman clad in a wisp of transparent drapery, a scroll in one hand and a miniature gallows complete with a hanged man in the other. She represents Security, and her scroll bids those entering the city to come in peace. The gallows is a sharp reminder of the consequences of not doing so.

Ambrogio's achievement in this fresco was twofold. First, despite the shifts in vantage point and scale, he maintained an overall visual coherence and kept all parts of the flowing composition intelligible. Second, he maintained a natural relationship between the figures and the environment. Ambrogio conveys a powerful vision of an orderly society, of peace and plenty, from the circle of young people dancing to a tambourine outside a shoemaker's shop to the well-off peasants tending fertile fields and lush vineyards. Sadly, plague struck in the next decade. Famine, poverty, and disease overcame Siena just a few years after this work was completed.

The world of the Italian city-states—which had seemed so full of promise in Ambrogio Lorenzetti's *Good Government* fresco—was transformed into uncertainty and desolation by epidemics of the plague. Yet as dark as those days must have seemed to the men and women living through them, beneath the surface profound, unstoppable changes were taking place. In a relatively short span of time, the European Middle Ages gave way to what is known as the Renaissance.

FRANCE

At the beginning of the fourteenth century the royal court in Paris was still the arbiter of taste in Western Europe, as it had been in the days of Saint Louis. During the Hundred Years' War, however, the French countryside was ravaged by armed struggles and civil strife. The power of the old feudal nobility, weakened significantly by warfare, was challenged by townsmen, who took advantage of new economic opportunities that opened up in the wake of the conflict. Leadership in the arts and architecture moved to the duchy of Burgundy, to England, and—for a brief golden moment—to the court of Prague.

Gothic sculptors found a lucrative new outlet for their work in the growing demand among wealthy patrons for religious art intended for homes as well as churches. Busy urban workshops produced large quantities of statuettes and reliefs in wood, ivory, and precious metals, often decorated with enamel and gemstones. Much of this art was related to the cult of the Virgin Mary. Architectural commissions were smaller—chapels rather than cathedrals, and additions to already existing buildings, such as towers, spires, and window tracery.

In the second half of the thirteenth century, architects working at the royal court in Paris (see Chapter 16) introduced a new style, which continued into the first part of the fourteenth century. Known as the French Court style, or Rayonnant style or Rayonnant Gothic in France, the art is characterized by elegance and refinement achieved through extraordinary technical virtuosity. In sculpture and painting, elegant figures move gracefully through a narrow stage space established by miniature architecture and elements of landscape. Sometimes a focus on the details of nature suggests the realism that appears in the fourteenth century.

Manuscript Illumination

By the late thirteenth century, literacy had begun to spread among laypeople. Private prayer books became popular among those who could afford them. Because they contained special prayers to be recited at the eight canonical "hours" between morning and night, an individual copy of one of these books came to be called a Book of Hours. Such a book included everything the lay person needed—psalms, prayers to the Virgin and the other saints, a calendar of feast days, the office of the Virgin, and even the offices of the dead. During the fourteenth century, a richly decorated Book of Hours was worn or carried like jewelry and was among a noble person's most important portable possessions.

THE BOOK OF HOURS OF JEANNE D'EVREUX.   Shortly after their marriage in 1325, King Charles IV gave his queen, Jeanne d'Evreux, a tiny, exquisite BOOK OF HOURS, the work of the illuminator Jean Pucelle (FIG. 17–16). This book was precious to the queen, who mentioned it in her will. She named its illuminator, Jean Pucelle, an unusual tribute.

In this manuscript, Pucelle worked in the *grisaille* technique—monochromatic painting in shades of gray with faint touches of color (here, blue and pink). The subtle shades emphasized his accomplished drawing. Queen Jeanne appears in the initial below the *Annunciation,* kneeling before a lectern and reading, perhaps, from her Book of Hours. This inclusion of the patron in prayer within a scene conveyed the idea that the scenes were visions inspired by meditation rather than records of historical events. In this case, the young queen would presumably have identified with Mary's joy at Gabriel's message.

Jeanne d'Evreux's Book of Hours combines two narrative cycles in its illuminations. One, the Hours of the Virgin, juxtaposes scenes from the Infancy and Passion of Christ, a form known as the Joys and Sorrows of the Virgin. The other is dedicated to the recently canonized king, Saint Louis. In the opening shown here, the joy of the *Annunciation* on the

17–16 | Jean Pucelle **PAGES WITH BETRAYAL AND ARREST OF CHRIST,** folio 15v. (left), and **ANNUNCIATION,** folio 16r. (right), **BOOK OF HOURS OF JEANNE D'EVREUX**
Paris c. 1325–28. *Grisaille* and color on vellum, each page 3½ × 2¼″ (8.9 × 6.2 cm).
The Metropolitan Museum of Art, New York. The Cloisters Collection 1954 (54.1.2).

right is paired with the "sorrow" of the *Betrayal and Arrest of Christ* on the left. In the *Annunciation,* Mary is shown receiving the archangel Gabriel in a Gothic building, while rejoicing angels look on from windows under the eaves. The group of romping children at the bottom of the page (known as the *bas-de-page* in French) at first glance seems to echo the joy of the angels. They might be playing "love tag," which would surely relate to Mary as the chosen one of the Annunciation. Folklorists have suggested, however, that the children are playing "froggy in the middle," or "hot cockles," games in which one child was tagged by the others. To the medieval reader the game symbolized the mocking of Christ or the betrayal of Judas, who "tags" his friend, and it evokes a darker mood by foreshadowing Jesus's death even as his life is beginning. In the *Betrayal* on the opposite page, Judas Iscariot embraces Jesus, thus identifying him to the Roman soldiers. The traitor sets in motion the events that lead to the Crucifixion. Saint Peter, on the left, realizing the danger, draws his sword to defend Jesus and slices off the ear of the high priest's servant Malchus. The *bas-de-page* on this side shows knights riding goats and jousting at a barrel stuck on a pole, a spoof of the military that may comment on the lack of valor of the soldiers assaulting Jesus.

Pucelle's work represents a sophisticated synthesis of contemporary French, English, and Italian art. From English illuminators he borrowed the merging of Christian narrative with allegory, the use of foliate borders filled with real and grotesque creatures (instead of the standard French vine scrolls), and his lively *bas-de-page* illustrations. His presentation of space, with figures placed within coherent architectural settings, suggests a firsthand knowledge of Sienese art: The small angels framed by the rounded arches of the attic are reminiscent of the half-length saints who appear above the front panel of Duccio's *Maestà.* Pucelle also adapted to manuscript illumination the Parisian Court style in sculpture, with its softly modeled, voluminous draperies gathered around tall, elegantly curved figures with curly hair and delicate features.

Sculpture

Sculpture in the fourteenth century is exemplified by its intimate character. Religious subjects became more emotionally expressive. In the secular realm, the cult of chivalry was revived just as the era of the knight on horseback was being rendered obsolete. Tales of love and valor were carved on luxury items to delight the rich, middle class, and aristocracy alike. Precious metals—gold, silver, and ivory—were preferred.

THE VIRGIN AND CHILD FROM SAINT-DENIS. A silver-gilt image of a standing **VIRGIN AND CHILD** (FIG. 17–17) was once among the treasures of the Abbey Church of Saint-Denis (see Chapter 16). An inscription on the base bears the date 1339 and the donor's name, Queen Jeanne d'Evreux. The Virgin holds Jesus in her left arm, her weight on her left leg, creating the graceful S-curve pose that became characteristic of the period. Fluid drapery, suggesting the consistency of heavy silk, covers her body. She originally wore a crown, and she holds a scepter topped with a large enameled and jeweled *fleur-de-lis,* the heraldic symbol of French royalty. The scepter served as a reliquary for a few strands of Mary's hair. The Virgin's sweet, youthful face and simple clothing, although based on thirteenth-century sculpture, anticipate the so-called Beautiful Mother imagery of fourteenth-century Prague (SEE FIG. 17–25), Flanders, and Germany. The Christ Child reaching out to touch his mother's lips is babylike in his proportions and gestures, a hint of realism. The image is not entirely joyous, however; on the enameled base, scenes of Christ's Passion remind us of the suffering to come.

COURTLY LOVE: AN IVORY BOX. A strong market also existed for personal items like boxes, mirrors, and combs with secular scenes inspired by popular literature and folklore. A box—perhaps a gift from a lover—made in a Paris workshop around 1330–50 provides a delightful example of such a work (FIG. 17–18). In its ivory panels, the God of Love shoots his arrows; knights and ladies throw flowers as missiles and joust with flowers. The subject is the **ATTACK ON THE CASTLE OF LOVE,** but what the owner kept in the box—jewelry? love tokens?—remains a mystery.

A tournament takes place in front of the Castle of Love. The tournament—once a mock battle, designed to keep knights fit for war—has become a lovers' combat. In the center panel, women watch jousting knights charge to the blare of the heralds' trumpets. In the scene on the left, knights use crossbows and a catapult to hurl roses at the castle, while the God of Love helps the women by aiming his arrows at the attackers. The action concludes in the scene on the right, where the tournament's victor and his lady love meet in a playful joust of their own.

Unlike the aristocratic marriages of the time, which were essentially business contracts based on political or financial exigencies, romantic love involved passionate devotion. Images of gallant knights serving ladies, who bestowed tokens of affection on their chosen suitors or cruelly withheld their love on a whim, captured the popular imagination. Tales of romance were initially spread by the musician–poets known as troubadours. Twelfth-century troubadour poetry marked a shift away from the usually negative way in which women had previously been portrayed as sinful daughters of Eve.

17–17 | **VIRGIN AND CHILD**
c. 1339. Silver gilt and enamel, height 27⅛" (69 cm).
Musée du Louvre, Paris.

Given by Jeanne d'Evreux to the Abbey Church of Saint-Denis, France.

17–18 | **ATTACK ON THE CASTLE OF LOVE**
Lid of a box. Paris. c. 1330–50. Ivory box with iron mounts, panel 4½ × 9¹¹⁄₁₆″ (11.5 × 24.6 cm).
The Walters Art Museum, Baltimore.

ENGLAND

Fourteenth-century England prospered in spite of the ravages of the Black Death and the Hundred Years' War with France. Life in medieval England is described in the rich store of Middle English literature. The brilliant social commentary of Geoffrey Chaucer in the *Canterbury Tales* (see "A New Spirit in Fourteenth-Century Literature," page 561) includes all classes of society. The royal family, especially Edward I—the castle builder—and many of the nobles and bishops were generous patrons of the arts.

Embroidery: Opus Anglicanum

An English specialty, pictorial needlework in colored silk and gold thread, gained such fame that it came to be called *opus anglicanum (English work)*. Among the collectors of this luxurious textile art were the popes, who had more than 100 pieces in the Vatican treasury. The names of several prominent embroiderers are known, but few names can be connected to specific pieces.

Opus anglicanum was employed for court dress, banners, cushions, bed hangings, and other secular items, as well as for the vestments worn by the clergy to celebrate the Mass (see Introduction Fig. 3, *Christine de Pizan Presenting a Book to the Queen of France*). Few secular pieces survive, since clothing and furnishings were worn out and discarded when fashions changed. But some vestments have survived, stored in church treasuries.

A liturgical vestment (that is, a special garment worn by the priest during mass), the red velvet **CHICHESTER-CONSTABLE**

CHASUBLE (FIG. 17–19) was embroidered with colored silk, gold threads forming the images as subtly as painting. Where gold threads were laid and couched (tacked down with colored silk), the effect resembles the burnished gold-leaf backgrounds of manuscript illuminations. The Annunciation, the Adoration of the Magi, and the Coronation of the Virgin are set in cusped, crocketed **ogee** (S-shaped) arches amid twisting branches sprouting oak leaves, seed-pearl acorns, and animal masks. Because the star and crescent moon in the Coronation of the Virgin scene are heraldic emblems of Edward III (ruled 1327–77), perhaps he or a family member ordered this luxurious vestment.

During the celebration of the Mass, garments of *opus anglicanum* would have glinted in the candlelight amid treasures on the altar. Court dress was just as rich and colorful, and at court such embroidered garments established the rank and

Sequencing Events

c. 1307–21	Dante writes *The Divine Comedy*
1309–77	Papacy transferred from Rome to Avignon
1348	Arrival of Black Death on European mainland
1378–1417	Great Schism in Catholic Church
1396	Greek studies instituted in Florence; beginning of the revival of Greek literature

17–19 | LIFE OF THE VIRGIN, BACK OF THE CHICHESTER-CONSTABLE CHASUBLE
From a set of vestments embroidered in *opus anglicanum* from southern England. 1330–50. Red velvet with silk and metallic thread and seed pearls; length 4′3″ (129.5 cm), width 30″ (76 cm). The Metropolitan Museum of Art, New York.
Fletcher Fund, 1927 (27.162.1).

status of the wearer. So heavy did such gold and bejeweled garments become that their wearers often needed help to move.

Architecture

In the later years of the thirteenth century and early years of the fourteenth, a distinctive and influential style, popularly known as the "Decorated style," which corresponded to the Rayonnant style in France (see Chapter 16), developed in England. This change in taste has been credited to Henry III's ambition to surpass his brother-in-law, Saint Louis (Louis IX) of France, as a royal patron of the arts.

THE DECORATED STYLE AT EXETER. The most complete Decorated style building is the **EXETER CATHEDRAL.** Thomas of Witney began work at Exeter in 1313 and was the master

mason from 1316 until 1342. He supervised construction of the nave and redesigned upper parts of the choir. He left the towers of the original Norman cathedral but turned the interior into a dazzling stone forest of colonnettes, moldings, and vault ribs (FIG. 17–20). From diamond-shaped piers covered with colonnettes rise massed moldings that make the arcade seem to ripple. Bundled colonnettes spring from sculptured **corbels** (supporting brackets that project from a wall) between the arches to support conical clusters of thirteen ribs that meet at the summit of the vault, a modest 69 feet above the floor. The basic structure here is the four-part vault with intersecting cross-ribs, but the designer added additional ribs, called **tiercerons,** to create a richer linear pattern. Elaborately carved **bosses** (decorative knoblike elements) cover the intersections where ribs meet. Large clerestory windows with bar-tracery mullions (slender vertical elements dividing the windows into subsections) illuminate the 300-foot-long nave. Unpolished gray marble shafts, yellow sandstone arches, and a white French stone, shipped from Caen, used in the upper walls add subtle graduations of color to the many-rayed space.

Detailed records survive for the building of Exeter Cathedral. They extend over the period from 1279 to 1514, with only two short breaks. Included is such mundane information as where the masons and carpenters were housed (in a hostel near the cathedral) and how they were paid (some by the day with extra for drinks, some by the week, some for each finished piece); how materials were acquired and transported (payments for horseshoes and fodder for the horses); and of course payments for the building materials (not only stone and wood but rope for measuring and parchment on which to draw forms for the masons). The bishops contributed generously to the building funds. Building was not an anonymous labor of love as imagined by romantic nineteenth-century historians.

Thomas of Witney also designed the bishop's throne. Richard de Galmeton and Walter of Memburg led a team of a dozen carpenters to build the throne and the intricate canopy, 57 feet high. The canopy is like a piece of embroidery translated into wood, revealing characteristic forms of the Decorated style: S-curves, nodding arches (called "nodding ogee arches" because they curve outward—and nod—as well as upward) lead the eye into a maze of pinnacles, bursting with leafy **crockets** and tiny carved animals and heads. To finish the throne in splendor, Master Nicolas painted and gilded the wood. When the bishop was seated on his throne wearing embroidered vestments like the *Chichester-Constable Chasuble,* he must have resembled a golden image in a shrine rather than a living man. Enthroned, he represented the power and authority of the Church.

THE PERPENDICULAR STYLE AT EXETER. During years following the Black Death, work at Exeter Cathedral came to a

17–20 | **EXETER CATHEDRAL**
Exeter, Devon, England. Thomas of Witney, Choir, 14th century and
Bishop's Throne, 1313–17; Robert Lesyngham, East Window, 1389–90.

standstill. The nave had been roofed but not vaulted, and the windows had no glass. When work could be resumed, taste had changed. The exuberance of the Decorated style gave way to an austere style in which rectilinear patterns and sharp angular shapes replaced intricate curves, and luxuriant foliage gave way to simple stripped-down patterns. This phase is known as the Perpendicular style.

In 1389–90, well-paid master mason Robert Lesyngham rebuilt the great East Window (FIG. 17–20), and he designed the window tracery in the new Perpendicular style. The window fills the east wall of the choir like a glowing altarpiece. A single figure in each light stands under a tall painted canopy that flows into and blends with the stone tracery. The Virgin with the Christ Child stands in the center over the high altar,

with four female saints at the left and four male saints, including Saint Peter, to whom the church is dedicated, on the right. At a distance the colorful figures silhouetted against the silver *grisaille* glass become a band of color, reinforcing the rectangular pattern of the mullions and transoms. The combination of *grisaille,* silver stain (creating shades of gold), and colored glass produces a cool silvery light.

The Perpendicular style produces a decorative scheme that heralds the Renaissance style (see Chapter 19) in its regularity, its balanced horizontal and vertical lines, and its plain wall or window surfaces. When Tudor monarchs introduced Renaissance art into the British Isles, builders did not have to rethink the form and structure of their buildings; they simply changed the ornament from the pointed cusped and crocketed arches of the Gothic style to the round arches and ancient Roman columns and capitals of the classical era. The Perpendicular style, used throughout the Late Gothic period in the British Isles, became England's national style. It remains popular today in the United States for churches and college buildings.

THE HOLY ROMAN EMPIRE

By the fourteenth century, the Holy Roman Empire existed more as an ideal fiction than a fact. The Italian territories had established their independence, and in contrast to England and France, Germany had become further divided into multiple states with powerful regional associations and princes. The Holy Roman Emperors, now elected by Germans, concentrated on securing the fortunes of their families. They continued to be patrons of the arts, promoting local styles.

The Supremacy of Prague

Charles IV of Bohemia (ruled 1346–75), whose admiration for the French king Charles IV was such that he changed his own name from Wenceslas to Charles, had been raised in France. He was officially crowned king of Bohemia in 1347 and Holy Roman Emperor in 1355.

Charles established his capital in Prague, which, in the view of its contemporaries, replaced Constantinople as the "New Rome." Prague had a great university, a castle, and a cathedral overlooking a town that spread on both sides of a river joined by a stone bridge, a remarkable structure itself.

When Pope Clement VI made Prague an archbishopric in 1344, construction began on a new cathedral in the Gothic style—to be named for Saint Vitus—which would also serve as the coronation church and royal pantheon. At Charles's first coronation, however, the choir remained unfinished. Charles, deeply involved in his projects, brought Peter Parler from Swabia to complete the building. Peter came from a distinguished family of architects.

THE PARLER FAMILY. In 1317 Heinrich Parler, a former master of works on the Cologne Cathedral, designed and began building the **CHURCH OF THE HOLY CROSS** in Schwäbisch Gmünd, in southwest Germany. In 1351, his son Peter (c. 1330–99), the most brilliant architect of this talented family, joined the shop. Peter designed the choir (FIG. 17–21) in the manner of a hall church in which a triple-aisled form was enlarged by a ring of deep chapels between the buttresses

17–21 | Heinrich and Peter Parler **CHURCH OF THE HOLY CROSS**
Schwäbisch Gmünd, Germany. Interior. Begun in 1317 by Henrich Parler; choir by Peter Parler begun in 1351; vaulting completed 16th century.

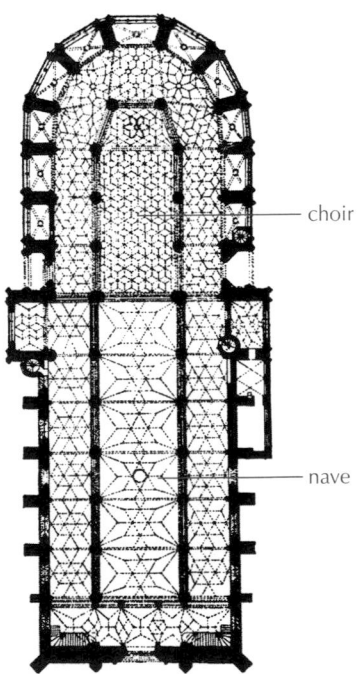

17–22 | **PLAN OF CHURCH OF THE HOLY CROSS**
Schwäbisch Gmünd.

— choir

— nave

of the choir. The unity of the entire space was enhanced by the complex net vault—a veritable web of ribs created by eliminating transverse ribs and ridge ribs. Seen clearly in the plan (FIG. 17–22), the contrast between Heinrich's nave and Peter's choir illustrates the increasing complexity of rib patterns, a complexity that in fact finally led to the unified interior space of the Renaissance.

Called by Charles IV to Prague in 1353, Peter turned the unfinished Saint Vitus Cathedral into a "glass house," adding a vast clerestory and glazed triforium supported by double flying buttresses, all covered by net vaults that created a continuous canopy over the space. Photos do not do justice to the architecture; but the small, gilded icon shrine suggests the richness and elaborateness of Peter's work. The shrine stands in the reliquary chapel of Saint Wenceslas (FIG. 17–23)—once a freestanding Romanesque chapel, now incorporated into the cathedral—on the south side of the church. The chapel itself, with walls encrusted with semiprecious stones, recalls a reliquary (c. 1370–71).

Peter, his family, and heirs became the most successful architects in the Holy Roman Empire. Their concept of space, luxurious decoration, and intricate vaulting dominated central European architecture for three generations.

MASTER THEODORIC AND THE "BEAUTIFUL STYLE." At Karlstejn Castle, a day's ride from Prague, the emperor built another chapel and again covered the walls with gold and precious stones as well as with paintings. One hundred thirty paintings of the saints also served as reliquaries, for they had relics inserted into their frames. Master Theodoric, the court painter, provided drawings on the wood panels, and he painted about thirty images himself (FIG. 17–24). These figures are crowded into—and even extend over—the frames,

17–23 | Peter Parler and workshop **SAINT WENCESLAS CHAPEL, CATHEDRAL OF SAINT VITUS**
Prague. Begun 1356. In 1370-71, the walls were encrusted with slabs of jasper, amethyst, and gold, forming crosses. Tabernacle, c. 1375: gilded iron. Height 81⅞" (208 cm).

The spires, pinnacles, and flying buttresses of the tabernacle may have been inspired by Peter Parler's drawings for the cathedral.

17–24 | Master Theodoric **SAINT LUKE**
Holy Cross Chapel, Karlstejn Castle, near Prague. 1360–64. Paint and gold on panel. 45¼ × 37" (115 × 94 cm).

emphasizing their size and power. Master Theodoric was head of the Brotherhood of Saint Luke, the patron saint of painters, and his painting of **SAINT LUKE,** accompanied by his symbol, the ox, looks out at the viewer, suggesting that this may really be a self-portrait of Master Theodoric. Master Theodoric's personal style—heavy bodies, oversized heads and hands, dour and haunted faces, and soft, deeply modeled drapery—merged with the French Gothic style to become what is known as the Beautiful style of the end of the century. The chapel, consecrated in 1365, so pleased the emperor that in 1367 he gave the artist a farm in appreciation for his work.

Like the architecture of the Parler family, the style created by Master Theodoric spread through central and northern Europe. Typical of this Beautiful style is the sweet-faced Virgin and Child, as seen in the **"BEAUTIFUL" VIRGIN AND CHILD** (FIG. 17–25), engulfed in swaths of complex drapery.

Cascades of V-shaped folds and clusters of vertical folds ending in rippling edges surround a squirming infant to create the feeling of a fleeting movement. Emotions are restrained, and grief as well as joy become lost in a naive piety. Yet, this art emerges against a background of civil and religious unrest. The Beautiful style seems like an escape from the realities of fourteenth-century life.

Mysticism and Suffering

The ordeals of the fourteenth century—famines, wars, and plagues—helped inspire a mystical religiosity that emphasized both ecstatic joy and extreme suffering. Devotional images, known as *Andachtsbilder* in German, inspired the worshiper to contemplate Jesus's first and last hours, especially during evening prayers, or vespers (giving rise to the term *Vesperbild* for the image of Mary mourning her son).

17–25 │ "BEAUTIFUL" VIRGIN AND CHILD
Probably from the Church of Augustinian Canons, Sternberk. c. 1390. Limestone with original paint and gilding; height 33⅛" (84 cm).

Through such religious exercises, worshipers hoped to achieve understanding of the divine and union with God. In the well-known example shown here (FIG. 17–26), blood gushes from the hideous rosettes that are the wounds of an emaciated Jesus. The Virgin's face conveys the intensity of her ordeal, mingling horror, shock, pity, and grief. Such images had a profound impact on later art, both within Germany and beyond.

Prague and the Holy Roman Empire under Charles IV had become a multicultural empire where people of different religions (Christians and Jews) and ethnic heritage (German and Slav) lived side by side. Charles died in 1378, and without his strong central government, political and religious dissent overtook the empire. Jan Hus, dean of the philosophy faculty at Prague University and a powerful reforming preacher, denounced the immorality he saw in the Church. He was burned at the stake, becoming a martyr and Czech national hero. The Hussite Revolution in the fifteenth century ended Prague's—and Bohemia's—leadership in the arts.

IN PERSPECTIVE

The emphasis on suffering and on supernatural power inspired many artists to continue the formal, expressive styles of earlier medieval and Byzantine art. At the same time, the humanism emerging in the paintings of Giotto and his school at the beginning of the fourteenth century could not be denied. Painters began to combine the flat, decorative, linear quality of Gothic art with the new representation of forms defined by light and space. In Italy they created a distinctive new Gothic style that continued through the fourteenth century. North of the Alps, Gothic elements survived in the arts well into the fifteenth century.

The courtly arts of manuscript illumination, embroidery, ivory carving, and of jewel, enamel, gold, and silver work flourished, becoming ever richer, more intricate and elaborate. Stained glass filled the ever-larger windows, while paintings or tapestries covered the walls. In Italy, artists inspired by ancient Roman masters and by Giotto looked with fresh eyes at the natural world. The full impact of their new vision was not fully assimilated until the beginning of the fifteenth century.

GIOTTO DI BONDONE
VIRGIN AND CHILD ENTHRONED
1305–10

AMBROGIO LORENZETTI.
ALLEGORY OF GOOD GOVERNMENT IN THE CITY
AND IN THE COUNTRY
SALA DELLA PACE, PALAZZO PUBBLICO, SIENA, ITALY
1338–40

LIFE OF THE VIRGIN
BACK OF THE
CHESTER-CONSTABLE CHASUBLE,
SOUTHERN ENGLAND
1330–50

PETER PARLER AND WORKSHOP.
ST. WENCESLAS CHAPEL
BEGUN 1356

MASTER THEODORIC
ST. LUKE
1360–64

FOURTEENTH-CENTURY ART IN EUROPE

1300

◀ **Papacy resides in Avignon** 1309–77

1320

◀ **Hundred Years' Wars** 1337–1453

1340

◀ **Black Death begins** 1348
◀ **Boccaccio begins writing**
The Decameron 1349–51

1360

◀ **Great Schism** 1378–1417

1380

◀ **Chaucer starts work on**
The Canterbury Tales 1387

1400

18–1 | Jan and Hubert van Eyck **GHENT ALTARPIECE (CLOSED). ANNUNCIATION WITH DONORS**
Completed 1432. Oil on panel, height 11′5″. Cathedral of Saint Bavo. Ghent.

CHAPTER EIGHTEEN

FIFTEENTH-CENTURY ART IN NORTHERN EUROPE AND THE IBERIAN PENINSULA

18

When Philip the Good, duke of Burgundy, entered Ghent in 1458, the entire Flemish city turned out. Townspeople made elaborate decorations and presented theatrical events, and local artists designed banners and made sets for the performances. That day in Ghent became an especially dramatic and fascinating example of the union of visual arts and performance, as groups of citizens welcomed Philip with *tableaux vivants* ("living pictures"). They dressed in costume and stood "absolutely frozen, like statues" to re-create scenes from their town's most celebrated work of art, Jan and Hubert van Eyck's *Ghent Altarpiece* (SEE FIG. 18–11), completed twenty six years earlier. The altarpiece had an enthroned figure of God, seated between the Virgin Mary and John the Baptist and flanked by angel musicians. Below, a depiction of the Communion of Saints, based on the biblical passage Revelation 14:1, described the Lamb of God receiving the veneration of a multitude of believers. The church fathers, prophets, martyrs, and other saints depicted in the altarpiece were among those scenes staged that day to greet Philip.

Closed, as we see it here (FIG. 18–1), the wings of the altarpiece present the ANNUNCIATION, with Gabriel and the Virgin on opposite sides of an upper room that overlooks a city. In panels above them, Old Testament prophets and seers from the ancient classical world foretell the coming of Christ.

Below, the donors are portrayed beside statues of the church's patron saints, Saint John the Baptist and Saint John the Evangelist, who, although painted to represent stone, seem to acknowledge the presence of their supplicants in glance and gesture. Before the altarpiece is even opened, as it was at Easter time, it signals the new interests of the fifteenth century: the intellectual change from religious symbolism to secular and ancient learning, a formal change to detailed realism and awareness of the world, and a social and economic change to middle-class power and patronage.

The vision of the Annunciation takes place in a domestic interior, and a prosperous Flemish city can be seen through the open windows. We are at once made aware of the remarkable rise of the middle class to wealth, power, and patronage. The donors are represented by true-to-life portraits, and the patron saints are sculptured figures on pedestals in niches, not visions. In fact, the two Saint Johns do not present the donors to God. Instead, the donors Jodocus Vijd and Elizabeth Borluut kneel in prayer, just as they must have knelt in front of the altarpiece in life.

Because of its monumental scale, complex iconography, and masterly painting techniques, the *Ghent Altarpiece* has continued to be one of the most studied and respected works of the early Renaissance in Europe since its creation in the early fifteenth century.

HUMANISM AND THE NORTHERN RENAISSANCE

Revitalized civic life and economic growth in the late fourteenth century gave rise to a prosperous middle class of artisans, merchants, and bankers who attained their place in the world through personal achievement, not inherited wealth. This newly rich middle class supported scholarship, literature, and the arts. Their patronage resulted in the explosion of learning and creativity known as the Renaissance. Though the actual term *Renaissance* (French for "rebirth") was applied by later historians, the characterization has its origins in the thinking of Petrarch and other fourteenth-century scholars, who believed in *humanism*—the power and potential of human beings.

Humanism is also fundamentally tied to the revival of classical learning and literature that appeared in fourteenth-century Italy with Petrarch, Boccaccio, and others (see "A New Spirit in Fourteenth-Century Literature," page 561). Beginning with Petrarch, humanists of the later fourteenth and fifteenth centuries looked back at the thousand years extending from the collapse of the Roman Empire to their own time, and they determined that human achievement of the ancient classical world was followed by a period of decline (a "middle age" or "dark age"). The third period—their own era—saw a revival, a rebirth, a renaissance, when humanity began to emerge from an intellectual and cultural stagnation and scholars again appreciated the achievements of the ancients.

Humanists extended education to the laity, investigated the natural world, and subjected philosophical and theological positions to logical scrutiny. They constantly invented new ways to extend humans' intellectual and physical reach. For all our differences, we still live in the modern era envisioned by these Renaissance thinkers—a time when human beings, their deeds, and their beliefs have primary importance.

The rise of humanism did not signify a decline in the importance of Christian belief, however. An intense Christian spirituality continued to inspire and pervade most European art. But despite the enormous importance of Christian faith, the established Western Church was plagued with problems. Its hierarchy was bitterly criticized for a number of practices, including a perceived indifference to the needs of common people. Strains within the Western Church exemplified the skepticism of the Renaissance mind. In the next century, these strains would give birth to the Protestant Reformation.

The new intense interest in the natural world manifested itself in the detailed observation and recording of nature. Artists depicted birds, plants, and animals with breathtaking accuracy. They looked at people and objects, and they modeled these forms with light and shadow, giving them three dimensions. In the north, artists such as Jan van Eyck (FIGS. 18–1, 18–11, 18–12, 18–13), Dirck Bouts (FIG. 18–19), and Hugo van der Goes (FIG. 18–20) used an **intuitive perspective** in order to approximate the appearance of things growing smaller and closer together in the distance. They coupled it with a masterful use of **atmospheric** or **aerial perspective**. This technique—applied to the landscape scenes that were a northern specialty—was based on observation that distant elements appear less distinct and less colorful than things close by: The sky becomes paler near the horizon and the distant landscape turns bluish-gray.

Along with the desire for accurate depiction of the world came a new interest in individual personalities. Fifteenth-century portraits have an astonishingly lifelike quality, combining careful—sometimes even unflattering—description with an uncanny sense of vitality. Indeed, the individual becomes important in every sphere. More names of artists survive from the fifteenth century, for example, than in the entire span from the beginning of the Common Era to the year 1400.

The new power of cities in the Flanders region and the greater Low Countries (present-day Belgium, Luxembourg, and the Netherlands; SEE MAP 18–1) provided a critical tension and balance with the traditional powers of royalty and the Church. Increasingly, the urban lay public sought to express personal and civic pride by sponsoring secular architecture, sculptured monuments, or paintings directed toward the community. The common sense values of the merchants formed a solid underpinning for humanist theories and enthusiasms.

But if the *Ghent Altarpiece* donors Jodocus Vijd and Elizabeth Borluut represent the new influence of the middle class, this influence nevertheless remained intertwined with the continuing power of the Church and the royal and noble

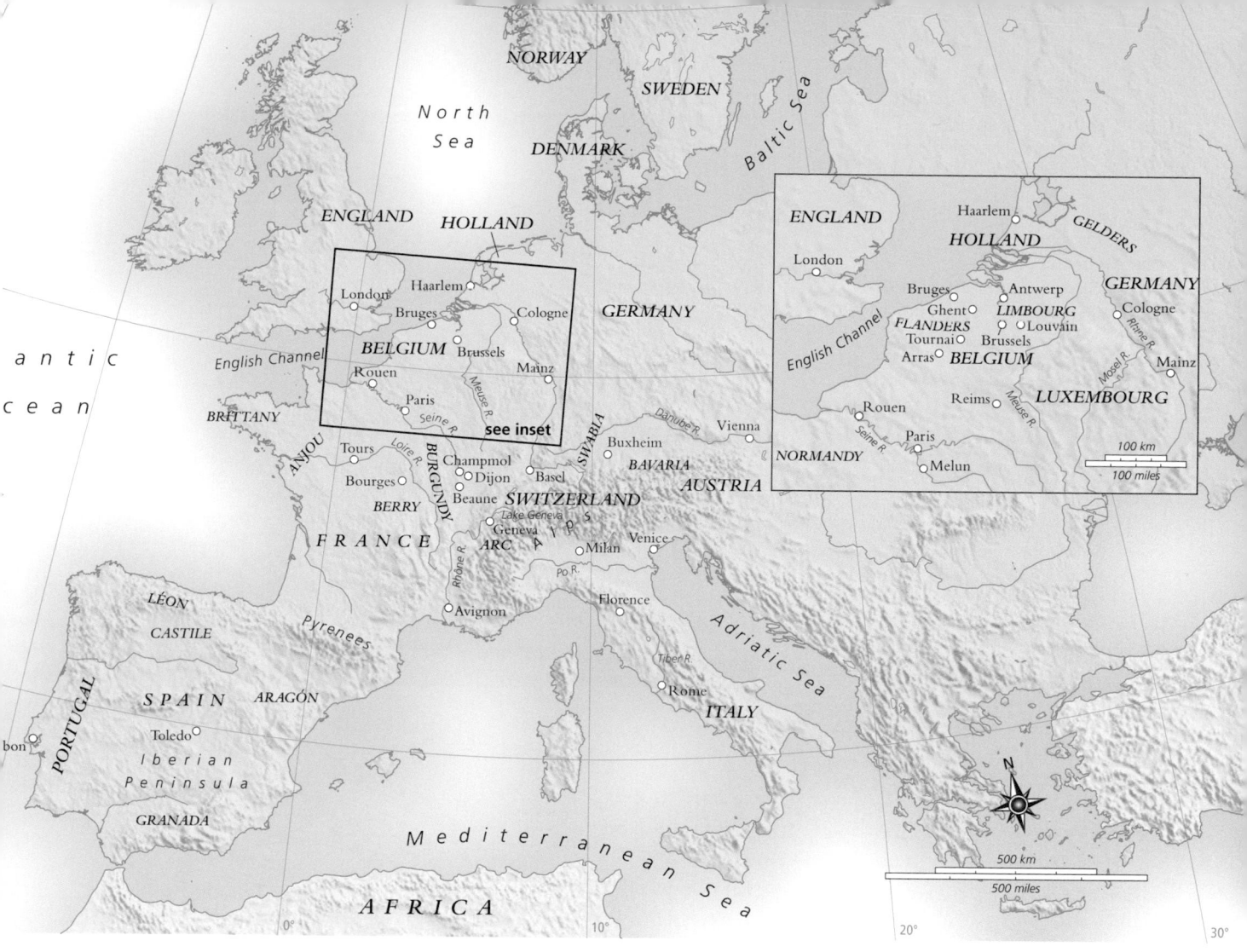

MAP 18–1 | **FIFTEENTH-CENTURY NORTHERN EUROPE AND THE IBERIAN PENINSULA**

The dukes of Burgundy, whose territory included much of present-day Belgium and Luxembourg, the Netherlands, and eastern France, became the cultural and political leaders of Western Europe. Their major cities of Bruges (Belgium) and Dijon (France) were centers of art and industry as well as politics.

courts. Like other wealthy individuals, Jodocus and Elizabeth sought eternal salvation with their donation to the Church; and though Jodocus eventually became the mayor of Ghent, he also served as a high official to the Burgundian duke Philip the Good (ruled 1419–67).

ART FOR THE FRENCH DUCAL COURTS

The dukes of Burgundy were the most powerful rulers in northern Europe for most of the fifteenth century, and a primary reason for this was their control not only of Burgundy but also of Flemish and Netherlandish centers of finance and trade, including the thriving cities of Ghent, Bruges, Tournai, and Brussels (FIG. 18–2). The major seaport, Bruges, was the commercial center of northern Europe and the rival of the Italian city-states of Florence, Milan, and Venice. In the late fourteenth century, Philip the Good's predecessor Philip the Bold (ruled 1363–1404) had acquired territory in the Nether-

lands—including the politically desirable region of Flanders— by marrying the daughter of the Flemish count. Though dukes Philip the Bold of Burgundy, John of Berry, and Louis of Anjou were brothers of King Charles V of France, their interests rarely coincided. Even the threat of a common enemy, England, during the Hundred Years' War was not a strong unifying factor. Burgundy and England were often allied because of common financial interests in Flanders.

While the French king held court in Paris, the dukes held even more splendid courts in their own cities. The dukes of Burgundy (including present-day east-central France, Belgium, Luxembourg, and the Netherlands) and Berry (central France), not the king in Paris, were arbiters of taste. The painting of the Duke of Berry in his great hall (FIG. 18–3), from an illuminated manuscript, which we will take up in more detail later, shows us how the dukes collected splendid robes and jewels, tapestry, goldsmithing, and monumental stone sculpture. Painting on panel also gained a place of importance, with early enthusiasm appearing in the ducal

18–2 | Robert Campin
A FLEMISH CITY
Detail of right wing of the *Mérode Altarpiece
(Triptych of the Annunciation)*, fig. 18–10.
c. 1425–28. Oil on wood panel, wing
approx. 25⅜ × 10¾″ (64.5 × 27.3 cm).
The Metropolitan Museum of Art, New
York.
The Cloisters Collection, 1956 (56.70)

The windows in Joseph's carpentry shop open
onto a view of a prosperous Flemish city. Tall,
well-kept houses crowd around churches,
whose towers dominate the skyline. People
gather in the open market square, walk up a
major thoroughfare, and enter the shops,
whose open doors and windows suggest security as well as commercial activity—an ideal to
be sure.

courts under Philip the Bold. The duke commissioned many
works from Flemish and Netherlandish painters. Those that
survive show a debt to the International Gothic style.

A new, composite style emerged in the late fourteenth
century from the papal court in Avignon in the south of
France, where artists from Italy, France, and Flanders worked
side by side. The International Gothic style, the prevailing
manner of the late fourteenth century, is characterized by
slender, gracefully posed figures whose delicate features are
framed by masses of curling hair and extraordinarily complex
headdresses. Noble men and women wear rich brocaded and
embroidered fabrics and elaborate jewelry. Landscape and
architectural settings are miniaturized; however, details of
nature—leaves, flowers, insects, birds—are rendered with
nearly microscopic detail. Spatial recession is represented by
rising tiled floors in buildings open at the front like stage sets,
by fanciful mountains and meadows having high horizon
lines, and some diminution in size of objects and lightening
of color near the horizon. Artists and patrons alike preferred
light, bright colors and a liberal use of gold in manuscript and
panel paintings, tapestries, and polychromed sculpture. The
International Gothic was so appealing that patrons throughout Europe continued to commission such works well into
the fifteenth century.

Painting and Sculpture for
the Chartreuse de Champmol

One of Philip the Bold's most lavish projects was the Carthusian monastery, or chartreuse ("chartrehouse"), at Champmol,
near Dijon, his Burgundian capital city. Land was acquired in
1377 and 1383 and construction began in 1385. The monastic

18–3 | Paul, Herman, and Jean Limbourg **JANUARY, THE
DUKE OF BERRY AT TABLE. TRÈS RICHES HEURES**
1411-16. Colors and ink on parchment, 8⅞ × 5⅜″
(22.5 × 13.7 cm). Musée Condé, Chantilly, France.

18–4 | Melchior Broederlam **CHAMPMOL ALTARPIECE**
Wings of the altarpiece for the Chartreuse de Champmol. 1393–99. Oil on wood panel, 5′5¾″ × 4′1¼″ (1.67 × 1.25 m).
Musée des Beaux-Arts, Dijon.

The paintings depict the Annunciation and Visitation at the left and the Presentation in the Temple and Flight into Egypt on the right.
The irregular shape of the paintings was determined by the sculpture they were meant to protect.

church was intended to house the family's tombs, and the monks were expected to pray continuously for the souls of Philip and his family. A Carthusian monastery was particularly expensive to maintain because the Carthusian monks did not provide for themselves by farming or other physical work but were dedicated to prayer and solitary meditation. In effect, Carthusians were a brotherhood of hermits.

MELCHIOR BROEDERLAM. The duke ordered a magnificent carved and painted altarpiece for the Chartreuse de Champmol (see "Altars and Altarpieces," page 591). The altarpiece, of gilded wood carved by Jacques de Baerze, depicts scenes of the Crucifixion flanked by the Adoration of the Magi and the Entombment. The primary interest today, however, is in the protective shutters, painted by Melchior Broederlam (active 1381–1410) with scenes from the life of the Virgin and the infancy of Christ (FIG. 18–4). In a personal style that carries the budding realism of the International Style further toward a faithful rendering of the natural world, Broederlam creates tangible figures in fanciful miniature architectural and landscape settings. Christian religious symbolism is present everywhere.

Under the benign eyes of God, the archangel Gabriel greets Mary with the news of her impending motherhood. A door leads into the dark interior of the tall pink rotunda meant

to represent the Temple of Jerusalem, a symbol of the Old Law. According to legend, Mary was an attendant in the Temple prior to her marriage to Joseph. The tiny enclosed garden and a pot of lilies are symbols of Mary's virginity. In International Gothic fashion, both the interior and exterior of the building are shown, and the floors are tilted up to give clear views of the action. Next, in the Visitation, just outside the temple walls, the now-pregnant Mary greets her older cousin Elizabeth, who is also pregnant and will soon give birth to John the Baptist.

On the right shutter, in the Presentation in the Temple, Mary and Joseph have brought the newborn Jesus to the temple for the Jewish purification rite. The priest Simeon takes him in his arms to bless him (Luke 2:25–32). At the far right, the Holy Family flees to Egypt to escape King Herod's order that all Jewish male infants be killed. The family travels along treacherous terrain similar to that in the Visitation scene. The landscape has been arranged to lead the eye up from the foreground and into the distance along a rising ground plane. Despite the imaginative architecture, fantastic mountains, miniature trees, and solid gold sky, the artist has created a sense of light and air around solid figures. Reflecting a new realism creeping into art, a hawk flies through the golden sky, and Joseph drinks from a flask and carries the family belongings in a satchel over his shoulder. The statue of

18–5 | Claus Sluter **WELL OF MOSES, DETAIL OF MOSES AND DAVID**
The Chartreuse de Champmol, Dijon, France. 1395–1406. Limestone with traces of paint, height of figures about 5′8″ (1.69 m).

The sculpture's original details included metal used for buckles and even eyeglasses. It was also painted: Moses wore a gold mantle with a blue lining over a red tunic; David's gold mantle had a painted lining of ermine, and his blue tunic was covered with gold stars and wide bands of ornament.

a pagan god, visible at the upper right, breaks and tumbles from its pedestal as the Christ Child approaches. A new era dawns and the New Law replaces the Old.

CLAUS SLUTER. Philip the Bold commissioned the Flemish sculptor Jean de Marville (active 1366–89) to direct the decoration of the monastery. When Jean died in 1389, he was succeeded by his assistant Claus Sluter (c. 1360–1406), from Haarlem, in Holland. Although the Chartreuse and its treasures were nearly destroyed during the French Revolution, the distinctive character of Sluter's work can still be seen in the surviving parts of a monumental well in the main cloister (FIG. 18–5). Begun in 1395, the **WELL OF MOSES** was unfinished at Sluter's death.

The concept of the *Well of Moses* is complex. A pier rose from the water and supported large freestanding figures of Christ on the cross mourned by the Virgin Mary, Mary Magdalen, and John the Evangelist. Forming a pedestal for this Crucifixion group are life-size stone figures of Old Testament men who foretold the coming of Christ: Moses (prophet and lawgiver), David (king of Israel and an ancestor of Jesus), and the prophets Jeremiah, Zachariah, Daniel, and Isaiah. These images and their texts may have been inspired by contemporary mystery plays such as *The Trial of Jesus* and *The Procession of Prophets*, in which prophets foretell and explain events of the Passion. *Meditations on the Life of Christ*, written between 1348 and 1368, by Ludolph of Saxony, provides another source.

Sluter depicted the Old Testament figures as physically and psychologically distinct individuals. Moses's sad old eyes blaze out from a memorable face entirely covered with a fine web of wrinkles. Even his horns—traditionally given to him because of a mistranslation in the Latin Bible—are wrinkled. A mane of curling hair and a beard cascade over his heavy shoulders and chest, and an enormous cloak envelops his body. Beside him stands David, in the voluminous robes of a medieval king, the personification of nobility.

Sluter looked at the human figure in a new way—as a ponderous mass defined by voluminous drapery. Drapery lies in deep folds falling in horizontal arcs and cascading lines; its heavy sculptural masses both conceal and reveal the body, creating strong highlights and shadows. With these vigorous, imposing, and highly individualized figures of the *Well of Moses,* Sluter introduced a radically new style in northern sculpture. He abandoned the idealized faces, elongated figures, and vertical drapery of the International Gothic style for surface realism and the broad horizontal movement of forms. Nevertheless, Sluter retained the detailed naturalism and rich colors (now almost lost but revealed in recent cleaning) and surfaces preferred by his patrons.

Manuscript Illumination

Of all the family, the duke of Burgundy's older brother Jean, duke of Berry, was the most enthusiastic art collector and bibliophile. In addition to commissioning religious art works for personal salvation and public devotion, he collected illuminated manuscripts, which signified both his worldly status and a commitment to learning.

Besides religious texts, wealthy patrons treasured richly illuminated secular writings such as herbals (encyclopedias of plants), health manuals, and both ancient and contemporary works of history and literature. Workshops in France and the Netherlands produced outstanding manuscripts to fill the demand. A typical manuscript page might have leafy tendrils framing the text, decorated opening initials, and perhaps a small inset picture, such as the illustration of Thamyris in Boccaccio's *Concerning Famous Women* (see "Women Artists

Art and Its Context
ALTARS AND ALTARPIECES

The altar in a Christian church symbolizes both the table of Jesus's Last Supper and the tombs of Christ and the saints. The front surface of a block altar is the *antependium*. Relics of the church's patron saint may be placed in a reliquary on the altar, beneath the floor on which the altar rests, or even within the altar itself.

Altarpieces are painted or carved constructions placed at the back or behind the altar in a way that makes altar and altar-piece appear to be visually joined. The altarpiece evolved into a large and elaborate architectural structure filled with images and protected by movable wings that function like shutters. An altarpiece may have a firm base, called a **predella**. A winged altarpiece can be a **diptych**, in which two panels are hinged together (SEE FIG. 18-22); a **triptych**, in which two wings fold over a center section (SEE FIG. 18-21); or a **polyptych**, consisting of many panels (SEE FIG. 18-16 AND 18-17).

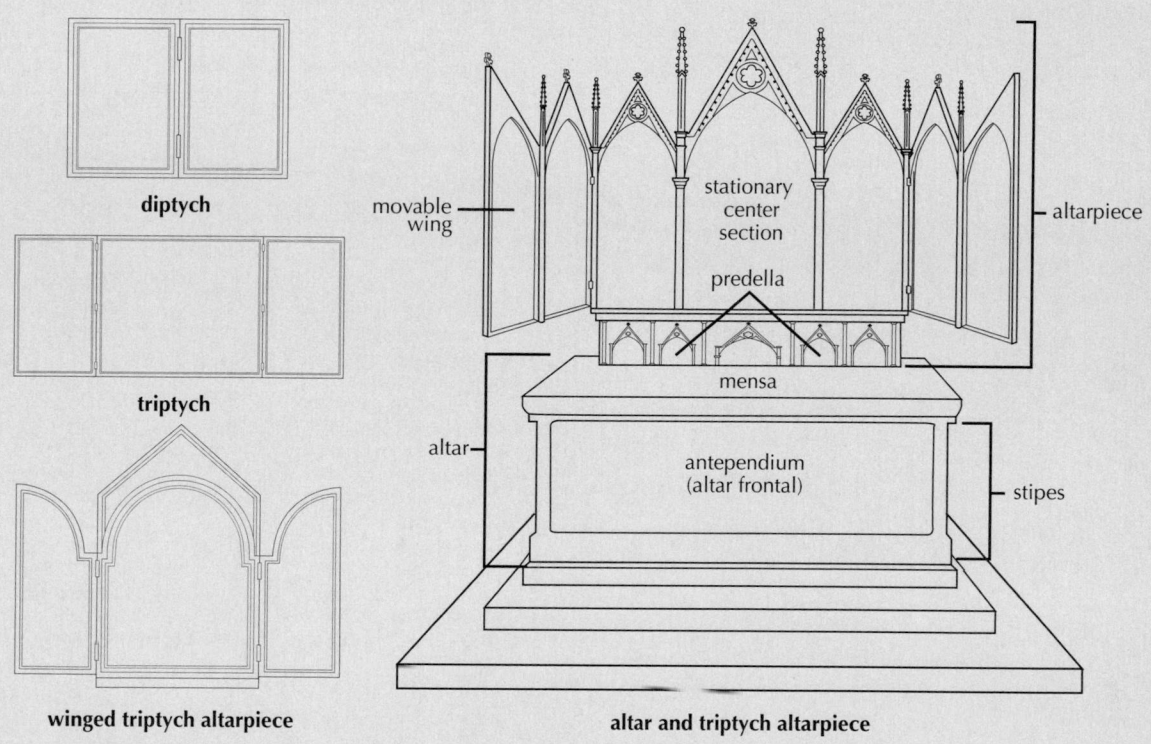

diptych

triptych

winged triptych altarpiece

movable wing

stationary center section

predella

altarpiece

mensa

altar

antependium (altar frontal)

stipes

altar and triptych altarpiece

in the Late Middle Ages and the Renaissance," page 592). The illustrations for the books made for the royal family might be large and lavish, as we see in the detail of the page where Christine de Pizan presents her work to the queen of France (Fig. 21, Introduction). Here the glimpse into the queen's private room displays tapestries on the walls and embroidered bed coverings.

The Flemish style that would influence all of fifteenth-century Europe originated in manuscript illumination of the late fourteenth century, when artists began to create full-page scenes set off with frames that functioned almost as windows looking into rooms or out onto landscapes with distant hori-zons. Painters in the Netherlands and Burgundy were especially skilled at creating an illusion of reality.

THE LIMBOURG BROTHERS. Among the finest Netherlandish illuminators at the beginning of the century were three brothers—Paul, Herman, and Jean Limbourg—commonly known as the Limbourg brothers, probably referring to their home region.

About 1404 the brothers entered the service of Duke John of Berry (1340–1416), for whom they produced their major work, the so-called *Très Riches Heures (Very Sumptuous Book of Hours)*, between 1413 and 1416 (see figs. 18–3, 18–6). A Book of Hours was a selection of prayers and readings to be

Art and Its Context

WOMEN ARTISTS IN THE LATE MIDDLE AGES AND THE RENAISSANCE

Medieval and Renaissance women artists typically learned to paint from their husbands and fathers because formal apprenticeships were not open to them. Noblewomen, who were often educated in convents, learned to draw, paint, and embroider. One of the earliest examples of a signed work by a woman painter is a tenth-century manuscript of the Apocalypse illustrated in Spain by a woman named Ende (SEE FIG. 14–10), who describes herself as "painter and helper of God." In Germany, women began to sign their work in the twelfth century. A collection of sermons was decorated by a nun named Guda (SEE FIG. 15–37), who not only signed her work but also included a self-portrait, one of the earliest in Western art.

Examples abound of women artists in the fourteenth and fifteenth centuries. In the fourteenth century, Jeanne de Montbaston and her husband, Richart, worked together as book illuminators under the auspices of the University of Paris. After Richart's death, Jeanne continued the workshop and, following the custom of the time, was sworn in as a *libraire* (publisher) by the university in 1353. In the fifteenth century, women could be admitted to the guilds in some cities, including the Flemish towns of Ghent, Bruges, and Antwerp, and by the 1480s one-quarter of the members of the painters' guild of Bruges were female.

Particularly talented women received major commissions. Bourgot, the daughter of the miniaturist Jean le Noir, illuminated books for King Charles V of France and Jean, duke of Berry. Christine de Pizan (1365–c. 1430), a well-known writer patronized by Philip the Bold of Burgundy and Queen Isabeau of France, described the work of an illuminator named Anastaise, "who is so learned and skillful in painting manuscript borders and miniature backgrounds that one cannot find an artisan . . . who can surpass her . . . nor whose work is more highly esteemed" (*Le Livre de la Cité des Dames*, I.41.4, translated by Earl J. Richards).

In a French edition of a book by the Italian author Boccaccio entitled *Concerning Famous Women*, the anonymous illuminator shows Thamyris, an artist of antiquity, at work in her studio. She is depicted in fifteenth-century dress, painting an image of the Virgin and Child. At the right, an assistant grinds and mixes the colors Thamyris will need to complete her painting. In the foreground, her brushes and paints are laid out conveniently on a table.

PAGE WITH THAMYRIS
From Giovanni Boccaccio's *De Claris Mulieribus (Concerning Famous Women)*. 1402. Ink and tempera on vellum. Bibliothèque Nationale de France, Paris.

used in daily prayer and meditation, and it included a calendar of holy days. The Limbourgs created full-page illustrations for the calendar in the International Gothic style, with subjects including both peasant labors and aristocratic pleasures. Like most European artists of the time, the Limbourgs showed the laboring classes in a light acceptable to aristocrats—that is, happily working for the nobles' benefit. But they also showed peasants enjoying their own pleasures.

In the **FEBRUARY** page (FIG. 18–6), farm people relax cozily before a blazing fire. This farm looks comfortable and well maintained, with timber-framed buildings, a row of beehives, a sheepfold, and tidy woven wattle fences. In the distance are a village and church. Most remarkably, the artists convey the feeling of cold winter weather: the breath of the bundled-up worker turning to steam as he blows on his hands, the leaden sky and bare trees, the snow covering the

18–6 | Paul, Herman, and Jean Limbourg
FEBRUARY, LIFE IN THE COUNTRY. TRÈS RICHES HEURES
1411-16. Colors and ink on parchment, 8⅞ × 5⅜"
(22.5 × 13.7 cm). Musée Condé, Chantilly, France.

table or buffet holds his collection of gold vessels. His chamberlain invites courtiers to approach (the words written overhead say "approach"). John is singled out visually by the red "cloth of honor" with his heraldic arms—swans and the lilies of France—and by a large fire screen that circles his head like a secular halo. Tapestries with battle scenes cover the walls and are rolled up around the fireplace. Rich clothing and jewels, embroidered fabrics and brocades, turbans, golden collars and chains attest to the wealth and lavish lifestyle of this great patron of the arts and brother of King Charles V.

THE MARY OF BURGUNDY PAINTER. By the end of the century, each scene on a manuscript page was a tiny image of the world rendered in microscopic detail. Complex compositions and ornate decorations were commonplace, with framed images surrounded by a fantasy of vines, flowers, insects, animals, shellfish, or other objects painted as if seen under a magnifying glass. Christine de Pizan's preferred artist, Anastaise, probably worked in this mode (see Fig. 21, Introduction).

One of the finest later painters was the anonymous artist known as the Mary of Burgundy Painter—so called because he painted a Book of Hours for Mary of Burgundy, daughter of Charles the Bold. Mary married the Habsburg heir, Maximilian of Austria, in 1477, and her grandson became both King of Spain as Charles I and Holy Roman Emperor as Charles V (see Chapter 20).

Within an illumination in a book only 7½ by 5¼ inches, reality and vision have been rendered equally tangible (FIG. 18–7). The painter has attained a new complexity in treating pictorial space. We look not only through the "window" of the illustration's frame but through another window in the wall of the room depicted in the painting. The spatial recession leads the eye into the far reaches of the church interior, past the Virgin and the gilded altarpiece in the sanctuary to two people conversing in the far distance.

Mary of Burgundy appears twice: once seated in the foreground by a window, reading from her Book of Hours; and again in the background, perhaps in a vision inspired by her reading. She kneels with attendants and angels in front of the Virgin and Child. On the window ledge is an exquisite

landscape, and the comforting smoke curling from the farmhouse chimney. The painting employs several International Gothic conventions: the high placement of the horizon line, the small size of trees and buildings in relation to people, and the cutaway view of the house showing both interior and exterior. The muted palette is sparked with touches of yellowish-orange, blue, and a patch of bright red on the man's turban at the lower left. The landscape recedes continuously from foreground to middle ground to background. An elaborate calendar device, with the chariot of the sun and the zodiac symbols, fills the upper part of the page.

In contrast, the illustration for the other winter month—January—depicts an aristocratic household (SEE FIG. 18–3). The Duke of Berry sits behind a table laden with food and rich tableware, including a huge gold standing salt. A second

18–7 | Mary of Burgundy Painter **MARY AT HER DEVOTIONS, HOURS OF MARY OF BURGUNDY**
Before 1482. Colors and ink on parchment, size of image 7½ × 5¼" (19.1 × 13.3 cm). Österreichische Nationalbibliothek, Vienna.

still life—a rosary (symbol of Mary's devotion), carnations (flowers symbolizing the nails of the Crucifixion), and a glass vase holding purple irises, representing the Virgin Mary's sorrows over the sacrifice of Christ (SEE FIG. 18–21). The artist has skillfully executed the filmy veil covering Mary's steeple headdress, the transparent glass vase, and the glass of the window (circular panes whose center "lump" was formed by the glassblower's pipe).

The Fiber Arts

The lavish detail with which textiles are depicted in Flemish manuscripts and paintings reflects their great importance in fifteenth-century society. In the fifteenth and sixteenth centuries, Flemish tapestry making was the finest in Europe. Major weaving centers at Brussels, Tournai, and Arras produced these intricately woven wall hangings for royal and aristocratic patrons, important church officials, and even town councils. Among the most common subjects were foliage and flower patterns, scenes from the lives of the saints, and themes from classical mythology and history, such as the Battle of Troy seen hanging on the Duke of Berry's walls. Tapestries provided both insulation and luxurious decoration for the stone walls of castle halls, churches, and municipal buildings.

Often they were woven for specific places or for festive occasions such as weddings, coronations, and other state events. Many were given as diplomatic gifts, and the wealth of individuals can often be judged by the number of tapestries listed in their household inventories.

The price of a tapestry depended on the work required and the materials used. Rarely was a fine, commissioned series woven only with wool; instead, tapestry producers enhanced the weaving with silk, silver, and gold threads. The richest kind of tapestry was made almost entirely of silk and gold. Because silver and gold threads were made of silk wrapped with real metal, people later burned many tapestries to retrieve the precious materials. As a result, few royal tapestries in France survived the French Revolution. Many existing works show obvious signs, however, that the metallic threads were painstakingly pulled out in order to get the gold but preserve the tapestries.

THE UNICORN TAPESTRY. Tapestries often formed series. One of the best-known surviving tapestry series is the *Hunt of the Unicorn*. Each piece exhibits many people and animals in a dense field of trees and flowers, with a distant view of a castle, as in the **UNICORN IS FOUND AT THE FOUNTAIN** (FIG. 18–8). The unusually fine condition of the tapestry allows us to appreciate its rich colors and the subtlety in modeling the faces, the tonal variations in the animals' fur, and even the depiction of reflections in the water. The unicorn, a mythical horselike animal with cloven hooves, a goat's beard, and a single long twisted horn, was said to be supernaturally swift and, in medieval belief, could only be captured by a virgin, to whom it came willingly. Thus, the unicorn became a symbol of the Incarnation (Christ is the unicorn captured by the Virgin Mary) and also a metaphor for romantic love.

Because of its religious connotations, the unicorn was an important animal in the medieval **bestiary**, an encyclopedia of real and imaginary animals that gave information of both moral and practical value. For example, the unicorn's horn (in fact, the narwhal's horn) was thought to be an antidote to poison. In the tapestry, the unicorn purifies the water by dipping its horn into the stream. This beneficent act, resulting in the capture and killing of the unicorn, was equated with Christ's death on the cross to save humanity. The prominence of the red roses (symbols both of the Passion and of Mary) growing behind the unicorn suggests that the tapestries may have celebrated Christian doctrine, but they could also have been a wedding gift.

All the woodland creatures included in the tapestry have symbolic meanings. For instance, lions, ancient symbols of power, represent valor, faith, courage, and mercy, and even—because they breathe life into their cubs—the Resurrection of Christ. The stag is another symbol of the Resurrection (it sheds and grows its antlers) and a protector against poisonous serpents and evil in general. Even today

18–8 UNICORN IS FOUND AT THE FOUNTAIN
From the *Hunt of the Unicorn* tapestry series.
c. 1495–1505. Wool, silk, and silver- and gilt-wrapped thread (13–21 warp threads per inch), 12′1″ × 12′5″
(3.68 × 3.78 m). The Metropolitan Museum of Art, New York.
Gift of John D. Rockefeller Jr., the Cloisters Collection, 1937 (37.80.2)

we expect the rabbits to symbolize fertility, and the dogs, fidelity. The pair of pheasants is an emblem of human love and marriage, and the goldfinch is another symbol of fertility and also of the Passion of Christ. Only the ducks swimming away have no apparent message.

The flowers and trees in the tapestry, identifiable from their botanically correct depictions, reinforce the theme of protective and curative powers. Each has both religious and secular meanings—as explained in herbals (encyclopedias of plants, their uses and significance)—but the theme of mar-

riage, in particular, is referred to by the presence of such plants as the strawberry, a common symbol of sexual love; the pansy, a symbol for remembrance; and the periwinkle, a cure for spiteful feelings and jealousy. The trees include oak for fidelity, beech for nobility, holly for protection against evil, hawthorn for the power of love, and pomegranate and orange for fertility. The parklike setting with its prominent fountain was inspired by the biblical love poem the Song of Songs (4:12, 13, 15–16): "You are an enclosed garden, my sister, my bride, an enclosed garden, a fountain sealed."

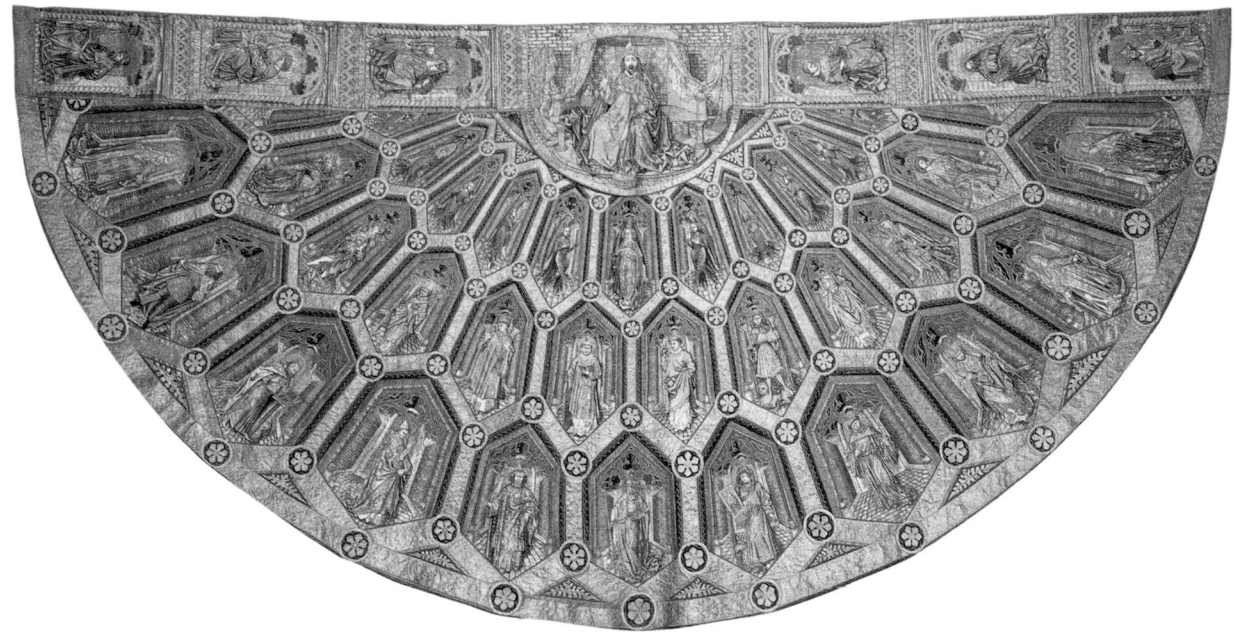

18–9 | **COPE OF THE ORDER OF THE GOLDEN FLEECE**
Flemish, mid-15th century. Cloth with gold and colored silk embroidery, 5′4⅜″ × 10′9⅜″ (1.64 × 3.3 m).
Imperial Treasury, Vienna.

COPE OF THE ORDER OF THE GOLDEN FLEECE. Remarkable examples of the Flemish fiber arts are the vestments of the Order of the Golden Fleece. The Order of the Golden Fleece was an honorary fraternity founded by Duke Philip the Good of Burgundy in 1430 with twenty-three knights chosen for their moral character and bravery. Religious services were an integral part of the order's meetings, and opulent liturgical and clerical objects were created for the purpose.

The surface of the sumptuous cope (cloak) in FIGURE 18–9 is divided into compartments filled with the standing figures of saints. At the top of the neck edge, as if presiding over the company, is an enthroned figure of Christ, flanked by scholar-saints in their studies. The embroiderers worked with great precision to create illusionistic effects of contemporary Flemish painting. The particular stitch used here is known as couching, that is, gold threads are tacked down using unevenly spaced colored silk threads to create images and an iridescent effect. (For the effect of a cope when worn, see the angels in the center panel of the *Portinari Altar*piece, FIG. 18–20.)

PAINTING IN FLANDERS

A strong economy based on wool, the textile industry, and international trade provided stability and money for the arts to flourish. Civic groups, town councils, and wealthy merchants were also important patrons in the Netherlands, where the cities were self-governing and largely independent of the landed nobility. Guilds oversaw nearly every aspect of their members' lives, and high-ranking guild members served on town councils and helped run city governments. Even experienced artists who moved from one city to another usually had to work as assistants in a local workshop until they met the requirements for guild membership.

The diversity of clientele encouraged artists to experiment with new types of images—with outstanding results. Throughout most of the fifteenth century, Flemish art and artists were greatly admired; artists from abroad studied Flemish works, and their influence spread throughout Europe, including Italy. Only at the end of the fifteenth century did a general preference for the Netherlandish painting style give way to a taste for the new styles of art and architecture developing in Italy.

The Founders of the Flemish School

Flemish artists were known for their exquisite illuminated manuscripts, tapestries, and stained glass. For works ranging from enormous altarpieces to small portraits, Flemish painters perfected the technique of painting with an oil medium rather than the tempera paint preferred by the Italians. Oil paint provided more flexibility: Slow to dry, it permitted artists to make changes as they worked. Most important, it had a luminous quality. Oil paint applied in thin glazes produced luminous effects that enabled the artists to capture rich jewel-like colors and subtle changes in textures and surfaces. Like manuscript illuminations, the panel paintings provided a window onto a scene, which fifteenth-century Flemish painters typically rendered with keen attention to individual features—whether of people, objects, or the natural world—in works laden with symbolic meaning.

ROBERT CAMPIN. One of the first outstanding exponents of the new Flemish style was Robert Campin (active 1406–44). His paintings reflect the Netherlandish taste for lively narrative and a bold three-dimensional treatment of figures reminiscent of the sculptural style of Claus Sluter. About 1425–28, Campin painted an altarpiece now known as the **MÉRODE ALTARPIECE** from the name of later owners (FIG. 18–10). Slightly over 2 feet tall and about 4 feet wide with the wings open, it was probably made for a small private chapel.

By depicting the Annunciation inside a Flemish home, Campin turned common household objects into religious symbols. The treatment is often referred to as "hidden symbolism" because objects are treated as an ordinary part of the scene, but their religious meanings would have been widely understood by contemporary people. The lilies in the **majolica** (glazed earthenware) pitcher on the table, for example, symbolize Mary's virginity, and were a traditional element of Annunciation imagery. The white towel and hanging waterpot in the niche symbolize Mary's purity and her role as the vessel for the Incarnation of God. Unfortunately, the precise meanings are not always clear today. The central panel may simply portray Gabriel telling Mary that she will be the Mother of Christ. Another interpretation suggests that the painting shows the moment immediately following Mary's

acceptance of her destiny. A rush of wind riffles the book pages and snuffs the candle as a tiny figure of Christ carrying a cross descends on a ray of light. Having accepted the miracle of the Incarnation (God assuming human form), Mary reads her Bible while sitting humbly on the footrest of the long bench. Her position becomes a symbol of her submission to God's will. But another interpretation of the scene suggests that it represents the moment just prior to the Annunciation. In this view, Mary is not yet aware of Gabriel's presence, and the rushing wind is the result of the angel's rapid entry into the room, where he appears before her, half kneeling and raising his hand in salutation.

The complex treatment of light in the *Mérode Altarpiece* is another Flemish innovation. Campin combines natural and supernatural light, with the strongest illumination coming from an unseen source at the upper left in front of the picture plane. The sun seems to shine through a miraculously transparent wall that allows the viewer to observe the scene. In addition, a few rays enter the round window at the left as the vehicle for the Christ Child's descent. More light comes from the window at the rear of the room, and areas of reflected light can also be detected, such as the right side of the brass waterpot.

Campin maintained some of the conventions typical of the International Gothic style: the abrupt recession of the bench toward the back of the room, the sharply uplifted floor and tabletop, and the disproportionate relationship between the figures and the architectural space. In an otherwise

18–10 | Robert Campin **MÉRODE ALTARPIECE (TRIPTYCH OF THE ANNUNCIATION) (OPEN)**
c. 1425–28. Oil on wood panel, center 25¼ × 24⅞″ (64.1 × 63.2 cm); each wing approx 25⅜ × 10¾″ (64.5 × 27.6 cm). The Metropolitan Museum of Art, New York.
The Cloisters Collection, 1956 (56.70)

intense effort to mirror the real world, this treatment of space may be a conscious remnant of medieval style, serving the symbolic purpose of visually detaching the religious realm from the world of the viewers. Unlike figures by such International Gothic painters as the Limbourg brothers (SEE FIGS. 18–3, 18–6), the Virgin and Gabriel are massive rather than slender, and their abundant draperies increase the impression of material weight.

Although in the biblical account Joseph and Mary were not married at the time of the Annunciation, this house clearly belongs to Joseph, who is shown in his carpentry shop. A prosperous Flemish city can be seen through the shop window, with people going about their business unaware of the drama taking place inside the carpenter's home (SEE FIG. 18–2). One clue indicates that this is not an everyday scene: the shop, displaying wooden wares—mousetraps, in this case—would have been on the ground floor, but Campin has the window apparently opening from the second floor. Furthermore, the significance of the mousetraps would have been recognized by knowledgeable people. They could refer to Saint Augustine's reference to Christ as the bait in a trap set by God to catch Satan. Joseph is drilling holes in a small board used as a drainboard for wine making, which would have been understood as symbolic of the Eucharistic wine and Christ's Passion.

Joseph's house has a garden planted with a rosebush; roses allude to both the Virgin and the Passion. Perhaps the man standing behind the open entrance gate, clutching his hat in one hand and a document in the other, is a self-portrait of the artist, but he has also been called the prophet Isaiah. Kneeling in front of the open door to the house are the donors of the altarpiece, Peter Inghelbrecht and his wife. Although they could observe the Annunciation through the door their eyes seem unfocused. Perhaps the scene of the Annunciation is a vision induced by their prayers.

JAN VAN EYCK. Campin's contemporary Jan van Eyck (active 1420s–41) was a trusted official as well as painter in the court of Philip the Good. His influence would extend through ducal Burgundy and into France, Spain, and Portugal, where he traveled on diplomatic missions for the duke. Duke Philip alluded to Jan's remarkable technical skills in a letter of 1434–35, saying that he could find no other painter equal to his taste or so excellent in art and science. Part of the secret of Jan's "science" was his technique of painting with oil glazes on wood panel. So brilliant were the results of his experiments that Jan has been mistakenly credited with being the inventor of oil painting. Actually, the medium had been known for several centuries, and medieval painters had used oil paint to decorate stone, metal, and occasionally plaster walls. Jan perfected the medium by building up his images in very thin transparent oil layers. This technique permitted a

precise, objective description of what he saw, with tiny, carefully applied brushstrokes so well blended that they are only visible at very close range.

The GHENT ALTARPIECE (FIG. 18–11), which we have already seen in closed form, presents questions of authorship. An inscription on the frame identifies both Jan and Hubert van Eyck as artists, but Hubert died in 1426. Perhaps Hubert left several unfinished panels in his studio when he died and Jan assembled them, repainting and adding to them to bring them into harmony. In addition to the visual evidence, modern scientific analysis—X-ray, infrared reflectography, and chemical analysis—supports this theory.

Dominating the altarpiece by size, central location, and brilliant red and gold color is the enthroned figure of God, wearing the triple crown of Saint Peter (the papal crown) and having an earthly crown at his feet. He is joined in his golden shrine by the Virgin Mary and John the Baptist, each enthroned and holding an open book. This divine trio (in Byzantine art, known as the Deësis) is flanked first by angel musicians and then by Adam and Eve. Van Eyck emphasizes humanity's fall from grace by depicting the murder of Abel by Cain, in the upper lunette (semicircular wall area), and Eve, who holds the forbidden fruit. In the upper register, each of the three themes—God with Mary and John, musical angels, and Adam and Eve—is represented in a different space and at a different scale. Angels stand on a tiled floor but against a blue sky. Adam and Eve stand in shallow stone niches.

The five lower panels present a unified field—a vast landscape with meadows, woods, and distant cities against a continuous horizon. All saints—apostles, martyrs, confessors and virgins, hermits, pilgrims, warriors, and judges—gather to adore the Lamb of God as described in the Book of Revelation. The Lamb stands on an altar, blood flowing into a chalice, ultimately leading to the fountain of life.

The three-dimensional mass of the figures, the voluminous draperies as well as the remarkable surface realism, even the faux sculpture, recall the art of Claus Sluter for the Burgundian court in Dijon. The extraordinary painting of brocades and jewels, the facial expressions (especially of the angels), the detailed rendering of plants, including Mediterranean palms and orange trees, and the concern with atmospheric perspective—all suggest Jan's unique contribution. Jan's technique is firmly grounded in the terrestrial world despite his visionary subject.

The portrait of a MAN IN A RED TURBAN of 1433 (FIG. 18–12) projects a strong sense of personality, and the signed and dated frame also bears Jan's personal motto, in Flemish, "As I can" ("The best that I am capable of doing"). This motto, derived from classical sources and written here in Greek letters, is a telling illustration of the humanist spirit of the age and the confident expression of an artist who

18–11 | Jan and Hubert van Eyck **GHENT ALTARPIECE (OPEN), ADORATION OF THE MYSTIC LAMB**
Completed 1432. Oil on panel, 11′5¾″ × 15′1½″ (3.5 × 4.6 m). Cathedral of Saint Bavo, Ghent.

On the frame of the altarpiece was written, "The painter Hubert van Eyck, greater than whom no one was found, began [this work]; and Jan, his brother, second in art, having carried through the task at the expense of Jodocus Vijd, invites you by this verse, on the sixth of May, to look at what has been done." (Translation by L. Silver)

knows his capabilities and is proud to display them. The *Man in a Red Turban* is a portrait in which the physical appearance seems recorded in a magnifying mirror. We see every wrinkle and scar, the stubble of a day's growth of beard on his chin and cheeks, and the tiny reflections of light from a studio window in the pupils of the eyes. The outward gaze of the subject is new in portraiture, and it suggests the subject's increased sense of self-confidence as he catches the viewer's eye.

Jan's best-known painting today is an elaborate portrait of a man and woman traditionally identified as **GIOVANNI ARNOLFINI AND HIS WIFE, GIOVANNA CENAMI (FIG. 18–13)**. This fascinating work continues to be subject to a number of interpretations, most of which suggest that it represents a wedding or betrothal. One remarkable detail is the artist's inscription above the mirror on the back wall: *Johannes de eyck fuit hic 1434* ("Jan van Eyck was present, 1434"). Normally, a work of art in fifteenth-century Flanders would have been signed "Jan

18–12 | Jan van Eyck **MAN IN A RED TURBAN**
1433. Oil on wood panel, 13⅛ × 10¼" (33.3 × 25.8 cm). The
National Gallery, London.

On the frame is written, "Als ich Kan. Joh. de Eyck me Fecit," Jan's
personal motto, which translates "As I can."

wealth, piety, and married life. The convex mirror reflecting the entire room and its occupants is a luxury object, but it may also symbolize the all-seeing eye of God. The roundels decorating its frame depict the Passion of Christ, a reminder of Christian redemption.

Many other details suggest the piety of the couple: the crystal prayer beads on the wall; the image of Saint Margaret, protector of women in childbirth, carved on the top of a high-backed chair next to the bed; and the single burning candle in the chandelier, a symbol of Christ's presence. The fruits shown at the left, seemingly placed there to ripen in the sun, may allude to fertility in a marriage, and also to the Fall of Adam and Eve in the Garden of Eden. The small dog may simply be a pet, but it serves also as a symbol of fidelity, and its rare breed—affenpinscher—suggests wealth.

The woman wears an aristocratic fur-lined overdress with a long train. Fashion dictated that the robe be gathered up and held in front of the abdomen, giving an appearance of pregnancy. This ideal of feminine beauty emphasized women's potential fertility. The merchant class copied the fashions of the court, and a beautifully furnished room containing a large bed hung with rich draperies was often a home's primary public space, not a private retreat.

Jan delighted in complex symbolism in the guise of ordinary objects. The paintings of his contemporaries and followers seem relatively straightforward by comparison.

ROGIER VAN DER WEYDEN. Little as we know about Jan van Eyck, we know less about the life of Rogier van der Weyden. Not a single existing work of art bears his name. He may have studied under Robert Campin, but this relationship is not altogether certain. At the peak of his career, Rogier maintained a large workshop in Brussels, where he was the official city painter. Apprentices and shop assistants came from as far away as Italy to study with him, adding to modern scholars' difficulties.

To establish the thematic and stylistic characteristics for Rogier's art, scholars have turned to a painting of the **DEPOSITION** (FIG. 18–14), an altarpiece commissioned by the Louvain Crossbowmen's Guild sometime before 1443, the date of the earliest known copy of it by another artist. The copy has wings painted with the four evangelists—Matthew, Mark, Luke, and John—and Christ's Resurrection. Perhaps the *Deposition* was once a triptych too.

The Deposition was a popular theme in the fifteenth century, in part because of its dramatic, emotionally moving nature. Rogier set the act of removing Jesus's body from the cross on a shallow stage closed off by a wooden backdrop that has been covered with a thin overlay of gold like a carved and painted altarpiece. The ten solid, three-dimensional figures seem to press forward into the viewer's space, forcing the viewer to identify with the grief of Jesus's friends—made palpably real by their portraitlike faces and elements of contem-

van Eyck made this." The wording is that of a witness to a legal document, and indeed, two witnesses to the scene are reflected in the mirror, a man in a red turban—perhaps the artist—and one other. The man in the portrait, identified by early sources as Giovanni Arnolfini, a member of an Italian merchant family living in Flanders, holds the hand of the woman and raises his right hand before the two witnesses. In the fifteenth century, a marriage was rarely celebrated with a religious ceremony. The couple signed a legal contract before two witnesses, after which the bride's dowry might be paid and gifts exchanged. However, it has been suggested that the painting might be a pictorial "power of attorney," giving the woman the right to act in her husband's absence. The recent discovery of a document showing that Arnolfini married in 1447, six years after Jan's death, adds to the mystery.

Whatever event or situation the painting depicts, the artist has juxtaposed secular and religious themes in a work that seems to have several levels of meaning. On the man's side of the painting, the room opens to the outdoors, the external "masculine" world, while the woman is silhouetted against a domestic interior, with its allusions to the roles of wife and mother. The couple is surrounded by emblems of

18–13 | Jan van Eyck   **DOUBLE PORTRAIT; TRADITIONALLY KNOWN AS GIOVANNI ARNOLFINI AND HIS WIFE, GIOVANNA CENAMI**
1434. Oil on wood panel, 33 × 22½" (83.8 × 57.2 cm).
The National Gallery, London.

"Johannes de eyck fuit hic [was present]." According to a later inventory, the original frame was inscribed with a quotation from Ovid, a Roman poet known for his celebration of romantic love.

porary dress—as they tenderly and sorrowfully remove his body from the cross for burial. Rogier has arranged Jesus, the life-size corpse at the center of the composition, in a graceful curve that is echoed in angular fashion by the fainting Virgin, thereby increasing the emotional identification between the Son and the Mother. The artist's compassionate sensibility is especially evident in the gestures of John the Evangelist, who supports the Virgin at the left, and Jesus's friend Mary Magdalen, who wrings her hands in anguish at the right. Rogier's

emotionalism links the Gothic past with the fifteenth-century humanistic concern for individual expressions of emotion. Although united by their sorrow, the mourning figures react in personal ways.

Rogier's choice of color and pattern balances and enhances his composition. For example, the complexity of the gold brocade worn by Joseph of Arimathea, who offered his new tomb for the burial, and the contorted pose and vivid dress of Mary Magdalen increase the visual impact of the

18–14 | Rogier van der Weyden **DEPOSITION**
From an altarpiece commissioned by the Crossbowmen's Guild, Louvain, Belgium. Before 1443,
possibly c. 1435-38. Oil on wood panel, 7′2⅜″ × 8′7⅛″ (2.2 × 2.62 m). Museo del Prado, Madrid.

right side of the panel and counter the pictorial weight of the larger number of figures at the left. The palette of subtle, slightly muted colors is sparked with red and white accents that focus the viewer's attention on the main subject. The whites of the winding cloth and the tunic of the youth on the ladder set off Jesus's pale body, as the white turban and shawl emphasize the ashen face of Mary.

Rogier painted his largest and most elaborate work, the altarpiece of the **LAST JUDGMENT**, for the hospital in Beaune, founded by the chancellor of the Duke of Burgundy, Nicolas Rolin (FIGS. 18–15, 18–16). Whether Rogier painted this altarpiece before or after he made a trip to Rome for the Jubilee of 1450 is debated by scholars. He would have known the iconography of the Last Judgment from medieval church tympana, but he could also have been inspired by the paintings and mosaics of the theme in Rome. The tall, straight figure of the archangel Michael, dressed in a white robe and cope, dominates the center of

the wide polyptych as he weighs souls under the direct order of God, who sits on the arc of a giant rainbow above him. The Virgin Mary and John the Baptist kneel at either end of the rainbow. Behind them on each side, six apostles and a host of saints (men at the right side of Christ and women at the left) witness the scene. The cloudy gold background serves, as it did in medieval art, to signify events in the heavenly realm or in a time remote from that of the viewer.

The bodily resurrection takes place on a narrow, barren strip of earth that runs across the bottom of all but the outer panels. Men and women climb out of their tombs, turning in different directions as they react to the call to Judgment. The scales of justice held by Michael tip in an unexpected direction; instead of Good outweighing Bad, the saved soul has become pure spirit and rises, while the damned soul sinks, weighed down by unrepented sins. The damned throw themselves into the flaming pit of hell—no demons drag them down; the saved greet the archangel Gabriel at the shining gate of heaven, depicted as a Gothic portal.

When the altarpiece's shutters are closed, they show Rogier's debt to Jan and the *Ghent Altarpiece*. The donors, Nicolas Rolin and Guigone de Salins, kneel in prayer before sculptures of the patron saints of the hospital chapel, Saint Sebastian and Saint Anthony. On the upper level the angel Gabriel greets the Virgin Mary, in yet another version of the Annunciation. The high status of the donors is indicated by their coats of arms and the gold brocade on the walls of their room. In contrast, the central images of Mary, Gabriel, and the two saints are represented in *grisaille* as unpainted stone sculpture set in shallow niches. As on the wings of the *Ghent Altarpiece*, the contrast of living and carved figures is dramatic and interactive. The popularity of *grisaille* in fifteenth-century northern panel painting goes back to Giotto's use of frescoed *grisaille* figures on the fictive marble base of the Arena Chapel (SEE FIG. 17–8), and is at odds with the actual fifteenth-century practice of adding polychromy to stone sculpture before it left the workshop. For Rogier (as for Jan van Eyck), perhaps leaving the stone "unfinished" was more effective and illusionary than depicting painted sculpture.

18–15 | Rogier van der Weyden
LAST JUDGMENT ALTARPIECE (OPEN)
After 1443, c. 1445–48. Oil on wood panel, open: 7'4⅝" × 17'11" (2.25 × 5.46 m). Musée de l'Hôtel-Dieu, Beaune, France.

18–16 | Rogier van der Weyden
LAST JUDGMENT ALTARPIECE (CLOSED)
Oil on panel, height 7'4⅝" (2.28 m). Donors: Nicolas Rolin and Guigone de Salins.

18–17 | Rogier van der Weyden **PORTRAIT OF A LADY**
c. 1455. Oil and tempera on wood panel, 14 1/16 × 10 5/8"
(37 × 27 cm). National Gallery of Art, Washington, D.C.
Andrew W. Mellon Collection (1937.1.44)

In his portraits, Rogier balanced a Flemish love of individual detail with a flattering idealization of the features of men and women. In **PORTRAIT OF A LADY** (FIG. 18–17), painted after his return from Italy, Rogier transformed the young woman into a vision of exquisite but remote beauty. Her long, almond-shape eyes, regular features, and smooth translucent skin appear in many portraits of women attributed to Rogier. He popularized the half-length pose that includes the woman's high waistline and clasped hands. Images of the Virgin and Child often formed diptychs with small portraits of this type. The woman is pious and humble, wealthy but proper and modest; nevertheless, her tense fingers convey a sense of inner controlled emotion. The portrait expresses the complex and often contradictory attitudes of both aristocratic and middle-class patrons of the arts, who balanced pride in their achievements with appropriate modesty.

Painting at Midcentury: The Second Generation

The extraordinary accomplishments of Robert Campin, Jan van Eyck, and Rogier van der Weyden attracted many followers in Flanders. The work of this second generation of Flemish painters was simpler, more direct, and easier to understand than that of their predecessors. These artists produced high-quality work of great emotional power, and they were in large part responsible for the rapid spread of the Flemish style throughout Europe.

PETRUS CHRISTUS. Among the most interesting of the second-generation painters was Petrus Christus (active 1444–c. 1475/76). He came from Holland, but nothing is known of his life before 1444, when he became a citizen of Bruges. He signed and dated six paintings.

In 1449 Christus painted a goldsmith, perhaps Saint Eligius, in his shop (FIG. 18–18). According to Christian tradition, Eligius, a seventh-century ecclesiastic, goldsmith, and mintmaster for the French court, used his wealth to ransom Christian captives. He became the patron saint of metalworkers. Here he weighs a jeweled ring, as a handsome couple looks on. The man wears a badge identifying him as a member of the court of the duke of Gelders; the young woman, dressed in Italian gold brocade, wears a jeweled double-horned headdress fashionable at midcentury (worn by Christine de Pisan and the ladies of the queen of France; see Fig. 21, Introduction).

The counter and shelves hold a wide range of metalwork and jewelry. The coins are Burgundian gold ducats and gold "angels" of Henry VI of England (ruled 1422–61, 1470–71), and on the bottom shelf are a box of rings, two bags with precious stones, and pearls. Behind them stands a crystal reliquary with a gold dome and a ruby and amethyst pelican. Many of the objects on the shelves had a protective function—for example, the red coral and the serpents' tongues (actually fossilized sharks' teeth) hanging above the coral could ward off the evil eye, and the coconut cup at the left neutralized poison. Slabs of porphyry and rock crystal were "touchstones," used to test gold and precious stones, such as the pendant and two brooches of gold with pearls and precious stones pinned to a dark fabric. Rosary beads and a belt end hang from the top shelf, where two silver flagons and a covered cup stand. A bridal belt, similar to the one worn in Rogier's *Portrait of a Lady*, curls across the counter. Such a combination of pieces suggests that the painting expresses the hope for health and well-being for the couple whose betrothal or wedding portrait this may be. Or perhaps the painting simply advertises the guild's wares.

As in Jan's *Giovanni Arnolfini and his wife Giovanna Cenami*, a convex mirror extends the viewer's field of vision, in this instance to the street outside, where two men appear. One is stylishly dressed in red and black, and the other holds a falcon, another indication of high status since only the nobility hunted with falcons. Whether or not the reflected image has symbolic meaning, the mirror has a practical value in allowing the goldsmith to observe the approach of a potential customer.

DIRCK BOUTS. Dirck Bouts (active c. 1444–75) is the best storyteller among the Flemish painters, skillful in direct narration rather than complex symbolism. The two remaining panels (FIG. 18–19) from a set of four on the subject of justice illustrate this skill. The town council of Louvain, for whom Bouts was the official painter, ordered these huge paintings for the city hall to be examples and warnings to city officials. The paintings depict an early moral tale, the **WRONGFUL EXECUTION OF THE COUNT**. The empress, seen standing with Emperor Otto III in her palace garden, falsely accuses a count of a sexual impropriety. Otto III has the count beheaded and the countess receives her husband's head, in the presence of the councilors. In the second panel, the countess successfully endures a trial by ordeal to prove her husband's innocence. Unscathed and still holding her husband's head, she lifts up a glowing iron bar before the shocked and repentant emperor. In the far distance, justice is done and the evil empress is executed by burning at the stake.

Dirck Bouts's paintings are notable for his use of spacious outdoor settings and his inclusion of contemporary portraits.

He is the first to create an illusion of space that recedes continuously and gradually from the picture plane to the far horizon. To achieve this effect, he employed devices such as walkways, walls, and winding roads along which characters in the scene are placed. His use of atmospheric perspective can be seen in the gradual lightening of the sky and the smoky blue hills at the horizon. Bouts is also credited with inventing

18–18 | Petrus Christus
A GOLDSMITH (SAINT ELIGIUS?) IN HIS SHOP 1449. Oil on oak panel, 38⅛ × 33½″ (98 × 85 cm). The Metropolitan Museum of Art, New York.
Robert Lehman Collection, 1975. (1975.1.110)

The artist signed and dated his work on the house reflected in the mirror.

18–19 | Dirck Bouts **WRONGFUL EXECUTION OF THE COUNT (LEFT), JUSTICE OF OTTO III (RIGHT)**
1470–75. Oil on wood panel, each 12′11″ × 6′7½″ (3.9 × 2 m). Musées Royaux des Beaux-Arts de Belgique,
Brussels, Belgium-Koninklijke Musea voor Schone Kunsten van Belgie, Brussels.

the official group portrait in which living individuals are integrated into a narrative scene along with fictional or religious characters. In the Louvain justice panels, the men observing the execution may have been members of the town council. Their impassive faces are realistic but their figures are impossibly tall and slender.

HUGO VAN DER GOES. Hugo van der Goes (c. 1440–82), dean of the painters guild in Ghent (1468–75), united the intellectual prowess of Jan van Eyck and the emotional sensitivity of Rogier van der Weyden. Hugo's major work was a large altarpiece of the Nativity (FIG. 18–20). The altarpiece was commissioned by Tommaso Portinari, head of the Medici bank in Bruges. Painted probably between 1474 and 1476, the triptych was sent to Florence and installed in 1483 in the Portinari fam-

ily chapel in the Church of Sant'Egidio. It had a noticeable impact on Florentine painters such as Ghirlandaio, whose own altarpiece in the Sassetti Chapel in the Church of Santa Trinita (SEE FIG. 19–35) reflects his study of Hugo's painting. Tommaso, his wife Maria Baroncelli, and their three oldest children are portrayed kneeling in prayer on the wings. On the left wing, looming larger than life behind Tommaso and his son Antonio, are the saints for whom they are named, Saint Thomas and Saint Anthony. The younger son, Pigello, born in 1474, was apparently added after the original composition was set. On the right wing, Maria and her daughter Margherita are presented by the saints Mary Magdalen and Margaret.

The theme of the altarpiece is the Nativity as told by Luke (2:10–19). The central panel represents the Adoration of the newborn Christ Child by Mary and Joseph, a host of angels, and the shepherds who have rushed in from the fields. In the middle ground of the wings are scenes invented by Hugo, a part of his personal vision. Winding their way through the winter landscape are two groups headed for Bethlehem. On the left wing, Mary and Joseph travel to their native city to take part in a census ordered by the region's Roman ruler, King Herod. Near term in her pregnancy, Mary has dismounted from her donkey and staggers, supported by Joseph. On the right wing, a servant of the three Magi, who are coming to honor the awaited Savior, asks directions from a peasant. The continuous landscape across the wings and central panel is the finest evocation of cold, barren winter since the Limbourg brothers' *February* (SEE FIG. 18–6).

Hugo's technique is firmly grounded in the terrestrial world despite the visionary subjects. Meadows and woods are painted meticulously. Like Bouts (SEE FIG. 18–19) and many other northern artists at this time, he used atmospheric perspective to approximate distance in the landscape. Although Hugo's brilliant palette and meticulous accuracy recall Jan van Eyck, and although the intense but controlled emotions he depicts suggest the emotional content of Rogier van der Weyden's works, the composition and interpretation of the altarpiece are entirely his own. He shifts figure size for emphasis: The huge figures of Joseph, Mary, and the shepherds are the same size as the patron saints on the wings, in contrast to the much smaller *Portinari* family and still smaller angels. Hugo also uses color, as well as the gestures and gazes of the figures, to focus our eyes on the center panel where the mystery of

the Incarnation takes place. Instead of lying swaddled in a manger or in his mother's arms, Jesus rests naked and vulnerable on the barren ground. Rays of light emanate from his body. The source of this image was the visionary writing of the Swedish mystic Saint Bridget (who composed her work c. 1360–70), which describes Mary kneeling to adore the Christ Child immediately after giving birth.

Hugo was also a master of disguised symbolism (FIG. 18–21). In the foreground the ceramic pharmacy jar (*albarello*), glass, flowers, and wheat have multiple meanings. The wheat sheaf refers both to the location of the event at Bethlehem, which in Hebrew means "house of bread," and to the Host, or bread, at Communion, which represents the Body of Christ. The majolica *albarello* is decorated with vines and grapes, alluding to the wine of Communion at the Eucharist, which represents the Blood of Christ. It holds a red lily for the Blood of Christ and three irises—white for purity and purple for Christ's royal ancestry. Every little flower has a meaning. The three irises may refer to the Trinity of Father (God), Son (Jesus), and Holy Ghost. The iris, or "little sword," also refers to Simeon's prophetic words to Mary at the Presentation in the Temple: "And you yourself a sword will pierce so that the thoughts of many hearts may be revealed" (Luke 2:35). The glass vessel symbolizes Mary and the entry of the Christ Child into the Virgin's womb, the way light passes through glass without breaking it. The seven blue columbines in the glass remind the viewer of the Virgin's future sorrows, and scattered on the ground are violets, symbolizing humility.

18–20 | Hugo van der Goes **PORTINARI ALTARPIECE (OPEN)**
c. 1474-76. Tempera and oil on wood panel; center 8'3½" × 10' (2.53 × 3.01 m), wings each 8'3½" × 4'7½" (2.53 × 1.41 m). Galleria degli Uffizi, Florence.

THE ⊙BJECT SPEAKS

HANS MEMLING'S SAINT URSULA RELIQUARY

Among the works securely assigned to Memling is the reliquary of Saint Ursula, a container in the form of a Gothic chapel, made in 1489 for the Hospital of Saint John in Bruges. According to legend, Ursula, the daughter of the Christian king of Brittany, was betrothed to a pagan English prince. She requested a three-year delay in the marriage to travel to Rome, during which time her husband-to-be was to convert to Christianity. On the trip home, she stopped in Cologne, which had been taken over by Attila the Hun and his nomadic warriors from Central Asia. When Ursula rejected an offer of marriage, they killed her with an arrow through the heart and also murdered her companions. The story of Ursula is told on the six side panels of the reliquary. Visible in the illustration are the pope bidding Ursula goodbye in Rome; the murder of her female companions in Cologne har-

bor; and Ursula's own death. On the reliquary's "roof" are roundels with musical angels flanking the Coronation of the Virgin. At the corners are carved saints, and on the end is Saint Ursula in the doorway of the "chapel," sheltering her followers under her mantle. In early stories, Ursula was accompanied on her trip by ten maidens. By the tenth century, however, she had become the leader of 11,000 young virgin martyrs.

Although the events supposedly took place in the fourth century, Memling has set them in contemporary Cologne: the city's Gothic cathedral, under construction (with the huge lifting wheel still visible), looms in the background of the Martyrdom panel. Memling created this deep space as a foil for his idealized female martyr, a calm aristocratic figure amid menacing men-at-arms. The surface pattern and intricately arranged folds of the drapery draw our attention to her.

Saints continued to play a role in the pre-Reformation Church although the need for personal intercessors began to be questioned by reformers. The possession of relics (remains) of the saints was an important source of prestige for a church, and relics attracted offerings from petitioners. The reliquary was commissioned presumably by the two women dressed in the white habits and black hoods worn by hospital sisters and depicted on the end of the reliquary not visible in the illustration. One hypothesis is that they are Jossine van Dudzeele and Anna van den Moortele, two nuns who were administrators of the hospital of Saint John in the fifteenth century. The reliquary of Saint Ursula, for all the beauty and interest of its paintings, is not a gold and jewel bedecked casket but a simple wooden shrine, an appropriate gift from the women who led the community and the hospital they served.

Hans Memling **SAINT URSULA RELIQUARY**
1489. Painted and gilded oak, 34 × 36 × 13″
(86.4 × 91.4 × 33 cm). Memling Museum,
Hospital of Saint John, Bruges, Belgium.

Hans Memling **MARTYRDOM OF SAINT URSULA**
Detail of the *Saint Ursula Reliquary*.
Panel 13¾ × 10″ (35 × 25.3 cm).

18–21 │ Hugo van der Goes **DETAIL OF STILL LIFE FROM THE CENTER PANEL OF THE PORTINARI ALTARPIECE**

Hugo's artistic vision goes far beyond this formal religious symbolism. For example, the shepherds, who stand in unaffected awe before the miraculous event, are among the most sympathetically rendered images of common people to be found in the art of any period. The portraits of the children are among the most sensitive studies of children's features.

HANS MEMLING. The artist who summarizes and epitomizes the end of the era in Flanders is Hans Memling (1430/35–94). Memling combines the intellectual depth and virtuoso rendering of his predecessors with a delicacy of feeling and exquisite grace. A German from the nearby Rhineland, Memling may have worked in Rogier van der Weyden's Brussels workshop in the 1460s, since Rogier's style remained the dominant influence on his art. Soon after Rogier's death in 1464, Memling moved to Bruges, where he developed an international clientele. In 1489 he produced the reliquary of Saint Ursula for the Hospital of Saint John (see "Hans Memling's Saint Ursula Reliquary," page 608). It has the form of a basilican church, and instead of gold, silver, and enamels, it is made of painted wood, modest materials in keeping with a commission from the nuns of the hospital.

EUROPE BEYOND FLANDERS

Flemish art—its complex symbolism, its realism and atmospheric space, its brilliant colors and sensuous textures—delighted wealthy patrons and well-educated courtiers both inside and outside of Flanders. At first, Flemish artists worked in foreign courts; later, many artists went to study in Flanders. Flemish manuscripts, tapestries, altarpieces, and portraits appeared in palaces and chapels throughout Europe. Soon local artists learned Flemish oil painting techniques and emulated the Flemish style. By the end of the fifteenth century, distinctive regional variations of Flemish art could be found throughout Europe, from the Atlantic Ocean to the Danube.

France

The centuries-long struggle for power and territory between France and England continued well into the fifteenth century. When King Charles VI of France died in 1422, England claimed the throne for the king's nine-month-old grandson, Henry VI of England. The plight of Charles VII, the late French king's son, inspired Joan of Arc to lead a crusade to return him to the throne. Thanks to Joan's efforts Charles was crowned at Reims in 1429. Although Joan was burned at the stake in 1431, the revitalized French forces drove the English from French lands. In 1461, Louis XI succeeded his father, Charles VII, as king of France. Under his rule the French royal court again became a major source of patronage for the arts.

JEAN FOUQUET. The leading court artist of the period in France, Jean Fouquet (c. 1420–81), was born in Tours and may have trained in Paris as an illuminator. He may have visited Italy in about 1445–47, but by about 1450 he was back in Tours, a renowned painter. Fouquet adapted contemporary Italian classical motifs in architectural decoration, and he was also strongly influenced by Flemish realism. He painted Charles VII, the royal family, and courtiers, and he illustrated manuscripts and designed tombs.

Among the court officials Fouquet painted is Étienne Chevalier, the treasurer of France under Charles VII. Fouquet painted a diptych showing Chevalier praying to the Virgin and Child (FIG. 18–22). According to an inscription, the painting was made to fulfill a vow made by Chevalier to the king's much-loved and respected mistress, Agnès Sorel, who died in 1450. Agnès Sorel, whom contemporaries described as a highly moral, extremely pious woman, was probably the model for the Virgin; her features were taken from her death mask, which is still preserved. Fouquet paints the figures of Virgin and angels as stylized, simplified forms, reducing the color to near-*grisaille,* then surrounds them with amazing jewels in the crown and the throne. The brilliant red and blue cherubs form a tapestrylike background.

In the other wing of the diptych, Fouquet uses a realistic style. Étienne Chevalier, who kneels in prayer with clasped hands and a meditative gaze, is presented to the Virgin by his name saint, Stephen (*Étienne* in French). Fouquet has followed the Flemish manner in depicting the courtier's ruddy features with a mirrorlike accuracy that is confirmed by other known portraits. Saint Stephen's features are also distinctive enough to

18–22 | Jean Fouquet **ÉTIENNE CHEVALIER AND SAINT STEPHEN** Left wing of the Melun Diptych c. 1450.
Oil on wood panel, 36½ × 33½″ (92.7 × 85.5 cm). Staatliche Museen zu Berlin, Preussischer Kulturbesitz, Gemäldegalerie.
VIRGIN AND CHILD Right wing of the Melun Diptych c. 1451. Oil on wood panel,
37¼ × 33½″ (94.5 × 85.5 cm). Koninklijk Museum voor Schone Kunsten, Antwerp, Belgium.

The diptych was separated long ago and the two paintings went to collections in different countries. They are reunited on this page.
The original frame was of blue velvet embroidered with pearls and gold and silver thread.

have been a portrait. According to legend and biblical accounts, Stephen, a deacon in the early Christian Church in Jerusalem, was the first Christian martyr, stoned to death for defending his beliefs. Here the saint wears liturgical, or ritual, vestments and carries a large stone on a closed Gospel book as evidence of his martyrdom. A trickle of blood can be seen on his tonsured head (male members of religious orders shaved their heads as a sign of humility). The two figures are shown in a hall decorated with the kind of marble paneling and classical architectural decoration Fouquet could have seen in Italy. Fouquet arranged the figures in an unusual spatial setting; the diagonal lines of the wall and uptilted tile floor recede toward an unseen vanishing point at the right. Despite his debt to Flemish realism and his nod to Italian architectural forms and to linear perspective (discussed in Chapter 19), Fouquet's austere geometric style is uniquely his own.

THE FLAMBOYANT STYLE. The great age of cathedral building that had begun about 1150 was over by the end of the fourteenth century, but the growing urban population needed houses, city halls, guild halls, and more parish churches. The richest patrons commissioned master masons to build light-filled spacious halls and sculptors to cover their buildings with elaborate Gothic architectural decoration. Like painters, sculptors also turned to the realistic depiction of nature, and they covered capitals and moldings with ivy, hawthorn leaves, and other vegetation. Called the Flamboyant style (meaning "flaming" in French) because of its repeated, twisted, flamelike tracery, this intricate, elegant decoration was used to cover new buildings and was added to older buildings being modernized with spires, porches, or window tracery. The forms often recall the earlier English Decorated style (see Chapter 17).

The **CHURCH OF SAINT-MACLOU** in Rouen, which was begun after a fund-raising campaign in 1432 and dedicated in 1521, is an outstanding example of the Flamboyant style (**FIG. 18–23**). It may have been designed by the Paris architect Pierre Robin. A projecting porch bends to enfold the façade of the church in a screen of tracery. Sunlight on the flame-shaped openings casts ever-changing shadows across the intentionally complex surface. Crockets—small, knobby leaflike ornaments that line the steep gables and slender buttresses—break every defining line. In the Flamboyant style, decoration sometimes seems divorced from structure. The strength of load-bearing

18–23 | Pierre Robin (?)
CHURCH OF SAINT-MACLOU, ROUEN
Normandy, France. West façade, 1432–1521; façade
c. 1500–14.

Sequencing Events

1416	Death of Jean, Duke of Berry
1431	Joan of Arc burned at the stake in Rouen
1455	Gutenberg prints the Bible
1453	Hundred Years' War ends
1492	Columbus reaches the West Indies and North America

Among the carved decorations are puns on the patron's sur-name, *Coeur* (meaning "heart" in French). The house was also Jacques Coeur's place of business, so it had large storerooms for goods and a strong room for treasure. (A well-stocked but lesser merchant's shop can be seen in the painting of Petrus Christus, *A Goldsmith in His Shop*; SEE FIG. 18–18.)

Spain and Portugal

Many Flemish and French artists traveled to Spain and Portugal, where they were held in high esteem. Queen Isabella of Castile, for example, assembled a large collection of Flemish paintings and illuminated manuscripts as well as a collection of tapestries, jewels, and gold- and silversmith's work. She was also a patron of architecture. In Toledo,

walls and buttresses is often disguised by an overlay of tracery; and traceried pinnacles, gables, and S-curve moldings combine with a profusion of ornament in geometric and natural shapes, all to dizzying effect. The interior of such a church, filled with light from huge windows, can be seen in the *Book of Hours of Mary of Burgundy* (SEE FIG. 18–7).

The **HOUSE OF JACQUES COEUR,** the fabulously wealthy merchant in Bourges, reflects the popularity of the Flamboy-ant style for secular architecture (**FIG. 18–24**). Built at great expense between 1443 and 1451, it survives almost intact, although it has been stripped of its rich furnishings. The ram-bling, palatial house is built around an irregular open court-yard, with spiral stairs in octagonal towers giving access to the rooms. Tympana over doors indicate the function of the rooms within; for example, over the door to the kitchen a cook stirs the contents of a large bowl. Flamboyant decora-tion enriches the cornices, balustrades, windows, and gables.

18–24 | **HOUSE OF JACQUES COEUR**
Bourges. France. Interior courtyard, 1443–51.

18–25 Juan Güas **SAN JUAN DE LOS REYES**
Interior, wall with carved coats-of-arms and saints. Toledo, Spain. Begun 1477.

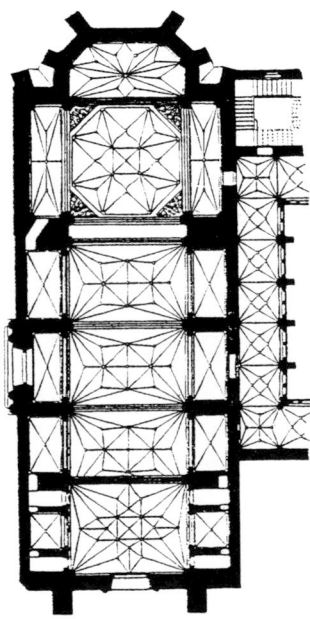

18–26 Juan Güas **PLAN OF SAN JUAN DE LOS REYES**
Begun 1477.

Isabella built a church for the Franciscans, which she intended to be the royal burial chapel.

SAN JUAN DE LOS REYES. Founded in 1477, **SAN JUAN DE LOS REYES** (Saint John of the Kings) was never used as intended, since the conquest of Granada in 1492 permitted Ferdinand and Isabella to build their pantheon in the former Moorish capital rather than in Toledo. Nevertheless, the church in Toledo established a new church type known as "Isabellan" (FIGS. 18–25, 18–26). The church had a single nave flanked by lateral chapels built between the wall buttresses, a raised choir over the western entrance (Spanish churches usually had the choir in the nave), and raised pulpits at the crossing. The transept did not extend beyond the line of the buttresses and chapels. A low lantern tower over the crossing focused the light on the space reserved for the tombs, which were never built. This simple compact design allowed ample space for the congregation, and the expanses of wall could be used for educational paintings, sculptures, or tapestries.

Lavish sculptural decoration at San Juan de los Reyes honored Ferdinand and Isabella. Heraldry—an art form in itself—became a major decorative feature in the fifteenth century. Huge shields with the royal coat of arms (chains and bars for King Ferdinand's Aragon and Catalunya and lions and castles for Queen Isabella's Leon and Castile) are held by the gigantic eagles of Saint John. They are flanked by saints standing on pedestals under flamboyant canopies. On moldings and piers the artists, led by Juan Güas, carved plants, insects, and animals as avidly and accurately as painters of manuscripts. Friezes with inscriptions mimic Moorish architectural inscriptions, and the luxurious surface decoration may also reflect the Moorish taste with which the Christians were well informed.

Isabellan art has a special relevance for the Americas. In 1492, when Isabella and Ferdinand entered the Moorish capital city of Granada in triumph, Spanish ships reached the Americas. Soon missionaries were sent to the New World, where they built churches in the Isabellan style, using local materials and workmen. The Mission style of California and the American Southwest (SEE FIG. 29–46) is a simplified version of the Isabellan style of San Juan de los Reyes.

NUÑO GONÇALVES. Local painters and sculptors quickly absorbed the Flemish style. They could have had firsthand experience, since Jan van Eyck, among others, visited Spain and Portugal. Jan was sent by the Duke of Burgundy to paint the portrait of a Portuguese princess who was a candidate for marriage to the duke. A little later Nuño Gonçalves (active 1450–71) painted the members of the Portuguese royal family. Gonçalves reflects Jan's influence in his monumental figures and intense interest in surfaces and rich colors, although the severity of the portraits recalls Dirck Bouts. Perhaps as early as 1465–67, Gonçalves painted a large multipanel altarpiece for the Convent of Saint Vincent de Fora in Lisbon (FIG. 18–27). The paintings are filled with remarkable portraits of people from all walks of life—the royal family, Cistercians, businessmen, fishermen—most of whom are identifiable. The central panel with the royal family holds a special interest for Americans. Here the painter has included a portrait of Prince Henry the Navigator, the man who inspired and financed Portuguese exploration. Prince Henry sent ships down the west coast of Africa and out into the Atlantic, but he died before Columbus's ships reached the Americas. Dressed in black, he kneels behind his nephew, King Alfonso V.

Saint Vincent, magnificent in red and gold vestments, stands in a tightly packed group of people, with members of the royal family at the front and courtiers forming a solid block across the rear. With the exception of the idealized features of the saint, all are portraits: At the right, King Alfonso V kneels before Saint Vincent, while his young son and his deceased uncle, Henry the Navigator, look on. Alfonso and his son rest their hands on their swords; Henry's hands are tented in prayer. At the left, Alfonso's deceased wife and mother hold rosaries. The appearance of Saint Vincent is clearly a vision, brought on by the intense prayers of the individuals around him.

Germany and Switzerland

Present-day Germany and Switzerland were situated within the Holy Roman Empire, a loose confederation of primarily German-speaking states. Industries, especially metalworking, developed in the Rhine Valley and elsewhere, and the artisan guilds grew powerful. Trade flourished under the auspices of the Hanseatic League, an association of cities and trading outposts, and both trade and manufacture were stimulated by the financial acumen of the rising merchant class. The Fugger family began their spectacular rise from simple textile workers and linen merchants to bankers for the Habsburgs and the popes. The Holy Roman Emperor and the pope continued their disputes, although a church council, held in Constance (1414–18), temporarily settled some of the problems of church-state relations. These problems would resurface, however, and lead to the Protestant Reformation in the next century.

Germanic artists worked in two very different styles. Some, working around Cologne, continued the International Gothic style with increased prettiness, softness, and sweetness of expression. The "Beautiful Style" of the fourteenth century continued, especially in the Rhineland, where artists perfected a soft, lyrical style. Other artists began an intense investigation and detailed description of the physical world. The major exponent of the latter style was Konrad Witz (active 1434–46). Witz, a native of Swabia in southern Germany, moved to Basel (in present-day Switzerland), where he found a rich source of patronage in the Church.

18–27 | Nuño Gonçalves **SAINT VINCENT WITH THE PORTUGUESE ROYAL FAMILY**
Panel from the *Altarpiece of Saint Vincent*. c. 1465–67.
Oil on wood panel, 6'9¼" × 4' 2⅝" (2.07 × 1.28 m).
Museu Nacional de Arte Antiga, Lisbon.

Witz's last large commission before his early death in 1446 was an altarpiece dedicated to Saint Peter for the Cathedral of Saint Peter in Geneva. Witz signed and dated his work in 1444. In the **MIRACULOUS DRAFT OF FISHES** (FIG. 18–28), a scene from the altarpiece which depicts Jesus's calling of the fishermen Peter and Andrew, Witz painted Lake Geneva, not Galilee. He has gone beyond the generic realism of the Flemings to paint a realistic portrait of a specific landscape: the dark mountain (the Mole) rising on the far shore of Lake Geneva and the snow-covered Alps shining in the distance. Witz records every nuance of light and water—the rippling surface, the reflections of boats, figures, and buildings, even the lake bottom. Peter's body and legs, visible through the water, are distorted by the refraction. The floating clouds above create shifting light and dark passages over the water. Perhaps for the first time in European art, the artist captures both the appearance and spirit of nature.

18–28 | Konrad Witz **MIRACULOUS DRAFT OF FISHES**
From an altarpiece from the Cathedral of Saint Peter, Geneva, Switzerland. 1444. Oil on wood panel, 4'3" × 5'1" (1.29 × 1.55 m). Musée d'Art et d'Histoire, Geneva.

18–29 | **THE BUXHEIM SAINT CHRISTOPHER**
1423. Hand-colored woodcut, 11⅜ × 8⅛" (28.85 × 20.7 cm).
Courtesy of the Director and Librarian, the John Rylands University Library, the University of Manchester, England.

The Latin verse reads, "Whenever you look at the face of Christopher, in truth, you will not die a terrible death that day." "1423"

THE GRAPHIC ARTS

Printmaking emerged in Europe at the end of the fourteenth century with the development of printing presses and the increased local manufacture and wider availability of paper. The techniques used by printmakers during the fifteenth century were woodcut and engraving (see "Woodcuts and Engravings on Metal," page 614). Woodblocks cut in relief had long been used to print designs on cloth, but only in the fifteenth century did the printing of images and texts on paper and the production of books in multiple copies of a single edition, or version, begin to replace the copying of each book by hand. Both handwritten and printed books were often illustrated, and printed images were sometimes hand colored.

Single Sheets

Single-sheet prints in the woodcut and engraving techniques were made in large quantities in the early decades of the fifteenth century. Initially, woodcuts were made primarily by woodworkers with no training in drawing, but soon artists began to draw the images for them to cut from the block.

THE BUXHEIM SAINT CHRISTOPHER. Devotional images were sold as souvenirs to pilgrims at holy sites. The **BUXHEIM SAINT CHRISTOPHER** was found in the Carthusian Monastery of Buxheim, in southern Germany, glued to the inside of the back cover of a manuscript (**FIG. 18–29**). Saint Christopher, patron saint of travelers, carries the Christ Child across the river. His efforts are witnessed by a monk holding out a light to guide him to the monastery door, but ignored by the hardworking millers on the opposite bank. Both the cutting of the block and the quality of the printing are very high. The artist and cutter vary the width of the lines to strengthen major forms. Delicate lines are used for inner modeling (facial features) and short parallel lines to indicate shadows (the inner side of draperies). Since the date 1423 is cut into the block, the print was thought to be among the earliest to survive. Recent studies have determined that the date refers to some event and the print was made at midcentury.

MARTIN SCHONGAUER. Engraving may have originated with goldsmiths and armorers, who recorded their work by rubbing lampblack into the engraved lines and pressing paper over the plate. German artist Martin Schongauer (c. 1435–91), who learned engraving from his goldsmith father, was an immensely skillful printmaker who excelled both in drawing and in the difficult technique of shading from deep blacks to faintest grays using only line. He was also a skilled painter. In **DEMONS TORMENTING SAINT ANTHONY,** engraved about 1470–75 (**FIG. 18–30**), Schongauer illustrated the original biblical meaning of temptation as a physical assault rather than a subtle inducement. Wildly acrobatic, slithery, spiky demons lift

WOODCUTS AND ENGRAVINGS ON METAL

Woodcuts are made by drawing on the smooth surface of a block of fine-grained wood, then cutting away all the areas around the lines with a sharp tool called a *gouge*, leaving the lines in high relief. When the block's surface is inked and a piece of paper pressed down hard on it, the ink on the relief areas transfers to the paper to create a reverse image. The effects can be varied by making thicker and thinner lines, and shading can be achieved by placing the lines closer or farther apart. Sometimes the resulting black-and-white images were then painted by hand.

Engraving on metal requires a technique called *intaglio*, in which the lines are cut into the plate with tools called *gravers* or *burins*. The engraver then carefully burnishes the plate to ensure a clean, sharp image. Ink is applied over the whole plate and forced down into the lines, then the plate's surface is carefully wiped clean of the excess ink. When paper and plate are held tightly together by a press, the ink in the lines transfers to the paper.

Woodblocks and metal plates could be used repeatedly to make nearly identical images. If the lines of the block or plate wore down, the artists could repair them. Printing large numbers of identical prints of a single version, called an *edition*, was usually a team effort in a busy workshop. One artist would make the drawing. Sometimes it was drawn directly on the block or plate with ink, in reverse of its printed direction, sometimes on paper to be transferred in reverse onto the plate or block by another person, who then cut the lines. Others would ink and print the images.

In the illustration of books, the plates or blocks would be reused to print later editions and even adapted for use in other books. A set of blocks or plates for illustrations was a valuable commodity and might be sold by one workshop to another. Early in publishing, there were no copyright laws, and many entrepreneurs simply had their workers copy book illustrations onto woodblocks and cut them for their own publications.

Anthony up off the ground to torment and terrify him in midair. The engraver intensified the horror of the moment by condensing the action into a swirling vortex of figures beating, scratching, poking, tugging, and no doubt shrieking at the stoical saint, who remains impervious to all by reason of his faith.

Printed Books

The explosion of learning in Europe in the fifteenth century encouraged experiments in faster and cheaper ways of producing books than by hand-copying them. The earliest printed books were block books, for which each page of text, with or without illustrations, was cut in relief on a single block of wood. Movable-type printing, in which individual letters could be arranged and locked together, inked, and then printed onto paper, was first achieved in the workshop of Johann Gutenberg in Mainz, Germany. More than forty copies of Gutenberg's Bible, printed around 1455, still exist. As early as 1465, two German printers were working in Italy, and by the 1470s there were presses in France, Flanders, Holland, and Spain. With the invention of this fast way to make a number of identical books, the intellectual and spiritual life of Europe—and with it the arts—changed forever.

WILLIAM CAXTON. England got its first printing press as the result of a second career launched by a former English cloth merchant, William Caxton (active c. 1441–91). Caxton had lived for thirty years in Bruges, where he came in contact with the humanist community as well as with local printing ventures. In 1476 Caxton moved back to London, where he

18–30 | Martin Schongauer
DEMONS TORMENTING SAINT ANTHONY
c. 1480–90. Engraving, 12¼ × 9″ (31.1 × 22.9 cm).
The Metropolitan Museum of Art, New York.
Rogers Fund, 1920 (20.5.2)

¶ Prologus

O Ret chere made our ost to be euerpchon
Andz to souper sette he vs anon
He serued vs wpth vptaplf at the beste
Stronge was the wpne & wel dzpnke vs tpste
A semelp man our ost was wpth alle
For to he a marchal in a lordes halle
A large man he was wpth epen steppe
A fopzer burgeps is ther non in chepe
Boldz of hps speche andz wel was p tanght
Andz of manhoodz lackedz he rpght nought
Else therto was he rpght a merp man
Andz after souper to plepen he bigan
Andz spak of mprthe among other thpnges
Whan that we hadde made our rekenpnges
He sapdz thus now lordpnges trewlp
Pe he to me rpght welcome hertlp
For hp mp trolbthe pf I shal not lpe
I satv not thps peer so merp a companpe

c iiij

18–31 | **PAGE WITH PILGRIMS AT TABLE, PROLOGUE TO CANTERBURY TALES**
By Geoffrey Chaucer, published by William Caxton, London, 1484 (second edition, the first with illustrations). Woodcut, 4⁷⁄₁₆ × 4⁷⁄₈″ (10.2 × 12 cm). The Pierpont Morgan Library, New York.
PML 693.

established the first English publishing house. He printed eighty books in the next fourteen years, including works by the fourteenth-century author Geoffrey Chaucer (see "A New Spirit in Fourteenth–Century Literature," page 561).

In the second edition of Chaucer's *Canterbury Tales*, published in 1484, Caxton added woodblock illustrations by an unknown artist (FIG. 18–31). The assembled pilgrims journeying to the shrine of Saint Thomas à Becket are seated around a table. Included in the group of storytellers is an engaging woman, Alice, the Wife of Bath. Some critics see the Wife of Bath as an example of a woman who good women should avoid, but Chaucer put words in the lively

Alice's mouth that are well understood by many women today. Simple woodcut illustrations such as this are typical of the popular art of the time.

New techniques for printing illustrated books in Europe at the end of the fifteenth century held great promise for the spread of knowledge and ideas in the following century.

IN PERSPECTIVE

The fifteenth century marks the end of the Middle Ages and the beginning of the modern world, our own era. The period has been called the Renaissance, for some people saw it as a period of "rebirth," but in fact Western Europeans built on the accomplishments of the twelfth century—a renaissance in its own right—and on the achievements of the thirteenth and fourteenth centuries. By the fifteenth century thoughtful people focused their attention on human beings and their accomplishments, on life in this world as well as the next. They held a sense of human history, including a new respect for ancient learning.

The fifteenth century saw the growth of a secular spirit, related to the growth of towns into cities where the stimulating hurly-burly of urban life encouraged verbal and intellectual exchange. Whereas towns had once revolved around a court or cathedral, the new cities were industrial and commercial centers. Business joined religion and politics as a powerful motivating force. While the church continued to be a major patron of the arts and architecture, new sources of patronage emerged in the cities.

Architects followed the basic Gothic principles and methods of construction, but they added increasingly elaborate carved decoration that turned solid stone into lacy confections. Sculpture was freed from architecture, and freestanding figures gave the impression of life, vitality, and even possibility of movement. This realism extended into all the arts. Painters and tapestry makers, like writers and sculptors, included images from daily life.

By the middle of the century, a new medium—the graphic arts—came into being. The rapid dissemination of information both in words and pictures now available through the printing press allowed people to read—and see—for themselves. The new empirical frame of mind that characterized the fifteenth century gave rise in the sixteenth century to an explosion of inquiry and new ways of looking at the world.

SLUTER.
WELL OF MOSES,
CHARTREUSE DE CHAMPMOL, DIJON
1395–1406

CAMPIN.
MÉRODE ALTARPIECE
C. 1425–28

HOUSE OF JACQUES COEUR
BOURGES
1443–51

ROGIER VAN DER WEYDEN.
PORTRAIT OF A LADY
C. 1455

MARTIN SCHONGAUER
ORMENTING SAINT ANTONY
C. 1480–90

HUNT OF THE UNICORN
TAPESTRY SERIES
C. 1495–1505

FIFTEENTH-CENTURY ART IN NORTHERN EUROPE AND THE IBERIAN PENINSULA

1400

◄ Great (Western) Schism Ends 1417

1420

◄ Duke Philip The Good of Burgundy
Founds The Order of the Golden
Fleece 1430

1440

◄ Habsburgs Begin Rule of Holy
Roman Empire 1452
◄ Hundred Year's War Ends 1453
◄ Gutenberg Prints *Bible* 1455

1460

◄ William Caxton Establishes First
English Publishing House 1476

1480

◄ Columbus Reaches the West Indies
1492

1500

19–1 | Paolo Uccello **THE BATTLE OF SAN ROMANO** 1438–40. Tempera on wood panel, approx. 6′ × 10′ 7″ (1.83 × 3.23 m). National Gallery, London.

CHAPTER NINETEEN

RENAISSANCE ART IN FIFTEENTH-CENTURY ITALY

19

The ferocious but bloodless battle we see in FIGURE 19–1 could take place only in our dreams. Under an elegantly fluttering banner, the Florentine general Niccolò da Tolentino leads his men against the Sienese at the Battle of San Romano, which took place on June 1, 1432. In the center foreground, Niccolò holds aloft a baton of command, the sign of his authority. His bold gesture, together with his white horse and fashionable crimson and gold damask hat, ensure that he dominates the scene. The general's knights charge into the fray, and when they fall, like the soldier at the lower left, they join the many broken lances on the ground—all arranged in conformity with the new mathematical depiction of space, **one-point (linear) perspective.**

The battle rages across a shallow stage defined by the debris of warfare arranged in a neat pattern on a pink ground and backed by a hedge of blooming orange trees and rosebushes. In the cultivated hills beyond, crossbowmen prepare their lethal bolts. A Florentine painter nicknamed Paolo Uccello ("Paul Bird"), whose given name was Paolo di Dono (c. 1397–1475), created this panel painting, housed today in London's National Gallery. It is one of three panels now separated; the other two are hanging in major museums in Florence and Paris.

The complete history of these paintings has only recently come to light. Lionardo Bartolini Salimbeni (1404–79), who led the Florentine city government during the war against Lucca and Siena, probably commissioned the paintings. Uccello's remarkable accuracy when depicting armor from the 1430s, heraldic banners, and even fashionable fabrics and crests surely would have appealed to civic pride.

The hedges of oranges, roses, and pomegranates—all ancient fertility symbols—make a tapestry-like background for the action. Lionardo and his wife Maddalena had six sons, two of whom inherited the paintings. According to a complaint brought by one of the heirs, Damiano, Lorenzo de' Medici, the powerful de facto ruler of Florence, "forcibly removed" the paintings from Damiano's house. The paintings were never returned, and Uccello's masterpieces are recorded in a 1492 inventory as hanging in Lorenzo's private chamber in the Medici palace. Perhaps Lorenzo, who was called "the Magnificent," saw Uccello's heroic pageant as a trophy worthy of a Medici merchant prince.

In the sixteenth century, the artist, courtier, and historian Giorgio Vasari devoted a chapter to Paolo Uccello in his book *The Lives of the Most Excellent Italian Architects, Painters, and Sculptors.* He described Uccello as a man so obsessed with the study of perspective that he neglected his painting, his family, and even his beloved birds, until he finally became "solitary, eccentric, melancholy, and impoverished" (Vasari, page 79). His wife "used to declare that Paolo stayed at his desk all night, searching for the vanishing points of perspective, and when she called him to bed, he dawdled, saying: 'Oh, what a sweet thing this perspective is!'" (Vasari, page 83; translation by J. C. and P. Bondanella, Oxford, 1991). Such passion for science is typical of fifteenth-century artists, who were determined to capture the appearance of the material world and to subject it to overriding human logic. Thus a battle scene becomes a demonstration of the science of perspective.

CHAPTER-AT-A-GLANCE

HUMANISM AND THE ITALIAN RENAISSANCE

By the end of the Middle Ages, the most important Italian cultural centers lay north of Rome in the cities of Florence, Milan, and Venice, and in the smaller duchies of Mantua, Ferrara, and Urbino. In the south, Naples, Apulia, and Sicily were under French and then Aragonese control. Much of the power and influential art patronage was in the hands of wealthy families: the Medici in Florence, the Montefeltro in Urbino, the Gonzaga in Mantua, the Visconti and Sforza in Milan, and the Este in Ferrara. Cities grew in wealth and independence as people moved to them from the countryside in unprecedented numbers. Commerce became increasingly important. In some of the Italian states a noble lineage was not necessary for—nor did it guarantee—political and economic success. Money conferred status, and a shrewd business or political leader could become very powerful. The period saw the rise of mercenary armies led by entrepreneurial (and sometimes brilliant) military commanders called *condottieri.* Unlike the knights of the Middle Ages, they owed allegiance only to those who paid them well; their employer might be a city-state, a lord, or even the pope. Some *condottieri*, like

Niccolò da Tolentino, became rich and famous. Others, like Federico da Montefeltro (SEE FIG. 19–29), were lords or dukes themselves, with their own territories in need of protection. Patronage of the arts was an important public activity with political overtones. As one Florentine merchant, Giovanni Rucellai, succinctly noted, he supported the arts "because they serve the glory of God, the honour of the city, and the commemoration of myself" (cited in Baxandall, page 2).

Like their northern counterparts (see Chapter 18), Italian humanists had a new sense of the importance of human thought and action, and they looked to the accomplishments of ages past for inspiration and instruction. For Italians, though, this had added significance. Although politically divided into many small entities, and therefore not resembling the country we know today, Italy existed as a geographic unit with a common heritage descended from ancient Rome. Ancient Rome therefore provided not only a unifying ideal of power and wealth but also a unifying culture based on ethical principles. Humanists sought the physical and literary records of the ancient world—assembling libraries, collecting sculpture and fragments of architecture, and beginning archaeological investigations of ancient Rome. They imagined a golden age of

Powerful families divided the Italian peninsula into city-states—the Medici in Florence, the Visconti and Sforza in Milan, the Montefeltro in Urbino, the Gonzaga in Mantua, and the Este in Ferrara. After 1420 the popes ruled Rome, while in the south Naples and Sicily were French and then Spanish (Aragonese) territories. Venice maintained her independence as a republic.

philosophy, literature, and the arts, which they hoped to recapture. Their aim was to live a rich, noble, and productive life—usually within the framework of Christianity but always adhering to a school of philosophy as a moral basis.

Artists, like the humanist scholars, turned to classical antiquity for inspiration even as they continued to fulfill commissions for predominantly Christian subjects. Secular works other than portraits do not survive in great numbers until the second half of the century. Much has been lost, especially painted home furnishings such as birth trays and marriage chests. Allegorical and mythological themes appeared, as patrons began to collect art for their personal enjoyment. Because few examples of ancient Roman painting were known in the fifteenth century, Renaissance painters looked to Roman sculpture and to literature. The male nude became an acceptable subject in Renaissance art, often justified as a religious image—Adam, Jesus on the cross, and martyrdoms of saints such as Sebastian. Other than representations of Eve or an occasional allegorical or mythological figure such as Venus, female nudes were rare until the end of the century.

Like the Flemish artists, Italian painters and sculptors moved gradually toward a greater precision in rendering the illusion of physical reality. They did so in a more analytical way than the northerners had, with the goal of achieving correct but perfected figures set within a rationally, rather than visually, defined space. Painters and sculptors developed a mathematical system called *linear perspective,* which achieved the illusion of a measured and continuously receding space (see "Brunelleschi, Alberti, and Renaissance Perspective," page 622). Italian architects also came to apply abstract, mathematically derived design principles to the plans and elevations of the buildings.

FLORENCE

In seizing Uccello's battle painting (SEE FIG. 19–1), Lorenzo de' Medici was asserting the role his family had come to play in the history of Florence. The fifteenth century witnessed the rise of the Medici from among the most successful of a newly rich middle class (comprising primarily merchants and

Technique
BRUNELLESCHI, ALBERTI, AND RENAISSANCE PERSPECTIVE

Artists such as Jan van Eyck refined intuitive perspective in order to approximate the appearance of things growing smaller and closer together in the distance, coupling it with atmospheric, or aerial, perspective. In Italy, the humanists' study of the natural world and their belief that "man is the measure of all things" led to the invention of a system of perspective that enabled artists to represent the visible world in a convincingly illusionistic way. This system—known variously as mathematical, linear, or one-point perspective—was first demonstrated by the architect Filippo Brunelleschi about 1420.

Brunelleschi's biographer, writing in the 1480s, describes two perspective panels that the architect created. One of them depicted the front of the Florentine Baptistry as if it were seen by someone standing three *braccia* inside the front door of the cathedral—a total of 60 *braccia* from the Baptistry. (In Florence, a *braccia*—meaning "arm," in Italian—measured about 2 feet.) To obtain this illusion, Brunelleschi pierced a hole in the back of the panel at the center point of the composition and placed a mirror one *braccia* length in front of it. Viewers could peep through the hole and see a reflection of the Baptistry that could be understood in actual space. The illusion was made even more striking by Brunelleschi's use of a burnished silver background, which reproduced real weather conditions.

Leon Battista Alberti developed and codified Brunelleschi's rules of perspective into a mathematical system for representing three dimensions on a two-dimensional surface in his treatise, in Latin, *De pictura (On Painting)* in 1435. A year later he published an Italian version, *Della pittura,* making a standardized, somewhat simplified method available to a larger number of draftspeople, painters, and relief sculptors. The goal he articulated is to make an image resemble a "view through a window," the view being the image represented, and the window, the picture plane.

In this highly artificial Italian system, the picture's surface was a flat plane that intersected the viewer's field of vision at a right angle. The system is based on a one-eyed viewer standing a prescribed distance from a work, dead center. From this fixed vantage point everything would appear to recede into the distance at the same rate, following imaginary lines called **orthogonals** that met at a single **vanishing point** on the horizon. Using orthogonals as a guide, artists could **foreshorten** objects, replicating the effect of perspective on individual objects. Despite its limitations, mathematical perspective seems to extend pictorial space into real space, providing the viewer with a direct, almost physical connection to the picture. It creates a compelling, even exaggerated sense of depth.

Early Renaissance artists relied on a number of mechanical methods. Many constructed devices with peepholes through which they sighted the figure or object to be represented. They used mathematical formulas to translate three-dimensional forms onto the picture plane, which they overlaid with a grid to provide reference points, or they emphasized the orthogonals created by tiled floors or buildings in the composition. As Italian artists became more comfortable with mathematical perspective over the course of the fifteenth century, they came to rely less on peepholes and formulas. Many artists adopted multiple vanishing points, which gave their work a more relaxed, less tunnel-like feeling.

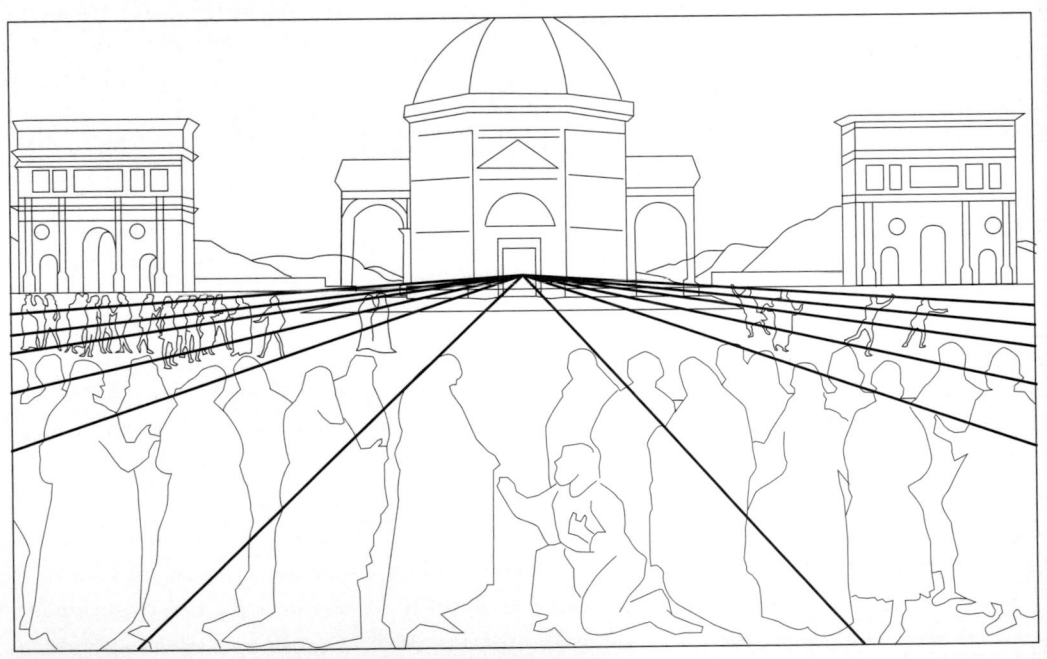

(Above) Perugino **THE DELIVERY OF THE KEYS TO SAINT PETER: SCHEMATIC DRAWING SHOWING THE ORTHOGONALS AND VANISHING POINT**

(Left) Perugino **THE DELIVERY OF THE KEYS TO SAINT PETER** Fresco on the right wall of the Sistine Chapel, Vatican, Rome. 1481. 11′5½″ × 18′ 8½″ (3.48 × 5.70 m).

bankers) to become the city's virtual rulers. Unlike hereditary aristocracy, the Medici rose up from obscure roots to make their fortune in banking. The competitive Florentine atmosphere that had fostered mercantile success and civic pride also cultivated competition in the arts and encouraged an interest in the ancient literary texts. These factors have led observers to consider Florence the cradle of the Italian Renaissance. Under Cosimo the Elder (1389–1464), the Medici became leaders in intellectual and artistic patronage. They sponsored philosophers and other scholars who wanted to study the classics, especially the works of Plato and his followers, the Neoplatonists. Neoplatonism distinguished between the spiritual (the ideal or Idea) and the physical (Matter) and encouraged artists to represent ideal figures. Writers, philosophers, and musicians dominated the Medici Neoplatonic circle. Few architects, sculptors, or painters were included, because most of them had learned their craft in apprenticeships and were considered little more than manual laborers. Nevertheless, interest in the ancient world rapidly spread beyond the Medici circle to artists and craftspeople, who sought to reflect the new interests of their patrons in their work. Gradually, artists began to see themselves as more than artisans, and society eventually recognized their best works as achievements of a very high order.

Although the Medici were the de facto rulers, Florence was considered to be a republic. The Council of Ten (headed for a time by Salimbeni, who commissioned Uccello's *Battle of San Romano*) was a kind of constitutional oligarchy where wealthy men formed the government. At the same time, the various guilds wielded tremendous power, and evidence of this is the fact that guild membership was a prerequisite for holding government office. Consequently, artists could look to the church and the state and civic groups—the city and the guilds—as well as private individuals for patronage, and the patrons expected the artists to reaffirm and glorify their achievements.

Architecture

The defining civic project of the early years of the fifteenth century was the completion of the Florence Cathedral with a magnificent dome over the high altar. The construction of the cathedral had begun in the late thirteenth century and had continued intermittently during the fourteenth century (see Chapter 17). As early as 1367, the builders had envisioned a very tall dome to span the huge interior space of the crossing, but they lacked the engineering know-how to construct it. When interest in completing the cathedral revived, around 1407, the technical solution was proposed by a young sculptor-turned-architect, Filippo Brunelleschi.

FILIPPO BRUNELLESCHI. Filippo Brunelleschi (1377–1446), whose father had been involved in the original plans for the cathedral dome in 1367, achieved what many considered impossible: He solved the problem of the dome. Brunelleschi originally had trained as a goldsmith. To further his education

19–2 | Filippo Brunelleschi **DOME OF FLORENCE CATHEDRAL**
1417–36; lantern completed 1471; the gallery, 1515.

The cathedral dome was a source of immense local pride. Renaissance architect and theorist Leon Battista Alberti described it as rising "above the skies, large enough to cover all the peoples of Tuscany with its shadow."

he traveled to Rome, probably with his friend, the sculptor Donatello. In Rome he studied ancient Roman sculpture and architecture. On his return to Florence, he tackled the problem of the cathedral. First he advised constructing a tall octagonal **drum**, as a base. The drum was finished in 1412, and in 1417, Brunelleschi was ready to design the dome itself (**FIG. 19–2**). From 1420 until 1436, workers built the dome. A revolutionary feat of engineering, the dome is a double shell of masonry 138 feet across. The octagonal outer shell is supported on eight large and sixteen lighter ribs. Instead of using a costly and even dangerous scaffold and centering, Brunelleschi devised a system in which temporary wooden supports were cantilevered out from the drum. He moved these supports up as building progressed. As the dome was built up course by course, each portion of the structure reinforced the next one. Vertical marble ribs interlocked with horizontal sandstone rings, connected and reinforced with iron rods and oak beams. The inner and outer shells were linked internally by a system of arches. When completed, this self-buttressed unit required no external support to keep it standing. Unsure of Brunelleschi's still theoretical approach to building, the men responsible for

19–3 Filippo Brunelleschi **OLD SACRISTY, CHURCH OF SAN LORENZO, FLORENCE**
1421–28, approx. 38 × 38′ (11.6 × 11.6 m).
Sculpture by Donatello.

Brunelleschi wanted simple architecture and protested the addition of sculpture.

the cathedral also appointed a respected master mason to assist with practical details of construction.

An **oculus** (round opening) in the center of the dome was surmounted by a **lantern** designed in 1436. After Brunelleschi's death, this crowning structure, made up of Roman architectural forms, was completed by another Florentine architect, Michelozzo di Bartolomeo (1396–1472). The final touch—a gilt bronzed ball—was added in 1468–71.

Other commissions came quickly after the cathedral dome project, as Brunelleschi's innovative designs were well received by Florentine patrons. From about 1418 until his death in 1446, Brunelleschi was involved in a series of influential projects. In 1419 he designed a foundling hospital for the city (see "The Foundling Hospital," page 626). For the Medici's parish church of San Lorenzo, he designed a sacristy (a room where ritual attire and vessels are kept), which also served as a burial chapel for Giovanni di Bicci de' Medici, who established the Medici fortune, and his wife (**FIG. 19–3**). Completed in 1428, it is called the **OLD SACRISTY** to distinguish it from the one built in the sixteenth century that lies opposite it on the other side of the church's choir. The Old Sacristy has a centralized plan, like a martyr's shrine in the Early Christian period. Later, Leon Battista Alberti, in his treatise on architecture (see page 622), wrote of the central plan as an ideal, derived from the

humanist belief that the circle was a symbol of divine perfection and that both the circle inscribed in a square and the cross inscribed in a circle were symbols of the cosmos.

The present church of San Lorenzo replaced an eleventh-century basilica. Brunelleschi conceived plans for the new church during the time that he designed and built the sacristy, that is, between 1421 and 1428, but Michelozzo, whose name appears in the construction documents, finished the building after Brunelleschi's death. The façade was never built.

The **CHURCH OF SAN LORENZO** has a basilican plan with a long nave flanked by side aisles that open into shallow lateral chapels (**FIG. 19–4**). A short transept and square crossing lead to a square sanctuary flanked by additional chapels opening off the transept. Projecting from the left transept, as one faces the altar, are Brunelleschi's sacristy and the older Medici tomb. The Church of San Lorenzo is notable for its mathematical regularity. Brunelleschi based his plan on a square **module**—a basic unit of measure that could be multiplied or divided and applied to every element of the design. Medieval builders had used modular plans, but Brunelleschi applied the module with greater consistency, and the result was a series of clear, harmonious spaces (**FIG. 19–5**). Ornamental details, all in a classical style, were carved in *pietra serena,* a grayish stone that became synonymous with Brunelleschi's interiors. Below the plain clerestory (upper-story wall of windows) with its unobtrusive openings, the arches of the nave arcade are carried on tall, slender Corinthian columns made even taller by the insertion of an **impost block** between the column capital and the springing of the round arches—one of Brunelleschi's favorite details. Flattened architectural forms in *pietra serena* repeat the arcade in the outer walls of the side aisles, and each bay is covered by its own shallow domical

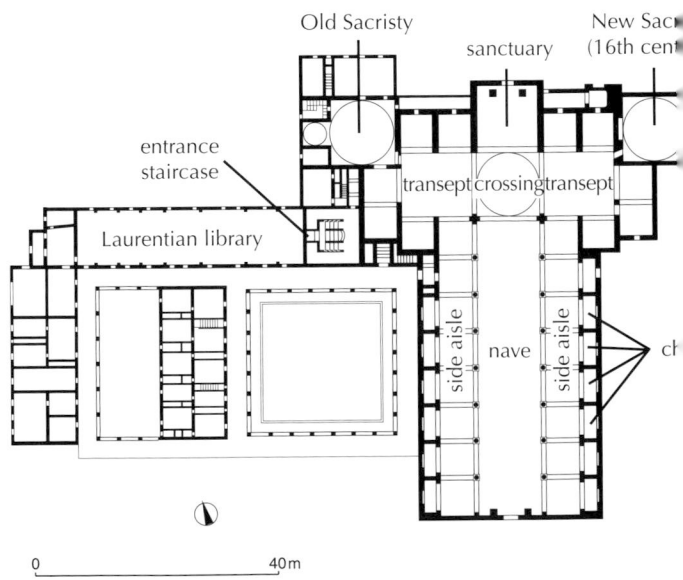

19–4 Filippo Brunelleschi **PLAN OF THE CHURCH OF SAN LORENZO, FLORENCE**
Includes later additions and modifications.

19–5 | Filippo Brunelleschi; continued by Michelozzo di Bartolomeo NAVE, CHURCH OF SAN LORENZO, FLORENCE
c. 1421–28, nave (designed 1434?) 1442–70.

vault. The square crossing is covered by a hemispherical dome; the nave and transept by flat ceilings. Brunelleschi's rational approach, unique sense of order, and innovative incorporation of classical motifs inspired later Renaissance architects, many of whom learned from his work firsthand by completing his unfinished projects.

THE MEDICI PALACE. Brunelleschi may have been involved in designing the nearby Medici Palace (now known as the **PALAZZO MEDICI-RICCARDI**) in 1446. According to sixteenth-century gossip recorded by Giorgio Vasari, Cosimo de' Medici the Elder rejected Brunelleschi's model for the *palazzo* as too grand (any large house was called a "palace"—*palazzo*). The courtyards of both buildings were the work of Michelozzo, whom many scholars have accepted as the designer of the building (**FIG. 19–6**). The austere exterior was in keeping with the republican political climate and Florentine religious attitudes, imbued with the Franciscan ideals of

19–6 | Attributed to Michelozzo di Bartolomeo
FAÇADE, PALAZZO MEDICI-RICCARDI, FLORENCE
Begun 1446.

For the palace site, Cosimo de' Medici the Elder chose the Via de' Gori at the corner of the Via Larga, the widest city street at that time. Despite his practical reasons for constructing a large residence and the fact that he chose simplicity and austerity over grandeur in the exterior design, his detractors commented and gossiped. As one exaggerated: "[Cosimo] has begun a palace which throws even the Colosseum at Rome into the shade."

THE ◉BJECT SPEAKS

THE FOUNDLING HOSPITAL

In 1419 the Guild of Silk Manufacturers and Goldsmiths in Florence undertook a significant public service: It established a large public orphanage and commissioned the brilliant young architect Filippo Brunelleschi to build it next to the Church of the Santissima Annunziata ("Most Holy Annunciation"), which housed a miracle-working painting of the Annunciation. Completed in 1444, the Foundling Hospital, the *Ospedale degli Innocenti*, was unprecedented in terms of scale and design innovation.

In the Foundling Hospital, Brunelleschi created a building that paid homage to traditional forms while introducing what came to be known as the Italian Renaissance style. Traditionally, a charitable foundation's building had a portico open to the street to provide shelter. Brunelleschi built an arcade of hitherto unimagined lightness and elegance, using smooth round columns and richly carved capitals—his own interpretation of the classical Corinthian order. The underlying mathematical basis for his design creates a sense of classical harmony. Each bay of the arcade encloses a cube of space defined by the 10-*braccia* (20-foot) height of the columns and the diameter of the arches. Hemispherical pendentive domes, half again as high as the columns, cover the cubes. The bays at the end of the arcade are slightly larger than the rest, creating a subtle frame for the composition. Brunelleschi defined the perfect squares and circles of his building with dark gray stone (*pietra serena*) against plain white walls. His training as a goldsmith and sculptor served him well as he led his artisans to carve crisp, elegantly detailed capitals and moldings for the open, covered gallery.

A later addition to the building seems eminently suitable: About 1487, Andrea della Robbia, who had inherited the family firm and its secret glazing formulas from his uncle Luca (see "Ceramics," page 634), created blue-and-white glazed terra-cotta medallions that signified the building's function. The babies in swaddling clothes, one in each medallion, are among the most beloved images of Florence.

The medallions seem to embody the human side of Renaissance humanism, reminding viewers that the city's wealthiest guild cared for the most helpless members of society. Perhaps the Foundling Hospital spoke to fifteenth-century Florentines of an increased sense of social responsibility. Or perhaps, by so publicly demonstrating social concerns, the wealthy guild that sponsored it solicited the approval and support of the lower classes in the cutthroat power politics of the day.

(ABOVE) Filippo Brunelleschi
FOUNDLING HOSPITAL, FLORENCE
Italy. Designed 1419; built 1421–44.

(LEFT) Andrea della Robbia
DETAIL OF TERRA-COTTA MEDALLION

poverty and charity. Like many other European cities, Florence had sumptuary laws, which forbade ostentatious displays of wealth—but they were often ignored. For example, private homes were supposed to be limited to a dozen rooms; Cosimo, however, acquired and demolished twenty small houses to provide the site for his new residence. The house was more than a dwelling place; it was his place of business, company headquarters. The *palazzo* symbolized the family and underscored the family's place in society. The building is linked to the seat of government, the Palazzo della Signoria (SEE FIG. 17–2), logistically by means of a straight line of connecting streets and symbolically through its imposing massiveness.

Huge in scale (each story is more than twenty feet high—today's builders calculate ten feet per story), the building has harmonious proportions and elegant, classically inspired details. On one side, the ground floor originally opened through large, round arches onto the street, creating in effect a loggia that provided space for the family business. These arches were walled up in the sixteenth century and given windows designed by Michelangelo. The façade of large, **rusticated** stone blocks—that is, blocks with their outer faces left rough, typical of Florentine town house exteriors—was derived from fortifications. On the façade, the stories are clearly set off from each other by the change in the stone surfaces from very rough at the ground level to almost smooth on the third.

The builders followed the time-honored tradition of placing rooms around a central courtyard. Unlike the still-medieval plan of the House of Jacques Coeur (SEE FIG. 18–24), however, the **MEDICI PALACE COURTYARD** is square in plan with rooms arranged symmetrically **(FIG. 19–7).** Round arches on slender columns form a continuous arcade and support an enclosed second story. Tall windows in the second story match the exterior windows. Disks bearing the Medici arms surmount each arch in a frieze decorated with swags in **sgraffito** work (tinted and engraved plaster). Such classical elements, inspired by the study of Roman ruins, gave the great house an aura of dignity and stability and undoubtedly enhanced the status of its owners. The Medici Palace inaugurated a new monumentality and regularity of plan in residential urban architecture. Wealthy Florentine families soon copied it in their own houses.

LEON BATTISTA ALBERTI. The relationship of the façade to the body of the building behind it was a continuing challenge for Italian Renaissance architects. Early in his architectural career, Leon Battista Alberti (1404–72), a lawyer turned humanist, architect, and author, devised a façade to be the unifying front for a planned merger of eight adjacent houses in Florence acquired by Giovanni Rucellai **(FIG. 19–8).** Work began about 1455, but the house was never finished, as is obvious on the right side of the view seen here. It has been suggested that Alberti designed a five-bay façade with a central door and that Bernardo Rossellino (1409–64), the builder on record, added two more bays and began the eighth but was unable to finish

19–7 | **COURTYARD WITH SGRAFFITO DECORATION, PALAZZO MEDICI-RICCARDI, FLORENCE**
Begun 1446.

19–8 | Leon Battista Alberti **PALAZZO RUCELLAI, FLORENCE**
Left five bays 1455-58; later extended but never finished.

19-9 | Nanni di Banco **THE FOUR CROWNED MARTYRS**
c. 1409-17. Marble, height of figures 6' (1.83 m). Orsanmichele, Florence (photographed before removal of figures to
museum). The sculpture has been cleaned and restored.

the Corinthian on the second floor, and a standard Corinthian on the third. The **PALAZZO RUCELLAI** provided a visual lesson for local architects in the use of classical elements and mathematical proportions, and Alberti's enthusiasm for classicism and his architectural projects in other cities were catalysts for the spread of the Renaissance movement.

Sculpture

The new architectural language inspired by ancient classical form was accompanied by a similar impetus in sculpture. By 1400, Florence had enjoyed internal stability and economic prosperity for over two decades. However, until 1428, the city and its independence were challenged by two great antire-publican powers: the Duchy of Milan and the Kingdom of Naples. In an atmosphere of wealth and civic patriotism, Florentines turned to commissions that would express their self-esteem and magnify the importance of their city. A new attitude toward realism, space, and the classical past set the stage for more than a century of creativity.

In the early fifteenth century the two principal sculptural commissions in Florence included the new set of bronze doors for the Baptistry of Florence Cathedral and the exterior niche decorations of Orsanmichele. Individual commissions for the Orsanmichele sculptures were awarded to a number of different artists. The competitive and distinctive nature of the works produced reveals a great deal about the artistic climate of early Renaissance Florence.

ORSANMICHELE. In the fourteenth century, the city's fourteen most powerful guilds had been assigned the ground floor niches that decorated the exterior of Orsanmichele and were asked to fill them with images of their patron saints (SEE FIG. 17-1). By 1400, only three had fulfilled this responsibility. In the new climate of republicanism and civic pride, the government pressured the guilds to furnish their niches with statuary. The assignment, with some replacements, took almost a century to reach its conclusion. In the meantime, Florence witnessed a dazzling sculptural exposition. Among the most important examples were two early commissions given to the sculptors Nanni di Banco and Donatello.

Nanni di Banco (c. 1385–1421), son of a sculptor in the Florence Cathedral workshop, produced statues for three of Orsanmichele's niches in his short but brilliant career. **THE FOUR CROWNED MARTYRS** was commissioned about 1409 by the stone carvers' and woodworkers' guild, to which Nanni himself belonged (FIG. 19-9). These martyrs, according to tradition, were third-century Christian sculptors who were executed for refusing to make an image of a pagan Roman god. Although the architectural setting resembles a small-scale Gothic chapel, Nanni's figures—with their solid bodies; heavy, form-revealing togas; stylized hair and beards; and naturalistic features—reveal Nanni's interest in ancient Roman sculpture, particularly portraiture, and are testimony to his role in the

the façade because Rucellai could not acquire the additional land. Alberti's design, influenced in its basic approach by the Palazzo Medici, was a simple rectangular front suggesting a coherent, cubical three-story building capped with an overhanging cornice, the heavy, projecting horizontal molding at the top of the wall. The double windows under round arches were a feature of Michelozzo's Palazzo Medici, but other aspects of the façade were entirely new. Inspired by the ancient Colosseum in Rome, Alberti created systematic divisions on the surface of the lightly rusticated wall with a horizontal-vertical pattern of pilasters and architraves. He superimposed the classically inspired orders on three levels: a novel type of the Doric on the ground floor (the first time this order is employed in Renaissance architecture), a modified version of

19—10 | Donatello **SAINT GEORGE**
1415-17. Marble, height 6'5" (1.95 m). Bargello, Florence.
Formerly Orsanmichele, Florence.

Sequencing Events
THE MEDICI OF FLORENCE

1360–1429	Giovanni di Bicci de' Medici founded family fortune
1389–1464	Cosimo de' Medici; later known as *Pater Patriae* ("Father of the Florentine state")
1416–69	Piero the Gouty
1449–92	Lorenzo the Magnificent
1471–1503	Piero the Unfortunate; driven out of Florence by Savonarola in 1494

revival of classicism. The saints convey a new spatial relationship to the building and to the viewer. They stand in a semicircle with forward feet and drapery protruding beyond the floor of the niche. The saints appear to be four individuals talking together, in an open arrangement that involves the passerby. Nanni's sense of a unified geometric composition is based on a circle completed in the space beyond the niche. In the relief panel below the niche, showing the four sculptors at work, Nanni has given the forms a similar solid vigor. He achieved this by deeply undercutting both figures and objects to cast shadows and enhance the illusion of three-dimensionality.

Another sculptor to receive guild commissions for the niches at Orsanmichele was Donatello (Donato di Niccolò di Betto Bardi, c. 1386/87–1466), the great genius of early Italian Renaissance sculpture and one of the most influential figures of the century in Italy. A member of the guild of stone carvers and woodworkers, he worked in both mediums. During his long and productive career, he rethought and executed each commission as if it were a new experiment. Donatello took a remarkably pictorial approach to relief sculpture. He developed a technique for creating the impression of very deep space by improving on the ancient Roman technique of varying heights of relief—high relief for foreground figures and very low relief, sometimes approaching engraving, for the background.

Commissioned by one of Florence's lesser guilds—the armorers and sword makers—to carve their patron saint for their niche, Donatello created a marble figure of **SAINT GEORGE** (FIG. 19—10). As originally conceived, Saint George would have been a standing advertisement for the guild. The figure carried a sword in his right hand and probably wore a metal helmet, a sword belt, and a sheath. The figure is remarkably successful even without these accoutrements. Saint George holds his shield squarely in front of his braced legs; he seems alert and ready as he turns to meet any challenge, yet the expression on his face is tense and worried. His rather sensitive features and wrinkled brow contrast with the serene confidence of medieval knights or aggressive *condottieri* (SEE FIG. 19—1).

The base of the niche, where Saint George is seen slaying a dragon to save the princess, is a remarkable feat of low-relief carving. The contours of the foreground figures are slightly undercut to emphasize their mass, while the landscape and architecture are in progressively lower relief until they are barely incised rather than carved. The result is a spatial setting in relief sculpture as believable as any illusionistic painting.

GATES OF PARADISE. In 1401, a competition was announced in order to determine who would design bronze relief panels for a new set of doors for the east—and most important—side of the Baptistry of San Giovanni. These doors faced the main entrance to the cathedral, and the commission carried enormous prestige—and expense. The commission was awarded to Lorenzo Ghiberti (1381?–1455), a young artist trained as a goldsmith, at the very beginning of

19–11 | Lorenzo Ghiberti **GATES OF PARADISE (EAST DOORS), BAPTISTRY OF SAN GIOVANNI, FLORENCE** 1425-52. Gilt bronze, height 15' (4.57 m). Museo dell'Opera del Duomo, Florence.

Ghiberti, whose bust portrait appears at the lower right corner of Jacob and Esau, wrote in his *Commentaries* (c. 1450-55): "I strove to imitate nature as clearly as I could, and with all the perspective I could produce, to have excellent compositions with many figures."

his career. His rival was none other than Brunelleschi, who claimed the competition ended in a tie.

Ghiberti's doors were such a success that in 1425 he was awarded the commission for the third set of doors for the east side of the baptistry, and his first set was moved to the north side. The door panels, commissioned by the Wool Manufacturers' Guild, were a significant conceptual leap from the older schemes of twenty-eight small scenes employed for Ghiberti's earlier doors and those of Andrea Pisano in the fourteenth century (SEE FIG. 17–5). The chancellor of Florence expressed the desire for a magnificent and memorable work. Ghiberti responded to the challenge by departing entirely from the old arrangement: He produced a set of ten Old Testament scenes, from the Creation to the reign of Solomon. Michelangelo reportedly said that those doors, installed in 1452, were worthy of being the **GATES OF PARADISE (FIG. 19–11)**. Overall gilding unites the ten large, square reliefs. Ghiberti organized the space either by a system

of linear perspective, with obvious orthogonal lines approximating the system described by Alberti in his 1435 treatise on painting (see "Brunelleschi, Alberti, and Renaissance Perspective," page 622) or sometimes more intuitively by a series of arches or rocks or trees leading the eye into the distance. Foreground figures are grouped in the lower third of the panel, while the other figures decrease gradually in size, suggesting deep space. The use of a system of perspective, with background and foreground clearly marked, also helped the artist to combine a series of related events within only one frame. In some panels, the tall buildings suggest ancient Roman architecture and illustrate the emerging antiquarian tone in Renaissance art.

The story of Jacob and Esau (Genesis 25 and 27) forms the relief in the center panel of the left door. Ghiberti creates a coherent and measurable space peopled by graceful, idealized figures (FIG. 19–12). He unifies the composition by paying careful attention to one-point perspective in the architectural setting. Squares marked out in the pavement establish the lines of the orthogonals that recede to a central vanishing point under the loggia, and towering arches supported on piers with Corinthian pilasters define the space above the figures. The story from Genesis unfolds in a series of individual episodes and begins in the background. On the rooftop (upper right) Rebecca stands, listening to God, who warns of her unborn sons' future conflict; under the left-hand arch she gives birth to the twins. The adult Esau sells his rights as oldest son to Jacob, and when he goes hunting (center right), Rebecca and Jacob plot against him. Finally, in the

19–12 | Lorenzo Ghiberti **JACOB AND ESAU, PANEL OF THE GATES OF PARADISE (EAST DOORS)** Formerly on the Baptistry of San Giovanni, Florence. c. 1435. Gilded bronze, 31¼" (79 cm) square. Museo dell'Opera del Duomo, Florence.

19–13 Donatello **DAVID**
c. 1446–60(?). Bronze, height 5′ 2¼″ (1.58 m). Museo
Nazionale del Bargello, Florence.

While still in the Medici courtyard, the base was inscribed:

"The victor is whoever defends the fatherland.
All-powerful God crushes the angry enemy.
Behold, a boy overcomes the great tyrant.
Conquer, O citizens!"

19–14 Donatello **EQUESTRIAN MONUMENT OF
ERASMO DA NARNI (GATTAMELATA)**
Piazza del Santo, Padua. 1443–53. Bronze, height approx.
12′2″ (3.71 m).

right foreground, Jacob receives Isaac's blessing, while in the center, Esau faces his father.

In the Renaissance interpretation, Esau symbolized the Jews and Jacob the Christians. The story explains conflict between the two religions and compositionally balances the panel on the opposite door valve. The vanishing point lies between the two panels. Therefore Jacob, who occupies the right foreground, is near the center of interest for the doors as a whole. Esau and his faithful hound complete the beautiful curve of figures that begins with the trio of women at the far left and shows Ghiberti's debt to the International Gothic. In the spirit of Renaissance individuality, Ghiberti not only signed his work, but also included his self-portrait in the medallion beside the lower right-hand corner of the panel.

DONATELLO: NEW EXPRESSIVENESS. Donatello excelled for three reasons: his constant exploration of human emotions and expressions; his vision and insight in representing the formal problems inherent in his subjects; and his ability to solve the technical problems posed by various mediums, from bronze and marble to polychromed wood. In bronze sculpture, he produced the first life-size male nude, **DAVID** (FIG. 19–13); one of the first life-size bronze equestrian portraits, **GATTAME-LATA** (FIG. 19–14); and the first statuettes since antiquity.

19–15 | Donatello **MARY MAGDALEN**
1450s(?). Polychromy and gold on wood, height 6′1″
(1.85 m). Museo dell'Opera del Duomo, Florence.

Since nothing is known about the circumstances of its creation, the sculpture of the *David* has been the subject of continuous inquiry and speculation. Although the statue clearly draws on the classical tradition of heroic nudity, this sensuous, adolescent boy in a jaunty laurel-trimmed shepherd's hat and boots has long piqued interest in its meaning. In one interpretation, the boy's angular pose, his underdeveloped torso, and the sensation of his wavering between childish interests and adult responsibility heighten his heroism in taking on the giant and destroying him. With Goliath's severed head now under his feet, David seems to have lost interest in warfare and now seems to be retreating into his dreams. The sculpture is first recorded in 1469 in the courtyard of the Medici palace, where it stood on a base engraved with an inscription extolling Florentine heroism and virtue. This inscription supports the suggestion that the sculpture celebrated the triumph of the Florentines over the Milanese in 1425. A peace treaty was signed in 1428. It ended the struggle with the despots of Milan, which had endured for over a quarter of a century, and helped give Florence a vision of itself as a strong, virtuous republic.

In 1443, Donatello was probably called to Padua to execute the equestrian statue commemorating the Paduan general of the Venetian army, Erasmo da Narni, nicknamed "Gattamelata" (meaning "Honeyed Cat"—a reference to his mother, Melania Gattelli). If one image were to characterize the self-made men of the Italian Renaissance, surely the most appropriate examples would be the *condottieri*—the brilliant generals (such as Tolentino, from Uccello's *Battle of San Romano*) who organized the armies and fought for any city-state willing to pay. The very word *chivalry* with all its connotations of honor, courage, and courtesy comes from the French word for "horse"—*cheval*. Italian Renaissance *condottieri* may have seen themselves as chivalric, as guardians of the state, although they were in fact tough, opportunistic mercenaries. But they, too, subscribed to an ideal of military and civic virtue.

Donatello's sources for this statue were two surviving Roman bronze equestrian portraits, one (now lost) in the north Italian city of Pavia, the other of the emperor Marcus Aurelius, which the sculptor certainly saw and probably sketched during his stay in Rome. Equestrian monuments of ancient Roman emperors demonstrated their virtues of bravery, nobility, and authority. Horsemanship was more than a necessary skill before the age of automobiles: It had symbolic meanings. The horse, a beast of enormous brute strength, symbolized the passions and man's physical animal nature. Consequently, skilled horsemanship demonstrated physical and intellectual control—self-control, as well as control of the animal—the triumph of the intellect, of "mind over matter."

Viewed from a distance, Donatello's man-animal juggernaut, installed on a high marble base in front of the Church of Sant'Antonio in Padua, seems capable of thrusting forward at the first threat. Seen up close, however, the man's sunken cheeks, sagging jaw, ropy neck, and stern but sad expression suggest a warrior grown old and tired from the constant need for military vigilance and rapid response.

During the decade that he remained in Padua, Donatello executed other commissions for the Church of Sant'Antonio, including a bronze crucifix and reliefs for the high altar and pulpits. His presence in the city introduced Renaissance ideas to northeastern Italy and gave rise to a new Paduan school of painting and sculpture. The expressionism of Donatello's late work inspired some artists to add psychological intensity even in public monuments. His **MARY MAGDALEN**, traditionally dated about 1455 (although it may have been executed before his stay in Padua), shows the saint, known for her physical beauty, as an emaciated, vacant-eyed hermit clothed by her own hair (FIG. 19–15). Few can look at this figure without a wrenching reaction to the physical deterioration caused by age and years of self-denial. Nothing is left for her but an ecstatic vision of the hereafter, and yet that is everything. Despite Donatello's total rejection of the classical ideal form in this figure, the powerful force of the Magdalen's personality makes this a masterpiece of Renaissance imagery.

VERROCCHIO'S *CONDOTTIERE*. In the early 1480s, the Florentine painter and sculptor Andrea del Verrocchio (1435–88) was commissioned by the government to produce an equestrian monument honoring the Venetian army general Bartolommeo Colleoni (d. 1475), who left money for a memorial to himself (FIG. 19–16). In contrast to the thoughtful and even tragic over-

19–17 Antonio del Pollaiuolo **HERCULES AND ANTAEUS**
c. 1475. Bronze, height with base 18" (45.7 cm).
Museo Nazionale del Bargello, Florence.

tones communicated by Donatello's *Gattamelata*, the impression conveyed by the tense forms of Verrocchio's equestrian monument is one of vitality and brutal energy. The general's ferocious determination is expressed in his clenched jaw and staring eyes. The taut muscles of the horse, the fiercely erect posture of the rider, and the complex interaction of the two make this image of will and domination a singularly compelling monument. It still presides over the square of Santi Giovanni e Paolo in Venice.

POLLAIUOLO. Sculptors in the fifteenth century worked not only on a monumental scale for the public sphere; they also created small works, each designed to inspire the mind and delight the eye of its private owner (see "Ceramics," page 634). The enthusiasm of European collectors in the latter part of the fifteenth century for small, easily transported bronzes contributed to the spread of classical taste. Antonio del Pollaiuolo, ambitious and multitalented—a goldsmith, embroiderer, printmaker, sculptor, and painter—came to work for the Medici family in Florence about 1460. His sculptures were mostly small bronzes; his **HERCULES AND ANTAEUS** of about 1475 is one of the largest (FIG. 19–17). This study of complex interlocking figures has an explosive energy that can best be appreciated by viewing it from every angle.

19–16 Andrea del Verrocchio **EQUESTRIAN MONUMENT OF BARTOLOMMEO COLLEONI, CAMPO SANTI GIOVANNI E PAOLO, VENICE**
Clay model 1486–88; cast after 1490; placed 1496. Bronze, height approx. 13' (4 m). Bronze cast by Alessandro Leopardi.

Technique
CERAMICS

Italian sculptors did not limit themselves to the traditional materials of wood, stone and marble, and bronze. They also returned to **terra cotta,** a clay medium whose popularity in Italy went back to Etruscan and ancient Roman times. Techniques of working with and firing clay had been kept alive by the ceramics industry and by a few sculptors, especially in northern Italy.

Typical of Renaissance ceramics in shape and decoration is the *albarello,* a jar designed especially for pharmacies: The tall concave shape made it easy to remove from a line of jars on pharmacy shelves, and the lip at the rim helped secure the cord that tied a parchment cover over the mouth. Sometimes the name of the owner or the contents of the jar were inscribed on a band around the center (the jar shown held syrup of lemon). The jars were glazed white and decorated in deep, rich colored enamel—orange, blue, green, and purple. The technique for making this lustrous, tin-glazed earthenware had been developed by Islamic potters and then by Christian potters in Spain. It spread to Italy from the Spanish island of Mallorca—known in Italian as Maiorca, which gave rise to the term *maiolica* to describe such wares. The painted decoration of broad scrolling leaves seen here is characteristic of the fifteenth century.

Ceramics were also used to supply the ever-increasing demand for architectural sculpture. Luca della Robbia (1399/1400–1482), although an accomplished sculptor in marble, began to experiment in 1441–42 with tin glazing to make his ceramic sculpture both weatherproof and decorative. As his inexpensive and rapidly produced sculpture gained an immediate popularity, he added color to the traditional white glaze. His workshop even made molds so that a particularly popular work could be replicated many times. The elegant and lyrical della Robbia style was continued by Luca's nephew Andrea and his children long after Luca's death (see "The Foundling Hospital," page 626).

ALBARELLO
Cylindrical pharmacy jar, from Faenza. c. 1480. Glazed ceramic, height 12⅜″ (31.5 cm). Getty Museum, Los Angeles.
Getty .84.DE.104

Statuettes of religious subjects were still popular, but humanist art patrons began to collect bronzes of Greek and Roman subjects. Many sculptors, especially those trained as goldsmiths, began to cast small copies after well-known classical works. Some artists also executed original designs *all'antica* ("in the antique style"). Although there were outright forgeries of antiquities at this time, works in the antique manner were intended simply to appeal to a cultivated humanist taste. Hercules was always a popular figure, as a patron of Florence. He was even used on the city seal. Among the many courageous acts by which Hercules gained immortality was the slaying of the evil Antaeus in a wrestling match by lifting him off the earth, the source of the giant's great physical power. Hercules had been attacked by Antaeus, the son of the earth goddess Ge (or Gaia), on his search for a garden that produced pure gold apples.

An engraving by Pollaiuolo, **THE BATTLE OF THE NUDES** (FIG. 19–18), reflects the interests of Renaissance scholars—the study of classical sculpture and the anatomical research that leads to greater realism—as well as the artist's technical skill in fine work on a metal plate. Pollaiuolo may have intended this, his only known—but highly influential—print, as a study in composition involving the human figure in action. The naked men, fighting each other ferociously against a tapestry-like background of foliage, seem to have been drawn from a single model in a variety of poses, many of which were taken from classical sources. Like the artist's *Hercules and Antaeus,* much of the engraving's fascination lies in how it depicts muscles of the male body reacting under tension.

Painting

Italian patrons generally commissioned murals and large altarpieces for their local churches and smaller panel paintings for their private chapels. Artists experienced in fresco, mural painting on wet plaster, were in great demand and traveled widely to execute wall and ceiling decorations. At first the Italians showed little interest in oil painting, for the most part

19–18 | Antonio del Pollaiuolo **BATTLE OF THE NUDES**
c. 1465–70. Engraving, 15⅛ × 23¼" (38.3 × 59 cm). Cincinnati Art Museum, Ohio.
Bequest of Herbert Greer French. 1943.118

using tempera even for their largest works. But, in the last decades of the century, Venetians began to use the oil medium for major panel paintings.

MASACCIO. The most innovative of the early Italian Renaissance painters was Tommaso di Ser Giovanni di Mone Cassai (1401–28/29?), nicknamed "Masaccio." In his short career of less than a decade, he established a new direction in Florentine painting, much as Giotto had a century earlier. Masaccio rejected the International Gothic style in favor of monumental forms that occupy rationally defined and unified space. Masaccio's interest in one-point perspective, the new architectural style, and classical sculpture allies him, especially, with his older contemporary Brunelleschi. Masaccio's fresco of the Trinity in the Church of Santa Maria Novella in Florence must have been painted around 1426, the date on the Lenzi family tombstone that was once in front of the fresco (FIG. 19–19). The **TRINITY** was meant to give the illusion of a stone funerary monument and altar table set below

a deep *aedicula* (framed niche) in the wall. The praying donors in front of the pilasters may be members of the Lenzi family. The red robes of the male donor at the left signify that he was a member of the governing council of Florence.

Masaccio created the unusual *trompe l'oeil* ("fool-the-eye") effect of looking up into a barrel-vaulted niche, made plausible through precisely rendered linear perspective. The eye and level of an adult viewer determined the horizon line on which the vanishing point was centered, just above the base of the cross. The painting demonstrates Masaccio's intimate knowledge of both Brunelleschi's perspective experiments and his architectural style (SEE FIG. 19–5). The painted architecture is an unusual combination of classical orders; on the wall surface, Corinthian pilasters support a plain architrave below a cornice, while inside the niche Renaissance variations on Ionic columns support arches on all four sides. The Trinity is represented by Jesus on the cross, the dove of the Holy Spirit poised in downward flight above his tilted halo, and God the Father, who stands behind the cross on a

the Trinity. Below, in an open sarcophagus, is a skeleton, a grim reminder that death awaits us all and that our only hope is redemption and life in the hereafter through Christian belief. The skeleton represents Adam, on whose tomb the cross was thought to have been set. The inscription above the skeleton reads: "I was once that which you are, and what I am you also will be."

THE BRANCACCI CHAPEL. Masaccio's brief career reached its height in his collaboration with another painter, Masolino (1383–c. 1440), on the fresco decoration of the **BRANCACCI CHAPEL** in the Church of Santa Maria del Carmine in Florence (**FIG. 19–20**). The project was ill-fated, however: The painters never finished their work—Masolino traveled to Hungary in 1425–27, and the two painters went to Rome in 1428. Masaccio died in Rome in 1428 or 1429. Felice Brancacci, the patron, was exiled in 1435. Eventually, another Florentine painter, Filippino Lippi, finished painting the chapel in the 1480s. The chapel was dedicated to Saint Peter, and the frescoes illustrate events in his life.

Masaccio combined a study of the human figure with an intimate knowledge of ancient Roman sculpture. In **THE EXPULSION FROM PARADISE,** he presented Adam and Eve as monumental nude figures (**FIG. 19–21**). In contrast to Flemish painters, who sought to record every visible hair or scratch (compare Adam and Eve from the *Ghent Altarpiece,* **FIG. 18–11**), Masaccio focused on the mass of bodies formed by the underlying bone and muscle structure to create a new realism. He used a generalized light shining on the figures from a single source and further emphasized their tangibility with cast shadows. Ignoring earlier interpretations of the event that emphasized wrongdoing and the fall from grace, Masaccio was concerned with the psychology of individual humans who have been cast mourning and protesting out of Paradise, and he captured the essence of humanity thrown naked into the world.

Adam and Eve lead to **THE TRIBUTE MONEY** (**FIG. 19–22**). The painting was done in thirty-one working days. Completed about 1427, it was rendered in a continuous narrative of three scenes within one setting (a medieval compositional technique). The painting illustrates an incident in which a collector of the Jewish temple taxes (the "tribute money") demands payment from Peter, shown in the central group with Jesus and the other disciples (Matt. 17:24–27). Saying "Render unto Caesar that which is Caesar's," Jesus instructs Peter to "go to the sea, drop in a hook, and take the first fish that comes up," which Peter does at the far left. In the fish's mouth is a coin worth twice the tax demanded, which Peter gives to the tax collector at the far right. The tribute story was especially significant for Florentines because in 1427, to raise money for defense against military aggression, the city enacted a graduated tax, based on the value of one's personal property.

19–19 | Masaccio **TRINITY WITH THE VIRGIN, SAINT JOHN THE EVANGELIST, AND DONORS**
Church of Santa Maria Novella, Florence. c. 1425–27/28. Fresco 21' × 10'5" (6.4 × 3.2 m).

high platform apparently supported on the rear columns. The "source" of the consistent illumination modeling the figures with light and shadow lies in front of the picture, casting reflections on the **coffers,** or sunken panels, of the ceiling. As in many scenes of the Crucifixion, Jesus is flanked by the Virgin Mary and John the Evangelist, who contemplate the scene. Mary gazes calmly out at us, her raised hand presenting

19—20 | **INTERIOR OF THE BRANCACCI CHAPEL, CHURCH OF SANTA MARIA DEL CARMINE, FLORENCE**
Frescoes by Masaccio and Masolino (1426–27) and Filippino Lippi (lower register) (c. 1482–84).

The Tribute Money is remarkable for its integration of figures, architecture, and landscape into a consistent scene. The group of Jesus and his disciples forms a clear central focus, from which the landscape seems to recede naturally into the far distance. To create this illusion, Masaccio used linear perspective in the depiction of the house and then reinforced it by diminishing the sizes of the trees and reducing Peter's size at the left. At the vanishing point established by the lines of the house is the head of Jesus. A second vanishing point determines the steps and stone rail at the right. Masaccio used atmospheric perspective as well as linear perspective in the distant landscape, where mountains fade from grayish green to grayish white and the houses and trees on their slopes are loosely sketched. Green leaves were painted on the branches *al secco* (meaning "on the dry plastered wall"; see Chapter 17, "Buon Fresco," page 569).

Masaccio modeled the foreground figures with strong highlights and cast their long shadows on the ground toward the left, implying a light source at the far right, as if the scene were lit by the actual window in the rear wall of the Brancacci Chapel. Not only does the lighting give the forms sculptural definition, but the colors vary in tone according to the strength of the illumination. Masaccio used a wide range of hues—pale pink, mauve, gold, blue green, apple green, peach—and a sophisticated color technique in which Andrew's green robe is shaded with red instead of darker green. All of the figures in *The Tribute Money,* except those of the temple tax collector, originally had gold-leaf halos, several of which had flaked off before the painting underwent restoration (1982–90). Rather than silhouette the heads against flat gold circles in the medieval manner, Masaccio conceived of the halo as a gold disk hovering in space above each head, and he subjected it to perspective foreshortening—shortening the lines of forms seen head-on to align them with the overall perspectival system—depending on the position of the figure.

19–21 | Masaccio **THE EXPULSION FROM PARADISE**
Brancacci Chapel. c. 1427. Fresco, 7′ × 2′ 11″ (214 × 90 cm).

Cleaning and restoration of the Brancacci Chapel paintings revealed the remarkable speed and skill with which Masaccio worked. He painted Adam and Eve in four *giornate* (each *giornata* of fresh plaster representing a day's work). Working from the top down and left to right, he painted the angel on the first day; on the second day, only the portal; the magnificent figure of Adam on the third day; and Eve on the fourth day.

Stylistic innovations take time to be fully accepted, and Masaccio's genius for depicting weight and volume, consistent lighting, and spatial integration was best appreciated by a later generation. Many important sixteenth-century Italian artists, including Michelangelo, studied and sketched from Masaccio's Brancacci Chapel frescoes. In the meantime, painting in Florence after Masaccio's death developed along lines somewhat different from that of *The Tribute Money* or *Trinity*, as other artists such as Paolo Uccello experimented in their own ways of conveying the illusion of a believably receding space (SEE FIG. 19–1).

Mural Painting in Florence After Masaccio

The tradition of covering walls with paintings in fresco continued through the fifteenth century. Walls of churches and chapels provided space for painters to combine Christian themes with local incidents and realistic portraits. Between 1438 and 1445, the decoration of the Dominican Monastery of San Marco in Florence, where Fra Angelico lived, was one of the most extensive projects.

FRA ANGELICO. Guido di Piero da Mugello (c. 1395/ 1400–55), known as Fra Giovanni da Fiesole, earned the designation "Fra Angelico" ("Angelic Brother") through his piety as well as his painting. He was beatified, the first step toward sainthood, in 1984. He is first documented as a painter in Florence in 1417–18, and he continued to be a very active painter after taking his vows as a Dominican monk (see "The Mendicant Orders," page 524).

Between 1438 and 1445, in the Monastery of San Marco, Fra Angelico and his assistants created a painting to inspire meditation in each monk's cell (forty-four in all), and they also added paintings to the chapter house (meeting room) and the corridors. The paintings were probably commissioned by Cosimo de' Medici. At the top of the stairs in the north corridor Fra Angelico painted the scene of the **ANNUNCIATION** (FIG. 19–23). Here the monks were to pause for prayer before going to their individual cells. The illusion of space created by the careful linear perspective seems to extend the stair and corridor out into a second cloister, the Virgin's home and verdant enclosed garden, where the angel Gabriel greets the modest, youthful Mary. The slender, graceful figures wearing flowing draperies assume modest poses. The natural light falling from the left models their forms and casts an almost supernatural radiance over their faces and hands. The scene is a vision that welcomes the monks to the most private areas of the monastery and prepares them for their meditations.

CASTAGNO. Another notable Florentine fresco, **THE LAST SUPPER**, is the work of Andrea del Castagno (c. 1417/19–57), painted for a convent of Benedictine nuns in 1447 (FIG. 19–24). The Last Supper was often painted in monastic refectories (dining halls) to remind the monks or nuns of

19–22 | Masaccio **THE TRIBUTE MONEY**
Brancacci Chapel. c. 1427. Fresco, 8′1″ × 19′7″ (1.87 × 1.57 m).

19–23 | Fra Angelico **ANNUNCIATION NORTH CORRIDOR, MONASTERY OF SAN MARCO, FLORENCE**
c. 1438–45. Fresco, 7′½″ × 19′6″ (230 × 297 m).

The shadowed vault of the portico is supported by a wall on one side and by slender Ionic and Corinthian columns on the other, a new building technique being used by Brunelleschi in the very years when the painting was being created.

19–24 | Andrea del Castagno **THE LAST SUPPER**
Refectory, Convent of Sant'Apollonia, Florence. 1447. Fresco, width approx. 16 × 32'
(4.6 × 9.8 m).

Christ's sacrifice and of the bread and wine as his Body and Blood. Here the scene takes place in the "upper room"—the biblical setting—but the humble house described in the Bible has become a great palace with sumptuous marble panels. A brilliantly colored and wildly patterned marble panel frames the heads of Christ and Judas. Judas is separated from the apostles and sits on the viewer's side of the table. Saint John sleeps, head on the table. The strong perspective lines of floor tiles, ceiling rafters, and paneled walls draw the viewer into the scene. The religious would have seen the painting as an extension of their hall. At first, the lines of the orthogonals seem to follow Alberti's perfect logic, but close examination reveals that only the lines of the ceiling converge, below the hands of Saint John; consequently, an uneasy situation is established, and we do not know why. Two windows light the room from the direction of the actual windows, further unifying the painted and actual spaces, and Castagno paints his figures in solid sculptured fashion with clear outlines and strong highlights. He worked quickly, completing the huge mural in at most thirty-two days.

ITALIAN ART IN THE SECOND HALF OF THE FIFTEENTH CENTURY

In the second half of the fifteenth century, the ideas and ideals of artists like Brunelleschi, Donatello, and Masaccio began to spread from Florence to the rest of Italy, combining with local styles. Artists who trained or worked in Florence then traveled to other cities to work, either temporarily or perma-

nently, carrying the style with them. Northern Italy embraced the new classical ideas swiftly, with the ducal courts at Mantua and Urbino taking the lead. The Republic of Venice and the city of Padua, which Venice had controlled since 1405, also emerged as innovative art centers in the last quarter of the century.

Urbino

East of Florence lay another outstanding cultural center, Urbino, where Count (later, in 1474, Duke) Federico da Montefeltro attracted writers, philosophers, and the finest artists of the day to his court. The palace at Urbino would have made a glorious backdrop for the courtly pageantry. The Renaissance book of manners, *The Book of the Courtier,* by Baldassare Castiglione, was written there.

THE PALACE AT URBINO. Construction of Federico's palace had begun about 1450, and in 1468 Federico hired Luciano Laurana (c. 1420/25–1479), who had been an assistant on the project, to direct the work. Among Laurana's major contributions to the palace were closing the courtyard with a fourth wing and redesigning the courtyard façades (FIG. 19–25). The result is a superbly rational solution to the problems of courtyard elevation design, particularly the awkward juncture of the arcades at the four corners. The ground-level portico on each side has arches supported by columns; the corner angles are bridged with piers having engaged columns on the arcade sides and pilasters facing the courtyard. This arrangement avoided the awkward visual effect of two arches springing from a single column and gave the corner a greater sense of stability. A variation of the composite capital (a Corinthian capital with added Ionic volutes) was used, perhaps for the first time, on the ground level. Corinthian pilasters flank the windows in the story above, forming divisions that repeat the bays of the portico. (The two short upper stories were added later.) The plain architrave was engraved with inscriptions lauding Federico's many virtues. Not visible in the photograph is an exceptionally magnificent monumental staircase leading from the courtyard to the main floor.

The interior of the Urbino palace likewise reflected its patron's embrace of new Renaissance ideas and interest in classical antiquity, seen in carved marble fireplaces and window and door surrounds. In creating luxurious home furnishings and interior decorations for educated clients such as Federico, Italian craft artists found freedom to experiment with new subjects, treatments, and techniques. Among these was the creation of *trompe l'oeil* effects, which had become more convincing with the development of linear perspective. *Trompe l'oeil,* commonly used in painting, was carried to its

ultimate expression in **intarsia** (wood inlay) decoration, exemplified by the walls of Federico da Montefeltro's "**STUDIOLO,**" or study, a room for private conversation and the collection of fine books and art objects (**FIG. 19–26**). The work was probably done by the architect and woodworker Giuliano da Maiano (1432–90) and carries a date of 1476.

The elaborate scenes in the small room are created entirely of wood inlaid on flat surfaces with scrupulously applied linear perspective and foreshortening. Each detail is rendered in *trompe l'oeil*: the illusionistic pilasters, carved cupboards with latticed doors, niches with statues, paintings, and built-in tables. Prominent in the decorative scheme is the prudent and industrious squirrel, a Renaissance symbol of the ideal ruler: in other words, of Federico da Montefeltro. A large window looks out onto an elegant marble loggia with a distant view of the countryside through its arches; and the shelves, cupboards, and tables are filled with all manner of fascinating things—scientific instruments, books, even the Duke's armor hanging like a suit in a closet. On the walls above were paintings of great scholars (whose books Federico

19–25 | Luciano Laurana **COURTYARD, DUCAL PALACE, URBINO**
Italy. Courtyard c. 1467-72; palace begun c. 1450.

The inscription extolling Federico's virtues—Justice, Clemency, Liberality, and Religion—was added in 1476 when he was made Duke of Urbino.

19–26 | **STUDIOLO OF FEDERICO DA MONTEFELTRO, DUCAL PALACE, URBINO**
1476. Intarsia, height 7′3″ (2.21 m). Woodwork probably by Giuliano da Maiano (1432–90).

owned) by Pedro Berruguete from Spain and Justus of Ghent from Flanders.

In 1472 Federico's wife Battista died, shortly after the birth of her ninth child, a son who would inherit the duchy. She was only 26, and Federico was disconsolate. Leaving the palace unfinished, he turned to building a funeral chapel, the church of San Bernardino, on a neighboring hilltop. The church can be seen in the background of Raphael's *Madonna and Child* (FIG. 20–5).

PIERO DELLA FRANCESCA. One artist Federico brought to Urbino was Piero della Francesca (c. 1415–92). Piero had worked in Florence in the 1430s before settling down in his native Borgo Sansepulcro, a Tuscan hill town under papal control. He knew current thinking in art and art theory—including Brunelleschi's system of spatial illusion and linear perspective, Masaccio's powerful modeling of forms and atmospheric perspective, and Alberti's theoretical treatises. Piero was one of the few practicing artists who also wrote about his own theories. Not surprisingly, in his treatise on perspective he emphasized the geometry and the volumetric construction of forms and spaces that were so apparent in his own work. He traveled widely—to Rome, to the Este court in Ferrara, and especially to Urbino.

From about 1454 to 1458, Piero was in Arezzo, where he decorated the Bacci Chapel of the Church of San Francesco

19–27 | Piero della Francesca **RECOGNITION AND PROVING OF THE TRUE CROSS**
San Francesco, Arezzo. 1450s. Fresco, 11′8″ × 24′6″ (3.56 × 7.47 m).

19–28 | Piero della Francesca **BATTISTA SFORZA AND FEDERICO DA MONTEFELTRO**
c. 1474. Oil on wood panel, each 18½ × 13″ (47 × 33 cm). Galleria degli Uffizi, Florence.

with a cycle of frescoes illustrating the legend of the True Cross, the cross on which Jesus was crucified. The Cross was buried after the Crucifixion, but Helena (the mother of Constantine, who was believed to be the first Christian Roman emperor) discovered and proved the authenticity of the cross when its touch brings to life a man being carried to his tomb.

In the **RECOGNITION AND PROVING OF THE TRUE CROSS,** (**FIG. 19–27**), Piero's analytical modeling and perspectival projection result in a highly believable illusion of space around his monumental figures. He reduced his figures to cylindrical and ovoid shapes and established a geometric patterned setting in marble veneered buildings. The building that forms a background is a brilliant example of the ideal Renaissance façade as designed by Alberti. Few such façades were ever finished. Particularly remarkable are the foreshortening of figures and objects such as the cross at the right and the anatomical accuracy of the revived youth's nude figure. Unlike many of his contemporaries, however, Piero gave his figures no expression of human emotion. They observe the miracle with an indifference born of complete confidence.

In about 1474 Piero painted the portraits of Federico and his recently deceased wife, Battista Sforza (**FIG. 19–28**). The small panels, painted in tempera in light colors, resemble Flemish painting in their detail and luminosity, their record of surfaces and textures, and their vast landscapes. In the traditional Italian fashion, the figures are portrayed in strict profile, as remote psychologically from the viewer as icons. The profile format also allowed for an accurate recording of Federico's likeness without emphasizing two disfiguring scars—the loss of his right eye from a sword blow and his broken nose. His good left eye is shown, and the angular profile of his nose seems like a distinctive family trait. Typically, Piero emphasized the underlying geometry of the forms. Dressed in the most elegant fashion (Federico wears his red ducal robe), Battista and Federico are silhouetted against a distant view recalling the hilly landscape around Urbino. The influence of Flemish art (which Piero would have known from Flemish and Spanish painters working with him in Urbino) is also strong in the careful record of Battista's jewels and in the well-observed atmospheric perspective, making the landscape as subtle and luminous as any Flemish panel or manuscript. Piero used another northern European device in the harbor view near the center of Federico's panel: The water narrows into a river that leads the eye into the distant landscape.

19–29 | Piero della Francesca **TRIUMPH OF FEDERICO AND BATTISTA**
Reverse of FIGURE 19–28.

Federico's inscription can be translated, "He that the perennial fame of virtues rightly celebrates holding the scepter, equal to the highest dukes, the illustrious, is borne in outstanding triumph." Battista had been dead two years when hers was written: "She that kept her modesty in favorable circumstances, flies on the mouths of all men, adorned with the praise of the acts of her great husband." (Translated by John Paolitti and Gary Radke, *Art in Renaissance Italy*. Prentice Hall, 2002, p. 288.)

The painting on the reverse of the portraits reflects the humanist interests of the court (FIG. 19–29). Engraved on the fictive parapets in letters inspired by ancient Roman inscriptions are stanzas praising the couple's respective virtues—Federico's moderation and the fame of his virtue; and Battista's restraint, shining in the reflected glory of her husband. Behind these laudatory inscriptions a wide landscape of hills and valleys appears to be nearly continuous across the two panels. Across the flat top of a jagged cliff in the foreground, triumphal carts roll, and we catch a glimpse of the kind of pageantry and spectacle that must have been enacted at court. The *Triumphs of Petrarch*—poetic allegories of love, chastity, fame, time, eternity (Christianized as Divinity), and death (see "A New Spirit in Fourteenth-Century Literature," page 561)—inspired many of these extravaganzas. White horses pull Federico's wagon. The Duke is crowned by a winged figure—either Victory or Fortune—and accompanied by personifications of Justice, Prudence, Fortitude, and Temperance. Battista's cart is controlled by a winged *putto* (nude little boy) driving a team of unicorns. The virtues standing behind her may be per-

sonifications of Chastity and Modesty. Seated in front of her are Faith and Charity, who holds a pelican. This bird, believed to feed its young from its own blood, may symbolize the recently deceased Battista's maternal sacrifices.

Mantua

Lodovico Gonzaga, the Marquis of Mantua, ruled a territory that lies on the north Italian plain between Venice and Milan. Like Federico, he made his fortune as a *condottiere*. Lodovico was schooled by humanist teachers and created a court where humanist ideas flourished in art as well as in literature. His relationship with Cosimo de' Medici led to a connection with Florentine artists and architects, including Alberti.

ALBERTI. The spread of Renaissance architectural style beyond Florence was due in significant part to Leon Battista Alberti, who traveled widely, wrote on architecture, and expounded his views to potential patrons. In 1470 Ludovico Gonzaga commissioned Alberti to enlarge the small **CHURCH**

19–30 | Leon Battista Alberti
FAÇADE, CHURCH OF SANT'ANDREA, MANTUA
Designed 1470, begun 1472.

19–32 | **NAVE, CHURCH OF SANT'ANDREA, MANTUA**
Designed 1470. Vault width 60′ (18.3 m).

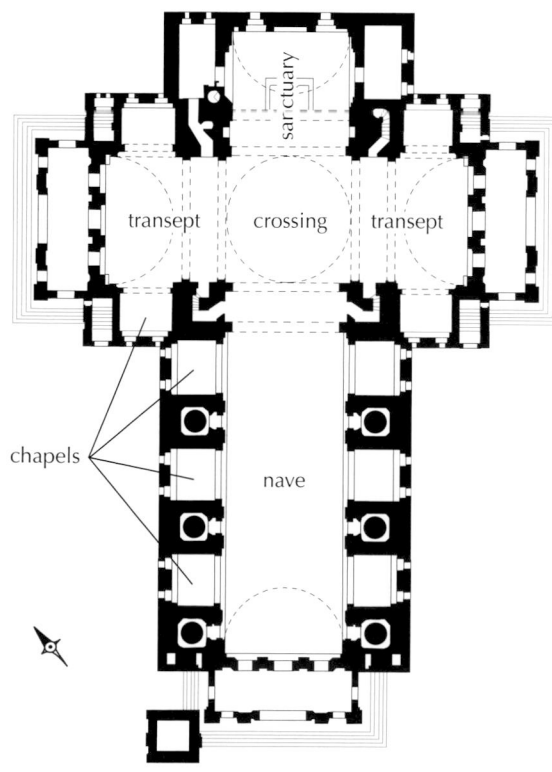

19–31 | Leon Battista Alberti **PLAN OF THE CHURCH OF SANT'ANDREA, MANTUA**
Designed 1470.

OF SANT'ANDREA, which housed a sacred relic believed to be the actual blood of Christ (**FIG. 19–30**). To satisfy his patron's desire for a sizable building to handle crowds coming to see the relic, Alberti proposed to build an "Etruscan temple." Work began on the new church in 1472, but Alberti died that summer. Construction went forward slowly, at first according to his original plan, but it was finally completed only at the end of the eighteenth century. Thus, it is not always clear which elements belong to Alberti's original design.

The Church of Sant'Andrea follows the Latin-cross plan, in which the transept intersects the nave high above the

19–33 | Andrea Mantegna **CAMERA PICTA, DUCAL PALACE, MANTUA**
1465-74. Frescoes. Diameter of false oculus 8'9" (2.7 m); room 62' 6" square (8 × 5 m square).

midpoint of the church. Here, the nave, nearly 60 feet wide, meets a transept of equal width at a square, domed crossing (FIGS. 19–31, 19–32). A rectangular sanctuary on axis with the nave is certainly in keeping with Alberti's ideas. Alberti was responsible, too, for the barrel-vaulted chapels at right angles to the nave that give the appearance of an arcade. Low chapel niches are carved out of the huge piers supporting the barrel vault of the nave. Light enters from chapel windows.

Alberti's design for the façade of Sant'Andrea (SEE FIG. 19–30) integrates two classical forms—a temple front and a triumphal arch with two sets of colossal Corinthian pilasters. The façade now has a clear volume of its own, which sets it off visually from the building behind. Pilasters flanking the barrel-vaulted triumphal-arch entrance are two stories high, whereas the others, raised on pedestals, run through three stories to support the entablature and pediment of the temple form. The arch itself has lateral barrel-vaulted spaces opening through two-story arches on the left and right.

Neither the simplicity of the plan nor the complexity of the façade hints at the grandeur of Sant'Andrea's interior. Its immense barrel-vaulted nave, extended on each side by tall chapels, was inspired by the monumental interiors of such ancient ruins as the Basilica of Maxentius and Constantine in the Roman Forum (SEE FIG. 6–75). This clear reference to Roman imperial art is put to Christian use. Alberti created a building of such colossal scale, spatial unity, and successful expression of Christian humanist ideals that it affected architectural design for centuries.

MANTEGNA. Andrea Mantegna (1431–1506) also worked at the court of Mantua. Mantegna, a painter, was trained in Padua and profoundly influenced by the sculptor Donatello, who arrived in Padua in 1443 and worked there for a decade. Mantegna absorbed such techniques as the Florentine linear perspective system, which Mantegna pushed to its limits with experiments in radical perspective views and foreshortenings. In 1460 Mantegna went to work for Ludovico Gonzaga, and he continued to work for the Gonzaga family for the rest of his life.

Mantegna's mature style is characterized by a virtuoso use of perspective, the skillful integration of figures into their settings, and a love of naturalistic details. His finest works are the frescoes of the **CAMERA PICTA** ("Painted Room"), a tower chamber in Ludovico Gonzaga's palace, which Mantegna decorated between 1465 and 1474 (FIG. 19–33). Around the walls the family receives its returning cardinal in scenes set in landscapes and loggias. (Ludovico's son, Cardinal Francesco, was head of the Church of Sant'Andrea; SEE FIG. 19–30). The paintings create a continuous scene with figures and countryside behind a fictive arcade. The people are all recognizable portraits of the family and court. On the domed ceiling, the artist painted a tour de force of radical perspective, a tech-

nique called *di sotto in sù* ("from below upwards"). The room appears to be open to a cloud-filled sky through a large oculus in a simulated marble- and mosaic-covered vault. On each side of a precariously balanced planter, three young women and an exotically turbaned African man peer over a marble balustrade into the room below. A fourth young woman in a veil looks dreamily upward. Joined by a large peacock, several *putti* play around the balustrade. The ceiling began a long tradition of illusionistic ceiling painting that culminated in the seventeenth century.

Although Mantegna made trips to Florence and Pisa in the 1460s and to Rome in 1488–90, he spent most of his time in Mantua. There he became a member of the humanist circle, whose interests in classical literature and archaeology he shared. He often signed his name using Greek letters.

Rome

Rome's establishment as a Renaissance center of the arts was enhanced by Pope Sixtus IV's decision to call to the city the best artists he could find to decorate the walls of his newly built chapel, named the Sistine Chapel after him. The resolution in 1417 of the Great Schism in the Western Church had secured the papacy in Rome, precipitating the restoration of not only the Vatican but the city as a whole.

PERUGINO. Among the artists who went to Rome was Pietro Vannucci, called "Perugino" (c. 1445–1523). Originally from near the town of Perugia in Umbria, Perugino worked for a while in Florence and by 1479 was in Rome. Two years later, he was working on the Sistine murals. One of his contributions, **DELIVERY OF THE KEYS TO SAINT PETER** (FIG. 19–34), portrayed the event that provided biblical support for the supremacy of papal authority, Christ's giving the keys of the kingdom of heaven to the apostle Peter (Matt. 16:19), who became the first bishop (pope) of Rome.

Delivery of the Keys is a remarkable work. Its carefully studied linear perspective reveals much about Renaissance ideals. In a light-filled piazza in which banded paving stones provide a geometric grid for perspectival recession, the figures stand like chess pieces on the squares, scaled to size according to their distance from the picture plane and modeled by a consistent light source from the upper left. The composition is divided horizontally between the lower frieze of massive figures and the band of widely spaced buildings above. Vertically, it is divided by the open space at the center between Christ and Peter and by the symmetrical architectural forms on each side of this central axis. Triumphal arches inspired by ancient Rome frame the church and focus the attention on the center of the composition, where the vital key is being transferred. The carefully calibrated scene is softened by the subdued colors, the distant idealized landscape and cloudy skies, and the variety of the

19—34 Perugino **DELIVERY OF THE KEYS TO SAINT PETER**
Fresco on the right wall of the Sistine Chapel, Vatican City, Rome. 1481. 11′5½″ × 18′8½″ (3.48 × 5.70 m).

figures' positions. Perugino's painting is, among other things, a representation of Alberti's ideal city, described in his treatise on architecture as having a "temple" (that is, a church) at the very center of a great open space raised on a dais and separate from any other buildings that might obstruct its view. His ideal church had a central plan, illustrated here as a domed octagon.

The Later Fifteenth Century in Florence

In the final decades of the fifteenth century, Florentine painting was characterized on one hand by a love of material opulence and an interest in describing the natural world, and on the other by a poetic, mystical spirit. The first trend was encouraged by the influence of Netherlandish art and the patronage of citizens who sought to advertise their wealth and position, the second by philosophic circles surrounding the Medici and the religious fervor that arose at the very end of the century.

GHIRLANDAIO. In Florence, the most prolific painting workshop of the later fifteenth century was that of the painter Domenico di Tommaso Bigordi (1449–94), known as Domenico "Ghirlandaio" ("Garland Maker"), a nickname adopted by his father, who was a goldsmith noted for his floral wreaths. A skilled painter of narrative cycles, Ghirlandaio reinterpreted the art of earlier fifteenth-century painters into a popular visual language of great descriptive immediacy.

19—35 Domenico Ghirlandaio **VIEW OF THE SASSETTI CHAPEL, CHURCH OF SANTA TRINITA, FLORENCE**
Frescoes of scenes from the Legend of Saint Francis; altarpiece with *Nativity and Adoration of the Shepherds*. 1483–86. Chapel: 12′2″ deep × 17′2″ wide (3.7 × 5.25 m).

19–36 | Domenico Ghirlandaio **NATIVITY AND ADORATION OF THE SHEPHERDS, SASSETTI CHAPEL PANEL, ALTARPIECE, SANTA TRINITÀ, FLORENCE**
1485. 65¾" square (1.67 m square).

The taste for Flemish painting in Florence grew noticeably after about 1450, and works such as Hugo van der Goes's *Portinari Altarpiece* (SEE FIG. 18–20), which Tommaso Portinari had sent home to Florence from Bruges in 1483, had considerable impact on Ghirlandaio's style.

Among Ghirlandaio's most effective narrative programs were frescoes of the life of Saint Francis created between 1483 and 1486 for the Sassetti family burial chapel in the Church of Santa Trinita, Florence (FIG. 19–35). In the uppermost tier of the paintings, Pope Honorius confirms the Franciscan order. The Loggia of the Lancers (see Chapter 17, FIG. 17–2) and the Palazzo della Signoria can be seen in the background. All the figures, including those coming up the stairs, are portraits of well-known Florentines. In the middle register, a small boy who has fallen from an upper window is resurrected by Saint Francis. The miracle is witnessed by contemporary Florentines, including members of the Sassetti family, and the scene takes place in the piazza outside the actual church. Thus, Ghirlandaio transferred the events of the traditional story from thirteenth-century

Rome to the Florence of his own day, painting views of the city and portraits of Florentines, taking delight in local color and anecdotes. Perhaps Renaissance painters represented events from the distant past in contemporary terms to emphasize their current relevance, or perhaps they and their patrons simply enjoyed seeing themselves in their fine clothes acting out the dramas in the cities of which they were justifiably proud.

The Sassetti Chapel altarpiece, **NATIVITY AND ADORA-TION OF THE SHEPHERDS** (FIG. 19–36), is still in its original frame and in the place for which it was painted. Ghirlandaio clearly was inspired by Hugo's *Portinari Altarpiece* (SEE FIG. 18–20), which had been placed on the high altar of the church of Sant'Egidio two years earlier in 1483. As in Hugo's painting, Domenico's Christ Child lies on the

19–37 | Sandro Botticelli **PRIMAVERA**
c. 1482. Tempera on wood panel, 6'8" × 10'4" (2.03 × 3.15 m). Galleria degli Uffizi, Florence.

ground, adored by the Virgin while shepherds—rugged countrymen—kneel at the right. He even copies some of Hugo's flowers—although here the iris, a symbol of the Passion, springs not from a vase, but from the earth in the lower right corner. Instead of elaborate late-medieval symbolism, Ghirlandaio includes references to classical Rome. First to catch the eye are the two classical pilasters with Corinthian capitals, one of which has the date 1485. The manger is an ancient sarcophagus with an inscription that promises resurrection (as in the fresco directly above the altarpiece where Saint Francis is reviving a child); and in the distance a classical arch inscribed with a reference to the Roman general Pompey the Great frames the road along which the Magi travel. Domenico replaces the psychological intensity of Hugo's figures with weighty, restrained actors. His mastery of linear perspective is revealed in the manner in which the diagonally placed wooden planks that support the thatched roof of the shed organize the space. A clear foreground, middle ground, and background are joined together in part by the road and in part by aerial perspective, which creates a seamless transition of color, from the sharp details and primary hues of the Adoration to the soft gray mountains in the distance.

BOTTICELLI. Like most artists in the second half of the fifteenth century, Sandro Botticelli (1445–1510) learned to draw and paint sculptural figures that were modeled by light from a consistent source and placed in a setting rendered with strict linear perspective. An outstanding portraitist, he, like Ghirlandaio, often included recognizable contemporary figures among the saints and angels in religious paintings. He worked in Florence, often for the Medici, then was called to Rome in 1481 by Pope Sixtus IV to help decorate the new Sistine Chapel along with Ghirlandaio, Perugino, and other artists.

Botticelli returned to Florence that same year and entered a new phase of his career. Like other artists working for patrons steeped in classical scholarship and humanistic speculation, he was exposed to a philosophy of beauty—as well as to the examples of ancient art in his employers' collections. For the Medici, Botticelli produced secular paintings of mythological subjects inspired by ancient works and by contemporary Neoplatonic thought, including **PRIMAVERA,** or **SPRING** (FIG. 19–37), and *Birth of Venus* (SEE FIG. 19–38).

The overall appearance of *Primavera* recalls Flemish tapestries, which were popular in Italy at the time. The decorative quality of the painting is deceptive, however, for it is a highly complex **allegory** (a symbolic illustration of a concept or principle), interweaving Neoplatonic ideas with esoteric references to classical sources. In simple terms, Neoplatonic philosophers and poets conceived of Venus, the goddess of love, as having two natures. The first ruled over earthly, human love and the second over universal divine love. In this way the philosophers could argue that Venus was a classical equivalent of the Virgin Mary. *Primavera* was painted at the time of the wedding of Lorenzo di Pierfrancesco de' Medici and Semiramide d'Appiano in 1482. The theme suggests love and fertility in marriage and provides in the image of Venus a model of the ideal woman. Venus is silhouetted and framed by an arching view through the trees. She is flanked by Flora, the Roman goddess of flowers and fertility, and by the Three Graces. Her son, Cupid, hovers above, playfully aiming an arrow at the Graces. At the far right is the wind god, Zephyr, in pursuit of the nymph Chloris, his breath causing her to sprout flowers from her mouth. At the far left, the messenger god, Mercury, uses his characteristic snake-wrapped wand, the caduceus, to dispel a patch of gray clouds drifting in Venus's direction. He is the sign of the month of May, and he looks out of the painting and onto summer. Venus, clothed in contemporary costume and wearing a marriage wreath on her head, here represents her terrestrial nature, governing wedded love. She stands in a grove of orange trees (a Medici

symbol) weighted down with lush fruit, suggesting human fertility; Cupid also embodies romantic desire. As practiced in central Italy in ancient times, the goddess Flora's festival had definite sexual overtones.

Several years later, some of the same mythological figures reappeared in Botticelli's **BIRTH OF VENUS** (FIG. 19–38), in which the central image represents the Neoplatonic idea of divine love and is based on an antique statue type known as the "modest Venus." The classical goddess of love and beauty, born of sea foam, floats ashore on a scallop shell, gracefully arranging her hands and hair to hide—or enhance—her sexuality. Her hair is highlighted with gold. Blown by the

19–38 | Sandro Botticelli **BIRTH OF VENUS**
c. 1484–86. Tempera and gold on canvas, 5′8⅞″ × 9′ 1⅞″ (1.8 × 2.8 m). Galleria degli Uffizi, Florence.

Art and Its Context
THE PRINTED BOOK

A book entitled *Hypnerotomachia Poliphili (The Love-Dream Struggle of Poliphilo)* tells of the search of Poliphilo through exotic places for his lost love, Polia. The book, written in the 1460s or 1470s by Fra Francesco Colonna, was published in 1499 by the noted Venetian printer Aldo Manuzio (Aldus Manutius in Latin), who had established a press in Venice in 1490 (known today as the Aldine Press). Many historians of the printed book consider Aldo's *Hypnerotomachia* to be the most beautiful book ever produced, from the standpoint of type and page design. The woodcut illustrations in the *Hypnerotomachia* incorporate pseudoclassical structures that would influence future architects and garden designers. *The Garden of Love*, illustrated here, provides a setting for music, story telling, and romance, while Venus as a fountain discreetly turns her back.

Although woodcuts, constantly refined and increasingly complex, would remain a popular medium of book illustration for centuries to come, books also came to be illustrated with engravings. The innovations in printing at the end of the 1400s held great promise for the spread of knowledge and ideas in the following century.

Fra Francesco Colonna **PAGE WITH GARDEN OF LOVE, HYPNEROTOMACHIA POLIPHILI**
Published by Aldo Manuzio (Aldus Manutius), Venice, 1499. Woodcut, image 5⅛ × 5⅛″ (13.5 × 13.5 cm). The Pierpont Morgan Library, New York.
PML 373.

wind, Zephyr (and his love, the nymph Chloris), Venus arrives at her earthly home. She is welcomed by a devotee—sometimes identified as one of the Hours—who holds a garment embroidered with flowers. The circumstances of this commission are uncertain. It is painted on canvas, which suggests that it is a banner or a painted tapestry-like wall hanging. The birth of Venus has been interpreted as the birth of the idea of beauty.

Botticelli's later career was affected by a profound spiritual crisis. While the artist was creating his mythologies, a Dominican monk, Fra Girolamo Savonarola (active in Florence 1490–98), had begun to preach impassioned sermons denouncing the worldliness of Florence. Many Florentines reacted with orgies of self-recrimination, and processions of weeping penitents wound through the streets. Botticelli, too, fell into a state of religious fervor. In a dramatic gesture of repentance, he burned many of his earlier paintings and began to produce highly emotional pictures pervaded by an intense religiosity.

In 1500, when many people feared that the end of the world was imminent, Botticelli painted **MYSTIC** nativity (FIG. 19–39) his only signed and dated painting. The Nativity takes place in a rocky, forested landscape in which the cave-stable follows the tradition of the Eastern Orthodox (Byzantine) Church, while the timber shed in front recalls the Western iconographic tradition (SEE FIG. 17–13). In the center of the painting, the Virgin Mary kneels in adoration of the Christ Child, who lies on the earth, as recorded in the vision of the fourteenth-century mystic Saint Bridget. Joseph crouches and hides his face, while the ox and the ass bow their heads to the Holy Child. The shepherds at the right and the Magi at the left also kneel before the Holy Family. A circle of singing angels holding golden crowns and laurel branches flies jubilantly above the central scene. Tiny devils, vanquished by the coming of Christ, try to escape from the bottom of the picture.

The most unusual element of the painting is the frieze of wrestling figures below the Holy Family. The men are ancient classical philosophers, who ceremonially struggle with angels. Each of the three pairs holds an olive branch, a symbol of peace, and a scroll—as do the angels circling above, whose scrolls are inscribed (in Greek) with the words: "Glory to God in the Highest; peace on earth to men of good will." (Palm Sunday in fifteenth-century Florence was called Olive Sunday, and olive branches, symbols of peace, rather than palms were carried in processions.) The inscription at the top of the painting (in Greek) begins: "I Alessandro made this picture. . . ." and goes on to reference the Book of Revelation, Chapter 11, which describes woes to come, and Chapter 12, which includes the vision of a woman crowned with stars and clothed by the sun (the woman of Revelations was interpreted by Christians as a portrayal of the Virgin Mary) and the description of the defeat of Satan. Thus, in spite of the troubles Botticelli saw all around him, he believed that Christ would come to save humankind.

Venice

In the last quarter of the fifteenth century, Venice emerged as a major Renaissance art center. Venice was an oligarchy (government by a select few) with an elected duke (*doge* in the Venetian dialect). The city government was founded at the end of the Roman empire and survived until the Napoleonic era. In building their city the Venetians had turned marshes into a commercial seaport, and they saw the sea as a resource, not a threat. They depended on naval power and on their lagoons rather than city walls. The city turned toward the east, especially after the Crusaders' conquest of Constantinople in 1204. Even earlier the Venetians were investing the Church of Saint Mark, a great Byzantine-inspired building, with the rich color of mosaics and gold liturgical decorations from the Eastern Christian empire. They excelled in the arts of textiles, gold and enamel, glass and mosaic, and fine printing (see "The Printed Book," page 652), as well as book binding.

THE VENETIAN PALACE.   Venice was a city of waterways with few large public spaces. Even palaces had only small interior courtyards and tiny gardens, and were separated by narrow alleys. They faced out on canals, whose waters gave protection and permitted the owners to build houses with large portals, windows, and loggias. This presented a sharp contrast to the fortresslike character of most Italian townhouses. But, as with the Florentine great houses, their owners combined in these structures a place of business with a dwelling.

The CA D'ORO (HOUSE OF GOLD), the home of the wealthy nobleman Marino Contarini, has a splendid front with three superimposed loggias facing the Grand Canal (FIG. 19–40). The house was constructed between 1421 and 1437, and its asymmetrical elevation is based on a traditional Byzantine plan. A wide central hall ran from front to back all the way through the building to a small inner courtyard with

19–39   Sandro Botticelli   **MYSTIC NATIVITY**
1500. Oil on canvas, 42 × 29½" (106.7 × 74.9 cm). The National Gallery, London.

This is the only work signed and dated by Botticelli; translated from the Greek, his inscription reads: "I Alessandro made this picture at the conclusion of the 1500th year" (National Gallery, London, files).

a well and garden. An outside stair led to the main floor on the second level. The entrance on the canal permitted goods to be delivered directly into the warehouse that constituted the ground floor. The principal floor, on the second level, had a salon and reception room opening on the richly decorated loggia. It was filled with light from large windows, and more light reflected off the polished terrazzo floor. Private family rooms filled the upper stories. In contrast to the massive stone façades of Florentine palaces (SEE FIGS. 19–6, 19–8), Contarini's instructions to his contractors and workers specified that the façade was to be painted with white enamel and ultramarine blue and that the red stones in the patterned wall should be oiled to make them even brighter. Details of carving, such as coats of arms and balls on the crest at the roof line, were to be gilded. Beautiful as the palace is today (it is now an art museum), in the fifteenth and sixteenth centuries it must have been truly spectacular.

19–40 | CA D'ORO, VENICE
1421-37. Contarini Palace, known as the Ca d'Oro.

THE BELLINI BROTHERS. The domes of the Church of Saint Mark dominated the city center, and the rich colors of its glowing mosaics captured painters' imaginations. The love of color encouraged the use of the oil medium. Venetian painters eagerly embraced the oil paint technique for both panel and canvas painting.

The most important Venetian artists of this period were two brothers, Gentile (c. 1429–1507) and Giovanni (c. 1430–1516) Bellini, whose father, Jacopo (c. 1400–70), had also been a central figure in Venetian art. Andrea Mantegna was also part of this circle, for he had married Jacopo's daughter in 1453.

Gentile Bellini celebrated the daily life of the city in large, lively narratives, such as the **PROCESSION OF THE RELIC OF THE TRUE CROSS BEFORE THE CHURCH OF SAINT MARK (FIG. 19–41).** Every year on the Feast of Saint Mark (April 25) the Confraternity of Saint John the Evangelist carried the miracle-working Relic of the True Cross in a procession through the square in front of the church. Bellini's painting of 1496 depicts an event that had occurred in 1444: the miraculous recovery of a sick child whose father, the man in red kneeling to the right of the relic, prayed for help as the relic passed by. Gentile has rendered the cityscape with great accuracy and detail. The mosaic-encrusted Byzantine Church of Saint Mark (SEE ALSO FIG. 7–44) forms a backdrop for the procession, and the *doge's* palace and base of the bell tower can be seen at the right. The relic, in a gold reliquary under a canopy, is surrounded by marchers with giant candles, led by a choir and followed at the far right by the *doge* and other officials. The procession and spectators bring the huge piazza to life.

Gentile's brother, Giovanni, amazed and attracted patrons with his artistic virtuosity for almost sixty years. The **VIRGIN**

19–41 | Gentile Bellini PROCESSION OF THE RELIC OF THE TRUE CROSS BEFORE THE CHURCH OF SAINT MARK
1496. Oil on canvas, 12' × 24'5" (3.67 × 7.45 m). Galleria dell'Accademia, Venice.

AND CHILD ENTHRONED WITH SAINTS FRANCIS, JOHN THE BAPTIST, JOB, DOMINIC, SEBASTIAN, AND LOUIS OF TOULOUSE (FIG. 19–42), painted about 1478 for the Chapel of the Hospital of San Giobbe (Saint Job), exhibits a dramatic perspectival view up into a vaulted apse. Certainly, Giovanni knew his father's perspective drawings well, and he may also have been influenced by his brother-in-law Mantegna's early experiments in radical foreshortening and the use of a low vanishing point. In Giovanni's painting, the vanishing point for the rapidly converging lines of the architecture lies at the center, on the feet of the lute-playing angel. Giovanni has placed his figures in a classical architectural interior with a coffered barrel vault, reminiscent of Masaccio's *Trinity* (SEE FIG. 19–19). The gold mosaic, with its identifying inscription and stylized **seraphim** (angels of the highest rank), recalls the art of the Byzantine Empire in the eastern Mediterranean and the long tradition of Byzantine-inspired painting and mosaics produced in Venice.

Giovanni Bellini also demonstrates the intense investigation and recording of nature associated with the early Renaissance. His early painting of **SAINT FRANCIS IN ECSTASY** (FIG. 19–43), painted in the 1470s, illustrates his command of an almost Flemish realism. The saint stands in communion with nature, bathed in early morning sunlight, his outspread hands showing the stigmata. Francis had moved to a cave in the barren wilderness in his search for communion with God, but in this landscape, the fields blossom and flocks of animals graze. The grape arbor over his desk and the leafy tree toward which he directs his gaze add to an atmosphere of sylvan delight. True to fifteenth-century religious art, however, Bellini unites Old and New Testament themes to associate Francis with Moses and Christ: The tree symbolizes the burning bush; the stream, the miraculous spring brought forth by Moses; the grapevine and the stigmata, Christ's sacrifice. The crane and donkey represent the monastic virtue of patience. The detailed realism, luminous colors, and symbolic elements suggest Flemish art, but the golden light suffusing the painting is associated with Venice, a city of mist, reflections, and above all, color.

Giovanni's career spanned the second half of the fifteenth century, but he produced many of his greatest paintings in the early years of the sixteenth, when his work matured into a grand, simplified, idealized style. It seems fitting to end our consideration of the first phase of Renaissance painting in Italy with Giovanni Bellini as an important and influential bridge to the future.

19–42 | Giovanni Bellini **VIRGIN AND CHILD ENTHRONED WITH SAINTS FRANCIS, JOHN THE BAPTIST, JOB, DOMINIC, SEBASTIAN, AND LOUIS OF TOULOUSE**
(computer reconstruction) Commissioned for the Chapel of the Hospital of San Giobbe, Venice. c. 1478. Oil on wood panel, 15′4″ × 8′4″ (4.67 × 2.54 m). Galleria dell'Accademia, Venice. The original frame is in the Chapel of the Hospital of San Giobbe, Venice. c. 1478.

Art historians have given the special name *sacra conversazione* ("holy conversation") to this type of composition that shows saints, angels, and sometimes even the painting's donors in the same pictorial space with the enthroned Virgin and Child. Despite the name, no "conversation" or other interaction among the figures takes place in a literal sense. Instead, the individuals portrayed are joined in a mystical and eternal communion occurring outside of time.

IN PERSPECTIVE

In many people's minds the Renaissance and Italy are synonymous—the Renaissance is the Italian Renaissance. Florence is its home, and the Medici family, its patrons. As we have seen, however, the fifteenth century witnessed changes throughout Western Europe—in Bruges as well as Florence.

The art of the fifteenth century reflects the values and worldview of the new social order. A spirit of inquiry was fueled by the study of classical texts begun in the fourteenth century. The kind of logical discourse formerly reserved for theological debate now was applied to the material world. Theories based on the close observation of

19–43 | Giovanni Bellini
SAINT FRANCIS IN ECSTASY
c. 1470's. Oil and tempera on wood
panel, 49 × 55⅞″ (125 × 142 cm).
The Frick Collection, New York.
Copyright the Frick Collection, New York.

phenomena were put forth to be challenged and defended. During this time individuals gained importance, not only as inquiring minds but as the subject of inquiry. Artists, too, emerged from anonymity and were recognized as distinct personalities.

Patrons wanted to see themselves and their possessions depicted as they were. Fifteenth-century portraits have an uncanny sense of vitality, in part because of their careful, even unflattering, representations of individuals. The patrons' desire for realism extended to their surroundings; they wanted identifiable views of the buildings and countryside where they worked and played, fought and died. Artists tacitly agreed to follow new ways of representing space and visually organizing a scene using linear and atmospheric perspective. By the end of the fifteenth century, the visual mastery of the material

world seemed complete; rational and scientific thought had triumphed in both secular and religious art.

Power was no longer the prerogative of divinely sanctioned elites; it now also lay in the hands of commoners—the merchants and bankers, the leaders of the major guilds and professions. The arts flourished as patronage extended beyond the church and the court to civic, mercantile, and religious associations, as well as to families grown powerful through business and banking.

The last decade of the century saw a sudden reversal of artistic fortunes as the fiery preacher Savonarola spread the fear of damnation and inspired a need for repentance. In great "bonfires of the vanities" people destroyed their finery and great works of art as well. The furor was brief but devastating, a dramatic prelude to the tumultuous sixteenth century.

NANNI DI BANCO
FOUR CROWNED MARTYRS
C. 1409–17

1400

MASACCIO
N FROM PARADISE,
BRANCACCI CHAPEL
C. 1427

CA D'ORO, VENICE
1421–37

1420

◄ **Great Schism Ends** 1417

◄ **Alberti Writes** *De Pictura*
(On Painting) 1435

1440

GHIBERTI
**EAST DOORS, FLORENCE
BAPTISTRY COMPLETED**
1452

◄ **Ghiberti Writes** *Commentaries*
C. 1450–55

1460

◄ **Lorenzo de' Medici Rules Florence**
1469–92

1480

ALBERTI
OF SANT'ANDREA DESIGNED
1470

BOTTICELLI
MYSTIC NATIVITY
1500

◄ **Savonarola Executed** 1498

1500

657

20–1 | Raphael **STANZA DELLA SEGNATURA** Vatican, Rome.
Fresco in the left lunette, *Parnassus*; in the right lunette, *School of Athens*. 1510–11. *School of Athens*,
19 × 27′ (5.79 × 8.24 m).

CHAPTER TWENTY

SIXTEENTH-CENTURY ART IN ITALY

20 Two young artists—Raphael (Raffaello Santi) and Michelangelo Buonarroti—although rivals in every sense, were both in the service of Pope Julius II in the early years of the sixteenth century. Raphael was painting the pope's private library (1509–11) while nearby Michelangelo painted the ceiling of his chapel (1508–12). The pope demanded an art that reflected his imperial vision of a new, worldwide Church based on humanistic ideas. In fulfilling this demand, Raphael and Michelangelo brought early Renaissance principles of harmony and balance together with a new monumentality based on classical ideals, and they knit these separate elements into a dynamic and synthetic whole. Together with the architect Donato Bramante and the multifaceted genius Leonardo da Vinci, they created a style we now think of as the High Renaissance.

Pope Julius II (ruled 1503–13) intended the **STANZA DELLA SEGNATURA,** or *Room of the Signature,* to be his library and study (**FIG. 20–1**). In painting the all-encompassing iconographic program we see here, Raphael created an ideal setting for the activities of a pope who believed that all human knowledge existed under the power of divine wisdom. Raphael based his mural program on the traditional organization of a library into divisions of theology, philosophy, the arts, and justice; and he created allegories to illustrate these themes. On one wall, churchmen discussing the sacraments represent theology, while across the room ancient philosophers debate in the *School of Athens,* led by Plato and Aristotle. Plato holds his book *Timaeus,* in which creation is seen in terms of geometry, and in which humanity encompasses and explains the universe. Aristotle holds his *Nicomachean Ethics,* a decidedly human-centered book concerned with relations between people. Ancient representatives of the academic curriculum—Grammar, Rhetoric, Dialectic, Arithmetic, Music, Geometry, and Astronomy—surround them. On a window wall, Justice, holding a sword and scales, assigns each his due. Across the room, Poetry and the Arts are represented by Apollo and the Muses, and the poet Sappho reclines against the fictive frame of an actual window. Raphael included his own portrait among the onlookers on the extreme lower right in the *School of Athens* and signed the painting with his initials—a signal that artists were increasingly aware of their individual significance.

Raphael achieved a lofty style in keeping with the papal ideals of classical grandeur, faith in human rationality and perfectibility, and the power of the pope as God's earthly administrator. But when Raphael died at the age of 37 on April 6, 1520, the grand moment was already passing: Luther and the Protestant Reformation were challenging papal authority.

CHAPTER-AT-A-GLANCE

EUROPE IN THE SIXTEENTH CENTURY

The sixteenth century was an age of social, intellectual, and religious ferment that transformed European culture. It was also marked by continual warfare triggered by the expansionist ambitions of the continent's various rulers. The humanism of the fourteenth and fifteenth centuries, with its medieval roots and its often uncritical acceptance of the authority of classical texts, slowly developed a critical spirit that led Europeans to further their exploration of new ideas, nature, and lands. New methods in cartography that took account of the earth's curvature and the degrees of distance undermined traditional views of the world and led to a more accurate understanding of Europe's distinct place in it. The use of the printing press caused an explosion in the number of books available, spreading new ideas through the translation and publication of ancient and contemporary texts, broadening the horizons of educated Europeans and encouraging more people to learn to read. Travel became more common than in earlier centuries; artists and their work became mobile; consequently, artistic styles became less regional and more international.

At the start of the sixteenth century, England, France, and Portugal were nation-states under strong monarchs. Central Europe (Germany) was divided into dozens of principalities, counties, free cities, and other small territories. But even states as powerful as Saxony and Bavaria acknowledged the overlordship of the Habsburg (Holy Roman) Empire—in

theory the greatest power in Europe. Charles V, elected Holy Roman Emperor in 1519, also inherited Spain, the Netherlands, and vast territories in the Americas. Italy, which was divided into many small states, was a diplomatic and military battlefield where, for much of the century, the Italian city-states, Habsburg Spain, France, and the papacy fought each other in shifting alliances. The popes themselves behaved like secular princes, using diplomacy and military force to regain control over central Italy and in some cases to establish family members as hereditary rulers. The popes' incessant demands for money, to finance the rebuilding of Saint Peter's as well as their self-aggrandizing art projects and luxurious lifestyles, aggravated the religious dissent that had long been developing, especially north of the Alps. Early in the century, religious reformers within the established Church challenged beliefs and practices—especially Julius II's sale of indulgences, which entailed a financial contribution to the Church in return for forgiveness of sins and insurance of salvation. Because they protested, these northern European reformers came to be called Protestants. Their demand for reform gave rise to a movement called the Reformation.

Although Italy remained staunchly Catholic, the Reformation had profound repercussions there. It drove the Catholic church not only to launch a fight against Protestantism but also to seek internal reform and renewal—a movement that became known as the Counter-Reformation. The Counter-Reformation would have a profound effect on artists and the works they created.

MAP 20–1 | SIXTEENTH-CENTURY ITALY

In the 16th century Italy remained a peninsula divided into city-states in the north and the Papal States in the center. In the south Naples and Sicily were part of the vast and powerful Hasburg domains.

The political maneuvering of Pope Clement VII (papacy 1523–34) led to a direct clash with Holy Roman Emperor Charles V. In May 1527, Charles's German mercenary troops attacked Rome, beginning a six-month orgy of killing, looting, and burning. The Sack of Rome, as it is called, shook the sense of stability and humanistic confidence that until then had characterized the Renaissance, and it sent many artists fleeing from the ruined city. Nevertheless, Charles saw himself as the leader of the Catholic forces—and he was the sole Catholic ally Clement had at the time. In 1530 Clement VII crowned Charles emperor in Bologna.

Sixteenth-century patrons valued artists highly and rewarded them well, not only with generous commissions but sometimes even with high social status. Charles V, for example, knighted the painter Titian. Some painters and sculptors became entrepreneurs, selling prints of their works on the side. The sale of prints was a means by which reputations and styles became widely known, and a few artists of stature became international celebrities. With their new fame and independence, the most successful artists could decide which commissions to accept or reject.

Many artists recorded their activities in private diaries, notebooks, and letters that have come down to us. In addition, contemporary writers reported on everything about artists, from their physical appearance to their personal reputation. In 1550, Giorgio Vasari wrote the first survey of Italian art history, *Lives of the Best Architects, Painters, and Sculptors*. Vasari included more than simple biographical details; he made value judgments on work, commented on the role of patrons, and argued that art had become more realistic and more beautiful over time. He described the art of his own age as the culmination of historical processes, with its fulfillment in the life and work of Michelangelo. From his characterization, in part, stems our notion of this time period as the High Renaissance—that is, as a high point in art since Cimabue and Giotto that marks a balanced synthesis of classical ideals and an ordered naturalism.

During this period, the fifteenth-century humanists' argument that the conception of a painting, sculpture, or work of architecture was not a manual art but a liberal (intellectual) art, which therefore required education in the classics and mathematics, became a topic of intense interest. The artist could express as much through painted, sculptural, and architectural forms as the poet could with words or the musician with melody. The myth of the divinely inspired creative genius—which arose during the Renaissance—is still with us today.

As with the business side of artistic production, however, the newly elevated status to which artists aspired favored men. Although few artists of either sex had access to the humanist education required for the sophisticated, often esoteric, subject matter used in paintings (most artists depended on outside sources for this aspect of their work), women were denied even the studio practice necessary to draw nude figures in foreshortened poses. Furthermore, it was almost impossible for an artist to achieve international status without traveling extensively and frequently relocating to follow commissions—something most women could not do. Still, women artists were active in European cultural life despite the obstacles to their entering any profession.

ITALY IN THE EARLY SIXTEENTH CENTURY: THE HIGH RENAISSANCE

Italian art from the 1490s to about the time of the Sack of Rome in 1527 has been called the "High Renaissance," the "Imperial style," and the "classical phase" of the Renaissance. It is characterized by a sense of gravity, a complex but balanced relationship of individual parts to the whole, and a deeper understanding of humanism and of ancient classical art than in the previous century. As before, outstanding Italian artists practicing in Rome, Florence, and other Italian cities spread this Italian Renaissance style throughout Europe.

Two important practical developments at the turn of the sixteenth century affected the arts in Italy: Technically, the use of tempera gave way to the more flexible oil medium in painting; and economically, commissions from private sources increased. Artists no longer depended so exclusively on the patronage of the Church, the aristocracy, or civic associations. Some members of the middle class in Italy and other European countries amassed wealth and became avid collectors of classical antiquities, paintings, and small bronzes, as well as coins, minerals, and fossils from the natural world.

Three Great Artists of the Early Sixteenth Century

Florence's renowned artworks and tradition of arts patronage attracted a stream of young artists to that city. The frescoes in the Brancacci Chapel there (SEE FIG. 19–20) inspired young artists, who went to study Masaccio's solid, monumental figures and eloquent facial features, poses, and gestures. For example, the young Michelangelo's sketches of the chapel frescoes clearly show the importance of Masaccio to his developing style. Michelangelo, Leonardo, and Raphael—the three leading artists of the classical phase of the Italian

Renaissance—all began their careers in Florence, although they soon moved to other centers of patronage and their influence spread far beyond that city.

LEONARDO DA VINCI.   Leonardo da Vinci (1452–1519) was twelve or thirteen when his family moved to Florence from the Tuscan village of Vinci. He was an apprentice in the shop of the painter and sculptor Verrocchio until about 1476. After a few years on his own, Leonardo traveled to Milan in 1481 or 1482 to work for the ruling Sforza family.

Leonardo spent much of his time in Milan on military and civil engineering projects, including both urban-renewal and fortification plans for the city, but he also created one of the key monuments of Renaissance art there: At Duke Ludovico Sforza's request, Leonardo painted THE LAST SUPPER (FIG. 20–2, AND Fig. 18, Introduction) in the refectory, or dining hall, of the Monastery of Santa Maria delle Grazie in Milan between 1495 and 1498. In fictive space defined by a coffered ceiling and four pairs of tapestries that seem to extend the refectory into another room, Jesus and his disciples are seated at a long table placed parallel to the picture plane and to the living diners seated in the hall. The stagelike space recedes from the table to three windows on the back wall, where the vanishing point of the one-point perspective lies behind Jesus's head. Jesus forms an equilateral pyramid at the center, his arms uniting the twelve disciples, who are grouped in four interlocking sets of three. As a narrative, the scene captures the moment when Jesus tells his companions that one of them will betray him. They react with shock, disbelief, and horror. Judas recoils, clutching his money bag in the shadows to the left of Jesus. Leonardo was an acute observer of human beings and his art vividly expressed human emotions.

On another level, *The Last Supper* is a symbolic evocation of both Jesus's coming sacrifice for the salvation of humankind and the institution of the ritual of the Mass. Breaking with traditional representations of the subject, such as the one by Andrea del Castagno (SEE FIG. 19–25), Leonardo placed the traitor Judas in the first triad to the left of Jesus, with the young John the Evangelist and the elderly Peter, rather than isolating him on the opposite side of the table. Judas, Peter, and John were each to play an essential role in Jesus's mission: Judas to set in motion the events leading to Jesus's sacrifice; Peter to lead the Church after Jesus's death; and John, the visionary, to foretell the Second Coming and the Last Judgment in the Apocalypse. By arranging the disciples and architectural elements into four groups of three, Leonardo incorporated a medieval tradition of numerical symbolism. He eliminated another symbolic element—the halo—and substituted the natural light from a triple window framing Jesus's head (compare Rembrandt's reworking of the composition, Fig. 19, Introduction).

20–2 | Leonardo **THE LAST SUPPER**
Wall painting in the refectory of the Monastery of Santa Maria delle Grazie, Milan, Italy. 1495–98. Tempera and oil on plaster, 15'2" × 28'10" (4.6 × 8.8 m). See Introduction, Fig. 18.

Instead of painting in fresco, Leonardo devised an experimental technique for this mural. Hoping to achieve the freedom and flexibility of painting on wood panel, he worked directly on dry *intonaco*—a thin layer of smooth plaster—with an oil-and-tempera paint for which the formula is unknown. The result was disastrous. Within a short time, the painting began to deteriorate, and by the middle of the sixteenth century its figures could be seen only with difficulty. In the seventeenth century, the monks saw no harm in cutting a doorway through the lower center of the composition. Since then the work has barely survived, despite many attempts to halt its deterioration and restore its original appearance. The painting narrowly escaped complete destruction in World War II, when the refectory was bombed to rubble around its heavily sandbagged wall. The coats of arms at the top are those of patron Ludovico Sforza, the Duke of Milan (ruled 1494–99), and his wife, Beatrice.

20–3 | Leonardo **VIRGIN AND SAINT ANNE WITH THE CHRIST CHILD AND THE YOUNG JOHN THE BAPTIST**
c. 1500. Charcoal heightened with white on brown paper,
55½ × 41" (141.5 × 104.6 cm). The National Gallery, London.

20–4 | Leonardo **MONA LISA**
c. 1503. Oil on wood panel, 30¼ × 21" (77 × 53 cm). Musée du Louvre, Paris.

The painting's careful geometry, the convergence of its perspective lines, the stability of its pyramidal forms, and Jesus's calm demeanor at the mathematical center of all the commotion together reinforce the sense of gravity, balance, and order. The work's qualities of stability, calm, and timelessness, coupled with the established Renaissance forms modeled after those of classical sculpture, characterize the art of the Renaissance at the beginning of the sixteenth century.

Leonardo returned to Florence in 1500, after the French, who had invaded Italy in 1494, claimed Milan. (They defeated Leonardo's Milanese patron, Ludovico Sforza, who remained imprisoned until his death in 1508.) Upon his return, Leonardo produced a large drawing of the **VIRGIN AND SAINT ANNE WITH THE CHRIST CHILD AND THE YOUNG JOHN THE BAPTIST** (FIG. 20–3). This work may be a full-scale model, called a **cartoon**, for a major painting, but no known painting can be associated with it. Scholars today believe it to be a finished work—perhaps one of the drawings artists often made as gifts. Mary sits on the knee of her mother, Anne, and turns to the right to hold the Christ Child, who strains away from her to reach toward his cousin, the young John the Bap-

tist. Leonardo created the illusion of high relief by modeling the figures with strongly contrasted light and shadow, a technique called **chiaroscuro** (Italian for "light-dark"). Rather than a central focus, carefully placed highlights create interlocking circular movements that activate the composition; they underscore the individual importance of each figure while making each of them an integral part of the whole. This effect emphasizes the figures' complex interactions, which are suggested by their exquisitely tender expressions, particularly those of Saint Anne and the Virgin.

Between about 1503 and 1506, Leonardo painted the renowned portrait known as **MONA LISA** (FIG. 20–4). The subject may have been 24-year-old Lisa Gherardini del Giocondo, the wife of a prominent merchant in Florence. Leonardo never delivered the painting and kept it with him for the rest of his life. Remarkably for the time, the young woman is portrayed without any jewelry, not even a ring. The solid pyramidal form of her half-length figure—a significant departure from the traditional portraits, which stopped at the upper torso—is silhouetted against distant mountains, whose desolate grandeur reinforces the painting's mysterious atmosphere.

Defining Art
THE VITRUVIAN MAN

A rtists throughout history have turned to geometric shapes and mathematical proportions to seek the ideal representation of the human form. Leonardo da Vinci, and before him Vitruvius, equated the ideal man with both circle and square. Ancient Egyptian artists laid out square grids as aids to design. Medieval artists adapted a variety of figures, from triangles to pentagrams. The Byzantines used circles centered on the bridge of the nose to create face, head, and halo.

The first-century BCE Roman architect and engineer Vitruvius, in his ten-volume *De architectura* (*On Architecture*), wrote: "For if a man be placed flat on his back, with his hands and feet extended, and a pair of compasses centered at his navel, the fingers and toes of his two hands and feet will touch the circumference of a circle described therefrom. And just as the human body yields a circular outline, so too a square figure may be found from it. For if we measure the distance from the soles of the feet to the top of the head, and then apply that measure to the outstretched arms, the breadth will be found to be the same as the height" (Book III, Chapter 1, Section 3). Vitruvius determined that the body should be eight heads high. Leonardo added his own observations in the reversed writing he always used for his notebooks when he created his well-known diagram for the ideal male figure, called the **VITRUVIAN MAN.**

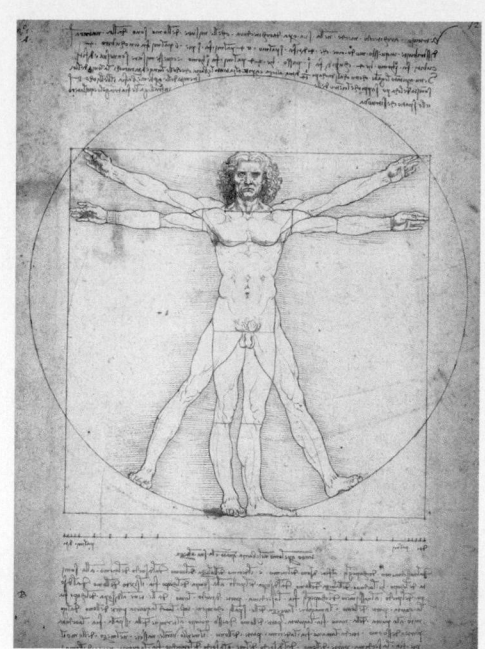

Leonardo   **VITRUVIAN MAN**
c. 1490. Ink, 13½ × 9⅝" (34.3 × 24.5 cm).
Galleria dell'Accademia, Venice.

Mona Lisa's expression has been called enigmatic because her gentle smile is not accompanied by the warmth one would expect to see in her eyes. The contemporary fashion for plucked eyebrows and a shaved hairline to increase the height of the forehead adds to her arresting appearance. Perhaps most unsettling is the bold and slightly flirtatious way her gaze has shifted toward the right to look straight out at the viewer. The implied challenge of her direct stare, combined with her apparent serenity and inner strength, has made the *Mona Lisa* one of the most haunting and consequently one of the most popular and best-known works in the history of art.

A fiercely debated topic in Renaissance Italy was the question of the superiority of painting or sculpture. Leonardo insisted on the supremacy of painting as the best and most complete means of creating an illusion of the natural world, while Michelangelo argued for sculpture. Yet in creating a painted illusion, Leonardo considered color to be secondary to the depiction of sculptural volume, which he achieved through his virtuosity in highlighting and shading. He also unified his compositions by covering them with a thin, lightly tinted varnish, which resulted in a smoky overall haze called *sfumato*. Because early evening light tends to produce a similar effect naturally, Leonardo considered dusk the finest time of day and recommended that painters set up their studios in a courtyard with black walls and a linen sheet stretched overhead to reproduce twilight.

Leonardo's fame as an artist is based on only a few works, for his many interests took him away from painting. Unlike his humanist contemporaries, he was not particularly interested in classical literature or archaeology. Instead, his passions were mathematics, engineering, and the natural world. He compiled volumes of detailed drawings and notes on anatomy, botany, geology, meteorology, architectural design, and mechanics. In his drawings of human figures, he sought not only the precise details of anatomy but also the geometric basis of perfect proportions (see "The Vitruvian Man," above). Leonardo's searching mind is evident in his drawings, not only of natural objects and human beings, but also of machines. His drawings are so clear and complete that modern engineers have been able to construct working models from them. He designed flying machines, a sort of automobile, a parachute, and all sorts of military equipment, including a mobile fortress. His imagination outran his means to bring his creations into being. For one thing, he lacked a source of power other than men and horses. For another, he may have lacked focus and follow-through: His contemporaries complained that he never finished anything and that his inventions distracted him from his painting.

20–5 | Raphael **THE SMALL COWPER MADONNA**
c. 1505. Oil on wood panel, 23⅜ × 17⅜″ (59.5 × 44.1 cm).
National Gallery of Art, Washington, D.C.
Widener Collection (1942.9.57)

RAPHAEL. About 1505, Raphael (Raffaello Santi or Sanzio, 1483–1520) arrived in Florence from his native Urbino. He had studied in Perugia with the leading artist of that city, Perugino (SEE FIG. 19–34). Raphael quickly became successful in Florence, especially with paintings of the Virgin and Child, such as **THE SMALL COWPER MADONNA** (named for a modern owner) of about 1505 (FIG. 20–5). Already a superb painter technically, the youthful Raphael shows his indebtedness to his teacher in the delicate tilt of the figures' heads and the tranquil, even mood that pervades the painting. But Raphael must have studied Leonardo's work to achieve the simple grandeur created by these monumental shapes, the pyramid activated by the spiraling movement of the child, and the figure-enhancing draperies of the Virgin. The solidly modeled forms are softened by the clear, even light of the outdoor setting.

In the distance on a hilltop, Raphael has painted a scene he knew well from his childhood, the domed Church of San Bernardino, two miles outside Urbino. The church contains the tombs of the dukes of Urbino, Federico and Guidobaldo da Montefeltro, and their wives (SEE FIG. 19–28). Donato Bramante, whose architecture was key in establishing the High Renaissance style (see page 677), may have designed the church.

Raphael left Florence about 1508 for Rome, where Pope Julius II put him to work almost immediately decorating rooms (*stanze*, singular *stanza*) in the papal apartments. In the *Stanza della Segnatura*—the papal library, which we saw at the beginning of the chapter (SEE FIG. 20–1)—Raphael painted the four branches of knowledge as conceived in the sixteenth century: Religion (the *Disputà*, depicting the disputation over the true presence of Christ in the Host, the Communion bread), Philosophy (the *School of Athens*), Poetry (*Parnassus*, home of the Muses), and Law (the *Cardinal Virtues under Justice*). The shape of the walls and vault of the room itself inspired the composition of the paintings—for example, the receding arches and vaults in the *School of Athens*, or the inclusion of the window as part of the rocky mountain in *Parnassus*.

Raphael's most outstanding achievement in the papal rooms was the **SCHOOL OF ATHENS,** painted about 1510–11 (FIG. 20–6). Here, the painter seems to summarize the ideals of the Renaissance papacy in his grand conception of harmoniously arranged forms in a rational space, as well as in the calm dignity of its figures. The learned Julius II may have actually devised the subjects painted; he certainly must have approved them.

Viewed through a *trompe l'oeil* arch, the Greek philosophers Plato and Aristotle—placed to the right and left of the compositional vanishing point—are silhouetted against the sky (the natural world) and command our attention. At the left, Plato gestures upward, indicating the "ideal" as impossible to attain on earth. Aristotle, with his outstretched hand palm down, seems to emphasize the importance of gathering empirical knowledge from observing the material world. Looking down from niches in the walls are sculptures of Apollo, the god of sunlight, rationality, poetry, music, and the fine arts; and Minerva, the goddess of wisdom and the mechanical arts. Around Plato and Aristotle are mathematicians, naturalists, astronomers, geographers, and other philosophers debating and demonstrating their theories to onlookers and to each other. The scene, flooded with a clear, even light from a single source, takes place in an immense barrel-vaulted interior, possibly inspired by the new design for Saint Peter's, under construction at the time. The grandeur of the building is matched by the monumental dignity of the philosophers themselves, each of whom has a distinct physical and intellectual presence. The sweeping arcs of the composition are activated by the variety and energy of the poses and gestures of these striking individuals. Such dynamic unity is an expression of the High Renaissance style.

Raphael continued to work for Julius II's successor, Leo X (papacy 1513–21), as director of all archaeological and architectural projects in Rome. Leo was born Giovanni de' Medici, the son of Lorenzo the Magnificent, and his driving ambition was the advancement of the Medici family—who had been exiled from Florence in 1494 and only returned to power there in 1512. Raphael's portrait of Leo X is, in effect,

20–6 | Raphael **SCHOOL OF ATHENS**
Fresco in the Stanza della Segnatura, Vatican, Rome. c. 1510–11. 19 × 27′ (5.79 × 8.24 m).

Raphael gave many of the figures in his imaginary gathering of philosophers the features of his friends and colleagues. It is speculated that Plato, standing immediately to the left of the central axis and pointing to the sky, was modeled after Leonardo da Vinci; Euclid, shown inscribing a slate with a compass at the lower right, was, according to Vasari, a portrait of Raphael's friend the architect Donato Bramante. Michelangelo, who was at work on the Sistine Chapel ceiling, only steps away from the *stanza* where Raphael was painting his fresco, may be the solitary figure at the lower left center, leaning on a block of marble and sketching, in a pose reminiscent of the figures of the sibyls and prophets on his great ceiling. Raphael's own features are represented on the second figure from the front group at the far right, as the face of a young man listening to a discourse by the astronomer Ptolemy.

a dynastic group portrait (FIG. 20–7). Facing the pope at the left is his cousin Giulio, Cardinal de' Medici, who governed Florence from 1519 to 1523 and then became Pope Clement VII (papacy 1523–34). Behind Pope Leo stands Luigi de' Rossi, a nephew whom he made a cardinal. Dressed in splendid brocades and enthroned in a velvet chair, the pope looks up from a richly illuminated fourteenth-century manuscript that he has been examining with a magnifying glass. He seems to stare into space, and, curiously, none of the three men look at each other. The mood seems uneasy, disconnected. Raphael carefully depicted the contrasting textures and surfaces in the picture, including the visual distortion caused by the magnifying glass on the book page. The polished brass knob on the

pope's chair reflects the window and the painter himself. In these telling details, Raphael acknowledges his debt—despite great stylistic differences—to fifteenth-century Flemish artists such as Jan van Eyck.

How could a man—even a brilliant artist—accomplish so much? Raphael was only 37 when he died. The answer lies partly in Raphael's genius for organizing his studio, which enabled him to accept numerous commissions. Retaining a flexible method, Raphael was able to assign assistants wherever he felt it was appropriate, even if that meant finishing major figures in a painting or making preparatory drawings—work generally assumed by the master. Raphael thus freed himself to concentrate on what he considered most necessary at any given

20–7 | Raphael **POPE LEO X WITH CARDINALS GIULIO DE' MEDICI AND LUIGI DE' ROSSI**
c. 1517. Oil on wood panel, 5'5⁄8" × 3'10⁷⁄8" (1.54 × 1.19 m). Galleria degli Uffizi, Florence.

time. This method sometimes resulted in uneven products, especially toward the end of the artist's short life, when he was overwhelmed with work. Yet, even then, Raphael's major pieces show his contribution to be the dominant one.

In 1515–16, Raphael and his shop provided cartoons on themes from the Acts of the Apostles to be made into tapestries to cover the wall below the fifteenth-century wall paintings of the Sistine Chapel (FIG. 20–8). This commission must have suited Raphael's method, accustomed as he was to teamwork. For the production of tapestries, which were woven in workshops in Flanders, artists made full-scale charcoal drawings, then painted over them with glue-based colors for the weavers to match. Pictorial weaving was the most prestigious and expensive kind of wall decoration. With murals by the leading painters of the fifteenth century above and Michelangelo circling over all, Raphael must have felt the challenge. The pope had given him the place of honor among the artists in the papal chapel.

The first tapestry in Raphael's series was the **MIRACULOUS DRAFT OF FISHES** on the Sea of Galilee (Matt. 4:18–22). The fisherman Simon, whom Christ called to be his first apostle, Peter, became the cornerstone on which the papal claims to authority rested. Andrew, James, and John would also become apostles. The two boats establish a friezelike composition, and

20–8 | Shop of Pieter van Aelst, Brussels, after cartoons by Raphael and assistants **MIRACULOUS DRAFT OF FISHES**
1515–16. From the nine-piece set, the *Acts of the Apostles* series; lower border, two incidents from the life of Giovanni de' Medici, later Pope Leo X. Woven 1517, installed 1519 in the Sistine Chapel. Wool and silk with silver-gilt wrapped threads, 16'1" × 21' (4.9 × 6.4 m). Musei Vaticani, Pinacoteca, Rome.

Raphael's *Acts of the Apostles* cartoons were used as the models for several sets of tapestries woven in van Aelst's Brussels shop, including one for Francis I of France and another for Henry VIII of England. In 1630, the Flemish painter Peter Paul Rubens (Chapter 22) discovered seven of the ten original cartoons in the home of a van Aelst heir and convinced his patron Charles I of England to buy them. Still part of the British royal collection today, they are exhibited at the Victoria & Albert Museum in London. The original tapestries were stolen during the Sack of Rome in 1527, returned in the 1530s, taken to Paris by Napoleon in 1798, purchased by a private collector in 1808, and returned to the Vatican as a gift that year. They are now displayed in the Raphael Room of the Vatican Painting Gallery.

20–9 | Michelangelo **PIETÀ**
c. 1500. Marble, height 5'8½"
(1.74 m). Saint Peter's, Vatican,
Rome.

the huge straining figures remind us that Raphael felt himself in clear competition with Michelangelo, whose Sistine ceiling had been completed only three years earlier. Raphael studied not only his contemporaries' paintings, but also antique sources in his efforts to achieve both monumentality and realism. For example, he copied the face of Christ from a fifteenth-century bronze copy of an ancient emerald cameo, which at the time was thought to be the true portrait of Jesus. The panoramic landscape behind the fishermen includes a crowd on the shore, and the city of Rome with its walls and churches. The three cranes in the foreground were not a simple pictorial device; in the sixteenth century they symbolized the ever-alert and watchful pope. The cranes proved to be a timely addition. When the tapestries were first displayed in the Sistine Chapel on December 26, 1519, papal authority was already being challenged by reformers like Martin Luther in Germany (see Chapter 21).

MICHELANGELO'S EARLY WORK. Michelangelo Buonarroti (1475–1564) was born in the Tuscan town of Caprese into an impoverished Florentine family that laid claim to nobility: a claim the artist carefully advanced throughout his life. He grew up in Florence, and spent his long career working there and in Rome. At thirteen, he was apprenticed to Ghirlandaio (SEE FIG. 19–36), in whose workshop he learned the rudiments of fresco painting and studied drawings of classical monuments. Soon the talented youth joined the household of Lorenzo the Magnificent, head of the ruling Medici family, where he came into contact with the Neoplatonic philosophers and studied sculpture with Bertoldo di Giovanni, a pupil of Donatello. Bertoldo worked primarily in bronze, and Michelangelo later claimed that he had taught himself to carve marble by studying the Medici collection of classical statues. After Lorenzo died in 1492, Michelangelo traveled to Venice and Bologna, then returned to Florence, where he fell under the spell of the charismatic preacher Fra Girolamo Savonarola (see Chapter 19). The preacher's execution for heresy in 1498 had a traumatic effect on Michelangelo, who said in his old age that he could still hear the sound of Savonarola's voice.

Michelangelo's major early work at the turn of the century was a **pietà** marble sculpture group, commissioned by a French cardinal and installed as a tomb monument in the Vatican basilica of Saint Peter (FIG. 20–9). The pietà—in

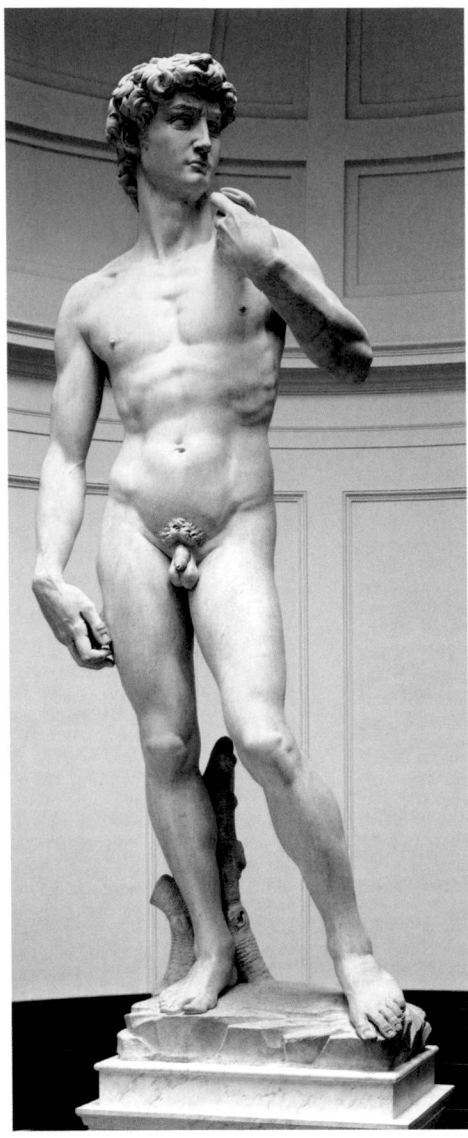

20–10 | Michelangelo **DAVID**
1501–04. Marble, height 17′ (5.18 m) without pedestal. Galleria dell'Accademia, Florence.

Michelangelo's most famous sculpture was cut from an 18-foot-tall marble block. The sculptor began with a small model in wax, then sketched the contours of the figure as they would appear from the front on one face of the marble. Then, according to his friend and biographer Vasari, he chiseled in from the drawn-on surface, as if making a figure in very high relief. The completed statue took four days to move on tree-trunk rollers down the narrow streets of Florence from the premises of the cathedral shop where he worked to its location outside the Palazzo della Signoria (SEE FIG. 17-2). In 1504, the Florentines gilded the tree stump and added a gilded wreath to the head and a belt of twenty-eight gilt-bronze leaves, since removed. In 1873 the statue was replaced by a copy, and the original was moved into the museum of the Florence Academy.

which the Virgin supports and mourns the dead Jesus—had long been popular in northern Europe but was an unusual theme in Italian art at the time. Michelangelo traveled to the marble quarries at Carrara in central Italy himself to select the block from which to make this large work, a practice he was to follow for nearly all of his sculpture. His choice of stone was important, for Michelangelo envisioned the statue as already existing within the marble and needing only to be "set free" from it. Michelangelo was a poet as well as an artist, and later wrote in his Sonnet 15:

"The greatest artist has no conception which a single block of marble does not potentially contain within its mass, but only a hand obedient to the mind can penetrate to this image" (1536–47).

Michelangelo's *Pietà* is a very young Virgin of heroic stature holding the lifeless, smaller body of her grown son. The seeming inconsistencies of age and size are forgotten in contemplating the sweetness of expression, the finely finished surfaces, and the softly modeled forms. Michelangelo's compelling vision of beauty is meant to be seen up close, from directly in front of the statue and on the statue's own level, so that the viewer can look into Jesus's face. The 25-year-old artist is said to have slipped into the church at night to sign the finished sculpture, to answer the many questions about its creator. It is the only signature of Michelangelo's that has not been disputed.

In 1501, Michelangelo accepted a commission for a statue of one of the symbols of Florence, the biblical **DAVID** (FIG. 20–10), to be placed high atop a buttress of the Cathedral. When it was finished in 1504, the David was so admired that the city council instead placed it at eye-level in the square next to the Palazzo Vecchio, the seat of Florence's government. There it stood as a reminder of Florence's republican status, which was briefly reinstated after the expulsion of the powerful Medici oligarchy in 1494. Although, in its muscular nudity, Michelangelo's *David* embodies the athletic ideal of antiquity—particularly of Hellenistic sculptures of Hercules (another symbol of Florence)—the emotional power of its expression and its concentrated gaze is entirely new. Unlike Donatello's bronze *David* (SEE FIG. 19–13), this is not a triumphant hero with the head of the giant Goliath under his feet. Instead, slingshot over his shoulder and a rock in his right hand, Michelangelo's *David* frowns and stares into space, seemingly preparing himself psychologically for the danger ahead, a mere youth confronting a gigantic experienced warrior. Here the male nude implies heroic or even divine qualities, as it did in classical antiquity. Traditionally no match for his opponent in experience, weaponry, or physical strength, Michelangelo's powerful *David* represents the supremacy of right over might—a perfect emblematic figure for the Florentines, who recently had fought the forces of Milan, Siena, and Pisa and still faced political and military pressure.

THE SISTINE CHAPEL. Despite Michelangelo's contractual commitment to the Florence Cathedral for statues of the apostles, in 1505 Pope Julius II, who saw Michelangelo as an ideal collaborator in the artistic aggrandizement of the papacy, arranged for him to come to Rome to work on the spectacular tomb-monument Julius planned for himself. Michelangelo began the new project, but two years later in 1506 the pope put this commission aside and ordered him to paint the **SISTINE CHAPEL CEILING** instead (FIG. 20–11).

Michelangelo considered himself a sculptor, but the strong-minded pope wanted his chapel painted and paid Michelangelo well for the work, which began in 1508. Michelangelo complained bitterly in a sonnet to a friend: "This miserable job has given me a goiter . . . The force of it has jammed my belly up beneath my chin. Beard to the sky . . . Brush splatterings make a pavement of my face . . . I'm not a painter." Despite his physical misery as he stood on a scaffold, painting the ceiling just above him, he achieved the

Sequencing Events
REIGNS OF THE GREAT PAPAL PATRONS OF THE SIXTEENTH CENTURY

1492–1503	Alexander VI (Borgia)
1503–13	Julius II (della Rovere)
1513–21	Leo X (Medici)
1523–34	Clement VII (Medici)
1534–49	Paul III (Farnese)
1585–90	Sixtus V (Peretti)

desired visual effects for viewers standing on the floor far below. His Sistine Chapel ceiling frescoes established a new and extraordinarily powerful style in Renaissance painting.

Julius's initial order for the ceiling was simple: *trompe l'oeil* coffers to replace the original star-spangled blue ceiling. Later he wanted the twelve apostles seated on thrones to be painted in the triangular walls between the lunettes framing the windows. According to Michelangelo, when he objected to the limitations of Julius's plan, the pope told him to paint whatever he liked. This Michelangelo presumably did, although a commission of this importance probably involved an adviser in theology. Certainly it required the pope's approval. Then, as master painter, Michelangelo assembled a team of expert assistants, who probably continued to work with him under close supervision.

In Michelangelo's final composition, illusionistic marble architecture establishes a framework for the figures on the vault of the chapel (FIG. 20–12). Running completely around the ceiling is a painted cornice with projections supported by short pilasters decorated with *putti*. Set within this frame are figures of Old Testament prophets and classical sibyls (female prophets) who were believed to have foretold Jesus's birth. Seated on the fictive cornice are heroic figures of nude young men, called *ignudi* (singular, *ignudo*), holding sashes attached to large gold medallions. Rising behind the *ignudi*, shallow bands of fictive stone span the center of the ceiling and divide it into compartments in which are painted scenes of the Creation, the Fall, and the Flood. The narrative sequence begins over the altar and ends near the chapel entrance (FIG. 20–13). God's earliest acts of creation are therefore closest to the altar, the Creation of Eve at the center of the ceiling, followed by the imperfect actions of humanity: the Temptation, the Fall, the Expulsion from Paradise, and God's eventual destruction of all people except Noah and his family by the Flood. The triangular spandrels contain paintings of the ancestors of Jesus; each is flanked by mirror-image nudes in reclining and seated poses.

According to discoveries during the most recent restoration, Michelangelo worked on the ceiling in two

20–11 | INTERIOR, SISTINE CHAPEL
Vatican, Rome. Built 1475–81; ceiling painted 1508–12; end wall, 1536–41. The ceiling measures
45 × 128′ (13.75 × 39 m).

Named after its builder, Pope Sixtus (Sisto) IV, the chapel is slightly more than 130 feet long and about 143½
feet wide, approximately the same measurements recorded in the Old Testament for the Temple of Solomon.
The floor mosaic was recut from the colored stones used in the floor of an earlier papal chapel. The walls were
painted in fresco between 1481 and 1483 with scenes from the lives of Moses and Jesus by Perugino (SEE FIG.
19-34), Botticelli, Ghirlandaio, and others. Below these are *trompe l'oeil* painted draperies, where Raphael's tapestries illustrating the Acts of the Apostles once hung (SEE FIG. 20-8). Michelangelo's famous ceiling frescoes begin
with the lunette scenes above the windows. On the end above the altar is his *Last Judgment* (SEE FIG. 20-28).

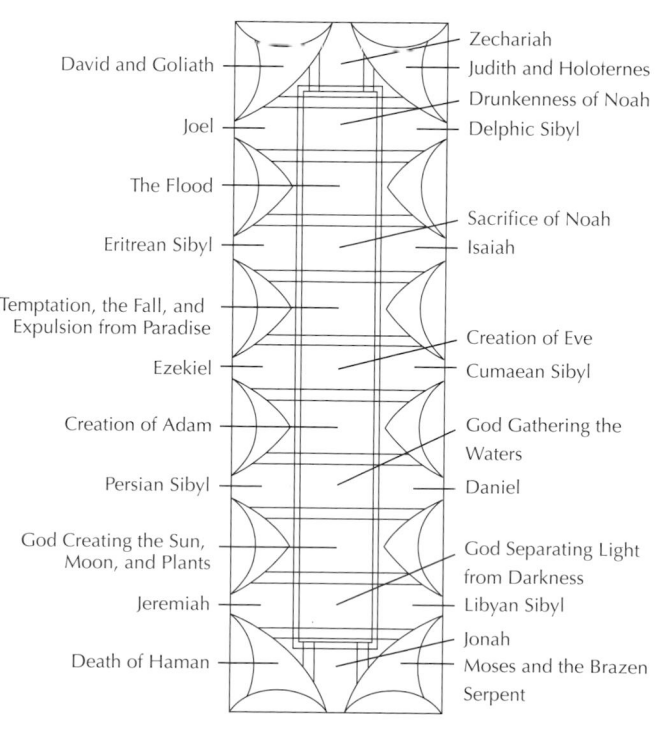

20–12 | Michelangelo
VIEW OF THE SISTINE CHAPEL CEILING FRESCOES
Vatican, Rome. 1508-12. 45′ × 128′
(13.75 × 39 m). Commissioned by Pope Julius II.

	Zechariah
David and Goliath	Judith and Holoternes
	Drunkenness of Noah
Joel	Delphic Sibyl
The Flood	
	Sacrifice of Noah
Eritrean Sibyl	Isaiah
Temptation, the Fall, and Expulsion from Paradise	
	Creation of Eve
Ezekiel	Cumaean Sibyl
Creation of Adam	God Gathering the Waters
Persian Sibyl	Daniel
God Creating the Sun, Moon, and Plants	God Separating Light from Darkness
Jeremiah	Libyan Sibyl
	Jonah
Death of Haman	Moses and the Brazen Serpent

20–13 | **DIAGRAM OF SCENES OF THE SISTINE CHAPEL CEILING**

20–14 | Michelangelo **CREATION OF ADAM, SISTINE CHAPEL CEILING**
1511–12.

The *Creation of Adam,* which opens the second stage of Michelangelo's fresco cycle, has the simplified background and the powerful male figures, and nude youths twisting into contrapposto poses characteristic of this phase of his work. Stylus marks above Adam's head show where the artist transferred his design onto the wet plaster.

stages, beginning in the late summer or fall of 1508 and moving from the chapel's entrance toward the altar, in reverse of the narrative sequence. The first half of the ceiling up to the Creation of Eve was unveiled in August 1511 and the second half in October 1512. His style became broader and the composition simpler as he progressed.

Perhaps the most familiar scene on the ceiling is the **CREATION OF ADAM** (FIG. 20–14). Here Michelangelo depicts the moment when God charges the languorous Adam with the spark of life. As if to echo the biblical text, Adam's

heroic body and pose mirror those of God, in whose image he has been created. Directly below Adam is an *ignudo* grasping a bundle of oak leaves and giant acorns, which refer to Pope Julius's family name (della Rovere, or "of the oak") and possibly also to a passage in the Old Testament prophecy of Isaiah (61:3): "They will be called oaks of justice, planted by the Lord to show his glory."

MICHELANGELO'S LATER SCULPTURE. Michelangelo's first papal sculpture commission, the tomb of Julius II, still incomplete at

Julius's death in 1513, was to plague him and his patrons for forty years. In 1505, he had presented his first designs to the pope for a huge freestanding structure crowned by the pope's sarcophagus and covered with more than forty statues and reliefs in marble and bronze. But Julius had halted the tomb project to divert money toward other ends. After Julius died, his heirs soon began to cut back on the expense and size of the tomb. At this time, between 1513 and 1516, and again from 1542 to 1545, Michelangelo worked on the figure of **MOSES** (FIG. 20–15), the only sculpture from the original design to be incorporated into the final, much-reduced monument to Julius II. No longer an actual tomb—Julius was buried elsewhere—the monument was installed in 1545, after decades of wrangling, in the Church of San Pietro in Vincoli, Rome, where Julius had been the cardinal. In the original design, Moses was to have been one of four seated figures; in the final configuration, however, Moses becomes the focus of the monument and a stand-in for the long-dead pope.

Moses is an inspired figure, a prophet holding the tablets of the Law, which he has just received from God on Mount Sinai. Like the prophets on the Sistine Chapel ceiling, his gigantic muscular figure, swathed in great sheets of drapery, is seated in a restless contrapposto that seems to strain the confines of the niche. Moses's beard is an extraordinary curling, flowing mass that covers his chest. Michelangelo's carving of this beard as it is drawn aside by a finger is a tour de force of marble sculpture.

After the Medici regained power in Florence in 1512, and Leo X succeeded Julius in 1513, Michelangelo became chief architect for Medici family projects at the Church of San Lorenzo in Florence—including a new chapel for the tombs of Lorenzo the Magnificent, his brother Giuliano, and two younger dukes, also named Lorenzo and Giuliano, ordered in 1519. The older men's tombs were never built to Michelangelo's designs, but the unfinished tombs for the younger relatives were placed on opposite side walls of the so-called New Sacristy (FIG. 20–16). The Old Sacristy, by Filippo Brunelleschi, is at the other end of the transept (SEE FIG. 19–3).

In the New Sacristy, each of the two monuments consists of an idealized portrait of the deceased, who turns to face the family's unfinished ancestral tomb. The men are dressed in a sixteenth-century interpretation of classical armor and seated in niches above pseudoclassical sarcophagi. Balanced precariously atop the sarcophagi are male and female figures representing the times of day. Their positions would not seem so unsettling had reclining figures of river gods been installed below them, as originally planned. Giuliano represents the Active Life, and his sarcophagus figures are allegories of Night and Day. Night is accompanied by her symbols: a star and crescent moon on her tiara; poppies, which induce sleep; and an owl under the arch of her leg. The huge mask at her back may allude to Death, since Sleep and Death were said to be the children of Night. Lorenzo, representing the

20–15 | Michelangelo **MOSES**

Tomb of Julius II. 1513–16, 1542–45. Marble, height 7'8½" (2.35 m). Church of San Pietro in Vincoli, Rome.

20-16 Michelangelo **NEW SACRISTY (MEDICI CHAPEL)**
1519-34. Church of San Lorenzo, Florence.

Looking from the altar, we see on the left the tomb of Giuliano de' Medici, with Giuliano seated in the niche and personifications of Day and Night reclining on the pseudo-classical sarcophagus; on the right, the tomb of Lorenzo with the personifications of Dusk and Dawn. Facing the altar is the unfinished tomb of Lorenzo the Magnificent with the "Medici Madonna" in the center and the Medici patron saints, Sts. Cosmas and Damian, at each side.

Contemplative Life, is supported by Dawn and Evening. The allegorical figures for the empty niches that flank the tombs were never carved. The walls of the sacristy are articulated with Brunelleschian *pietra serena* pilasters and architraves in the Corinthian order.

Ongoing political struggles in Florence interrupted Michelangelo's work. In 1534, detested by the new Duke of Florence and fearing for his life, Michelangelo returned to Rome, where he settled permanently. He had left the Medici chapel unfinished. Many years later, in 1545, his students assembled the tomb sculptures, including unfinished figures of the times of day, into the composition we see today. The figures of the dukes are finely finished, but the times of day are notable for their contrasting areas of rough unfinished and polished marble. These are the only unfinished sculptures Michelangelo may have permitted to be put in place, and we do not know what his reasons were. Michelangelo specialists call this his *nonfinito* ("unfinished") quality, suggesting that he had begun to view his artistic creations as symbols of human imperfection. Indeed, Michelangelo's poetry often expressed his belief that humans could achieve perfection only in death. The lack of finish may also reflect his belief that the block of marble held the image prisoner within it. Some of

Michelangelo's unfinished sculptures were placed in the Great Grotto of the Boboli Gardens in Florence (see "The Grotto," right).

Michelangelo's style continued to evolve throughout his career in sculpture, painting, and architecture, and he produced significant works until his death in 1564. We will return to him later in this chapter to examine his further development and his direct influence on artists of the later sixteenth century.

Architecture in Rome and the Vatican

The election of Julius II as pope in 1503 crystallized a resurgence of the papal power. France, Spain, and the Holy Roman Empire all had designs on Italy. The political turmoil that beset Florence, Milan, and other northern cities left Rome as Italy's most active artistic and intellectual center. During the ten years of his reign, Julius fought wars and formed alliances to consolidate his power. And in addition to commissioning large painting programs and sculpture projects, he also enlisted the artists Bramante, Raphael, and Michelangelo as architects to carry out his vision of revitalizing Rome and the Vatican, the pope's residence, as the center of a new Christian art based on classical forms and principles.

Inspired by the achievements of their fifteenth-century predecessors as well as the monuments of antiquity, architects working in Rome created a new ideal classical style typified by the architecture of Bramante. The first-century Roman architect and engineer Vitruvius wrote a treatise on classical architecture (see "The Vitruvian Man," page 665) that became an important source for sixteenth-century Italian architects. Although most commissions were for churches, opportunities also arose to build urban palaces and country villas.

BRAMANTE.   Donato Bramante (1444–1514) was born near Urbino and trained as a painter, but turned to architectural design early in his career. Earlier in this chapter, we saw a church attributed to him, the Church of San Bernardino near Urbino, in the landscape background of Raphael's *Small Cowper Madonna* (SEE FIG. 20–5). About 1481, he became attached to the Sforza court in Milan, where he would have known Leonardo da Vinci. In 1499, Bramante settled in Rome, but work came slowly. The architect was nearing sixty when, according to a dedicatory inscription, the Spanish rulers Queen Isabella and King Ferdinand commissioned a small shrine over the spot in Rome where the apostle Peter was believed to have been crucified (FIG. 20–17). In this tiny building, known as the TEMPIETTO ("Little Temple"), Bramante combined his interpretation of the principles of Vitruvius and the fifteenth-century architect Leon Battista Alberti, from the stepped base to the Doric columns and frieze (Vitruvius had advised that the Doric order be used for temples to gods of particularly forceful character) to the elegant balustrade. The centralized plan and the tall drum, or

Elements of Architecture
THE GROTTO

Of all the enchanting features of Renaissance gardens, none is more intriguing than a *grotto*, a recess typically constructed of irregular stones and shells and covered with fictive foliage and slime to suggest a natural cave. The fancifully decorated grotto usually included a spring, pool, fountain, or other waterworks. Sculpture of earth giants might support its walls, and depictions of nymphs might suggest the source of the water that nourished the garden. Great Renaissance gardens had at least one grotto where one could commune with nymphs and Muses and escape the summer heat. Alberti recommended that the contrived grotto be covered "with green wax, in imitation of mossy Slime which we always see in moist grottoes" (Alberti, *On Architecture*, 9.4).

The Great Grotto of the Boboli Gardens of the Pitti Palace in Florence, designed by Bernardo Buontalenti in 1583 and constructed in 1587-93, contained four marble captives (originally conceived for the tomb of Pope Julius II) carved by Michelangelo and, in its inner cave, a 1592 copy of *Astronomy* (or *Venus Urania* by Giovanni da Bologna (SEE FIG. 20–41). Flowing water operated fountains, hydraulic organs, and other devices, such as mechanical birds that fluttered their wings and chirped or sang, filling the grotto with noise, if not music. Water jets concealed in the floor, stairs, or crevasses in the rockwork could be turned on by the owner to drench his guests, to the great amusement of all.

Bernardo Buontalenti   **THE GREAT GROTTO, BOBOLI GARDENS, PITTI PALACE, FLORENCE**
1583-93. Sculpture by Michelangelo.

20–17 | Donato Bramante **TEMPIETTO, CHURCH OF SAN PIETRO IN MONTORIO**
Rome. 1502–10; dome and lantern were restored in the 17th century.

20–18 | Antonio da Sangallo the Younger and Michelangelo
PALAZZO FARNESE, ROME
1517–50. When Sangallo died in 1546, Michelangelo added the third floor and cornice.

circular wall, supporting a hemispheric dome recall early Christian shrines built over martyrs' relics, as well as ancient Roman circular temples. Especially notable is the sculptural effect of the building's exterior, with its deep wall niches creating contrasts of light and shadow, and the Doric frieze of carved papal emblems. Bramante's design called for a circular cloister around the church, but the cloister was never built.

Shortly after Julius II's election as pope, he commissioned Bramante to renovate the Vatican Palace. Julius also appointed him chief architect of a project to replace Saint Peter's Basilica (see "Saint Peter's Basilica," right).

THE ROMAN PALACE. Sixteenth-century Rome was more than a city of churches and public monuments. Wealthy families, many of whom had connections with the pope or the cardinals—the "princes of the church"—commissioned architects to design residences to enhance their prestige. For example, Cardinal Alessandro Farnese (who became Pope Paul III in 1534) set Antonio da Sangallo the Younger (1484–1546) the task of rebuilding the **PALAZZO FARNESE** into the largest, finest palace in Rome (FIG. 20–18). The main façade of the great rectangular building faces a public square—which was created by tearing down blocks of

houses. The massive central door is emphasized by elaborate rusticated stonework (as are the building's corners, where the shaped stones are known as **quoins**) and is surmounted by a balcony suitable for ceremonial appearances, over which is set the **cartouche** (a decorative plaque) with the Farnese coat of arms—lilies. The palace's three stories are clearly defined by two horizontal bands of stonework, or stringcourses. Windows are treated differently on each story: on the ground floor, the twelve windows sit on supporting brackets. The story directly above is known in Italy as the *piano nobile*, or first floor (Americans would call it the second floor), which contains large and richly decorated reception rooms. Its twelve windows are decorated with alternating triangular and arched pediments supported by pairs of engaged half-columns in the Corinthian order. The second floor (or American third floor) has windows all with triangular pediments whose supporting Ionic half columns are set on brackets echoing those under the windows on the ground floor. At the back, a loggia overlooks a garden and the Tiber River. Annibale Carracci painted the loggia in 1597–1601 (SEE FIG. 22–13). When Sangallo died, the pope turned work on the palace over to Michelangelo, who added focus to the building by emphasizing the portal and gave it added dignity by increasing the height of the top story, capping the building with a magnificent cornice.

Great patrons of the arts were also great collectors of antiquities, none greater than Farnese, and none more generous to artists wanting to study. The Farnese *Hercules* stood in the courtyard, to impress visitors with the extensive collection of antiquities—and the erudition—of the owner (Figs. 23, 24, Introduction). Imagine walking into the Farnese Palace; then identify with the two "tourists" who come upon the colossal figure. The Farnese *Hercules,* along with the *Laocoön* and other discoveries by sixteenth-century art excavators, created new

Elements of Architecture
SAINT PETER'S BASILICA

The history of Saint Peter's in Rome is an interesting case of the effects of individual and institutional demands on the practical congregational needs of a major religious building. The original church, now referred to as Old Saint Peter's, was built in the fourth century CE by Constantine, the first Christian Roman emperor, to mark the grave of the apostle Peter, the first bishop of Rome and therefore the first pope. Because the site was considered the holiest in Europe, Constantine's architect had to build a structure large enough to house Saint Peter's tomb and to accommodate the crowds of pilgrims who came to visit it. To provide a platform for the church, a huge terrace was cut into the side of the Vatican Hill, across the Tiber River from the city. Here Constantine's architect erected a basilica, with a new feature, a transept, to allow large numbers of visitors to approach the shrine at the front of the apse. The rest of the church was, in effect, a covered cemetery, carpeted with the tombs of believers who wanted to be buried near the apostle's grave. When it was built, Constantine's basilica, as befitted an imperial commission, was one of the largest buildings in the world (interior length 368 feet; width 190 feet), and for more than a thousand years it was the most important pilgrim shrine in Europe.

In 1506, Pope Julius II made the astonishing decision to demolish the Constantinian basilica, which had fallen into disrepair, and to replace it with a new building. That anyone, even a pope, had the nerve to pull down such a venerated building is an indication of the extraordinary sense of assurance of the age—and of Julius himself. To design and build the new church, the pope appointed Donato Bramante. Bramante envisioned the new Saint Peter's as a central-plan building, in this case a Greek cross (with four arms of equal length) crowned by an enormous dome. This design was intended to continue the tradition of domed and round *martyria* (martyrs' shrines). In Renaissance thinking, the central plan and dome symbolized the perfection of God.

The deaths of pope and architect in 1513 and 1514 put a temporary halt to the project. Successive plans by Raphael, Antonio da Sangallo, and others changed the Greek cross to a Latin cross (with three shorter arms and one long one) to provide the church with a full-length nave. However, when Michelangelo was appointed architect in 1546, he returned to the Greek-cross plan. Michelangelo simplified Bramante's design to create a single, unified space covered with a hemispherical dome. The dome was finally completed some years after Michelangelo's death by Giacomo della Porta, who retained Michelangelo's basic design but gave the dome a taller profile (SEE FIG. 20–29).

During the Counter-Reformation, the Church emphasized congregational worship, so more space was needed to house the congregation and allow for processions. To expand the church—and to make it more closely resemble Old Saint Peter's—Pope Paul V in 1606 commissioned the architect Carlo Maderno to change Michelangelo's Greek-cross plan to a Latin-cross plan. Maderno extended the nave to its final length of slightly more than 636 feet and added a new façade, thus completing Saint Peter's as it is today. Later in the seventeenth century, the sculptor and architect Gianlorenzo Bernini changed the approach to the basilica by creating an enormous piazza. In the twentieth century a wide avenue was built joining the piazza and the Tiber River.

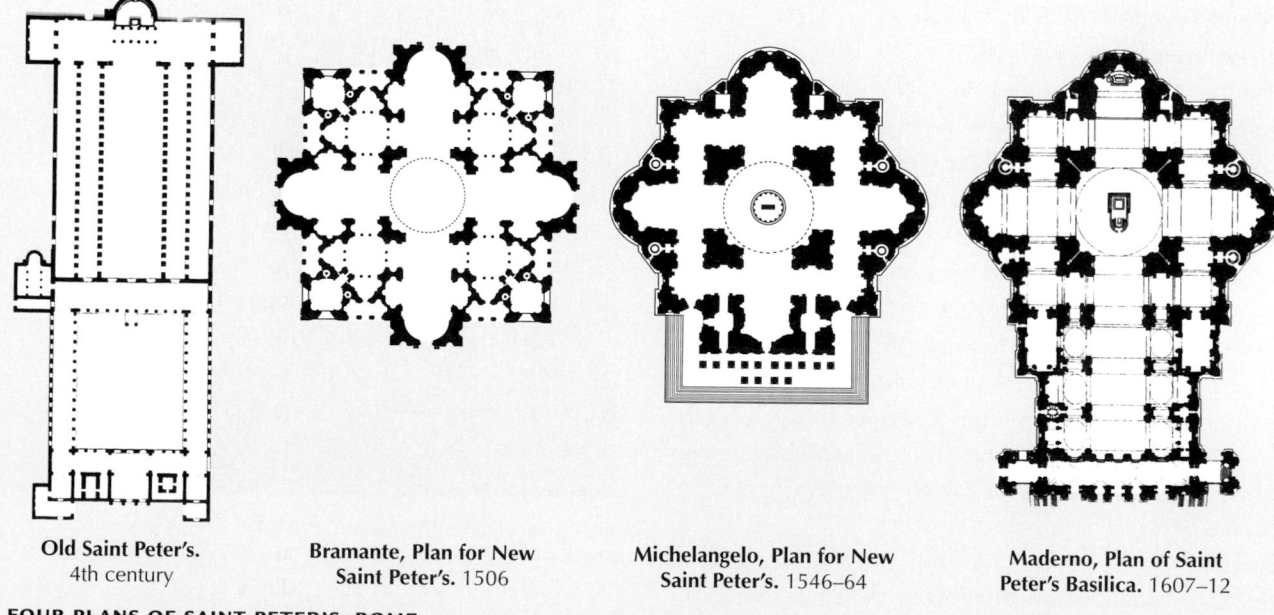

Old Saint Peter's.
4th century

Bramante, Plan for New Saint Peter's. 1506

Michelangelo, Plan for New Saint Peter's. 1546–64

Maderno, Plan of Saint Peter's Basilica. 1607–12

FOUR PLANS OF SAINT PETER'S, ROME

ideals for the contemporary artists. Like our two gentlemen, once having seen these extraordinary muscle men their view of art would be forever changed. Who could return to the bony figure of Jan van Eyck's Adam?

Architecture and Painting in Northern Italy

While Rome ranked as Italy's preeminent arts center at the beginning of the sixteenth century, wealthy and powerful families elsewhere in Italy also patronized the arts and letters, just as the Montefeltro had in Urbino and the Gonzaga had in Mantua during the fifteenth century. Their architects created fanciful structures and their painters developed a new colorful, illusionistic style—witty, elegant, and finely executed art designed to appeal to the jaded taste of the intellectual elite of Mantua, Parma, and Venice.

GIULIO ROMANO. In Mantua, Federigo II Gonzaga (ruled 1519–40) continued the family tradition of patronage when in 1524 he lured a Roman architect and follower of Raphael, Giulio Romano (c. 1499–1546), to Mantua to build a pleasure palace. The **PALAZZO DEL TÈ** (FIG. 20–19) is not "serious" architecture and was never meant to be. Giulio Romano devoted more space in his design to gardens, pools, and stables than he did to rooms for living—and partying. Federigo and his erudite friends would have known classical orders and proportions so well that they could appreciate this travesty of classical ideals—visual jokes such as lintels masquerading as arches and dropped triglyphs. The building itself is skillfully constructed. Later architects and scholars have studied the palace, with its sophisticated humor and exquisite craft, as a precursor to Mannerism or as Mannerist itself (see page 692).

Giulio Romano continued his witty play on the classics in the decoration of the two principal rooms. One, dedicated to the loves of the gods, depicted the marriage of Cupid and Psyche. The other room is a remarkable feat of *trompe l'oeil* painting in which the entire building seems to be collapsing about the viewer as the gods defeat the giants (FIG. 20–20). Here, Giulio Romano accepted the challenge Andrea Mantegna had laid down in the Camera Picta of the Gonzaga palace (SEE FIG. 19–33), painted for Federigo's grandfather. Like the building itself, the mural paintings display brilliant craft in the service of lighthearted, even superficial, goals: to distract, amuse, and enchant the viewer.

CORREGGIO. At about the same time that Giulio Romano was building and decorating the Palazzo del Tè in Mantua, in nearby Parma an equally skillful master, Correggio, was creating just as theatrical effects through dramatic foreshortening in the Parma Cathedral dome. In his brief but prolific career, Correggio (Antonio Allegri, c. 1489–1534) produced most of his work for patrons in Parma and Mantua. Correggio's great work, the **ASSUMPTION OF THE VIRGIN** (FIG. 20–21),

20–19 | Giulio Romano **COURTYARD FAÇADE, PALAZZO DEL TÈ, MANTUA**
1527-34.

20–20 | Giulio Romano **FALL OF THE GIANTS**
Fresco in the Sala dei Giganti, Palazzo del Tè. 1530-32.

a fresco painted between 1526 and 1530 in the dome of Parma Cathedral, distantly recalls the illusionism of Mantegna's ceiling in the Gonzaga palace. But Leonardo da Vinci also clearly inspired Correggio's use of softly modeled forms,

20–21 | Correggio **ASSUMPTION OF THE VIRGIN**
Fresco in main dome, interior, Parma Cathedral, Italy. c. 1526–30. Diameter of base of dome approx. 36′ (11 m).

spotlighting effects of illumination, and a slightly hazy over-all appearance (*sfumato*). Correggio also assimilated Raphael's idealism into his personal style. In the *Assumption*, Correggio created a dazzling illusion: The architecture of the dome seems to dissolve and the forms seem to explode through the building, drawing the viewer up into the swirling vortex of saints and angels who rush upward, amid billowing clouds, to accompany the Virgin as she soars into heaven. Correggio's painting of the sensuous flesh and clinging draperies of the figures contrasts with the spirituality of the theme (the Virgin's miraculous transport to heaven at the moment of her death). The viewer's strongest impression is of a powerful, spiraling upward motion of alternating cool clouds and warm, sensuous figures. Illusionistic painting directly derived from this work became a hallmark of ceiling decoration in Italy in the following century.

20–22 | Properzia de' Rossi
JOSEPH AND POTIPHAR'S WIFE
San Petronio, Bologna. 1525-26. Marble, 1'9" × 1'11"
(54 × 58 cm). Museo de S. Petronio, Bologna.

PROPERZIA DE' ROSSI. Very few women had the opportunity or inclination to become sculptors. Properzia de' Rossi (c. 1490–1529/30), who lived in Bologna, was an exception. She mastered many arts, including engraving, and was famous for her miniature carvings, including an entire Last Supper carved on a peach pit! She carved several pieces in marble—two sibyls, two angels, and this relief of **JOSEPH AND POTIPHAR'S WIFE**—for the cathedral of San Petronio in Bologna (**FIG. 20–22**). The contemporary historian Vasari wrote that a rival male sculptor prevented her from being paid fairly and from getting more commissions. This particular relief, according to Vasari, was inspired by her own love for a young man, which she got over by carving this panel. Joseph escapes, running, as the partially clad seductress snatches at his cloak. Properzia is the only woman Vasari includes in the 1550 edition of the *Lives*.

Venice and the Veneto

In the sixteenth century the Venetians did not see themselves as rivals of Florence and Rome, but rather as superiors. Their city was the greatest commercial sea power of the Mediterranean; they had challenged Byzantium and now they confronted the Muslim Turks. Favored by their unique geographical situation—protected by water and controlling sea routes in the Adriatic Sea and the eastern Mediterranean—the Venetians became wealthy and secure patrons of the arts. Their Byzantine heritage, preserved by their natural conservatism, encouraged an art of rich patterned surfaces emphasizing light and color.

The idealized style and oil painting technique initiated by the Bellini family in the late fifteenth century (see Chapter 19) were developed further by sixteenth-century painters in Venice and the Veneto region, the part of northeastern Italy ruled by Venice. Venetians were the first Italians to use oils for painting on both wood panel and canvas. Possibly because they were a seafaring people accustomed to working with large sheets of canvas, and possibly because of humidity problems in their walls, the Venetians were also the first to use large canvas paintings instead of frescoes. Because oils dried slowly, errors could be corrected and changes made easily during the work. The flexibility of the canvas support, coupled with the radiance and depth of oil-suspended color pigments, eventually made oil painting an almost universally preferred medium. Oil paint was particularly suited to the rich color and lighting effects employed by Giorgione and Titian, two of the city's major painters of the sixteenth century. (Two others, Veronese and Tintoretto, will be discussed later in this chapter.)

GIORGIONE. The career of Giorgione (Giorgio da Castelfranco, c. 1475–1510) was brief—he died from the plague—and most scholars accept only four or five paintings as entirely by his hand. Nevertheless, his importance to Venetian painting is critical, as he introduced new, enigmatic pastoral themes, known as *poesie* (or painted poems), that were inspired by the contemporary literary revival of ancient pastoral poetry. He is significant for his sensuous nude figures, and, above all, an appreciation of nature in his landscape painting. His early life and training are undocumented, but his work suggests that he studied with Giovanni Bellini. Perhaps Leonardo da Vinci's subtle lighting system and mysterious, intensely observed landscapes also inspired him.

Giorgione's most famous work, called today **THE TEMPEST** (**FIG. 20–23**), was painted shortly before his death. It is an example of the imaginative and sensual (rather than historical and intellectual) aspects of the *poesie*. Simply trying to understand what is happening in the picture piques our interest. At the right, a woman is seated on the ground, nude except for the end of a long white cloth thrown over her shoulders. Her nudity seems maternal rather than erotic as she nurses the baby at her side. Across the dark, rock-edged spring stands a man wearing the uniform of a German mercenary soldier. His head is turned toward the woman, but he appears to have paused for a moment before continuing to turn toward the viewer. X-rays of the painting show that Giorgione altered his composition while he was still at work on it—the soldier replaces a second woman. Inexplicably, a spring gushes forth between the figures to feed a lake surrounded by

20–23 | Giorgione **THE TEMPEST**
c. 1506. Oil on canvas, 32 × 28¾″ (82 × 73 cm). Galleria dell'Accademia, Venice.

The subject of this enigmatic picture preoccupied twentieth-century art historians, many of whom came up with well-reasoned possible solutions to the mystery. However, the painting's subject seems not to have particularly intrigued sixteenth-century observers, one of whom described it in 1530 simply as a small landscape in a storm with a gypsy woman and a soldier.

substantial houses, and in the far distance a bolt of lightning splits the darkening sky. Indeed, the artist's attention seems focused on the landscape and the unruly elements of nature rather than on the figures. By making the landscape central to the composition, Giorgione gave nature an importance that is new in Western painting.

Although he may have painted *The Tempest* for purely personal reasons, most of Giorgione's known works were of traditional subjects, produced on commission for clients: portraits, altarpieces, and paintings on the exteriors of Venetian buildings. When commissioned in 1507 to paint the exterior of the Fondaco dei Tedeschi, the warehouse and offices of German merchants in Venice, Giorgione hired Titian (Tiziano Vecellio, c. 1489–1576) as an assistant. For the next three years, before Giorgione's untimely death, the two artists' careers were closely bound together.

20–24 | Titian
THE PASTORAL CONCERT OR ALLEGORY ON THE INVENTION OF PASTORAL POETRY
c. 1510. Oil on canvas, 41¼ × 54¾" (105 × 136.5 cm). Musée du Louvre, Paris.

The painting known as **THE PASTORAL CONCERT** (FIG. 20–24) has been attributed to both Giorgione and Titian, although today scholarly opinion favors Titian. As in Giorgione's *The Tempest*, the idyllic, fertile landscape, here bathed in golden, hazy late-afternoon sunlight, seems to be the true subject of the painting. In this mythic world, two men—an aristocratic musician in rich red silks and a barefoot, singing peasant in homespun cloth—turn toward each other, ignoring the two women in front of them. One woman plays a pipe and the other pours water into a well, oblivious of the swaths of white drapery sliding to the ground that enhance rather than hide their nudity. Are they the musicians' muses? Behind the figures the sunlight illuminates another shepherd and his animals near lush woodland. The painting evokes a mood, a golden age of love and innocence recalled in ancient Roman pastoral poetry. In fact, the painting is now interpreted as an allegory on the invention of poetry. *The Pastoral Concert* had a profound influence on later painters—even into the nineteenth century, when Édouard Manet (SEE FIG. 30–49) reinterpreted it.

TITIAN. Everything about Titian's early life is obscure, including his birth, probably about 1489. He supposedly began an apprenticeship as a mosaicist, then studied painting under Gentile and Giovanni Bellini (see page 654). He was about 20 when he began work with Giorgione, and whatever Titian's early work had been, he had completely absorbed Giorgione's style by the time Giorgione died two years later. Titian completed paintings that they had worked on together, and when Giovanni Bellini died in 1516, Titian became the official painter to the Republic of Venice.

In 1519, Jacopo Pesaro, commander of the papal fleet that had defeated the Turks in 1502, commissioned Titian to commemorate the victory in a votive altarpiece for a side-aisle chapel in the Franciscan Church of Santa Maria Gloriosa dei Frari in Venice. Titian worked on the painting for seven years and changed the concept three times before he finally came up with a revolutionary composition—one that complemented the viewer's approach from the left: He created an asymmetrical setting of huge columns on high bases soaring right out of the frame (FIG. 20–25). Into this architectural setting, he placed the Virgin and Child on a high throne at one side and arranged saints and the Pesaro family at the sides and below on a diagonal axis, crossing at the central figure of Saint Peter (a reminder of Jacopo's role as head of the papal forces in 1502). The red of Francesco Pesaro's brocade garment and of the banner diagonally across sets up a contrast of primary colors against Saint Peter's blue tunic and yellow mantle and the red and blue draperies of the Virgin. Saint Maurice (behind Jacopo at the left) holds the banner with the coat of arms of the pope, and a cowering Turkish captive reminds the viewer of the Christian victory. Light floods in from above, illuminating not only the faces, but also the great columns, where *putti* in the clouds carry a cross. Titian was famous for his mastery of light and color even in his own day, but this altarpiece demonstrates that he also could draw and model as solidly as any Florentine. The composition, perfectly balanced but built on diagonals instead of a vertical and horizontal grid, looks forward to the art of the seventeenth century.

20–25 | Titian **PESARO MADONNA**
1519–26. Oil on canvas, 16′ × 8′10″ (4.9 × 2.7 m). Side-aisle altarpiece, Santa Maria Gloriosa dei Frari, Venice.

In 1529, Titian, who was well-known outside Venice, began a long professional relationship with Emperor Charles V, who vowed to let no one else paint his portrait. Charles ennobled Titian in 1533. The next year Titian was commissioned to paint a portrait of Isabella d'Este (see "Women Patrons of the Arts," page 688). Isabella was past 60 when Titian portrayed her in 1534–36, but she asked to appear as she had in her twenties. A true magician of portraiture, Titian was able to satisfy her wish by referring to an early portrait by another artist while also conveying the mature Isabella's strength, self-confidence, and energy.

No photograph can convey the vibrancy of Titian's paint surfaces, which he built up in layers of pure colors, chiefly red, white, yellow, and black. A recent scientific study of Titian's paintings revealed that he ground his pigments much finer than had earlier wood-panel painters. The complicated process by which he produced many of his works began with a charcoal drawing on the prime coat of lead white that was used to seal the pores and smooth the surface of the rather coarse Venetian canvas. The artist then built up the forms with fine glazes of different colors, sometimes in as many as ten to fifteen layers. Titian and others had the

20–26 | Titian **VENUS OF URBINO**
c. 1538. Oil on canvas, 3'11" × 5'5" (1.19 × 1.65 m). Galleria degli Uffizi, Florence.

advantage of working in Venice, the first place to have professional retail "color sellers." These merchants produced a wide range of specially prepared pigments, even mixing their oil paints with ground glass to increase its glowing transparency. Not until the second half of the sixteenth century did color sellers open their shops in other cities.

According to a contemporary, Titian could make "an excellent figure appear in four brushstrokes." His technique was admirably suited to the creation of female nudes, whose flesh seems to glow with an incandescent light. Paintings of nude reclining women became especially popular in sophisticated court circles, where male patrons could enjoy and appreciate the "Venuses" under the cloak of respectable classical mythology. Typical of such paintings is the Venus Titian painted about 1538 for the Duke of Urbino (FIG. 20–26). The sensuous quality of this work suggests that Titian was as inspired by flesh-and-blood beauty as by any source from mythology or the history of art. Here, a beautiful Venetian courtesan—whose gestures seem deliberately provocative—

stretches languidly on her couch in a spacious palace, white sheets and pillows setting off her glowing flesh and golden hair. A spaniel, symbolic of fidelity, sleeping at her feet and maids assembling her clothing in the background lend a comfortable domestic air. The **VENUS OF URBINO** inspired artists as distant in time as Manet (SEE FIG. 30–50).

Over the course of his lengthy career, Titian continued to explore art's expressive potential. In his late work he sought the essence of the form and idea, not the surface perfection of his youthful works. Beset by failing eyesight and a trembling hand, Titian left the **PIETÀ** he was painting for his tomb unfinished at his death in 1576 (FIG. 20–27). Against a monumental arched niche, the Virgin mourns her son. Titian painted himself as Saint Jerome kneeling before Christ. The figures emerge out of darkness, their forms defined by the broken brushstrokes that activate the dynamic diagonal of the composition. Titian, like Michelangelo, outlived the classical phase of the Renaissance and his new style profoundly influenced Italian art of the later years of the sixteenth century.

20—27 | Titian (finished by Palma Giovane) **PIETÀ**
c. 1570–76. Oil on canvas, 11′6″ × 12′9″ (3.5 × 3.9 m). Galleria dell'Accademia, Venice.

ART AND THE COUNTER-REFORMATION

Pope Clement VII, whose miscalculations had spurred Emperor Charles V to attack and destroy Rome in 1527, also misjudged the threat to the Church and to papal authority posed by the Protestant Reformation. His failure to address the issues raised by the reformers enabled the movement to spread. His successor, the rich and worldly Roman noble Alessandro Farnese, who was elected Pope Paul III (papacy 1534–49), was the first pope to grapple directly with the rise of Protestantism and vigorously pursue Church reform. In 1536, he appointed a commission to investigate charges of corruption within the Church. He convened the Council of Trent (1545–63) to define Catholic dogma, initiate disciplinary reforms, and regulate the training of clerics.

Pope Paul III also addressed Protestantism through repression and censorship. In 1542, he instituted the Inquisition, a papal office that sought out heretics for interrogation, trial, and sentencing. The enforcement of religious unity extended to the arts. Traditional images of Christ and the saints continued to be used to inspire and educate, but art was scrutinized for traces of heresy and profanity. Guidelines issued by the Council of Trent limited what could be represented in Christian art and led to the destruction of some works. At the same time, art became a powerful weapon of propaganda, especially in the hands of members of the Society of Jesus, a new religious order

Art and Its Context

WOMEN PATRONS OF THE ARTS

In the sixteenth century, many wealthy women, from both the aristocracy and the merchant class, were enthusiastic patrons of the arts. The Habsburg princesses Margaret of Austria and Mary of Hungary presided over brilliant humanist courts. The Marchesa of Mantua, Isabella d'Este (1474–1539), became a patron of painters, musicians, composers, writers, and literary scholars. Married to Francesco II Gonzaga at age 15, she had great beauty, great wealth, and a brilliant mind that made her a successful diplomat and administrator. A true Renaissance woman, her motto was the epitome of rational thinking—"Neither through Hope nor Fear." An avid collector of manuscripts and books, she sponsored the publication of an edition of Virgil while still in her twenties. She also collected ancient art and objects, as well as works by contemporary Italian artists such as Mantegna, Leonardo, Perugino, Correggio, and Titian. Her study in the Mantuan palace was a veritable museum for her collections. The walls above the storage and display cabinets were painted in fresco by Mantegna, and the carved wood ceiling was covered with mottoes and visual references to Isabella's impressive literary interests.

Titian **ISABELLA D'ESTE**
1534–36. Oil on canvas, 40⅛ × 25³⁄₁₆" (102 × 64.1 cm). Kunsthistorisches Museum, Vienna.

founded by the Spanish nobleman Ignatius of Loyola (1491–1556) and confirmed by Paul III in 1540. The Jesuits, dedicated to piety, education, and missionary work, spread worldwide from Il Gesù, their headquarters church in Rome (SEE FIG. 20–31). They came to lead the Counter-Reformation movement and the revival of the Catholic Church.

The Reformation and Counter-Reformation inspired the papacy to promote the Church's preeminence by undertaking an extensive program of building and art commissions. Under such patronage, religious art of the Italian late Renaissance flourished in the second half of the sixteenth century.

Art and Architecture in Rome and the Vatican

To restore the heart of the city of Rome, Paul III began rebuilding the Capitoline Hill as well as continuing work on Saint Peter's. His commissions include some of the finest art and architecture of the late Italian Renaissance. His first major commission brought Michelangelo, after a quarter of a century, to the Sistine Chapel.

MICHELANGELO'S LATE WORK. In his early sixties, Michelangelo complained bitterly of feeling old, but he nonetheless began the important and demanding task of painting the **LAST JUDGMENT** on the 48-foot-high end wall above the chapel altar (FIG. 20–28).

Abandoning the clearly organized medieval conception of the Last Judgment, in which the saved are neatly separated from the damned, Michelangelo painted a writhing swarm of rising and falling humanity. At the left (the right side of Christ), the dead are dragged from their graves and pushed up into a vortex of figures around Christ, who wields his arm like a sword of justice. The shrinking Virgin represents a change from Gothic tradition, where she sat enthroned beside, and equal in size to, her son. To the right of Christ's feet is Saint Bartholomew, who in legend was martyred by being skinned alive. He holds his flayed skin, the face of which may be painted with Michelangelo's own distorted features. Despite the efforts of several saints to save them at the last minute, the rejected souls are plunged toward hell on the right, leaving the elect and still-unjudged in a dazed, almost uncomprehending state. On the lowest level of the mural is the gaping, fiery entrance to hell, toward which Charon, the ferryman of the dead to the underworld, propels his craft. Conservative clergy criticized the painting for its nudity, and after Michelangelo's death they ordered bits of drapery to be added. The painting was long interpreted as a grim and constant reminder to the celebrants of the Mass—the pope and his cardinals—that ultimately they would be judged for their deeds. However, the brilliant colors revealed by recent cleaning contrast with the grim message.

Another of Paul III's ambitions was to complete the new Saint Peter's, a project that had been under way for forty years (see "Saint Peter's Basilica," page 679). Michelangelo was well

20—28 | Michelangelo **LAST JUDGMENT, SISTINE CHAPEL**
1536–41 (cleaning finished 1994). Fresco, 48 × 44′(14.6 × 13.4 m).

Dark, rectangular patches left by the restorers (visible, for example, in the upper left and right corners) contrast with the vibrant colors of the chapel's frescoes. These dark areas show just how dirty the walls had become over the centuries before their recent cleaning.

20–29 | Michelangelo **SAINT PETER'S BASILICA, VATICAN**
c. 1546-64; dome completed 1590 by Giacomo della Porta;
lantern 1590-93. View from the west.

height, narrowing its segmental bands, and changing the shape of its openings.

Michelangelo—often described by his contemporaries as difficult and even arrogant—alternated between periods of depression and frenzied activity. Yet he was devoted to his friends and helpful to young artists. He believed that his art was divinely inspired; later in life, he became deeply absorbed in religion and dedicated himself to religious works.

Michelangelo's last days were occupied by an unfinished sculpture now known, from the name of a modern owner, as the **RONDANINI PIETÀ** (FIG. 20–30). The *Rondanini Pietà* is the final artistic expression of a lonely, disillusioned, and physically debilitated man who struggled to end his life as he had lived it—working. In his youth, the stone had released the *Pietà* in Saint Peter's as a perfect, exquisitely finished work (SEE FIG. 20–9), but this block resisted his best efforts to shape it. He was still working on the sculpture six days before his death. The ongoing struggle between artist and medium is nowhere more apparent than in this moving example of Michelangelo's *nonfinito* creations. In his late work, Michelangelo subverted Renaissance ideals of human perfectability and denied his own youthful idealism, uncovering new forms that mirrored the tensions in Europe during the second half of the sixteenth century.

20–30 | Michelangelo **PIETÀ (KNOWN AS THE RONDANINI PIETÀ)**
1559-64. Marble, height 5'3⅜" (1.61 m). Castello Sforzesco, Milan. Intended for his own tomb.

Shortly before his death in 1564, Michelangelo resumed work on this sculpture group, which he had begun some years earlier. He cut down the massive figure of Jesus, merging the figure's now elongated form with that of the Virgin, who seems to carry her dead son upward toward heaven.

aware of the work done by his predecessors—from Bramante to Raphael to Antonio da Sangallo the Younger. The 71-year-old sculptor, confident of his architectural expertise, demanded the right to deal directly with the pope, rather than through a committee of construction deputies. Michelangelo further shocked the deputies—but not the pope—by tearing down or canceling parts of Sangallo's design and returning to Bramante's central plan, long associated with Christian martyr shrines. Although seventeenth-century additions and renovations dramatically changed the original plan of the church and the appearance of its interior, Michelangelo's **SAINT PETER'S BASILICA** (FIG. 20–29) still can be seen in the contrasting forms of the flat and angled walls and the three **hemicycles** (semicircular structures), in which colossal pilasters, blind windows (having no openings), and niches form the sanctuary of the church. The level above the heavy entablature was later given windows of a different shape. The dome that was erected by Giacomo della Porta in 1588–90 retains Michelangelo's basic design: a segmented dome with regularly spaced openings, resting on a high drum with pedimented windows between paired columns, and surmounted by a tall lantern reminiscent of Bramante's Tempietto (SEE FIG. 20–17). Della Porta's major changes were raising the dome

The elderly artist Michelangelo, like Titian, secure in the techniques gained over decades of masterful craft, could abandon the knowledge of a lifetime as he attempted to express ultimate truths through art. In his late work, he discovered new stylistic directions that would inspire succeeding generations of artists.

VIGNOLA. Michelangelo alone could not satisfy the demand for architects. One young artist who helped meet the need for new churches was Giacomo Barozzi (1507–73), known as Vignola after his native town. He worked in Rome in the late 1530s surveying ancient Roman monuments and providing illustrations for an edition of Vitruvius. From 1541 to 1543 he was in France with Francesco Primaticcio at the Château of Fontainebleau (see Chapter 21). After returning to Rome, he secured the patronage of the Farnese family.

Vignola profited from the Counter-Reformation program of church building. The Church's new emphasis on individual, emotional participation brought a focus on sermons and music. It also required churches to have wide naves and unobstructed views of the altar instead of the complex interiors of medieval and earlier Renaissance churches. Ignatius of Loyola was determined to build the Jesuit headquarters church in Rome under these precepts, although he did not live to see his church finished (**FIG. 20–31**). The cornerstone was laid in 1540, but construction of the **CHURCH OF IL GESÙ** did not begin until 1568, as the Jesuits had to raise considerable funds. Cardinal Alessandro Farnese (Paul III's namesake and grandson) donated funds to the project in 1561 and selected Vignola as architect. After Vignola died in 1573, Giacomo della Porta finished the dome and façade.

Il Gesù was admirably suited for its congregational purpose. Vignola designed a wide, barrel-vaulted nave, shallow connected side chapels but not aisles, and short transepts that

20–31 | Giacomo della Porta **FAÇADE OF THE CHURCH OF IL GESÙ, ROME**
c. 1573-84.

did not extend beyond the line of the outer walls—enabling all worshipers to gather in the central space. A single huge apse and dome over the crossing (**FIG. 20–32**) directed their attention to the altar. The building fit compactly into the city block—a requirement that now often overrode the desire to orient a church along an east-west axis. The façade design emphasized the central portal with classical pilasters, engaged

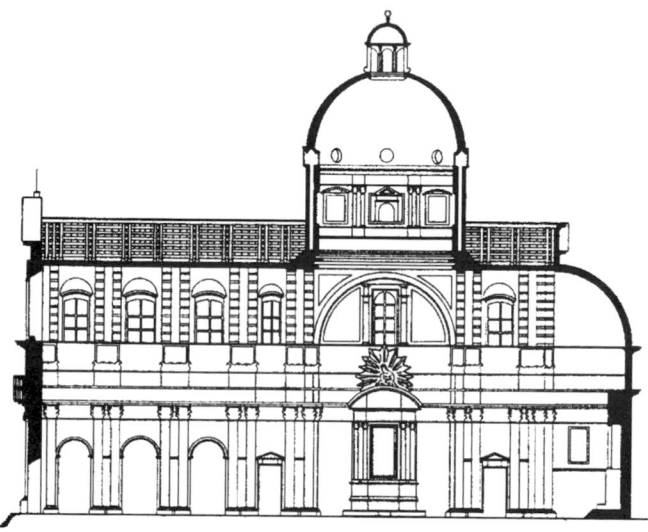

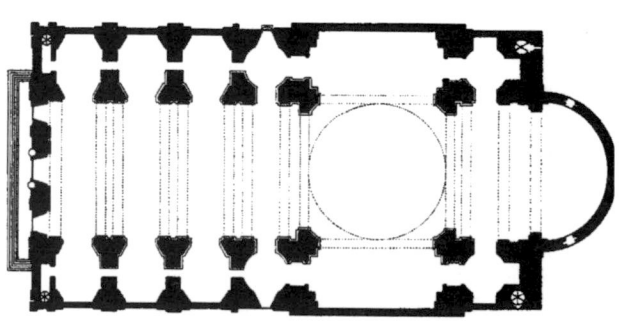

20–32 | Giacomo da Vignola **PLAN AND SECTION OF THE CHURCH OF IL GESÙ, ROME**
Cornestone laid in 1540; Project begun in 1550; Giacomo da Vignola's design begun in 1563; building begun in 1568; completed by Giacomo della Porta in 1584.

20–33 | **CAPPONI CHAPEL, CHURCH OF SANTA FELICITÀ, FLORENCE**
Chapel by Filippo Brunelleschi for the Barbadori family, 1419–23; acquired by the Capponi family, who ordered paintings by Pontormo, 1525–28.

One of the few surviving early Mannerist interiors—fresco, stained-glass window, and altarpiece in an early Renaissance structure.

columns and pediments, and volutes scrolling out to hide the buttresses of the central vault and to link the tall central section with the lower sides.

As finally built by Giacomo della Porta, the design, in its verticality and centrality, would have significant influence on church design well into the next century. The façade abandoned the early Renaissance grid of classical pilasters and entablatures for a two-story design of paired colossal order columns that reflected and tied together the two stories of the nave elevation. Each of these stories was further subdivided by moldings, niches, and windows. The entrance of the church, with its central portal and tall window, became the focus of the composition. Pediments at every level break into the level above, leading the eye upward to the cartouches

with coats of arms. Both Cardinal Farnese, the patron, and the Jesuits (whose arms entail the initials IHS, the monogram of Christ) are commemorated here on the façade.

MANNERISM

A word that has inspired controversy—sometimes even rancorous debate—among historians of Italian art is *Mannerism*. The term comes from the Italian word *maniera*, used in the sixteenth century to suggest self-aware elegance and grace to the point of artifice. When modern critics began to use the term, some defined it as a style opposed to the principles of High Renaissance art; others treated it as an historical period in art between the early sixteenth-century High Renais-

20–34 | Pontormo **ENTOMBMENT**
1525-28. Oil and tempera on wood panel, 10′3″ × 6′4″
(3.1 × 1.9 m). Altarpiece in Capponi Chapel, Church of Santa
Felicità, Florence.

unfathomable secondary scenes. Mannerist artists admired the great artists of the earlier generation, and the late styles of Michelangelo and Titian also became a source of inspiration.

Elements of Mannerism, stimulated and supported by aristocratic, sophisticated, and courtly patrons, began to appear in Florence and Rome at the height of the High Renaissance around 1510. The term has been interpreted as an artistic expression of the unsettled political and religious conditions in Europe. Furthermore, a formal relationship between new art styles and aesthetic theories began to appear at this time—especially the elevation of "grace" as an ideal.

Painting

Examples of early Mannerism are the frescoes and altarpieces painted between 1525 and 1528 by Jacopo da Pontormo (1494–1557) for the hundred-year-old **CAPPONI CHAPEL** in the Church of Santa Felicità in Florence (FIG. 20–33). Open on two sides, the chapel forms an interior loggia. The altarpiece depicts the **ENTOMBMENT** (FIG. 20–34), and frescoes depict the Annunciation. The Virgin accepts the angel's message, but the juxtaposition with the altarpiece also seems to present her with a vision of her future sorrow, as she sees her son's body lowered from the cross. Pontormo's ambiguous composition in the altarpiece enhances the visionary quality of the painting. The bare ground and cloudy sky give little sense of physical location. Some figures press into the viewer's space, while others seem to levitate or stand on the smooth boulders. Pontormo chose a moment just after Jesus's removal from the cross, when the youths who have lowered him have paused to regain their hold. The emotional atmosphere of the scene is expressed in the odd poses, and drastic shifts in scale, but perhaps most poignantly in the use of secondary colors and colors shot through with contrasting colors, like iridescent silks. The palette is predominantly blue and pink with accents of olive green, gray, scarlet, and creamy white. The overall tone of the picture is set by the color treatment of the crouching youth, whose skintight bright pink shirt is shaded in iridescent, pale gray-green.

sance and the seventeenth-century Baroque. Today many critics would like to drop the term altogether, but it has entered the standard art historical vocabulary. Certainly one can agree that different styles existed at the same time in sixteenth-century Italy.

Today, in the visual arts, Mannerism has come to mean intellectually intricate subjects, highly skilled techniques, and art concerned with beauty for its own sake. Mannerism is an attitude, a point of view, as much as a "style." Certain characteristics do occur regularly: extraordinary virtuosity; intricate compositions; sophisticated, elegant figures; and fearless manipulations or distortions of accepted formal conventions. Some artists and patrons favored obscure, unsettling, and often erotic imagery; unusual colors and juxtapositions; and

20–35 | Parmigianino **MADONNA WITH THE LONG NECK**
1534-40. Oil on wood panel, 7'1" × 4'4"
(2.16 × 1.32 m). Galleria degli Uffizi, Florence.

PARMIGIANINO. Parmigianino (Francesco Mazzola, 1503–40) created equally intriguing variations on the classical style. Until he left his native Parma in 1524 for Rome, the strongest influence on his work had been Correggio. In Rome, Parmigianino met Giulio Romano, and he also studied the work of Raphael and Michelangelo. He assimilated what he saw into a distinctive style of Mannerism, calm but strangely unsettling. After the Sack of Rome in 1527, he moved to Bologna and then back to Parma.

Left unfinished at the time of his early death is a painting known as the **MADONNA WITH THE LONG NECK** (FIG. 20–35). The elongated figure of the Madonna, whose massive legs and lower torso contrast with her narrow shoulders and long neck and fingers, resembles the large metal vase inexplicably being carried by the youth at the left. The sleeping Christ Child recalls the pose of the pietà, and in the background Saint Jerome unrolls a scroll beside tall white columns that

have no more substance than theater sets in the middle distance. Like Pontormo, Parmigianino presents a well-known image in a manner calculated to unsettle viewers. The painting challenges the viewer's intellect while it exerts its strange appeal to aesthetic sensibility.

BRONZINO. Agnolo di Cosimo (1503–72), whose nickname of "Bronzino" means "Copper-colored" (just as we might call someone "Red"), was born near Florence. About 1522, he became Pontormo's assistant. (He probably helped with the tondos in the corners of the Capponi Chapel.) In 1530, he established his own workshop, though he continued to work occasionally with Pontormo on large projects. In 1540, Bronzino became the court painter to the Medici. Although he was a versatile artist who produced altarpieces, fresco decorations, and tapestry designs over his long career, he is best known today for his courtly portraits. Bronzino's virtuosity in rendering costumes and settings creates a rather cold and formal effect, but the self-contained demeanor of his subjects admirably conveys their haughty personalities. The **PORTRAIT**

20–36 | Bronzino **PORTRAIT OF A YOUNG MAN**
c. 1540-45. Oil on wood panel, 37½ × 29½"
(95.5 × 74.9 cm). The Metropolitan Museum of Art, New York.
The H. O. Havemeyer Collection (29.100.16).

OF A YOUNG MAN (FIG. 20–36) demonstrates Bronzino's characteristic portrayal of his subjects as intelligent, aloof, elegant, and self-assured. The youth toys with a book, suggesting his scholarly interests, but his walleyed stare creates a slightly unsettling effect and seems to associate his portrait with the carved masks surrounding him.

Bronzino's **ALLEGORY WITH VENUS AND CUPID**, one of the strangest paintings in the sixteenth century, contains all the formal, iconographical, and psychological characteristics of Mannerist art (FIG. 20–37). The painting could stand alone as a summary of the period. Seven figures, two masks, and a dove interweave in an intricate formal composition pressed breathlessly into the foreground plane. Taken as individual images, they display the apparent ease of execution and grace of form, ideal perfection of surface and delicacy of color that characterize Mannerist art. Together they become a disturbingly erotic and inexplicable composition.

The painting defies easy explanation for it is one of the complex allegories that delighted the sophisticated courtiers who enjoyed equally esoteric wordplay and classical references. Nothing is quite what it seems. Venus and her son Cupid engage in lascivious dalliance, encouraged by a *putto* representing Folly, Jest, or Playfulness, who is about to throw pink roses at them. Cupid kisses his mother and squeezes her breast and nipple while Venus lifts up an arrow from Cupid's quiver, leading some scholars to suggest that the painting's title should be "*Venus Disarming Cupid*." Venus holds the golden apple of discord given to her by Paris; her dove seems to support Cupid's feet, while a pair of ugly red masks lying at her feet reiterates the theme of duplicity. An old man, Time or Chronos, assisted by an outraged Truth, pulls back a curtain to expose the couple. Lurking just behind Venus a monstrous serpent with a lion's legs and claws and the head of a beautiful young girl crosses her hands to hold a honeycomb and scorpion's stinger. She has been called Inconstancy and Fraud but also Pleasure. In the shadows a screaming head tears its hair—if female, she is Jealousy or Envy, but if male, he would be Pain. The complexity of the painting and the

20–38 | Giulio Clovio (Jura Klovic, born in Croatia) **THE FARNESE HOURS: ADORATION OF THE MAGI AND THE MEETING OF SOLOMON AND THE QUEEN OF SHEBA**
1546. Vellum, each folio 6 × 4″ (17.3 × 11 cm). The Pierpont Morgan Library, New York.
M69 fl 380-3912

possibilities for multiple meanings are typical of the games enjoyed by sixteenth-century intellectuals. Perhaps the allegory tells of the impossibility of constant love and the folly of lovers, which will become apparent in time. But perhaps it is an allegory on sin and a condemnation of vice. In any event, Duke Cosimo ordered the painting himself, and he presented it to King Francis I of France.

Manuscripts and Miniatures

THE FARNESE HOURS. In spite of the increasing use of the printing press (see Chapter 19), luxury manuscripts continued to be made by hand. **THE FARNESE HOURS,** a book of hours commissioned by Cardinal Alessandro Farnese from Guilio Clovio (1498–1578), is a masterpiece among Italian Renaissance manuscripts (**FIG. 20–38**). The colophon (at the end of the manuscript) dates it at 1546, and the contemporary historian Giorgio Vasari wrote that Giulio worked for nine years painting the miniatures. Vasari perceptively calls him a "new, if small, Michelangelo." Small indeed, each page measures only 7 by 4 inches, but the paintings encompass every aspect of Mannerist art—the "serpentine figures" in graceful poses and the elongated proportions so noticeable in the nudes support the frames and the extraordinarily elongated figures in the narra-

tives. Brilliant colors combine with pale atmospheric space. The Old Testament supports the New, in a way typical of medieval manuscripts. Thus the Queen of Sheba's visit and homage to Solomon prefigures the Magi's journey with gifts for the Christ Child. King Solomon has the features of the patron, Cardinal Farnese, and beside him is a dwarf in painter's clothes making a typical sixteenth-century visual pun—he is a small man, a "miniature" painter.

ANGUISSOLA. Northern Italy, more than any other part of the peninsula, produced a number of gifted women artists. Sofonisba Anguissola (c. 1532–1625), born into a noble family in Cremona, was unusual as a woman artist in that she was not the daughter of an artist. Her father gave all his children a humanistic education and encouraged them to pursue careers in literature, music, and especially painting. He consulted Michelangelo about Sofonisba's artistic talents in 1557, asking for a drawing that she might copy and return to be critiqued. Michelangelo evidently obliged because Sofonisba Anguissola's father wrote an enthusiastic letter of thanks.

Anguissola was also skilled at miniatures and portraits, an important kind of painting in the sixteenth century, when people had few means of recording a lover, friend, or family

member's features. Anguissola painted herself holding a medallion, the border of which spells out her name and home town, Cremona (FIG. 20–39). Such visual and verbal games delighted sixteenth-century viewers. The interlaced letters at the center of the medallion are a riddle; they seem to form a monogram with the first letters of her sisters' names: Minerva, Europa, Elena. Such names are further evidence of the Anguissola family's enthusiasm for the classics.

Contemporaries especially admired Sofonisba Anguissola's self-portraits. One wrote that he liked to show off her painting as "two marvels, one the work, the other the artist" (quoted in Hartt/Wilkins, page 629). In 1560, Anguissola accepted the invitation of the queen of Spain to become a lady-in-waiting and court painter, a post she held for twenty years. In a 1582 Spanish inventory, Anguissola is described as "an excellent painter of portraits above all the painters of this time"—extraordinary praise in a court that patronized Titian.

CELLINI. The Florentine goldsmith and sculptor Benvenuto Cellini (1500–71), who wrote a dramatic—and scandalous—autobiography and a practical handbook for artists, worked in the French court at Fontainebleau, where he made the famous **SALTCELLAR OF KING FRANCIS I** (FIG. 20–40)—a table accessory transformed into an elegant sculptural ornament by fanciful imagery and superb execution. In gold and enamel, the Roman sea god Neptune, representing the source of salt, sits next to a tiny boat-shaped container that carries the seasoning, while a personification of Earth guards the plant-derived

20–39 | Sofonisba Anguissola **SELF-PORTRAIT**
c. 1552. Oil on parchment on cardboard, 2½ × 3¼″ (6.4 ×8.3 cm). Museum of Fine Arts, Boston.
Emma F. Munroe Fund (60.155)

20–40 | Benvenuto Cellini **SALTCELLAR OF KING FRANCIS I OF FRANCE**
1540–43. Gold and enamel, 10½ × 13⅛″ (26.67 × 33.34 cm). Kunsthistorisches Museum, Vienna.

20–41 | Giovanni da Bologna (Giambologna)
ASTRONOMY, or VENUS URANIA
c. 1573. Bronze gilt, height 15¼" (38.8 cm). Kunsthistorisches Museum, Vienna.

pepper, contained in the triumphal arch to her right. Representations of the seasons and the times of day on the base refer to both daily meal schedules and festive seasonal celebrations. The two main figures, their poses mirroring each other with one bent and one straight leg, lean away from each other at impossible angles yet are connected and visually balanced by glances and gestures. Their supple, elongated bodies and small heads reflect the Mannerist conventions of artists like Parmigianino. Cellini wrote, "I represented the Sea and the Land, both seated, with their legs intertwined just as some branches of the sea run into the land and the land juts into the sea. . ." (quoted in Hartt/Wilkins, page 669).

Late Mannerism

In the second half of the sixteenth century, probably the most influential sculptor in Italy was Jean de Boulogne, better known by his Italian name, Giovanni da Bologna or Giambologna (1529–1608). Born in Flanders, he settled by 1557 in Florence, where both the Medici family and the sizable Netherlandish community there were his patrons. He not only influenced a later generation of Italian sculptors, he also spread the Mannerist style to the north through artists who came to study his work. Although inspired by Michelangelo, Giovanni was more concerned with graceful forms and poses, as in his gilded-bronze **ASTRONOMY**, or **VENUS URANIA** (**FIG. 20–41**) of about 1573. The figure's identity is suggested by the astronomical device on the base of the plinth. Designed with a classical prototype of Venus in mind, the sculptor twisted Venus's upper torso and arms to the far right and extended her neck in the opposite direction so that her chin was over her right shoulder, straining the limits of the human body. Consequently, Giambologna's statuette may be seen from any viewpoint. The elaborate coiffure of tight ringlets and the detailed engraving of drapery texture contrast strikingly with the smooth, gleaming flesh of Venus's body. Following the common practice for cast-metal sculpture, Giambologna replicated this statuette several times for different patrons.

The northern Italian city of Bologna was especially hospitable to accomplished women. In the latter half of the sixteenth century it boasted of some two dozen women painters and sculptors, as well as a number of women scholars who lectured at the university. There, Lavinia Fontana (1552–1614) learned to paint from her father. By the 1570s, her success was so well rewarded that her husband, the painter Gian Paolo Zappi, gave up his own painting career to care for their large family and help his wife with the technical aspects of her work, such as framing. In 1603 Fontana moved to Rome as an official painter to the papal court. She also soon came to the attention of the Habsburgs, who became major patrons of her work.

While still in her twenties, Fontana painted the **NOLI ME TANGERE** (**FIG. 20–42**), illustrating the biblical story of Christ

20–42 | Lavinia Fontana **NOLI ME TANGERE**
1581. Oil on canvas, 47⅞ × 36⅝″ (120.3 × 93 cm).
Galleria degli Uffizi, Florence.

revealing himself before his Ascension to Mary Magdalen and warning her not to touch him (John 20:17). Christ's costume refers to the passage in the Gospel of John that tells us that Mary Magdalen at first thought Christ was the gardener.

Christ steps forward like a classical god—but dressed in a short tunic and wearing a gardener's hat. His graceful gesture echoes that of the Magdalen. In the middle distance a second confrontation is taking place: the earlier meeting of the women with the angel at the empty tomb. Like a medieval artist, Fontana ignores the sequence of earthly time and contrasts the large foreground figures with the tiny figures at the tomb, creating a striking plunge into depth. This unsettling spatial and temporal disconnect is a typical Mannerist conceit.

LATER SIXTEENTH-CENTURY ART IN VENICE AND THE VENETO

By the second half of the sixteenth century, Venice ruled supreme as "Queen of the Adriatic." Her power was not, however, unchallenged, and the Turks remained a threat to commerce. In 1571, allied with Spain and the pope, the Christian fleet with Venetian ships defeated the Turkish fleet at the Battle of Lepanto and so established Christian power for future generations. Victorious and wealthy Venetians entered on a lavish lifestyle, building palaces and villas, which they hung with lush oil paintings. The *Triumph of Venice* (see Fig. 12, Introduction), commissioned by the city government from the artist Veronese for the Hall of the Great Council in the Doge's palace, captures the splendor of Venice.

Oil Painting

Rather than the cool, formal, technical perfection sought by the Mannerists, painters in Venice expanded upon the techniques initiated there by Giorgione and Titian, concerning themselves above all with color, light, and expressively loose brushwork.

VERONESE. Paolo Caliari (1528–88) took his nickname—"Veronese"—from his hometown, Verona, but he worked mainly in Venice. His paintings are nearly synonymous today with the popular image of Venice as a splendid city of

THE ◉BJECT SPEAKS

VERONESE IS CALLED BEFORE THE INQUISITION

Jesus among his disciples at the Last Supper was an image that spoke powerfully to believers during the sixteenth century. So it was not unusual when, in 1573, the highly esteemed painter Veronese revealed an enormous canvas that seemed at first glance to depict this scene. The Church officials of Venice were shocked and offended by the impiety of placing near Jesus a host of extremely unsavory characters. Veronese was called before the Inquisition to explain his painting.

Venice, July 18, 1573. The minutes of the session of the Inquisition Tribunal of Saturday, the 18th of July, 1573. . . .*

Q: What picture is this of which you have spoken?

A: This is a picture of the Last Supper that Jesus Christ took with His apostles in the house of Simon . . .

Q: At this supper of Our Lord have you painted other figures?

A: Yes, milords.

Q: Tell us how many people and describe the gestures of each.

(Veronese describes the painting.)

Q: What is the significance of those armed men dressed as Germans, each with a halberd in his hand?

A: We painters take the same license the poets and the jesters take and I have represented these two halberdiers, one drinking and the other eating nearby on the stairs. They are placed there so that they might be of service because it seemed to me fitting, according to what I have been told, that the master of the house, who was great and rich, should have such servants.

Q: And that man dressed as a buffoon with a parrot on his wrist, for what purpose did you paint him on that canvas?

A: For ornament, as is customary . . .

Q: Who do you really believe was present at that Supper?

A: I believe one would find Christ with His Apostles. But if in a picture there is some space to spare I enrich it with figures according to the stories.

Q: Did anyone commission you to paint Germans, buffoons, and similar things in that picture?

A: No, milords, but I received the commission to decorate the picture as I saw fit. It is large and, it seemed to me, it could hold many figures.

Q: Are not the decorations which you painters are accustomed to add to paintings or pictures supposed to be suitable and proper to the subject and the principal figures or are they for pleasure—simply what comes to your imagination without any discretion or judiciousness?

A: I paint pictures as I see fit and as well as my talent permits.

Q: Does it seem fitting at the Last Supper of the Lord to paint buffoons, drunkards, Germans, dwarfs, and similar vulgarities?

A: No, milords . . .

(The questions continue in this vein.)

The judges decreed that Veronese must change the painting within three months or be liable to penalties. Veronese changed the picture's title so that it referred to another banquet, given by the tax collector Levi. The "buffoons, drunkards . . . and similar vulgarities" remained, and Veronese noted his new source—Luke 5—on the balustrade. That Gospel reads that "Levi gave a great banquet for him [Jesus] in his house, and a large crowd of tax collectors and others were at table with them" (Luke 5:29). In changing the declared subject of the painting, Veronese also had modest revenge on the Inquisitors: When Jesus was criticized for associating with such people, he replied, "I have not come to call the righteous to repentance but sinners" (Luke 5:32).

* E. G. Holt, *Literary Sources of Art History.* Princeton, NJ: Princeton University Press, 1947. pp. 245–48.

Veronese **FEAST IN THE HOUSE OF LEVI**
From the refectory of the Dominican Monastery of Santi Giovanni e Paolo, Venice. 1573. Oil on canvas, 18'3" × 42' (5.56 × 12.8 m). Galleria dell'Accademia, Venice.

20–43 | Tintoretto **THE LAST SUPPER**
1592–94. Oil on canvas, 12′ × 18′8″ (3.7 × 5.7 m). Church of San Giorgio Maggiore, Venice.

Tintoretto, who had a large workshop, often developed a composition by creating a small-scale model like a miniature stage set, which he populated with wax figures. He then adjusted the positions of the figures and the lighting until he was satisfied with the entire scene. Using a grid of horizontal and vertical threads placed in front of this model, he could easily sketch the composition onto squared paper for his assistants to copy onto a large canvas. His assistants also primed the canvas, blocking in the areas of dark and light, before the artist himself, free to concentrate on the most difficult passages, finished the painting. This efficient working method allowed Tintoretto to produce a large number of paintings in all sizes.

pleasure and pageantry sustained by a nominally republican government and great mercantile wealth. Veronese's elaborate architectural settings and costumes, still lifes, anecdotal vignettes, and other everyday details, often unconnected with the main subject, proved immensely appealing to Venetian patrons. His vision of the glorious Venice reached an apogee in the ceiling of the council chamber in the ducal palace (Fig. 12, Introduction).

Veronese's most famous work is a Last Supper that he renamed **FEAST IN THE HOUSE OF LEVI** (see opposite), painted in 1573 for the Dominican Monastery of Santi Giovanni e Paolo. At first glance, the subject of the painting seems to be architecture and only secondarily Christ seated at the table. An enormous loggia framed by colossal triumphal arches and reached by balustraded stairs symbolizes Levi's house. Beyond the loggia an imaginary city of white marble gleams. Within this grand setting, realistic figures in splendid costumes assume exaggerated, theatrical poses. The huge size of the painting

allowed Veronese to include the sort of anecdotal vignettes beloved by the Venetians—the parrots, monkeys, and Germans—but detested by the Church's Inquisitors, who saw in them profane undertones.

TINTORETTO. Another Venetian master, Jacopo Robusti (1518–94), called "Tintoretto" ("Little Dyer," because his father was a dyer), worked in a style that developed from, and exaggerated, the techniques of Titian, in whose shop he reportedly apprenticed. Tintoretto's goal, declared on a sign in his studio, was to combine Titian's color with the drawing of Michelangelo. Like Veronese, Tintoretto often received commissions to decorate huge interior spaces. He painted **THE LAST SUPPER** (FIG. 20–43) for the choir of the Church of San Giorgio Maggiore, a building designed by Palladio (SEE FIG. 20–44). Comparison with Leonardo da Vinci's painting of almost a century earlier is instructive (see Figs. 20–2 and fig. 18, Introduction). Instead of Leonardo's closed

20–44 | Palladio **CHURCH OF SAN GIORGIO MAGGIORE, VENICE**
Plan 1565; construction 1565–80; façade, 1597–1610; campanile 1791.
Finished by Vincenzo Scamozzi following Palladio's design.

and logical space with massive figures reacting in individual ways to Jesus's statement, Tintoretto's view is from a corner, with the vanishing point on a high horizon line at the far right side. The table, coffered ceiling, and inlaid floor all seem to plunge dramatically into the distance. The figures, although still large bodies modeled by flowing draperies, turn and move in a continuous serpentine line that unites apostles, servants, and angels. Tintoretto used two light sources: one real, the other supernatural. Light streams from the oil lamp flaring dangerously over the near end of the table; angels seem to swirl out from the flame and smoke. A second light emanates from Jesus himself and is repeated in the glow of the apostles' halos. The mood of intense spirituality is enhanced by deep colors flashed with bright highlights, as well as by the elongated figures—treatments that reflect both the Byzantine art of Venice and the Mannerist aesthetic. The still lifes on the tables and the homey detail of a cat and basket emphasize the reality of the viewers' experience. At the same time, the deep chiaroscuro and brilliant dazzling lights catching forms in near-total darkness enhance the convincingly otherworldly atmosphere. The

interpretation of *The Last Supper* also has changed—unlike Leonardo's more secular emphasis on personal betrayal, Tintoretto has returned to the religious institution of the Eucharist: Jesus offers bread and wine, a model for the priest administering the sacraments at the altar next to the painting.

The speed with which Tintoretto drew and painted was the subject of comment in his own time, and the brilliance and immediacy so admired today (his slashing brushwork was fully appreciated by the gestural painters of the twentieth century) were derided as evidence of carelessness. His rapid production may be attributed to the efficiency of his working methods: Tintoretto had a large workshop of assistants and he usually provided only the original conception, the beginning drawings, and the final brilliant touches on the finished painting. Tintoretto's workshop included members of his family—of his eight children, four became artists. His oldest daughter, Marietta Robusti, worked with him as a portrait painter, and two or perhaps three of his sons also joined the shop. So skillfully did Marietta capture her father's style and technique that today art historians cannot identify her work in the shop.

20–45 NAVE, CHURCH OF SAN GIORGIO MAGGIORE, VENICE
Begun 1566. Tintoretto's *Last Supper* (not visible) hangs to the left of the altar.

Architecture: Palladio

Just as Veronese and Tintoretto expanded upon the rich Venetian tradition of oil painting established by Giorgione and Titian, Andrea Palladio dominated architecture during the second half of the century by expanding upon principles of Alberti and of ancient Roman architecture. His work—whether a villa, palace, or church—was characterized by harmonious symmetry and a rejection of ornamentation. Over the years, Palladio became involved in several publishing ventures, including a guide to Roman antiquities, an illustrated edition of Vitruvius, and books on architecture that for centuries would be valuable resources for architectural design.

Born Andrea di Pietro della Gondola (1508–80), probably in Padua, Palladio began his career as a stonecutter. After moving to Vicenza, he was hired by the nobleman, humanist scholar, and amateur architect Giangiorgio Trissino. Trissino gave him the nickname "Palladio" for the Greek goddess of wisdom, Pallas Athena, and the fourth-century Roman writer Palladius. Palladio learned Latin at Trissino's small academy and accompanied his benefactor on three trips to Rome, where he made drawings of Roman monuments.

SAN GIORGIO MAGGIORE. By 1559, when he settled in Venice, Palladio was one of the foremost architects of Italy. In 1565, he undertook a major architectural commission: the monastery CHURCH OF SAN GIORGIO MAGGIORE (FIG. 20–44). His design for the Renaissance façade to the traditional basilica-plan elevation—a wide lower level fronting the nave and side aisles surmounted by a narrower front for the nave clerestory—is ingenious. Inspired by Alberti's solution for Sant'Andrea in Mantua (SEE FIG. 19–31), Palladio created the illusion of two temple fronts of different heights and widths, one set inside the other. At the center, colossal columns on high pedestals, or bases, support an entablature and pediment that front the narrower clerestory level of the church. The lower temple front, which covers the triple-aisle width and slanted side-aisle roofs, consists of pilasters supporting an entablature and pediment running behind the columns of the taller clerestory front. Palladio retained Alberti's motif of the triumphal-arch entrance. Although the façade was not built until after the architect's death, his original design was followed.

The interior of San Giorgio (FIG. 20–45) is a fine example of Palladio's harmoniously balanced geometry, expressed here in strong verticals and powerful arcs. The tall engaged columns and shorter pairs of pilasters of the nave arcade echo the two levels of orders on the façade, thus unifying the building's exterior and interior.

THE VILLA ROTONDA. Palladio's versatility can best be seen in numerous villas built early in his career. In the 1560s, he started his most famous and influential villa just outside Vicenza (FIGS. 20–46, 20–47). Although traditionally villas were working farms, Palladio designed this one as a retreat for relaxation (a party house). To afford views of the countryside on each face of the building, he placed a porch, with four columns, arched openings in the walls, and a wide staircase. The main living quarters are on this second level, as is usual in European palace architecture, and the lower level is reserved for the kitchen, storage, and other utility rooms. Upon its completion in 1569, the villa was dubbed the **VILLA ROTONDA** because it had been inspired by another round hall, the Roman Pantheon. After its purchase in 1591 by the Capra family, it became known as the Villa Capra. The villa's plan shows the geometric clarity of Palladio's conception: a circle inscribed in a small square inside a larger square, with symmetrical rectangular compartments and identical rectangular projections from each of its faces. The use of a central dome on a domestic building was a daring innovation that effectively secularized the dome. The Villa Rotonda was the first of what was to become a long tradition of domed country houses, particularly in England and the United States.

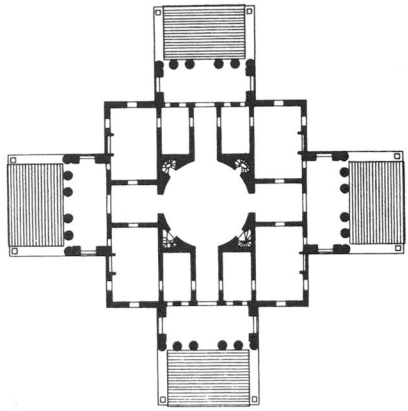

20–46 | **PLAN OF THE VILLA ROTONDA**
c. 1550.

Palladio was a scholar and an architectural theorist as well as a designer of buildings. His books on architecture provided ideal plans for country estates, using proportions derived from ancient Roman structures. Despite their theoretical bent, his writings were often more practical than earlier treatises. Perhaps his early experience as a stonemason provided him with the knowledge and self-confidence to approach technical problems and discuss them as clearly as he did theories of ideal proportion and uses of the classical orders. By the eighteenth century, Palladio's *Four Books of Architecture* had been included in the library of most educated people. Thomas Jefferson had one of the first copies in America.

IN PERSPECTIVE

In spite of ongoing struggles between the Holy Roman emperor and the pope, and in spite of the scandals beginning to envelop the Church, the early sixteenth century emerged as a golden age for the arts. As sixteenth-century artists built on the past, they carried the investigation of nature, classics, and humanistic learning further than their fifteenth-century predecessors. Art went beyond realism to idealism. Artists not only reproduced the surface appearances, they sought underlying forms. In painting a figure, for example, their study of anatomy had to be more than skin deep; their knowledge of the skeletal and muscular structure of the human body was on display, and the observation of a face led to the study of a personality. The ideal of the dignity of all human beings as creatures made by God, expounded by the philosophers and forcefully elucidated in Michelangelo's paintings in the Sistine Chapel, informed the art of this period.

As classicists, their fascination with the tangible remains of ancient Rome—inscriptions, fragments of architecture and sculpture—turned into full-scale archaeological excavation and the discovery of major pagan artworks such as the *Laocoön*. Like the ancient Greeks (whose sculpture they knew only in Roman copies), the Italian painters of the High Renaissance sought perfection. They, too, developed an ideal canon of proportions and a kind of spiritual geometry that underlies their painting and sculpture. This classical equilibrium in the arts, balancing physical and spiritual forces, proved to be fleeting.

By 1530 change was in the air, and an anticlassical style emerged in works of art that later critics defined as "Mannerist." A high level of technical skill could be assumed and was used to achieve dazzling displays of grace, elegance, and "manner." As complex in their compositions as they were in their subjects, the Mannerist artworks stimulate an uneasy imagination, and today they often defy analysis or explication. Social institutions might be crumbling but artists, secure in their technical achievements and admired by their patrons, continued to paint, carve, and build.

20–47 | Palladio
VILLA ROTONDA (VILLA CAPRA), VICENZA
Italy. Begun, 1560s.

MICHELANGELO
DAVID
1501–4

GIULIO ROMANO
COURTYARD FAÇADE , PALAZZO DEL TÈ, MANTUA
1527–34

BENVENUTO CELLINI
**OF KING FRANCIS I
OF FRANCE**
1540–43

SOFONISBA ANGUISSOLA
SELF PORTRAIT
C. 1552

TINTORETTO
THE LAST SUPPER
1592–94

1500

1520

1540

1560

1580

1600

SIXTEENTH-CENTURY ART IN ITALY

◄ **Luther Officially Protests Church's Sale of Indulgences** 1517

◄ **Charles V Holy Roman Emperor** 1519–56

◄ **Charles V Orders Sack of Rome** 1527

◄ **Jesuit Order Confirmed** 1540

◄ **Pope Paul III Institutes Inquisition** 1542

◄ **Council of Trent** 1545–63

◄ **Vasari's *Lives* Published** 1550

◄ **Veronese Appears Before the Inquisition** 1573

21–2 | Tilman Riemenschneider **ALTARPIECE OF THE HOLY BLOOD (WINGS OPEN)**
Center, *Last Supper*. c. 1499–1505. Limewood, glass, height of tallest figure 39″ (99.1 cm); height of altar 29′6″ (9 m). Sankt Jakobskirche, Rothenburg ob der Tauber, Germany.

TILMAN RIEMENSCHNEIDER. Tilman Riemenschneider (c. 1460–1531) became a master in 1485 and soon had the largest workshop in Würzburg. His shop included specialists in both wood and stone sculpture. Riemenschneider attracted patrons from other cities, and in 1501 he signed a contract with the Church of Saint James in Rothenburg, where a relic said to be a drop of Jesus's blood was preserved. The **ALTARPIECE OF THE HOLY BLOOD** (FIG. 21–2) is a spectacular limewood construction standing nearly 30 feet high. A specialist in architectural shrines had begun work on the elaborate Gothic frame in 1499. The frame cost fifty florins. Riemenschneider was commissioned to provide the figures and scenes to be placed within this frame, and Riemenschneider was paid sixty florins for the sculpture (a suggestive commentary on the value assigned the work by the patrons).

In the main scene of the altarpiece, the *Last Supper*, Riemenschneider depicted the moment when Christ revealed that one of his followers would betray him. Unlike Leonardo da Vinci, who chose the same moment (see Introduction, Fig. 18), Riemenschneider made Judas the central figure in the composition and placed Jesus off-center at the left. The disciples sit around the table. As the event is described in the Gospel of John (13:21–30), Jesus extends a morsel of food to Judas, signifying that Judas will be the traitor who sets in motion the events leading to the Crucifixion. An apostle points down, a strange gesture until one realizes that he points to the Crucifix in the predella, to the relic of Christ's blood, and to the altar table, the symbolic representation of the table of the Last Supper and the tomb of Christ.

Rather than creating individual images in his sculptures, Riemenschneider repeated a limited number of facial types. In this way he could make effective use of his workshop. His figures have large heads, prominent features, sharp cheekbones, sagging jowls, baggy eyes, and elaborate hair with thick wavy locks and deeply drilled curls. The muscles, tendons, and raised veins of hands and feet are also especially lifelike. His assistants and apprentices copied these faces and figures, either from drawings or from three-dimensional models made by the master. In the altarpiece, deeply hollowed folds and active patterned draperies create strong highlights and dark shadows that unite the figures with the intricate carving of the framework. In the *Last Supper* the scene is set in a real room with actual benches for the figures, with windows in the back wall glazed with bull's-eye glass. Natural light shining through both the church and altarpiece windows illuminates the scene, creating changing effects depending on the time of day and the weather.

In addition to producing an enormous number of religious images for churches, Riemenschneider was politically active in the city's government, and he even served as mayor in 1520. His career ended during the Peasants' War (1524–26), an early manifestation of the Protestant movement. His support for the peasants led to a fine and imprisonment in 1525, and he died in 1531.

VEIT STOSS. Riemenschneider's contemporary Veit Stoss (1450–1533) spent his early years (1477–96) in Cracow, Poland, where he became wealthy from his sculpture and architectural commissions, as well as from financial investments. After returning to his native Nuremberg, he too began to specialize in limewood sculpture, probably because established artists already dominated commissions in other mediums. He had a small shop whose output was characterized by an easily recognizable realistic style. Following the lead of Riemenschneider and others, Stoss shows in his unpainted limewood sculptures a special appreciation for the wood itself, which he exploited for its inherent colorations, grain patterns, and range of surface finishes.

Stoss carved the **ANNUNCIATION AND VIRGIN OF THE ROSARY** **(FIG. 21–3)** for the choir of the Church of Saint Lawrence in Nuremberg in 1517–18. Gabriel's greeting to Mary takes place within a wreath of roses symbolizing the prayers of the rosary, which was being popularized by the Dominicans. Disks are carved with scenes of the Joys of the Virgin, to which are added her death (Dormition) and Coronation. Mary and Gabriel are adored and supported by angels. Their dignified figures are encased in elaborate crinkled and fluttering drapery that seems to blend with the delicate angels and to cause the entire work to float like an apparition in the upper reaches of the choir. The sculpture continues the expressive, mystical tradition prevalent since the Middle Ages in the art of Germany, where the recitation of prayers to the Virgin (the rosary) had become an important part of personal devotion.

NIKOLAUS HAGENAUER. Prayer was also the principal source of solace and relief to the ill before the advent of modern medicine. About 1505, the Strasbourg sculptor Nikolaus Hagenauer (active 1493–1530s) carved an altarpiece for the Abbey of Saint Anthony in Isenheim near Colmar **(FIG. 21–4)**. The Abbey's hospital specialized in the care of patients with skin diseases, including the plague, leprosy, and Saint Anthony's Fire (a terrible disease caused by eating rye and other grains infected with the ergot fungus). The shrine includes images of Saint Anthony, Saint Jerome, and Saint Augustine. Three men kneel at the feet of the saints: the donor, Jean d'Orliac, and two men offering a rooster and a piglet. The three are tiny figures, as befits their subordinate status.

In the predella below, Jesus and the apostles bless the altar, Host, and assembled patients in the hospital. The limewood sculpture was painted in lifelike colors, and the shrine itself was gilded to enhance its resemblance to a precious reliquary. Later, Matthias Grünewald painted wooden shutters to cover the shrine (SEE FIGS. 21–5, 21–6).

Painting

German art during the first decades of the sixteenth century was dominated by two very different artists, Matthias Grünewald and Albrecht Dürer. Grünewald's unique style expressed the

21–3 | Veit Stoss **ANNUNCIATION AND VIRGIN OF THE ROSARY**
1517-18. Painted and gilt limewood, 12′2″ × 10′6″ (3.71 × 3.20 m). Church of Saint Lawrence, Nuremberg.

continuing currents of medieval German mysticism and emotional spirituality, while Dürer's intense observation of the natural world represented the scientific Renaissance interest in empirical observation, including mathematical perspective to create the illusion of space, and the use of a reasoned canon of proportions for depicting the human figure.

MATTHIAS GRÜNEWALD. As an artist in the court of the archbishop of Mainz, Matthias Grünewald (Matthias Gothart Neithart, c. 1470/75–1528) was a man of many talents, who worked as an architect and hydraulic engineer as well as a painter. He is best known today for painting the wings of the **ISENHEIM ALTARPIECE** (SEE FIGS. 21–5, 21–6), built to protect the shrine carved by Nikolaus Hagenauer. In his realism and intensity of feeling, Grünewald may have been inspired by the visions of Saint Bridget of Sweden, a fourteenth-century mystic whose works were published in Germany beginning in 1492. She described the Crucifixion in morbid detail.

21–4 | Nikolaus Hagenauer **SAINT ANTHONY ENTHRONED BETWEEN SAINTS AUGUSTINE AND JEROME,
SHRINE OF THE** *ISENHEIM ALTARPIECE* **(OPEN, SHOWING GRÜNEWALD WINGS.)**
From the Community of Saint Anthony, Isenheim, Alsace, France. c. 1500. Painted and gilt limewood,
center panel 9′9½″ × 10′9″ (2.98 × 3.28 m); predella 2′5½″ × 11′2″ (0.75 × 3.4 m). Wings 8′2½″ × 3′½″
(2.49 × 0.93 m). Predella: *Christ and the Apostles.* Wings *Saint Anthony and Saint Paul* (left); *The Temptation of
Saint Anthony* (right). 1510–15. Musée d'Unterlinden, Colmar, France.

The altarpiece is impressive in size and complexity. Grünewald painted one set of fixed wings and two sets of movable ones, plus one set of sliding panels to cover the predella. The altarpiece could be exhibited in different configurations depending upon the Church calendar. The wings and carved wooden shrine complemented one another, the inner sculpture seeming to bring the surrounding paintings to life, and the painted wings protecting the precious carvings.

On weekdays, when the altarpiece was closed, viewers saw a shocking image of the Crucifixion in a darkened landscape, a Lamentation below it on the predella, and life-size figures of Saints Sebastian and Anthony Abbot—saints associated with the plague—standing on *trompe l'oeil* pedestals on the fixed wings (FIG. 21–5). Grünewald represented in the most horrific details the tortured body of Jesus, covered with gashes from being beaten and pierced by the thorns used to form a crown for his head. His ashen body, open mouth, and blue lips indicate that he is dead. In fact, he appears already to be decaying, an effect enhanced by the palette of putrescent green, yellow, and purplish red—all described by Saint Bridget; she wrote, "The color of death spread through his flesh. . ." A ghostlike Virgin Mary has collapsed in the arms of an emaciated John the Evangelist, and Mary Magdalen has fallen in anguish to her knees; her

clasped hands with outstretched fingers seem to echo Jesus's fingers, cramped in rigor mortis. At the right John the Baptist points at Jesus and repeats his prophecy, "He shall increase." The Baptist and the lamb, holding a cross and bleeding from its breast into a golden chalice, allude to baptism, the Eucharist, and to Christ as the sacrificial Lamb of God (recalling the *Ghent Altarpiece;* SEE FIG. 18–12). In the predella below, Jesus's bereaved mother and friends prepare his body for burial—an activity that must have been a common sight in the abbey's hospital.

In contrast to these grim scenes, the first opening displays events of great joy—the Annunciation, the Nativity, and the Resurrection—appropriate for Sundays and Church festivals (FIG. 21–6). Praying in front of these images, the patients hoped for miraculous recovery. Unlike the awful darkness of the Crucifixion, the inner scenes are illuminated with clear natural daylight, phosphorescent auras and halos, and the glitter of stars in a night sky. Fully aware of contemporary formal achievements in Italy, Grünewald created the illusion of three-dimensional space and volumetric figures, and he simplified and idealized the forms. Underlying this attempt to arouse a sympathetic emotional response in the viewer is a complex religious symbolism, undoubtedly the result of close collaboration with his monastic patrons.

21–5 | Matthias Grünewald   **ISENHEIM ALTARPIECE (CLOSED)**
From the Community of Saint Anthony, Isenheim, Alsace, France. Center panels: *Crucifixion*; predella: *Lamentation*; side panels: *Saints Sebastian* (left) and *Anthony Abbot* (right). c. 1510–15. Date 1515 on ointment jar. Oil on wood panel, center panels 9'9½" × 10'9" (2.97 × 3.28 m) overall; each wing 8'2½" × 3'½" (2.49 × 0.93 m); predella 2'5½" × 11'2" (0.75 × 3.4 m). Musée d'Unterlinden, Colmar, France.

21–6 | Matthias Grünewald   **ISENHEIM ALTARPIECE (FIRST OPENING)**
Left to right: *Annunciation, Virgin and Child with Angels, Resurrection*. c. 1510–15. Oil on wood panel, center panel 9'9½" × 10'9" (2.97 × 3.28 m), each wing 8'2½" × 3'½" (2.49 × 0.92 m). Musée d'Unterlinden, Colmar, France.

Materials and Techniques
GERMAN METALWORK: A COLLABORATIVE VENTURE

In Nuremberg, a city known for its master metalsmiths, Hans Krug (d. 1519) and his sons Hans the Younger and Ludwig were among its finest gold- and silversmiths. They created marvelous display pieces for the wealthy, such as this silver-gilt apple cup. Made about 1510, a gleaming apple, in which the stem forms the handle of the lid, balances on a leafy branch that forms its base.

The Krug family was responsible for the highly refined casting and finishing of the final product, but several artists worked together to produce such pieces—one drawing designs, another making the models, and others creating the final piece in metal. A drawing by Dürer may have been the basis for the apple cup. Though we know of no piece of goldwork by the artist himself, Dürer was a major catalyst in the growth of Nuremberg as a key center of German goldsmithing. He accomplished this by producing designs for metalwork throughout his career, evidence of the essential role of designers in the metalwork process. With design in hand, the model maker created a wooden form for the goldsmith to follow. The result of this artistic collaboration was a technical tour de force, an intellectual conceit, and a very beautiful object.

Workshop of Hans Krug (?) **APPLE CUP**
c. 1510–15. Gilt silver, height 8½" (21.5 cm).
Germanisches Nationalmuseum, Nuremberg.

The *Annunciation* on the left wing may have been inspired by a special liturgy called the Golden Mass, which celebrated the divine motherhood of the Virgin. The Mass included a staged reenactment of the angel's visit to Mary, as well as readings from the story of the Annunciation (Luke 1:26–38) and the Old Testament prophecy of the Savior's birth (Isaiah 7:14–15), which is inscribed in Latin on the pages of the Virgin's open book.

The central panels show the heavenly and earthly realms joined in one space. In a variation on the northern European visionary tradition, the new mother adores her miraculous Christ Child while envisioning her own future as Queen of Heaven amid angels and cherubs. Grünewald portrayed three distinct types of angels in the foreground—young, mature, and a feathered hybrid with a birdlike crest on its human head—and a range of ethnic types in the heavenly realm. Perhaps this latter was intended to emphasize the global dominion of the Church, whose missionary efforts were expanding as a result of European exploration. Saint Bridget describes the jubilation of the angels as "the glowing flame of love."

The panels are also filled with traditional imagery of the Annunciation: Marian symbols such as the enclosed garden, the white towel on the tub, and the clear glass cruet behind it, which signify Mary's virginity; the water pot next to the tub, which alludes both to purity and to childbirth; and the fig tree in the background, suggesting the Virgin Birth, since figs were thought to bear fruit without pollination. The bush of red roses at the right alludes not only to Mary but also to the Passion of Jesus, thus recalling the Crucifixion on the outer wings and providing a transition to the Resurrection on the right wing. There, the shock of Christ's explosive emergence from his stone sarcophagus tumbles the guards about, and his new state of being—no longer material but not yet entirely spiritual—is vibrantly evident in his dissolving, translucent figure.

The second opening of the altarpiece (SEE FIG. 21–4) reveals Hagenauer's sculpture and was reserved for the special festivals of Saint Anthony. The wings in this second opening show Saint Anthony attacked by horrible demons—perhaps inspired by the horrors of the diseased patients—and the meeting of Saint Anthony with the hermit Saint Paul. The meeting of the two hermits in the desert glorifies the monastic life, and in the wilderness Grünewald depicts medicinal plants used in the hospital's therapy. Grünewald painted his self-portrait as the face of Saint Paul, and Saint Anthony is a portrait of the donor and administrator of the hospital, the Italian Guido Guersi, whose coat of arms Grünewald painted on the rock.

Like Riemenschneider, Grünewald's career may have been damaged by his active support of the peasants in the Peasants' War. He left Mainz and spent his last years in Frankfurt and then Halle.

ALBRECHT DÜRER. Studious, analytical, observant, and meticulous—and as self-confident as Michelangelo—

21–7 | Albrecht Dürer **SELF-PORTRAIT**
1500. Signed "Albrecht Dürer of Nuremberg...age 28." Oil on wood panel, 26¼ × 19¼" (66.3 × 49 cm). Alte Pinakothek, Munich.

21–8 | Albrecht Dürer **FOUR HORSEMEN OF THE APOCALYPSE**
From *The Apocalypse.* 1497–98. Woodcut, 15½ × 11⅛" (39.4 × 28.3 cm). The Metropolitan Museum of Art, New York.
Gift of Junius S. Morgan, 1919 (19.73.209)

Albrecht Dürer (1471–1528) was the foremost artist in the northern part of the Holy Roman Empire. He made his home in Nuremberg, where he became a prominent citizen. Its university made Nuremberg a center of learning as well as business, with an active group of humanists and internationally renowned artists. With the new scholarship the city became a leading publishing center.

Dürer's father was a goldsmith and must have expected his son to follow in his trade. Dürer did complete an apprenticeship in goldworking, as well as in stained-glass design, painting, and the making of woodcuts, but it was ultimately as a painter and graphic artist that he found his artistic fame (see "German Metalwork: A Collaborative Venture," p. 714).

In 1490, Dürer began traveling to extend his education. He went to Basel, Switzerland, hoping to meet Martin Schongauer, but arrived after the master's death. Dürer remained in Basel until 1494, providing drawings for woodcut illustrations for books. His first trip to Italy (1494–95) introduced him to Italian Renaissance ideas and attitudes and, as we considered at the beginning of this chapter, to the concept of the artist as an independent creative genius. In the **SELF-PORTRAIT** of 1500 (FIG. 21–7), Dürer represents himself as an idealized, almost Christlike, figure in a severely frontal pose, like an icon. He stares directly at the viewer. His rich fur-lined robes and flowing locks create an equilateral triangle, the timeless symbol of unity.

On his return to Nuremberg, Dürer began to publish his own prints to bolster his income, and ultimately the prints, not his paintings, made his fortune. His first major publication, *The Apocalypse*, appeared simultaneously in German and Latin editions in 1497–98. It consisted of a woodcut title page and fourteen full-page illustrations with the text printed on the back of each. The best-known of the woodcuts is the **FOUR HORSEMEN OF THE APOCALYPSE** (FIG. 21–8), based on figures described in Revelation 6:1–8: a crowned rider, armed with a bow, on a white horse (Conquest); a rider with a sword, on a red horse (War); a rider with a set of scales, on a black horse (Plague and Famine); and a rider on a sickly pale horse (Death). Earlier artists had simply lined up the horsemen in the landscape. Dürer created a compact overlapping group of wild riders charging across the land and trampling the cowering men.

21–9 | Albrecht Dürer **ADAM AND EVE**
1504. Engraving, 9⅞ × 7⅝″ (25.1 × 19.4 cm). Philadelphia
Museum of Art.

Purchased: Lisa Nora Elkins Fund

Dürer embedded the landscape with symbolic content reflecting the medieval theory that after Adam and Eve disobeyed God, they and their descendants became vulnerable to imbalances in the body fluids that controlled human temperament. As we saw in *Melencolia I* (FIG. 20–1), an excess of black bile from the liver produced melancholy, despair, and greed. Yellow bile caused anger, pride, and impatience; phlegm in the lungs resulted in lethargy and disinterest; and an excess of blood made a person unusually optimistic but also compulsively interested in pleasures of the flesh. These four human temperaments, or personalities, are symbolized here by the melancholy elk, the choleric cat, the phlegmatic ox, and the sensual rabbit. The mouse is a symbol of Satan (see the mousetrap in FIG. 18–2), whose earthly power, already manifest in the Garden of Eden, was capable of bringing perfect human beings to a life of woe through their own bad choices. The parrot may symbolize false wisdom, since it can only repeat mindlessly what it hears. Dürer's pride in his engraving can be seen in the prominence of his signature—a placard bearing his full name and date hung on a branch of the tree of life.

Dürer's familiarity with Italian art was greatly enhanced by a second, leisurely trip over the Alps in 1505–06. Thereafter, he seems to have resolved to reform the art of his own country by publishing theoretical writings and manuals that discussed Renaissance problems of perspective, ideal human proportions, and the techniques of painting. Between 1513 and 1515, Dürer used images, not words, to define a philosophy of Christian life. He created what are known today as his master prints—three engravings having profound themes, but also demonstrating his skill as a graphic artist who could imply color, texture, and space by black lines alone.

Dürer admired Martin Luther, but they never met. In 1526, the artist openly professed his Lutheranism in a pair of inscribed panels, the **FOUR APOSTLES** (FIG. 21–10). On the left panel, the elderly Peter, who normally has a central position as the first pope, has been displaced by Luther's favorite evangelist, John, who holds an open Gospel that reads "In the beginning was the Word," reinforcing the Protestant emphasis on the Bible. On the right panel, Mark stands behind Paul, whose teachings and epistles were particularly admired by the Protestants. A long inscription on the frame warns the viewer not to be led astray by "false prophets" but to heed the words of the New Testament as recorded by these "four excellent men." Below each figure are excerpts from their letters and from the Gospel of Mark warning against those who do not understand the true word of God. In the inscriptions, Dürer used Luther's German translation of the New Testament. The paintings were surely meant to demonstrate that a Protestant art was possible.

Dürer presented the panels to the city of Nuremberg, which had already adopted Lutheranism as its official religion. Dürer wrote, "For a Christian would no more be led to superstition by a picture or effigy than an honest man to commit murder because he carries a weapon by his side. He must

Dürer probably did not cut his own woodblocks but employed a skilled carver who followed his drawings faithfully. Dürer's dynamic figures show affinities with Schongauer's *Temptation of Saint Anthony* (SEE FIG. 18–30). He adapted Schongauer's metal engraving technique to the woodcut medium, using a complex pattern of lines to model the forms. Dürer's early training as a goldsmith is evident in his meticulous attention to detail, and in his decorative cloud and drapery patterns. He fills the foreground with large, active figures just as late fifteenth-century artists had done.

Perhaps as early as the summer of 1494, Dürer began to experiment with engravings, cutting the metal plates himself with artistry equal to Schongauer's. His growing interest in Italian art and his theoretical investigations are reflected in his 1504 engraving **ADAM AND EVE** (FIG. 21–9), which represents his first documented use of ideal human proportions based on Roman copies of ancient Greek sculpture. He may have seen figures of Apollo and Venus in Italy, and he would have known ancient sculpture from contemporary prints and drawings. But behind his idealized human figures he represents plants and animals with typically northern European naturalistic detail.

indeed be an unthinking man who would worship picture, wood, or stone. A picture therefore brings more good than harm, when it is honourably, artistically, and well made" (cited in Snyder, 2nd ed., page 333).

LUCAS CRANACH THE ELDER. One of Dürer's friends, and Martin Luther's favorite painter, Lucas Cranach the Elder (1472–1553), had moved his workshop to Wittenberg in 1504, after a number of years in Vienna. In addition to the humanist milieu of its university and library, Wittenberg offered the patronage of the Saxon court. Appointed court painter to Elector Frederick the Wise, Cranach created woodcuts, altarpieces, and many portraits.

At the humanistic court Cranach met Italian artists who evidently inspired him to paint female nudes himself. Just how far the German artist's style and conception of the figure differ from Italian Renaissance idealism is easily seen in his **NYMPH OF THE SPRING**, a painting that characterizes the Renaissance in the north (FIG. 21–11; compare Titian's *Venus of Urbino,* FIG. 20–26). The sleeping nymph was a Renaissance theme, not an ancient one. Cranach was inspired by a fifteenth-century inscription on a fountain beside the Danube. Translated from the Latin, the text reads, "I am the nymph of the sacred font. Do not interrupt my sleep for I am at peace." Cranach records the Danube landscape with northern fidelity and turns his nymph into a highly provocative young woman, who glances

21–10 | Albrecht Dürer **FOUR APOSTLES**
1526. Oil on wood panel, each panel 7′½″ × 2′6″ (2.15 × 0.76 m). Alte Pinakothek, Munich.

FONTIS NYMPHA SACRI SOM:
NVM NE RVMPE QVIESCO ·

21–11 | Lucas Cranach the Elder **NYMPH OF THE SPRING**
c. 1537. Oil on panel, 19 × 28½" (48.5 × 72.9 cm). National Gallery of Art, Washington, D.C.

In 1537 Cranach adopted as his device a dragon with folded wings, seen on the rock above the fountain.

slyly out at the viewer through half-closed eyes. She has cast aside a fashionable red velvet gown, but still wears her jewelry, which together with her transparent veil enhances rather than conceals her nudity. Unlike other artists working for Protestant patrons, many of whom looked on earthly beauty as a sinful vanity, Cranach seems delighted by earthly things—the lush foliage that provides the nymph's couch, the pair of partridges (symbols of Venus and married love), and Cupid's bow and quiver of arrows hanging on the tree. The *Nymph of the Spring* seems to depict a beauty from the Wittenburg court rather than a follower of the classical Venus.

ALBRECHT ALTDORFER. Landscape, with or without figures, became a popular theme in the sixteenth century. In the fifteenth century, northern artists had examined and recorded nature with the care and enthusiasm of biologists, but they painted their landscapes as backgrounds for figural compositions, usually with religious themes. In the 1520s, however, religious art found little favor among Protestants. Landscape painting, on the other hand, had no overt religious imagery, although

it could be seen as a reflection or even glorification of God's works on earth. The most accomplished German landscape painter of the period was Albrecht Altdorfer (c. 1480–1538).

Altdorfer probably received his early training in Bavaria from his father; he then became a citizen in 1505 of the city of Regensburg in the Danube River valley. He remained there painting the Danube Valley for the rest of his life. The **DANUBE LANDSCAPE** of about 1525 (**FIG. 21–12**) is an early example of pure landscape painting—one without a narrative subject or human figures, and with no religious significance. A small work on vellum laid down on a wood panel, the landscape seems to be a minutely detailed view of the natural terrain, but the forest seems far more poetic and mysterious than Dürer's or Cranach's carefully observed views of nature. The low mountains, gigantic lacy pines, neatly contoured shrubberies, and fairyland castle with red-roofed towers at the end of a winding path announce a new sensibility. The eerily glowing yellow-white horizon below moving gray and blue clouds in a sky that takes up more than half the composition foretell the Romanticism that will characterize later German landscape painting.

21-12 | Albrecht Altdorfer   **DANUBE LANDSCAPE**
c. 1525. Oil on vellum on wood panel, 12 × 8½″ (30.5 × 22.2 cm). Alte Pinakothek, Munich.

RENAISSANCE ART IN FRANCE

France in the early sixteenth century took a different road than did Germany. Pope Leo X came to an agreement with the French king Francis I (ruled 1515–47) in 1519 that spared the country the turmoil suffered in Germany. Furthermore, whereas Martin Luther had devoted followers among the political leaders as well as the people, the French reformer John Calvin (1509–64) fled to Switzerland in 1534, where he led a theocratic state in Geneva. Nevertheless, wars of religion between political factions favoring either Catholics or Huguenots (Protestants), who each wished to exert power over the French crown, also devastated France in the second half of the century.

In 1560, the devoutly Catholic Catherine de' Medici, widow of Henry II (ruled 1547–59), became regent for her young son, Charles IX. She tried, but failed, to balance the warring factions, and her machinations ended in religious polarization and a bloody conflict that began in 1562. Her successor and third son Henry III (ruled 1574–89) was murdered by a fanatical Dominican friar, and his Protestant cousin, Henry, king of Navarre, the first Bourbon king, inherited the throne. Henry converted to Catholicism and ruled as Henry IV. Backed by a country sick of bloodshed, he quickly settled the religious question by granting toleration to Protestants in the Edict of Nantes in 1598.

The Introduction of Italian Art

The greatest French patron of Italian artists was King Francis I. Immediately after his ascent to the throne, Francis showed his desire to "modernize" the French court by acquiring the versatile talents of Leonardo da Vinci. Leonardo moved to France in 1516, officially to advise the king on royal architectural projects and, the king said, for the pleasure of his conversation. Francis continued to support the arts throughout his reign despite the distraction of continual wars against his brother-in-law, Emperor Charles V. Under his patronage, an Italian-inspired Renaissance blossomed in France.

JEAN CLOUET. The Flemish artist Jean Clouet (c. 1485–c. 1540) found great favor as the royal portrait painter. Clouet was in France as early as 1509, and in 1527 he moved to Paris as principal court painter. In his official portrait of the king (FIG. 21–13), Clouet created a flattering image by modeling Francis's distinctive features with subtle shading, a technique that may have been partially inspired by exposure to the work of Leonardo. At the same time he created an image of pure power. The depiction of the king's thick neck and huge body seems at odds with the nervous movement of his fingers. Elaborate, puffy sleeves broadened his shoulders to more than fill the panel, much as parade armor turned scrawny men into giants. The delicately worked costume of silk, satin, velvet, jewels, and gold embroidery could be painted separately from

21–13 | Jean Clouet **FRANCIS I**
1525–30. Oil and tempera on wood panel, 37¾ × 29⅛"
(95.9 × 74 cm). Musée du Louvre, Paris.

the portrait itself. The clothing was often loaned to the artist or modeled by a servant to spare the "sitter" the boredom of posing. In creating such official portraits, the artist sketched the subject, then painted a prototype that, upon approval, was the model for numerous replicas made for diplomatic and family purposes.

THE CHÂTEAU OF CHENONCEAU. With the enthusiasm of Francis for things Italian and the widening distribution of Italian books on architecture, the Italian Renaissance style soon appeared in French architecture. Builders of elegant rural palaces, called châteaux, were quick to introduce Italianate decoration to otherwise Gothic buildings, but French architects soon adapted classical principles of building design as well.

One of the most beautiful of these Renaissance palaces was not built as a royal residence, although it soon became one. In 1512 Thomas Bohier, a royal tax collector, bought the castle of Chenonceau on the River Cher, a tributary of the Loire River (FIG. 21–14). He demolished the old castle, leaving only a tower. Using the piers of a water mill on the river bank as part of the foundations, he and his wife erected a new Renaissance home. The plan reflects the classical principles of geometric regularity and symmetry—a rectangular building with rooms arranged on each side of a wide central hall. Only the library and chapel, which are corbelled out over the water, break the line of the walls. In the upper story, the builders used traditional features of medieval castles—battlements, corner turrets, steep roofs, and dormer windows. The château was finished in 1521. When the owners died soon after, their son gave the château to the king, who turned it into a hunting lodge (see "Chenonceau: The Castle of the Ladies," p. 722).

Later, the foremost French Renaissance architect, the Roman-trained Philibert de l'Orme (d. 1570), designed a gallery on a bridge across the river for Catherine de' Medici. The extension was completed about 1581 and incorporated contemporary Italianate window treatments, wall molding, and cornices that harmonized almost perfectly with the forms of the original turreted building. Chenonceau remains today one of the most important—and beautiful—examples of classical influence on French Renaissance architecture.

FONTAINEBLEAU.   Francis I also began renovating royal properties. Having chosen as his primary residence the medieval hunting lodge at Fontainebleau, Francis began transforming it into a grand palace. Most of the exterior structure was altered or destroyed by later renovations, but parts of the interior decoration, the work of artists and artisans from Italy, have been preserved and restored. The first artistic director at

Sequencing Events
KEY EVENTS IN THE PROTESTANT REFORMATION

1517	Martin Luther propounds his Ninety-Five Theses at Wittenberg.
1534	Henry VIII of England breaks from Rome; founds Church of England.
1555	Lutheranism recognized in Germany by the Holy Roman Emperor at the Peace of Augsburg.

Fontainebleau, the Mannerist painter Rosso Fiorentino (d. 1540), arrived in 1530. Francesco Primaticcio (1504–70), who had worked with Giulio Romano in Mantua (SEE FIG. 20–19), joined Rosso in 1532 and succeeded him in 1540. Primaticcio worked on the decoration of Fontainebleau from 1532 until his death in 1570. During that time, he also commissioned and imported a large number of copies and casts of original Roman sculpture, from the newly discovered *Laocoön* (see Introduction, Fig. 10) to the relief decoration on the Column of Trajan. These works provided an invaluable visual source of figures and techniques for the northern European artists employed on the Fontainebleau project.

21–14 | **CHÂTEAU OF CHENONCEAU**
Touraine, France. 1513–21; gallery on bridge, finished c. 1581.

Art and Its Context
CHENONCEAU: THE CASTLE OF THE LADIES

Women played an important role in the patronage of the arts during the Renaissance. Nowhere is their influence stronger than in the castle-palaces (châteaux) built in the Loire River valley. At Chenonceau, built beside and literally over the River Cher, a tributary of the Loire, women built, saved, and restored the château. Catherine Briconnet and her husband Thomas Bohier originally acquired the property, including a fortified mill, on which they built their country residence. Catherine supervised the construction, which included such modern conveniences as a straight staircase (an Italian and Spanish feature) instead of traditional medieval spiral stairs, and a kitchen inside the château instead of in a distant outbuilding. When Thomas died in 1524 and Catherine in 1526, their son gave Chenonceau to King Francis I.

King Henry II, Francis's son, gave Chenonceau to his mistress Diane de Poitiers in 1547. She managed the estate astutely, increased revenue, developed the vineyards, added intricately planted gardens in the Italian style, and built a bridge across the Cher. When Henry died in a tournament, the queen Catherine de' Medici (1519-89) appropriated the château for herself.

Catherine, like so many of her family a great patron of the arts, added the two-story gallery to the bridge at Chenonceau, as well as outbuildings and additional formal gardens. Her parties were famous—mock naval battles on the river, fireworks, banquets, dances, and on one occasion two choruses of young women dressed as mermaids in the moat and nymphs in the shrubbery—who were then chased about by young men costumed as satyrs! When Catherine's third son became king as Henry III in 1574, she gave Chenonceau to his wife, Louise of Lorraine.

Louise of Lorraine lived in mourning at Chenonceau after Henry III was assassinated in 1589. She wore only white and covered the walls, windows, and furniture in her room with black velvet and damask. She gave Chenonceau to her niece when she died.

In the eighteenth and nineteenth centuries the ladies continued to determine the fate of Chenonceau. During the French Revolution (1789-93) the owner, Madame Dupin, was so beloved by the villagers that they protected her and saved her home. Then in 1864 Madame Pelouze bought Chenonceau and restored it by removing Catherine de' Medici's Italian "improvements."

Chenonceau continued to play a role in the twentieth century. During World War I it was used as a hospital. During the German occupation in World War II (1940-42), when the River Cher formed the border with Vichy "Free" France, the gallery bridge at Chenonceau became an escape route. In 2000 the Valley of the Loire and its châteaux became a UNESCO World Heritage site.

21–15 | Primaticcio **STUCCO AND WALL PAINTING, CHAMBER OF THE DUCHESS OF ÉTAMPES, CHÂTEAU OF FONTAINEBLEAU**
France. 1540s.

Following ancient tradition, the king maintained an official mistress—Anne, the duchess of Étampes, who lived at Fontainebleau. Among Primaticcio's first projects was the redecoration of Anne's rooms (FIG. 21–15). The artist combined woodwork, stucco relief, and fresco painting in his complex but lighthearted and graceful interior design. The lithe figures of stucco nymphs, with their long necks and small heads, recall Parmigianino's paintings (see fig. 20–35). Their spiraling postures are playfully sexual. The wall surface is almost overwhelmed with garlands, mythological figures, and Roman architectural ornament, yet the visual effect is extraordinarily confident and joyous. The first School of Fontainebleau, as this Italian phase of the palace decoration is called, established a tradition of Mannerism in painting and interior design that spread to other centers in France and into the Netherlands.

Art in the Capital

Before the defeat of King Francis I at Pavia by the Holy Roman Emperor Charles V, and the king's subsequent imprisonment in Spain in 1525, the French court was a mobile unit, and the locus of French art resided outside of Paris in the Loire valley. After 1525, Francis made Paris his bureaucratic seat; and the capital and region around it—the Île de France—took the artistic lead with an attendant shift in style.

21–16 | Pierre Lescot
WEST WING OF THE COUR CARRÉ, PALAIS DU LOUVRE
Paris. Begun 1546.

RENOVATING THE LOUVRE. Paris saw the birth of a French classical style when the kings Francis I and Henry II decided to modernize the medieval castle of the Louvre. The work began in 1546, with the replacement of the west wing of the square court, the **COUR CARRÉ (FIG. 21–16)**, by the architect Pierre Lescot (c. 1510–78). Working with the sculptor Jean Goujon (1510–68), Lescot designed a building incorporating Renaissance ideals of balance and regularity with classical architectural details and rich sculptural decoration. The irregular roof lines of a château, such as at Chenonceau, gave way to discreetly rounded arches and horizontal balustrades. Classical pilasters and entablatures replaced Gothic buttresses and stringcourses. Pediments topped a round-arched arcade on the ground floor, suggesting an Italian loggia. The sumptuous decoration recalls the French medieval Flamboyant style, but with classical pilasters and acanthus replacing Gothic colonnettes and cusps.

FRENCH GARDENS AND GROTTOS. Gardens played an important role in architectural designs, usually intended to be viewed from the owners' rooms on the principal (second) floor. Elaborate flower beds bordered with clipped evergreen yews were planted in generally symmetrical patterns. Long avenues enlivened by sculpture and sculptured fountains led to witty surprises such as trick waterworks and grottos. One of the most brilliant must have been the grotto created by Bernard Palissy for the Tuileries Palace facing the Louvre.

Bernard Palissy (1510–90) created a false earthenware grotto made of glazed ceramic rocks and shells, to which he added crumbling statues, a cat stalking birds, ferns, garlands of fruits and vegetation, fish and crayfish seeming to swim in the pool, and reptiles slithering or creeping over mossy rocks—all of which glistened with water and surely achieved Alberti's

21–17 | Attributed to Bernard Palissy
OVAL PLATE IN *"STYLE RUSTIQUE"*
1570-80/90 (?). Polychromed tin and glazed earthenware, length 20½" (52 cm). Musée du Louvre, Paris.

ideal Slime (see "The Grotto," page 677). Reportedly, he made all the figures from casts of actual animals and plants. In 1563, Palissy had been appointed the court's "inventor of rustic figurines." A Protestant, he was repeatedly arrested during periods of persecution, and he died in prison. Although his Tuileries grotto was destroyed, we can imagine its appearance from the distinctive ceramic designs attributed to him (FIG. 21–17). Platters decorated in high relief with plants, reptiles, and insects resemble descriptions of the grotto. Existing examples are best called "Palissy-style" works, because their authenticity is nearly impossible to prove.

THE ⬤BJECT SPEAKS

SCULPTURE FOR THE KNIGHTS OF CHRIST AT TOMAR

One of the strangest—and in its own way most beautiful—sixteenth-century sculptures in Portugal seems to float over the cloisters of the Convent of Christ in Tomar. Unexpectedly, in the heart of the castle-monastery complex, one comes face to face with the Old Man of the Sea. He supports on his powerful shoulders an extraordinary growth—part roots and trunk of a gnarled tree, part tangled mass of seaweed, algae, ropes, and anchor chains. Barnacle- and coral-encrusted piers lead the eye upward, revealing a large lattice-covered window, the great west window of the Church of the Knights of Christ.

When in 1314 Pope Clement V disbanded the Templars (a monastic order of knights founded in Jerusalem in 1118 after the First Crusade), King Dinis of Portugal offered them a renewed existence as the Knights of Christ. In 1356, they made the former Templar castle and monastery in Tomar their headquarters. When Prince Henry the Navigator (1394–1460) became the Grand Master of the Order, he invested their funds in the exploration of the African coast and the Atlantic Ocean. The Templar insignia, the squared cross, became the emblem used on the sails of Portuguese ships.

King Manuel I of Portugal (ruled 1495–1521) commissioned the present church, with its amazing sculpture from Diogo de Arruda, in 1510. It reflects the wealth and power of sixteenth-century Portugal and the Knights of Christ. So distinctive is the style developed under King Manuel by artists like the Arruda brothers, Diogo (active 1508–31) and Francisco (active 1510–47), that Renaissance art in Portugal is called "Manueline." Architecture became more and more sculptural; piers and columns were carved to resemble twisted ropes; vaulting ribs multiplied into treelike branches. In the window of Tomar, Manueline sculpture reached the pinnacle of

Diogo de Arruda
WEST WINDOW, CHURCH IN THE CONVENT OF CHRIST
Tomar, Portugal. c. 1510. Commissioned by King Manuel I of Portugal.

complexity. Every surface is carved with architectural and natural detail associated with the sea. Twisted ropes form the corners of the window; the coral pillars support great swathes of seaweed. Chains and cables drop through the watery depths to the place where the head of a man—some see him as the Old Man of the Sea; others see a self-portrait of Diogo de Arruda—emerges from the roots of a tree. Trees with generations of ancestors seated in their branches became an important theme in Portuguese art. Here, the idea of a male figure as the foundation block recalls the biblical Tree of Jesse.

Above the window more ropes, cables, and seaweed support the emblems of the patron—the armillary spheres and the coat of arms of Manuel I with its Portuguese castles framing the five wounds of Christ.

Topping the composition is the square cross of the Order of Christ—clearly delineated against the wall of the chapel.

The armillary sphere became a symbol of the era. This complex form of celestial globe, with the sun at the center surrounded by rings marking the paths of the planets, acknowledges the new scientific theory that the sun, not the earth, is the center of the solar system. (Copernicus, teaching in Germany at this time, only published his theories in 1531 and 1543.) Although the armillary sphere had no practical value in navigation, it was a teaching device, a way to demonstrate and learn astronomy. King Manuel's continued use of the armillary sphere as his emblem indicates his determination to make Portugal the leader in the exploration of the sea. Indeed, in Manuel's reign the Portuguese reached India and Brazil.

RENAISSANCE ART IN SPAIN AND PORTUGAL

The sixteenth century saw the high point of Spanish political power. The country had been united in the fifteenth century by the marriage of Isabella of Castile and Ferdinand of Aragon. Only Navarre (in the Pyrenees) and Portugal remained outside the union of the crowns (see "Sculpture for the Knights of Christ at Tomar," page 724).

When Isabella and Ferdinand's grandson Charles V abdicated in 1556, his son Philip II (1556–98) became the king of Spain, the Netherlands, and the Americas, as well as ruler of Milan, Burgundy, and Naples. Philip made Spain his permanent residence. From an early age, Philip was a serious art collector, and for more than half a century, he supported artists in Spain, Italy, and the Netherlands. His navy, the famous Spanish Armada, halted the advance of Islam in the Mediterranean and secured control of most American territories. Despite enormous effort and wealth, however, Philip could not suppress the revolt of the northern provinces of the Netherlands, nor could he prevail in his war against the English, who destroyed his navy in 1588. He was able to gain control of the entire Iberian Peninsula, however, by claiming Portugal when the king died in 1580. Portugal remained part of Spain until 1640.

Architecture

Philip built **EL ESCORIAL** (FIG. 21–18), the great monastery-palace complex outside Madrid, partly to comply with his father's direction to construct a "pantheon" in which all Spanish kings might be buried and partly to house his court and government. To build the palace, in 1559 Philip summoned from Italy Juan Bautista de Toledo (d. 1567), who had been Michelangelo's supervisor of work at Saint Peter's from 1546 to 1548. Juan Bautista's design reflected his indoctrination in Bramante's classical principles in Rome, but the king himself dictated the severity and size of the structure. El Escorial's grandeur comes from its overwhelming size, fine proportions, and excellent masonry. The complex includes not only the royal residence but also the Royal Monastery of San Lorenzo, a school, a library, and a church, its crypt serving as the royal burial chamber. The plan was said to resemble a gridiron, the instrument of martyrdom of its patron saint, Lawrence, who was roasted alive.

In 1572, Juan Bautista's assistant, Juan de Herrera, was appointed architect, and he immediately changed the design, adding second stories on all wings and breaking the horizontality of the main façade with a central frontispiece that resembled superimposed temple fronts. Before beginning the church in the center of the complex, Philip solicited the advice of Italian architects—including Vignola and Palladio (see p. 690 and p. 703). The final design combined ideas that Philip approved and Herrera carried out. Although not a replica of any Italian design, the building embodies Italian classicism in its geometric clarity and symmetry and the use of superimposed orders on the temple-front façade. In its sober and severe character, however, it embodies the austere and deeply religious spirit of the Spanish Philip II.

Painting

The arts continued to be sponsored by the Church and the nobles. Pageantry—including the sign language of heraldry, luxurious armor, and textiles—answered the aesthetic desires of the patrons. Philip II was a great patron of the Venetian painter Titian, and he collected Netherlandish artists such as Bosch (see page 728).

21–18 | Juan Bautista de Toledo and Juan de Herrera
EL ESCORIAL
Madrid. 1563-84. Detail from an anonymous 18th-century painting.

EL GRECO. Today the most famous Spanish painter from the last quarter of the sixteenth century is Domenikos Theotokopoulos (1541–1614), who arrived in Spain in 1577 after working for ten years in Italy. "El Greco" ("The Greek"), as he is called, was trained as an icon painter in the Byzantine manner in his native Crete, then under Venetian rule. In about 1566, he went to Venice and entered Titian's studio, where he also studied the paintings of Tintoretto and Veronese. From about 1570 to 1577, he worked in Rome, apparently without finding sufficient patronage, although he lived for a time in the Farnese Palace. Probably encouraged by Spanish Church officials whom he met in Rome, El Greco settled in Toledo, Spain, the seat of the archbishop. He had apparently hoped for a court appointment, but Philip II disliked the painting he had commissioned from El Greco for El Escorial and never gave him work again.

In Toledo, El Greco joined the circle of humanist scholars. His annotations in his own copies of Vitruvius and Vasari demonstrate his concern with the issues of the day. He wrote that the artist's goal should be to copy nature, that Raphael relied too heavily on the ancients, and that the Italians' use of mathematics to achieve ideal proportions hindered their painting of nature. At the same time an intense religious revival was under way in Spain, expressed in the impassioned preaching of Ignatius of Loyola, as well as in the poetry of the two great Spanish mystics: Saint Teresa of Ávila (1515–82), founder of the Discalced ("unshod") Carmelites, and her follower Saint John of the Cross (1542–91). El Greco's style—rooted in Byzantine icon painting and strongly reflecting Venetian artists' rich colors and loose brushwork—expressed in paint the intense spirituality of these mystics.

21–19 | El Greco **BURIAL OF COUNT ORGAZ**
1586. Oil on canvas, 16' × 11'10" (4.88 × 3.61 m).
Church of Santo Tomé, Toledo, Spain.

21–20 | El Greco
VIEW OF TOLEDO
c. 1610. Oil on
canvas, 47¾ × 42¾"
(121 × 109 cm).
The Metropolitan
Museum of Art,
New York.
The H. O. Havemeyer
Collection. Bequest of
Mrs. H. O. Havemeyer,
1929 (29.100.6)

In 1586, the Orgaz family commissioned El Greco to paint a large altarpiece honoring an illustrious fourteenth-century ancestor. Count Orgaz had been a great benefactor of the Church, and at his funeral in 1323 the saints Augustine and Stephen were said to have appeared to lower his body into his tomb as his soul was seen ascending to heaven. El Greco's painting the **BURIAL OF COUNT ORGAZ** (FIG. 21–19) reenacts the miraculous burial. An angel lifts Orgaz's tiny ghostly soul along the central axis of the painting through the heavenly hosts toward the enthroned Christ at the apex of the canvas. El Greco filled the space around the burial scene with portraits of the local aristocracy and religious notables. He placed his own eight-year-old son at the lower left next to Saint Stephen and signed the painting on the boy's white kerchief. El Greco may also have put his own features on the man just above the saint's head, the only one who looks straight out at the viewer.

In composing the painting, El Greco used Mannerist devices reminiscent of Pontormo (SEE FIG. 20–34), filling the pictorial field with figures and eliminating specific reference to the spatial setting. Yet he has distinguished between heaven and earth by the elongation of the heavenly figures and the light emanating from Christ, who sheds an otherworldly luminescence quite unlike the natural light below. The two realms are connected, however, by the descent of the light from heaven to strike the priestly figure in the white vestment at the lower right.

Late in his life, El Greco painted one of his rare landscapes, **VIEW OF TOLEDO** (FIG. 21–20), a topographical cityscape transformed into a mystical illusion by a stormy sky and a narrowly restricted palette of greens and grays. This conception is very different from Altdorfer's peaceful, idealized *Danube Landscape* (SEE FIG. 21–12). If any precedent comes to mind, it is the lightning-rent sky and prestorm atmosphere in Giorgione's *The Tempest* (SEE FIG. 20–23). In El Greco's painting, the precisely accurate portrayal of Toledo's geography and architecture seems to have been overridden by the artist's desire to convey the power of nature. In this, El Greco looks forward to the art of the Baroque period.

RENAISSANCE PAINTING IN THE NETHERLANDS

In the Netherlands the sixteenth century was an age of bitter religious and political conflict. Despite the opposition of the Spanish Habsburg rulers, the Protestant Reformation took hold in the northern provinces. Seeds of unrest were sown still deeper over the course of the century by continued religious persecution, economic hardship, and control by inept governors. A long battle for independence began with a revolt in 1568 and lasted until Spain relinquished all claims to the region eighty years later. As early as 1579, when the seven northern Protestant provinces declared themselves the United Provinces, the discord split the Netherlands, eventually dividing it along religious lines into the northern provinces—United Provinces (present-day Netherlands)—and Catholic Flanders (present-day Belgium).

Even with the turmoil, the Netherlanders found the resources to pay for art, and Antwerp and other cities developed into art centers. The Reformation led artists to seek patrons outside the Church. While courtiers and burghers alike continued to commission portraits, the demand arose for small paintings with interesting secular subjects appropriate for homes. For example, some artists became specialists known for their landscapes or satires. In addition to painting, textiles, ceramics, and sculpture in wood and metal flourished in the Netherlands. Flemish tapestries were sought after, as they had been in the fifteenth century. In Italy fine Netherlandish tapestries were highly prized and leading Italian artists made paintings (cartoons) to be woven. For example, Raphael's cartoons for the tapestries of the Sistine Chapel were woven in Brussels by the workshop of Pieter van Aelst (SEE FIG. 20–8).

The graphic arts emerged as an important medium and provided many artists with another source of income. Pieter Bruegel began his career drawing amusing and moralizing images to be printed and published by At the Four Winds, an Antwerp publishing house. Artists such as Hendrick Goltzius, who traveled sketchbook in hand, turned their experiences to profit when they returned home. Goltzius, who had spent 1591–92 in Rome, recorded the awestruck wonder of his Dutch friends at the sight of the recently discovered 10-foot-tall Hercules displayed in the Farnese Palace (see Fig. 24, Introduction). Surely he meant to inform and amuse—and sell prints.

Netherlandish artists had their biographer. Like Vasari in Italy, Carel van Mander (1548–1606) recorded the lives of his contemporaries in lively stories that mix fact and gossip. He,

too, intended his book *Het Schilderbock (The Painter's Book)* to be a survey of the history of art, and he included material from the ancient Roman writers Pliny and Vitruvius as well as from Vasari, his contemporary. Vasari's revised and expanded *Lives* had been published in 1568 and served as a source and a model for Van Mander and others.

Art for Aristocratic and Noble Patrons

Artistic taste among the wealthy bourgeoisie and noble classes in early sixteenth-century Netherlands was characterized by a striking diversity: the imaginative and difficult visions of Hieronymus Bosch, as well as the more Italian-influenced compositions of Jan Gossaert. In the later years of his life (after 1500), Bosch's membership in a local but prestigious confraternity called the Brotherhood of Our Lady seems to have opened doors to noble patrons such as Count Hendrick III of Nassau and Duke Philip the Fair. His younger contemporary, Gossaert, left the city of Antwerp as a young man to spend the majority of his active years as the court painter for the natural son of Duke Philip the Good. His art also attracted members of the Habsburgs, including Charles V, who were seduced by Gossaert's combination of northern European and Italian styles.

HIERONYMUS BOSCH. One of the most fascinating of the Netherlandish painters to viewers today is Hieronymus Bosch (1450–1516), whose work depicts a world of fantastic imagination more often associated with medieval than Renaissance art. A superb colorist and technical virtuoso, Bosch spent his career in the town whose name he adopted, 's-Hertogenbosch. Bosch's religious devotion is certain, and his range of subjects shows that he was well educated.

Challenging and unsettling paintings such as the triptych GARDEN OF EARTHLY DELIGHTS (FIG. 21–21) have led modern critics to label Bosch both a mystic and a social critic. The subject of the painting seems to be the Christian belief in human beings' natural state of sinfulness. Because only the damned are shown in the Last Judgment on the right, the work seems to caution that damnation is the natural outcome of a life lived in ignorance and folly, that people ensure their damnation through their self-centered pursuit of pleasures of the flesh—the sins of gluttony, lust, greed, and sloth.

In the left wing, God introduces Adam and Eve, under the watchful eye of the owl of perverted wisdom. The owl symbolizes both wisdom and folly. Folly had become an important concept to the northern European humanists, who believed in the power of education. They believed that people would choose to follow the right way if they knew it. Here the owl peers out from a fantastic pink fountain in a lake from which vicious creatures creep out into the world. Their hybrid forms result from unnatural unions. In the central panel, the earth teems with revelers, monstrous birds, and huge fruits, symbolic of fertility and sexual abandon. In hell, at the right, the sensual pleasures—eating, drinking, music, and dancing—become torture in a dark

2I–2I Hieronymus Bosch **GARDEN OF EARTHLY DELIGHTS**
c. 1505–15. Oil on wood panel, center panel 7′2½″ × 6′4¾″ (2.20 × 1.95 m), each wing 7′2½″ × 3′2″
(2.20 × 0.97 m). Museo del Prado, Madrid.

world of fire and ice. A creature with stump legs balanced unsteadily on rowboats watches his own stomach, filled with lost souls in the proverbial "tavern on the road to hell."

One scholar has proposed that the central panel is a parable on human salvation in which the practice of alchemy—the process that sought to turn common metals into gold—parallels Christ's power to convert human dross into spiritual gold. In this theory, the bizarre fountain at the center of the lake in the middle distance can be seen as an alchemical "marrying chamber," complete with the glass vessels for collecting the vapors of distillation. Others see the theme known as "the power of women." In this interpretation the central pool is the setting for a display of seductive women and sex-obsessed men. Women frolic alluringly in the pool while men dance and ride in a mad circle trying to attract them. In this strange garden, men are slaves to their own lust. Yet another critic focused on the fruit, writing (c. 1600) that the triptych was known as *The Strawberry Plant* because it represented the "vanity and glory and the passing taste of strawberries or the strawberry plant and its pleasant odor that is hardly remembered once it has passed." Luscious fruits having sexual symbolism—strawberries, cherries, grapes, and pomegranates—appear everywhere in the

Garden, serving as food, as shelter, and even as a boat. Is human life as fleeting and insubstantial as the taste of a strawberry? Meaning clearly lies in the eye of the beholder of these very private paintings.

The *Garden of Earthly Delights* was commissioned by an aristocrat (probably Count Hendrick III of Nassau) for his Brussels town house, and the artist's choice of a triptych format, which suggests an altarpiece, may have been an understated irony. In a private home the painting may have inspired lively discussion and even ribald comment, much as it does today in its museum setting. Despite—or perhaps because of—its bizarre subject matter, the triptych was copied in 1566 into tapestry versions, one for a cardinal (now in the Escorial) and another for the French king Francis I. At least one painted copy was made as well. Bosch's original triptych was sold at the onset of the Netherlands revolt and sent in 1568 to Spain, where it entered the collection of Philip II.

JAN GOSSAERT. In contrast to the private visions of Bosch, Jan Gossaert (c. 1478–c. 1533) took a conservative line in subject matter and also embraced the new classical art of Italy. Gossaert (who later called himself "Mabuse" after his native

21–22 | Jan Gossaert   **SAINT LUKE PAINTING THE VIRGIN MARY**
1520. Oil on panel, 43⅜ × 32¼″ (110.2 × 81.9 cm). Kunsthistorisches Museum, Vienna.

city Maubeuge) entered the service of Philip, the illegitimate son of the Duke of Burgundy. In 1508 he traveled to Italy with Philip, and on their return Gossaert continued to work for Philip—who became archbishop of Utrecht in 1517.

After a period when he had been influenced by Jan van Eyck, Gossaert settled into what has been called a "Romanizing" style, inspired by Italian Mannerist paintings with a strong interjection of decorative details based on ancient Roman art.

In **SAINT LUKE PAINTING THE VIRGIN MARY** (FIG. 21–22), the artist's studio is an extraordinary structure of barrel vaults and classical piers and arches, which are carved with a dense ornament of foliage and medallions. Mary and the Christ Child appear to Saint Luke in a vision of golden light and clouds. The saint kneels at a desk, drawing, his hand guided by an angel. Luke's crumpled red robe recalls fifteenth-century drapery conventions. Behind the saint, seated on a round, columnar structure, Moses holds the tablets of the Law, having seen the burning bush (which, as with Mary's virginity, was not consumed) on Mount Sinai. Moses removed his shoes in the presence of God's manifestation and so has Saint Luke in the presence of his vision. In short, the artist is divinely inspired. Gossaert, like Dürer before him, emphasizes the divine inspiration of the artist.

Antwerp

In the sixteenth century the city of Antwerp was the commercial and artistic center of the southern Netherlands. Antwerp's deep port made it an international center of trade (it was one of the European centers for trade in spices), and it was the financial center of Europe. Painting, printmaking, and book production flourished in this environment, attracting artists and craftsmen from all over Europe. The demand for luxury goods (including art) fostered the birth of the art market, in which art was transformed into a commodity both for local and international consumption. In responding to this market, many artists became specialists in one area, such as portraiture or landscape. Eventually, art dealers emerged as middlemen, further shaping the nascent art market and the professions it includes.

Sequencing Works of Art
THE CLASSICIZING INFLUENCE

1504	Albrecht Dürer, *Adam and Eve*
1520	Jan Gossaert, *Saint Luke Painting the Virgin Mary*
1546	Pierre Lescot, west wing of the Cour Carré, Louvre, Paris, begun
1563–84	Juan Bautista de Toledo and Juan de Herrera, El Escorial, Madrid, Spain
1591–97	Robert Smythson, Hardwick Hall, Shrewsbury, England

MARINUS VAN REYMERSWAELE. In contrast to Gossaert's inspired *Saint Luke*, Marinus van Reymerswaele from Zeeland (c. 1493–after 1567) painted "Everyman" going about his daily affairs. In his popular Antwerp workshop he produced secular panel paintings featuring such characters as the universally despised money-lenders and tax collectors. **THE BANKER AND HIS WIFE** (FIG. 21–23), painted in 1540, is

21–23 | Marinus van Reymerswaele **THE BANKER AND HIS WIFE**
1540. Oil on panel, 33¾ × 45⅞" (85.7 × 116.5 cm). Museo Nazionale del Bargello, Florence.

21—24 | Caterina van Hemessen SELF-PORTRAIT
1548. Oil on wood panel, 12¼ × 9¼″ (31.1 × 23.5 cm).
Öffentliche Kunstsammlung, Basel, Switzerland.

The panel on the easel already has its frame. Caterina holds a small palette and brushes and steadies her right hand with a mahlstick, an essential tool for an artist doing fine, detailed work.

almost a caricature of *A Goldsmith (Saint Eligius?) in His Shop* by Petrus Christus (SEE FIG. 18–18). In contrast to the pious saint, the banker greedily counts coins, avidly watched by his young wife, whose thin, clawlike fingers turn the pages of the account book. Two other popular themes emerge: "the power of women," a variation of "the world turned upside down," and the "mismatched couple"—the old man with a young wife. Virtuoso painting technique has been applied to a less-than-worthy subject, but the artist probably intended more than mere illustration. The painting recalls the sins of lust and greed—the folly of ill-matched lovers, and the sin caused by the love of money. The cluttered table and filled shelves suggest the emerging specialty of still-life painting—which, along with landscape painting, will become an important theme in the art of the next century.

CATERINA VAN HEMESSEN. As religious art declined in the face of Protestant disapproval, portraits became a major source of work for artists. Caterina van Hemessen (1528–87)

of Antwerp had an illustrious international reputation as a portraitist. She had learned to paint from her father, the Flemish Mannerist Jan Sanders van Hemessen, but her quiet realism and skilled rendering also had its roots in the Italian High Renaissance, whose ideas were brought back to the Netherlands by painters who had visited Italy. To maintain the focus on the foreground subject, van Hemessen painted her portraits against even, dark-colored backgrounds, on which she identified the sitter by name and age, signing and dating each work. The inscription in her **SELF-PORTRAIT** (FIG. 21–24) reads: "I Caterina van Hemessen painted myself in 1548. Her age 20." In delineating her own features, van Hemessen presented a serious young person without personal vanity yet seemingly already self-assured about her artistic abilities.

During her early career in Antwerp, van Hemessen became a favored court artist to Mary of Hungary, sister of Emperor Charles V and regent of the Netherlands, for whom she painted not only portraits but also religious works. In 1554, Caterina married the organist of Antwerp Cathedral, and when Mary ceased to be regent in 1556 (at the time of Charles's abdication), the couple accompanied Mary to Spain.

PIETER BRUEGEL THE ELDER. So popular did the works of Hieronymus Bosch remain that, nearly half a century after his death, Pieter Bruegel (c. 1525–69) began his career by imitating them. Fortunately, Bruegel's talents went far beyond those of an ordinary copyist. Like Bosch he often painted large narrative works crowded with figures, and he chose moralizing or satirical subject matter. He traveled throughout Italy, but, unlike many Renaissance artists, he did not record the ruins of ancient Rome or the wonders of the Italian cities. Instead, he seems to have been fascinated by the landscape, particularly the formidable jagged rocks and sweeping panoramic views of Alpine valleys, which he recorded in detailed drawings. Back home in his studio, he made an impressive leap of the imagination as he painted the flat and rolling lands of Flanders as broad panoramas, even adding imaginary mountains on the horizon (SEE FIG. 21–26).

In 1563, after his first career as a draftsman for the engravers in At the Four Winds publishing house, he moved to Brussels. Bruegel's style and subjects found great favor with local scholars, merchants, and bankers, who appreciated the beautifully painted, artfully composed works that also reflected contemporary social, political, and religious conditions. Bruegel visited country fairs to sketch the farmers and townspeople who became the focus of his paintings, whether religious or secular. He depicted characters not as unique individuals but as well-observed types, whose universality makes them familiar even today. Bruegel presented Flemish farmers vividly and sympathetically while also exposing their very human faults.

Clearly Bruegel knew the classics; he had been a member of the humanistic circles in Antwerp. He could only have

21–25 | Pieter Bruegel the Elder **THE FALL OF ICARUS**
c. 1555–56. Oil on panel transferred to canvas. 29 × 44⅛" (73.6 × 112 cm). Konenklijke Musea voor Schone Kunsten van Belgie, Brussels.

painted **THE FALL OF ICARUS** (FIG. 21–25) after reading Ovid, so closely does he follow the ancient Roman's description of Icarus's fall. Icarus—thrilled by the experience and filled with exuberant self-confidence—ignored his father's warning and flew too near the sun, melting his wings of feathers and wax. As Ovid tells the story, in Book 8 of his *Metamorphoses*, no one noticed as the youth plunged into the sea—neither the fisherman, the shepherd, nor the plowman. Bruegel's painting of these workers indicates a very close observation of real people going about their normal activities. That he was as aware of local folklore as he was of the classics is demonstrated by his inclusion of a half-hidden corpse in the underbrush. A Flemish proverb says, "No plow stops at the death of any man."

But where is Icarus, the fallen hero? Amid rippling waves near the shore two tiny legs thrash madly as the boy plunges to his death. Man's great achievement—flight—and man's pride in accomplishment—and death because of this pride—all are irrelevant to the simple people whose goal is day-to-day survival in the continuous cycle of nature.

Bruegel was not only a great landscape painter, he could depict nature in all seasons and in all moods. His **RETURN OF THE HUNTERS** (FIG. 21–26) is one of a cycle of six panels, each representing two months of the year. In this December–January scene, Bruegel has captured the atmosphere of the damp, cold winter, with its early nightfall, in the same way that his compatriots the Limbourgs did 150 years earlier in the *February* calendar illustration (see fig. 18–6). At first, the *Hunters* appears neutral and realistic, but the sharp plunge into space, the juxtaposition of near and far without middle ground, is a typically sixteenth-century device. The viewer seems to hover with the birds slightly above the ground, looking down first on the busy foreground scene, then suddenly across the valley to the snow-covered village and frozen ponds. The main subjects of the painting, the hunters, have their backs turned and do not reveal their feelings as they slog through the snow, trailed by their dogs. They pass an inn, at the left, where a worker moves a table to receive a pig that others are singeing in a fire. But this is clearly not an accidental image; it is a slice of everyday life

21–26 | Pieter Bruegel the Elder **RETURN OF THE HUNTERS**
1565. Oil on wood panel, 3'10½" × 5'3¾" (1.18 × 1.61 m). Kunsthistorisches Museum, Vienna.

faithfully reproduced within the carefully calculated composition. The sharp diagonals sweeping into space are countered by the pointed gables and roofs at the lower right as well as by the jagged mountain peaks along the right edge. Their rhythms are deliberately slowed and stabilized by a balance of vertical tree trunks and horizontal rectangles of water frozen over in the distance. As a depiction of Netherlandish life, this scene represents a relative calm before the storm. Three years after it was painted, the anguished struggle of the northern provinces for independence from Spain began.

Pieter the Elder died in 1569, leaving two children, Pieter the Younger and Jan, both of whom became successful painters in the next century. The dynasty continued with Jan's son, Jan the Younger. In the seventeenth century, the spelling of the family name was changed from Bruegel to Brueghel.

RENAISSANCE ART IN ENGLAND

England, although facing the disruption of the Reformation, was economically and politically stable enough to provide sustained support for architecture and the decorative arts during the Tudor dynasty. Music and literature also flourished, but painting was left to foreigners. Henry VIII was known for his love of music (he was himself a composer of considerable

accomplishment), and he also hoped to compete with the wealthy, sophisticated court of Francis I in the visual arts.

As a young man Henry VIII (ruled 1509–47) was loyal to the Church. When he wrote a book attacking Luther in 1520, the pope declared him "Defender of the Faith." But when the pope refused to annul his marriage to Catherine of Aragon, Henry broke with Rome. By action of Parliament in 1534 he became the "Supreme Head on earth of the Church and Clergy of England." He ordered an English translation of the Bible to be put in every church. In 1536 and 1539, he went further and dissolved the monasteries, confiscating their great wealth and rewarding his followers with monastic lands and buildings. Henry's need for money had disastrous effects on the arts as his men stripped shrines and altars of their jewels and precious metals. The final blow to religious art came during the reign of Henry's son Edward VI when in 1548 all images were officially prohibited and two years later altars were replaced by wooden tables.

During the brief reign of Mary (ruled 1553–58), England officially returned to Catholicism, but the accession of Elizabeth in 1558 confirmed England as a Protestant country. So effective was Elizabeth, who ruled until 1603, that the last decades of the sixteenth century in England are called the Elizabethan Age.

Artists in the Tudor Court

Religious painting had no place in England, but a remarkable record of the appearance of Tudor monarchs survives in portraiture. Because direct contacts with Italy became difficult after Henry's break with the Roman Catholic Church, the Tudors favored Netherlandish and German artists. Thus, it was a German-born painter, Hans Holbein the Younger (c. 1497–1543), who shaped the taste of the English court and upper classes, and a Flemish artist who held the title of "King's Painter."

HANS HOLBEIN. Holbein first visited London from 1526 to 1528 and was introduced by the Dutch scholar Erasmus to the humanist circle around the statesman Thomas More. He returned to England in 1532 and was appointed court painter to Henry VIII about four years later. One of Holbein's official portraits of Henry (FIG. 21–27), shown at age 49 according to the inscription on the dark blue-green background, was painted in 1540, although the king's appearance had already been established in an earlier prototype. Henry, who envied the

21–27 | Hans Holbein the Younger **HENRY VIII**
1540. Oil on wood panel, 32½ × 29½″ (82.6 × 75 cm). Galleria Nazionale d'Arte Antica, Rome.

21–28 | Attributed to Levina Bening Teerlinc
PRINCESS ELIZABETH
c. 1559. Oil on oak panel, 42¾ × 32¼" (109 × 81.8 cm). The Royal Collection, Windsor Castle, England.
(RCIN 404444, OM 46 WC 2010)

French king Francis I and attempted to outdo him in every way, imitated French fashions and even copied the style of the French king's beard. Henry's huge frame—he was well over 6 feet tall and had a 54-inch waist—is covered by the latest style of dress: a short puffed-sleeve coat of heavy brocade trimmed in dark fur; a narrow, stiff white collar fastened at the front; and a doublet, encrusted with gemstones and gold braid, which was slit to expose his silk shirt. Holbein used the English king's great size to advantage for this official portrait, enhancing Henry's majestic figure with embroidered cloth, fur, and jewelry to create one of the most imposing images of

power in the history of art. He is dressed for his wedding to his fourth wife, Anne of Cleves, on April 5, 1540.

LEVINA BENING TEERLINC. Holbein was not the highest-paid painter in Henry VIII's court. That status belonged to a Netherlandish woman, Levina Bening Teerlinc. Since Teerlinc worked in England for thirty years, her near-anonymity is an art-historical mystery. At Henry's invitation to become "King's Paintrix," she and her husband arrived in London in 1545 from Bruges, where her father was a leading manuscript illuminator. She maintained her court appointment

Art and Its Context
ARMOR FOR ROYAL GAMES

The medieval tradition of holding tilting, or jousting, competitions at English festivals and public celebrations continued during Renaissance times. Perhaps the most famous of these, the Accession Day Tilts, were held annually to celebrate the anniversary of Elizabeth I's coronation. The gentlemen of the court, dressed in armor made especially for the occasion, held mock battles in the queen's honor. They rode their horses from opposite directions, trying to strike each other with long lances. Each pair of competitors made six passes and the judges rated their performances.

The elegant armor worn by George Clifford, third Earl of Cumberland, at the Accession Day Tilts has been preserved in the collection of the Metropolitan Museum of Art in New York. Tudor roses and back-to-back capital E's in honor of the queen decorate the armor's surface. As the Queen's Champion beginning in 1590, Clifford also wore her jeweled glove attached to his helmet as he met all comers in the tiltyard of Whitehall Palace in London.

Made by Jacob Halder in the royal armories at Greenwich, the 60-pound suit of armor is recorded in the sixteenth-century Almain Armourers' Album along with its "exchange pieces." These allowed the owner to vary his appearance by changing mitts, side pieces, or leg protectors, and also provided backup pieces if one were damaged.

Jacob Halder **ARMOR OF GEORGE CLIFFORD, THIRD EARL OF CUMBERLAND**
Made in the royal workshop at Greenwich, England. c. 1580–85. Steel and gold, height 5'9½" (1.77 m). The Metropolitan Museum of Art, New York.
Munsey Fund, 1932 (32.130.6)

until her death about 1576, in the reign of Elizabeth I. Because Teerlinc was the granddaughter and daughter of Netherlandish manuscript illuminators, she is assumed to have painted miniature portraits or scenes on vellum and ivory. Certainly, she designed Elizabeth's first official seal of 1559, which included the queen's likeness. One life-size portrait frequently attributed to her—but by no means securely—depicts Elizabeth Tudor as a young princess (FIG. 21–28). Elizabeth's pearled cap, an adaptation of the so-called French hood popularized by her mother, Anne Boleyn, is set back to expose her famous red hair. Her brocaded outer dress, worn over a rigid hoop, is split to expose an underskirt of cut velvet. Although her features are softened by youth and no doubt are idealized as well, her long, high-bridged nose and the fullness below her small lower lip give her a distinctive appearance. The prominently displayed books were no doubt included to signify Elizabeth's well-known love of learning.

21–29 | Nicholas Hilliard **GEORGE CLIFFORD, THIRD EARL OF CUMBERLAND (1558–1605)**
c. 1595. Watercolor on vellum on card, oval 2¾ × 2⁷⁄₁₆″ (7.1 × 5.8 cm). The Nelson-Atkins Museum of Art, Kansas City, Missouri.
Gift of Mr. and Mrs. John W. Starr through the Starr Foundation. F58-60/188

NICHOLAS HILLIARD. In 1570, while Levina Teerlinc was still active at Elizabeth's court, Nicholas Hilliard (1547–1619) arrived in London from southwest England to pursue a career as a jeweler, goldsmith, and painter of miniatures. Hilliard never received a court appointment but worked instead on commission, creating miniature portraits of the queen and court notables, including **GEORGE CLIFFORD, THIRD EARL OF CUMBERLAND** (FIG. 21–29). Cumberland was a regular participant in the annual tilts and festivals celebrating the anniversary of Elizabeth I's ascent to the throne. In Hilliard's miniature, Cumberland wears a richly engraved and gold-inlaid suit of armor, forged for his first appearance, in 1583, at the tilts (see "Armor for Royal Games," page 737). Hilliard had a talent for giving his male subjects an appropriate air of courtly jauntiness. Cumberland, a man of about thirty with a stylish beard, mustache, and curled hair, is humanized by his direct gaze and unconcealed receding hair-

line. Cumberland's motto, "I bear lightning and water," is inscribed on a stormy sky, with a lightning bolt in the form of a caduceus (the classical staff with two entwined snakes), one of his emblems. After all, he was that remarkable Elizabethan type—a naval commander and a gentleman pirate.

Architecture

Henry VIII, as the newly declared head of the Church of England, sold or gave church land to favored courtiers. Many properties were bought by speculators who divided and resold them. To increase support for the Tudor dynasty, Henry and his successors also granted titles to rich landowners. To display their wealth and status, many of these newly created aristocrats embarked on extensive building projects. They built lavish country residences, which sometimes surpassed the French châteaux in size and grandeur. At this time, Elizabethan architecture still reflected the Perpendicular Gothic style (SEE FIG. 17–20), with its severe walls and broad expanses of glass, although designers modernized the forms by replacing medieval ornament with classical motifs copied from architectural handbooks and pattern books. The first architectural manual in English, published in 1563, was written by John Shute, one of the few builders who had spent time in Italy. But books by Flemish, French, and German architects were readily available. Most influential were the treatises on architectural design by the Italian architect Sebastiano Serlio.

HARDWICK HALL. One of the grandest of all the Elizabethan houses was **HARDWICK HALL**, the home of Elizabeth, Countess of Shrewsbury, known as "Bess of Hardwick" (FIG. 21–30). When she was in her seventies, the redoubtable countess—who inherited riches from all four of her deceased husbands—employed Robert Smythson (c. 1535–1614), England's first Renaissance professional architect, to build Hardwick Hall (1591–97).

Smythson's—and Bess's—plan for Hardwick was new. The medieval great hall became a two-story entrance hall, with rooms arranged symmetrically around it—a nod to classical balance. A sequence of rooms leads to a grand stair up to the Long Gallery and **HIGH GREAT CHAMBER** on the second floor (FIG. 21–31), where the countess received guests, entertained, and sometimes dined. The High Great Chamber was designed to display a set of six Brussels tapestries with the story of Ulysses. The room had enormous windows, ornate fireplaces, and a richly carved and painted plaster frieze around the room. The frieze, by the master Abraham Smith, depicts Diana and her maiden hunters in a forest where they pursue stags and boars. In the window bay, the frieze turns into an allegory on the seasons; Venus whipping Cupid represents spring, and the goddess Ceres, summer. Smith based his allegories on Flemish prints. Graphic arts transmitted images from artist to artist and country to country much as photography does today.

21–30 | Robert Smythson **HARDWICK HALL, SHREWSBURY**
England. 1591–97.

Elizabeth, Countess of Shrewsbury, who commissioned Smythson, participated actively in the design of her houses. She embellished the roofline with her initials, ES, in letters 4 feet tall.

21–31 | Robert Smythson **HIGH GREAT CHAMBER, HARDWICK HALL**
Shrewsbury, England. 1591–97. Brussels tapestries, 1550s; painted plaster sculpture by Abraham Smith.

IN PERSPECTIVE

In the sixteenth century people faced many challenges—political, religious, and aesthetic. Humanistic learning, based on the written word, was dominant—Germany was, after all, the home of the first printed book—and an increasingly literate public gained access not only to practical information but also to new ideas. Germany was also the center of the Reformation within the Christian Church. In many places, the reformers' zeal led to the destruction first of religious art and then sometimes of all the arts. People worshiped in stark shells of church buildings. With no call to paint religious themes, the artists found new themes and focused on worldly subjects, especially on portraits.

Artists were well aware of the new forces at work across the Alps in Italy, and study tours were an essential part of education. Traveling artists could copy ancient classical art in Rome, study mural painting in Florence, and admire the dazzling lush oil painting in Venice. The idea took hold that artists could express as much through painted, sculptural, and architectural forms as poets could with words or musicians with melody. The notion of divinely inspired creativity supplanted manual artistry.

Intense religiosity vied with materialistic enterprise early in the century. The crafts also emerged as splendid fine arts, as seen in pictorial tapestries, gold and silver show-piece tableware, and glazed ceramics, among other mediums. All the arts of personal display—cut velvet and brocade gowns and robes, chains and jewels of state—can be studied in portraits.

The Protestants carried on the tradition of using the visual arts to promote a cause, to educate, and to glorify with grand palaces and portraits—just as the Catholic Church had over the centuries used great church buildings and religious art for its didactic as well as aesthetic values. The effects of the Reformation and the Counter-Reformation would continue to reverberate in the arts of the following century throughout Europe and, across the Atlantic, in America.

VEIT STOSS
**ANNUNCIATION AND
VIRGIN OF THE ROSARY**
1517–18

ALBRECHT DÜRER
SELF-PORTRAIT
1500

SIXTEENTH-CENTURY ART IN NORTHERN EUROPE AND THE IBERIAN PENINSULA

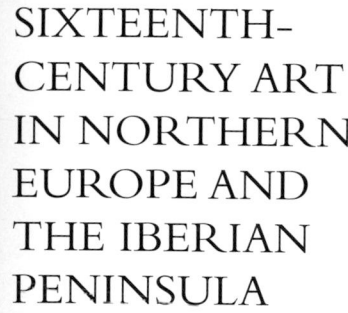

1500

PIERRE LESCOT
WEST WING. COUR CARRÉ,
PALAIS DU LOUVRE, PARIS
BEGUN 1546

◀ Luther Protests Church's Sale of Indulgences 1517

◀ Charles V Holy Roman Emperor 1519–56

1520

◀ First Circumnavigation of Earth 1522

◀ Peasants' War 1524–26

◀ Charles V Orders Sack of Rome 1527

◀ Church of England Separates from Roman Church   1534

1540

◀ Council of Trent 1545–63

PIETER BRUEGEL THE ELDER
RETURN OF THE HUNTERS
1565

1560

◀ Elizabeth I Queen of England 1558–1603

EL GRECO
BURIAL OF COUNT ORGAZ
1586

1580

◀ Dutch Unite against Spanish Rule 1579

◀ English Defeat Spanish Navy in Spanish Armada 1588

1600

ROBERT SMYTHSON
T CHAMBER, HARDWICK
SHREWSBURY, ENGLAND
1591–97

22–1 | Hyacinthe Rigaud **LOUIS XIV** 1701. Oil on canvas, 9′2″ × 7′10¾″ (2.19 × 2.4 m). Musée du Louvre, Paris.

CHAPTER TWENTY-TWO

BAROQUE ART

22

In Hyacinthe Rigaud's 1701 portrait of **LOUIS XIV (FIG. 22–1)**, the richly costumed monarch known as *le Roi Soleil* ("the Sun King"; ruled 1643–1715) is presented to us by an unseen hand that pulls aside a huge billowing curtain. Showing off his elegant legs, of which he was very proud, the 63-year-old French monarch poses in an elaborate robe of state, decorated with gold *fleurs-de-lis* and white ermine, and he wears the red-heeled built-up shoes he had invented to compensate for his short stature. At first glance, the face under the huge wig seems almost incidental to the overall grandeur of the presentation. Yet the directness of Louis XIV's gaze makes him movingly human despite the pompous pose and the overwhelming magnificence that surrounds him. Rigaud's genius in portraiture was always to capture a good likeness while idealizing his subjects' less attractive features and giving minute attention to the virtuoso rendering of textures and materials of the costume and setting.

Louis XIV had ordered this portrait as a gift for his grandson Philip, but when Rigaud finished the painting, Louis liked it so much that he kept it. Three years later, Louis ordered a copy from Rigaud to give his grandson, now King Philip V of Spain (ruled 1700–46). The request for copies of

portraits was not unusual, for the royal and aristocratic families of Europe were linked through marriage, and paintings made appropriate gifts for relatives. Rigaud's workshop produced between thirty and forty portraits a year. His portraits varied in price according to whether the entire figure was painted from life or whether Rigaud merely added a portrait head to a stock figure in a composition he had designed for his workshop to execute.

Rigaud's long career spanned a time of great change in Western art. Not only did new manners of representation emerge, but, whereas art had once been under the patronage of the Church and the aristocracy, a kind of broad-based commercialism arose that was reflected both by portrait workshops such as Rigaud's and by the thousands of still-life and landscape painters producing works for the middle-class households that could now afford to decorate their homes. These changes of the seventeenth and eighteenth centuries—the Baroque period in Europe—took place in a cultural context in which individuals and organizations were grappling with the effects of religious upheaval, economic growth, colonial expansion, political turbulence, and a dramatic explosion of scientific knowledge.

THE BAROQUE PERIOD

The word *baroque* was initially used in the late 1700s as a derogatory term to characterize the exuberant and extravagant aspects of some of the art of the preceding century and a half. Today, *Baroque* can designate certain formal characteristics of style, as well as refer to a period in the history of art lasting from the end of the sixteenth into the eighteenth century. Baroque style is characterized by an emotional rather than intellectual response to a work of art and by an interest in exploiting the dramatic moment through choice of subject and style. Artists created open compositions in which elements are placed or seem to move diagonally, expand upward, or overlap their supposed frames. Many artists developed a loose, free technique using rich colors and dramatic contrasts of light and dark, producing what one critic called an "absolute unity" of form. This unified concept extends to the more expansive unity between architecture, sculpture, and painting and the theatrical effects that could be created by what we would term a multimedia approach. Although many of the formal characteristics of the Baroque have been applied to other periods, like Hellenistic Greek styles, the term *Baroque* will be used here to refer to the complex of styles—including a more restrained, classical stream—that developed against the historical backdrop of the Counter-Reformation, the advancement of science, the expanding world of exploration and trade, and the rise of private patronage in the arts.

By the seventeenth century, the permanent division within Europe between Roman Catholicism and Protestantism had a critical effect on European art. As part of the Counter-Reformation program that came to fruition in the seventeenth century, the Church used art to encourage piety among the faithful and to persuade those it regarded as heretics to return to the fold. Patronage of art in Catholic as well as Protestant countries was spurred by economic growth that helped to support not only the aristocracy, but a large, affluent middle class eager to build and furnish fine houses and even palaces. Buildings ranged from magnificent churches and palaces to stage sets for plays and ballets, while painting and sculpture varied from large religious works and history paintings to portraits, still lifes, and **genre** paintings (scenes of everyday life). At the same time, scientific advances compelled people to question their worldview. Of great importance was the growing understanding that Earth was not the center of the universe but was a planet revolving around the sun (see "Science and the Changing Worldview," page 746).

Within these historical parameters, artists achieved spectacular technical virtuosity and an impressive ability to produce for their patrons and the market. Painters manipulated their mediums from the thinnest glazes to heavy **impasto** (thickly applied pigments), taking pleasure in the very quality of the material. A desire for realism led some artists to reach for a verisimilitude that went against the idealization of classical and Renaissance styles. The English leader Oliver Cromwell supposedly demanded that his portrait be painted "warts and all." Leading artists such as Rubens and Rembrandt organized their studios into veritable picture factories. Artists were admired for the originality of a concept or design, and their shops produced paintings on demand—including copy after copy of popular themes or portraits. The respect for the "original," or first edition, is a modern concept.

The role of viewers also changed. Earlier, Renaissance painters and patrons had been fascinated with the visual possibilities of perspective, but even such displays as Mantegna's ceiling fresco at Mantua (SEE FIG. 19–34) remained an intellectual conceit. Seventeenth-century masters, on the other hand, treated viewers as participants in the artwork, and the space of the work included the world beyond the frame. In Catholic countries, representations of horrifying scenes of martyrdom or the passionate spiritual life of a mystic in religious ecstasy inspired a renewed faith (SEE FIG. 22–6). In Protestant countries, images of civic parades and city views inspired pride in accomplishment (SEE FIGS. 22–45, 22–49). Viewers participated in art like audiences in a theater—vicariously but completely—as the work of art reached out visually and emotionally to draw them into its orbit. The seventeenth-century French critic Roger de Piles described this exchange when he wrote: "True painting . . . calls to us; and has so powerful an effect, that we cannot help coming near it, as if it had something to tell us" (quoted in Puttfarken, page 55).

MAP 22—1 | THE SEVENTEENTH CENTURY IN EUROPE AND NORTH AMERICA

Protestantism dominated in northern Europe, while Roman Catholicism remained strong after the Counter-Reformation in southern Europe.

ITALY

Italy in the seventeenth century remained a divided land in spite of a common history, language, and geography with borders defined by the seas. The Kingdom of Naples and Sicily was Spanish; the Papal States crossed the center; Venice maintained its independence as a republic; and the north remained divided among small principalities. In spite of religious wars raging in Germany and France, churchmen remained powerful patrons of the arts, especially as they recognized the visual arts' role in propaganda campaigns. The popes, cardinals, and their families turned to artists to enhance their status. Additionally, the Church had set down rules for art at the Council of Trent (1563) that went against the arcane, worldly, and often lascivious trends exploited by Mannerism. The clergy's call for clarity, simplicity, chaste subject matter, and the ability to rouse a very Catholic piety in the face of Protestant revolt found a response in the fresh approaches to subject matter and style offered by a new generation of artists.

Architecture and Sculpture in Rome

A major goal of the Counter-Reformation was to properly embellish the Church and its mother city. Pope Sixtus V (papacy 1585–90) had begun the renewal by cutting long straight avenues through the city to link the major pilgrimage churches with one another and with the main gates of Rome. Sixtus also ordered open spaces—piazzas—cleared in front of major churches, marking each site with an Egyptian obelisk. (His chief architect, Domenico Fontana, performed remarkable feats of engineering to move the huge monoliths.) In a practical vein, Sixtus also reopened one of the ancient aqueducts to stabilize the city's water supply. Unchallengeable power and vast financial resources were required to carry out such an extensive plan of urban renewal and to materially fashion Rome—which had been the victim of rapacity and neglect since the Middle Ages—once more into the center of spiritual and worldly power.

The Counter-Reformation popes had great wealth, although eventually they nearly bankrupted the Church with

Science and Technology
SCIENCE AND THE CHANGING WORLDVIEW

Investigations of the natural world that had begun during the Renaissance changed the way people of the seventeenth and eighteenth centuries—including artists—saw the world. Some of the new discoveries brought a sense of the grand scale of the universe, while others focused on the minute complexity of the microscopic world of nature. As frames of reference expanded and contracted, artists found new ways to mirror these changing perspectives in their own works.

The philosophers Francis Bacon (1561–1626) of England and René Descartes (1596–1650) of France established a new scientific method of studying the world by insisting on scrupulous objectivity and logical reasoning. Bacon proposed that facts be established by observation and tested by controlled experiments. Descartes argued for the deductive method of reasoning, in which a conclusion was arrived at logically from basic premises—the most fundamental example being "I think, therefore I am."

In 1543, the Polish scholar Nicolaus Copernicus (1473–1543) published *On the Revolutions of the Heavenly Spheres*, which contradicted the long-held view that Earth is the center of the universe (the Ptolemaic theory) by arguing that Earth and other planets revolve around the sun. The Church put the book on its Index of Prohibited Books in 1616, but Johannes Kepler (1571–1630) continued demonstrating that the planets revolve around the sun in elliptical orbits. Galileo Galilei (1564–1642), an astronomer, mathematician, and physicist, developed the telescope as a tool for observing the heavens. His findings provided further confirmation of the Copernican theory, but since the Church prohibited teaching that theory, Galileo was tried for heresy by the Inquisition and forced to recant his views. As the first person to see the craters of the moon through a telescope, Galileo began the exploration of space that eventually led humans to take their first steps on the moon in 1969.

Seventeenth-century science explored not only the vastness of outer space but also the smallest elements of inner space, thanks to the invention of the microscope by the Dutch lens maker and amateur scientist Antoni van Leeuwenhoek (1632–1723). Although embroiderers, textile inspectors, manuscript illuminators, and painters had long used magnifying glasses in their work, Leeuwenhoek perfected grinding techniques and increased the power of his lenses far beyond what those uses required. Ultimately, he was able to study the inner workings of plants and animals and even see microorganisms. Soon, scientists learned to draw, or depended on artists to draw, the images revealed by the microscope for further study

and publication. Not until the discovery of photography in the nineteenth century could scientists communicate their discoveries without an artist's help.

Maria Sibylla Merian **PLATE 9 FROM DISSERTATION IN INSECT GENERATIONS AND METAMORPHOSIS IN SURINAM** 1719. Hand-colored engraving, 18⅞ × 13" (47.9 × 33 cm). National Museum of Women in the Arts, Washington, D.C. Gift of Wallace and Wilhelmina Holladay Collection, funds contributed by Mr. and Mrs. George G. Anderman and an anonymous donor (1976.56)

Maria Sibylla Merian (1647–1717) was unusual in making noteworthy contributions as both researcher and artist. German by birth and Dutch by training, Merian was once described by a Dutch contemporary as a painter of flowers, fruit, birds, worms, flies, mosquitoes, spiders, "and other filth." At the time, it was believed that insects emerged spontaneously from the soil, but Merian's research on the life cycles of insects proved otherwise, findings she published in 1679 and 1683 as *The Wonderful Transformation of Caterpillars and (Their) Singular Plant Nourishment*. In 1699, Amsterdam subsidized Merian's research on plants and insects in the Dutch colony of Surinam in South America; her results were published as *Dissertation in Insect Generations and Metamorphosis in Surinam*, illustrated with sixty large plates engraved after her watercolors. Each plate is scientifically precise, accurate, and informative, presenting insects in various stages of development, along with the plants they live on.

their building programs. Sixtus began to renovate the Vatican and its library. He completed the dome of Saint Peter's and built splendid palaces. The Renaissance ideal of the central-plan church continued to be used for the shrines of saints, but Counter-Reformation thinking called for churches with long, wide naves to accommodate large congregations assembled to hear firm sermons as well as to participate in the Mass. In the sixteenth century, the decoration of new churches had been generally austere, but seventeenth- and eighteenth-century Catholic taste favored opulent and spectacular visual effects to heighten the emotional involvement of worshipers.

22–2 | SAINT PETER'S BASILICA AND PIAZZA, VATICAN, ROME
Carlo Maderno, façade, 1607–26; Gianlorenzo Bernini, piazza design, c. 1656–57.

Perhaps only a Baroque artist of Bernini's talents could have unified the many artistic periods and styles that come together in Saint Peter's Basilica (starting with Bramante's original design for the building in the sixteenth century). The basilica in no way suggests a piecing together of parts made by different builders at different times but rather presents itself as a triumphal unity of all the parts in one coherent whole.

SAINT PETER'S BASILICA IN THE VATICAN. Half a century after Michelangelo had returned Saint Peter's Basilica to Bramante's original vision of a central-plan building, Pope Paul V (papacy 1605–21) commissioned Carlo Maderno (1556–1629) to provide the church with a longer nave and a new façade (FIG. 22–2). Construction began in 1607, and everything but the façade bell towers was completed by 1615 (see "Saint Peter's Basilica," Chapter 20, page 679). In essence, Maderno took the concept of Il Gesù's façade (SEE FIG. 20–31) and enlarged it to befit the most important church of the Catholic world. Maderno's façade for Saint Peter's "steps out" in three progressively projecting planes: from the corners to the doorways flanking the central entrance area, then the entrance area, then the central doorway itself. Similarly, the colossal orders connecting the first and second stories are flat pilasters at the corners but fully round columns where they flank the doorways. These columns support a continuous entablature that also steps out—following the columns—as it moves toward the central door. A triangular pediment provides vertical movement, as does the superimposition of pilasters on the relatively narrow attic story above the entablature.

When Maderno died in 1629, he was succeeded as Vatican architect by his collaborator of five years, Gianlorenzo Bernini (1598–1680). Gianlorenzo was taught by his father,

and part of his training involved sketching the Vatican collection of ancient sculpture, such as *Laocoön and His Sons* and the Farnese Hercules (see Introduction, Fig. 23), as well as the many examples of Renaissance painting in the papal palace. Throughout his life, Bernini admired antique art and, like other artists of this period, considered himself a classicist. Today, we not only appreciate his strong debt to the Renaissance tradition but also consider his art a breakthrough that takes us into a new, Baroque style.

When Urban VIII was elected pope in 1623, he unhesitatingly gave the young Bernini the demanding task of designing an enormous bronze **baldachin,** or canopy, for the high altar of Saint Peter's. The church was so large that a dramatic focus on the altar was essential. The resulting **BALDACCHINO** (FIG. 22–3), completed in 1633, stands almost 100 feet high and exemplifies the Baroque artists' desire to combine architecture and sculpture—and sometimes painting as well—so that works no longer fit into a single category or a single medium. The twisted columns symbolize the union of Old and New Testaments—the vine of the Eucharist climbing the columns of the Temple of Solomon. The fanciful Composite capitals, combining elements of both the Ionic and the Corinthian orders, support an entablature with a crowning element topped with an orb (a sphere representing the

belonged to Saint Peter as the first bishop of Rome. The Chair of Peter symbolized the direct descent of Christian authority from Peter to the current pope, a belief rejected by Protestants and therefore deliberately emphasized in Counter-Reformation Catholicism. In Bernini's work, the chair is carried by four theologians and is lifted even farther by a surge of gilded clouds moving upward to the Holy Spirit, who materializes in the stained-glass window in the form of a dove surrounded by an oval of golden rays. Adoring, gilded angels and gilt-bronze rays fan out around the window and seem to extend the penetration of the natural light—and the Holy Spirit—into the apse of the church. The gilding also reflects the light back to the window, creating a dazzling, ethereal effect that the seventeenth century, with its interest in mystics and visions, would equate with the activation of divinity—and the sort of effect that present-day artists achieve by resorting to electric spotlights.

At approximately the same time that he was at work on the Chair of Peter, Bernini designed and supervised the building of a colonnade to form a huge double piazza in front of the entrance to Saint Peter's (SEE FIG. 22–2). The open space that he had to work with was irregular, and an Egyptian obelisk and a fountain already in place (part of

22–3 | Gianlorenzo Bernini **BALDACCHINO**
1624-33. Gilt bronze, height approx. 100' (30.48 m).
Chair of Peter shrine, 1657-66. Gilt bronze, marble, stucco, and glass. Pier decorations, 1627-41. Gilt bronze and marble. Crossing, Saint Peter's Basilica, Vatican, Rome.

universe) and a cross (symbolizing the reign of Christ). Figures of angels and *putti* decorate the entablature, which is hung with tasseled panels in imitation of a cloth canopy. These symbolic elements, both architectural and sculptural, not only mark the site of the tomb of Saint Peter but also serve as a monument to Urban VIII and his family, the Barberini, whose emblems—including honeybees and suns on the tasseled panels, and laurel leaves on the climbing vines—are prominently displayed.

Between 1627 and 1641, Bernini and several other sculptors, again combining architecture and sculpture, rebuilt Bramante's crossing piers as giant reliquaries. Statues of saints Helena, Veronica, Andrew, and Longinus stand in niches below alcoves containing their relics, to the left and right of the *baldacchino*. Visible through the *baldacchino*'s columns in the apse of the church is another reliquary: the gilded stone, bronze, and stucco shrine made by Bernini between 1657 and 1666 for the ancient wooden throne thought to have

22–4 | Gianlorenzo Bernini **DAVID**
1623. Marble, height 5'7" (1.7 m). Galleria Borghese, Rome.

Sixtus V's plan for Rome) had to be incorporated into the overall plan. Bernini's remarkable design frames the oval piazza with two enormous curved porticoes, or covered walkways, supported by Doric columns. These curved porticoes are connected to two straight porticoes, which lead up a slight incline to the two ends of the church façade. Bernini spoke of his conception as representing the "motherly arms of the Church" reaching out to the world. He had intended to build a third section of the colonnade closing the side of the piazza facing the church so that pilgrims, after crossing the Tiber River bridge and passing through narrow streets, would suddenly emerge into the enormous open space before the church. Even without the final colonnade section, the great church, colonnade, and piazza with its towering obelisk and monumental fountains—Bernini added the second one to balance the first—are an awe-inspiring vision.

BERNINI AS SCULPTOR. Even after Bernini's appointment as Vatican architect in 1629, he was able to accept outside commissions by virtue of his large workshop. In fact, Bernini first became famous as a sculptor, and he continued to work as a sculptor throughout his career, for both the papacy and private clients. A man of many talents, he was also a painter and even a playwright—an interest that dovetailed with his genius for theatrical and dramatic aspects in his sculpture and architecture.

Bernini's **DAVID (FIG. 22–4),** made for a nephew of Pope Paul V in 1623, introduced a new type of three-dimensional composition that intrudes forcefully on the viewer's space. Inspired by the athletic figures Annibale Carracci had painted in the Farnese gallery some twenty years earlier (SEE, for example, the Giant preparing to heave a boulder at the far end of the gallery, FIG. 22–13), Bernini's *David* bends at the waist and twists far to one side, ready to launch the lethal rock. Unlike Michelangelo's cool and self-confident youth (SEE FIG. 20–10), this more mature *David,* with his lean, sinewy body, is all tension and determination, a frame of mind emphasized by his ferocious expression, tightly clenched mouth, and straining muscles. Bernini's energetic, twisting figure includes the surrounding space as part of the composition by implying the presence of an unseen adversary somewhere behind the viewer. Thus, the viewer becomes part of the action that is taking place at that very moment. This immediacy, the emphasis on the climactic moment, and the inclusion of the viewer in the work of art represent an important new direction for art.

From 1642 until 1652, Bernini worked on the decoration of the funerary chapel of Venetian cardinal Federigo Cornaro (FIG. 22–5) in the Church of Santa Maria della Vittoria, designed by Carlo Maderno earlier in the century. Like Il Gesù (SEE FIG. 20–32), the church had a single nave with shallow side chapels. Santa Maria della Vittoria was built by the order of the Discalced (unshod) Carmelite Friars, and the chapel of the Cornaro family was dedicated to one of the

22–5 | Gianlorenzo Bernini **CORNARO CHAPEL, CHURCH OF SANTA MARIA DELLA VITTORIA, ROME** 1642-52.

order's great figures, the Spanish saint Teresa of Ávila, canonized only twenty years earlier. Bernini designed the chapel to be a rich and theatrical setting in which to portray an event in Teresa's life that contributed to her sainthood. To accomplish this, he covered the walls with colored marble panels

22–6 | Gianlorenzo Bernini **SAINT TERESA OF ÁVILA IN ECSTASY**
1645–52. Marble, height of the group 11′6″ (3.5 m). Cornaro Chapel, Church of Santa Maria della Vittoria, Rome.

and crowned them with a projecting cornice supported by marble pilasters.

In the center of the chapel and framed by columns in the huge oval niche above the altar, Bernini's marble group **SAINT TERESA OF ÁVILA IN ECSTASY** (FIG. 22–6) represents a vision described by the Spanish mystic in which an angel pierced her body repeatedly with an arrow, transporting her to a state of indescribable pain, religious ecstasy, and a sense of oneness with God. Saint Teresa and the angel, who seem to float upward on moisture-laden stucco clouds, are cut from a heavy mass of solid marble supported on a hidden pedestal and by hidden metal bars sunk deep into the chapel wall. Bernini's skill at capturing the movements and emotions of these figures is matched by his virtuosity in simulating different textures and colors in the pure white medium of marble; the angel's gauzy, clinging draperies seem silken in contrast with Teresa's heavy woolen robe, the habit of her order. Yet Bernini effectively used the configuration of the garment's folds to convey the swooning, sensuous body beneath, even though only Teresa's face, hands, and bare feet are actually visible.

As he would later do for the Chair of Peter (SEE FIG. 22–3), Bernini used a directed light source to announce the divine presence that enfolds the saint's ecstasy and spiritual martyrdom. Above the cornice on the back wall, the curved ceiling surrounds a concealed window that mysteriously illuminates the niche that houses Saint Teresa and dissolves the descending rays of gilt bronze, the solid marble figures, and the clouds on which they are suspended into a painterly vision. Kneeling at what appear to be *prie-dieux* on both sides of the chapel are marble portraits of Federigo, his deceased father (a Venetian doge), and six cardinals of the Cornaro family. The figures are informally posed and naturalistically portrayed. Two read from their prayer books, others exclaim at the miracle taking place in the light-infused realm above the altar, and one leans out from his seat, apparently to look at someone entering the chapel—perhaps the viewer, whose space these figures share. The frescoed vault, above, executed by another artist, depicts the dove of the Holy Spirit hovering over angels and stuccoed scenes of the saint's life.

Gianlorenzo Bernini was deeply religious and held fast to the tenets espoused by the Counter-Reformation. Although he created a "stage" for his subject, his purpose was not to produce a mere spectacle but to capture a critical, dramatic moment at its emotional and sensual height and by doing so guide the viewer to identify totally with the event— and perhaps be transformed in the process.

Bernini's complex, theatrical interplay of media— sculpture, architecture, and painting—and of the various levels of illusion in the chapel—divine, mystical, and actual—invite the beholder to identify with Teresa's experience. His brilliant solution to the problem of transfixing the momentary in physical materials was imitated by sculptors throughout Europe.

BORROMINI'S CHURCH OF SAN CARLO. The intersection of two of the wide straight avenues created by Pope Sixtus V inspired city planners to add a special emphasis, with fountains marking each of the four corners of the crossing. In 1634, the Trinitarian monks decided to build a new church at the site and awarded the commission for **SAN CARLO ALLE QUATTRO FONTANE** (Saint Charles at the Four Fountains) to Francesco Borromini (1599–1667). Borromini, a nephew of architect Carlo Maderno, had arrived in Rome in 1619 from northern Italy to enter his uncle's workshop. Later, he worked under Bernini's supervision on the decoration of Saint Peter's, and some details of the *Baldacchino,* as well as the structural engineering, are now attributed to him, but San Carlo was his first independent commission. Unfinished at

22–7 | Francesco Borromini **FAÇADE, CHURCH OF SAN CARLO ALLE QUATTRO FONTANE, ROME** 1665-67.

Borromini's death, the church was nevertheless completed according to his design.

San Carlo stands on a narrow piece of land, with one corner cut off to accommodate one of the four fountains that give the church its name (FIG. 22–7). To fit the irregular site, Borromini created an elongated central-plan interior space with undulating walls (FIG. 22–8), whose powerful, sweeping curves create an unexpected feeling of movement, as if the walls were heaving in and out. Robust pairs of columns support a massive entablature, over which an oval dome, supported on pendentives, seems to float. The coffers (inset panels in geometric shapes) filling the interior of the oval-shaped dome form an eccentric honeycomb of crosses, elongated hexagons, and octagons (FIG. 22–9). These coffers decrease sharply in size as they approach the apex, or highest point, where the dove of the Holy Spirit hovers in a climax that brings together geometry used in the chapel: oval, octagon, circle, and—very important—a triangle, symbol of the Trinity as well as of the church's patrons. The dome appears be shimmering and inflating, thanks to light sources placed in the lower coffers and the lantern.

22–8 | Francesco Borromini
INTERIOR, CHURCH OF SAN CARLO ALLE QUATTRO FONTANE, ROME
1638–41

22–9 | **DOME INTERIOR, CHURCH OF SAN CARLO ALLE QUATTRO FONTANE**
1638–41.

It is difficult today to appreciate how audacious Borromini's design for this small church was. In it he abandoned the modular, additive system of planning taken for granted by every architect since Brunelleschi. He worked instead from an overriding geometrical scheme for the ideal, domed, central-plan church. Borromini looked at his buildings in terms of geometrical units as a Gothic architect might, subdividing the units to obtain more complex, rational shapes. For example, the elongated, octagonal plan of San Carlo is composed of two triangles set base to base along the short axis of the plan (FIG. 22–10). This diamond shape is then subdivided into secondary triangular units made by calculating the distances between what will become the concave centers of the four major and five minor niches. Yet Borromini's conception of the whole is not medieval. The chapel is dominated horizontally by a classical entablature that breaks any surge upward toward the dome, allowing the eye to play with the rhythm of paired Corinthian columns. Borromini's treatment of the architectural elements as if they were malleable was also unprecedented. His contemporaries understood immediately what an extraordinary innovation the church represented; the Trinitarian monks who had commissioned it received requests for plans from visitors from all over Europe. Although Borromini's invention had little influence on the architecture of classically minded Rome, it was widely imitated in northern Italy and beyond the Alps.

Borromini's design for San Carlo's façade (SEE FIG. 22–7), done more than two decades later, was as innovative as his plan for its interior had been. He turned the building's front into an undulating, sculpture-filled screen punctuated with large columns and deep concave and convex niches that create dramatic effects of light and shadow. Borromini also gave his façade a strong vertical thrust in the center by placing over the tall doorway a statue-filled niche, then a windowed niche covered with a canopy, then a giant, forward-leaning cartouche held up by angels carved in such high relief that they appear to hover in front of the wall. The entire façade is crowned with a balustrade broken by the sharply pointed frame of the cartouche. Borromini's façade was enthusiastically imitated in northern Italy and especially in northern and eastern Europe.

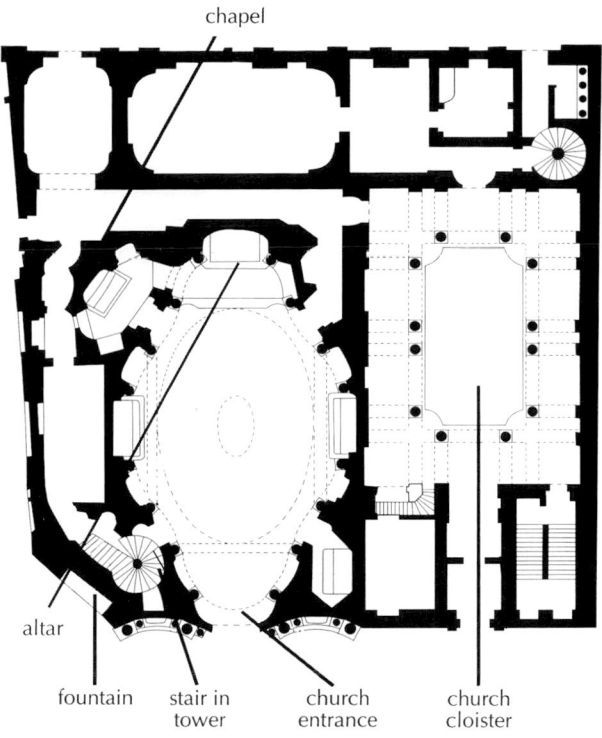

chapel

altar

fountain   stair in   church   church
          tower   entrance   cloister

22–10 | Francesco Borromini   **PLAN OF THE CHURCH OF SAN CARLO ALLE QUATTRO FONTANE, ROME** 1638–41.

PIAZZA NAVONA. Rome's **PIAZZA NAVONA,** a popular site for festivals and celebrations, became another center of urban renewal with the election of Innocent X as pope (papacy 1644–55). Both the palace and parish church of his family, the Pamphilis, fronted on the piazza, which had been the site of a stadium built by Emperor Domitian in 86 CE, and it still retains the shape of the ancient racetrack. The stadium, in ruins, had been used for festivals during the Middle Ages and as a marketplace since 1477. A modest shrine to Saint Agnes stood on the site of her martyrdom.

The Pamphilis enlarged their palace in 1644–50 and in 1652 decided to rebuild their parish church, the Church of Sant'Agnese (Saint Agnes). In 1653–57 Francesco Borromini took the commission, altered the interior, and designed the façade, conceiving a plan that unites church and piazza (**FIG. 22–11**). The façade sweeps inward from two flanking towers to a monumental portal approached by broad stairs. The inward curve of the façade brings the dome nearer the entrance than usual, making it clearly visible from the piazza. The templelike design of columns and pediment around the door also leads the eye to the steeply rising dome on its tall drum. As the pope had wished, the church truly dominates the urban space.

22–11 | **PIAZZA NAVONA, ROME**
In the middle ground, Gianlorenzo Bernini's Four Rivers Fountain, 1648–51. To the left of the fountain, Franceso Borromini's Church of Sant'Agnese, 1653–57. In the foreground, Giacomo della Porta's fountain of 1576. Giuseppe Vasi, *The Flooding of the Piazza Navona,* 18th century, engraving.

22–16 | Caravaggio **THE CALLING OF SAINT MATTHEW**
1599–1600. Oil on canvas, 10′7½″ × 11′2″ (3.24 × 3.4 m). Contarelli Chapel, Church of San Luigi dei Francesi, Rome.

Caravaggio's first public commission, paintings for the Contarelli Chapel in the French community's Church of Saint Louis (Church of San Luigi dei Francesi), included **THE CALLING OF SAINT MATTHEW (FIG. 22–16)**, painted about 1599–1600 and meant to suggest conversion, one of the tasks of the Church. The work is painted in oils. (Caravaggio had a very short apprenticeship and never seemed to have mastered the technique of fresco—nor, perhaps, skill in painting figures in depth.) The painting depicts Jesus calling Levi, the tax collector, to join his apostles (Mark 2:14). Levi sits at a table, counting out gold coins for a boy at the left, surrounded by overdressed young men in plumed hats, velvet doublets, and satin shirts. Nearly hidden behind the cloaked apostle Peter, at the right, the gaunt-faced Jesus points dramatically at Levi, a gesture that is repeated by the tax collector's surprised response of pointing to himself. An intense raking light enters the painting from a high, unseen source at the right, above the altar, and spotlights the faces of the men. The viewpoint of the chapel visitor is the empty space across from Saint Matthew, so that she or he directly participates in the dramatic moment of conversion. For all of his realism and claims of independence, Caravaggio also used antique and Renaissance sources. Jesus's outstretched arm, for example, recalls God's gesture giving life to Adam in Michelangelo's *Creation of Adam* on the Sistine Chapel ceiling (SEE FIG. 20–14). It is now restated as Jesus's command to Levi to begin a new life by becoming his disciple Matthew.

The emotional power of Baroque realism combines with a solemn monumentality in Caravaggio's **ENTOMBMENT** (**FIG. 22–17**), painted in 1603–4 for a chapel in Santa Maria in Vallicella, the church of Neri's Congregation of the Oratory. With almost physical force, the size and immediacy of this painting strike the viewer, whose perspective is from within the burial pit into which Jesus's lifeless body is being lowered. The figures form a large off-center triangle, within which angular elements are repeated: the projecting edge of the stone slab; Jesus's bent legs; the akimbo arm, bunched coat, and knock-kneed stance of the man on the right; and even the spaces between the spread fingers of the raised hands. The Virgin and Mary Magdalen barely intrude on the scene, which, through the careful placing of the light, focuses on the dead Jesus, the sturdy-legged laborer supporting his body at the right, and the young John the Evangelist at the triangle's apex.

Despite the great esteem in which Caravaggio was held by some, especially the younger generation of artists, his violent temper repeatedly got him into trouble. During the last decade of his life, he was frequently arrested, generally for minor offenses such as street brawling. In 1606, however, he killed a man in a fight over a tennis match and had to flee Rome. He went first to Naples, then to Malta, finding work in both places. The Knights of Malta awarded him the cross of their religious and military order in July 1608, but in October he was imprisoned for insulting one of their number, and again he escaped and fled. The aggrieved knight's agents tracked him to Naples in the spring of 1610 and severely wounded him. The artist recovered and moved north to Port'Ercole, where he died of a fever on July 18, 1610, just short of his thirty-ninth birthday. Caravaggio's intense realism and tenebrist lighting influenced nearly every important European artist of the seventeenth century.

GENTILESCHI. One of Caravaggio's most successful Italian followers was Artemisia Gentileschi (1593–c. 1652/53), whose international reputation helped spread the Caravaggesque style beyond Rome. Born in Rome, Artemisia first studied and worked under her father, one of the early followers of Caravaggio. In 1616, she moved to Florence, where she worked for the grand duke of Tuscany and was elected, at the age of twenty-three, to the Florentine Academy of Design. As a resident of Florence, Artemisia was well aware of the city's identification with the Jewish hero David and heroine Judith (both subjects of sculpture by Donatello and Michelangelo), and she painted several versions of Judith triumphant over the Assyrian general Holofernes (**FIG. 22–18**). Artemisia brilliantly uses Baroque naturalism and tenebrist effects, dramatically showing Judith still holding the bloody sword and hiding the candle's light as her maid stuffs the general's head into a sack. Tension mounts—enhanced by the dramatic use of light—as the women listen for the sounds of guards.

22–17 | Caravaggio **ENTOMBMENT**
Vittrici Chapel, Church of Santa Maria in Vallicella, Rome. 1603–4. Oil on canvas, 9′10⅛″ × 6′7¹⁵⁄₁₆″ (3 × 2.03 m). Musei Vaticani, Pinacoteca, Rome.

The *Entombment* was one of many paintings confiscated from Rome's churches and taken to Paris during the French occupation by Napoleon's troops in 1798 and 1808–14. It was one of the few to be returned after 1815 through the negotiations of Pius VII and his agents, who were assisted greatly by the Neoclassical sculptor Antonio Canova, a favorite of Napoleon. The decision was made not to return the works to their original churches and chapels but instead to assemble them in a gallery where the general public could enjoy them. Today, Caravaggio's painting is one of the most important in the collections of the Vatican Museums.

Religious subjects have dominated Western art since the medieval period. Beginning in the Renaissance, however, themes drawn from mythology, literature, daily life, and folklore began to play a significant role. Starting with Mannerism, and continuing into the Baroque period, artists and patrons delighted in iconography that was often complex and extremely subtle. A sourcebook, the *Iconologia,* by Cesare Ripa (1593), became an essential tool for creating and deciphering architectural division. It is impossible to understand which figures are three-dimensional and which are painted, and some paintings are on real panels that extend over the actual architectural frame. Gaulli, who arrived in Rome from Genoa in 1657, had worked in his youth for Bernini, from whom he absorbed a taste for drama and for multimedia effects. The elderly Bernini, who worshiped daily at Il Gesù, may well have offered his personal advice to his former assistant, and Gaulli was certainly familiar with other illusionistic paintings in Rome as well, including Pietro da Cortona's Barberini ceiling.

Gaulli's astonishing creation went beyond anything that had preceded it in unifying architecture, sculpture, and painting. Every element is dedicated to creating the illusion that clouds and angels have floated down through an opening in the church's vault into the upper reaches of the nave. The extremely foreshortened figures are projected as if seen from below, and the whole composition is focused off-center on the golden aura around the letters *IHS*, the monogram of Jesus and the insignia of the Jesuits. The subject is, in fact, a Last Judgment, with the elect rising joyfully toward the name of God and the damned plummeting through the ceiling toward the nave floor. The sweeping inclusion in the work of the space of the nave, the powerful and exciting appeal to the viewer's emotions, and the nearly total unity of visual effect have never been surpassed.

THE HABSBURG LANDS

When the Holy Roman Emperor Charles V abdicated in 1556 (see Chapter 21), he left Spain and its American colonies, the Netherlands, Burgundy, Milan, and the Kingdom of Naples and Sicily to his son Philip II and the Holy Roman Empire (Germany and Austria) to his brother Ferdinand. Ferdinand and the Habsburg emperors who succeeded him ruled their territories from Vienna in Austria, but much of German-speaking Europe remained divided into small units in which local rulers decided on the religion of their territory. Catholicism prevailed in southern and western Germany and in Austria, while the north was Lutheran.

The Spanish Habsburg kings Philip III (ruled 1598–1621), Philip IV (ruled 1621–65), and Charles II (ruled 1665–1700) reigned over a weakening empire. After repeated local rebellions, Portugal reestablished its independence in 1640. The Kingdom of Naples remained in a constant state of unrest. After eighty years of war, the Protestant northern Netherlands—which had formed the United Dutch Republic—gained independence in 1648. Amsterdam grew into one of the wealthiest cities of Europe, and the Dutch Republic became an increasingly serious threat to Spanish trade and colonial possessions. The Catholic southern Netherlands (Flanders), discussed separately below, remained under Spanish and then Austrian Habsburg rule.

What had seemed an endless flow of gold and silver from the Americas to Spain diminished, as precious-metal production in Bolivia and Mexico lessened. Agriculture, industry, and trade at home also suffered. As they tried to defend the Roman Catholic Church and their empire on all fronts, the Spanish kings squandered their resources and finally went bankrupt in 1692. Nevertheless, despite the decline of the Habsburgs' Spanish empire, seventeenth-century writers and artists produced much of what is considered the greatest Spanish literature and art, and the century is often called the Spanish Golden Age.

Painting in Spain's Golden Age

The primary influence on Spanish painting in the fifteenth century had been the art of Flanders; in the sixteenth, it had been the art of Florence and Rome. Seventeenth-century Spanish painting, profoundly influenced by Caravaggio's powerful art, was characterized by an ecstatic religiosity combined with intense realism whose surface details emerge from the deep shadows of tenebrism. This influence is not surprising, since the Kingdom of Naples was ruled by Spanish monarchs, and contact between Naples and the Iberian peninsula was strong and productive.

JUAN SÁNCHEZ COTÁN.   Late in the sixteenth century, Spanish artists developed a significant interest in paintings of artfully arranged objects rendered with intense attention to detail. Juan Sánchez Cotán (1561–1627) was one of the earliest painters of these pure still lifes in Spain. In **STILL LIFE WITH**

22–24 | Juan Sánchez Cotán **STILL LIFE WITH QUINCE, CABBAGE, MELON, AND CUCUMBER**
c. 1602. Oil on canvas, 27⅛ × 33¼" (68.8 × 84.4 cm). San Diego Museum of Art.
Gift of Anne R. and Amy Putnam

22–25 | Jusepe de Ribera **MARTYRDOM OF SAINT BARTHOLOMEW**
1634. Oil on canvas, 41¼ × 44⅞" (1.05 × 1.14 m). National Gallery of Art, Washington, D.C.
Gift of the 50th Anniversary Gift Committee (1990.137.1)

QUINCE, CABBAGE, MELON, AND CUCUMBER (FIG. 22–24), of about 1602, he plays off the irregular, curved shapes of the fruits and vegetables against the angular geometry of the ledge. His precisely ordered subjects—two of which are suspended from strings—form a long arc from the upper left to the lower right. It is not clear whether the seemingly airless space is a wall niche or a window ledge or why these objects have been arranged in this way. Set in a strong light against impenetrable darkness, this highly artificial arrangement portrayed in an intensely realistic manner suggests not only a fascination with spatial ambiguity but a contemplative sensibility and interest in the qualities of objects that look forward to the work of Zurbarán and Velázquez.

JUSEPE DE RIBERA. José or Jusepe de Ribera (c. 1591–1652), born in Seville but living in Naples, has been claimed by both Spain and Italy; however, Naples was ruled by Spain, and in Italy he was known as "Lo Spagnoletto" ("the Little

Spaniard"). He combined the classical and Caravaggesque styles he had learned in Rome, and after settling in Naples in 1620, he created a new Neapolitan—and eventually Spanish—style. Ribera became the link extending from Caravaggio in Italy to the Spanish masters Zurbarán and Velázquez. Ribera was once thought to epitomize Spanish religiosity.

Scenes of martyrdom became popular as the church—aiming to draw people back to Catholicism—ordered art depicting heroic martyrs who had endured shocking torments as witness to their faith. Others, like Saint Teresa (SEE FIG. 22–6), reinforced the importance of personal religious experience and intuitive knowledge. A striking response to this call for relevance and passion is Ribera's painting of Saint Bartholomew, an apostle who was martyred by being skinned alive (FIG. 22–25). The bound Bartholomew looks heavenward as his executioner tests the knife that he will soon use on his still-living victim. Ribera has learned the lessons of Caravaggio well, as he highlights the intensely realistic aged

22–26 | Francisco de Zurbarán **SAINT SERAPION**
1628. Oil on canvas, 47½ × 40¾" (120.7 × 103.5 cm).
Wadsworth Atheneum, Hartford, Connecticut.
Ella Gallup Sumner and Mary Catlin Sumner Collection Fund

faces with the dramatic light of tenebrism and depicts the aging wrinkled flesh with almost painful naturalism. The compression of the figures into the foreground space heightens their immediacy and horror.

FRANCISCO DE ZURBARÁN. Equally horrifying in its depiction of martyrdom, but represented with understated control, is the 1628 painting of **SAINT SERAPION** (FIG. 22–26) by Francisco de Zurbarán (1598–1664). Little is known of his early years before 1625, but Zurbarán too came under the influence of the Caravaggesque taste prevalent in Seville, the major city in southwestern Spain. His own distinctive style incorporated a taste for abstract design, which some critics see as part of the heritage of centuries of Islamic Moorish occupation.

Zurbarán executed his major commissions for the monastic orders. In the painting shown here, he portrays the martyrdom of Serapion, who was a member of the thirteenth-century Mercedarians, a Spanish order founded to rescue the Christian prisoners of the Moors. Following the vows of his order, Serapion sacrificed himself in exchange for Christian captives. The dead man's pallor, his rough hands,

and the coarse ropes contrast with the off-white of his creased Mercedarian habit, its folds carefully arranged in a pattern of highlights and varying depths of shadow. The only colors are the red and gold of the insignia. This composition, almost timeless in its immobility, is like a tragic still life, a study of fabric and flesh.

DIEGO VELÁZQUEZ. Diego Rodríguez de Silva y Velázquez (1599–1660), the greatest painter to emerge from the Caravaggesque school of Seville, shared this fascination with objects. Velázquez entered Seville's painters' guild in 1617. Like Ribera, he began his career as a tenebrist and naturalist. During his early years, he painted figural works set in taverns, markets, and kitchens and emphasized still lifes of various foods and kitchen utensils. His early **WATER CARRIER OF SEVILLE** (FIG. 22–27) is a study of surfaces and textures of the splendid ceramic pots that characterized folk art through the centuries. Velázquez was devoted to studying and sketching from life, and the man in the painting was a well-known Sevillian water seller. Like Sánchez Cotán, Velázquez arranged the elements of his paintings with almost mathematical rigor. The objects and figures allow the artist to exhibit his virtuosity in rendering sculptural volumes and contrasting textures illuminated by dramatic natural light. Light reacts to the surfaces: reflecting off the glazed waterpot at the left and the coarser clay jug in the foreground; being absorbed by the rough wool and dense velvet of the costumes; and reflecting, being refracted, and passing through the clear glass held by the man and through the waterdrops on the jug's surface.

In 1623, Velázquez moved to Madrid, where he became court painter to young King Philip IV, a prestigious position that he held until his death in 1660. The opportunity to study paintings in the royal collection, as well as to travel, enabled the development of his distinctive personal style. The Flemish painter Peter Paul Rubens (see pages 774–777), during a 1628–29 diplomatic visit to the Spanish court, convinced the king that Velázquez should visit Italy. Velázquez made two trips, the first in 1629–31 and a second in 1649–51. He was profoundly influenced by contemporary Italian painting, and on the first trip seems to have taken a special interest in narrative paintings with complex figure compositions.

Velázquez's Italian studies and his growing skill in composition are apparent in both figure and landscape painting. In **THE SURRENDER AT BREDA** (FIG. 22–28), painted in 1634–35, Velázquez treats the theme of triumph and conquest in an entirely new way—far removed from traditional gloating military propaganda. Years earlier, in 1625, the duke of Alba, the Spanish governor, had defeated the Dutch at Breda. In Velázquez's imagination, the opposing armies stand on a hilltop overlooking a vast valley where the city of Breda burns and soldiers are still deployed. The Dutch commander, Justin of Nassau, hands over the keys of Breda to the

22–27 | Diego Velázquez **WATER CARRIER OF SEVILLE**
c. 1619. Oil on canvas, 41½ × 31½″ (105.3 × 80 cm). Victoria & Albert Museum,
London.

In the hot climate of Seville, Spain, where this painting was made, water vendors walked
the streets selling cool drinks from large clay jars like the one in the foreground. In this
scene, the clarity and purity of the water are proudly attested to by its seller, who offers the
customer a sample poured into a glass goblet. The jug contents were usually flavored with
the addition of a piece of fresh fruit or a sprinkle of aromatic herbs.

victorious Spanish commander, Ambrosio Spinola, the duke
of Alba. The entire exchange seems extraordinarily gracious;
the painting represents a courtly ideal of gentlemanly conduct. The victors stand at attention, holding their densely
packed lances upright in a vertical pattern—giving the painting its popular name, "The Lances"—while the defeated
Dutch, a motley group, stand out of order, with pikes and
banners drooping. The painting is memorable as a work of

art, not as history. According to reports, no keys were
involved and the Dutch were more presentable in appearance
than the Spaniards. The victory was short-lived: The Dutch
retook Breda in 1637.

In *The Surrender at Breda,* Velázquez displays his ability to
arrange a large number of figures to tell a story effectively. A
strong diagonal starting in the sword of the Dutch soldier in
the lower left foreground and ending in the checked banner

on the upper right unites the composition and moves the viewer thematically from the defeated to the victorious soldiers. Portraitlike faces, meaningful gestures, and brilliant control of color and texture convince us of the reality of the scene. The landscape painting is almost startling. Across the huge canvas, Velázquez painted an entirely imaginary Netherlands in greens and blues worked with flowing, liquid brushstrokes. Luminosity is achieved by laying down a thick layer of lead white and then flowing the layers of color over it. The silvery light forms a background for dramatically silhouetted figures and weapons. Velázquez revealed a breadth and intensity unsurpassed in his century; his painting has inspired modern artists such as Manet and Picasso.

Although complex compositions became characteristic of many of Velázquez's paintings, perhaps his most striking and enigmatic work is the enormous multiple portrait, nearly 10½ feet tall and over 9 feet wide, known as **LAS MENINAS (THE MAIDS OF HONOR)** (FIG. 22–29). Painted in 1656, near the end of the artist's life, this painting continues to challenge the viewer and stimulate debate. Like Caravaggio's *Entombment* (SEE FIG. 22–17), it draws the viewer directly into its action, for in one interpretation, the viewer is apparently standing in the space occupied by King Philip and the queen, whose reflections can be seen in the large mirror on the back wall. (Others say the mirror reflects the canvas on which Velázquez is working.) The central focus, however, is not on the royal couple or on the artist but on the 5-year-old *infanta* (princess) Margarita, who is surrounded by her attendants, most of whom are identifiable portraits.

The cleaning of *Las Meninas* in 1984 revealed much about Velázquez's methods. He used a minimum of underdrawing, building up his forms with layers of loosely applied paint and finishing off the surfaces with dashing highlights in white, lemon yellow, and pale orange. Velázquez tried to depict the optical properties of light rather than using it to model volumes in the classical time-honored manner. While his technique captures the appearance of light on surfaces, at close inspection his forms dissolve into a maze of individual strokes of paint.

No consensus exists today on the meaning of this monumental painting. Yes, it is a royal portrait; it is also a self-portrait of Velázquez standing at his easel. But more than that, *Las Meninas* seems to have been a personal statement. Throughout his life, Velázquez had sought respect and acclaim for himself and for the art of painting. Here, dressed as a courtier, the Order of Santiago on his chest (added later) and the keys of the palace in his sash, Velázquez proclaimed the dignity and importance of painting as one of the liberal arts.

22–28 | Diego Velázquez **THE SURRENDER AT BREDA (THE LANCES)**
1634–35. Oil on canvas, 10'7⅞" × 12'½" (3.07 × 3.67 m). Museo del Prado, Madrid.

22–29 | Diego Velázquez **LAS MENINAS (THE MAIDS OF HONOR)**
1656. Oil on canvas, 10′5″ × 9′½″ (3.18 × 2.76 m). Museo del Prado, Madrid.

BARTOLOMÉ ESTEBAN MURILLO. The Madrid of Velázquez was the center of Spanish art; Seville declined after an outbreak of plague in 1649. Still living and working in Seville, however, was Bartolomé Esteban Murillo (1617–82). Seville was a center for trade with the Spanish colonies, where Murillo's work had a profound influence on art and religious iconography. Many patrons wanted images of the Virgin Mary and especially of the Immaculate Conception, the controversial idea that Mary was born free from original sin. Although the Immaculate Conception became Catholic dogma only in 1854, the concept, as well as devotion to Mary, was widespread during the seventeenth and eighteenth centuries.

Counter-Reformation authorities provided specific instructions for artists painting the Virgin: Mary was to be dressed in blue and white, her hands folded in prayer, as she is carried upward by angels, sometimes in large flocks. She may be surrounded by an unearthly light ("clothed in the sun") and may stand on a crescent moon in reference to the woman of the apocalypse. Angels often carry palms and symbols of the Virgin, such as a mirror, a fountain, roses, and lilies, and

22–30 | Bartolomé Esteban Murillo **THE IMMACULATE CONCEPTION**
c. 1645–50. Oil on canvas, 7′8″ × 6′5″ (2.35 × 1.96 m). State Hermitage Museum,
St. Petersburg, Russia.

they may vanquish the serpent, Satan. Today, Murillo's paintings are admired for his skill as a draftsman and colorist. His version of ideal beauty—in Mary, Jesus, or the cherubs that surround Mary—is never cloying. The Church exported many paintings by Murillo, Zurbarán, and others to the New World. When the native population began to visualize the Christian story, paintings such as Murillo's **THE IMMACULATE CONCEPTION** provided the imagery (FIG. 22–30).

Architecture in Spain and Austria

THE CATHEDRAL OF SANTIAGO DE COMPOSTELA. Turning away from the severity displayed in the sixteenth-century El Escorial monastery-palace (SEE FIG. 21–19), Spanish architects again embraced the lavish decoration that had characterized

their art since the fourteenth century. The profusion of ornament typical of Moorish and Gothic architecture in Spain swept back into fashion, first in huge retablos (altarpieces), then in portals (main doors often embellished with sculpture), and finally in entire buildings.

In the seventeenth century, the role of Saint James as patron saint of Spain was challenged by the supporters of Saint Teresa of Ávila and then by supporters of Saint Michael, Saint Joseph, and other popular saints. It became important to the archbishop and other leaders in Santiago de Compostela, where the Cathedral of Saint James was located, to establish their primacy. They reinforced their efforts to revitalize the yearly pilgrimage to the city, undertaken by Spaniards since the ninth century, and used architecture as part of their campaign.

Renewed interest in pilgrimages to the shrines of saints in the seventeenth century brought an influx of pilgrims, and consequently financial security, to the city and the church. The cathedral chapter ordered a façade of almost unparalleled splendor to be added to the twelfth-century pilgrimage church (FIG. 22–31). The twelfth-century portal had already been closed with doors in the sixteenth century and a staircase built that incorporated the western crypt. A south tower was built in 1667–80 and then later copied as the north tower.

The last man to serve as architect and director of works, Fernando Casas y Nóvoas (active 1711–49), tied the disparate elements together at the west—towers, portal, stairs—in a grand design focused on a veritable wall of glass, popularly called "The Mirror." His design culminates in a freestanding gable soaring above the roof, visually linking the towers, and framing a statue of Saint James. The extreme simplicity of the cloister walls and the archbishop's palace at each side of the portal heighten the dazzling effect of this enormous expanse of glass windows, glittering jewel-like in their intricately carved granite frame.

THE BENEDICTINE ABBEY, MELK. The arts suffered in seventeenth-century Germanic lands, including Austria, during and after the Protestant Reformation. Wars over religion ravaged the land. When peace finally returned in the eighteenth century, Catholic Austria and Bavaria (southern Germany) saw a remarkable burst of building activity, including the creation and refurbishing of churches and palaces with exuberant interior decoration. Emperor Charles VI (ruled 1711–40) inspired building in his capital, Vienna, and throughout Austria.

22–31 | **WEST FAÇADE, CATHEDRAL OF SAINT JAMES, SANTIAGO DE COMPOSTELA, SPAIN.**
South tower 1667–1680; north tower and central block finished mid-18th century by Fernando de Casas y Nóvoas.

22–32 | Jakob Prandtauer **BENEDICTINE MONASTERY CHURCH, MELK**
Austria. 1702–36 and later.

Church architecture looked to Italian Baroque developments, which were then added to German medieval forms such as tall bell towers. With these elements, German Baroque architects gave their churches an especially strong vertical emphasis. One of the most imposing buildings of this period is the Benedictine Abbey of Melk, built high on a promontory overlooking the Danube River on a site where there had been a Benedictine monastery since the eleventh century. The complex combines church, monastery, library, and—true to the Benedictine tradition of hospitality—guest quarters that evolved into a splendid palace to house the traveling court (FIG. 22–32). The architect, Jakob Prandtauer (1660–1726), oversaw its construction from 1702 until his death in 1726. The buildings were finished in 1749.

Seen from the river, the monastery appears to be a huge twin-towered church, but it is in fact a complex of buildings. Two long (1,050 feet) parallel wings flank the church; one contains a great hall and the other, the monastery's library. The wings are joined by a curving building and terrace overlooking the river in front of the church. Large windows and open galleries take advantage of the river view. Colossal pilasters and high, bulbous-domed towers emphasize the building's verticality. Its grand and palacelike appearance is a reminder that the monastery was an ancient foundation enjoying imperial patronage.

Spectacular as it is, even the Danube River view does not prepare one for the interior of the church (FIG. 22–33). People descending the spiral staircase from the hall and library emerge into an amazing yellow and pink confection. Every surface moves. Huge deep red pilasters support a massive undulating entablature. They establish the semblance of a wall behind which the chapels, galleries, and screens curve and disappear in a maze of gilded sculpture. Light from huge clerestory windows, reminiscent of ancient Roman architecture, enhance the effect of detachment. One cannot distinguish actual from fictive architecture. Figures seem to spill out over the architecture which—as in Gaulli's ceiling for Il Gesù (SEE FIG. 22–23)—sometimes is actually built and sometimes is fiction. Overhead white, gold, and pastel colors cause the frescoed vault to seem to float upward, detached from architecture below. The painting is the work of the first great Austrian Baroque muralist, Johann Michael Rottmayr (c. 1654–1750).

FLANDERS AND THE NETHERLANDS

After a period of relative autonomy from 1598 to 1621 under a Habsburg regent, Flanders, the southern—and predominantly Catholic—part of the Netherlands, returned to direct Spanish rule. Led by the nobleman Prince William of Orange, the Netherlands' Protestant northern provinces (present-day Holland) rebelled against Spain in 1568. The seven provinces joined together as the United Provinces in 1579 and began the long struggle for independence, achieved in the seventeenth century. The king of Spain considered the Dutch heretical rebels, but finally the Dutch prevailed. In

22–33 | **INTERIOR, BENEDICTINE MONASTERY CHURCH, MELK**

Austria. Completed after 1738, after designs by Prandtauer, Antonio Beduzzi, and Joseph Munggenast.

1648, the United Provinces joined emissaries from Spain, the Vatican, the Holy Roman Empire, and France on equal footing in peace negotiations. The resulting Peace of Westphalia recognized the independence of the northern Netherlands.

Flanders

With the southern Netherlands remaining under Catholic Habsburg rule, churches were restored and important commissions went to religious subject matter. As Antwerp, the capital city and major arts center of the southern Netherlands, gradually recovered from the turmoil of the religious wars, artists of great talent flourished there. Painters like Peter Paul Rubens and Anthony Van Dyck established international reputations that brought them important commissions from foreign as well as local patrons.

RUBENS.   Peter Paul Rubens (1577–1640), whose painting has become synonymous with Flemish Baroque art, was born in Germany, where his father, a Protestant, had fled from his native Antwerp to escape religious persecution. In 1587, after her husband's death, Rubens's mother and her children returned to Antwerp and to Catholicism. Rubens decided in his late teens to become an artist and at age twenty-one was accepted into the Antwerp painters' guild, a testament to his energy, intelligence, and skill. Shortly thereafter, in 1600,

Rubens left for Italy. In Venice, Rubens's work came to the attention of the duke of Mantua, who offered him a court post. His activities on behalf of the duke over the next eight years did much to prepare him for the rest of his long and successful career. Surprisingly, other than designs for court entertainments and occasional portraits, the duke never acquired an original painting by Rubens. Instead, he had him copy famous paintings in collections all over Italy to add to the ducal collection.

Rubens visited every major Italian city, went to Madrid as the duke's emissary, and spent two extended periods in Rome, where he studied the great works of Roman antiquity and the Italian Renaissance. While in Italy, Rubens studied the paintings of two contemporaries, Caravaggio and Annibale Carracci. Hearing of Caravaggio's death in 1610, Rubens encouraged the duke of Mantua to buy the artist's *Death of the Virgin,* which the patron had rejected because of the shocking realism. The duke eventually bought the painting.

In 1608, Rubens returned to Antwerp, where he accepted employment by the Habsburg governors of Flanders, Archduke Albert and Princess Isabella Clara Eugenia, the daughter of Philip II. Shortly after his return he married and in 1611 built a house, studio, and garden in Antwerp (FIG. 22–34). Rubens lived in a large typical Flemish house. He added a studio in the

22–34 | Peter Paul Rubens RUBENS HOUSE
Built 1610-15. Looking toward the garden: house at left, studio at right. From an engraving of 1684. British Museum, London. The house was restored and opened as a museum in 1946.

22–35 | Peter Paul Rubens **THE RAISING OF THE CROSS**
Church of Saint Walpurga, Antwerp, Belgium. 1610–11. Oil on canvas, center panel 15′1⅞″ × 11′1½″
(4.62 × 3.39 m); each wing 15′1⅞″ × 4′11″ (4.62 × 1.52 m). Cathedral of Our Lady, Antwerp.
©IRPA-KIK, Brussels

Italian manner across a courtyard, joining the two buildings by a second-floor gallery over the entrance portal. Beyond the courtyard lay the large formal garden, laid out in symmetrical beds. The living room permitted access to a gallery overlooking Rubens's huge studio, a room designed to accommodate large paintings and to house what became virtually a painting factory. The large arched windows provided ample light for the single, two-story room, and a large door permitted the assistants to move finished paintings out to their designated owners. Across the courtyard, one can see the architectural features of the garden, which inspired the architecture of the painting *Garden of Love* (SEE FIG. 22–37).

Rubens's first major commission in Antwerp was a large canvas triptych for the main altar of the Church of Saint Walpurga, **THE RAISING OF THE CROSS** (FIG. 22–35), painted in 1610–11. Rubens continued the Flemish tradition of uniting the triptych by extending the central action and the landscape through all three panels (see Rogier van der Weyden's Last Judgment Altarpiece, FIG. 18–16). At the center, Herculean figures strain to haul upright the wooden cross with Jesus already stretched upon it. At the left, the followers of Jesus join in mourning, and at the right, indifferent soldiers

supervise the execution. All the drama and intense emotion of Caravaggio and the virtuoso technique of Annibale Carracci are transformed and reinterpreted according to Rubens's own unique ideal of thematic and formal unity. The heroic nude figures, dramatic lighting effects, dynamic diagonal composition, and intense emotions show his debt to Italian art, but the rich colors and surface realism, with minute attention given to varied textures and forms, belong to his native Flemish tradition.

Rubens had created a powerful, expressive visual language that was as appropriate for the secular rulers who engaged him as it was for the Catholic Church. Moreover, his intelligence, courtly manners, and personal charm made him a valuable and trusted courtier to his royal patrons, who included Philip IV of Spain, Queen-Regent Marie de' Medici of France, and Charles I of England. In 1621, Marie de' Medici, who had been regent for her son Louis XIII, asked Rubens to paint the story of her life, to glorify her role in ruling France, and also to commemorate the founding of the new Bourbon royal dynasty. In twenty-four paintings, Rubens portrayed Marie's life and political career as one continuous triumph overseen by the ancient gods of Greece and Rome.

22–36 | Peter Paul Rubens **HENRI IV RECEIVING THE PORTRAIT OF MARIE DE' MEDICI**
1621–25. Oil on canvas, 12′11⅛″ × 9′8⅛″ (3.94 × 2.95 m). Musée du Louvre, Paris.

In the painting depicting the royal engagement (FIG. 22–36), Henri IV falls in love at once with Marie's portrait, shown to him—at the exact center of the composition—by Cupid and Hymen, the god of marriage, while the supreme Roman god, Jupiter, and his wife, Juno, look down from the clouds. Henri, wearing his steel breastplate and silhouetted against a landscape in which the smoke of a battle lingers in the distance, is encouraged by a personification of France to abandon war for love, as *putti* play with the rest of his armor. The ripe colors, multiple tex-

tures, and dramatic diagonals give a sustained visual excitement to these enormous canvases, making them not only important works of art but also political propaganda of the highest order.

In 1630, while Rubens was in England on a peace mission, Charles I knighted him and commissioned him to decorate the ceiling of the new Banqueting House at Whitehall Palace, London (SEE FIG. 22–65). There, he painted the apotheosis of James I (Charles's father) and the glorification of the Stuart dynasty.

For all the grandeur of his commissioned paintings, Rubens was a sensitive, innovative painter, as the works he created for his own pleasure clearly demonstrate. His greatest joys seem to have been his home in Antwerp and his home in the country, Castle Steen, a working farm with gardens, fields, woods, and streams.

In **GARDEN OF LOVE**—a garden reminiscent of his own—Rubens may have portrayed his second wife, Helene Fourment, as the leading lady among a crowd of beauties (**FIG. 22–37**). *Putti* encourage the lovers, and one pushes a hesitant young woman into the garden. The couple joins the ladies and gentlemen who are already enjoying the pleasures of nature. The sculpture and architectural setting recall Italian Mannerist conceits. For example, the nymph presses water from her breasts to create the fountain. Herms flank the entrance and columns banded with rough-hewn rings support the pavilion that forms the entrance to the grotto of Venus. All is lush color, shimmering satin, falling water, and sunset sky—the visual and tactile effects so appreciated by seventeenth-century viewers achieved through masterful brushwork.

To satisfy his clients all over Europe, Rubens employed dozens of assistants, many of whom were, or became, important painters in their own right. Using workshop assistants was standard practice for a major artist, but Rubens was par-

ticularly methodical, training or hiring specialists in costumes, still lifes, landscapes, portraiture, and animal painting who together could complete a work from his detailed sketches. Among his friends and collaborators were Anthony Van Dyck and his friend and neighbor Jan Brueghel.

PORTRAITS AND STILL LIFES. One of Rubens's collaborators, Anthony Van Dyck (1599–1641), had an illustrious independent career as a portraitist. Son of an Antwerp silk merchant, he was listed as a pupil of the dean of Antwerp's Guild of Saint Luke at age 10. He had his own studio and roster of pupils at age 16 but was not made a member of the guild until 1618, the year after he began his association with Rubens as a painter of heads. The need to blend his work seamlessly with that of Rubens enhanced Van Dyck's technical skill; his independent work shows an elegance and aristocratic refinement that seems to express his own character. After a trip to the English court of James I (ruled 1603–25) in 1620, Van Dyck traveled to Italy and worked as a portrait painter for seven years before returning to Antwerp. In 1632, he returned to England as the court painter to Charles I (ruled 1625–49), by whom he was knighted and given a studio, a summer home, and a large salary.

22–37 | Peter Paul Rubens **GARDEN OF LOVE**
1630-32. Oil on canvas, 6'6" × 9'3½" (1.98 × 2.83 m). Museo del Prado, Madrid.

THE ⬤BJECT SPEAKS

BRUEGHEL AND RUBENS'S *ALLEGORY OF SIGHT*

In 1599, the Spanish Habsburg princess Isabel Clara Eugenia married the Austrian Habsburg archduke Albert, uniting two branches of the family. Together they ruled the Habsburg Netherlands for the king of Spain. They were patrons of the arts and sciences and friends of artists—especially Peter Paul Rubens. Their interests and generous patronage were abundantly displayed in five allegorical paintings of the senses by Rubens and Jan Brueghel. The two artists were neighbors and frequently collaborated; Rubens painted the figures, and Brueghel created the settings. Such collaboration between major artists was not unusual in Antwerp.

Of the five paintings, the **ALLEGORY OF SIGHT** is the most splendid: It is like an illustrated catalog of the ducal collection.

Gathered in a huge vaulted room are paintings, sculpture, furniture, objects in gold and silver, and scientific equipment—all under the magnificent double-headed eagle emblems of the Habsburgs. We explore the painting inch by inch, as if reading a book or scanning a palace inventory. There on the table are Brueghel's copies of Rubens's portraits of Archduke Albert and Princess Isabel Clara Eugenia; another portrait of the duke rests on the floor. Besides the portraits, we can find Rubens's *Daniel in the Lions' Den* (upper left corner), *The Lion and Tiger Hunt* (top center), and *The Drunken Silenus* (lower right), as well as the *Madonna and Child in a Wreath of Flowers* (far right), a popular seventeenth-century subject, for which Rubens painted the Madonna and Brueghel created the wreath. Brueghel

also included Raphael's *Saint Cecilia* (behind the globe) and Titian's *Venus and Psyche* (over the door).

In the foreground, the classical goddess Venus, attended by Cupid (both painted by Rubens), has put aside her mirror to contemplate a painting of *Christ Healing the Blind*. She is surrounded by the equipment needed to see and to study: The huge globe at the right and the armillary sphere with its gleaming rings at the upper left—the Earth and the solar system—symbolize the extent of humanistic learning, an image that speaks to viewers of our day as clearly as it did to those of its own. The books and prints, ruler, compasses, magnifying glass, and the more complex astrolabe, telescope, and eyeglasses may also refer to spiritual blindness—to those who look but do not see.

Jan Brueghel and Peter Paul Rubens **ALLEGORY OF SIGHT**
From *Allegories of the Five Senses*. c. 1617–18. Oil on wood panel, 25⅝ × 43″ (65 × 109 cm). Museo del Prado, Madrid.

PORTRAITS. Dutch Baroque portraiture took many forms, ranging from single portraits in sparsely furnished settings to allegorical depictions of people in elaborate costumes surrounded by appropriate symbols. Although the accurate portrayal of facial features and costumes was the most important gauge of a portrait's success, the best painters went beyond pure description to convey a sense of mood or emotion in the sitter. (We cannot know if it was an accurate representation of their personality in the modern sense, however.) Group portraiture documenting the membership of corporate organizations was a Dutch specialty. These large canvases, filled with many individuals who shared the cost of the commission, challenged painters to present a coherent, interesting composition that nevertheless gave equal attention to each individual portrait.

Frans Hals (c. 1581/85–1666), the leading painter of Haarlem, developed a style grounded in the Netherlandish love of realism and inspired by the Caravaggesque style introduced by artists such as ter Brugghen. Like Velázquez, he tried to re-create the optical effects of light on the shapes and textures of objects. He painted boldly, with slashing strokes and angular patches of paint. When his work is seen at a distance, however, all the colors merge into solid forms over which a flickering light seems to move. In Hals's hands, this seemingly effortless technique suggests a boundless joy in life.

22–41 | Frans Hals **CATHARINA HOOFT AND HER NURSE**
c. 1620. Oil on canvas, 33¾ × 25½″ (85.7 × 64.8 cm).
Staatliche Museen zu Berlin, Preussischer Kulturbesitz,
Gemäldegalerie.

In his painting **CATHARINA HOOFT AND HER NURSE** (FIG. 22–41), of about 1620, Hals captured the vitality of a gesture and a fleeting moment in time. While the portrait records for posterity the great pride of the parents in their child, the painting also records their wealth in its study of rich fabrics, laces, and expensive toys (a golden rattle). Hals depicted the heartwarming delight of a child, who seems to be acknowledging the viewer as a loving family member while her doting nurse tries to distract her with an apple.

In contrast to this intimate individual portrait are Hals's official group portraits, such as his **OFFICERS OF THE HAARLEM MILITIA COMPANY OF SAINT ADRIAN** (FIG. 22–42), of about 1627. Less imaginative artists had arranged their sitters in neat rows to depict every face clearly. Instead, Hals's dynamic composition turned the group portrait into a lively social event. The composition is based on a strong underlying geometry of diagonal lines—gestures, banners, and sashes—balanced by the stabilizing perpendiculars of table, window, tall glass, and striped banner. The black suits and hats make the white ruffs and sashes of rose, white, and blue even more brilliant.

The company, made up of several guard units, was charged with the military protection of Haarlem. Officers came from the upper middle class and held their commissions for three years, whereas the ordinary guards were tradespeople and craftworkers. Each company was organized like a guild, under the patronage of a saint. When the men were not on war alert, the company functioned as a fraternal order, holding archery competitions, taking part in city processions, and maintaining an altar in the local church (SEE ALSO FIG. 22–45.)

22–42 | Frans Hals **OFFICERS OF THE HAARLEM MILITIA COMPANY OF SAINT ADRIAN**
c. 1627. Oil on canvas, 6′ × 8′8″ (1.83 × 2.67 m). Frans Halsmuseum, Haarlem.

A painting long praised as one of Hals's finest works was recently discovered to be by Judith Leyster (c. 1609–60), Hals's contemporary. A cleaning uncovered her distinctive signature, the monogram *JL* with a star, which refers to her surname, meaning "pole star." Leyster's work shows clear echoes of her exposure to the Utrecht painters who had enthusiastically adopted Caravaggio's realism, dramatic tenebrist lighting effects, large figures pressed into the foreground plane, and, especially, theatrically presented themes. Since in 1631 Leyster signed as a witness at the baptism in Haarlem of one of Hals's children, it is assumed they were close; she may also have worked in Hals's shop. She entered Haarlem's Guild of Saint Luke in 1633, which allowed her to take pupils into her studio, and her competitive relationship with Frans Hals around that time is made clear by the complaint she lodged against him in 1635 for luring away one of her apprentices.

Leyster is known primarily for her informal scenes of daily life, which often carry an underlying moralistic theme. In her lively **SELF-PORTRAIT** of 1635 (FIG. 22–43), the artist has paused momentarily in her work to look back, as if the viewer had just entered the room. Her elegant dress and the fine chair in which she sits are symbols of her success as an artist whose popularity was based on the very type of painting underway on her easel. (One critic has suggested that her subject—a man playing a violin—may be a visual pun on the painter with palette and brush.) Leyster's understanding of light and texture is truly remarkable. The brushwork she used to depict her own flesh and delicate ruff is finer than Hals's technique and forms an interesting contrast to the broad strokes of thick paint used to create her full, stiff skirt. She further emphasized the difference between her portrait and her painting by executing the image on her easel in lighter tones and soft, loose brushwork. The narrow range of colors sensitively dispersed in the composition and the warm spotlighting are typical of Leyster's mature style.

REMBRANDT VAN RIJN. The most important painter working in Amsterdam in the seventeenth century was Rembrandt van Rijn (1606–69). Rembrandt, one of nine children born in Leiden to a miller and his wife, enrolled at the University of Leiden in 1620 at age 14 but chose instead to study painting with a local artist. Later he studied briefly under

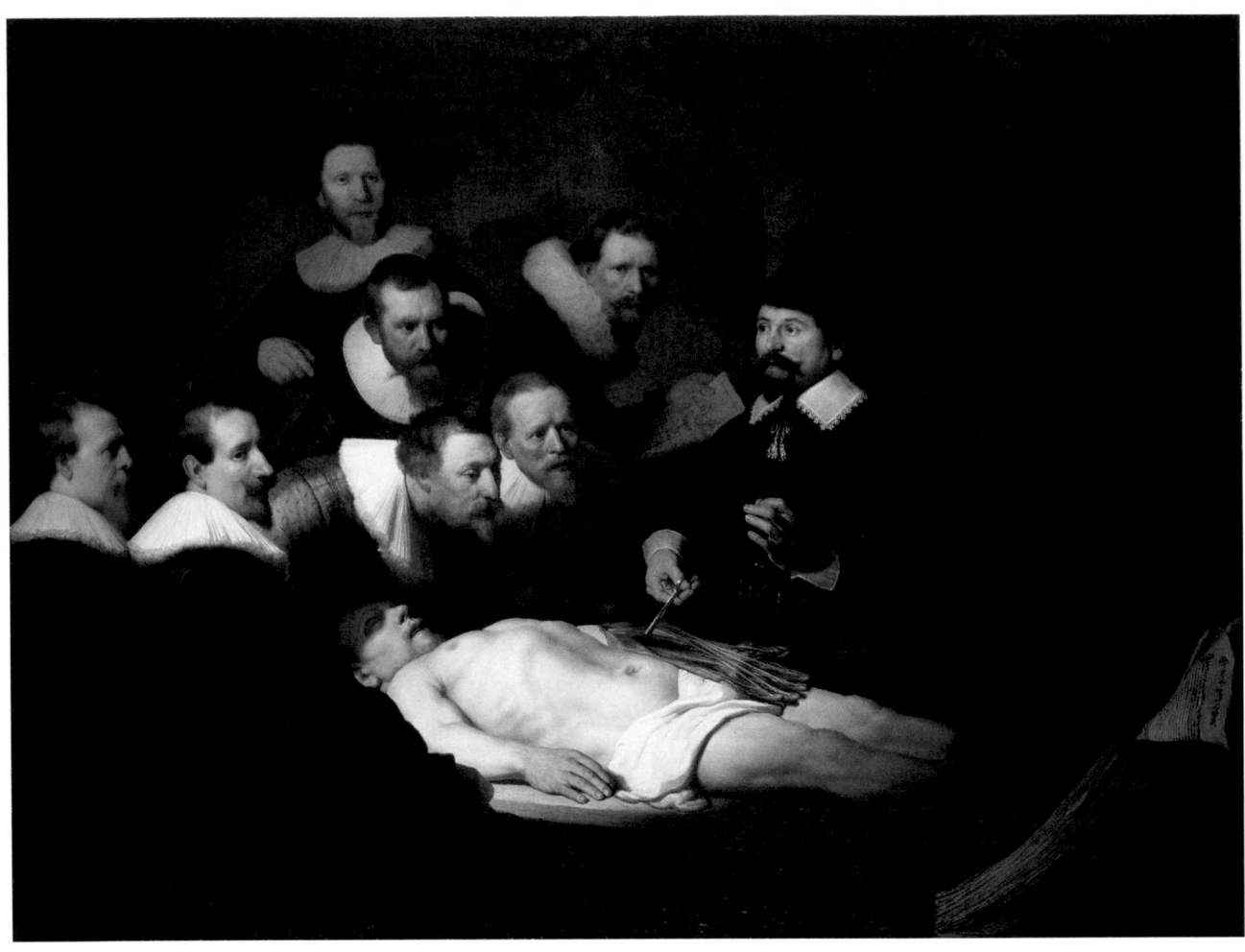

22–44 | Rembrandt van Rijn **THE ANATOMY LESSON OF DR. NICOLAES TULP**
1632. Oil on canvas, 5′3¾″ × 7′1¼″ (1.6 × 2.1 m). Mauritshuis, The Hague, Netherlands.

Pieter Lastman (1583–1633), the principal painter in Amsterdam at the time. From Lastman, a history painter who had worked in Rome, Rembrandt learned the new styles developed in Rome by Annibale Carracci and Caravaggio: naturalism, drama, and extreme tenebrism. He was back in Leiden by 1626, painting religious and historical scenes as well as fantasy portraits from models likely drawn from his family and acquaintances. Late in 1631 he returned to Amsterdam to work primarily as a portrait painter, although he continued to paint a wide range of narrative themes and landscapes.

In his first group portrait, **THE ANATOMY LESSON OF DR. NICOLAES TULP** (FIG. 22-44) of 1632, Rembrandt combined his scientific and humanistic interests. Frans Hals had activated the group portrait rather than conceiving it as a simple reproduction of figures and faces; Rembrandt transformed it into a dramatic narrative scene. Doctor Tulp, who was head of the surgeons' guild from 1628 to 1653, sits right of center, and the other doctors gather around to observe the cadaver and listen to the famed anatomist. Rembrandt built his composition on a sharp diagonal that pierces space from right to left, uniting the cadaver on the table, the calculated arrangement of speaker and listeners, and the open book into a climactic event. Rembrandt makes effective use of Caravaggio's tenebrist technique. The figures emerge from a dark and undefined ambience with their faces framed by brilliant white ruffs. Radiant light from an unknown source streams down on the juxtaposed arms and hands, as Dr. Tulp flexes his own left hand to demonstrate the action of the cadaver's arm muscles. Unseen by the viewers are the illustrations of the huge book. It must be an edition of Andreas Vesalius's study of human anatomy, published in Basel in 1543, which was the first attempt at accurate anatomical illustrations in print. Rembrandt's painting has been seen as an homage to Vesalius and to science, as well as a portrait of the members of the Amsterdam surgeons' guild.

Prolific and popular with Amsterdam clientele, Rembrandt ran a busy studio producing works that sold for high prices. The prodigious output of his large workshop and of many followers who imitated his manner has made it difficult for scholars to define his body of work, and many paintings by students and assistants formerly attributed to Rembrandt have recently been assigned to other artists. Rembrandt's

22–45 | Rembrandt van Rijn **CAPTAIN FRANS BANNING COCQ MUSTERING HIS COMPANY (THE NIGHT WATCH)**
1642. Oil on canvas, 11′11″ × 14′4″ (3.63 × 4.37 m). (Cut down from the original size.)
Rijksmuseum, Amsterdam.

mature work reflected his cosmopolitan city environment, his study of science and nature, and the broadening of his artistic vocabulary by the study of Italian Renaissance art, chiefly from engravings and paintings. Thanks to prints imported by the busy Amsterdam art market, he could study such works as Leonardo's *Last Supper* (see Introduction, Fig. 18).

In 1642, Rembrandt was one of several artists commissioned by a wealthy civic-guard company to create large group portraits of its members for its new meeting hall. The result, **CAPTAIN FRANS BANNING COCQ MUSTERING HIS COMPANY** (FIG. 22–45), carries the idea of the group portrait as drama even further. Because of the dense layer of grime and darkened varnish on it and its dark background architecture, this painting was once thought to be a night scene and was therefore called "The Night Watch." After cleaning and restoration in 1975–76 it now exhibits a natural golden light that sets afire the palette of rich colors—browns, blues, olive green, orange, and red—around a central core of lemon yellow in the costume of a lieutenant. To the dramatic group composition, showing a company forming for a parade in an Amsterdam street, Rembrandt added several colorful but

seemingly unnecessary figures While the officers stride purposefully forward, the rest of the men and several mischievous children mill about. The radiant young girl in the left middle ground, carrying a chicken and wearing a money pouch, may be a pun on the kind of guns *(klower)* that gave the name (the Kloveniers) to the company. Chicken legs with claws *(klauw* in Dutch) also are part of their coat of arms. She may stand as a kind of symbolic mascot of the militia company.

In his enthusiasm for printmaking as an important art form with its own aesthetic qualities, Rembrandt was remarkably like Albrecht Dürer (SEE FIGS. 21–9, 21–10). He focused on etching, which uses acid to inscribe a design on metal plates. His earliest etchings date from 1627. About a decade later, he began to experiment with making additions to his compositions in the **drypoint** technique, in which the artist uses a sharp needle to scratch shallow lines in a plate. Because etching and drypoint allow the artist to work directly on the plate, the style of the finished print can have the relatively free and spontaneous character of a drawing. Rembrandt's commitment to the full exploitation of the medium is indicated by the fact that in these works he alone

some cultivated activity, such as writing, reading letters, or playing a musical instrument. Most of his accepted works are of a similar type—quiet interior scenes, low-key in color, and asymmetrical but strongly geometric in organization. Vermeer achieved his effects through a consistent architectonic construction of space in which every object adds to the clarity and balance of the composition. An even light from a window often gives solidity to the figures and objects in a room.

All emotion is subdued, as Vermeer evokes the stillness of meditation. Even the brushwork is so controlled that it becomes invisible, except when he paints reflected light as tiny droplets of color.

In **WOMAN HOLDING A BALANCE** (FIG. 22–50), perfect equilibrium creates a monumental composition and a moment of supreme stillness. The woman contemplates the balance and so calls our attention to the act of weighing and

22–50 | Jan Vermeer **WOMAN HOLDING A BALANCE**
c. 1664. Oil on canvas, 15⅞ × 14″ (39 × 35 cm). National Gallery of Art, Washington, D.C.
Widener Collection (1942.9.97)

22–51 | Gerard ter Borch
THE SUITOR'S VISIT
c. 1658. Oil on canvas,
32½ × 29⅞" (82.6 × 75.3 cm).
National Gallery of Art,
Washington, D.C.

Andrew W. Mellon Collection
(1937.1.58).

judging. Her hand and the scale are central, but directly over her head, on the wall of the room, an image of Christ in a gold aureole appears in a large painting of the Last Judgment. Thus, Vermeer's painting becomes a metaphor for eternal judgment. The woman's moment of quiet introspection before she touches the gold or pearls, shimmering with the reflected light from the window, also recalls the *vanitas* theme of the transience of life, allowing the painter to comment on the ephemeral quality of material things.

LIFE IN THE CITY, GENRE SCENES. Continuing a long Netherlandish tradition, genre paintings of the Baroque period—generally painted for private patrons and depicting scenes of contemporary daily life—were often laden with symbolic references, although their meaning is not always clear. A clean house might indicate a virtuous housewife and mother while a messy household suggested laziness and the sin of sloth. Ladies dressing in front of mirrors certainly could be succumbing to vanity, and drinking parties led to overindulgence and lust.

One of the most refined of the genre painters was Gerard ter Borch (1617–81). In his painting traditionally known as **THE SUITOR'S VISIT** (FIG. 22–51), from about 1658, a well-dressed man bows gracefully to an elegant woman arrayed in white satin, who stands in a sumptuously furnished room in which another woman plays a lute. Another man, in front of a fireplace, turns to observe the newcomer. The painting appears to represent a prosperous gentleman paying a call on a lady of equal social status, possibly a courtship scene. The dog in the painting and the musician seem to be simply part of the scene, but we are already familiar with the dog as a symbol of fidelity, and stringed instruments were said to symbolize, through their tuning, the harmony of souls and thus, possibly, a loving relationship. On the other hand, it has been suggested that the theme is not so innocent: that the gestures here suggest a liaison. The dog could be interpreted sexually, as sniffing around, and the music making could be associated with sensory pleasure. Ter Borch was renowned for his exquisite rendition of lace, velvet, and especially satin, and such wealth could be seen as a symbol of excess. One critic has even suggested that the white satin is a metaphor for the women's skin. If there is a moral lesson, it is presented discreetly and ambiguously.

Another important genre painter is Jan Steen (1626–79), whose larger brushstrokes contrast with the meticulous treatment of ter Borch. Steen painted over 800 (mostly undated) works but never achieved financial success. Most of his scenes used everyday life to portray moral tales, illustrate proverbs and folk sayings, or make puns to amuse the spectator. Steen moved about the country for most of his life, and from 1670 until his death he kept a tavern in Leiden. He probably found inspiration and models all about him. Early in his career Steen was influenced by Frans Hals, and his work, in turn, influenced a **school,** or circle of artists working in a related style, of Dutch artists who emulated his ever-changing style and subjects. Steen could be very summary or extremely detailed in his treatment of forms. His paintings of often riotous and disorderly interiors gave rise to the saying "a Jan Steen household."

Jan Steen's paintings of children are especially remarkable, for he captured not only their childish physiques but also their fleeting moods and expressions with rapid and fluid brushstrokes. His ability to capture such transitory dispositions was well expressed in his painting **THE DRAWING LESSON** (Introduction, Fig. 17). Here, youthful apprentices—a boy and a well-dressed young woman—observe the master artist correct an example of drawing, a skill widely believed to be the foundation of art. The studio is cluttered with all the supplies the artists need. On the floor at the lower right, objects such as a lute, wine jug, book, and skull also remind the viewer of the transitory nature of life in spite of the permanence art may seem to offer.

Emanuel de Witte (1617–92) of Rotterdam specialized in architectural interiors, first in Delft in 1640 and then in Amsterdam after settling there permanently in 1652. Although many of his interiors were composites of features from several locations combined in one idealized architectural view, de Witte also painted faithful "portraits" of actual buildings. One of these is his **PORTUGUESE SYNAGOGUE, AMSTERDAM** (FIG. 22–52), of 1680. The synagogue, which still stands and is one of the most impressive buildings in Amsterdam, is shown here as a rectangular hall divided into one wide central aisle with narrow side aisles, each covered with a wooden barrel vault resting on lintels supported by columns. De Witte's shift of the viewpoint slightly to one side has created an interesting spatial composition, and strong contrasts of light and shade add dramatic movement to the simple interior. The caped figure in the foreground and the dogs provide a sense of scale for the architecture and add human interest.

Today, the painting is interesting both as a record of seventeenth-century synagogue architecture and as evidence of Dutch religious tolerance in an age when Jews were often persecuted. Ousted from Spain and Portugal in the late fifteenth and early sixteenth centuries, many Jews had settled first in

22–52 | Emanuel de Witte **PORTUGUESE SYNAGOGUE, AMSTERDAM**
1680. Oil on canvas, 43½ × 39″ (110.5 × 99.1 cm). Rijksmuseum, Amsterdam. Architect Daniel Stalpaert built the synagogue in 1670–75.

Flanders and then in the Netherlands. The Jews in Amsterdam enjoyed religious and personal freedom, and their synagogue was considered one of the outstanding sights of the city.

LANDSCAPE. The Dutch loved the landscapes and vast skies of their own country, but those who painted them were not slaves to nature as they found it: The concept was foreign to this time period. The artists constructed and refined their work in the confines of their studio and were never afraid to remake a scene by rearranging, adding, or subtracting to give their compositions formal organization or a desired mood. Starting in the 1620s, view painters generally adhered to a convention in which little color was used beyond browns, grays, and beiges. After 1650, they tended to be more individualistic in their styles, but nearly all brought a broader range of colors into play. One continuing motif was the emphasis on cloud-filled expanses of sky dominating a relatively narrow horizontal band of earth below. Painters specialized in the sea, the countryside, the city, and its buildings. Paintings of architectural interiors also became popular and seem to have been painted for their own beauty, just as exterior views of the land, cities, and harbors were.

The Haarlem landscape specialist Jacob van Ruisdael (1628/29–82), whose popularity drew many pupils to his workshop, was especially adept at both the invention of

22–53 | Jacob van Ruisdael
THE JEWISH CEMETERY
1655–60. Oil on canvas,
4′ 6″ × 6′2½″ (1.42 × 1.89 m).
The Detroit Institute of Arts.
Gift of Julius H. Haass in memory of
his brother Dr. Ernest W. Haass (24.3)

dramatic compositions and the projection of moods in his canvases. His **JEWISH CEMETERY** (FIG. 22–53), of 1655–60, is a thought-provoking view of silent tombs, crumbling ruins, and stormy landscape, with a rainbow set against dark, scudding clouds. Ruisdael was greatly concerned with spiritual meanings of the landscape, which he expressed in his choice of such environmental factors as the time of day, the weather, the appearance of the sky, or the abstract patterning of sun and shade. The barren tree points its branches at the tombs. Here the tombs, ruins, and fallen and blasted trees suggest an allegory of transience. The melancholy mood is mitigated by the rainbow, a traditional symbol of renewal and hope.

STILL LIFES AND FLOWER PIECES. The Dutch were so proud of their artists' still-life paintings that they presented one (a flower piece by Rachel Ruysch) to the French queen Marie de' Medici when she made a state visit to Amsterdam. A still-life painting might carry moralizing connotations and commonly had a *vanitas* theme, reminding viewers of the transience of life, material possessions, and even art.

One of the first Dutch still-life painters was Pieter Claesz (1596/97–1660) of Haarlem, who, like the Antwerp artist Clara Peeters, painted "breakfast pieces," that is, a meal of bread, fruits, and nuts. In subtle, nearly monochromatic paintings, such as **STILL LIFE WITH A WATCH** (FIG. 22–54), Claesz seems to give life to inanimate objects. He organizes dishes in diagonal positions to give a strong sense of space, and he gives the maximum contrast of textures within a color scheme of white, grays, and browns. The brilliant yellow lemon provides visual excitement with its rough curling peel, juicy flesh, and soft pulpy inner skin. The tilted silver tazza contrasts with the half-filled glass that becomes a towering monumental presence and permits Claesz to display his skill at transparencies

22–54 | Pieter Claesz **STILL LIFE WITH A WATCH**
1636. Oil on panel, Royal Picture Gallery, Maurithuis,
The Hague.

The heavy round glass is a Roemer, an inexpensive, everyday item, as are the pewter plates. The gilt cup (tazza) was a typical ornamental piece. Painters owned and shared such valuable props, and this and other show pieces appear in many paintings.

22–55 | Rachel Ruysch **FLOWER STILL LIFE**
After 1700. Oil on canvas, 30 × 24″ (76.2 × 61 cm). The Toledo Museum of Art, Ohio.
Purchased with funds from the Libbey Endowment. Gift of Edward Drummond Libbey (1956.57)

and reflections. No longer are inanimate objects represented for their symbolic value as in fifteenth-century Flemish painting, yet meaning is not entirely lost, for such paintings suggest the prosperity of Claesz's patrons. The food might be simple, but the lemon is a luxury imported from Mediterranean lands, and the silver ornamental cup graced the tables of only the wealthy. Finally, the meticulously painted timepiece suggests a deeper meaning—perhaps human achievement in science and technology, or perhaps it also becomes a *vanitas* symbol of the inexorable passage of time and the fleet-

ing life of human beings, thoughts also suggested by the interrupted breakfast.

Still-life paintings in which cut-flower arrangements predominate are referred to simply as "flower pieces." Significant advances were made in botany during the seventeenth century through the application of orderly scientific methods and objective observation (see "Science and the Changing Worldview," page 746). The Dutch were major growers and exporters of flowers, especially tulips, which appear in nearly every flower piece in dozens of exquisite variations. The Dutch tradition of flower painting peaked in the long career of Rachel Ruysch (1664–1750) of Amsterdam. Her flower pieces were highly prized for their sensitive, free-form arrangements and their unusual and beautiful color harmonies. During her seventy-year career, she became one of the most sought-after and highest-paid still-life painters in Europe—her paintings brought twice what Rembrandt's did.

In her **FLOWER STILL LIFE** (FIG. 22–55), painted after 1700, Ruysch placed the container at the center of the canvas's width, then created an asymmetrical floral arrangement of pale oranges, pinks, and yellows rising from lower left to top right of the picture, offset by the strong diagonal of the tabletop. To further balance the painting, she placed highlighted blossoms and leaves against the dark left half of the canvas and silhouetted them against the light wall area on the right. Ruysch often emphasized the beauty of curving flower stems and enlivened her compositions with interesting additions, such as casually placed pieces of fruit or insects, in this case a large gray moth (lower left) and two snail shells.

Flower painting, a much-admired specialty in the seventeenth- and eighteenth-century Netherlands, was almost never a straightforward depiction of actual fresh flowers. Instead, artists made color sketches of fresh examples of each type of flower and studied scientifically accurate color illustrations in botanical publications. Using their sketches and notebooks, in the studio they would compose bouquets of perfect specimens of a variety of flowers that could never be found blooming at the same time. The short life of blooming flowers was a poignant reminder of the fleeting nature of beauty and of human life.

FRANCE

The early seventeenth century in France was marked by almost continuous foreign and civil wars. The assassination of King Henri IV in 1610 left France in the hands of the queen, Marie de' Medici (regency 1610–17; SEE FIG. 22–36), as regent for her 9-year-old son, Louis XIII (ruled 1610–43). When Louis came of age, the brilliant and unscrupulous Cardinal Richelieu became chief minister and set about increasing the power of the Crown at the expense of the French nobility. The death of Louis XIII again left France with a child king, the five-year-old Louis XIV (ruled 1643–1715). His mother, Anne of Austria, became regent, with the assistance of another powerful minister, Cardinal Mazarin. At Mazarin's death in 1661, Louis XIV (SEE FIG. 22–1) began his long personal reign, assisted by yet another able minister, Jean-Baptiste Colbert.

An absolute monarch whose reign was the longest in European history, Louis XIV expanded royal art patronage, making the French court the envy of every ruler in Europe. The arts, like everything else, came under royal control. In

1635, Cardinal Richelieu had founded the French Royal Academy, directing the members to compile a definitive dictionary and grammar of the French language. In 1648, the Royal Academy of Painting and Sculpture was founded, which, as reorganized by Colbert in 1663, maintained strict control over the arts (see "Grading the Old Masters," page 799). Although it was not the first European arts academy, none before it had exerted such dictatorial authority—an authority that lasted in France until the late nineteenth century. Membership in the academy assured an artist of royal and civic commissions and financial success, but many talented artists did well outside it.

Architecture and Its Decoration at Versailles

French architecture developed along classical lines in the second half of the seventeenth century under the influence of François Mansart (1598–1666) and Louis Le Vau (1612–70). When the Royal Academy of Architecture was founded in 1671, its members developed guidelines for architectural design based on the belief that mathematics was the true basis of beauty. Their chief sources for ideal models were the books of Vitruvius and Palladio (see Chapter 20).

In 1668, Louis XIV began to enlarge the small château built by Louis XIII at Versailles, not far from Paris. Louis moved to the palace in 1682 and eventually required his court to live in Versailles; 5,000 aristocrats lived in the palace itself, together with 14,000 servants and military staff members. The town had another 30,000 residents, most of whom were employed by the palace. The designers of the palace and park complex at Versailles (FIG. 22–56) were Le Vau, Charles Le Brun (1619–90), who oversaw the interior decoration, and André Le Nôtre (1613–1700), who planned the gardens (see "French Baroque Garden Design," page 796). For both political and sentimental reasons, the old Versailles château was left standing, and the new building went up around it. This project consisted of two phases: the first additions by Le Vau, begun in 1668; and an enlargement completed after Le Vau's death by his successor, Jules Hardouin-Mansart (1646–1708), from 1670 to 1685.

Hardouin-Mansart was responsible for the addition of the long lateral wings and the renovation of Le Vau's central block on the garden side to match these wings (FIG. 22–57). The three-story elevation has a lightly rusticated ground floor, a main floor lined with enormous arched windows separated by Ionic pilasters, an attic level whose rectangular windows are also flanked by pilasters, and a flat, terraced roof. The overall design is a sensitive balance of horizontals and verticals relieved by a restrained overlay of regularly spaced projecting blocks with open, colonnaded porches.

In his renovation of Le Vau's center-block façade, Hardouin-Mansart enclosed the previously open gallery on the main level, creating the famed **HALL OF MIRRORS** (FIG. 22–58), which is about 240 feet (73 meters) long and

22–56 Louis Le Vau and Jules Hardouin-Mansart **PALAIS DE VERSAILLES, VERSAILLES**
France. 1668–85. Gardens by André Le Nôtre.

22–57 **CENTRAL BLOCK OF THE GARDEN FAÇADE, PALAIS DE VERSAILLES**

22–58 | Jules Hardouin-Mansart and Charles Le Brun   **HALL OF MIRRORS, PALAIS DE VER-SAILLES**
Begun 1678. Length approx. 240′ (73 cm).

In the seventeenth century, mirrors and clear window glass were enormously expensive. To furnish the Hall of Mirrors, hundreds of glass panels of manageable size had to be assembled into the proper shape and attached to one another with glazing bars, which became part of the decorative pattern of the vast room.

47 feet (13 meters) high. He achieved architectural symmetry and extraordinary effects by lining the interior wall opposite the windows with Venetian glass mirrors the same size and shape as the arched windows. (Mirrors were tiny and extremely expensive in the seventeenth century, and these huge walls of glass were created by fitting eighteen-inch panels together.) The mirrors reflect the natural light from the windows and give the impression of an even larger space; at night, the reflections of flickering candles must have turned the mirrored gallery into a veritable painting in which the king and courtiers saw themselves as they promenaded. Inspired by Carracci's Farnese ceiling (SEE FIG. 22–13), Le Brun decorated the vaulted ceiling with paintings (on canvas, which is more stable in the damp northern climate) glorify-

ing the reign of Louis XIV and Louis's military triumphs, assisted by the classical gods. In 1642, he had studied in Italy, where he came under the influence of the classical style of his compatriot Nicolas Poussin (discussed later in this chapter). As "First Painter to the King" and director of the Royal Academy, Le Brun controlled art education and patronage from 1661/63 until his death in 1690. He tempered the more exuberant Baroque ceilings he had seen in Rome with Poussin's classicism to produce spectacular decorations for the king. The underlying theme for the design and decoration of the palace was the glorification of the king as Apollo the Sun God, with whom Louis identified. Louis XIV thought of the duties of kingship, including its pageantry, as a solemn performance, so it is most appropriate that Rigaud's portrait

Elements of Architecture
FRENCH BAROQUE GARDEN DESIGN

Wealthy landowners commissioned garden designers to transform their large properties into gardens extending over many acres. The challenge for garden designers was to unify diverse elements—buildings, pools, monuments, plantings, natural land formations—into a coherent whole. At Versailles, André Le Nôtre imposed order upon the vast expanses of palace gardens and park by using broad, straight avenues radiating from a series of round focal points. He succeeded so thoroughly that his plan inspired generations of urban designers as well as landscape architects.

In Le Nôtre's hands, the palace terrain became an extraordinary work of art and a visual delight for its inhabitants. Neatly contained stretches of lawn and broad, straight vistas seemed to stretch to the horizon, while the formal gardens became an exercise in precise geometry. The Versailles gardens are classically harmonious in their symmetrical, geometric design but Baroque in their vast size and extension into the surrounding countryside, where the gardens thickened into woods cut by straight avenues.

The most formal gardens lay nearest the palace, and plantings became progressively less elaborate and larger in scale as the distance from the palace increased. Broad, intersecting paths separated reflecting pools and planting beds, which are called embroidered **parterres** for their colorful patterns of flowers outlined with trimmed hedges. After the formal zone of parterres came lawns, large fountains on terraces, and trees planted in thickets to conceal features such as an open-air ballroom and a colonnade. Statues carved by at least seventy sculptors also adorned the park. A mile-long canal, crossed by a sec-

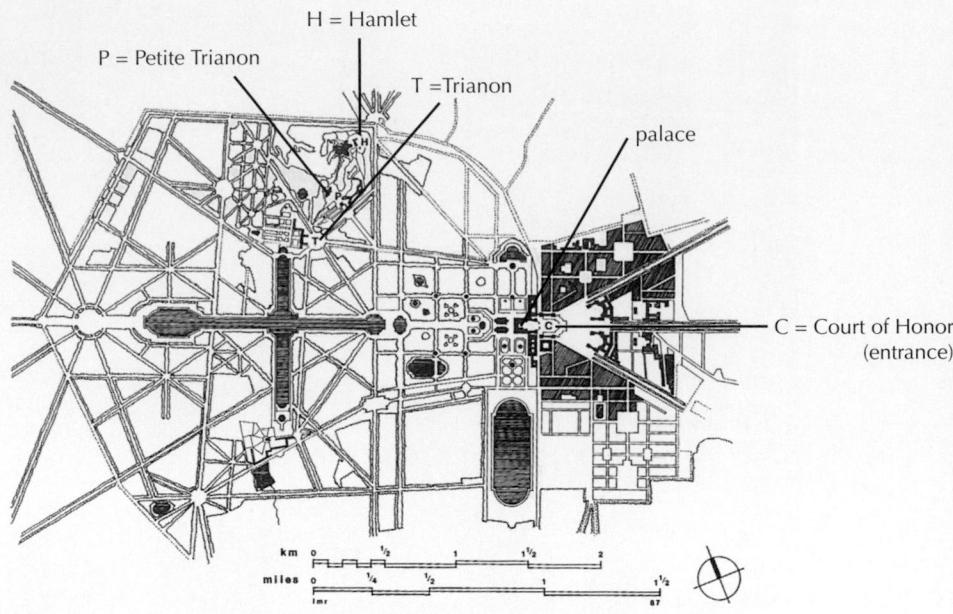

Louis Le Vau and André Le Nôtre   **PLAN OF THE PALAIS DE VERSAILLES**
Versailles, France. c. 1661–1785. Drawing by Leland M. Roth after Delagrive's engraving of 1746.

ond canal nearly as large, marked the main axis of the garden. Fourteen waterwheels brought the water from the river to supply the canals and the park's 1,400 fountains. Only the fountains near the palace played all day; the others were turned on only when the king approached.

At the north of the secondary canal, a smaller pavilion-palace, the Trianon, was built in 1669. To satisfy the king's love of flowers year-round, the gardens of the Trianon were bedded out with blooming plants from the south, shipped in by the French navy. Even in midwinter, the king and his guests could stroll through a summer garden. The head gardener is said to have had nearly 2 million flowerpots at his disposal. In the eighteenth century, Louis XV added greenhouses and a botanical garden. The facilities of the fruit and vegetable garden that supplied the palace in 1677–83 today house the National School of Horticulture.

---

presents him on a raised, stagelike platform, with a theatrical curtain (SEE FIG. 22–1). Versailles was the splendid stage on which the king played this grandiose drama.

In the seventeenth century, French taste in sculpture tended to favor classicizing works inspired by antiquity and the Italian Renaissance. A highly favored sculptor in this classical style, François Girardon (1628–1715) had studied the monuments of classical antiquity in Rome in the 1640s.

He had worked with Le Vau and Le Brun before he began working to decorate Versailles. In keeping with the repeated identification of Louis XIV with Apollo, Girardon created the sculpture group **APOLLO ATTENDED BY THE NYMPHS OF THETIS** (FIG. 22–59), executed about 1666–75, for the central niche of the so-called Grotto of Thetis—a formal, triple-arched pavilion named after a sea nymph beloved by the Sun God. In Girardon's circular grouping, Apollo, after his long journey across the heavens, is attended by the graceful nymphs of Thetis. As in classical or Renaissance sculpture, the composition is best understood from a fixed viewpoint. The original setting was destroyed in 1684, and in 1776, Louis XVI had the painter Hubert Robert design a "natural" rocky cavern for Girardon's sculpture.

Painting

The lingering Mannerism of the sixteenth century in France gave way as early as the 1620s to Baroque classicism and Caravaggism—the use of strong chiaroscuro (tenebrism) and raking light—and the placement of large-scale figures in the foreground. Later in the century, under the control of the academy and inspired by studies of the classics and the surviving antiquities in Rome, French painting was dominated by the classical influences propounded by Le Brun.

THE INFLUENCE OF CARAVAGGIO. One of Caravaggio's most important followers in France, Georges de La Tour (1593–1652) received major royal and ducal commissions and became court painter to Louis XIII in 1639. La Tour may have traveled to Italy in 1614–16, and in the 1620s he almost certainly visited the Netherlands, where Caravaggio's style was being enthusiastically emulated. Like Caravaggio, La Tour filled the foreground of his canvases with monumental figures, but in place of Caravaggio's detailed naturalism he used a simplified setting and a light source within the picture so intense that it often seems to be his real subject. La Tour painted Mary Magdalen many times. In **MARY MAGDALEN WITH THE SMOKING FLAME** (FIG. 22–60), as in many of his paintings, the light emanates from a candle. The hand and skull, symbols of mortality, act as devices to establish a foreground plane, and the compression of the figure within the pictorial space lends a sense of intimacy. The light is the unifying element of the painting and conveys the somber mood. Mary Magdalen has put aside her rich clothing and jewels and meditates on the frailty and vanity of human life. She sighs, and the candle flickers.

Something of this same feeling of timelessness pervades the paintings of the Le Nain brothers, Antoine (c. 1588–1648), Louis (c. 1593–1648), and Mathieu (1607–1677). Although the brothers were working in Paris by about 1630, little else is known about their lives and careers. Because they collaborated closely with each other, art historians have only recently begun to distinguish their individual styles. They painted genre scenes imbued with a strange sense of foreboding and enigmatic meaning. **THE VILLAGE PIPER** (FIG. 22–61) of 1642, by Antoine Le Nain, is typical of the brothers' work. Peasant children gather around the figure of a flute player. The simple homespun garments and undefined setting turn the painting into a study in neutral colors and rough textures, with soft young

22–59 | François Girardon **APOLLO ATTENDED BY THE NYMPHS OF THETIS**
From the Grotto of Thetis, Palais de Versailles, Versailles, France. c. 1666–75. Marble, life-size. Grotto by Hubert Robert in 1776; sculpture reinstalled in a different configuration in 1778.

faces that contrast with the old man, who seems lost in his simple music. Why the brothers chose to paint these peasants and who bought the paintings are questions still not resolved.

THE CLASSICAL LANDSCAPE: POUSSIN AND CLAUDE LORRAIN. The painters Nicolas Poussin (1594–1665) and Claude Gellée (called "Claude Lorrain" or simply "Claude," 1600–82) pursued their careers in Italy although they usually worked for French patrons. They perfected the ideal "classical" landscape and profoundly influenced painters for the next two centuries. Poussin and Claude were classicists in that they organized natural elements and figures into idealized compositions. Both were influenced by Annibale Carracci and to some extent by Venetian painting, yet each evolved an unmistakable personal style that conveyed an entirely different mood from that of their sources and from each other.

Nicolas Poussin, born in Normandy, settled in Paris, where his career as a painter was unremarkable. Determined to go to Rome, he finally arrived there in 1624. The Barberini became his foremost patrons, and Bernini considered Poussin to be one of the greatest painters in Rome. Poussin's landscapes with figures are the epitome of the orderly, arranged, classical landscape. In his **LANDSCAPE WITH SAINT JOHN ON PATMOS** (FIG. 22–62), from 1640, Poussin created a consistent perspective progression from the picture plane back into the distance through a clearly defined foreground, middle ground, and background. These zones are

22–60 | Georges de La Tour **MARY MAGDALEN WITH THE SMOKING FLAME**
c. 1640. Oil on canvas, 46¼ × 36⅛" (117 × 91.8 cm). Los Angeles County Museum of Art.
Gift of the Ahmanson Foundation (M. 77.73)

marked by alternating sunlight and shade, as well as by architectural elements. Surrounded by the huge, tumbled ruins of ancient Rome—and by extension all earthly empires—Saint John writes the Book of Revelation, describing the end of the world, the Last Judgment, and the Second Coming of Christ: a renewal of life suggested by the flourishing vegetation. This grand theme is represented in the highly intellectualized format of Poussin's classical composition. In the middle distance are a ruined temple and an obelisk, and the round building in the distant city is

Hadrian's Tomb, which Poussin knew from Rome. Precisely placed trees, hills, mountains, water, and even clouds take on a solidity of form that seems almost as structural as architecture. The reclining evangelist and the eagle, his symbol, seem immobile—locked into this perfect landscape. The triumph of the rational mind takes on moral overtones. The subject of Poussin's painting is not the story of John the Evangelist but rather the balance and order of nature.

In the second half of the seventeenth century, the French Academy took Poussin's paintings and notes on

Defining Art
GRADING THE OLD MASTERS

The members of the French Royal Academy of Painting and Sculpture considered ancient classical art to be the standard by which contemporary art should be judged. By the 1680s, however, younger artists of the academy began to argue that modern art might equal and even surpass the art of the ancients—a radical thought that sparked controversy.

A debate arose over the relative merits of drawing and color in painting. The conservatives argued that drawing was superior to color because drawing appealed to the mind while color appealed to the senses. They saw Nicolas Poussin as embodying perfectly the classical principles of subject and design. But the young artists who admired the vivid colors of Titian, Veronese, and Rubens claimed that painting should deceive the eye, and since color achieves this deception more convincingly than drawing, application of color should be valued over drawing. Adherents to the two positions were called *poussinistes* (in honor of Poussin) and *rubénistes* (for Rubens).

The portrait painter and critic Roger de Piles (1635–1709) took up the cause of the *rubénistes* in a series of pamphlets. In *The Principles of Painting*, Piles evaluated the most important painters on a scale of 0 to 20 in four categories. He gave no score higher than 72 (18 in each category), since no mortal artist could achieve perfection. Caravaggio received the lowest grade, a 0 in expression and 6 in drawing for a low of 28, while Michelangelo and Leonardo both got a 4 in color and Rembrandt a 6 in drawing.

Most of the painters we have studied don't do very well. Raphael and Rubens get 65 points, Van Dyck comes close with 55. Poussin and Titian earn 53 and 51, while Rembrandt slips by with 50. Leonardo da Vinci gets 49, and Michelangelo and Dürer with 37 and Caravaggio with 28 all are resounding failures in Piles's view.

22–61 | Antoine Le Nain **THE VILLAGE PIPER**
1642. Oil on copper, 8¾ × 11½" (21.3 × 29.2 cm). Detroit Institute of Arts.

painting as a final authority. From then on, whether as a model to be followed or one to be reacted against, Poussin influenced French art.

When Claude Lorrain went to Rome in 1613, he first studied with Agostino Tassi, an assistant of Guercino and a specialist in architectural painting. Claude, however, preferred landscape. He sketched outdoors for days at a time, then returned to his studio to compose his paintings. Claude was fascinated with light, and his works are often studies of the effect of the rising or setting sun on colors and the atmosphere. A favorite and much imitated device was to place one or two large objects in the foreground—a tree, building, or hill—past which the viewer's eye enters the scene and proceeds, often by zigzag paths, into the distance.

Claude used this compositional device to great effect in paintings such as **EMBARKATION OF THE QUEEN OF SHEBA** **(FIG. 22–63)**. Instead of balanced, symmetrically placed elements, Claude leads the viewer into the painting in a zigzag fashion. A ruined building with Corinthian cornice and columns frames the composition at the left; light catching the seashore leads the eye to the right, where a handsome palace with a grand double staircase and garden with trees establishes a middle ground. Across the water the sails and rigging of ships provide extra visual interest. More distant still are the

harbor fortification with town and lighthouse and finally the breakwater (at the left). On the horizon the sun illuminates the clouds in a clearing sky and catches the waves to make a glowing sea path to shore. The small figures—workers and onlookers in the foreground, the queen and her courtiers waiting on the quay and about to board—seem incidental, added to give the painting a subject. Claude's meticulous one-point perspective focuses on the sun with the same driving force with which earlier painters focused on Christ and the saints.

HYACINTHE RIGAUD. Hyacinthe Rigaud (1659–1743), trained by his painter father, won the Royal Academy's prestigious Prix de Rome in 1682, which would have paid his expenses for study at the Academy's villa in Rome. Rigaud rejected the prize, however, and opened his own Paris studio. After painting a portrait of Louis XIV's brother in 1688, he became a favorite of the king himself. His representation of the monarch (SEE FIG. 22–1) reveals a more extravagant style than the restrained classicism of Le Brun. In fact, Louis favored a more theatrical presentation for himself and his court, and Rigaud's representation of the Sun King embodies official portraiture as the height of royal propaganda.

22–62 | Nicolas Poussin **LANDSCAPE WITH SAINT JOHN ON PATMOS**
1640. Oil on canvas, 40 × 53½″ (101.8 × 136.3 cm). The Art Institute of Chicago.
A. A. Munger Collection, 1930.500

22–63 Claude Lorrain **EMBARKATION OF THE QUEEN OF SHEBA**
1648. Oil on canvas, 4′ 10″ × 6′ 4″ (1.48 × 1.93 m). National Gallery, London.
Reproduced by courtesy of the Trustees of the National Gallery, London

ENGLAND

England and Scotland were joined in 1603 with the ascent to the English throne of James VI of Scotland, who reigned over Great Britain as James I (ruled 1603–25). James increased royal patronage of British artists, especially in literature and architecture. William Shakespeare wrote *Macbeth,* featuring the king's legendary ancestor Banquo, in tribute to the new royal family, and the play was performed at court in December 1606.

Although James's son Charles I was an important collector and patron of painting, religious and political tensions that erupted into civil wars cost Charles his throne and his life in 1649. A succession of republican and monarchical rulers who alternately supported Protestantism or Catholicism followed, until the Catholic king James II was deposed in the Glorious Revolution of 1689 by his Protestant son-in-law and daughter, William and Mary. After Mary's death in 1694, William (the Dutch great-grandson of William of Orange, who had led the Netherlands' independence movement) ruled on his own until his death in 1702. He was succeeded by Mary's sister Anne (ruled 1702–14).

Architecture and Landscape Design

In sculpture and painting, the English court patronized foreign artists. The field of architecture, however, was dominated in the seventeenth century by the Englishmen Inigo Jones, Christopher Wren, and Nicholas Hawkmoor. They replaced the country's long-lived Gothic style with a classical one and were followed in a more Baroque mode by another English architect, John Vanbrugh. Major changes in landscape architecture took place during the eighteenth century, led by the innovative designer Lancelot "Capability" Brown.

INIGO JONES. In the early seventeenth century, the architect Inigo Jones (1573–1652) introduced his version of Renaissance classicism—an architectural design based on the style of the architect Andrea Palladio—into England. Jones had studied Palladio's work in Venice, and he filled his copy of Palladio's *Four Books of Architecture* (which has been preserved) with notes. Appointed surveyor-general in 1615, Jones was commissioned to design the Queen's House in Greenwich and the Banqueting House for the royal palace of Whitehall.

The **BANQUETING HOUSE, WHITEHALL PALACE** (FIG. 22-64), built in 1619–22 to replace an earlier hall destroyed by fire, was used for court ceremonies and entertainments such as the popular masques—dance-dramas combining theater, music, and dance in a spectacle in which professional actors, courtiers, and even members of the royal family participated. The west front shown here, consisting of what appears to be two upper stories with superimposed Ionic and Composite orders raised over a plain basement level, exemplifies the understated elegance of Jones's interpretation of Palladian design. Pilasters flank the end bays, and engaged columns subtly emphasize the three bays at the center. These vertical elements are repeated in the balustrade along the roofline. A rhythmic effect was created in varying window treatments from triangular and segmental (semicircular) pediments on the first level to cornices with volute (scroll-form) brackets on the second. The sculpted garlands just below the roofline add an unexpected decorative touch, as does the use of a different-color stone—pale golden, light brown, and white—for each story (no longer visible after the building was refaced in uniformly white Portland stone).

Although the exterior suggests two stories, the interior of the Banqueting House (FIG. 22-65) is actually one large hall divided by a balcony, with antechambers at each end. Ionic pilasters suggest a colonnade but do not impinge on the ideal, double-cube space, which measures 55 feet in width by 110 feet in length by 55 feet in height. In 1630, Charles I commissioned Peter Paul Rubens to decorate the ceiling. Jones had divided the flat ceiling into nine compartments, for which Rubens painted canvases glorifying the reign of James I. Installed in 1635, the paintings show the triumph of the Stu-

art dynasty with the king carried to heaven in clouds of glory. The large rectangular panel beyond it depicts the birth of the new nation, flanked by allegorical paintings of heroic strength and virtue overcoming vice. In the long paintings on each side, *putti* holding the fruits of the Earth symbolize the peace and prosperity of England and Scotland under Stuart rule. So proud was Charles of the result that, rather than allow the smoke of candles and torches to harm the ceiling decoration, he moved evening entertainments to an adjacent pavilion.

CHRISTOPHER WREN. After Jones's death, English architecture was dominated by Christopher Wren (1632–1723). Wren began his professional career in 1659 as a professor of astronomy; architecture was a sideline until 1665, when he traveled to France to further his education. While there, he met with French architects and with Bernini, who was in Paris to consult on his designs for the Louvre. Wren returned to England with architectural books, engravings, and a greatly increased admiration for French classical Baroque design. In 1669, he was made surveyor-general, the position once held by Inigo Jones; in 1673, he was knighted.

After the Great Fire of 1666 demolished central London, Wren was continuously involved in rebuilding the city. He built more than fifty Baroque churches. His major project from 1675 to 1710, however, was the rebuilding of **SAINT PAUL'S CATHEDRAL** (FIG. 22-66). Attempts to salvage the burned-out medieval church on the site failed, and a new cathedral was needed. Wren's famous second design for Saint Paul's (which survives in the so-called Great Model of 1672–73) was for a centrally planned building with a great dome in the manner of Bramante's plan for Saint Peter's. This was rejected, but Wren ultimately succeeded both in satisfying Reformation tastes for a basilica and in retaining the unity inherent in the dome. Saint Paul's has a long nave and equally long sanctuary articulated by small, domed bays. Semicircular, colonnaded porticoes open into short transepts that compress themselves against the crossing, where the dome rises 633 feet from ground level. Wren's dome for Saint Paul's has an interior masonry vault with an oculus and an exterior sheathing of lead-covered wood but also has a brick cone rising from the inner oculus to support a tall lantern. (The ingenuity of the design and engineering remind one that Wren was mathematician and professor of astronomy at Oxford.) The columns surrounding the drum on the exterior recall Bramante's Tempietto in Rome (SEE FIG. 20-17), although Wren never went to Italy and knew Italian architecture only from books.

On the façade of Saint Paul's, two stages of paired Corinthian columns support a carved pediment. The deep-set porticoes and columned pavilions atop the towers create dramatic areas of light and shadow. Not only the huge size of the cathedral but also its triumphant verticality, complexity of form, and chiaroscuro effects make it a major monument of the English Baroque. Wren recognized the importance of the

22-64 | Inigo Jones **BANQUETING HOUSE, WHITEHALL PALACE**
London. 1619-22.

22–65 | INTERIOR, BANQUETING
HOUSE, WHITEHALL PALACE
Ceiling paintings of the apotheosis
of King James and the glorification
of the Stuart monarchy by Peter Paul
Rubens. 1630–35.

building. On the simple marble slab that forms his tomb in the crypt of the cathedral, he had engraved: "If you want to see his memorial, look around you."

BLENHEIM PALACE. Like Wren, Sir John Vanbrugh (1664–1726) came late to architecture. His heavy, angular style, utterly unlike Wren's, was well suited to buildings intended to express power and domination. Wren's assistant Nicholas Hawksmoor (1661–1736) also worked in a bolder style. Perhaps the most important achievement of the two was **BLENHEIM PALACE** (FIG. 22–67), built in two phases (1705–12 and 1715–25) in Woodstock, just northwest of London. Van-

brugh was an amateur, a soldier and playwright whose architectural designs are indeed theatrical. Hawksmoor was an established professional who understood building and engineering. The two combined to create the imposing and impractical monument to the glory of England—an architectural challenge to Louis XIV and Versailles. Built by Queen Anne, with funds from Parliament, for John Churchill, duke of Marlborough, after his 1704 victory over the armies of Louis XIV at Blenheim, the palace was made a national monument as well as the residence of the dukes of Marlborough. Except for the formal gardens at each side of the center block, the informal and natural landscaping is the work of

22–66 | Christopher Wren **SAINT PAUL'S CATHEDRAL, LONDON**
Designed 1673, built 1675–1710.

Lancelot "Capability" Brown. Blenheim's enormous size and symmetrical plan, with service and stable wings flanking an entrance court, recall Versailles as they reach out to encompass the surrounding terrain.

Blenheim's grounds originally comprised a practical kitchen garden, an avenue of elm trees, and another garden. In the 1760s, the grounds were redesigned by Lancelot "Capability" Brown (1716–83) according to his radical new style now called, appropriately, "landscape architecture." In contrast to the geometric rigor of the French and Italian gardens, Brown's designs appeared to be both informal and natural. The "natural" appearance was created by feats of engineering, as the land was reformed to create views inspired by the paintings of Claude Lorrain. In order to accomplish this at Blenheim, Brown dammed the small river flowing by the palace to form two lakes and a rockwork cascade, then created sweeping lawns and vistas with artfully arranged trees. (Gardeners and their patrons thought of the future, as they planted trees that they would never see grow to maturity.) The formal gardens in the French style now seen at each side of Blenheim's center block were added in the twentieth century.

22–67 | John Vanbrugh **BLENHEIM PALACE, WOODSTOCK**
Oxfordshire, England. 1705–12 and 1715–25.

English Colonies in North America

In the seventeenth century, the art of North America reflected the tastes of the European rulers—England on the East Coast, France in Canada and Louisiana, Spain in the Southwest. Not surprisingly, much of the colonial art was the work of immigrant artists, and styles often lagged behind the European mainstream. The rigors of colonial life meant that few people could afford to think of fine houses and art collections. Furthermore, the Puritans, religious dissenters who had left England and settled in the Northeast beginning in 1620, wanted simple, functional buildings for homes and churches. Architecture and crafts responded more quickly than sculpture and painting in the development of native styles. Although by the last decades of the seventeenth century a market for fine furniture and portraits had developed, native artists of outstanding talent often found it advantageous to resettle in Europe.

ARCHITECTURE. Early architecture in the British North American colonies was derived from European timber construction. Wood, so easily obtained in the Northeast, was used to create the same kinds of houses and churches then being built in rural England (as well as in Holland and France, which also had colonies in North America). In seventeenth-century New England, many buildings reflected the adapta-

tion of contemporary English country buildings, which were appropriate to the severe North American winters—framed-timber construction with steep roofs, massive central fireplaces and chimneys, overhanging upper stories, and small windows with tiny panes of glass or parchment screens. Following a time-honored tradition, walls consisted of wooden frames filled with **wattle and daub** (woven branches packed with clay) or brick in more expensive homes. Instead of leaving this construction exposed, as was common in Europe, colonists usually weatherproofed it with horizontal plank siding, called **clapboard**. The **PARSON CAPEN HOUSE** in Topsfield, Massachusetts (**FIG. 22–68**), built in 1683, is a well-preserved example. The earliest homes generally consisted of a single

22–68 | **PARSON CAPEN HOUSE**
Topsfield, Massachusetts. 1683.

22–69 | Anonymous ("Freake Painter") **MRS. FREAKE AND BABY MARY**
c. 1674. Oil on canvas, 42¼ × 36¼" (108 × 92.1 cm).
Worcester Museum of Art, Worcester, Massachusetts.
Gift of Mr. and Mrs. Albert W. Rice

"great room" and fireplace, but the Capen House has two stories, each with two rooms flanking the central fireplace and chimney. The main fireplace was the center of domestic life; all the cooking was done there, and the firelight provided illumination for reading and sewing.

PAINTING.   Painting and sculpture had to wait for more settled and affluent times in the eastern seacoast colonies. For a long time, the only works of sculpture were carved or engraved tombstones. Painting, too, was sponsored as a necessary part of family record keeping, and portraits done by itinerant "face painters," called **limners**, have a charm and sincerity that appeal to the modern eye. The anonymous painter of **MRS. FREAKE AND BABY MARY** (FIG. 22–69), dated about 1674, seems to have known Dutch portraiture, probably

through engraved copies that were imported and sold in the colonies. Even though the "Freake Painter" was clearly self-taught and lacked skills in illusionistic, three-dimensional composition, emotionally this portrait has much in common with Frans Hals's *Catharina Hooft and Her Nurse* (SEE FIG. 22–41). Maternal pride in an infant and hope for her future are universal ideals that apply to little Mary as well as to Catharina, even though their worlds were far apart.

IN PERSPECTIVE

Cataclysmic forces unleashed in the sixteenth century came to fruition in the arts only in the seventeenth century, as political and religious factions attacked each other with lethal fanaticism and enlisted art—as well as God—on their side. Spectacular visions, brilliant state portraits, and grandiose palaces and churches proclaimed the power of church and state. In papal Rome, Bernini, Borromini, and Gaulli worked their visual magic while Caravaggio revolutionized painting with his new naturalism. In Spain, France, and England, artists such as Rigaud and Van Dyck created portraits that were miracles of royal propaganda while Velázquez and Rubens glorified political and military victories.

Florence, Venice, and even Antwerp lost their economic and hence cultural advantage while papal Rome, Louis XIV's Paris and Versailles, and the commercial center of Amsterdam became the economic engines of the arts. In the Protestant countries, religious art was replaced by secular subject matter and a strong realistic style as the arts found a new economic basis—the open art market. Artists like Vermeer or Ruisdael painted themes considered "lesser" by the critics but with sales in mind: still lifes, landscapes, and scenes of daily life. As the universities became the centers of intellectual life, curriculum changed from religion and philosophy to science and mathematics. Artists like Maria Sibylla Merian joined scientists in the exploration and recording of nature, and Rembrandt probed the human mind and spirit.

Trade became global, and fortunes were to be made as ships replaced the overland routes between Europe and Asia and new trade routes crossed the Atlantic. The fascinating phenomenon today referred to as "core and periphery"—cultural transference between colonial power and colony—is epitomized by the comparison of two portraits, Hals's *Catharina Hooft* and the "Freake Painter's" *Baby Mary*—as a new art center arose in the New World.

BAROQUE ART

PEETERS
**L LIFE WITH FLOWERS, GOBLET,
DRIED FRUIT AND PRETZLES**
1611

BERNINI
BALDACCHINO
SAINT PETER'S BASILICA, VATICAN
1624–1633

LA TOUR
**MARY MAGDALEN WITH
THE SMOKING FLAME**
C. 1640

VELAZQUEZ
LAS MENINAS
1656

WREN
ST. PAUL'S CATHEDRAL
DESIGNED 1673

DE WITTE
PORTUGUESE SYNAGOGUE, AMSTERDAM
1680

1600

1620

1640

1660

1680

1700

◀ **Thirty Year's War** 1618–48

◀ **Mayflower Lands in North America**
1620

◀ **Galileo Forced to Recant** 1633

◀ **Louis XIV of France Ruled** 1643–1715

◀ **French Royal Academy of Painting
and Sculpture** 1648

◀ **Spanish Habsburgs Recognize
Independence of United Provinces**
1648

◀ **Charles I of England Beheaded;
England a Commonwealth** 1649

◀ **Restoration of Charles II and
Monarchy in England** 1660

◀ **Great Fire of London** 1666

◀ **French Royal Academy of
Architecture** 1671

◀ **Newton Publishes Laws of Gravity
and Motion** 1687

◀ **Glorious Revolution in England** 1689

◀ **Steam Engine Invented** 1698

807

23–1 | **TAJ MAHAL** Agra, India. Mughal period, reign of Shah Jahan, c. 1631–48.

CHAPTER TWENTY-THREE

ART OF SOUTH AND SOUTHEAST ASIA AFTER 1200

23

Visitors catch their breath. Ethereal, weightless, the building before them barely seems to touch the ground. Its reflection shimmers in the pools of the garden meant to evoke a vision of paradise as described in the Qur'an, the holy book of Islam. Its façades are delicately inlaid with inscriptions and arabesques in semiprecious stones—carnelian, agate, coral, turquoise, garnet, lapis, and jasper. Above, its luminous, white marble dome reflects each shift in light, flushing rose at dawn, dissolving in its own brilliance in the noonday sun. One of the most celebrated buildings in the world, the **TAJ MAHAL** (FIG. 23–1) was built in the seventeenth century by the Mughal ruler Shah Jahan as a mausoleum for his favorite wife, Mumtaz-i-Mahal, who died in childbirth.

Inside, the Taj Mahal invokes the *hasht behisht*, or "eight paradises," a plan named for the eight small chambers that ring the interior—one at each corner and one behind each *iwan*, a vaulted opening with an arched portal. In two stories (for a total of sixteen chambers), the rooms ring the octagonal central area, which rises the full two stories to a domed ceiling that is lower than the outer dome. In this central chamber, surrounded by a finely carved octagonal openwork marble screen, are the exquisite inlaid cenotaphs of Shah Jahan and his wife, whose actual tombs lie in the crypt below.

A dynasty of Central Asian origin, the Mughals were the most successful of the many Islamic groups that established themselves in India beginning in the tenth century. Under their patronage, Persian and Central Asian influences mingled with older traditions of the South Asian subcontinent, adding yet another dimension to the already ancient and complex artistic heritage of India.

INDIA AFTER 1200

By 1200 India was already among the world's oldest civilizations (see "Foundations of Indian Culture," page 815). The art that survives from its earlier periods is almost exclusively sacred, most of it inspired by the three principal religions: Buddhism, Hinduism, and Jainism. These three religions continued as the principal focus for Indian art, even as invaders from the northwest began to establish the new religious culture of Islam.

Buddhist Art

After many centuries of prominence, Buddhism had been in decline as a cultural force in India since the seventh century C.E. By 1200, the principal Buddhist centers were concentrated in the northeast, in the region that had been ruled by the Pala dynasty (c. 750–1199). There, in great monastic universities that attracted monks from as far away as China, Korea, and Japan, was cultivated a form of Buddhism known as Tantric (Vajrayana) Mahayana.

ICONOGRAPHY OF A TANTRIC BODHISATTVA. The practices of Tantric Buddhism, which included techniques for visualizing deities, encouraged the development of images with precise iconographic details such as the gilt-bronze sculpture of the **BODHISATTVA AVALOKITESHVARA** in FIGURE 23–2. *Bodhisattvas* are beings who are well advanced on the path to buddhahood (enlightenment), the goal of Mahayana Buddhists, and who have vowed out of compassion to help others achieve enlightenment. Avalokiteshvara, the *bodhisattva* of greatest compassion, whose vow is to forgo buddhahood until all others become *buddhas*, became the most popular of these saintly beings in India and in East Asia.

Characteristic of *bodhisattvas*, Avalokiteshvara is distinguished in art by his princely garments, unlike a *buddha*, who wears a monk's robes. Avalokiteshvara is specifically recognized by the lotus flower he holds and by the presence in his crown of his "parent" *buddha*, in this case Amitabha, *buddha* of the Western Pure Land (the Buddhist paradise). Other marks of Avalokiteshvara's extraordinary status are the third eye (symbolizing the ability to see in miraculous ways) and the wheel on his palm (signifying the ability to teach the Buddhist truth).

Avalokiteshvara is shown here in the relaxed pose known as the posture of royal ease. One leg angles down; the other is drawn up onto the lotus seat, itself considered an emblem of spiritual purity. His body bends gracefully, if a bit stiffly, to one side. The chest scarf and lower garment cling to his body, fully revealing its shape. Delicate floral patterns enliven the textiles, and closely set parallel folds provide a wiry, linear tension that contrasts with the hard but silken surfaces of the body. Linear energy continues in the sweep of the tightly pleated hem emerging from under the right thigh, in the sinuous lotus stalks on each side, and in the fluttering ribbons of the elaborate crown. A profusion of details and varied textures creates an ornate effect—the lavish jewelry, the looped hair piled high and cascading over the shoulders, the ripe blossoms, the rich layers of the lotus seat. Though still friendly and human, the image is somewhat formalized. The features of the face, where we instinctively look for a human echo, are treated abstractly, and despite its reassuring smile, the statue's expression remains remote. Through richness of ornament and tension of line, this style expresses the heightened power of a perfected being.

With the fall of the Pala dynasty in the late twelfth century, the last centers of Buddhism in northern India collapsed, and the monks dispersed, mainly into Nepal and Tibet (SEE MAP 23–1). From that time, Tibet has remained the principal stronghold of Tantric Buddhist practice and its arts. The artistic style perfected under the Palas, however, became an influential international style throughout East and Southeast Asia.

Jain Art

The Jain religion traces its roots to a spiritual leader called Mahavira (c. 599–527 BCE), whom it regards as the final in a series of twenty-four saviors known as pathfinders, or *tirthankaras*. Devotees seek through purification to become worthy of rebirth in the heaven of the pathfinders, a zone of pure existence at the zenith of the universe. Jain monks live a life of austerity, and even laypersons avoid killing any living creature.

A MANUSCRIPT LEAF FROM THE *KALPA SUTRA.* As Islamic, or Muslim, territorial control over northern India expanded,

MAP 23–1 | **INDIA**

Throughout its history, the Indian subcontinent was subject to continual invasion that caused the borders of its kingdoms to contract and expand until the establishment of modern-day India in the mid-twentieth century.

non-Islamic religions resorted to more private forms of artistic expression, such as illustrating sacred texts, rather than public activities, such as building temples. In these circumstances, the Jains of western India, primarily in the region of Gujarat, created many illustrated manuscripts, such as this *Kalpa Sutra*, which explicates the lives of the pathfinders **(FIG. 23–3)**. Produced during the late fourteenth century, it is one of the first Jain manuscripts on paper rather than palm leaf, the material which had previously been used for written documents.

With great economy, the illustration, inserted between blocks of Sanskrit text, depicts the birth of Mahavira. He is shown cradled in his mother's arms as she reclines in her bed under a canopy connoting royalty, attended by three ladies-in-waiting. Decorative pavilions and a shrine with peacocks on the roof suggest a luxurious palace setting. Everything appears two-dimensional against the brilliant red or blue

ground. Vibrant colors and crisp outlines impart an energy to the painting that suggests the arrival of the divine in the mundane world. Transparent garments with variegated designs reveal the swelling curves of the figures, whose alert postures and gestures convey a sense of the importance and excitement of the event. Strangely exaggerated features, such as the protruding eyes, contribute to the air of the extraordinary. With its angles and tense curves, the drawing is closely linked to the aesthetics of Sanskrit **calligraphy**, and the effect is as if the words themselves had suddenly flared into color and image.

Hindu Art

Hinduism became the dominant religious tradition of India. With the increasing popularity of Hindu sects came the rapid development of Hindu temples. Spurred by the ambitious building programs of wealthy rulers, well-formulated

23–2 | THE BODHISATTVA AVALOKITESHVARA
Kurkihar, Bihar. Pala dynasty, 12th century. Gilt-bronze, height 10″ (25.5 cm). Patna Museum, Patna.

23–3 | DETAIL OF A LEAF WITH THE BIRTH OF MAHAVIRA
Kalpa Sutra. Western Indian school (probably Gujarat), c. 1375–1400. Gouache on paper, 3⅜ × 3″ (8.5 × 7.6 cm). Prince of Wales Museum, Bombay.

regional styles had evolved by about 1000 CE. The most spectacular structures of the era were monumental, with a complexity and grandeur of proportion unequaled even in later Indian art.

Emphasis on monumental individual temples gave way to the building of vast temple complexes and more moderately scaled yet more richly ornamented individual temples. These developments took place largely in the south of India, for temple building in the north virtually ceased with the consolidation of Islamic rule there from the beginning of the thirteenth century. The mightiest of the southern Hindu kingdoms was Vijayanagar (c. 1336–1565), whose rulers successfully countered the southward progress of Islamic forces for more than 200 years. Viewing themselves as defenders and preservers of Hindu faith and culture, Vijayanagar kings lavished donations on sacred shrines. Under the patronage of the Vijayanagar and their successors, the Nayaks, the principal monuments of later Hindu architecture were created.

TEMPLE AT MADURAI. The enormous temple complex at Madurai, one of the capitals of the Nayaks, is an example of this fervent expression of Hindu faith. Founded around the thirteenth century, it is dedicated to the goddess Minakshi (the local name for Parvati, the consort of the god Shiva) and to Sundareshvara (the local name for Shiva himself). The temple complex stands in the center of the city and is the focus of Madurai life. At its heart are the two oldest shrines, one to Minakshi and the other to Sundareshvara. Successive additions over the centuries gradually expanded the complex around these small shrines and came to dominate the visual landscape of the city. The most dramatic features of this and similar "temple cities" of the south were the thousand-pillar halls, large ritual-bathing pools, and especially entrance gateways, called *gopuras*, which tower above the temple site and the surrounding city like modern skyscrapers (FIG. 23–4).

Gopuras proliferated as a temple city grew, necessitating new and bigger enclosing walls, and thus new gateways. Successive rulers, often seeking to outdo their predecessors, donated taller and taller *gopuras*. As a result, the tallest structures in temple cities are often at the periphery, rather than at the central temples, which are sometimes totally overwhelmed by the height of the surrounding structures. The temple complex at Madurai has eleven *gopuras*, the largest over 160 feet tall.

Formally, the *gopura* has its roots in the *vimana*, the pyramidal tower characteristic of the seventh-century southern temple style. As the *gopura* evolved, it took on the graceful concave silhouette shown here. The exterior is embellished with thousands of sculpted figures, evoking a teeming world of gods and goddesses. Inside, stairs lead to the top for an extraordinary view.

Myth and Religion
TANTRIC INFLUENCE IN THE ART OF NEPAL AND TIBET

The legacy of India's Tantric Buddhist art can be traced in the regions of Nepal and Tibet. Artistic expression of esoteric Buddhist ideals reached a high point in the seventeenth and eighteenth centuries. Indeed, even today, artists worldwide continue to explore aspects of this tradition.

Inlaid Devotional Sculpture. In Nepal, where Hinduism intermingled with Buddhism, sculptors developed a metalwork style in which a traditional artistic use of polished stones became prevalent in devotional sculptures as well. Inlaid gems and semiprecious stones often enlivened their copper or bronze sculptures, which were almost always brightly gilded. Complex representations of deities, often multiarmed and adorned with celestial attributes, predominated, but some themes from early Buddhism were revived. In one particularly fine eighteenth-century example, Maya, the Mother of Buddha, holds the legendary tree branch while the Buddha emerges from her side. The cast and chased details of the regal costume of Queen Maya, including fluttering scarves, elaborate jewelry, and a large crown, are studded with real jewels, pearls, and semiprecious stones. The tree, also, is richly inlaid, symbolizing the auspicious nature of the event. Both the tree and the figure rise from a pedestal shaped to suggest the blossoming lotus, a reference to the appearance of the Buddha's purity in the muddy pond of the material world.

***Tangka* Painting.** Buddhism was established relatively late in Tibet but the region has since become almost wholly identified with the religion. With the rule of a lineage of Dalai Lamas established in the seventeenth century and continuing through to the twentieth century, and a related expansion of monasteries, the arts associated with Tantric Buddhism flourished. Wrathful manifestations of deities, mysterious and powerful, were evoked in sculpted and painted forms, with the scroll-like *tangka* emerging as a major format. A nineteenth-century painting of Achala, one of a group of wrathful deities associated with truth, resolve, and the overcoming of obstacles, exemplifies this major aspect of Tibetan art. The deity exudes brilliant red flames while brandishing a sword and posing as if to strike. Following traditional practice, the artist—or artists, as these may have employed highly specialized craftsmen—positions the terrifying figure on a lotus pedestal, establishing his ethereal nature. The background suggests the green hills and blue sky of the material world as well as the cosmic geometry envisioned in Tantric Buddhism. Repeated representations of the deity emphasize the efficacious function and conspicuous power of the image.

MAYA, MOTHER OF BUDDHA, HOLDING A TREE BRANCH
Nepal. 18th century. Gilt bronze with inlaid precious stones, height 22" (56 cm). Musée Guimet, Paris.

ACHALA
Tibet. 19th century. Gouache on cotton, 33½ × 23⅔"
(85 × 60 cm). Musée Guimet, Paris.
Photo Réunion des Musées Nationaux; Art Resource, New York

23-4 | **OUTER *GOPURA* OF THE MINAKSHI-SUNDARESHVARA TEMPLE**
Madurai, Tamil Nadu, South India. Nayak dynasty, mostly 13th to mid-17th century, with modern renovations.

THE BUDDHIST AND HINDU INHERITANCE IN SOUTHEAST ASIA

India's Buddhist and Hindu traditions influenced Southeast Asia (discussed in Chapter 9), where they were absorbed by newly rising kingdoms in the regions now comprising Burma (Myanmar), Thailand, Cambodia (Kampuchea), Vietnam, and Indonesia.

Theravada Buddhism in Burma and Thailand

In northern Burma, from the eleventh to the thirteenth century, rulers raised innumerable religious monuments—temples, monasteries, and stupas—in the Pagan plain, following the scriptures of Theravada Buddhism (or Hinayana Buddhism, see Chapter 9). To the south arose the port city

23-5 | **SHWE-DAGON STUPA (PAGODA)**
Terrace, 15th century. Construction at the site from at least the 14th century, with replastering and redecoration continuously to the present.

Art and Its Context
FOUNDATIONS OF INDIAN CULTURE

The earliest civilization on the Indian subcontinent flourished toward the end of the third millennium BCE along the Indus River in present-day Pakistan. Remains of its expertly engineered brick cities have been uncovered, together with works of art that intriguingly suggest spiritual practices and reveal artistic traits known in later Indian culture.

The decline of the Indus Valley civilization during the mid-second millennium BCE coincides with (and may be related to) the arrival from the northwest of a seminomadic warrior people known as the Indo-European Aryans. Over the next millennium they were influential in formulating the new civilization that gradually emerged. The most important Aryan contributions to this new civilization included the Sanskrit language and the sacred texts called the Vedas. The evolution of Vedic thought under the influence of indigenous Indian beliefs culminated in the mystical, philosophical texts called the Upanishads, which took shape sometime after 800 BCE.

The Upanishads teach that the material world is illusory; only Brahman, the universal soul, is real and eternal. We—that is, our individual souls—are trapped in this illusion in a relentless cycle of birth, death, and rebirth. The ultimate goal of religious life is to liberate ourselves from this cycle and to unite our individual soul with Brahman.

Buddhism and Jainism are two of the many religions that developed in the climate of Upanishadic thought. Buddhism (see "Buddhism" page 317) is based on the teachings of Shakyamuni Buddha, who lived in central India about 500 BCE; Jainism was shaped about the same time by the followers of the spiritual leader Mahavira. Both religions acknowledged the cyclical nature of existence and taught a means of liberation from it, but they rejected the authority, rituals, and social strictures of Vedic religion. Whereas the Vedic religion was in the hands of a hereditary priestly class, Buddhist and Jain communities welcomed all members of society, which gave them great appeal. The Vedic tradition eventually evolved into the many sects now collectively known as Hinduism (see "Hinduism" page 318).

Through most of its history India was a mosaic of regional dynastic kingdoms, but from time to time, empires emerged that unified large parts of the subcontinent. The first was the Maurya dynasty (c. 322–185 BCE), whose great king Ashoka patronized Buddhism. From this time Buddhist doctrines spread widely and its artistic traditions were established.

In the first century CE the Kushans, a Central Asian people, created an empire extending from present-day Afghanistan down into central India. Buddhism prospered under Kanishka, the most powerful Kushan king, and spread into Central Asia and to East Asia. At this time, under the evolving thought of Mahayana Buddhism, traditions first evolved for depicting the image of the Buddha in art.

Later, under the Gupta dynasty (c. 320–486 CE) in central India, Buddhist art and culture reached their high point. However, Gupta monarchs also patronized the Hindu religion, which from this time grew to become the dominant Indian religious tradition, with its emphasis on the great gods Vishnu (the Creator), Shiva (the Destroyer), and the Goddess—all with multiple forms.

After the tenth century, numerous regional dynasties prevailed, some quite powerful and long-lasting. During the early part of this period, to roughly 1200, Buddhism continued to decline as a cultural force, while artistic achievement under Hinduism soared. Hindu temples, in particular, developed monumental and complex forms that were rich in symbolism and ritual function, with each region of India producing its own variation.

of Rangoon (in Burmese Yangon, called Dagon in antiquity), now the nation's capital. Established by Mon rulers (SEE FIG. 9–29) at least by the eleventh century, Rangoon is site of the Shwe-dagon stupa (FIG. 23–5), which enshrines relics of the Buddha. The modern structures of Shwe-dagon (which means "Golden Dagon") rise from an ancient core—fourteenth century or earlier—and reflect centuries of continual restoration and enhancement. The site continues to be a center of Theravada devotion amid symbolic ornamentation—especially lotus elements symbolic of the Buddha's purity—and splendid decoration in gilding and precious stones supplied by pious contributions. Images of the Buddha, and sometimes his footprints alone, provide focal points for devotion.

In Thailand, the Sukhothai kingdom (mid-thirteenth to late fourteenth century) also embraced Theravada Buddhism, although Hindu shrines were constructed as well in its capital city called Sukhothai (ancient name Sukhodaya). Artisans working under royal patrons developed a classic statement of Theravada ideals in bronze sculptures of the Buddha. Notable was their development of a free-standing walking Buddha. The highest expression of the ascetic simplicity of Theravada Buddhism, however, may be found in their many renditions of the **BUDDHA CALLING THE EARTH TO WITNESS** (FIG. 23–6).

Inspired by devotional texts and poetry, and further refined through reference to models from Sri Lanka, the iconographical and stylistic elements reached a height of perfection. The Buddha's cranial protuberance is interpreted as a flame of divine knowledge, and details of his ecclesiastical costume are reduced to a few elegant lines. The *mudras* (see p. 325), or hand gestures, are quietly eloquent.

23–6 | **BUDDHA CALLING THE EARTH TO WITNESS**
Sukhothai style. Bronze. Height 37″ (94 cm). Collection of H.R.H. Prince Chalermbol Yugala, Bangkok.

Vietnamese Ceramics

Both the Burmese and the Thai kingdoms produced ceramics, often inspired by the stonewares and porcelains from China. Sukhothai potters, for example, made green-glazed and brown-glazed wares, called Sawankhalok wares. Even more widespread were the wares of Vietnamese potters. For example, excavation of the Hoi An "hoard" (SEE FIG. 23–7), actually the contents of a sunken ship laden with ceramics for export, brought to light an impressive variety of ceramic forms made by Vietnamese potters of the late fifteenth to early sixteenth century. Painted in underglaze cobalt blue and further embellished with overglaze enamels, these wares were shipped throughout Southeast Asia and beyond, as far east as Japan and as far west as England and The Netherlands.

23–7 | **GROUP OF CERAMICS FROM THE HOI AN HOARD, VIETNAMESE**
Late 15th to early 16th century, porcelain with underglaze blue decoration, barbed-rim dishes:
(left) diam. 14″ (35.1 cm); (right) diam. 13¼″ (34.7 cm). Phoenix Art Museum, 2000.105–109.

More than 150,000 blue-and-white ceramics were found in the hold of a sunken ship excavated in the late 1990s under commission from the Vietnamese government, which later sent many of the retrieved items to public auction. Among the works shown here, the twenty-three small cups were found packed inside the jar.

23–8 | RAMAYANA SCENE
Candi Panataran, Java. Stone relief, height 29½″ (70 cm).
Early 14th century.

MUGHAL PERIOD

Islam first touched the South Asian subcontinent in the eighth century, when Arab armies captured a small territory near the Indus River. Later, beginning around 1000, Turkic factions from Central Asia, relatively recent converts to Islam, began military campaigns into North India, at first purely for plunder, then seeking territorial control. From 1206, various Turkic dynasties ruled portions of the subcontinent from the northern city of Delhi. These sultanates, as they are known, constructed forts, **mausoleums**, monuments, and **mosques**. Although these early dynasties left their mark, it was the Mughal Dynasty that made the most inspired and lasting contribution to the art of India.

The Mughals, too, came from Central Asia. Muhammad Zahir-ud-Din, known as Babur ("Lion" or "Panther"), was the first Mughal emperor of India (ruled 1526–30). He emphasized his Turkic heritage, though he had equally impressive Mongol ancestry. After some initial conquests in Central Asia, he amassed an empire stretching from Afghanistan to Delhi, which he conquered in 1526. Akbar (ruled 1556–1605), the third ruler, extended Mughal control over most of North India, and under his two successors, Jahangir and Shah Jahan, northern India was generally unified by 1658. The Mughal Empire lasted until 1858, when the last Mughal emperor was deposed and exiled to Burma by the British.

Mughal Architecture

Mughal architects were heir to a 300-year-old tradition of Islamic building in India. The Delhi sultans who preceded them had great forts housing government and court buildings. Their architects had introduced two fundamental Islamic structures, the mosque and the tomb, along with construction based on the arch and the dome. (Earlier Indian architecture had been based primarily on post-and-lintel construction. They had also drawn freely on Indian architecture, borrowing both decorative and structural elements to create a variety of hybrid styles, and had especially benefited from the centuries-old Indian virtuosity in stone carving and masonry. The Mughals followed in this tradition, synthesizing Indian, Persian, and Central Asian elements for their forts, palaces, mosques, tombs, and **cenotaphs** (tombs or monuments to someone whose remains are actually somewhere else).

Akbar, an ambitious patron of architecture and city planning, constructed a new capital at a place he named *Fatehpur Sikri* ("City of Victory at Sikri"), celebrating his military conquests and the birth of his son Jahangir. The palatial and civic buildings, built primarily during Akbar's residence there from about 1572 to 1585, have drawn much admiration from modern and contemporary architects. Akbar's congregational mosque (Jami Masjid), completed about 1571–72, is one of

Indonesian Traditions

Indonesia experienced a Hindu revival in the centuries following its Buddhist period, which came to a close in the eighth or ninth century (see Chapter 9). As a consequence, it has maintained unique traditions that build upon the Hindu epics, especially the Ramayana. Javanese versions of these epics can be found illustrated in narrative reliefs from shrines of the fourteenth century (FIG. 23–8). Here modeling is reduced and rhythmic surface ornamentation increased. This style is often called the *wayang* style because of its similarities to the leather shadow puppets of Indonesia's *wayang* theater, still popular today. During the fifteenth century, Islam spread over Indonesia and subsequent religious monuments avoided figural representation. In their portrayal of botanical motifs and other ornaments, however, Indonesian sculptors preserved some elements of the relief style seen here.

23-9 | BULAND DARVAZA (THE LOFTY GATE)
Fatehpur Sikri, approaching the Congregational Mosque
(Jami Masjid), 1573-74.

the largest and most ornately finished mosques in India. Built on a high plinth, its vast central courtyard is approached from the south through the **BULAND DARVAZA (THE LOFTY GATE)**, as seen in FIGURE 23–9. This gateway is dignified in proportion but monumental in scale, rising more than 150 feet above the road below. An inscription dated 1601 cites Akbar's triumphant return from the Deccan; however, many scholars maintain a date in the 1570s or 1580s for the monumental gateway itself.

THE TAJ MAHAL.   Perhaps the most famous of all Indian Islamic structures, the Taj Mahal is sited on the bank of the Yamuna River at Agra, in northern India. Built between 1631 and 1648, it was commissioned as a mausoleum for his wife by the emperor Shah Jahan (ruled 1628–58), who is believed to have taken a major part in overseeing its design and construction.

Visually, the Taj Mahal never fails to impress (SEE FIG. 23–1). As visitors enter through a monumental, hall-like gate, the tomb rises before them across a spacious garden set with long reflecting pools. Measuring some 1,000 by 1,900 feet, the enclosure is unobtrusively divided into quadrants planted with trees and flowers and framed by broad walkways and stone inlaid in geometric patterns. In Shah Jahan's time, fruit trees and cypresses—symbolic of life and death, respectively—lined the walkways, and fountains played in the shal-

low pools. One can imagine the melodies of court musicians that wafted through the garden. Truly, the senses were beguiled in this earthly evocation of paradise.

Set toward the rear of the garden, the tomb is flanked by two smaller structures not visible here, one a mosque and the other a hall designed in mirror image. They share a broad base with the tomb and serve visually as stabilizing elements. Like the entrance hall, they are made mostly of red sandstone, rendering even more startling the full glory of the tomb's white marble. The tomb is raised higher than these structures on its own marble platform. At each corner of the platform, a **minaret**, or slender tower, defines the surrounding space. The minarets' three levels correspond to those of the tomb, creating a bond between them. Crowning each minaret is a *chattri*, or pavilion. Traditional embellishments of Indian palaces, *chattris* quickly passed into the vocabulary of Indian Islamic architecture, where they appear prominently. Minarets occur in architecture throughout the Islamic world; from their heights, the faithful are called to prayer.

A lucid geometric symmetry pervades the tomb. It is basically square, but its **chamfered**, or sliced-off, corners create a subtle octagon. Measured to the base of the **finial** (the spire at the top), the tomb is almost exactly as tall as it is wide. Each façade is identical, with a central *iwan* flanked by two stories of smaller *iwans*. (A typical feature of eastern Islamic architecture, an *iwan* is a vaulted opening with an arched portal.) By creating voids in the façades, these *iwans* contribute markedly to the building's sense of weightlessness. On the roof, four octagonal *chattris*, one at each corner, create a visual transition to the lofty, bulbous dome, the crowning element that lends special power to this structure. Framed but not obscured by the *chattris*, the dome rises more gracefully and is lifted higher by its **drum** than in earlier Mughal tombs, allowing the swelling curves and lyrical lines of its beautifully proportioned, surprisingly large form to emerge with perfect clarity.

By the seventeenth century, India was well known for exquisite craftsmanship and luxurious decorative arts (see "Luxury Arts," page 827). The pristine surfaces of the **TAJ MAHAL** are embellished with utmost subtlety (FIG. 23–10). Even the sides of the platform on which the Taj Mahal stands are carved in relief with a **blind arcade** motif and carved relief panels of flowers. The portals are framed with verses from the Qur'an inlaid in black marble, while the **spandrels** are decorated with floral **arabesques** inlaid in colored semiprecious stones, a technique known by its Italian name, *pietra dura*. Not strong enough to detract from the overall purity of the white marble, the embellishments enliven the surfaces of this impressive yet delicate masterpiece.

Mughal Painting

Probably no one had more control over the solidification of the Mughal Empire and the creation of Mughal art than the emperor Akbar. A dynamic, humane, and just leader, Akbar

23–10 | TAJ MAHAL
Agra, India. Mughal period, reign of Shah Jahan, c. 1631–48.

enjoyed religious discourse and loved the arts, especially painting. He created an imperial **atelier** (workshop) of painters, which he placed under the direction of two artists from the Persian court. Learning from these two masters, the Indian painters of the atelier soon transformed Persian styles into the more vigorous, naturalistic styles that mark the Mughal school (see "Indian Painting on Paper," page 820). At Akbar's cosmopolitan court, pictorial sources from Europe also became inspiration for Mughal artists.

PAINTING IN THE COURT OF AKBAR. Akbar's court painters also produced paintings documenting Akbar's own life and accomplishments in the *Akbarnama*. Among the most fascinating in the series are those which record Akbar's supervision of the construction of Fatehpur Sikri. One painting (FIG. 23–11) documents Akbar's inspection of the stone masons and other craftsmen, and includes an ambitious rendering of the Buland Darwaza (The Lofty Gate), shown above in FIGURE 23–9.

One of the most famous and extraordinary works produced in Akbar's atelier is an illustrated manuscript of the *Hamzanama*, a Persian classic about the adventures of Hamza, uncle of the Prophet Muhammad. Painted on cotton cloth, each illustration is more than 2½ feet high. The entire project gathered 1,400 illustrations into twelve volumes and took fifteen years to complete.

One illustration shows Hamza's spies scaling a fortress wall and surprising some men as they sleep (FIG. 23–12). One man climbs a rope; another has already beheaded a figure in yellow and lifts his head aloft—realistic details are not avoided in paintings from the Mughal atelier. The receding lines of the architecture, viewed from a slightly elevated vantage point, provide a reasonably three-dimensional setting. Yet the

23–11 | AKBAR INSPECTING THE CONSTRUCTION OF FATEHPUR SIKRI
Akbarnama, c. 1590. Opaque watercolor on paper, 14¾ × 10″ (37.5 × 25 cm). Victoria & Albert Museum, London. (I.S.2-1896 91/117)

Many of the painters in the Mughal imperial workshops are recorded in texts of the period. Based on those records and on signatures that occur on some paintings, scholars have attributed the design of this work to Tulsi Kalan (Tulsi the Elder), the painting to Bandi, and the portraits to Madhu Kalan (Madhu the Elder) or Madhu Khurd (Madhu the Younger).

Technique
INDIAN PAINTING ON PAPER

Before the fourteenth century most painting in India had been on walls or palm leaves. With the introduction of paper, Indian artists adapted painting techniques from Persia and over the ensuing centuries produced jewel-toned works of surpassing beauty on paper.

Painters usually began their training early. As young apprentices, they learned to make brushes and grind pigments. Brushes were made from the curved hairs of a squirrel's tail, arranged to taper from a thick base to a single hair at the tip. Paint came from pigments of vegetables and minerals—lapis lazuli to make blue, malachite for pale green—that were ground to a paste with water, then bound with a solution of gum from the acacia plant. Paper was made by crushing fibers of cotton and jute to a pulp, pouring the mixture onto a woven mat, drying, and then burnishing with a smooth piece of agate, often achieving a glossy finish.

Artists frequently worked from a collection of sketches belonging to a master painter's atelier. Sometimes, to transfer the drawing to a blank sheet beneath, sketches were pricked with small, closely spaced holes that were then daubed with wet color. The resulting dots were connected into outlines, and the process of painting began.

First, the painter applied a thin wash of a chalk-based white, which sealed the surface of the paper while allowing the underlying sketch to show through. Next, outlines were filled with thick washes of brilliant, opaque, unmodulated color. When the colors were dry, the painting was laid facedown on a smooth marble surface and burnished with a rounded agate stone, rubbing first up and down, then side to side. The indirect pressure against the marble polished the pigments to a high luster. Then outlines, details, and modeling—depending on the style—were added with a fine brush.

Sometimes certain details were purposely left for last, such as the eyes, which were said to bring the painting to life. Gold and raised details were applied when the painting was nearly finished. Gold paint, made from pulverized, 24-karat gold leaf bound with acacia gum, was applied with a brush and burnished to a high shine. Raised details such as the pearls of a necklace were made with thick, white, chalk-based paint, with each pearl a single droplet hardened into a tiny raised mound.

sense of depth is boldly undercut by the richly variegated geometric patterns of the tilework, which are painted as though they had been set flat on the page. Contrasting with the flat geometric patterns are the large human figures, whose rounded forms and softened contours create a convincing sense of volume. The energy exuded by the figures is also characteristic of painting under Akbar—even the sleepers seem active. This robust, naturalistic figure style is quite different from the linear style seen earlier in Jain manuscripts (SEE FIG. 23–3) and even from the Persian styles that inspired Mughal paintings.

Nearly as prominent as the architectural setting with its vivid human adventure is the sensuous landscape in the foreground, where monkeys, foxes, and birds inhabit a grove of trees that shimmer and glow against the darkened background like precious gems. The treatment of the gold-edged leaves at first calls to mind the patterned geometry of the tilework, yet a closer look reveals a skillful naturalism born of careful observation. Each tree species is carefully distinguished—by the way its trunk grows, the way its branches twist, the shape and veining of its leaves, the silhouette of its overall form. Pink and blue rocks with lumpy, softly outlined forms add still further interest to this painting, whose every inch is full of intriguing elements.

PAINTING IN THE COURT OF JAHANGIR. Painting from the reign of Jahangir (ruled 1605–27) presents a different tone. Like his father, Jahangir admired painting and, if anything, paid even more attention to his atelier. Indeed, he boasted that he could recognize the hand of each of his artists even in collaborative paintings, which were common. Unlike Akbar, however, Jahangir preferred the courtly life to the adventurous one, and paintings produced for him reflect his subdued and refined tastes and his admiration for realistic detail.

One such painting is **JAHANGIR IN DARBAR** (FIG. 23–13). The work, probably part of a series on Jahangir's reign, shows the emperor holding an audience, or *darbar*, at court. Jahangir himself is depicted at top center, seated on a balcony under a canopy. Members of his court, including his son, the future emperor Shah Jahan, stand somewhat stiffly to each side. The audience, too, is divided along the central axis, with figures lined up in profile or three-quarter view. In the foreground, an elephant and a horse complete the symmetrical format.

Jahangir insisted on fidelity in portraiture, including his own in old age. The figures in the audience are a medley of portraits, possibly taken from albums meticulously kept by the court artists. Some represent people known to have died before Jahangir's reign, so the painting may represent a symbolic gathering rather than an actual event. Standing out amid the bright array of garments is the black robe of a Jesuit priest from Europe. Both Akbar and Jahangir were known for their interest in things foreign, and many foreigners flocked to the courts of these open-minded rulers.

23–12 | **HAMZA'S SPIES SCALE THE FORTRESS**
Hamzanama, North India. Mughal period, Mughal, reign of Akbar, c. 1567–82.
Gouache on cotton, 30 × 24″ (76 × 61 cm). Museum of Applied Arts, Vienna.

The scene is formal, the composition static, and the treatment generally two-dimensional. Nevertheless, the sensitively rendered portraits and the fresh colors, with their varied range of pastel tones, provide the aura of a keenly observed, exquisitely idealized reality that marks the finest paintings of Jahangir's time.

Rajput Painting

Outside of the Mughal strongholds at Delhi and Agra, much of northern India was governed regionally by local Hindu princes, descendants of the so-called Rajput warrior clans, who were allowed to keep their lands in return for allegiance to the Mughals. Like the Mughals, Rajput princes frequently supported painters at their courts, and in these settings, a variety of strong, indigenous Indian painting styles were perpetu-ated. Rajput painting, more abstract and poetic than the Mughal style, included subjects like those treated by Mughal painters, royal portraits and court scenes, as well as indigenous subjects such as Hindu myths, love poetry, and the Ragamala (illustrations relating to musical modes).

The Hindu devotional movement known as *bhakti*, which had done much to spread the faith in the south from around the seventh century, now experienced a revival in the north. As it had earlier in the south, *bhakti* inspired an outpouring of poetic literature, this time devoted especially to Krishna, the popular human incarnation of the god Vishnu. Most renowned is the *Gita Govinda*, a cycle of rhapsodic poems about the love between God and humans expressed metaphorically through the love between the young Krishna and the cowherd Radha.

23-13 | Abul Hasan and Manohar **JAHANGIR IN DARBAR**
Jahangirnama. North India. Mughal period, Mughal, reign of Jahangir, c. 1620. Gouache on paper,
13¾ × 7⅞" (35 × 20 cm). Museum of Fine Arts, Boston.

Frances Bartlett Donation of 1912 and Picture Fund (14, 654)

The illustration here is from a manuscript of the *Gita Govinda* produced in the region of Rajasthan about 1525–50. The blue god Krishna sits in dalliance with a group of cowherd women. Standing with her maid and consumed with love for Krishna, Radha peers through the trees, overcome by jealousy. Her feelings are indicated by the cool blue color behind her, while the crimson red behind the Krishna grouping suggests passion (FIG. 23–14). The curving stalks and bold patterns of the flowering vines and trees express not only the exuberance of springtime, when the story unfolds, but also the heightened emotional tensions of the scene. Birds, trees, and flowers are brilliant as fireworks against the black, hilly landscape edged in an undulating white line. As in the Jain manuscript earlier (SEE FIG. 23–3), all the figures are of a single type, with plump faces in profile and oversized eyes. Yet the resilient line of the drawing gives them life, and the variety of textile patterns provides some individuality. The intensity and resolute flatness of the scene seem to thrust all of its energy outward, irrevocably engaging the viewer in the drama.

Quite a different mood pervades **HOUR OF COWDUST**, a work from the Kangra school in the Punjab Hills, foothills of the Himalayas north of Delhi (FIG. 23–15). Painted around 1790, some 250 years later than the previous work, it shows the influence of Mughal naturalism on the later schools of Indian painting. The theme is again Krishna.

23–14 : KRISHNA AND THE GOPIS
From the *Gita Govinda*, Rajasthan, India. Mughal period, Rajput, c. 1525-50. Gouache on paper, 4⅞ × 7½″ (12.3 × 19 cm). Prince of Wales Museum, Bombay.

The lyrical poem *Gita Govinda*, by the poet-saint Jayadeva, was probably written in eastern India during the latter half of the twelfth century. The episode illustrated here occurs early in the relationship of Radha and Krishna, which in the poem is a metaphor for the connection between humans and god. The poem traces the progress of their love through separation, reconciliation, and fulfillment. Intensely sensuous imagery characterizes the entire poem, as in the final song, when Krishna welcomes Radha to his bed. (Narayana is the name of Vishnu in his role as cosmic creator.)

> Leave lotus footprints on my bed of tender shoots, loving Radha!
> Let my place be ravaged by your tender feet!
>   Narayana is faithful now. Love me Radhika!
> I stroke your feet with my lotus hand—you have come far.
> Set your golden anklet on my bed like the sun.
>   Narayana is faithful now. Love me Radhika!
> Consent to my love. Let elixir pour from your face!
> To end our separation I bare my chest of the silk that bars your breast.
>   Narayana is faithful now. Love me Radhika!
>
>   (Translated by Barbara Stoler Miller)

Wearing his peacock crown, garland of flowers, and yellow garment—all traditional iconography of Krishna-Vishnu—he returns to the village with his fellow cowherds and their cattle. All eyes are upon him as he plays his flute, said to enchant all who hear it. Women with water jugs on their heads turn to look; others lean from windows to watch and call out to him. We are drawn into this charming village scene by the diagonal movements of the cows as they surge through the gate and into the courtyard beyond. Pastel houses and walls create a sense of space, and in the distance we glimpse other villagers going about their work or peacefully sitting in their houses. A rim of dark trees softens the horizon, and an atmospheric sky completes the aura of enchanted naturalism. Again, all the figures are similar in

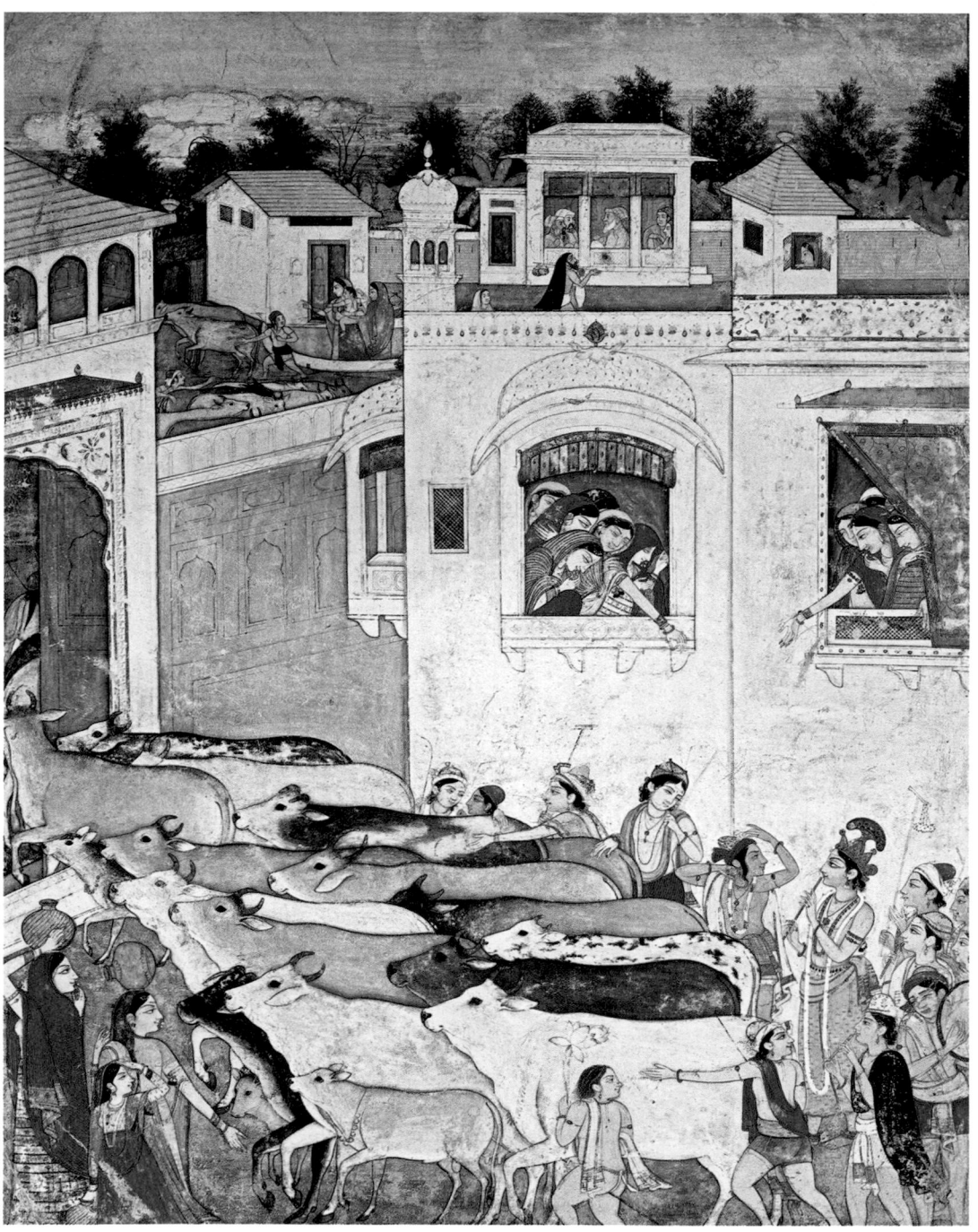

23–15 | **HOUR OF COWDUST**
From Punjab Hills, India. Mughal period, Rajput, Kangra school, c. 1790. Gouache on paper, 14¹⁵⁄₁₆ × 12⅜₁₆″ (36 × 31.9 cm). Museum of Fine Arts, Boston.
Denman W. Ross Collection (22.683)

type, this time with a perfection of proportion and a gentle, lyrical movement that complement the idealism of the setting. The scene embodies the sublime purity and grace of the divine, which, as in so much Indian art, is evoked into our human world to coexist with us as one.

INDIA'S ENGAGEMENT WITH THE WEST

By the time *Hour of Cowdust* was painted, India's regional princes had reasserted themselves, and the vast Mughal Empire had shrunk to a small area around Delhi. At the same time, however, a new power, Britain, was making itself felt, inaugurating a markedly different period in Indian history.

British Colonial Period

First under the mercantile interests of the British East India Company in the seventeenth and eighteenth centuries, and then under the direct control of the British government as a part of the British Empire in the nineteenth century, India was brought forcefully into contact with the West and its culture. The political concerns of the British Empire extended even to the arts, especially architecture. Over the course of the nineteenth century, the great cities of India, such as Calcutta, Madras, and Bombay (now Mumbai), took on a European aspect as British architects built in the revivalist styles favored in England.

NEW DELHI. In 1911 the British announced their intention to move the seat of government from Calcutta to a newly constructed Western-style capital city to be built at New Delhi. Two years later, Sir Edwin Lutyens (1869–1944) was appointed joint architect for New Delhi (with Herbert Baker), and was charged with laying out the new city and designing the Viceroy's House (now Rashtrapati Bhavan or President's House). Drawing inspiration from Classical antiquity—as well as from more recent urban models, such as Washington, D.C.—Lutyens sited the Viceroy's House as a focal point along with the triumphal arch that he designed as the All India War Memorial, now called the INDIA GATE (FIG. 23–16). In these works Lutyens sought to maintain the tradition of Classical architecture—he developed a "Delhi order" based on the Roman Doric—while incorporating massing, detail, and ornamentation derived from Indian architecture as well. The new capital was inaugurated in 1931.

MOTHER INDIA. Far prior to Britain's consolidation of imperial power in New Delhi a new spirit asserting Indian independence and pan-Asiatic solidarity was awakening. For example, working near Calcutta, the painter Abanindranath Tagore (1871–1951)—nephew of the poet Rabindranath Tagore (1861–1941), who went on to win the Nobel Prize for Litera-

23–16 | Sir Edwin Lutyens **INDIA GATE**
(Originally the All India War Memorial), New Delhi. British Colonial Period, 20th century.

ture in 1913—deliberately rejected the medium of oil painting and the academic realism of Western art. Like the Nihonga artists of Japan (SEE FIG. 25–16) with whom he was in contact, Tagore strove to create a style that reflected his ethnic origins. In **BHARAT MATA (MOTHER INDIA)** he invents a nationalistic icon by using Hindu symbols while also drawing upon the format and techniques of Mughal painting (FIG. 23–17).

The Modern Period

In the wake of World War II, the imperial powers of Europe began to shed their colonial domains. The attainment of self-rule had been five long decades in the making, when finally—chastened by the non-violent example of Mahatma Gandhi (1869–1948)—the British Empire relinquished its "Jewel in the Crown," which was partitioned to form two modern nations: India and Pakistan.

MODERNISM AT CHANDIGARH. After Indian independence in 1947, a modern, internationalist approach was welcomed by the exuberant young nation. One example of this new spirit is the **GANDHI BHAVAN** at Punjab University in Chandigarh, in North India (FIG. 23–18). Used for both lectures and prayer, the hall was designed in the late 1950s by Indian architect B. P. Mathur in collaboration with Pierre Jeanneret, cousin of the French Modernist architect Le Corbusier (Chapter 31), who had drawn plans for the new city at Chandigarh and whose version of the International Style had become influential in India.

The Gandhi Bhavan's three-part, pinwheel plan and abstract sculptural qualities reflect the modern vision of the International Style. Yet other factors speak to India's heritage. Its robust combinations of angles and curves recall ancient Sanskrit letterforms, while the pools surrounding the building evoke Mughal tombs, as well as the ritual-bathing pools of Hindu temples. Yet the abstract style is free of specific religious associations.

A MODERN INDIAN PAINTER. Artists working after Indian independence have continued to study and work abroad, but often draw upon India's distinctive literary and religious traditions as well as regional and folk art traditions. One example is Manjit Bawa (born 1941), who worked in Britain as a silkscreen artist before returning to India to settle in New Delhi. His distinctive canvases, painted meticulously in oil, juxtapose illusionistically modeled figures and animals against brilliantly colored backgrounds of flat, unmodulated color. The composite result, for example in **DHARMA AND THE GOD** (**FIG. 23–19**), brings a strikingly new interpretation to the heroic figures of Indian tradition.

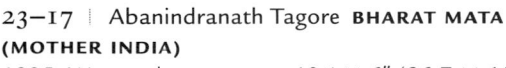

23–17 | Abanindranath Tagore **BHARAT MATA** (**MOTHER INDIA**)
1905. Watercolor on paper, 10½ × 6″ (26.7 × 15.3 cm). Rabindra Bharati Society, Calcutta.

23–18 | B. P. Mathur and Pierre Jeanneret **GANDHI BHAVAN** Punjab University, Chandigarh, North India. Modern period, 1959-61.

THE OBJECT SPEAKS

LUXURY ARTS

The decorative arts of India represent the height of opulent luxury. Ornament embellishes even the invisible backs of pendants and bottoms of containers. Technically superb and crafted from precious materials, tableware, jewelry, furniture, and containers enhance the prestige of their owners and give visual pleasure as well. Metalwork and work in rock crystal, agate, and jade, carving in ivory, and intricate jewelry are all characteristic Indian arts. Because of the intrinsic value of their materials, however, pieces have been disassembled, melted down, and reworked, making the study of Indian luxury arts very difficult. Many pieces, like the carved ivory panel illustrated here, have no date or records of manufacture or ownership. And, like it, many such panels have been removed from a larger container or piece of furniture.

Frozen in timeless delight, carved in ivory against a golden ground, where openwork, stylized vines with spiky leaves, weave an elegant arabesque; loving couples dally under the arcades of a palace courtyard, the thin columns and cusped arches of which resemble the arcades of the palace of Tirumala Nayak (reigned 1623–59) in Madurai (Tamil Nadu). Their huge eyes under heavy brows suggest the intensity of their gaze, and the artist's choice of the profile view shows off their long noses and sensuously thick lips. Their hair is tightly controlled; the men have huge buns and the women, long braids hanging down their backs. Are they divine lovers? After all, Krishna lived and loved on earth among the cowherd maidens. Or are we observing scenes of courtly romance?

The rich jewelry and well-fed look of the couples indicate a high station in life. Men as well as women have voluptuous figures—rounded buttocks and thighs, abdomens hanging over jeweled belts, and sharply indented slim waists that emphasize seductive breasts. Their smooth flesh contrasts with the diaphanous fabrics that swath their plump legs, and their long arms and elegant gestures seem designed to show off their rich jewelry—bracelets, armbands, necklaces, huge earrings, and ribbons. Such amorous couples symbolize harmony as well as fertility.

The erotic imagery suggests that the panel illustrated here might have adorned a container for personal belongings such as jewelry, perfume, or cosmetics. In any event, the ivory relief is a brilliant example of South Indian secular arts.

PANEL FROM A BOX
Nayak dynasty, Tamil Nadu, South India. Late 17th–18th century. Ivory backed with gilded paper, 6 × 12⅜ × ⅛" (15.2 × 31.4 × 0.3 cm). Virginia Museum of Fine Arts.
The Arthur and Margaret Glasgow Fund. 80.171

23–19 | Manjit Bawa **DHARMA AND THE GOD**
1984. Oil on canvas, 216 x 185.4 cm. Peabody
Essex Museum. Salem, Massachusetts.

The Davida and Chester Hervitz Collection

IN PERSPECTIVE

India's voluptuous figurative art, together with her rich religious traditions, had already reached a high point when the Mughals gained control of North India in the sixteenth century, and these traditions continued to thrive under regional patrons throughout the subcontinent. Within the Mughal empire, however, styles introduced from Persia mingled with these sensibilities, and Islamic ideals imparted a new emphasis to nonfigural art forms.

Under their Mughal patrons, architects developed vast building programs based on symmetrical plans and proportionate elevations. The pointed arches and complex vaults in their interiors were matched by the corresponding shapes of their open pavilions and exterior elements, thus providing graceful notes of repetition throughout the imperial complexes. Craftsmen embellished the surfaces of these buildings with intricate inlays of colored, hard stones portraying floral motifs inspired by nature's rhythms, thus perfecting the architectural whole to the pinnacle of refinement.

In the nineteenth century, as the British imposed their rule throughout India, Western academic painting attracted followers in the major cities. Gradually, British architects found opportunity in the construction of civic buildings in India, first in Calcutta and Bombay, and later culminating in the design of the modern capital at New Delhi.

Simultaneously, however, a move for independence from Britain, together with a search for modernity, led artists first to embrace Western artistic ideals and then to modify them, all the while aiming to identify and develop a tradition drawn from India's own history. As elsewhere in Asia, this search for a modern identity occasionally required the conscientious rejection of Western influences. On the one hand, modern Indian artists have drawn inspiration from sources in their "folk art," admired for its directness and the variety of its local characteristics. At the same time, India's sophisticated literary and religious traditions continue to inspire its art at the highest level.

RAMAYANA SCENE,
CANDI PANATARAN
EARLY 14TH CENTURY

CERAMICS FROM THE HOI AN HOARD
LATE 15TH–EARLY 16TH CENTURY

TAJ MAHAL
C. 1631–48

HOUR OF COWDUST
C. 1790

TAGORE
MATA (MOTHER INDIA)
1905

MATHUR AND JEANNERET
GANDHI BHAVAN
1959–61

1200

1300

1400

1500

1600

1700

1800

1900

2000

ART OF SOUTH AND SOUTHEAST ASIA AFTER 1200

◀ **Fall of Pala Dynasty** c. 1199

◀ **Turkic Dynasties Begin to Rule Portions of Indian Subcontinent** c. 1206

◀ **Sukhothai Kingdom, Thailand** Mid 13th–late 14th century

◀ **Vijayanagar Dynasties** c. 1336–1565

◀ **Babur, First Mughal Emperor, Begins Rule** 1526

◀ **British East India Company Begins Activity in India** c. 1600

◀ **Unfied Mughal Empire in Northern India** c.1658

◀ **End of Mughal Empire** 1858
◀ **Peak of British Imperial Power in India** 1858–1947

◀ **Independent India** 1947

24–1 | **GARDEN OF THE CESSATION OF OFFICIAL LIFE** (also known as the Humble Administrator's Garden) Suzhou, Jiangsu. Ming dynasty, early 16th century.

CHAPTER TWENTY-FOUR

CHINESE AND KOREAN ART AFTER 1279

24 Early in the sixteenth century, an official in Beijing, frustrated after serving in the capital for many years without promotion, returned to his home near Shanghai. Taking an ancient poem, "The Song of Leisurely Living," for his model, he began to build a garden. He called his retreat the Garden of the Cessation of Official Life (FIG. 24–1) to indicate that he had exchanged his career as a bureaucrat for a life of leisure. By leisure, he meant that he could now dedicate himself to calligraphy, poetry, and painting, the three arts dear to scholars in China.

The scholar class of imperial China was a phenomenon unique in the world, the product of an examination system designed to recruit the finest minds in the country for government service. Instituted during the Tang dynasty (618–907) and based on even earlier traditions, the civil service examinations were excruciatingly difficult, but for the tiny percentage that passed at the highest level, the rewards were prestige, position, power, and wealth. During the Song dynasty (960–1279) the examinations were expanded and regularized, and more than half of all government positions came to be filled by scholars.

Steeped in the classic texts of philosophy, literature, and history, China's scholars—often called *wenren* or literati—shared a common bond in education and outlook. Their lives typically moved between the philosophical poles of Confucianism and Daoism (see "Foundations of Chinese Culture," page 834). Following Confucianism, they became officials to fulfill their obligation to the world; pulled by Daoism, they retreated from society in order to come to terms with nature and the universe: to create a garden, to write poetry, to paint.

Under a series of remarkably cultivated emperors, the literati reached the height of their influence during the Song dynasty. Their world was about to change dramatically, however, with lasting results for Chinese art.

CHAPTER-AT-A-GLANCE

- ■ THE MONGOL INVASIONS

- ■ YUAN DYNASTY

- ■ MING DYNASTY | Court and Professional Painting | Decorative Arts | Architecture and City Planning | The Literati Aesthetic

- ■ QING DYNASTY | Orthodox Painting | Individualist Painting

- ■ THE MODERN PERIOD

- ■ ARTS OF KOREA: THE JOSEON DYNASTY TO THE MODERN ERA | Joseon Ceramics | Joseon Painting | Modern Korea

- ■ IN PERSPECTIVE

THE MONGOL INVASIONS

At the beginning of the thirteenth century the Mongols, a nomadic people from the steppes north of China, began to amass an empire. Led first by Jenghiz Khan (c. 1162–1227), then by his sons and grandsons, they swept westward into central Europe and overran Islamic lands from Central Asia through present-day Iraq. To the east, they quickly captured northern China, and in 1279, led by Kublai Khan, they conquered southern China as well. Grandson of the mighty Jenghiz, Kublai proclaimed himself emperor of China and founder of the Yuan dynasty (1279–1368).

The Mongol invasions were traumatic, and their effect on China was long lasting. During the Song dynasty, China had grown increasingly introspective. Rejecting foreign ideas and influences, intellectuals had focused on defining the qualities that constituted true "Chinese-ness." They drew a clear distinction between their own people, whom they characterized as gentle, erudite, and sophisticated, and the "barbarians" outside China's borders, whom they regarded as crude, wild, and uncivilized. Now, faced with the reality of barbarian occupation, China's inward gaze intensified in spiritual resistance. For centuries to come, long after the Mongols had gone, leading scholars continued to seek intellectually more challenging, philosophically more profound, and artistically more subtle expressions of all that could be identified as authentically Chinese.

YUAN DYNASTY

The Mongols established their capital in the northern city now known as Beijing (MAP 24–1). The cultural centers of China, however, remained the great cities of the south, where the Song court had been located for the previous 150 years. Combined with the tensions of Yuan rule, this separation of China's political and cultural centers created a new situation dynamic in the arts.

Throughout most of Chinese history, the imperial court had set the tone for artistic taste; artisans attached to the court produced architecture, paintings, gardens, and objects of jade, lacquer, ceramics, and silk especially for imperial use. Over the centuries, painters and calligraphers gradually moved higher up the social scale, for these "arts of the brush" were often practiced by scholars and even emperors, whose high status reflected positively on whatever interested them. With the establishment of an imperial painting academy during the Song dynasty, painters finally achieved a status equal to that of court officials. For the literati, painting came to be grouped with **calligraphy** and poetry as the trio of accomplishments suited to members of the cultural elite.

But while the literati elevated the status of painting by virtue of practicing it, they also began to develop their own ideas of what painting should be. Not needing to earn an income from their art, they cultivated an amateur ideal in which personal expression counted for more than "mere" professional skill. They created for themselves a status as artists totally separate from and superior to professional painters, whose art they felt was inherently compromised, since it was done to please others, and impure, since it was tainted by money.

The conditions of Yuan rule now encouraged a clear distinction between court taste, ministered to by professional artists and artisans, and literati taste. The Yuan dynasty continued the imperial role as patron of the arts, commissioning buildings, murals, gardens, paintings, and decorative arts. Western visitors such as the Italian Marco Polo were impressed by the magnificence of the Yuan court (see "Marco Polo," page 836). But scholars, profoundly alienated from the new government, took little notice of these accomplishments, and thus wrote nothing about them. Nor

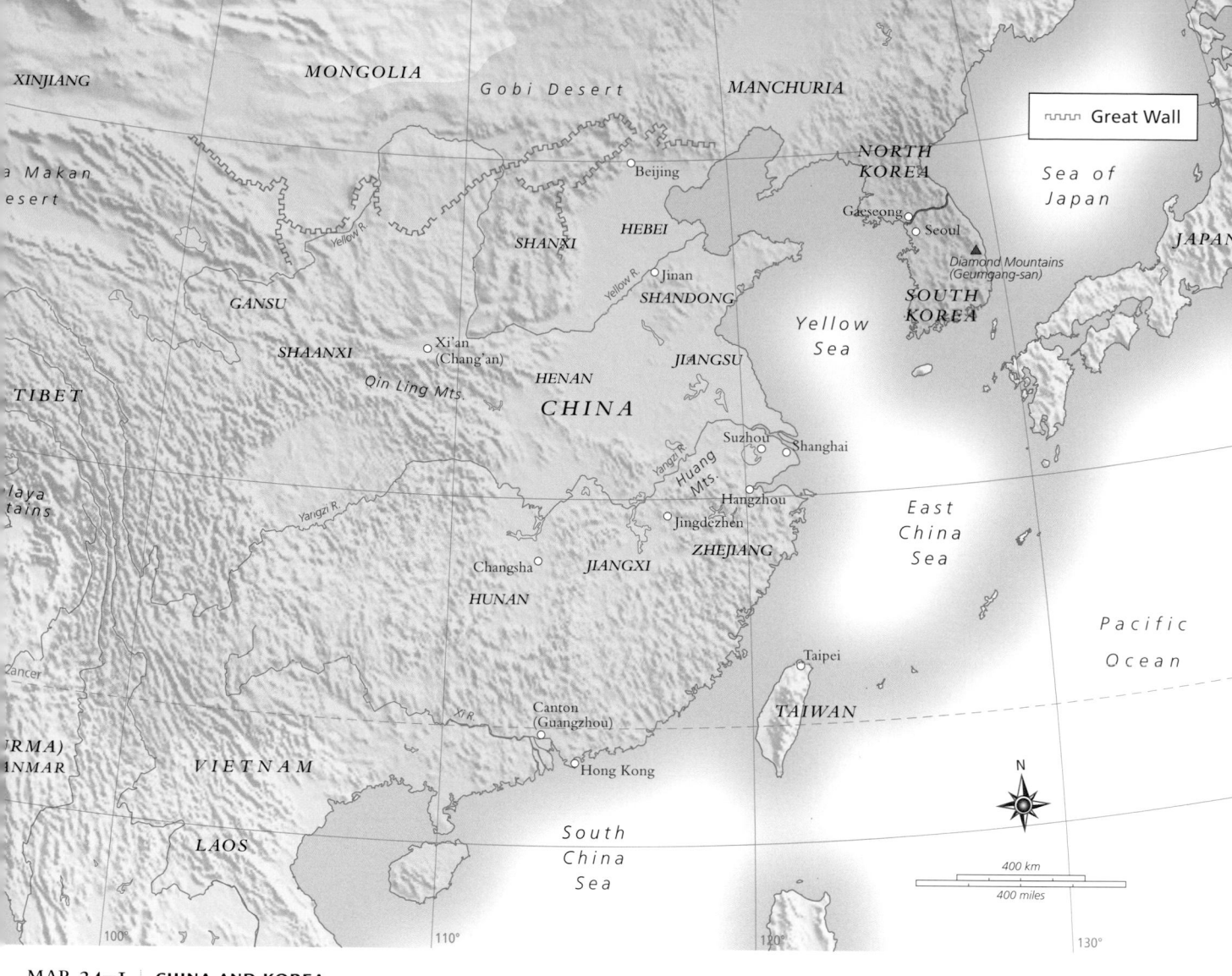

MAP 24–1 | **CHINA AND KOREA**

The Qinling Mountains divide China into northern and southern regions with distinctively different climates and cultures.

did Yuan rulers have much use for scholars, especially those from the south. The civil service examinations were abolished, and the highest government positions were bestowed, instead, on Mongols and their foreign allies. Scholars now tended to turn inward, to search for solutions of their own and to try to express themselves in personal and symbolic terms.

ZHAO MENGFU. Typical of this trend was Zhao Mengfu (1254–1322), a descendant of the imperial line of Song. Unlike many scholars of his time, he eventually chose to serve the Yuan government and was made a high official. A painter, calligrapher, and poet, all of the first rank, Zhao was especially known for his carefully rendered paintings of horses. But he also cultivated another manner, most famous in his landmark painting **AUTUMN COLORS ON THE QIAO AND HUA MOUNTAINS** (FIG. 24–2).

Zhao painted this work for a friend whose ancestors came from Jinan, the present-day capital of Shandong province, and the painting supposedly depicts the landscape there. Yet the mountains and trees are not painted in the accomplished naturalism of Zhao's own time but rather in the archaic yet oddly elegant manner of the earlier Tang dynasty (618–907). The Tang dynasty was a great era in Chinese history, when the country was both militarily strong and culturally vibrant. Through his painting Zhao evoked a nostalgia not only for his friend's distant homeland but also for China's past.

This educated taste for the "spirit of antiquity" became an important aspect of **literati painting** in later periods. Also typical of literati taste are the unassuming brushwork, the subtle colors sparingly used (many literati paintings forgo color altogether), the use of landscape to convey personal meaning, and even the intended audience—a close friend. The literati did not paint for public display but for each other. They favored small formats such as **handscrolls, hanging scrolls,** or **album leaves** (book pages), which could easily be shown to friends or shared at small gatherings (see "Formats of Chinese Painting," page 837).

Art and Its Context
FOUNDATIONS OF CHINESE CULTURE

Chinese culture is distinguished by its long and continuous development. Between 6000 and 2000 BCE a variety of Neolithic cultures flourished across China. Through long interaction these cultures became increasingly similar and they eventually gave rise to the three Bronze Age dynastic states with which Chinese history traditionally begins: the Xia, the Shang (c. 1700–1100 BCE), and the Zhou (1100–221 BCE).

The Shang developed traditions of casting ritual vessels in bronze, working jade in ceremonial shapes, and writing consistently in scripts that directly evolved into the modern Chinese written language. Society was stratified, and the ruling group maintained its authority in part by claiming power as intermediaries between the human and spirit worlds. Under the Zhou a feudal society developed, with nobles related to the king ruling over numerous small states.

During the latter part of the Zhou dynasty, states began to vie for supremacy through intrigue and increasingly ruthless warfare. The collapse of social order profoundly influenced China's first philosophers, who largely concerned themselves with the pragmatic question of how to bring about a stable society.

In 221 BCE, rulers of the state of Qin triumphed over the remaining states, unifying China as an empire for the first time. The Qin created the mechanisms of China's centralized bureaucracy, but their rule was harsh and the dynasty was quickly overthrown. During the ensuing Han dynasty (206 BCE–220 CE), China at last knew peace and prosperity. Confucianism was made the official state ideology, in the process assuming the form and force of a religion. Developed from the thought of Confucius (551–479 BCE), one of the many philosophers of the Zhou, Confucianism is an ethical system for the management of society based on establishing correct relationships among people. Providing a counterweight was Daoism, which also came into its own during the Han dynasty. Based on the thought of Laozi, a possibly legendary contemporary of Confucius, and the philosopher Zhuangzi (369–286 BCE), Daoism is a view of life that seeks to harmonize the individual with the *Dao*, or Way, the process of the universe. Confucianism and Daoism have remained central to Chinese thought—the one addressing the public realm of duty and conformity, the other the private world of individualism and creativity.

Following the collapse of the Han dynasty, China experienced a centuries-long period of disunity (220–589 CE). Invaders from the north and west established numerous kingdoms and dynasties, while a series of six precarious Chinese dynasties held sway in the south. Buddhism, which had begun to filter over trade routes from India during the Han dynasty, now spread widely. The period also witnessed the economic and cultural development of the south (all previous dynasties had ruled from the north).

China was reunited under the Sui dynasty (581–618 CE), which quickly fell to the Tang (618–907 CE), one of the most successful dynasties in Chinese history. Strong and confident, Tang China fascinated and, in turn, was fascinated by the cultures around it. Caravans streamed across Central Asia to the capital, Chang'an, then the largest city in the world. Japan and Korea sent thousands of students to study Chinese culture, and Buddhism reached the height of its influence before a period of persecution signaled the start of its decline.

The mood of the Song dynasty (960–1279 CE) was quite different. The martial vigor of the Tang gave way to a culture of increasing refinement and sophistication, and Tang openness to foreign influences was replaced by a conscious cultivation of China's own traditions. In art, landscape painting emerged as the most esteemed genre, capable of expressing both philosophical and personal concerns. With the fall of the north to invaders in 1126, the Song court set up a new capital in the south, which became the cultural and economic center of the country.

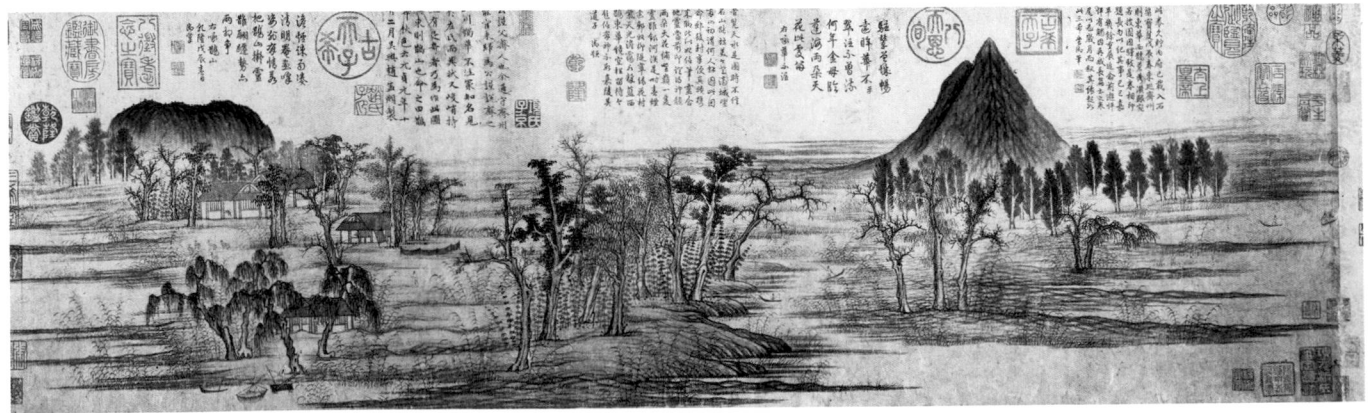

24–2 | Zhao Mengfu **AUTUMN COLORS ON THE QIAO AND HUA MOUNTAINS**
Yuan dynasty, 1296. Handscroll, ink and color on paper, 11¼ × 36¾" (28.6 × 9.3 cm).
National Palace Museum, Taipei, Republic of China.

24–3 | Ni Zan THE RONGXI STUDIO
Yuan dynasty, 1372. Hanging scroll, ink on paper, height 29⅜″ (74.6 cm). National Palace Museum, Taipei, Republic of China.

The idea that a painting is not done to capture a likeness or to satisfy others but is executed freely and carelessly for the artist's own amusement is at the heart of the literati aesthetic. Ni Zan once wrote this comment on a painting: "What I call painting does not exceed the joy of careless sketching with a brush. I do not seek formal likeness but do it simply for my own amusement. Recently I was rambling about and came to a town. The people asked for my pictures, but wanted them exactly according to their own desires and to represent a specific occasion. [When I could not satisfy them,] they went away insulting, scolding, and cursing in every possible way. What a shame! But how can one scold a eunuch for not growing a beard?" (cited in Bush and Shih, page 266).

NI ZAN. Of the considerable number of Yuan painters who took up Zhao's ideas, several became models for later generations. One such was Ni Zan (1301–74), whose most famous surviving painting is **THE RONGXI STUDIO** (FIG. 24–3). Done entirely in ink, the painting depicts the lake region in Ni's home district. Mountains, rocks, trees, and a pavilion are sketched with a minimum of detail using a dry brush technique—a technique in which the brush is not fully loaded with ink but rather about to run out, so that white paper "breathes" through the ragged strokes. The result is a painting with a light touch and a sense of simplicity and purity. Literati styles were believed to reflect the painter's personality. Ni's spare, dry style became associated with a noble spirit, and many later painters adopted it or paid homage to it.

Ni Zan was one of those eccentrics whose behavior has become legendary in the history of Chinese art. In his early years he was one of the richest men in the region, the owner of a large estate. His pride and his aloofness from daily affairs often got him into trouble with the authorities. His cleanliness was notorious. In addition to washing himself several times daily, he also ordered his servants to wash the trees in his garden and to clean the furniture after his guests had left. He was said to be so unworldly that late in life he gave away most of his possessions and lived as a hermit in a boat, wandering on rivers and lakes.

Whether these stories are true or not, they were important elements of Ni's legacy to later painters, for Ni's life as well as his art served as a model. The painting of the literati was bound up with certain views about what constituted an appropriate life. The ideal, as embodied by Ni Zan and others, was of a brilliantly gifted scholar whose spirit was too refined for the dusty world of government service and who thus preferred to live as a recluse, or as one who had retired after having become frustrated by a brief stint as an official.

MING DYNASTY

The founder of the next dynasty, the Ming (1368–1644), came from a family of poor uneducated peasants. As he rose through the ranks in the army, he enlisted the help of scholars to gain

China under Kublai Khan was one of four Mongol khanates that together extended west into present-day Iraq and through Russia to the borders of Poland and Hungary. For roughly a century, travelers moved freely across this vast expanse, making the era one of unprecedented cross-cultural exchange. Diplomats, missionaries, merchants, and adventurers flocked to the Yuan court, and Chinese envoys were dispatched to the West. The most celebrated European traveler of the time was a Venetian named Marco Polo (c. 1254–1324), whose descriptions of his travels were for several centuries the only firsthand account of China available in Europe.

Marco Polo was still in his teens when he set out for China in 1271. He traveled with his uncle and father, both merchants, bearing letters for Kublai Khan from Pope Gre-

gory X. After a four-year journey the Polos arrived at last in Beijing. Marco became a favorite of the emperor and spent the next seventeen years in his service, during which time he traveled extensively throughout China. He eventually returned home in 1295.

Imprisoned later during a war between Venice and Genoa, rival Italian city-states, Marco Polo passed the time by dictating an account of his experiences to a fellow prisoner. The resulting book, *A Description of the World*, has fascinated generations of readers with its depiction of prosperous and sophisticated lands in the East. Translated into almost every European language, it was an important influence in stimulating further exploration. When Columbus set sail across the Atlantic in 1492, one of the places he hoped to find was a country Marco Polo called Zipangu—Japan.

---

power and solidify his following. Once he had driven the Mongols from Beijing and firmly established himself as emperor, however, he grew to distrust intellectuals. His rule was despotic, even ruthless. Throughout the nearly 300 years of Ming rule, most emperors shared his attitude, so although the civil service examinations were reinstated, scholars remained alienated from the government they were trained to serve.

Court and Professional Painting

The contrast between the luxurious world of the court and the austere ideals of the literati continued through the Ming dynasty.

A typical example of Ming court taste is **HUNDREDS OF BIRDS ADMIRING THE PEACOCKS**, a large painting on silk by Yin Hong, an artist active during the late fifteenth and early sixteenth centuries (**FIG. 24–4**). A pupil of some well-known courtiers, Yin most probably served in the court at Beijing. The painting is an example of the birds-and-flowers **genre**, which had been popular with artists of the Song academy. Here the subject takes on symbolic meaning, with the homage of the birds to the peacocks representing the homage of court officials to the emperor. The style goes back to Song academy models, although the large format and multiplication of details are traits of the Ming.

A related, yet bolder and less constrained, landscape style was also popular during this period. Sometimes called the Zhe style since its roots were in Hangzhou, Zhejiang province, where the Southern Song court had been located, this manner especially influenced painters in Korea and Japan. A major

24–4 | Yin Hong **HUNDREDS OF BIRDS ADMIRING THE PEACOCKS**
Ming dynasty, late 15th–early 16th century. Hanging scroll, ink and color on silk, 7'10½" × 6'5" (2.4 × 1.96 m). The Cleveland Museum of Art.
Purchase from the J. H. Wade Fund, 74.31

Technique
FORMATS OF CHINESE PAINTING

With the exception of large wall paintings that typically decorated palaces, temples, and tombs, most Chinese paintings were done in ink and water-based colors on silk or paper. Finished works were generally mounted as **handscrolls, hanging scrolls**, or leaves in an **album**.

An album comprises a set of paintings of identical size mounted in a book. (A single painting from an album is called an **album leaf**.) The paintings in an album are usually related in subject, such as various views of a famous site or a series of scenes glimpsed on one trip.

Album-sized paintings might also be mounted as a handscroll, a horizontal format generally about 12 inches high and anywhere from a few feet to dozens of feet long. More typically, however, a handscroll would be a single continuous painting. Handscrolls were not meant to be displayed all at once, the way they are commonly presented today in museums. Rather, they were unrolled only occasionally, to be savored in much the same spirit as we might view a favorite film. Placing the scroll on a flat surface such as a table, a viewer would unroll it a foot or two at a time, moving gradually through the entire scroll from right to left, lingering over favorite details. The scroll was then rolled up and returned to its box until the next viewing.

Like handscrolls, hanging scrolls were not displayed permanently but were taken out for a limited time—a day, a week, a season. Unlike a handscroll, however, the painting on a hanging scroll was viewed as a whole, unrolled and put up on a wall,

with the roller at the lower end acting as a weight to help the scroll hang flat. Although some hanging scrolls are quite large, they are still fundamentally intimate works, not intended for display in a public place.

Creating a scroll was a time-consuming and exacting process accomplished by a professional mounter. The painting was first backed with paper to strengthen it. Next, strips of paper-backed silk were pasted to the top, bottom, and sides, framing the painting on all four sides. Additional silk pieces were added to extend the scroll horizontally or vertically, depending on the format. The assembled scroll was then backed again with paper and fitted with a half-round dowel, or wooden rod, at the top of a hanging scroll or on the right end of a handscroll, with ribbons for hanging and tying, and with a wooden roller at the other end. Hanging scrolls were often fashioned from several patterns of silk, and a variety of piecing formats were developed and codified. On a handscroll, a painting was generally preceded by a panel giving the work's title and often followed by a long panel bearing **colophons**—inscriptions related to the work, such as poems in its praise or comments by its owners over the centuries. A scroll would be remounted periodically to better preserve it, and colophons and inscriptions would be preserved in each remounting. **Seals** added another layer of interest. A treasured scroll often bears not only the seal of its maker but also those of collectors and admirers through the centuries.

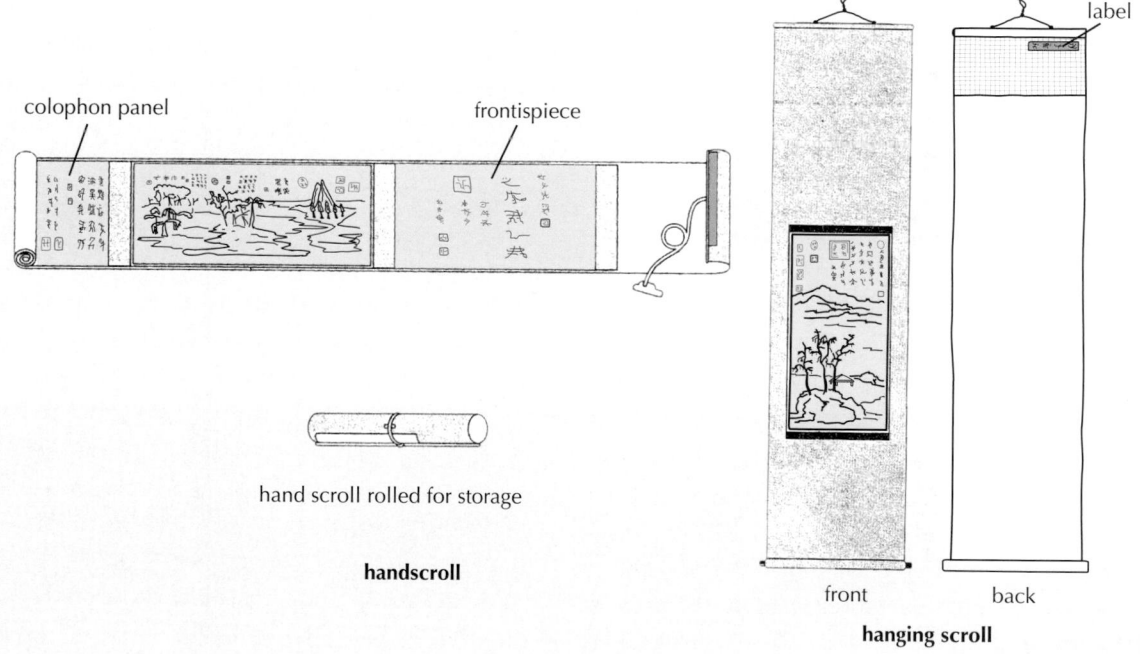

colophon panel

frontispiece

label

hand scroll rolled for storage

handscroll

front

back

hanging scroll

example is **RETURNING HOME LATE FROM A SPRING OUTING** (**FIG. 24–5**), unsigned but attributed to Dai Jin (1388–1462). This work reflects the Chinese sources for such artists as An Gyeon (SEE FIG. 24–17) and Sesshu (SEE FIG. 25–3).

QIU YING. The preeminent professional painter in the Ming period was Qiu Ying (1494–1552), who lived in Suzhou, a prosperous southern city. He inspired generations of imitators with exceptional works, such as a long handscroll

24–5 | Dai Jin **RETURNING HOME LATE FROM A SPRING OUTING**
Ming dynasty. Hanging scroll, ink on silk, 167.9 × 83.1 cm. National Palace Museum, Taipei, Republic of China.

known as **SPRING DAWN IN THE HAN PALACE** (FIGS. 24–6, 24–7). The painting is based on Tang-dynasty depictions of women in the court of the Han dynasty (206 BCE–220 CE). While in the service of a well-known collector, Qiu Ying had the opportunity to study many Tang paintings, whose artists usually concentrated on the figures, leaving out the background entirely. Qiu's graceful and elegant figures—although modeled after those in Tang works—are portrayed in a setting of palace buildings, engaging in such pastimes as chess, music, calligraphy, and painting. With its antique subject matter, refined technique, and flawless taste in color and composition, *Spring Dawn in the Han Palace* brought professional painting to a new high point.

Decorative Arts

Qiu Ying painted to satisfy his patrons in Suzhou. The cities of the south were becoming wealthy, and newly rich merchants collected paintings, antiques, and art objects. The court, too, was prosperous and patronized the arts on a lavish scale. In such a setting, the decorative arts thrived.

MING BLUE-AND-WHITE WARES. The Ming became famous the world over for its exquisite ceramics, especially **porcelain** (see "The Secret of Porcelain," page 840). The imperial **kilns** in Jingdezhen, in Jiangxi province, became the most renowned center for porcelain not only in all of China, but in all the world. Particularly noteworthy are the blue-and-white wares

24–6 | Qiu Ying **SECTION OF SPRING DAWN IN THE HAN PALACE**
Ming dynasty, first half of the 16th century. Handscroll, ink and color on silk, 1′ × 18′13⁄16″ (0.30 × 5.7 m). National Palace Museum, Taipei, Republic of China.

24–7 | **DETAIL OF SECTION OF SPRING DAWN IN THE HAN PALACE**

24-8 | **FLASK**
Ming dynasty, 1426-35. Porcelain with decoration painted in underglaze cobalt blue. Collection of the Palace Museum, Beijing.

Dragons have featured prominently in Chinese folklore from earliest times—Neolithic examples have been found painted on pottery and carved in jade. In Bronze Age China, dragons came to be associated with powerful and sudden manifestations of nature, such as wind, thunder, and lightning. At the same time, dragons became associated with superior beings such as virtuous rulers and sages. With the emergence of China's first firmly established empire during the Han dynasty, the dragon was appropriated as an imperial symbol, and it remained so throughout Chinese history. Dragon sightings were duly recorded and considered auspicious. Yet even the Son of Heaven could not monopolize the dragon. During the Tang and Song dynasties the practice arose of painting pictures of dragons to pray for rain, and for Chan (Zen) Buddhists, the dragon was a symbol of sudden enlightenment.

produced there during the ten-year reign of the ruler known as the Xuande Emperor (ruled 1426-35), such as the flask in FIGURE 24-8. The subtle shape, the refined yet vigorous decoration of dragons writhing above the sea, and the flawless **glazing** embody the high achievement of Ming artisans.

Architecture and City Planning

Centuries of warfare and destruction have left very few Chinese architectural monuments intact. The most important remaining example of traditional Chinese architecture is the Forbidden City, the imperial palace compound in Beijing, whose principal buildings were constructed during the Ming dynasty (FIG. 24-9).

THE FORBIDDEN CITY. The basic plan of Beijing was the work of the Mongols, who laid out their capital city accord-

ing to traditional Chinese principles. City planning began early in China—in the seventh century, in the case of Chang'an (present-day Xi'an), the capital of the Sui and Tang emperors. The walled city of Chang'an was laid out on a rectangular grid, with evenly spaced streets that ran north-south and east-west. At the northern end stood a walled imperial complex.

Beijing, too, was developed as a walled, rectangular city with streets laid out in a grid. The palace enclosure occupied the center of the northern part of the city, which was reserved for the Mongols. Chinese lived in the southern third of the city. Later, Ming and Qing emperors preserved this division, with officials living in the northern or Inner City and commoners living in the southern or Outer City. Under the third Ming emperor, Yongle (ruled 1403-24), the Forbidden City was rebuilt as we see it today.

The approach to the Forbidden City was impressive. Visitors entered through the Meridian Gate, a monumental gate with side wings (at the center in FIG. 24-9). Inside the Meridian Gate a broad courtyard is crossed by a bow-shaped waterway that is spanned by five arched marble bridges. At the opposite end of the courtyard is the Gate of Supreme Harmony, opening onto an even larger courtyard that houses three ceremonial halls raised on a broad platform. First is the Hall of Supreme Harmony, where, on the most important state occasions, the emperor was seated on his throne, facing south. Beyond is the smaller Hall of Central Harmony, then the Hall of Protecting Harmony. Behind these vast ceremonial spaces, still on the central axis, is the inner court, again with a progression of three buildings, this time more intimate in scale. In its balance and symmetry the plan of the Forbidden City reflects ancient Chinese beliefs about the harmony of the universe, and it emphasizes the emperor's role as the Son of Heaven, whose duty was to maintain the cosmic order from his throne in the middle of the world.

24-9 | **THE FORBIDDEN CITY**
Now the Palace Museum, Beijing
Mostly Ming dynasty. View from the southwest.

Technique
THE SECRET OF PORCELAIN

Marco Polo, it is said, was the one who named a new type of ceramic he found in China. Its translucent purity reminded him of the smooth whiteness of the cowry shell, *porcellana* in Italian. **Porcelain** is made from kaolin, an extremely refined white clay, and petuntse, a variety of the mineral feldspar. When properly combined and fired at a sufficiently high temperature, the two materials fuse into a glasslike, translucent ceramic that is far stronger than it looks.

Porcelaneous stoneware, fired at lower temperatures, was known in China by the seventh century, but true porcelain was perfected during the Song dynasty. To create blue-and-white porcelain such as the flask in FIGURE 24-8, blue pigment was made from cobalt oxide, finely ground and mixed with water. The decoration was painted directly onto the unfired porcelain vessel, then a layer of clear glaze was applied over it. (In this technique, known as *underglaze painting*, the pattern is painted beneath the glaze.) After firing, the piece emerged from the kiln with a clear blue design set sharply against a snowy white background.

Entranced with the exquisite properties of porcelain, European potters tried for centuries to duplicate it. The technique was finally discovered in 1709 by Johann Friedrich Böttger in Dresden, Germany, who tried—but failed—to keep it a secret.

The Literati Aesthetic

In the south, particularly in the district of Suzhou, literati painting, associated with the educated men who served the court as government officials, remained the dominant trend. One of the major literati figures from the Ming period is Shen Zhou (1427–1509), who had no desire to enter government service and spent most of his life in Suzhou. He studied the Yuan painters avidly and tried to recapture their spirit in such works as *Poet on a Mountaintop* (see "Poet on a Mountaintop," page 842). Although the style of the painting recalls the freedom and simplicity of Ni Zan (SEE FIG. 24–3), the motif of a poet surveying the landscape from a mountain plateau is Shen's creation.

LITERATI INFLUENCE ON FURNITURE, ARCHITECTURE, AND GARDEN DESIGN. The taste of the literati came to influence furniture and architecture, and especially the design of gardens. Chinese furniture made for domestic use reached the height of its development in the sixteenth and seventeenth centuries. Characteristic of Chinese furniture, the chair in FIGURE 24–10 is constructed without the use of glue or nails. Instead, pieces fit together based on the principle of the **mortise-and-tenon joint**, in which a projecting element (tenon) on one piece fits snugly into a cavity (mortise) on another. Each piece of the chair is carved, as opposed to being bent or twisted, and the joints are crafted with great precision. The patterns of the wood grain provide subtle interest unmarred by any painting or other embellishment. The style, like that of Chinese architecture, is one of simplicity, clarity, symmetry, and balance. The effect is formal and dignified but natural and simple—virtues central to the Chinese view of proper human conduct as well.

The art of landscape gardening also reached a high point during the Ming dynasty, as many literati surrounded their homes with gardens. The most famous gardens were created in the southern cities of the Yangzi River (Chang Jiang) delta, especially in Suzhou. The largest surviving garden of the era is the Garden of the Cessation of Official Life, with which this chapter opened (SEE FIG. 24–1). Although modified and reconstructed many times through the centuries, it still reflects many of the basic ideas of the original Ming owner. About a third of the garden is devoted to water through artificially created brooks and ponds. The landscape is dotted with pavilions, kiosks, libraries, studios, and corridors. Many

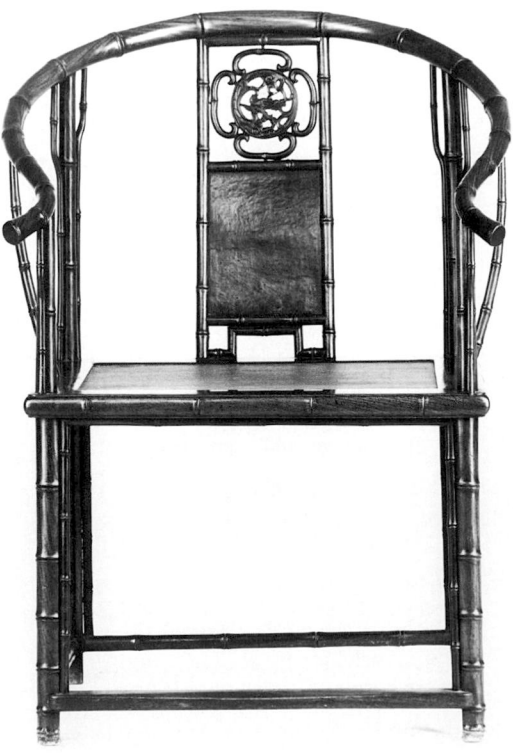

24–10 | ARMCHAIR
Ming dynasty, 16th–17th century. Huanghuali wood (hardwood), 39⅜ × 27¼ x 20″ (100 × 69.2 x 50.8 cm). The Nelson-Atkins Museum of Art, Kansas City, Missouri.
Purchase, Nelson Trust (46-78/1)

of the buildings have poetic names, such as Rain Listening Pavilion and Bridge of the Small Flying Rainbow.

DONG QICHANG, LITERATI THEORIST.   The ideas underlying literati painting found their most influential expression in the writings of Dong Qichang (1555–1636). A high official in the late Ming period, Dong Qichang embodied the literati tradition as poet, calligrapher, and painter. He developed a view of Chinese art history that divided painters into two opposing schools, northern and southern. The names have nothing to do with geography—a painter from the south might well be classed as northern—but reflect a parallel Dong drew to the northern and southern schools of Chan (Zen) Buddhism in China. The southern school of Chan, founded by the eccentric monk Huineng (638–713), was unorthodox, radical, and innovative; the northern school was traditional and conservative. Similarly, Dong's two schools of painters represented progressive and conservative traditions. In Dong's view the conservative northern school was dominated by professional painters whose academic, often decorative, style emphasized technical skill. In contrast, the progressive southern school preferred ink to color and free brushwork to meticulous detail. Its painters aimed for poetry and personal expression. In promoting this theory, Dong gave his unlimited sanction to literati painting, which he positioned as the culmination of the southern school, and he fundamentally influenced the way the Chinese viewed their own tradition.

Dong Qichang summarized his views on the proper training for literati painters in the famous statement "Read ten thousand books and walk ten thousand miles." By this he meant that one must first study the works of the great masters, then follow "heaven and earth," the world of nature. These studies prepared the way for greater self-expression through brush and ink, the goal of literati painting. Dong's views rested on an awareness that a painting of scenery and the actual scenery are two very different things. The excellence of a painting does not lie in its degree of resemblance to reality—that gap can never be bridged—but in its expressive power. The expressive language of painting is inherently abstract and lies in its nature as a construction of brushstrokes. For example, in a painting of a rock, the rock itself is not expressive; rather, the brushstrokes that add up to a "rock" are expressive.

With such thinking Dong brought painting close to the realm of calligraphy, which had long been considered the highest form of artistic expression in China. More than a thousand years before Dong's time, a body of critical terms and theories had evolved to discuss calligraphy in light of the formal and expressive properties of brushwork and composition. Dong introduced some of these terms—ideas such as opening and closing, rising and falling, and void and solid—to the criticism of painting.

Dong's theories are fully embodied in his painting **THE QINGBIAN MOUNTAINS** (**FIG. 24–11**). According to Dong's own inscription, the painting was based on a work by the tenth-century artist Dong Yuan. Dong Qichang's style, however, is quite different from the master's he admired. Although there is some indication of foreground, middle ground, and distant

24–11 | Dong Qichang
THE QINGBIAN MOUNTAINS
Ming dynasty, 1617. Hanging scroll, ink on paper, 21'8" × 7'4⅜" (6.72 × 2.25 m). The Cleveland Museum of Art.

Leonard C. Hanna, Jr., Fund (1980.10)

THE OBJECT SPEAKS

POET ON A MOUNTAINTOP

In earlier landscape paintings, human figures were typically shown dwarfed by the grandeur of nature. Travelers might be seen scuttling along a narrow path by a stream, while overhead towered mountains whose peaks conversed with the clouds and whose heights were inaccessible. Here, the poet has climbed the mountain and dominates the landscape. Even the clouds are beneath him. Before his gaze, a poem hangs in the air, as though he were projecting his thoughts.

The poem, composed by Shen Zhou himself, and written in his distinctive hand, reads:

White clouds like a scarf enfold the
mountain's waist;
Stone steps hang in space—a long,
narrow path.
Alone, leaning on my cane, I gaze
intently at the scene,
And feel like answering the murmuring
brook with the music of my flute.
(Translation by Jonathan Chaves, *The Chinese
Painter as Poet*, New York, 2000, page 46.)

Shen Zhou composed the poem and wrote the inscription at the time he painted the album. The style of the calligraphy, like the style of the painting, is informal, relaxed, and straightforward—

qualities that were believed to reflect the artist's character and personality.

The painting reflects Ming philosophy, which held that the mind, not the physical world, was the basis for reality. With its perfect synthesis of poetry, calligraphy, and painting, and with its harmony of mind and landscape, *Poet on a Mountaintop* represents the essence of Ming literati painting.

Shen Zhou   **POET ON A MOUNTAINTOP**
Leaf from an album of landscapes; painting mounted as part of a handscroll. Ming dynasty,
c. 1500. Ink and color on paper, 15¼ × 23¾" (40 × 60.2 cm).
The Nelson-Atkins Museum of Art, Kansas City, Missouri.

mountains, the space is ambiguous, as if all the elements were compressed to the surface of the picture. With this flattening of space, the trees, rocks, and mountains become more readily legible in a second way, as semiabstract forms made of brushstrokes.

Six trees arranged diagonally define the extreme foreground and announce themes that the rest of the painting repeats, varies, and develops. The tree on the left, with its outstretched branches and full foliage, is echoed first in the shape of another tree just across the river and again in a tree farther up and toward the left. The tallest tree of the foreground grouping anticipates the high peak that towers in the distance almost directly above it. The forms of the smaller foreground trees, especially the one with dark leaves, are repeated in numerous variations across the painting. At the same time, the simple and ordinary-looking boulder in the foreground is transformed in the conglomeration of rocks, ridges, hills, and mountains above. This double reading, both abstract and representational, parallels the work's double nature as a painting of a landscape and an interpretation of a traditional landscape painting.

The influence of Dong Qichang on the development of Chinese painting of later periods cannot be overstated. Indeed, nearly all Chinese painters since the early seventeenth century have reflected his ideas in one way or another.

QING DYNASTY

In 1644, when the armies of the Manchu people to the northeast of China marched into Beijing, many Chinese reacted as though their civilization had come to an end. Yet, the Manchus had already adopted many Chinese customs and institutions before their conquest. After gaining control of all of China, a process that took decades, they showed great respect for Chinese tradition. In art, all the major trends of the late Ming dynasty eventually continued into the Manchu, or Qing, dynasty (1644–1911).

Orthodox Painting

Literati painting was by now established as the dominant tradition; it had become orthodox. Scholars followed Dong Qichang's recommendation and based their approach on the study of past masters, and they painted large numbers of works in the manner of Song and Yuan artists as a way of expressing their learning, technique, and taste.

WANG HUI. The grand, symphonic composition A THOUSAND PEAKS AND MYRIAD RAVINES (FIG. 24–12), painted by Wang Hui (1632–1717) in 1693, exemplifies all the basic elements of Chinese landscape painting: mountains, rivers, waterfalls, trees, rocks, temples, pavilions, houses, bridges, boats, wandering scholars, fishers—the familiar and much-loved cast of actors from a tradition now many centuries old. At the upper right corner, the artist has written:

24–12 | Wang Hui A THOUSAND PEAKS AND MYRIAD RAVINES
Qing dynasty, 1693. Hanging scroll, ink on paper, 8′2½″ × 3′4½″ (2.54 × 1.03 m). National Palace Museum, Taipei, Republic of China.

Moss and weeds cover the rocks and mist hovers over the water.
The sound of dripping water is heard in front of the temple gate.
Through a thousand peaks and myriad ravines the spring flows,
And brings the flying flowers into the sacred caves.
In the fourth month of the year 1693, in an inn in the capital, I painted this based on a Tang-dynasty poem in the manner of [the painters] Dong [Yuan] and Ju[ran].

(Translated by Chu-tsing Li)

This inscription shares Wang Hui's complex thoughts as he painted this work. In his mind were both the lines of a Tang-dynasty poem, which offered the subject, and the paintings of the tenth-century masters Dong Yuan and Juran, which inspired his style. The temple the poem asks us to imagine is nestled on the right bank in the middle distance, but the painting shows us the scene from afar, as when a camera pulls slowly away from some small human drama until its actors can barely be distinguished from the great flow of nature. Giving viewers the experience of dissolving their individual identity in the cosmic flow had been a goal of Chinese landscape painting since its first era of greatness during the Song dynasty.

The Qing emperors of the late seventeenth and eighteenth centuries were painters themselves. They collected literati painting, and their taste was shaped mainly by artists such as Wang Hui. Thus literati painting, long associated with reclusive scholars, ultimately became an academic style practiced at court.

Individualist Painting

The first few decades of Qing rule had been both traumatic and dangerous for those who were loyal—or worse, related—to the Ming. Some committed suicide, while others sought refuge in monasteries or wandered the countryside. Among them were several painters who expressed their anger, defiance, frustration, and melancholy in their art. They took Dong Qichang's idea of painting as an expression of the artist's personal feelings very seriously and cultivated highly original styles. These painters have become known as the *individualists*.

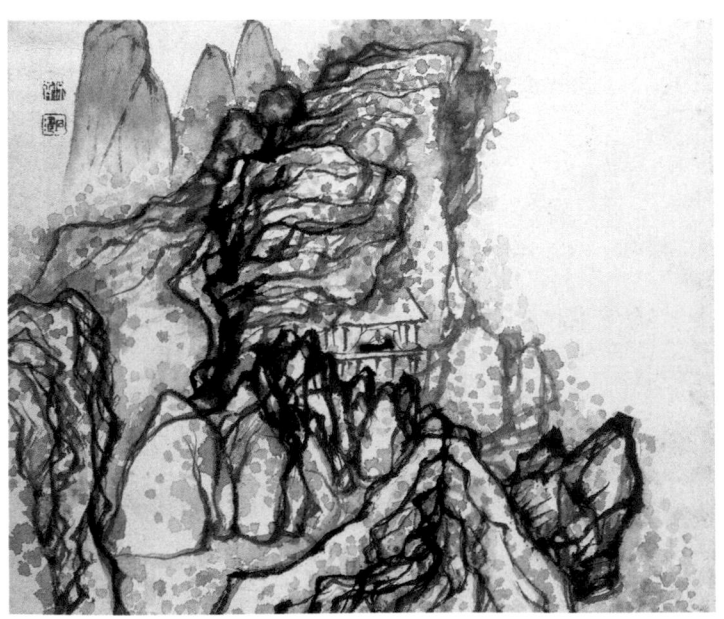

24–13 | Shitao **LANDSCAPE**
One leaf from *An Album of Landscapes*. Qing dynasty, c. 1700.
Ink and color on paper, 9½ × 11″ (24.1 × 28 cm).
Collection C. C. Wang family

SHITAO. One of the individualists was Shitao (1642–1707), who was descended from the first Ming emperor and who took refuge in Buddhist temples when the dynasty fell. In his later life he brought his painting to the brink of abstraction in such works as **LANDSCAPE** (FIG. 24–13). A monk sits in a small hut, looking out onto mountains that seem to be in turmoil. Dots, used for centuries to indicate vegetation on rocks, here seem to have taken on a life of their own. The rocks also seem alive—about to swallow up the monk and his hut. Throughout his life Shitao continued to identify himself with the fallen Ming, and he felt that his secure world had turned to chaos with the Manchu conquest.

THE MODERN PERIOD

In the mid- and late nineteenth century, China was shaken from centuries of complacency by a series of humiliating military defeats at the hands of Western powers and Japan. Only then did the government finally realize that these new rivals were not like the Mongols of the thirteenth century. China was no longer at the center of the world, a civilized country surrounded by "barbarians." Spiritual resistance was no longer sufficient to solve the problems brought on by change. New ideas from Japan and the West began to filter in, and the demand arose for political and cultural reforms. In 1911 the Qing dynasty was overthrown, ending 2,000 years of imperial rule, and China was reconceived as a republic.

During the first decades of the twentieth century Chinese artists traveled to Japan and Europe to study Western art. Returning to China, many sought to introduce the ideas and techniques they had learned, and they explored ways to synthesize the Chinese and the Western traditions. After the establishment of the present-day Communist government in 1949, individual artistic freedom was curtailed as the arts were pressed into the service of the state and its vision of a new social order. After 1979, however, cultural attitudes began to relax, and Chinese painters again pursued their own paths.

WU GUANZHONG. One artist who emerged during the 1980s as a leader in Chinese painting is Wu Guanzhong (b. 1919). Combining his French artistic training and Chinese background, Wu Guanzhong has developed a semiabstract style to depict scenes from the Chinese landscape. His usual method is to make preliminary sketches on site, then, back in his studio, he develops these sketches into free interpretations based on his feeling and vision. An example of his work, **PINE SPIRIT**, depicts a scene in the Huang (Yellow) Mountains (FIG. 24–14). The technique, with its sweeping gestures of paint, is clearly linked to Abstract Expressionism, an influential Western movement of the post–World War II years (Chapter 32); yet the painting also claims a place in the long tradition of Chinese landscape as exemplified by such masters as Shitao.

24–14 | Wu Guanzhong
PINE SPIRIT
1984. Ink and color on paper,
2′3⅝″ × 5′3½″
(0.70 × 1.61 m). Spencer
Museum of Art, The University
of Kansas, Lawrence.
Gift of the E. Rhodes and Leonard B.
Carpenter Foundation

Like all aspects of Chinese society, Chinese art has felt the strong impact of Western influence, and the question remains whether Chinese artists will absorb Western ideas without losing their traditional identity. Interestingly, landscape remains an important subject, as it has been for more than a thousand years, and calligraphy continues to play a vital role. Using the techniques and methods of the West, some of China's artists have joined an international avant-garde (see, for example, Wenda Gu in Chapter 32) while other painters still seek communion with nature through their ink brushstrokes as a means to come to terms with human life and the world.

ARTS OF KOREA: THE JOSEON DYNASTY TO THE MODERN ERA

In 1392, General Yi Seonggye (1335–1408) overthrew the the Goryeo dynasty (918–1392), establishing the Joseon dynasty (1392–1910), sometimes called the Yi dynasty. He first maintained his capital at Gaeseong, the old Goreyo capital, but moved it to Seoul in 1394, where it remained through the end of the dynasty. The Joseon regime rejected Buddhism, espousing Neo-Confucianism as the state philosophy. Taking Ming-dynasty China as its model, the new government patterned its bureaucracy on that of the Ming emperors, even adopting as its own such outward symbols of Ming imperial authority as blue-and-white porcelain. The early Joseon era was a period of cultural refinement and scientific achievement, during which Koreans invented Han'geul (the Korean alphabet) and moveable type, not to mention the rain gauge, astrolabe, celestial globe, sundial, and water clock.

Joseon Ceramics

Like their Silla and Goryeo forebears, Joseon potters excelled in the manufacture of ceramics, taking their cue from contemporaneous Chinese wares, but seldom copying them directly.

BUNCHEONG CERAMICS. Descended from Goryeo celadons, Joseon-dynasty stonewares, known as *buncheong* wares, enjoyed widespread usage throughout the peninsula. Their decorative effect relies on the use of white slip that makes the humble stoneware resemble more expensive white porcelain. In fifteenth-century examples, the slip is often seen inlaid into repeating design elements stamped into the body.

Sixteenth-century *buncheong* wares are characteristically embellished with wonderfully fluid, calligraphic brushwork painted in iron-brown slip on a white slip ground. Most painted *buncheong* wares have stylized floral décor, but rare pieces, such as the charming wine bottle in FIGURE 24–15, feature pictorial decoration. In fresh, lively brushstrokes, a bird with outstretched wings grasps a fish that it has just caught in its talons; waves roll below, while two giant lotus blossoms frame the scene.

Japanese armies repeatedly invaded the Korean peninsula between 1592 and 1597, destroying many of the *buncheong* kilns, and essentially bringing the ware's production to a halt. Tradition holds that the Japanese took many *buncheong* potters

24–15 | **HORIZONTAL WINE BOTTLE WITH DECORATION OF A BIRD CARRYING A NEWLY CAUGHT FISH**
Korean. Joseon dynasty, 16th century. *Buncheong* ware: light gray stoneware with decoration painted in iron-brown slip on a white slip ground. 6⅒ × 9½″ (15.5 × 24.1 cm). Museum of Oriental Ceramics, Osaka, Japan.
Gift of the Sumitomo Group [20773]

24–16 | **BROAD-SHOULDERED JAR**
With Decoration of a Fruiting Grapevine. Korean. Joseon dynasty, 17th century. Porcelain with decoration painted in underglaze iron-brown slip. Height 22⅛" (53.8 cm). Ehwa Women's University Museum, Seoul, Republic of Korea.

Chinese potters invented porcelain during the Tang dynasty, probably in the eighth century. Generally fired in the range of 1300° to 1400° centigrade, porcelain is a high-fired, white-bodied ceramic ware. Its unique feature is its translucency. Korean potters learned to make porcelain during the Goryeo dynasty, probably as early as the eleventh or twelfth century, though few Goryeo examples remain today. For many centuries, the Chinese and Koreans were the only peoples able to produce porcelains.

home with them to produce *buncheong*-style wares, which were greatly admired by connoisseurs of the tea ceremony. In fact, the spontaneity of Korean *buncheong* pottery has inspired Japanese ceramics to this day.

PAINTED PORCELAIN. Korean potters produced porcelains with designs painted in underglaze cobalt blue as early as the

fifteenth century, inspired by Chinese porcelains of the early Ming period (SEE FIG. 24–8). The Korean court dispatched artists from the royal painting academy to the porcelain kilns—located some thirty miles southeast of Seoul—to train porcelain decorators. As a result, from the fifteenth century onward, the painting on the best Korean porcelains closely approximated that on paper and silk, unlike in China, where ceramic decoration followed a path of its own with but scant reference to painting traditions.

In another unique development, Korean porcelains from the sixteenth and seventeenth centuries often feature designs painted in underglaze iron-brown rather than the cobalt blue customary in Ming porcelain. Also uniquely Korean are porcelain jars with bulging shoulders, slender bases and short, vertical necks, which appeared by the seventeenth century and came to be the most characteristic ceramic shapes in the later Joseon period. Painted in underglaze iron-brown, the seventeenth-century jar shown here depicts a fruiting grape branch around its shoulder (FIG. 24–16). In typical Korean fashion, the design spreads over a surface unconstrained by borders, resulting in a balanced but asymmetrical design that incorporates the Korean taste for unornamented spaces.

Joseon Painting

Korean secular painting came into its own during the Joseon dynasty. Continuing Goryeo traditions, early Joseon examples employ Chinese styles and formats, their range of subjects expanding from botanical motifs to include landscapes, figures, and a variety of animals.

Painted in 1447 by An Gyeon (b. 1418), **DREAM JOURNEY TO THE PEACH BLOSSOM LAND** (FIG. 24–17) is the earliest extant and dated Joseon secular painting. It illustrates a fanciful tale by China's revered nature poet Tao Qian (365–427) and recounts a dream about chancing upon a utopia secluded from the world for centuries while meandering among the peach blossoms of spring.

24–17 | An Gyeon **DREAM JOURNEY TO THE PEACH BLOSSOM LAND**
Korean. Joseon dynasty, 1447. Handscroll, ink and light colors on silk, 15¼ × 41⅞" (38.7 × 106.1 cm). Central Library, Tenri University, Tenri (near Nara), Japan.

24–18 | Jeong Seon **PANORAMIC VIEW OF THE DIAMOND MOUNTAINS (GEUMGANG-SAN)**
Korean. Joseon dynasty, 1734. Hanging scroll, ink and colors on paper, 40⅝ × 37″ (130.1 × 94.0 cm). Lee'um, Samsung Museum, Seoul, Republic of Korea.

The monumental mountains and vast, panoramic vistas of such fifteenth-century Korean paintings, as with their Goryeo forebears, echo Northern Song painting styles. Chinese paintings of the Southern Song (1127–1279) and Ming periods (1368–1644) also influenced Korean painting of the fifteenth, sixteenth, and seventeenth centuries, though these styles never completely supplanted the imprint of the Northern Song masters.

THE SILHAK MOVEMENT. In the eighteenth century, a truly Korean style emerged, inspired by the *silhak,* or "practical learning," movement, which emphasized the study of things Korean in addition to the Chinese classics. The impact of the *silhak* movement is exemplified by the painter Jeong Seon (1676–1759), who chose well-known Korean vistas as the subjects of his paintings, rather than the Chinese themes favored by earlier artists. Among Jeong Seon's paintings are numerous representations of the Diamond Mountains (Geumgang-san), a celebrated range of craggy peaks along Korea's east coast. Painted in 1734, the scroll reproduced here aptly captures the Diamond Mountains' needlelike peaks (**FIG. 24–18**). The subject is Korean, and so is the energetic spirit and the intensely personal style, with its crystalline mountains, distant clouds of delicate ink wash, and individualistic brushwork.

Among figure painters, Sin Yunbok (b. 1758) is an important exemplar of the *silhak* attitude. Active in the late eighteenth and early nineteenth centuries, Sin typically depicted aristocratic figures in native Korean garb. Entitled **PICNIC AT THE LOTUS POND,** the album leaf illustrated here (**FIG. 24–19**) represents a group of Korean gentlemen enjoying themselves in the countryside on an autumn day in the

24–19 | Sin Yunbok **PICNIC AT THE LOTUS POND**
From an *Album of Genre Scenes.* Korean. Joseon dynasty, late 18th century. Leaf from an album of thirty leaves; ink and colors on paper, 11⅛ × 13⅞″ (28.3 × 35.2 cm). Kansong Museum of Art, Seoul, Republic of Korea.

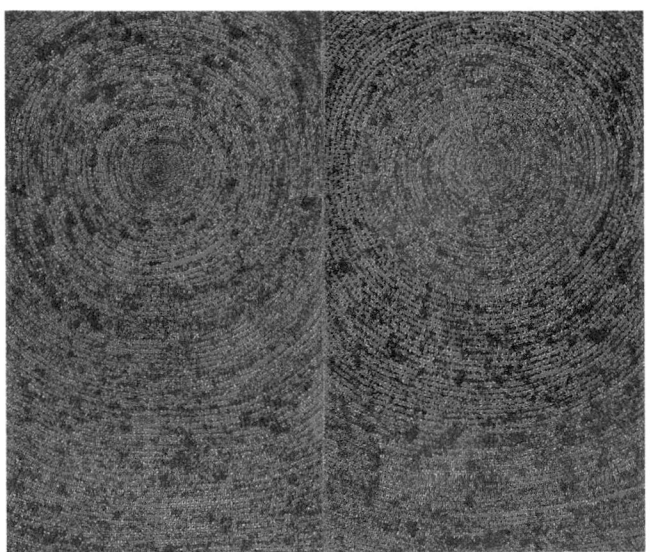

24–20 | Gim Hwangi **5-IV-71**,
Korean. 1971. Oil on canvas, 39½ × 39½"
(100 × 100 cm). Whanki Museum.

company of several *gisaeng,* or female entertainers. The figures are recognizably Korean—the women with their full coiffures, short jackets, and generous skirts, and the men with their beards, white robes, and wide-brimmed hats woven of horse hair and coated with black lacquer. The stringed instrument played by the gentleman seated in the lower right corner is a *gayageum,* or Korean zither, the most hallowed of all Korean musical instruments.

Modern Korea

Long known as "the Hermit Kingdom," the Joseon dynasty pursued a policy of isolationism, closing its borders to most of the world, except China, until 1876. Japan's annexation of Korea in 1910 brought the Joseon dynasty to a close, but effectively prolonged Korea's seclusion from the outside world. The legacy of self-imposed isolation compounded by colonial occupation (1910–45)—not to mention the harsh circumstances imposed by World War II (1939–45), followed by the even worse conditions of the Korean War (1950–53)—impeded Korea's artistic and cultural development during the first half of the twentieth century.

A MODERNIST PAINTER FROM KOREA. Despite these privations, some modern influences did reach Korea indirectly via China and Japan, and beginning in the 1920s and 1930s a few Korean artists experimented with contemporary Western styles, typically painting in the manner of Cézanne or Gauguin, but sometimes trying abstract, nonrepresentational styles. Among these, Gim Hwangi (1913–1974) was influenced by Constructivism and geometric abstraction and would become one of twentieth-century Korea's influential painters. Like many Korean artists after the Korean War, Gim wanted to examine Western modernism at its source. He visited Paris in

1956 and then, from 1964 to 1974, lived and worked in New York, where he produced his best-known works. His painting **5-IV-71** presents a large pair of circular radiating patterns composed of small dots and squares in tones of blue, black, and gray (FIG. 24–20). While appearing wholly Western in style, medium, concept, and even title—Gim Hwangi typically adopted the date of a work's creation as its title—*5-IV-71* also seems related to Asia's venerable tradition of monochrome ink painting, while suggesting a transcendence that seems Daoist or Buddhist in feeling. Given that the artist was Korean, that he learned the Chinese classics in his youth, that he studied art in Paris, and that he then worked in New York, it is possible that his painting embodies all of the above. Gim's painting illustrates the paradox that the modern artist faces while finding a distinctive, personal style: whether to paint in an updated version of a traditional style, in a wholly international style, in an international style with a distinctive local twist, or in an eclectic, hybrid style that incorporates both native and naturalized elements from diverse traditions. By addressing these questions, Gim Hwangi blazed a trail for subsequent Korean-born artists, such as the renowned video artist Nam June Paik (1932–2006), whose work can be seen in figure 32–86.

IN PERSPECTIVE

Invading from the steppes of Asia, the Mongols conquered China and established there the Yuan dynasty. While maintaining their foreign connections, Mongol leaders also adopted the values of Chinese dynastic rule, becoming patrons and collectors of art. Scholars educated for government service preserved and further developed the literati ideals that had coalesced during the earlier Song dynasty.

When the Yuan period of foreign rule came to an end, the new Ming ruling house revived the court traditions of the Song, including Southern Song court painting styles, and they commissioned decorated porcelains of exquisite quality. The Ming also became the model for the rulers of Korea's Joseon dynasty, under whose patronage these styles achieved a distinctive and austere beauty.

In the Qing era, China was again ruled by an outside group, this time the Manchus. While maintaining their traditional connections to Tibet and inner Asia through their patronage of Tibetan Buddhism, the Manchu rulers also embraced Chinese ideals, especially those of the literati. Practicing painting and calligraphy, composing poetry in Chinese, and collecting esteemed Chinese works of art, these rulers amassed the great palace collections that can now be seen in Beijing and Taipei.

By the twentieth century, China gradually embraced modern international trends. Chinese artists, and those in neighboring Korea, strove to choose among ideals of Western art, attracted first to its documentary qualities and then to its increasing abstraction, all the while maintaining ties to their own traditions.

NI ZAN
THE RONGXI STUDIO
1372

◀ **Yuan Dynasty** 1279–1368

◀ **Ming Dynasty** 1368–1644

◀ **Joseon Dynasty, Korea** 1392–1910

I300

I400

MING FLASK
1426–35

I500

I600

◀ **Qing Dynasty** 1644–1911

**GARDEN OF CESSATION OF
OFFICIAL LIFE**
EARLY 16TH CENTURY

I700

SIN YUNBOK
LATE 18TH CENTURY

I800

I900

◀ **Korea a Japanese Colony** 1910–1945
◀ **Republic of China: Mainland**
1912–1949
◀ **South Korea** 1945–Present
◀ **North Korea** 1945–Present
◀ **Republic of China: Taiwan**
1949–Present
◀ **People's Republic of China**
1949–Present
◀ **Korean War** 1950–1953

WU GUANZHONG
PINE SPIRIT
1984

2000

25–1 | Katsushika Hokusai **THE GREAT WAVE** From *Thirty-Six Views of Mt. Fuji*. Edo period, c. 1831.
Polychrome woodblock print on paper, 9 ⅞ × 14 ⅝″ (25 × 37.1 cm). Honolulu Academy of Arts, Honolulu, Hawaii.
James A. Michener Collection (HAA 13, 695)

CHAPTER TWENTY-FIVE

JAPANESE ART AFTER 1392

25 The great wave rears up like a dragon with claws of foam, ready to crash down on the figures huddled in the boat below. Exactly at the point of imminent disaster, but far in the distance, rises Japan's most sacred peak, Mount Fuji, whose slopes, we suddenly realize, swing up like waves and whose snowy crown is like foam—comparisons the artist makes clear in the wave nearest us, caught just at the moment of greatest resemblance. This woodblock print (FIG. 25-1), known as **THE GREAT WAVE**—from a series called *Thirty-Six Views of Mt. Fuji* by Katsushika Hokusai (1760–1849)—has inspired countless imitations and witty parodies, yet its forceful composition remains ever fresh.

Today, Japanese color woodblock prints of the eighteenth and nineteenth centuries are collected avidly around the world, but in their own day they were barely considered art. Commercially produced by the hundreds for ordinary people to buy, they were the fleeting secular souvenirs of their era—an era that was one of the most fascinating in Japanese history. When seen in Europe and America, these and other Japanese prints were immediately acclaimed, and they strongly influenced late nineteenth- and early twentieth-century Western art (Chapter 30). **Japonisme**, or *japonism*, became the vogue, and Hokusai and Hiroshige (1797–1858) became as famous in the West as in Japan. Indeed, their art was taken more seriously in the West; the first book on Hokusai was published in France, and according to one estimate, by the early twentieth century more than 90 percent of Japanese prints had been sold to Western collectors.

MUROMACHI PERIOD

By the year 1392, Japanese art had already developed a long and rich history (see "Foundations of Japanese Culture," page 854). Beginning with prehistoric pottery and tomb art, then expanding through cultural influences from China and Korea, Japanese visual expression reached high levels of sophistication in both religious and secular arts. Very early in the tradition, a particularly Japanese aesthetic emerged, including a love of natural materials, a taste for asymmetry, a sense of humor, and a tolerance for qualities that may seem paradoxical or contradictory—characteristics that continue to distinguish Japanese art, appearing and reappearing in ever-changing guises.

By the end of the twelfth century, the political and cultural dominance of the emperor and his court had given way to rule by warriors, or samurai, under the leadership of the shogun, the general-in-chief. In 1338 the Ashikaga family gained control of the shogunate and moved its headquarters to the Muromachi district in Kyoto. In 1392 they reunited northern and southern Japan and retained their grasp on the office for more than 150 years. The Muromachi period after the reunion (1392–1573) is also known as the Ashikaga era.

The Muromachi period is especially marked by the ascendance of Zen Buddhism, whose austere ideals particularly appealed to the highly disciplined samurai. While Pure Land Buddhism, which had spread widely during the latter part of the Heian period (794–1185), remained popular, Zen, patronized by the samurai, became the dominant cultural force in Japan.

Ink Painting

Several forms of visual art flourished during the Muromachi period, but **ink painting**—monochrome painting in black ink and its diluted grays—reigned supreme. Muromachi ink painting was heavily influenced by the aesthetics of Zen, yet

it also marked a shift away from the earlier Zen painting tradition. As Zen moved from an "outsider" sect to the chosen sect of the ruling group, the fierce intensity of earlier masters gave way to a more subtle and refined approach. And whereas earlier Zen artists had concentrated on rough-hewn depictions of Zen figures such as monks and teachers, now Chinese-style ink landscapes became the most important theme. Traditionally, the monk-artist Shubun (active c. 1418–63) is regarded as Japan's first great master of the ink landscape. Unfortunately, no works survive that can be proven to be his. Two landscapes by Shubun's pupil Bunsei (active c. 1450–60) have survived, however. In the one shown here (**FIG. 25–2**),

25–2 | Bunsei
LANDSCAPE
Muromachi period, mid-15th century. Hanging scroll, ink, and light colors on paper, 28 ¾ × 13″ (73.2 × 33 cm). Museum of Fine Arts, Boston.
Special Chinese and Japanese Fund (05.203)

MAP 25–1 | JAPAN

Ideas and artistic influences from the Asian continent flowed to Japan before and after the island nation's self-imposed isolation from the 17th to the 19th century.

the foreground reveals a spit of rocky land with an overlapping series of motifs—a spiky pine tree, a craggy rock, a poet seated in a hermitage, and a brushwood fence holding back a small garden of trees and bamboo. In the middle ground is space—emptiness, the void.

We are expected to "read" the empty paper as representing water, for subtle tones of gray ink suggest the presence of a few people fishing from their boats near the distant shore. The two parts of the painting seem to echo each other across a vast expanse. A depiction of nature echoing the human spirit, the painting illustrates well the pure, lonely, and ultimately serene spirit of the Zen-influenced poetic landscape tradition.

SESSHU.   Ink painting soon took on a different spirit. Zen monks painted—just as their Western counterparts illuminated manuscripts—but gave away their artworks. By the turn of the sixteenth century, temples were being asked for so many paintings that they formed ateliers staffed by monks

who specialized in art rather than religious ritual or teaching. Some painters even found they could survive on their own as professional artists. Nevertheless, many of the leading masters remained monks, at least in name, including the most famous of them all, Sesshu (1420–1506). Although he lived his entire life as a monk, Sesshu devoted himself primarily to painting. Like Bunsei, he learned from the tradition of Shubun, but he also had the opportunity to visit China in 1467. Sesshu traveled extensively there, viewing the scenery, stopping at Zen monasteries, and seeing whatever Chinese paintings he could. He does not seem to have had access to works by contemporary **literati** masters such as Shen Zhou (see Chapter 24), but saw instead the works of professional painters. Sesshu later claimed that he learned nothing from Chinese artists, but only from the mountains and rivers he had seen. When Sesshu returned from China, he found his homeland rent by the Onin Wars, which devastated the capital of Kyoto. Japan was to be torn apart by further civil warfare for the next hundred years. The refined art patronized by a secure society in

Art and Its Context
FOUNDATIONS OF JAPANESE CULTURE

With the end of the last Ice Age roughly 15,000 years ago, rising sea levels submerged the lowlands connecting Japan to the Asian landmass, creating the chain of islands we know today as Japan (SEE MAP 25–1). Not long afterward, early Paleolithic cultures gave way to a Neolithic culture known as Jomon (c. 11,000–400 BCE), after its characteristic cord-marked pottery. During the Jomon period, a sophisticated hunter-gatherer culture developed. Agriculture supplemented hunting and gathering by around 5000 BCE, and rice cultivation began some 4,000 years later.

A fully settled agricultural society emerged during the Yayoi period (c. 400 BCE–300 CE), accompanied by hierarchical social organization and more centralized forms of government. As people learned to manufacture bronze and iron, use of those metals became widespread. Yayoi architecture, with its unpainted wood and thatched roofs, already showed the Japanese affinity for natural materials and clean lines, and the style of Yayoi granaries in particular persisted in the design of shrines in later centuries. The trend toward centralization continued during the Kofun period (c. 300–552 CE), an era characterized by the construction of large royal tombs, following the Korean practice. Veneration of leaders grew into the beginnings of the imperial system that has lasted to the present day.

The Asuka era (552–645 CE) began with a century of profound change as elements of Chinese civilization flooded into Japan, initially through the intermediary of Korea. The three most significant Chinese contributions to the developing Japanese culture were Buddhism (with its attendant art and architecture), a system of writing, and the structures of a centralized bureaucracy. The earliest extant Buddhist temple compound in Japan—the oldest currently existing wooden building in the world—dates from this period.

The arrival of Buddhism also prompted some formalization of Shinto, the loose collection of indigenous Japanese beliefs and practices. Shinto is a shamanistic religion that emphasizes cere-

monial purification. Its rituals include the invocation and appeasement of spirits, including those of the recently dead. Many Shinto deities are thought to inhabit various aspects of nature, such as particularly magnificent trees, rocks, and waterfalls, and living creatures such as deer. Shinto and Buddhism have in common an intense awareness of the transience of life, and as their goals are complementary—purification in the case of Shinto, enlightenment in the case of Buddhism—they have generally existed comfortably alongside each other to the present day.

The Nara period (645–794 CE) takes its name from Japan's first permanently established imperial capital. During this time the founding works of Japanese literature were compiled, among them an important collection of poetry called the *Manyoshu*. Buddhism advanced to become the most important force in Japanese culture. Its influence at court grew so great as to become worrisome, and in 794 the emperor moved the capital from Nara to Heian-kyo (present-day Kyoto), far from powerful monasteries.

During the Heian period (794–1185) an extremely refined court culture thrived, embodied today in an exquisite legacy of poetry, calligraphy, and painting. An efficient method for writing the Japanese language was developed, and with it a woman at the court wrote the world's first novel, *The Tale of Genji*. Esoteric Buddhism, as hierarchical and intricate as the aristocratic world of the court, became popular.

The end of the Heian period was marked by civil warfare as regional warrior (samurai) clans were drawn into the factional conflicts at court. Pure Land Buddhism, with its simple message of salvation, offered consolation to many in troubled times. In 1185 the Minamoto clan defeated their arch rivals, the Taira, and their leader, Minamoto Yoritomo, assumed the position of shogun (general-in-chief). While paying respects to the emperor, Minamoto Yoritomo kept actual military and political power to himself, setting up his own capital in Kamakura. The Kamakura era (1185–1333) began a tradition of rule by shogun that lasted in various forms until 1868.

---

peacetime was no longer possible. Instead, the violent spirit of the times sounded its disturbing note, even in the world of landscape painting.

This new spirit is evident in Sesshu's **WINTER LANDSCAPE,** which makes full use of the forceful style that he developed (FIG. 25–3). A cliff descending from the mist seems to cut the composition in two. Sharp, jagged brushstrokes delineate a series of rocky hills, where a lone figure makes his way to a Zen monastery. Instead of a gradual recession into space, flat overlapping planes fracture the composition into crystalline facets. The white of the paper is left to indicate snow, while the sky is suggested by tones of gray. A few trees cling desperately to the rocky land, and the harsh chill of winter is boldly expressed.

IKKYU. A third important artist of the Muromachi period was a monk named Ikkyu (1394–1481). A genuine eccentric and one of the most famous Zen masters in Japanese history, Ikkyu derided the Zen of his day, writing, "The temples are rich but Zen is declining, there are only false teachers, no true teachers." Ikkyu recognized that success was distorting the spirit of Zen. Originally, Zen had been a form of counterculture for those who were not satisfied with prevailing ways. Now, however, Zen monks acted as government advisers, teachers, and even leaders of merchant missions to China. Although true Zen masters were able to withstand all outside pressures, many monks became involved with political matters, with factional disputes among the temples, or with their reputations as poets or artists. Ikkyu did not hesitate to mock what he regarded as "false Zen." He even paraded through the streets with a wooden sword, claiming that his sword would be as much use to a samurai as false Zen to a monk.

Ikkyu's **calligraphy**, which is especially admired, has a spirit of spontaneity. To write out the classic Buddhist couplet "Abjure evil, practice only the good," he created a pair of single-line scrolls (FIG. 25–4). At the top of each scroll—first the right scroll and then the left—Ikkyu began with standard script, in which each stroke of a character is separate and distinct. As his brush moved down a scroll, he grew more excited and wrote in increasingly cursive script, until finally his frenzied brush did not leave the paper at all. This calligraphy displays the intensity that is the hallmark of Zen.

The Zen Dry Garden

Elegant simplicity—profound and personal—was the result of disciplined meditation coupled with manual labor, as practiced in the Zen Buddhism introduced into Japan in the late twelfth century. Zen monasteries aimed at self-sufficiency. Monks were expected to be responsible for their physical as well as spiritual needs. Consequently, the performance of

Sequencing Events
PERIODS IN JAPANESE ART AFTER 1392

1336–1573	Muromachi Period
1568–1615	Momoyama Period
1615–1868	Edo Period
1868–Present	Meiji and Modern Periods

simple tasks—weeding the garden, cooking meals, mending garments—became occasions for meditation in the search for enlightenment. Zen monks turned to their gardens not as the focus of detached viewing and meditation but as the objects of constant vigilance and work—pulling weeds, tweaking unruly shoots, and raking the gravel of the dry gardens. This philosophy profoundly influenced Japanese art.

The dry landscape gardens of Japan, *karesansui* (literally "dried-up mountains and water"), exist in perfect harmony with Zen Buddhism. The dry garden in front of the abbot's quarters in the Zen temple of Ryoan-ji is one of the most

25–3 | Sesshu **WINTER LANDSCAPE**
Muromachi period, c. 1470s. Ink on paper, 18 ¼ × 11 ½″ (46.3 × 29.3 cm). Collection of the Tokyo National Museum.

25–4 | Ikkyu **CALLIGRAPHY COUPLET**
Daitoku-ji, Kyoto. Muromachi period, c. mid-15th century. Ink on paper, each 10′2 ⅞″ × 1′4 ½″ (3.12 × 0.42 m).

renowned Zen creations in Japan (FIG. 25–5). A flat rectangle of raked gravel, about 29 by 70 feet, surrounds fifteen stones of different sizes in islands of moss. The stones are set in asymmetrical groups of two, three, and five. Low, plaster-covered walls establish the garden's boundaries, but beyond the perimeter wall, maple, pine, and cherry trees add color and texture to the scene. Called "borrowed scenery," these elements are a considered part of the design even though they grow outside the garden. The garden is celebrated for its severity and emptiness.

Dry gardens began to be built in the fifteenth and sixteenth centuries in Japan. By the sixteenth century, Chinese landscape painting influenced the gardens' composition, and miniature clipped plants and beautiful stones were arranged to resemble famous paintings. Especially fine and unusual stones were coveted and even carried off as war booty, such was the cultural value of these seemingly mundane objects.

The Ryoan-ji garden's design, as we see it today, probably dates from the mid-seventeenth century, since earlier written sources refer only to cherry trees, not to a garden. By the time this garden was created, such stone and gravel gardens had become highly intellectualized, abstract reflections of nature. This garden has been interpreted as representing islands in the sea, or mountain peaks rising above the clouds, perhaps even a swimming tigress with her cubs, or constellations of stars and planets. All or none of these interpretations may be equally satisfying—or irrelevant—to a monk seeking clarity of mind through contemplation. The austere beauty of the naked gravel has led many people to meditation.

MOMOYAMA PERIOD

The civil wars sweeping Japan laid bare the basic flaw in the Ashikaga system, which was that samurai were primarily loyal to their own feudal lord, or *daimyo*, rather than to the central government. Battles between feudal clans grew more frequent, and it became clear that only a *daimyo* powerful and bold enough to unite the entire country could control Japan. As the Muromachi period drew to a close, three leaders emerged who would change the course of Japanese history.

The first of these leaders was Oda Nobunaga (1534–82), who marched his army into Kyoto in 1568, signaling the end of the Ashikaga family as a major force in Japanese politics. A ruthless warrior, Nobunaga went so far as to destroy a Buddhist monastery because the monks refused to join his forces. Yet he was also a patron of the most rarefied and refined arts. Assassinated in the midst of one of his military campaigns, Nobunaga was succeeded by the military commander Toyotomi Hideyoshi (1537–98), who soon gained complete power in Japan. He, too, patronized the arts when not leading his army, and he considered culture a vital adjunct to his rule. Hideyoshi, however, was overly ambitious. He believed that he could conquer both Korea and China, and he wasted much of his resources on two ill-fated invasions. A stable government finally emerged in 1600 with the triumph of a third leader, Tokugawa Ieyasu (1543–1616), who established his shogunate in 1603. But despite its turbulence, the era of Nobunaga and Hideyoshi, known as the Momoyama period (1568–1615), was one of the most creative eras in Japanese history.

25–5 | **ROCK GARDEN, RYOAN-JI, KYOTO**
Photographed spring 1993. Muromachi period, c. 1480.
Photograph by Michael S. Yamashita

The American composer John Cage once exclaimed that every stone at Ryoan-ji was in just the right place. He then said, "And every other place would also be just right." His remark is thoroughly Zen in spirit. There are many ways to experience Ryoan-ji. For example, we can imagine the rocks as having different visual "pulls" that relate them to one another. Yet there is also enough space between them to give each one a sense of self-sufficiency and permanence.

25–6 | **HIMEJI CASTLE**
Hyogo, near Osaka. Momoyama period, 1601–09.

Architecture

Today the very word *Momoyama* conjures up images of bold warriors, luxurious palaces, screens shimmering with **gold leaf**, and magnificent ceramics. The Momoyama period was also the era when Europeans first made an impact in Japan. A few Portuguese explorers had arrived at the end of the Muromachi era in 1543, and traders and missionaries were quick to follow. It was only with the rise of Nobunaga, however, that Westerners were able to extend their activities beyond the ports of Kyushu, Japan's southernmost island. Nobunaga welcomed foreign traders, who brought him various products, the most important of which were firearms.

European muskets and cannons soon changed the nature of Japanese warfare and influenced Japanese architecture. In response to the new weapons, monumental fortified castles were built in the late sixteenth century. Some were eventually lost to warfare or torn down by victorious enemies, and others have been extensively altered over the years. One of the most beautiful of the surviving castles is Himeji, not far from the city of Osaka (FIG. 25–6). Rising high on a hill above the plains, Himeji has been given the name White Heron. To reach the upper fortress, visitors must follow angular paths beneath steep walls, climbing from one area to the next past stone ramparts and through narrow fortified gates, all the while feeling as though lost in a maze, with no sense of direction or progress. At the main building, a further climb up a series of narrow ladders leads to the uppermost chamber.

There, the footsore visitor is rewarded with a stunning 360-degree view of the surrounding countryside. The sense of power is overwhelming.

Kano School Decorative Painting

Castles such as Himeji were sumptuously decorated, offering artists unprecedented opportunities to work on a grand scale. Large murals on **fusuma**—paper-covered sliding doors—were particular features of Momoyama design, as were folding screens with gold-leaf backgrounds, whose glistening surfaces not only conveyed light within the castle rooms but also displayed the wealth of the warrior leaders. Temples, too, commissioned large-scale paintings for their rebuilding projects after the devastation of the civil wars.

The Momoyama period produced a number of artists who were equally adept at decorative golden screens and broadly brushed *fusuma* paintings. Daitoku-ji, a celebrated Zen monastery in Kyoto, has a number of subtemples that are treasure troves of Japanese art. One, the Juko-in, possesses *fusuma* by Kano Eitoku (1543–90), one of the most brilliant painters from the professional school of artists founded by the Kano family and patronized by government leaders for several centuries. Founded in the Muromachi period, the Kano school combined training in the ink-painting tradition with new skills in decorative subjects and styles. The illustration here shows two of the three walls of *fusuma* panels painted when the artist was in his mid-twenties (FIG. 25–7). To the

25–7 | Kano Eitoku **FUSUMA**
Depicting pine and cranes (left) and plum tree (right) from the central room of the Juko-in, Daitoku-ji, Kyoto. Momoyama period, c. 1563–73. Ink and gold on paper, height 5′9 ⅛″ (1.76 m).

left, the subject is the familiar Kano school theme of cranes and pines, both symbols of long life; to the right is a great gnarled plum tree, symbol of spring. The trees are so massive they seem to extend far beyond the panels. An island rounding both walls of the far corner provides a focus for the out-reaching trees. Ingeniously, it belongs to both compositions at the same time, thus uniting them into an organic whole. Eitoku's vigorous use of brush and ink, his powerfully jagged outlines, and his dramatic compositions all hark back to the style of Sesshu, but the bold new sense of scale in his works is a leading characteristic of the Momoyama period.

The Tea Ceremony

Japanese art is never one-sided. Along with castles, golden screens, and massive *fusuma* paintings there was an equal interest during the Momoyama period in the quiet, the restrained, and the natural. This was expressed primarily through the tea ceremony.

The term "tea ceremony," a phrase now in common use, does not convey the full meaning of *cha no yu*, the Japanese ritual drinking of tea, which has no counterpart in Western culture. Tea itself had been introduced to Japan from the Asian continent hundreds of years earlier. At first, tea was molded into cakes and boiled. However, the advent of Zen in the late Kamakura period (1185–1392) brought to Japan a different way of preparing tea, with the leaves crushed into powder and then whisked in bowls with hot water. Zen monks used such tea as a mild stimulant to aid meditation, and it also was considered a form of medicine.

SEN NO RIKYU. The most famous tea master in Japanese history was Sen no Rikyu (1522–91). He conceived of the tea ceremony as an intimate gathering in which a few people would enter a small rustic room, drink tea carefully prepared in front of them by their host, and quietly discuss the tea utensils or a Zen scroll hanging on the wall. He did a great

deal to establish the aesthetic of modesty, refinement, and rusticity that permitted the tearoom to serve as a respite from the busy and sometimes violent world outside. A traditional tearoom is quite small and simple. It is made of natural materials such as bamboo and wood, with mud walls, paper windows, and a floor covered with tatami—mats of woven straw. One tearoom that preserves Rikyu's design is named Tai-an (FIG. 25–8). Built in 1582, it is distinguished by its tiny door (guests must crawl to enter) and its alcove, or **tokonoma,** where a Zen scroll or a simple flower arrangement may be

25–8 | Sen no Rikyu **TAI-AN TEAROOM**
Myoki-an Temple, Kyoto. Momoyama period, 1582.

displayed. At first glance, the room seems symmetrical. But the disposition of the *tatami* does not match the spacing of the *tokonoma*, providing a subtle undercurrent of irregularity. A longer look reveals a blend of simple elegance and rusticity. The walls seem scratched and worn with age, but the tatami are replaced frequently to keep them clean and fresh. The mood is quiet; the light is muted and diffused through three small paper windows. Above all, there is a sense of spatial clarity. All nonessentials have been eliminated, so there is nothing to distract from focused attention. The tearoom aesthetic became an important element in Japanese culture, influencing secular architecture through its simple and evocative style (see "Shoin Design," page 860).

EDO PERIOD

Three years after Tokugawa Ieyasu gained control of Japan, he proclaimed himself shogun. His family's control of the shogunate was to last more than 250 years, a span of time known as the Edo period (1615–1868) or the Tokugawa era.

Under the rule of the Tokugawa family, peace and prosperity came to Japan at the price of an increasingly rigid and often repressive form of government. The problem of potentially rebellious *daimyo* was solved by ordering all feudal lords to spend either half of each year or every other year in the new capital of Edo (present-day Tokyo), where their wives and children were sometimes required to live permanently. Zen Buddhism was supplanted as the prevailing intellectual force by a form of neo-Confucianism, a philosophy formulated in Song-dynasty China that emphasized loyalty to the state. More drastically, Japan was soon closed off from the rest of the world by its suspicious government. Japanese were forbidden to travel abroad, and with the exception of small Chinese and Dutch trading communities on an island off the southern port of Nagasaki, foreigners were not permitted in Japan.

Edo society was officially divided into four classes. Samurai officials constituted the highest class, followed by farmers, artisans, and finally merchants. As time went on, however, merchants began to control the money supply, and in Japan's increasingly mercantile economy they soon reached a high, if unofficial, position. Reading and writing became widespread at all levels of society. Many segments of the population—samurai, merchants, intellectuals, and even townspeople—were now able to patronize artists, and a pluralistic cultural atmosphere developed unlike anything Japan had experienced before.

The Tea Ceremony

The rebuilding of temples continued during the first decades of the Edo period, and for this purpose government officials, monks, and wealthy merchants needed to cooperate. The tea ceremony was one way that people of different classes could come together for intimate conversations. Every utensil connected with tea, including the waterpot, the kettle, the bam-

boo spoon, the whisk, the tea caddy, and, above all, the teabowl, came to be appreciated for their aesthetic qualities, and many works of art were created for use in *cha no yu*.

The age-old Japanese admiration for the natural and the asymmetrical found full expression in tea ceramics. Korean-style rice bowls made for peasants were suddenly considered the epitome of refined taste, and tea masters urged potters to mimic their imperfect shapes. But not every misshapen bowl would be admired. An extremely rarified appreciation of beauty developed that took into consideration such factors as how well a teabowl fit into the hands, how subtly the shape and texture of the bowl appealed to the eye, and who had previously used and admired it. For this purpose, the inscribed box became almost as important as the ceramic that fit within it, and if a bowl had been given a name by a leading tea master, it was especially treasured by later generations.

One of the finest teabowls extant is named **MOUNT FUJI** after Japan's most sacred peak **(FIG. 25–9)**. (Mount Fuji is

25–9 | Hon'ami Koetsu **TEABOWL, CALLED MOUNT FUJI**
Edo period, early 17th century. Raku ware, height 3 ⅜"
(8.5 cm). Sakai Collection, Tokyo.

Connoisseurs developed a subtle vocabulary to discuss the aesthetics of tea. A favorite term was *sabi* (literally, "loneliness"), which refers to the tranquility found when feeling alone. Other virtues were *wabi* (literally, "poverty"), which suggests the artlessness of humble simplicity, and *shibui*, (literally, "bitter" or "astringent"), meaning elegant restraint, and said to be exemplified by the color of the inside of an old teapot.

Elements of Architecture
SHOIN DESIGN

Of the many expressions of Japanese taste that reached great refinement in the Momoyama period, **shoin** architecture has had perhaps the most enduring influence. *Shoin* are upper-class residences that combine a number of traditional features in more-or-less standard ways, always asymmetrically. These features include wide verandas, wood posts as framing and defining decorative elements, woven straw **tatami** mats as floor and ceiling covering, several shallow alcoves for prescribed purposes, *fusuma* (sliding doors) as fields for painting or textured surfaces, and **shoji** screens—wood frames covered with translucent rice paper. The *shoin* illustrated here was built in 1601 as a guest hall, called Kojo-in, at the great Onjo-ji monastery. *Tatami, shoji*, alcoves, asymmetry, and other features of *shoin* are still seen in Japanese interiors today.

In the original *shoin*, one of the alcoves would contain a hanging scroll, an arrangement of flowers, or a large painted screen. Seated in front of that alcove, called a **tokonoma**, the owner of the house would receive guests, who could contemplate the object above the head of their host. Another alcove contained staggered shelves, often for writing instruments. A writing space fitted with a low writing desk was on the veranda side of the room, with *shoji* that could open to the outside.

The architectural harmony of *shoin* was based on the proportionate disposition of basic units, or **modules**. In Japanese carpentry, the common module of design and construction is the **bay**, reckoned as the distance from the center of one post to the center of another, which is governed in turn by the standard size of *tatami* floor mats. Although varying slightly from region to region, the size of a single *tatami* is about 3 by 6 feet. Room area in Japan is still expressed in terms of the number of *tatami* mats, so that, for example, a room may be described as an eight-mat room.

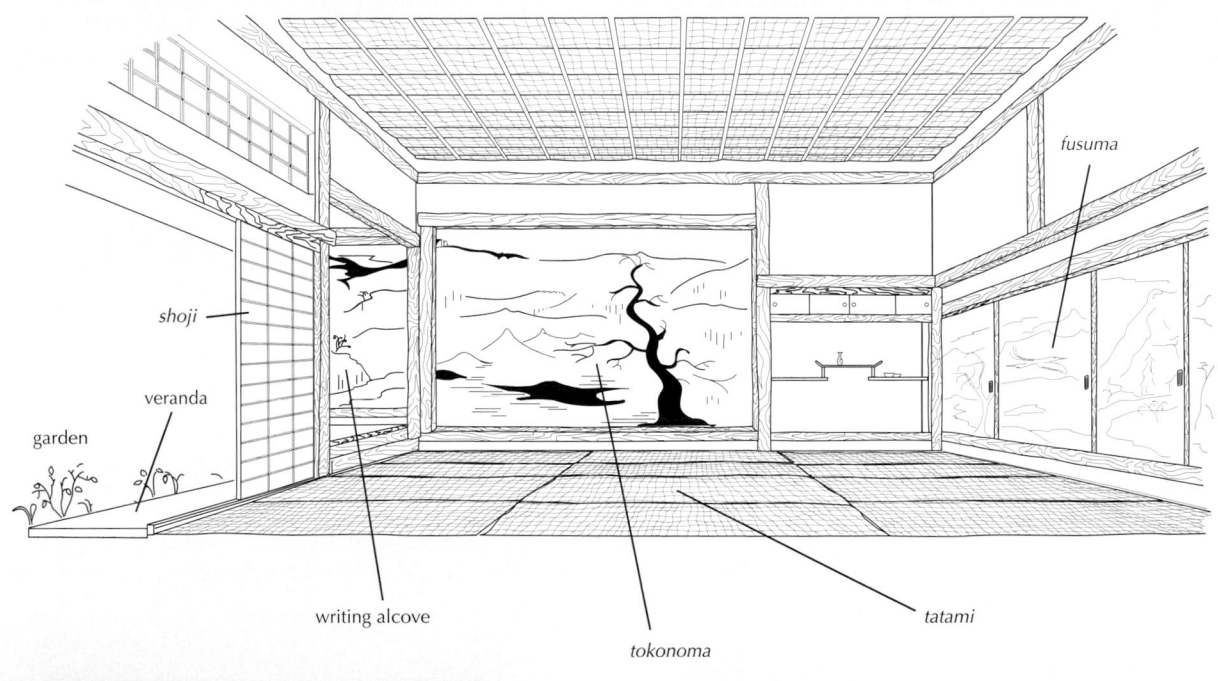

GUEST HALL, KOJO-IN, ONJO-JI MONASTERY
Shiga prefecture. Momoyama period. 1601.

depicted in FIGURE 25–1.) An example of **raku** ware—a hand-built, low-fired ceramic developed especially for use in the tea ceremony—the bowl was crafted by Hon'ami Koetsu (1558–1637), a leading cultural figure of the early Edo period. Koetsu was most famous as a calligrapher, but he was also a painter, lacquer designer, poet, landscape gardener, connoisseur of swords, and potter. With its small foot, straight sides, slightly irregular shape, and crackled texture, this bowl

exemplifies tea taste. In its rough exterior we sense directly the two elements of earth and fire that create pottery. Merely looking at it suggests the feeling one would get from holding it, warm with tea, cupped in one's hands.

Rimpa School Painting

One of Koetsu's friends was the painter Tawaraya Sotatsu (active c. 1600–40), with whom he collaborated on several magnificent handscrolls. Sotatsu is considered the first great painter of the Rimpa school, a grouping of artists with similar tastes rather than a formal school, such as the Kano school. Rimpa masters excelled in decorative designs of strong expressive force, and they frequently worked in several mediums.

Sotatsu painted some of the finest golden screens that have survived. The splendid pair here depict the celebrated islands of Matsushima near the northern city of Sendai

(FIG. 25–10). Working in a boldly decorative style, the artist has created asymmetrical and almost abstract patterns of waves, pines, and island forms. On the right screen (shown here on top), mountainous islands echo the swing and sweep of the waves, with stylized gold clouds in the upper left. The left screen continues the gold clouds until they become a sand spit from which twisted pines grow. Their branches seem to lean toward a strange island in the lower left, composed of an

25–10 | Tawaraya Sotatsu **PAIR OF SIX-PANEL SCREENS, KNOWN AS THE MATSUSHIMA SCREENS**
Edo period, 17th century. Ink, mineral colors, and gold leaf on paper; each screen 4′9 ⅞″ × 11′8 ½″ (1.52 × 3.56 m). Freer Gallery of Art, Smithsonian Institution, Washington, D.C.

Gift of Charles Lang Freer (F1906.231 & 232)

The six-panel screen format was a triumph of scale and practicality. Each panel consisted of a light wood frame surrounding a latticework interior covered with several layers of paper. Over this foundation was pasted a high-quality paper, silk, or gold-leaf ground, ready to be painted by the finest artists. Held together with ingenious paper hinges, a screen could be folded for storage or transportation, resulting in a mural-size painting light enough to be carried by a single person, ready to be displayed as needed.

THE OBJECT SPEAKS

LACQUER BOX FOR WRITING IMPLEMENTS

Ogata Korin (1658–1716), another great master of the Rimpa school, originated many remarkable works, including colorful golden screens, monochrome scrolls, and paintings in glaze on his brother Kenzan's pottery. He also designed some highly prized works in **lacquer**. His writing box is a lidded container designed to hold tools and materials for calligraphy. Korin's design for this black lacquer box sets a motif of irises and a plank bridge in a dramatic combination of mother-of-pearl, silver, lead, and gold lacquer. For Japanese viewers the decoration immediately recalls a famous passage from the tenth-century *Tales of Ise*, a classic of Japanese literature. A nobleman poet, having left his wife in the capital, pauses at a place called Eight Bridges, where a river branches into eight streams, each covered with a plank bridge. Irises are in full bloom, and his traveling companions urge the poet to write a *tanka*—a five-line, thirty-one-syllable poem—beginning each line with a syllable from the word for "iris": *Kakitsubata* (*ka-ki-tsu-ba-ta*). The poet responds (substituting *ha* for *ba*):

> **Ka**ragoromo
> **ki**tsutsu narenishi
> **tsu**ma shi areba
> **ha**rubaru kinuru
> **ta**bi o shi zo omou.

When I remember
my wife, fond and familiar
as my courtly robe,
I feel how far and distant
my travels have taken me.

(Translated by Stephen Addiss)

The poem brought tears to all their eyes, and the scene became so famous that any painting of a group of irises, with or without a plank bridge, immediately calls it to mind.

Lacquer is derived in Asia from the sap of the lacquer tree, *Rhus Verniciflua*. The tree is indigenous to China, where examples of lacquerware have been found dating back to the Neolithic period. Knowledge of lacquer spread early to Korea and Japan, and the tree came to be grown commercially throughout East Asia.

Gathered by tapping into a tree and letting the sap flow into a container, lacquer is then strained to remove impurities and heated to evaporate excess moisture. The thickened sap can be colored with vegetable or mineral dyes and lasts for several years if carefully stored. Applied in thin coats to a surface such as wood or leather, lacquer hardens into a smooth, glasslike, protective coating that is waterproof, heat- and acid-resistant, and airtight. Lacquer's practical qualities made it ideal for storage containers and vessels for food and drink. In Japan the leather scales

of samurai armor were coated in lacquer, as were leather saddles. The decorative potential of lacquer was developed in the manufacture of expensive luxury items.

The creation of a piece of lacquer is a painstaking process that can take a sequence of specialized artisans several years. First, the item is fashioned of wood and sanded smooth. Next, layers of lacquer are built up. In order to dry properly, lacquer must be applied in extremely thin coats. (If the lacquer is applied too thickly, the exterior surface dries first, forming an airtight seal that prevents the lacquer below from drying.) Optimal temperature and humidity are also essential to drying, and artisans quickly learned to control them artificially. Up to thirty coats of lacquer, each dried and polished before the next is brushed on, are required.

In China, lacquer was often applied to a thickness of up to 300 coats, then elaborately carved. In Japan and Korea, inlay with mother-of-pearl and precious metals was brought to a high point of refinement. Japanese artisans also perfected a variety of methods known collectively as *maki-e* ("sprinkled design"), in which flaked or powdered gold or silver was embedded in a still-damp coat of lacquer.

Ogata Korin   LACQUER BOX FOR WRITING IMPLEMENTS
Edo period, late 17th–early 18th century. Lacquer, lead, silver, and mother-of-pearl, 5 ⅝ × 10 ¾ × 7 ¾″
(14.2 × 27.4 × 19.7 cm). Tokyo National Museum, Tokyo.

organic, amoebalike form in gold surrounded by mottled ink. This mottled effect was a specialty of Rimpa school painters.

As one of the "three famous beautiful views of Japan," Matsushima was often depicted in art. Most painters, however, emphasized the large number of pine-covered islands that make the area famous. Sotatsu's genius was to simplify and dramatize the scene, as though the viewer were passing the islands in a boat on the roiling waters. Strong, basic mineral colors dominate, and the sparkling two-dimensional richness of the gold leaf contrasts dramatically with the three-dimensional movement of the waves.

Nanga School Painting

Rimpa artists such as Sotatsu and Korin are considered quintessentially Japanese in spirit, both in the expressive power of their art and in their use of poetic themes from Japan's past. Other painters, however, responded to the new Confucian atmosphere by taking up some of the ideas of the literati painters of China. These painters are grouped together as the Nanga ("Southern") school. Nanga was not a school in the sense of a professional workshop or a family tradition. Rather, it took its name from the southern school of amateur artists described by the Chinese literati theorist Dong

Qichang (Chapter 24). Educated in the Confucian mold, Nanga masters were individualists, creating their own variations of literati painting from unique blendings of Chinese models, Japanese aesthetics, and personal brushwork. They were often experts at calligraphy and poetry as well as painting, but one, Uragami Gyokudo (1745–1820), was even more famous as a musician, an expert on the seven-string Chinese zither called the *qin*. Most instruments are played for entertainment or ceremonial purposes, but the *qin* has so deep and soft a sound that it is played only for oneself or a close friend. Its music becomes a kind of meditation, and for Gyokudo it opened a way to commune with nature and his own inner spirit.

Gyokudo was a hereditary samurai official, but midway through his life he resigned from his position and spent seventeen years wandering through Japan, absorbing the beauty of its scenery, writing poems, playing music, and beginning to paint. During his later years Gyokudo produced many of the strongest and most individualistic paintings in Japanese history, although they were not appreciated by people during his lifetime. **GEESE ASLANT IN THE HIGH WIND** is a leaf from an album Gyokudo painted in 1817, three years before his death (FIG. 25–11). The creative power in this painting is remarkable. The wind seems to have the force of a hurricane, sweeping the tree branches and the geese into swirls of action. The greatest force comes from within the land itself, which mushrooms out and bursts forth in peaks and plateaus as though an inner volcano were erupting.

Zen Painting

Deprived of the support of the government and samurai officials, who now favored neo-Confucianism, Zen initially went into something of a decline during the Edo period. In the early eighteenth century, however, it was revived by a monk named Hakuin Ekaku (1685–1769), who had been born in a small village not far from Mount Fuji and who resolved to become a monk after hearing a fire-and-brimstone sermon in his youth. For years he traveled around Japan seeking out the strictest Zen teachers. After a series of enlightenment experiences, he eventually became an important teacher himself.

In his later years Hakuin turned more and more to painting and calligraphy as forms of Zen expression and teaching. Since the government no longer sponsored Zen, Hakuin reached out to ordinary people, and many of his paintings portray everyday subjects that would be easily understood by farmers and merchants. The paintings from his sixties have great charm and humor, and by his eighties he was creating works of astonishing force. Hakuin's favorite subject was Daruma (Bodhidharma), the semilegendary Indian monk who had begun the Zen tradition in China

25–11 | Uragami Gyokudo **GEESE ASLANT IN THE HIGH WIND**
Edo period, 1817. Ink and light colors on paper, 12 ³⁄₁₆ × 9 ⅞" (31 × 25 cm). Takemoto Collection, Aichi.

Technique
INSIDE A WRITING BOX

The interior of a writing box is fitted with compartments for holding an ink stick, an ink stone, brushes, and paper—tools and materials not only for writing but also for **ink painting**.

Ink sticks are made by burning wood or oil inside a container. Soot deposited by the smoke then is collected, bound into a paste with resin, heated for several hours, kneaded and pounded, and finally pressed into small stick-shaped or cake-shaped molds to harden. Molds are often carved to produce an ink stick (or ink cake) decorated in low relief. The tools of writing and painting are also beautiful objects in their own right.

Fresh ink is made for each writing or painting session by grinding the hard, dry ink stick in water against a fine-grained stone. A typical ink stone has a shallow well at one end sloping up to a grinding surface at the other. The artist fills the well with water from a waterpot. The ink stick, held vertically, is dipped into the well to pick up a small amount of water, then is rubbed in a circular motion firmly on the grinding surface. The process is repeated until enough ink has been prepared. Grinding ink is viewed as a meditative task, time for collecting one's thoughts and concentrating on the painting or calligraphy ahead.

Brushes are made from animal hair set in simple bamboo or hollow-reed handles. Brushes taper to a fine point that responds with great sensitivity to any shift in pressure. Although great painters and calligraphers do eventually develop their own styles of holding and using the brush, all begin by learning the basic position for writing. The brush is held vertically, grasped firmly between the thumb and first two fingers, with the fourth and fifth fingers often resting against the handle for more subtle control.

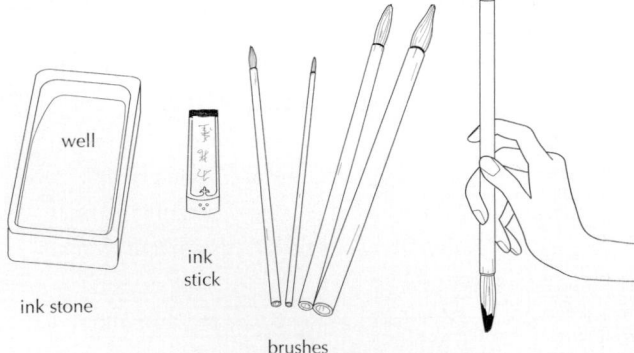

well

ink stone

ink stick

brushes

25–12 | Hakuin Ekaku **BODHIDHARMA MEDITATING**
Edo period, 18th century. Ink on paper, 49 ½ × 21 ¾″ (125.7 × 55.3 cm). On extended loan to the Spencer Museum of Art, The University of Kansas, Lawrence.

Hakuin had his first enlightenment experience while meditating upon the *koan* (mysterious Zen riddle) about *mu*. One day a monk asked a Chinese Zen master, "Does a dog have the *buddha* nature?" Although Buddhist doctrine teaches that all living beings have *buddha* nature, the master answered, "*Mu*," meaning "has not" or "nothingness." The riddle of this answer became a problem that Zen masters gave their students as a focus for meditation. With no logical answer possible, monks were forced to go beyond the rational mind and penetrate more deeply into their own being. Hakuin, after months of meditation, reached a point where he felt "as though frozen in a sheet of ice." He then happened to hear the sound of the temple bell, and "it was as though the sheet of ice had been smashed." Later, as a teacher, Hakuin invented a *koan* of his own that has since become famous: "What is the sound of one hand clapping?"

(FIG. 25–12). Here he has portrayed the wide-eyed Daruma during his nine years of meditation in front of a temple wall in China. Intensity, concentration, and spiritual depth are conveyed by broad and forceful brushstrokes. The inscription is the ultimate Zen message, attributed to Daruma himself: "Pointing directly to the human heart, see your own nature and become Buddha."

Hakuin's pupils followed his lead in communicating their vision through brushwork. The Zen figure once again became the primary subject of Zen painting, and the painters were again Zen masters rather than primarily artists.

Maruyama-Shijo School Painting

Zen paintings were given away to all those who wished them, including poor farmers as well as artisans, merchants, and samurai. Many merchants, however, were more concerned with displaying their increasing wealth than with spiritual matters, and their aspirations fueled a steady demand for golden screens and other decorative works of art.

MARUYAMA OKYO. One school that arose to satisfy this demand was the Maruyama-Shijo school, formed in Kyoto by Maruyama Okyo (1733–95). Okyo had studied Western-style "perspective pictures" in his youth, and he was able in his mature works to incorporate shading and perspective into a decorative style, creating a sense of volume that was new to East Asian painting. Okyo's new style proved very popular in Kyoto, and it soon spread to Osaka and Edo (present-day Tokyo) as well. The subjects of Maruyama-Shijo painting were seldom difficult to understand. Instead of legendary Chinese themes, Maruyama-Shijo painters portrayed the birds, animals, hills, trees (FIG. 25–13), farmers, and townsfolk of Japan. Although highly educated people might make a point of preferring Nanga painting, Maruyama-Shijo works suited the tastes of the emerging upper middle class.

NAGASAWA ROSETSU. The leading pupil of Okyo was Nagasawa Rosetsu (1754–99), a painter of great natural talent who added his own boldness and humor to the Maruyama-Shijo tradition. Rosetsu delighted in surprising his viewers with odd juxtapositions and unusual compositions. One of his finest works is a pair of screens, the left one depicting a bull and a puppy (FIG. 25–14). The bull is so immense that it fills almost the entire six panels of the screen and still cannot be contained at the top, left, and bottom. The puppy, white

25–13 | Maruyama Okyo **PINE TREE IN SNOW**
Edo period, 1765. Hanging scroll, ink and color on silk, 48 ½ × 28 ¼" (123 × 71.75 cm). Tokyo National Museum.

25–14 | Nagasawa Rosetsu **BULL AND PUPPY**
Edo period, 18th century. One of a pair of six-panel screens, ink and gold wash on paper, 5'7 ¼ × 12'3" (1.70 × 3.75 m). Los Angeles County Museum of Art, California.
Joe and Etsuko Price Collection (L.83.45.3a)

against the dark gray of the bull, helps to emphasize the huge size of the bull by its own smallness. The puppy's relaxed and informal pose, looking happily right out at the viewer, gives this powerful painting a humorous touch that increases its charm. In the hands of a master such as Rosetsu, plebeian subject matter could become simultaneously delightful and monumental, equally pleasing to viewers with or without much education or artistic background.

Ukiyo-E: Pictures of the Floating World

Not only did newly wealthy merchants patronize painters in the middle and later Edo period, but even artisans and trades-people could purchase works of art. Especially in the new capital of Edo, bustling with commerce and cultural activities, people savored the delights of their peaceful society. Buddhism had long preached that pleasures were fleeting; the cherry tree, which blossoms so briefly, became the symbol for the transience of earthly beauty and joy. Commoners in the Edo period did not dispute this transience, but they took a new attitude: Let's enjoy it to the full as long as it lasts. Thus the Buddhist phrase *ukiyo* ("floating world") became positive rather than negative.

There was no world more transient than that of the pleasure quarters, set up in specified areas of every major city. Here were found restaurants, bathhouses, and brothels. The heroes of the day were no longer famous samurai or aristocratic poets. Instead, swashbuckling actors and beautiful courtesans were admired. These paragons of pleasure soon became immortalized in paintings and—because paintings were too expensive for common people—in **woodblock prints** known as *ukiyo-e*, "pictures of the floating world" (see "Japanese Woodblock Prints," page 867).

HARUNOBU. At first prints were made in black ink, then colored by hand when the public so desired. The first artist to design prints to be printed in many colors was Suzuki Harunobu (1724–70). His exquisite portrayals of feminine beauty quickly became so popular that soon every artist was designing multicolored *nishiki-e* ("brocade pictures").

One print that displays Harunobu's charm and wit is **GEISHA AS DARUMA CROSSING THE SEA** (FIG. 25–15). Harunobu has portrayed a young woman in a red cloak crossing the water on a reed, a reference to one of the legends about Daruma. To see a young woman peering ahead to the other shore, rather than a grizzled Zen master staring off into space, must have greatly amused the Japanese populace. There was also another layer of meaning in this image because geishas were sometimes compared to Buddhist teachers or deities in their ability to bring ecstasy, akin to enlightenment, to humans. Harunobu's print suggests these meanings, but it also succeeds simply as a portrait of a beautiful woman, with the gently curving lines of drapery suggesting the delicate feminine form beneath.

25–15 | Suzuki Harunobu   **GEISHA AS DARUMA CROSSING THE SEA**   Edo period, mid-18th century. Polychrome woodblock print on paper, 10 ⅞ × 8 ¼″ (27.6 × 21 cm). Philadelphia Museum of Art.
Gift of Mrs. Emile Geyelin, in memory of Anne Hampton Barnes

The second great subject of *ukiyo-e* were the actors of the new form of popular theater known as *kabuki*. Because women had been banned from the stage after a series of scandalous incidents, male actors took both male and female roles. Much as people today buy posters of their favorite sports, music, or movie stars, so, too, in the Edo period people clamored for images of their pop idols.

HIROSHIGE AND HOKUSAI. During the nineteenth century, landscape joined courtesans and actors as a major theme—not the idealized landscape of China, but the actual sights of Japan. The two great masters of landscape prints were Utagawa Hiroshige (1797–1858) and Katsushika Hokusai (1760–1849). Hiroshige's *Fifty-Three Stations of the Tōkaido* and Hokusai's *Thirty-Six Views of Mt. Fuji* became the most successful sets of graphic art the world has known. The woodblocks were printed and printed again until they wore out. They were then recarved, and still more copies were printed. This process continued for decades, and thousands of prints from the two series are still extant.

The Great Wave (SEE FIG. 25–1) is the most famous of the scenes from *Thirty-Six Views of Mt. Fuji*. Hokusai was already

Technique
JAPANESE WOODBLOCK PRINTS

Woodblock prints are called ***ukiyo-e*** in Japanese, which can be translated as "pictures of the floating world." They represent the combined expertise of three people: the artist, the carver, and the printer. Coordinating and funding the endeavor was a publisher, who commissioned the project and distributed the prints to stores or itinerant peddlers, who would sell them.

The artist supplied the master drawing for the print, executing its outlines with brush and ink on tissue-thin paper. Colors might be indicated, but more often they were understood or decided on later. The drawing was passed on to the carver, who pasted it facedown on a hardwood block, preferably cherrywood, so that the outlines showed through the paper in reverse. A light coating of oil might be brushed on to make the paper more transparent, allowing the drawing to stand out with maximum clarity. The carver then cut around the lines of the drawing with a sharp knife, always working in the same direction as the original brushstrokes. The rest of the block was chiseled away, leaving the outlines standing in relief. This block, which reproduced the master drawing, was called the **key block**. If the print was to be **polychrome**, having multiple colors, prints made from the key block were in turn pasted facedown on blocks that would be used as guides for the carver of the color blocks. Each color generally required a separate block, although both sides of a block might be used for economy.

Once the blocks were completed, the printer took over. Paper for printing was covered lightly with animal glue (gelatin). A few hours before printing, the paper was lightly moistened so that it would take ink and color well. Water-based ink or color was brushed over the block, and the paper placed on top and rubbed with a smooth, padded device called a *baren*, until the design was completely transferred. The key block was printed first, then the colors one by one. Each block was carved with two small marks called **registration marks**, in exactly the same place in the margins, outside of the image area—an L in one corner, and a straight line in another. By aligning the paper with these marks before letting it fall over the block, the printer ensured that the colors would be placed correctly within the outlines. One of the most characteristic effects of later Japanese prints is a grading of color from dark to pale. This was achieved by wiping some of the color from the block before printing, or by moistening the block and then applying the color gradually with an unevenly loaded brush—a brush loaded on one side with full-strength color and on the other with diluted color.

Totoya Hokkei (1780–1850)
RAIKO ATTACKS A DEMON KITE
Edo period, c. 1825. Polychrome woodblock print on paper, 8 ⅛ × 7 ⅓" (21.4 × 18.6 cm) Collection of the Frank Lloyd Wright Archives, Scottsdale, Arizona. This print, of a luxurious limited-edition type called *surimono*, celebrates the hero Raiko, legendary slayer of demons, and suggests a message for the new year: vanquishing bad luck and ushering in good. The poem in the print reads:

A demon kite
trails its string
so high in the sky
that even young eyes
lose sight of it in the mist

(Translated by John T. Carpenter)

25–16 | Yokoyama Taikan **FLOATING LIGHTS**
Meiji period, 1909. One from a pair of hanging scrolls, ink, colors, and gold on silk, 56 ½ × 20 ½ " (143 × 52 cm). The Museum of Modern Art, Ibaraki.

in his seventies, with a fifty-year career behind him, when he designed this image. Such was his modesty that he felt that his Fuji series was only the beginning of his creativity, and he wrote that if he could live until he was 100, he would finally learn how to become an artist.

THE MEIJI AND MODERN PERIODS

Pressure from the West for entry into Japan mounted dramatically in the mid-nineteenth century, and in 1853 the policy of national seclusion was ended. Resulting tensions precipitated the downfall of the Tokugawa shogunate, however, and in 1868 the emperor was formally restored to power, an event known as the Meiji Restoration. The court moved from Kyoto to Edo, which was renamed Tokyo, meaning "Eastern Capital."

Meiji

The Meiji period marked a major change for Japan. After its long isolation, Japan was deluged by the influx of the West. Western education, governmental systems, clothing, medicine, industrialization, and technology were all adopted rapidly into Japanese culture. Teachers of sculpture and oil painting were imported from Italy, while adventurous Japanese artists traveled to Europe and America to study.

A MEIJI PAINTER. Ernest Fenollosa (1853–1908), an American who had recently graduated from Harvard, traveled to Japan in 1878 to teach philosophy and political economy at Tokyo University. Within a few years, he and a former student Okakura Kakuzo (1862–1913) began urging artists to study traditional Japanese arts rather than to focus exclusively on Western art styles and media. Yokoyama Taikan (1868–1958) subsequently developed his personal style within the *Nihonga* (Japanese painting) genre promoted by Okakura. Drawing from Japanese tradition, notably the Rimpa style, Yokoyama avoided outlines and instead defined forms in fields of color. His pictorial space, however, owes something to the Western tradition. Like Okakura, Yokoyama traveled widely. His **FLOATING LIGHTS** (FIG. 25–16) was inspired by a visit to India in 1903, where he observed women engaged in divination on the banks of the Ganges.

Modern Japan

In the push to become a modern industrialized country, Japan did not lose its sense of tradition, even in the days of the strongest Western influence. In modern Japan, artists still choose whether to work in an East Asian style, a Western style, or some combination of the two. Just as Japanese art in earlier periods had both Chinese style and native traditions, so Japanese art today has both Western and native aspects.

A MODERN CERAMICIST. Perhaps the liveliest contemporary art is ceramics. Japan has retained a widespread appreciation for pottery. Many people still practice the traditional arts of the tea ceremony and flower arranging, both of which require ceramic vessels, and most people own at least one fine ceramic piece. In this atmosphere, many potters earn a comfortable living by making art ceramics, an opportunity not available in other countries. Some ceramicists continue to create raku teabowls and other traditional wares, while others experiment with new styles and new techniques.

Miyashita Zenji (b. 1939), who lives in Kyoto, creates an initial form by constructing an undulating shape out of pieces of cardboard; he then builds up the surface with clay of many different colors, using torn paper to create irregular shapes. When fired, the varied colors of the clay seem to form a landscape, with layers of mountains leading up to the sky. Miyashita's work is modern in shape, yet traditional in its evocation of nature.

Miyashita is representative of the high level of contemporary ceramics in Japan, which is supported by a broad spectrum of educated and enthusiastic collectors and admirers. Objects useful for the tea ceremony or for flower arranging, such as Miyashita's flower vase entitled **WIND** (FIG. 25–17), reflect a continued refinement of traditional taste. There is also strong public interest in contemporary painting, prints, calligraphy, textiles, lacquer, architecture, and sculpture.

A CONTEMPORARY SCULPTOR. One of the most adventurous and original sculptors currently working is Chuichi Fujii (b. 1941). Born into a family of sculptors in wood, Fujii found himself as a young artist more interested in the new materials of plastic, steel, and glass. However, in his mid-

thirties he took stock of his progress and decided to begin again, this time with wood. At first he carved and cut into the wood, but he soon realized that he wanted to allow the material to express its own natural spirit, so he devised an ingenious new technique that preserved the individuality of each log while making of it something new. Fujii first studies the log to come to terms with its basic shape. Next, he inserts hooks into the log and runs wires between them. Every day he tightens the wires, over a period of months gradually pulling the log into a new shape. When he has bent the log to the shape he envisioned, Fujii makes a cut and sees whether his sculpture will stand. If he has miscalculated, he discards the work and begins again.

Here, Fujii has created a circle, one of the most basic forms in nature but never before seen in such a thick tree trunk (FIG. 25–18). The work strongly suggests the *enso*, the circle that Zen monks painted to express the universe, the all, the void, the moon—and even a tea cake. Yet Fujii does not try to proclaim his links with Japanese culture. He says that while his works may seem to have some connections with traditional Japanese arts, he is not conscious of them.

The artist has achieved something entirely new, yet his work also embodies the love of asymmetry, respect for natural materials, and dramatic simplicity encountered throughout the history of Japanese art.

A CONTEMPORARY PAINTER. In the 1990s, art in Japan merged with that in the West, with tradition and creativity playing out in new ways. Takashi Murakami (b. 1962), who lives and works in New York as well as in Japan, is prominent among artists who have taken Japan's *manga* and *anime* art forms, derived from the *ukiyo-e* tradition, as an inspiration for

25–17 | Miyashita Zenji **WIND**
c. 1989. Stoneware, 21⅞ × 12¾ × 5⅛″ (55.4 × 32.4 × 13 cm).
Spencer Museum of Art, The University of Kansas, Lawrence.
Gift of the Friends of the Art Museum/Helen Foresman Spencer Art Acquisition Fund

25–18 | Chuichi Fujii **UNTITLED '90**
1990. Cedar wood, height 7′5 ½″ (2.3 m).
Hara Museum of Contemporary Art, Tokyo.

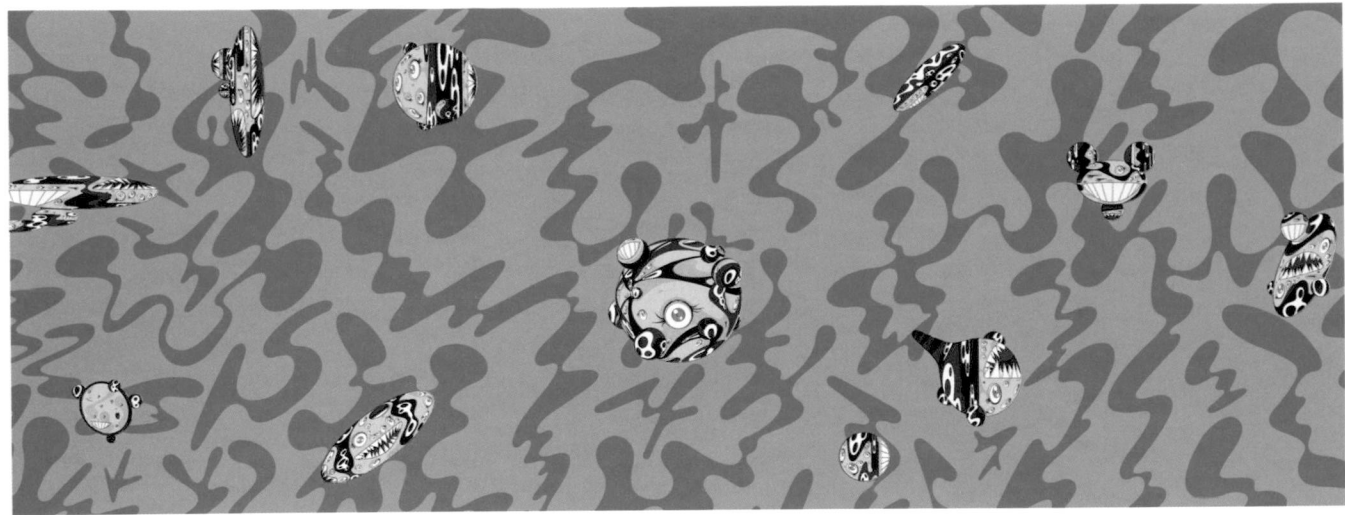

25–19 | Takashi Murakami **MAGIC BALL (POSITIVE)**
1999. Seven panels, acrylic on canvas mounted on board, 94 ½ × 248 ¼ × 2 ¾″ (240 × 630 × 7 cm).
Collection: Galerie 20.21, Essen.

painting and sculpture. These forms' close involvement with popular culture has a strong precedent in the *ukiyo-e* tradition. The emphasis on undulating lines and flat forms—to the point of a denial of pictorial space—also has its root in that Edo period style. Murakami's floating motifs (**FIG. 25–19**) reference *anime* and at the same time satirize its international consumer culture.

IN PERSPECTIVE

Muromachi, Momoyama, and Edo—six hundred years of Japanese culture—saw profound social and political changes. The arts felt these shifts through changing patterns of patronage of arts, yet all the while distinctive aesthetic orientations matured.

Evocative ink landscapes and Zen dry gardens, based on traditions imported from China, developed as the deeply artistic expressions in Japan. In these art forms the bold brushstrokes or subtle washes, and the general aesthetic of monochrome ink complements a strong appreciation of nature, its materials, and its forms. Wood, clay, and straw, or naturally shaped rocks provide patterns and textures with no need of obvious embellishment.

During the same periods, Japanese art inspired exquisite and exacting craftsmanship. Decoration in gold played a distinctive role in the painted screens that defined interior spaces as well as in the ornamentation of lacquer ware and other useful objects. Forms from nature became abstract and stylized patterns. Representation was often distilled to the simplicity of fluctuating line and flat shapes of color.

Japanese art of these periods was also invested with whimsy or even paradox. A sense of humor shows: sometimes easily accessible and at other times in works of art so sophisticated that they could only be understood by those with a deep knowledge of both Japanese and Chinese literature. In Japan, the patronage of art has long reflected a pluralistic cultural atmosphere. With that has come an ability to refine forms to greater and greater subtlety or, in contrast, to startle the viewer with audacious surprises.

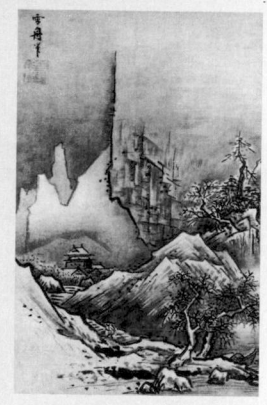

JAPANESE ART AFTER 1392

1300

◄ **Muromachi (Ashikaga)** 1392–1573

1500

◄ **Momoyama** 1568–1615

◄ **Edo (Tokugawa)** 1615–1868

1700

◄ **Meiji** 1868–1912

1900

◄ **Taisho** 1912–1926
◄ **Showa** 1926–1989

◄ **Occupation** 1945–1952

◄ **Heisei** 1989–Present

2000

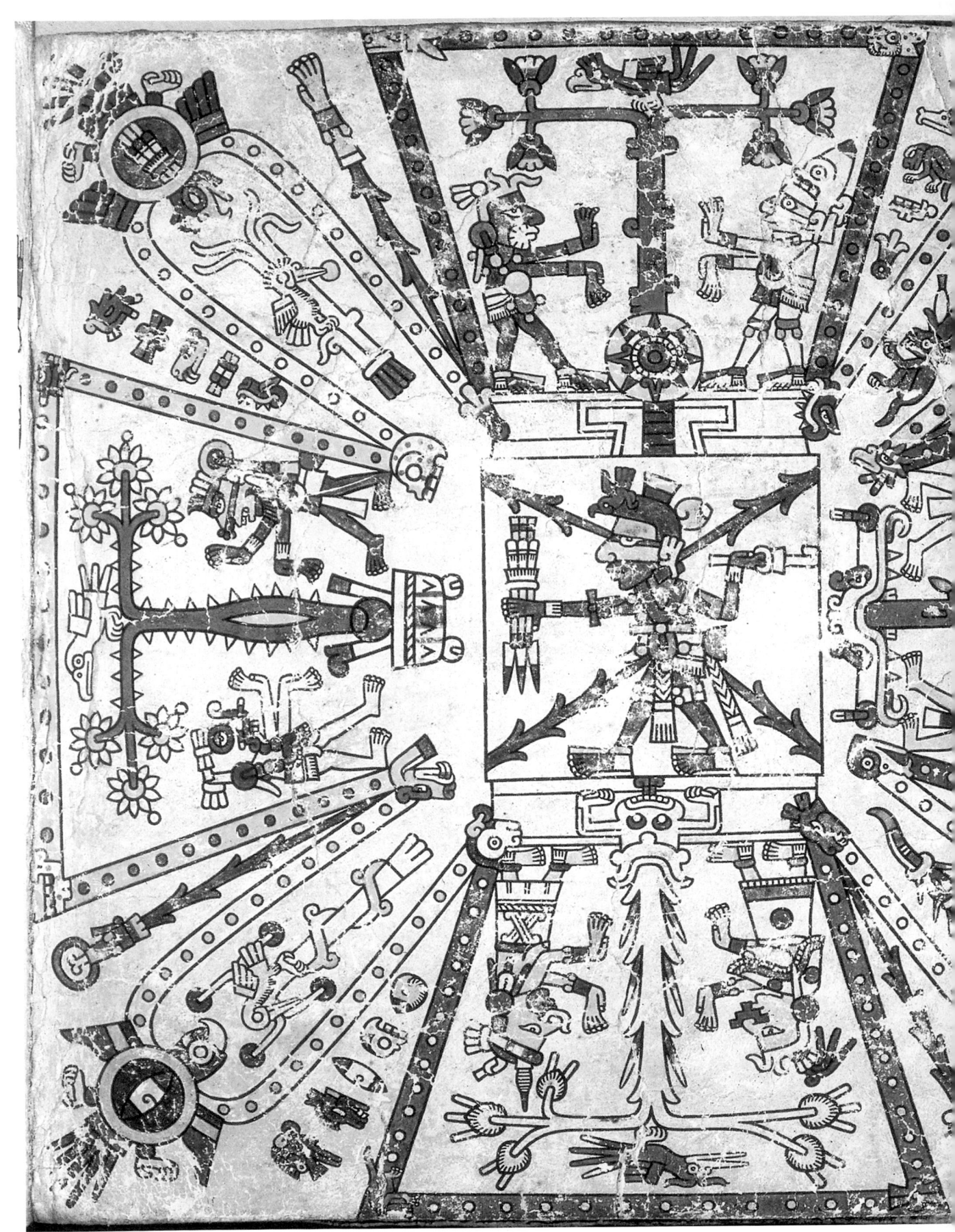

26–1 | **A VIEW OF THE WORLD**   Page from Codex Fejervary-Mayer. Aztec, c. 1400–1519/21. Paint on animal hide, each page 6⅞ × 6⅞" (17.5 × 17.5 cm), total length 13'3" (4.04 m). The National Museums and Galleries on Merseyside, Liverpool, England.

CHAPTER TWENTY-SIX

ART OF THE AMERICAS AFTER 1300

26 Early in November 1519, the army of the Spanish conquistador Hernán Cortés beheld for the first time the great Aztec capital of Tenochtitlan. The shimmering city, which seemed to be floating on the water, was built on islands in the middle of Lake Texcoco in the Valley of Mexico, and linked by broad causeways to the mainland. One of Cortés's companions later recalled the wonder the Spanish felt at that moment: "When we saw so many cities and villages built on the water and other great towns and that straight and level causeway going towards [Tenochtitlan], we were amazed . . . on account of the great towers and [temples] and buildings rising from the water, and all built of masonry. And some of our soldiers even asked whether the things that we saw were not a dream" (cited in Berdan, page 1).

The startling vision that riveted Cortés's soldiers was indeed real, a city of stone built on islands—a city that held many treasures and many mysteries. Much of the period before the conquistadors' arrival remains enigmatic, but a rare manuscript that survived the Spanish conquest of Mexico depicts the preconquest worldview of the native peoples. At the center of the image is the ancient fire god Xiuhtecutli (FIG. 26–1). Radiating from him are the four directions—each associated with a specific color, a deity, and a tree with a bird in its branches. In each corner, to the right of a U-shaped band, is an attribute of Tezcatlipoca, the Smoking Mirror, an omnipotent, primal deity who could see humankind's thoughts and deeds—in the upper right a head, in the upper left an arm, in the lower left a foot, and in the lower right bones. Streams of blood flow from these attributes back to the fire god in the center. Such images are filled with important, symbolically coded information—even the dots refer to the number of days in one aspect of the Mesoamerican calendar—and they were integral parts of the culture of the Americas.

When the first European explorers and adventurers arrived in 1519, the Western Hemisphere was already inhabited from the Arctic Circle to Tierra del Fuego by peoples with long and complex histories and rich and varied cultural traditions. This chapter focuses on the arts of the indigenous peoples of the Americas (MAP 26–1) just prior to, and in the wake of, their encounter with an expansionist Europe.

Two great empires—the Aztec in Mexico and the Inca in South America—had risen to prominence in the fifteenth century at about the same time that European adventurers began to explore the oceans in search of new trade routes to Asia. In the encounter that followed, the Aztec and Inca empires were destroyed.

THE AZTEC EMPIRE

The Mexica people who lived in the remarkable city that Cortés found in the early sixteenth century were then rulers of much of the land that took their name, Mexico. Their rise to power had been recent and swift. Only 400 years earlier, according to their own legends, they had been a nomadic people living northwest of the Valley of Mexico on the shores of the mythical Aztlan. The term *Aztec* derives from the word *Aztlan*.

After a period of migration, the Aztecs arrived in the Valley of Mexico in the thirteenth century. They eventually settled on an island in Lake Texcoco where they had seen an eagle perching on a prickly pear cactus (tenochtli), a sign that their legends told them would mark the end of their wandering. They called the place Tenochtitlan. The city was situated on a collection of islands linked by human-made canals in a grid pattern.

In the fifteenth century, the Aztecs—joined by allies in a triple alliance—began an aggressive campaign of expansion. The tribute they exacted from all over central Mexico transformed Tenochtitlan into a glittering capital. As the Spanish conquistador Hernán Cortés approached Tenochtitlan in November 1519, he and his soldiers marveled at the stone buildings, towers, and temples that seemed from a distance to rise from the water like a mirage.

Religion

Aztec religion was based on a complex pantheon that combined the Aztec deities with more ancient ones that had long been worshiped in central Mexico. According to Aztec belief, the gods had created the current universe at the ancient city of Teotihuacan in the Valley of Mexico (see Chapter 12). The continued existence of the world depended on human actions, including rituals of bloodletting and human sacrifice. The end of each round of fifty-two years in the Mesoamerican calendar was a particularly dangerous time that required a special fire-lighting ritual. Sacrificial victims sustained the sun god, Huitzilopochtli, in his daily course through the sky. Huitzilopochtli was the son of the Earth mother Coatlicue. When Coatlicue conceived Huitzilopochtli by holding within her chest a ball of hummingbird feathers (the soul of a fallen warrior) that had dropped from the sky, her other children—the stars and the moon—jealously conspired to kill her. When they attacked, Huitzilopochtli emerged from his mother's body

fully grown and armed, drove off his half brothers, and destroyed his half sister, the moon goddess Coyolxauhqui. Every day at dawn, the Sun God fights off the darkness, killing the stars (his 400 brothers) and the moon (his sister).

Tenochtitlan

An idealized representation of the city of Tenochtitlan and its sacred ceremonial precinct (**FIG. 26–2**) was drawn by Aztec scribes for Spanish administrators. It forms the first page of the *Codex Mendoza*, prepared for the Spanish viceroy in the sixteenth century. An eagle perched on a prickly pear cactus—the symbol of the city—fills the center of the page.

26–2 | **THE FOUNDING OF TENOCHTITLAN**
Page from *Codex Mendoza*. Aztec, 16th century. Ink and color on paper, 12⅜ × 8⁷⁄₁₆″ (21.5 × 31.5 cm). The Bodleian Library, University of Oxford, England.
MS. Arch Selden. A.1.fol. 2r

MAP 26–1 | **THE AMERICAS AFTER 1300**

Diverse peoples spread throughout the Americas, each shaping a distinct culture in the area it settled.

Waterways divide the city into four quarters, which are further subdivided into wards, as represented by the seated figures. The victorious warriors at the bottom of the page represent Aztec conquests.

The focal point of the sacred precinct—symbolized in FIGURE 26–2 by the temple or house at the top of the page—was the Great Pyramid, a 115- to 130-foot-high, four-tiered pyramid with two temples on top: a red and black temple dedicated to Huitzilopochtli and a blue temple for Tlaloc, the god of rain and fertility. Two steep staircases led up the west face of the pyramid from the plaza in front. Sacrificial victims climbed these stairs to the Temple of Huitzilopochtli, where priests threw them over a stone, quickly cut open their chests, and pulled out their still-throbbing hearts, hearts whose beating insured the survival of the sun, the gods, and the Aztecs. Their bodies were then rolled down the stairs and dismembered. Thousands of severed heads were said to have been kept on a skull rack in the plaza, represented in FIGURE 26–2 by the rack with a single skull to the right of the eagle.

During the winter rainy season the sun rose behind the Temple of Tlaloc, and during the dry season it rose

behind the Temple of Huitzilopochtli. The double temple thus united two natural forces, sun and rain, or fire and water. During the spring and autumn equinoxes, the sun rose between the two temples, illuminating the Temple of Quetzalcoatl, the feathered serpent, an ancient creator god associated with time (the calendar), civilization, and the arts.

TWO GODDESSES. Sculptures of serpents and serpent heads on the Great Pyramid in Tenochtitlan associated it with the place where the Sun God slew the moon goddess, Coyolxauhqui. A huge circular relief of the dismembered goddess lay at the foot of the temple stairs, as if the enraged and triumphant Huitzilopochtli had cast her there like a sacrificial victim (FIG. 26–3). Her torso is in the center, surrounded by her head and limbs. A rope around her waist is attached to a skull. She has bells on her cheeks and balls of down in her hair. She wears a magnificent headdress and has distinctive ear ornaments composed of disks, rectangles, and triangles. The sculpture is two-dimensional in concept—a flat surface with a deeply cut background.

26-3 | **THE MOON GODDESS COYOLXAUHQUI ("SHE OF THE GOLDEN BELLS")**
The Sacred Precinct, now the Museo Templo Mayor, Tenochtitlan. Aztec, 1469 (?). Stone, diameter 10'10" (3.33 m). Museo Templo Mayor, Mexico City.

This disk was discovered in 1978 by workers from a utility company who were excavating in central Mexico City.

26-4 | **THE GODDESS COATLICUE**
Aztec, 1487–1520. Basalt, height 8'6" (2.65 m). Museo Nacional de Antropología, Mexico City.

Standing high above the disk of the vanquished moon goddess was an imposing statue of Coatlicue, mother of Huitzilopochtli (FIG. 26–4). A sixteenth-century Spaniard described seeing such a statue covered with blood inside the Temple of the Sun. Coatlicue means "she of the serpent skirt," and this broad-shouldered figure with clawed hands and feet has a skirt of twisted snakes. A pair of serpents, symbols of gushing blood, rise from her neck to form her head. Their eyes are her eyes; their fangs, her tusks. The writhing serpents of her skirt also form her body. Around her stump of a neck hangs a necklace of sacrificial offerings—hands, hearts, and a dangling skull. Despite the surface intricacy, the sculpture's simple, bold, and blocky forms create an impression of solidity. The colors with which it was originally painted would have heightened its dramatic impact.

Indeed Aztec art was colorful. An idea of its iridescent splendor is captured in the feather headdress said to have been given by Moctezuma to Cortés, and thought to be the one listed in the inventory of treasures Cortés shipped to Charles V, the Habsburg emperor in Spain in 1519. Featherwork was one of the glories of Mesoamerican art but very few of these extremely fragile artworks survive. "Moctezuma's Crown," as it was called, was originally a conqueror's trophy, and only recognized as "art" in recent times (FIG. 26–5). It is made of brilliant green, red, white, and blue feathers of the quetzal bird, macaw parrot, and other lesser birds, fastened to a reed frame. The feathers were gathered in small bunches, their quills reinforced with reed tubes, and then sewn to the frame in overlapping layers. Featherworkers were esteemed craftspersons. A song in praise of the feather artist says, "He is whole; he has a face and a heart. The good feather artist is skillful, is master of himself; it is his duty to humanize the desires of the people. He works with feathers, chooses them, arranges them, paints them with different colors, joins them together." (Sorge Gruziriski, *The Aztecs, Discoveries*, New York: Abrams. English translation, 1992, p. 153.)

The Aztec empire was short lived. Within two years of their arrival in Mexico, the Spanish conquistadors overran Tenochtitlan. They built their own capital, Mexico City, over its ruins and established their own cathedral on the site of Tenochtitlan's sacred precinct.

THE INCA EMPIRE IN SOUTH AMERICA

At the beginning of the sixteenth century the Inca Empire was one of the largest states in the world. It extended more than 2,600 miles along western South America, encompassing most of modern Peru, Ecuador, Bolivia, and northern Chile and reaching into present-day Argentina. Like the Aztec Empire, its rise was rapid and its destruction sudden.

The Incas called their empire the "Land of the Four Quarters." At its center was their capital, Cuzco, "the navel of

26–5 | **FEATHER HEADDRESS OF MOCTEZUMA**
Before 1519. Quetzal, macaw, and other feathers on a reed frame.
Museum für Völkerkunde, Vienna.

the world," located high in the Andes Mountains. The Inca state was one of many small competing kingdoms that emerged in the highlands. In the fifteenth century the Incas began to expand, suddenly and rapidly, and had subdued most of their vast domain—through conquest, alliance, and intimidation—by 1500.

To hold this linguistically and ethnically diverse empire together, the Inca ("Inca" refers to both the ruler and to the people) relied on religion, an efficient bureaucracy, and various forms of labor taxation, in which the payment was a set amount of time spent performing tasks for the state. As part of their labor tax, people were required to work the lands of the gods and the state for part of each year. In return the state provided gifts through their local leaders and sponsored lavish ritual entertainments. Men might serve periodically on public-works projects—building roads and terracing hillsides, for example—or in the army. Women wove cloth, a commodity that Inca people considered more precious than gold. The Inca might relocate whole communities to best exploit the resources of the empire. Ranks of storehouses at Inca administrative centers assured the state's ability to feed its armies and supply its workers. No Andean civilization ever developed writing, but the Inca kept detailed accounts on knotted and colored cords, called *quipu*.

THE INCA ROAD SYSTEM. To move their armies and speed transport and communication within the empire, the Incas built more than 23,000 miles of roads. These varied from 50-

foot-wide thoroughfares to 3-foot-wide paths. Two main north–south roads, one along the coast and the other through the highlands, were linked by east–west roads. Travelers journeyed on foot, using llamas as pack animals. Stairways helped them negotiate steep mountain slopes, and rope suspension bridges allowed river gorge crossings. The main road through the Pacific coastal desert had walls to protect it from blowing sand. All along the roads, storehouses and lodgings—more than a thousand have been found—were spaced a day's journey apart. A relay system of runners could carry messages between Cuzco and the farthest reaches of the empire in about a week.

Masonry

Cuzco, a capital of great splendor, was home to the Inca, ruler of the empire. The city was a showcase of the finest Inca masonry, some of which can still be seen in the present-day city. This masonry has survived earthquakes that have destroyed later structures. Fine **INCA MASONRY** consisted of either rectangular blocks or irregular polygonal blocks (FIG. 26–6). In both types, adjoining blocks were painstakingly shaped to fit tightly together without mortar (see "Inca Masonry," page 878). Their stone faces might be slightly beveled along their edges so that each block presented a "pillowed" shape expressing its identity, or walls might be smoothed into a continuous flowing surface in which the individual blocks form a seamless whole. In contrast to the massive walls, Inca buildings had gabled, thatched roofs.

Elements of Architecture
INCA MASONRY

Working with the simplest of tools—mainly heavy stone hammers—and using no mortar, Inca builders created stonework of great refinement and durability: roads and bridges that linked the entire empire, built-up terraces for growing crops, and structures both simple and elaborate. At Machu Picchu (SEE FIGS. 26–6, 26–7), all buildings and terraces within its 3-square-mile extent were made of granite, the hard stone occurring at the site. Commoners' houses and some walls were constructed of irregular stones that were carefully fitted together. Some walls and certain domestic and religious structures were erected using squared-off, smooth-surfaced stones laid in even rows. At a few Inca sites, the stones used in construction were boulder-size: up to 27 feet tall.

irregular-stone wall   smooth-surfaced wall

26–6 | **INCA MASONRY, DETAIL OF A WALL IN MACHU PICCHU**
Peru. Inca, 1450–1530.

Doors, windows, and niches were trapezoid shaped, narrower at the top than the bottom. The effort expended on stone construction by the Inca was prodigious.

MACHU PICCHU. **MACHU PICCHU**, one of the most spectacular archaeological sites in the world, provides an excellent example of Inca architectural planning (FIG. 26–7). At 9,000 feet above sea level, it straddles a ridge between two high peaks in the eastern slopes of the Andes and looks down on the Urubamba River. Stone buildings, today lacking only their thatched roofs, occupy terraces around central plazas, and narrow agricultural terraces descend into the valley. The site, near the eastern limits of the empire, was the estate of the Inca Pachacuti (ruled 1438–71). Its temples and sacred stones—some, left natural, were erected in courtyard shrines—suggest that the site also had an important religious function.

Textiles

The production of fine textiles had been an important art in the Andes from the time of the Paracas culture (see Chapter 12), beginning about 1000 BCE. Among the Incas, textiles of cotton and camelid fibers (from llama, vicuna, and alpaca) were a primary form of wealth. One form of labor taxation required the manufacture of fibers and cloth, and textiles as well as agricultural products filled Inca storehouses. Cloth was deemed a fitting offering for the gods, so fine garments were draped around golden statues, and even three-dimensional images were constructed of cloth.

TUNICS. The patterns and designs on garments were not simply decorative but also carried symbolic messages, including indications of a person's ethnic identity and social rank. In the elaborate **TUNIC** in FIGURE 26–8, each square represents a miniature tunic, but the meanings of the individual patterns

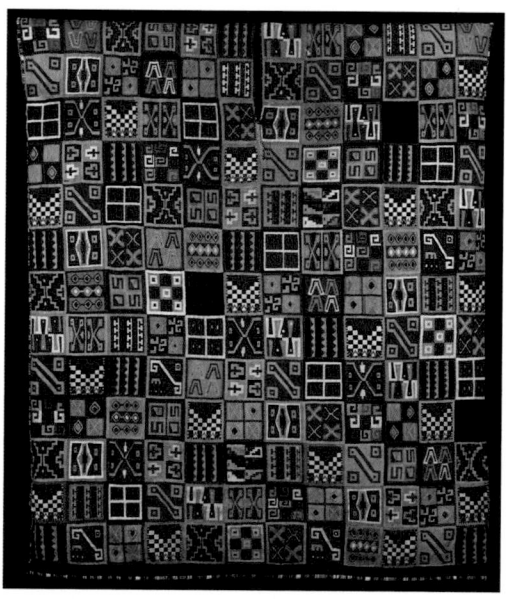

26–7 | **MACHU PICCHU**
Peru. Inca, 1450–1530.

are not yet completely understood. The four-part motifs may refer to the Land of the Four Quarters. The diagonal key motif is often found on tunics with horizontal border stripes but its meaning is not known. The checkerboard patterns are thought to designate military officers and royal escorts. While we may not be sure what was meant in every case, patterns and colors appear to have been standardized like uniforms in order to convey information at a glance.

Metalwork

Following Cortés's example, Francisco Pizarro led an expedition to South America in 1532. He and his men seized the Inca ruler, Atahualpa, held him for ransom, and then treacherously strangled him. They marched on to Cuzco and seized it in 1533.

The Spanish were far less interested in Inca cloth than in their vast quantities of gold and silver. The Inca valued objects made of gold and silver not for their precious metal, but because they saw in them symbols of the sun and the moon. They are said to have called gold the "sweat of the sun" and silver the "tears of the moon." On the other hand, the

26–8 | **TUNIC**
Peru. Inca, c. 1500. Wool and cotton, 35⅞ × 30″ (91 × 76.5 cm). Dumbarton Oaks Research Library and Collections, Pre-Columbian Collection, Washington, D.C.

26–9 | LLAMA
From Bolivia or Peru, found near Lake Titicaca, Bolivia. Inca, 15th century. Cast silver with gold and cinnabar, 9 × 8½ × 1¾" (22.9 × 21.6 × 4.4 cm). American Museum of Natural History, New York.

Spanish exploration of the New World was propelled by fever-ish tales of native treasure. Whatever gold and silver objects the Spanish could lay their hands on, they melted down to enrich their royal coffers. Only a few small figures buried as offerings, like the little llama (FIG. 26–9), escaped the conquerors. The llama was thought to have a special connection with the sun, with rain, and with fertility, and a llama was sacrificed to the sun every morning and evening in Cuzco. A white llama was kept as the symbol of the Inca. Dressed in a red tunic and wear-ing gold jewelry, this llama passed through the streets of Cuzco during April celebrations. According to Spanish commenta-tors, these processions included life-size gold and silver images of llamas, people, and gods.

The Aftermath of the Spanish Conquest

Native American populations in Mexico and Peru declined sharply after the conquest because of the exploitative policies of the conquerors and the ravages of smallpox and other dis-eases that spread from Europe and against which the indige-nous people had no immunity. European missionaries suppressed local beliefs and practices and worked to spread Roman Catholicism throughout the Americas. While increas-ing numbers of Europeans began to settle and dominate the land, native arts did not end with the Spanish conquest. Tradi-tional arts, including fine weaving, continue to this day.

NORTH AMERICA

In America north of Mexico, from the upper reaches of Canada and Alaska to the southern tip of Florida, existed many different peoples with widely varying cultures. Much of their artwork was small, portable, fragile, and imperma-nent. In previous times these artworks were not appreciated for their aesthetic qualities, but were collected as anthropo-logical artifacts or curiosities. As a consequence, one often must visit anthropology and natural history museums to view works of indigenous art. Today this attitude has changed, and Native American artworks have entered col-lections as art and are displayed in such prestigious places as the National Museum of the American Indian in Washing-ton, D.C. Today work of an increasing number of young Native American artists can be seen alongside Euro-American artists in mainstream art galleries. We will look at art from only four North American cultural areas: the East-ern Woodlands, the Great Plains, the Northwest Coast, and the Southwest (SEE MAP 26–2).

The Eastern Woodlands

In the eastern woodlands, most tribes lived in stable villages, and they combined hunting, gathering, and agriculture for their livelihood. In the sixteenth century, skilled politicians appeared among them. The Iroquois formed a powerful con-federation of five northeastern Native American nations, and they played a prominent military and political role until after the American Revolution. The Huron and Illinois also formed sizable confederacies.

The arrival in the seventeenth century on the Atlantic coast of a few boatloads of Europeans seeking religious free-dom, land to farm, and a new life for themselves brought major changes. Trade with these settlers gave the Woodlands peoples access to things they valued, while on their part, the colonists learned native forms of agriculture, hunting, and fishing—skills they needed in order to survive. The arrival of the Europeans also had a negative impact, since they brought diseases, espe-cially smallpox, with them. Disease wiped out entire Native populations. The lands seemed an untended wilderness to the Europeans, although in the first years of colonization some peo-ple remarked on the presence of abandoned fields and villages.

Native Americans traded furs for such useful items as metal tools, cookware, needles, and cloth, and they especially prized European glass beads and silver. They associated glass beads, and other shiny, reflective objects and materials, with ancient cul-tural values of self-knowledge, introspection, and understand-ing. These trade items largely replaced older materials, such as crystal, copper, and shell. The traditional meanings and values of

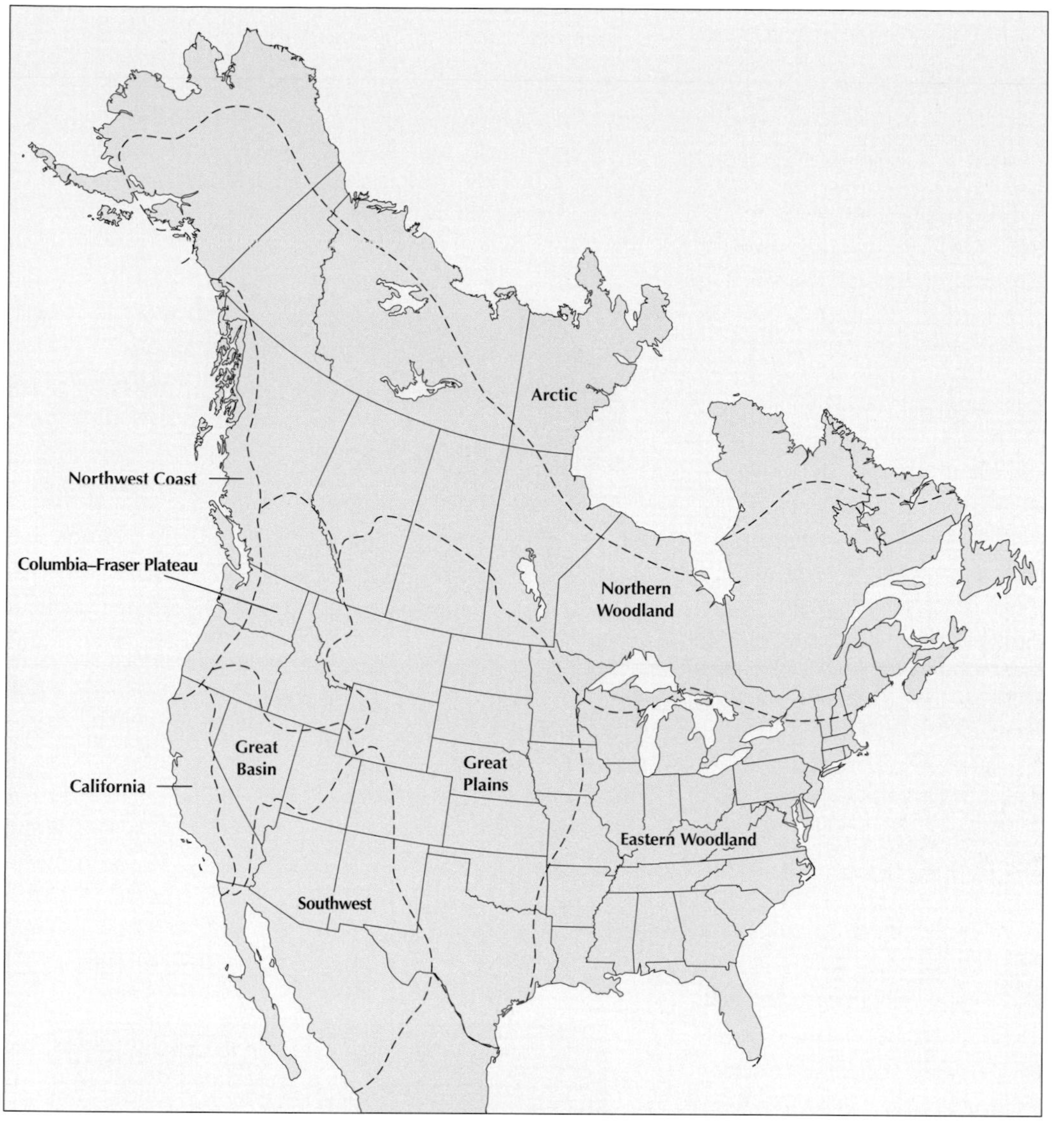

MAP 26—2 | NORTH AMERICAN CULTURAL AREAS

beads and similar items survive today from the ancestral mound-building civilizations of Eastern North America in contemporary celebratory and ceremonial powwow dress.

WAMPUM. Woodlands peoples made belts and strings of cylindrical purple and white shell beads called *wampum*. The Iroquois and Delaware peoples used wampum to keep records (the purple and white patterns served as memory devices) and exchanged belts of wampum to conclude treaties (FIG. 26–10). Few actual wampum treaty belts have survived, so this one associated with an unwritten treaty when the land now comprising the State of Pennsylvania was

26–10 | **WAMPUM BELT, TRADITIONALLY CALLED WILLIAM PENN'S TREATY WITH THE DELAWARE**
1680's. Shell beads. Royal Ontario Museum, Canada.
HD6364

Technique
BASKETRY

Basketry is the weaving of reeds, grasses, and other plant materials to form containers. In North America the earliest evidence of basketwork, found in Danger Cave, Utah, dates to as early as 8400 BCE. Over the subsequent centuries, Native American women, notably in California and the American Southwest, developed basketry into an art form that combined utility with great beauty.

There are three principal basket-making techniques: coiling, twining, and plaiting. *Coiling* involves sewing together a spiraling foundation of rods with some other material. *Twining* is the sewing together of a vertical warp of rods. *Plaiting* employs weaving strips over and under each other.

The coiled basket shown here was made by the Pomo of California. According to Pomo legend, the Earth was dark until their ancestral hero stole the sun and brought it to Earth in a basket. He hung the basket first just over the horizon, but, dissatisfied with the light it gave, he kept suspending it in different places across the dome of the sky. He repeats this process every day, which is why the sun moves across the sky from east to west. In the Pomo basket, the structure of coiled willow and bracken fern root produces a spiral surface into which the artist worked sparkling pieces of clamshell, trade beads, and the soft tufts of woodpecker and quail feathers. The underlying basket, the glittering shells, and the soft, moving feathers make this an exquisite container. Such baskets were treasured possessions, cremated with their owners at death.

FEATHERED WEDDING BASKET
Pomo. c. 1877. Willow, bulrush, fern, feather, shells, glass beads. Height 5½" (14 cm), diameter 12" (36.5 cm). Philbrook Museum, Tulsa, Oklahoma.
Clark Field Collection (1948.39.37)

---

ceded by the Delawares in 1682 is especially prized. The belt with two figures of equal size holding hands suggests the mutual respect enjoyed by the Delaware and Penn's Society of Friends (Quakers), a respect that later collapsed into land fraud and violence. In general, wampum strings and belts had the power of legal agreement and also symbolized a moral and political order.

QUILLWORK. Woodlands art focused on personal adornment—tattoos, body paint, elaborate dress—and fragile arts such as quillwork. Quillwork involved dyeing porcupine and bird quills with a variety of natural dyes, soaking the quills to soften them, and then working them into rectilinear, ornamental surface patterns on deerskin clothing and on birchbark items like baskets and boxes. A Sioux legend recounts how a mythical ancestor, Doublewoman ("double" because she was both beautiful and ugly, benign and dangerous), appeared to a woman in a dream and taught her the art of quillwork. As the legend suggests, quillwork was a woman's art form, as was basketry (see "Basketry," above). The Sioux **BABY CARRIER** (FIG. 26–11) is richly decorated with symbols of protection and well-being, including bands of antelopes in profile and thunderbirds—flying with their heads turned and tails outspread. The thunderbird was an especially beneficent symbol, thought to be capable of protecting against both human and supernatural adversaries.

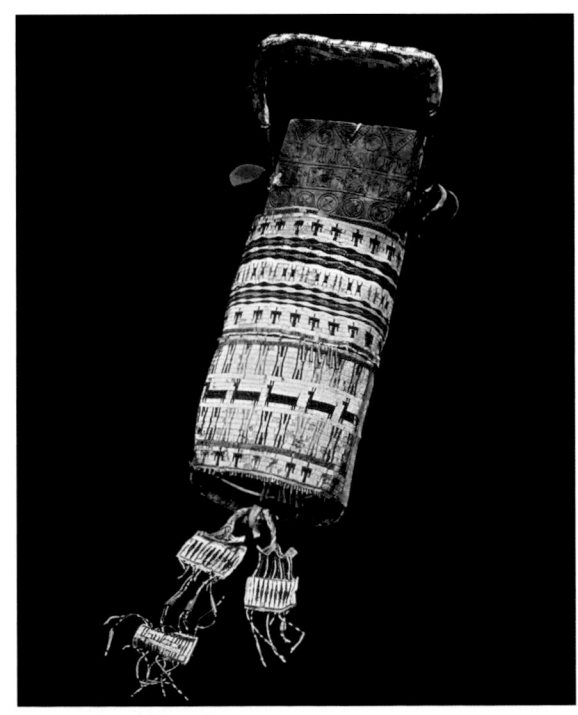

26–11 | BABY CARRIER
The Upper Missouri River area. Eastern Sioux, 19th century. Board, buckskin, porcupine quill, length 31" (78.8 cm). Department of Anthropology, Smithsonian Institution Libraries, Washington, D.C.
(Catalogue No. 7311)

26–12 | SHOULDER BAG
Delaware people. Kansas. c. 1860. Wool fabric, cotton fabric and thread, silk ribbon, and glass beads, 23 × 7¾" (58.5 × 19.8 cm). The Detroit Institute of Arts.
Founders Society Purchase (81.216)

BEADWORK. In spite of the use of shell beads in wampum, decorative beadwork did not become commonplace until after European contact. In the late eighteenth century, Native American artists began to acquire European colored-glass beads, and in the nineteenth century they favored the tiny seed beads from Venice and Bohemia. Early beadwork mimicked the patterns and colors of quillwork. In the nineteenth century it largely replaced quillwork and incorporated European designs. About 1830 Canadian nuns introduced the young women in their schools to embroidered European floral motifs, and the native embroiderers began to adapt these designs as well as European needlework techniques and patterns from European garments into their own work. Functional aspects of garments might be transformed into purely decorative motifs; for example, a pocket would be replaced by an area of beadwork shaped like a pocket. A **SHOULDER BAG** from Kansas, made by a Delaware woman (**FIG. 26–12**), is covered with curvilinear plant motifs in contrast to the

26–13 | **BLACKFOOT WOMEN RAISING A TEPEE**
Photographed c. 1900. Montana Historical Society, Helena, Montana.

rectilinear patterns of traditional quillwork. White lines outline brilliant pink and blue leaf-shaped forms, heightening the intensity of the colors, which alternate within repeated patterns. The Delaware bag exemplifies the evolution of beadwork design.

The Great Plains

Between the Eastern Woodlands region and the Rocky Mountains to the west lay an area of prairie grasslands called the Great Plains. On the Great Plains, two differing ways of life developed, one a relatively recent and short lived (1700–1870) nomadic lifestyle—dependent on the region's great migrating herds of buffalo for food, clothing, and shelter—and the other, a much older sedentary and agricultural lifestyle. Horses, from wild herds descended from feral horses brought to America by Spanish explorers in the sixteenth and seventeenth centuries, made travel and a nomadic life easier for the dispossessed eastern groups that moved to the plains.

European settlers on the eastern seaboard put increasing pressure on the Eastern Woodlands peoples, seizing their farmlands and forcing them westward. Both Native Americans and backcountry settlers were living in loosely village-based, farming societies and thus were competing for the same resources. The resulting interaction of Eastern Woodlands artists with one another and with Plains artists led in some cases to the emergence of a new hybrid style, while other artists consciously fought to maintain their own cultures.

PORTABLE ARCHITECTURE. The nomadic Plains peoples hunted buffalo for food and hides from which they created clothing and a light, portable dwelling known as a TEPEE (FIG. 26–13). The tepee was well adapted to withstand the strong and constant wind, and the dust and violent storms of

the prairies. The framework of a tepee consisted of a stable pyramidal frame of three or four long poles, filled out with about twenty additional poles, in a roughly egg-shaped plan. The framework was covered with hides (or, later, with canvas) to form a conical structure. The hides were specially prepared to make them flexible and waterproof. A typical tepee required about eighteen hides; the largest, about thirty-eight hides. An opening at the top served as the smoke hole for a central hearth. The tepee leaned slightly into the prevailing west wind while the flap-covered door and smoke hole faced east, away from the wind. An inner lining covered the lower part of the walls and the perimeter of the floor to protect the occupants from drafts.

Tepees were the property and responsibility of women, who set them up at new encampments and lowered them when the group moved on. Blackfoot women could set up their huge tepees in less than an hour. Women painted, embroidered, quilled, and beaded tepee linings, backrests, clothing, and equipment. The patterns with which tepees were decorated, as well as their proportions and colors, varied from nation to nation, family to family, and individual to individual. In general, the bottom was covered with the traditional motifs of the people, and the center section held personal images. When disassembled and packed to be dragged by a horse to another location, the tepee served as a platform for transporting other possessions. The Sioux arranged their tepees in two half circles—one for the sky people and one for the earth people—divided along an east–west axis. When the Blackfoot people gathered in the summer for their ceremonial Sun Dance, their encampment contained hundreds of tepees in a circle a mile in circumference.

PLAINS INDIAN PAINTING. Plains men recorded their exploits in paintings on tepee linings and covers and on buffalo-hide robes. The earliest surviving painted buffalo-hide robe illustrates a battle fought in 1797 by the Mandan (of what is now North Dakota) and their allies against the Sioux (FIG. 26–14). The painter, trying to capture the full extent of a conflict in which five nations took part, shows a party of warriors in twenty-two separate episodes. The party is led by a man with a pipe and an elaborate eagle-feather headdress, and the warriors are armed with bows and arrows, lances, clubs, and flintlock rifles. Details of equipment and emblems of rank—headdresses, sashes, shields, feathered lances, powder horns for the rifles—are depicted carefully. Horses are shown in profile with stick legs, C-shaped hooves, and either clipped or flowing manes.

The figures stand out clearly against the light-colored background of the buffalo hide. The painter pressed lines into the hide, then filled in with black, red, green, yellow, and brown pigments. He drew the warriors as stick figures with rectangular torsos and tiny round heads. A strip of colored porcupine quills runs down the spine of the buffalo hide. The robe would have been worn draped over the shoulders of the powerful warrior whose deeds it commemorates. As the wearer moved, the painted horses and warriors would seem to come alive, transforming the warrior into a living representation of his exploits.

Life on the Great Plains changed abruptly in 1869, when the Euro-Americans finished the transcontinental railway linking the east and west coasts of the United States and providing easy access to Native American lands. Between

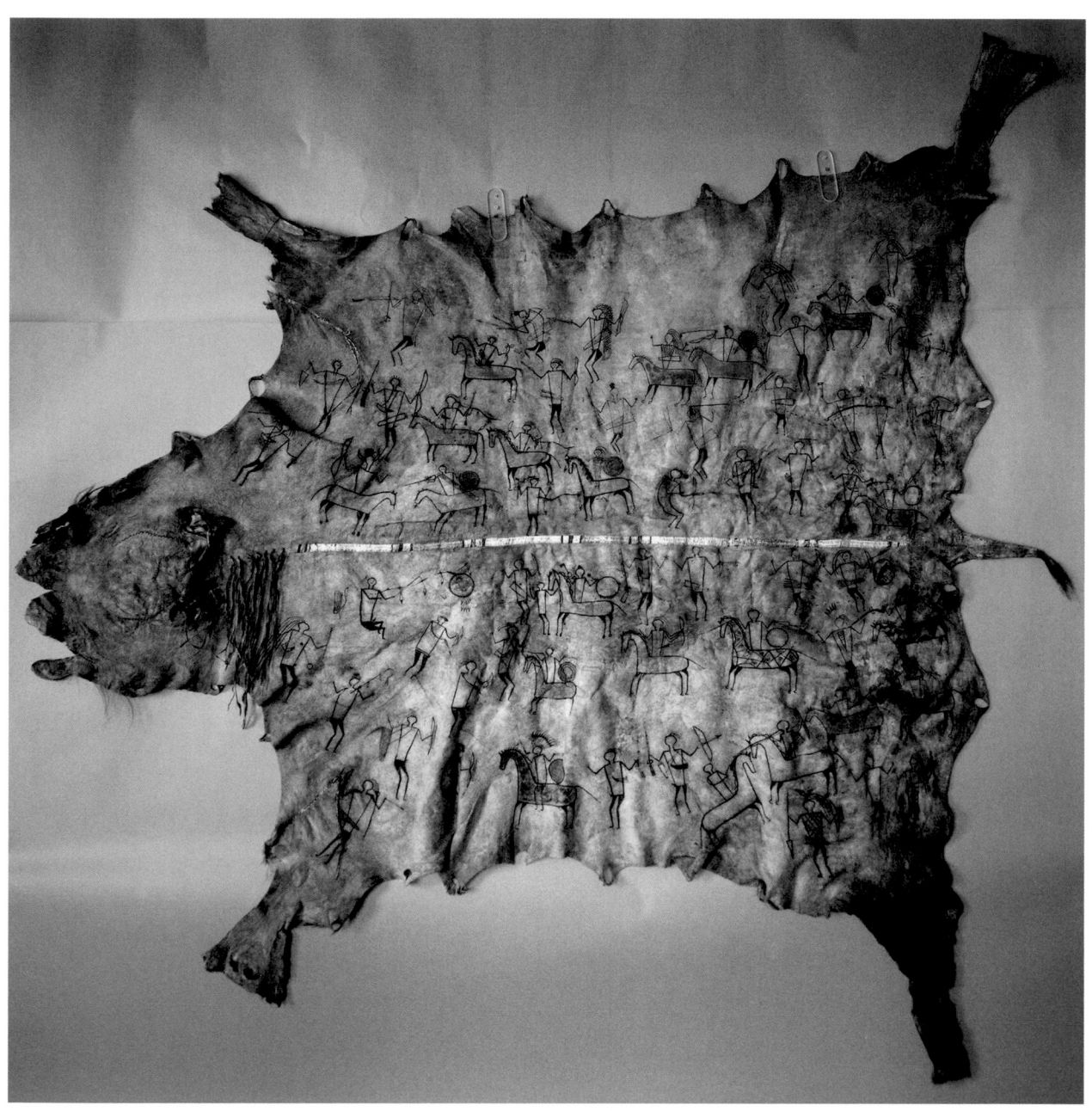

26–14 | **BATTLE-SCENE, HIDE PAINTING**
Mandan. North Dakota. 1797–1800. Tanned buffalo hide, dyed porcupine quills, and black, red, green, yellow, and brown pigment, 7'10" × 8'6" (2.44 × 2.65 m). Peabody Museum of Archaeology, Harvard University, Cambridge, Massachusetts.
(99-12-10/53121)

This robe, collected in 1804 by Meriwether Lewis and William Clark on their 1804–06 expedition into western lands acquired by the United States in the Louisiana Purchase, is the earliest documented example of Plains painting. It was one of a number of Native American artworks that Lewis and Clark sent to President Thomas Jefferson. Jefferson displayed the robe in the entrance hall of his home at Monticello, Virginia.

1871 and 1890, Euro-American hunters had killed off most of the buffalo, and soon ranchers and then farmers moved into the Great Plains. The U.S. government forcibly moved the outnumbered and outgunned Native Americans to reservations, land considered worthless until the later discovery of oil and, in the case of the Black Hills, gold.

The Northwest Coast

From southern Alaska to northern California, the Pacific coast of North America is a region of unusually abundant resources. Its many rivers fill each year with salmon returning to spawn. Harvested and dried, the fish could sustain large populations throughout the year. The peoples of the Northwest Coast—among them the Tlingit, the Haida, and the Kwakwaka'wakw (formerly spelled Kwakiutl)—exploited this abundance to develop a complex and distinctive way of life in which the arts played a central role.

ANIMAL IMAGERY. Northwest Coast people lived in extended family groups (clans) that claimed descent from a mythic animal or animal-human ancestor. A family derived its name and the right to use certain animals and spirits as totemic emblems, or crests, from its mythic ancestor. These emblems appeared prominently in Northwest Coast art, notably in carved cedar house poles and the tall, freestanding poles (mortuary poles) erected to memorialize dead chiefs. Chiefs, who were males in the most direct line of descent from the mythic ancestor, administered a family's spiritual and material resources. They validated their status and garnered prestige for themselves and their families by holding ritual feasts known as potlatches, during which they gave valuable gifts to the invited guests. Shamans, who were sometimes also chiefs, mediated between the human and spirit worlds. Some shamans were female, giving them unique access to specific aspects of the spiritual world.

The people lived in large, elaborately decorated communal houses made of massive timbers and thick planks. Carved and painted partition screens separated the chief's quarters from the rest of the house. The Tlingit screen illustrated here (FIG. 26–15) came from the house of Chief Shakes of Wrangell (d. 1916), whose family crest was the grizzly bear. The image of a rearing grizzly painted on the screen is itself made up of smaller bears and bear heads that appear in its ears, eyes, nostrils, joints, paws, and body. The images within the image enrich the monumental symmetrical design. The oval door opening is a symbolic vagina; passing through it reenacts the birth of the family from its ancestral spirit.

TEXTILES. Blankets and other textiles produced by the Chilkat Tlingit had great prestige among the Northwest Coast people (FIG. 26–16). Both men and women worked on the blankets. Men drew the patterns on boards, and women wove the patterns into the blankets, using shredded cedar

26–15 | **GRIZZLY BEAR HOUSE-PARTITION SCREEN**
The house of Chief Shakes of Wrangell, Canada. Tlingit people. c. 1840. Cedar, native paint, and human hair, 15 × 8′ (4.57 × 2.74 m). Denver Art Museum, Denver, Colorado.

bark and mountain-goat wool. The weavers did not use looms; instead, they hung cedar warp threads from a rod and twisted colored goat wool back and forth through them to make the pattern. The ends of the warp formed the fringe at the bottom of the blanket.

The small face in the center of the blanket shown here represents the body of a large stylized creature, perhaps a sea bear (a fur seal) or a standing eagle. Above the body are the creature's large eyes; below it and to the sides are its legs and claws. Characteristic of Northwest painting and weaving, the images are composed of two basic elements: the **ovoid**, a slightly bent rectangle with rounded corners, and the **formline**, a continuous, shape-defining line. Here, subtly swelling black formlines define shapes with gentle curves, ovoids, and rectangular C shapes. When the blanket was worn, its two-dimensional shapes would have become three-dimensional, with the dramatic central figure curving over the wearer's back and the intricate side panels crossing over his shoulders and chest.

MASKS. Many Native American cultures stage ritual dance ceremonies to call upon guardian spirits. The participants in Northwest Coast dance ceremonies wore elaborate costumes and striking carved and painted wooden masks. Among the most elaborate masks were those used by the Kwakwaka'wakw in their Winter Ceremony, in which they initiated members into the shamanistic Hamatsa society (see "Hamatsa Masks," page 888). The dance reenacted the taming of Hamatsa, a cannibal spirit, and his three attendant bird spirits. Magnificent carved and painted masks transformed the dancers into Hamatsa and the bird attendants who searched for victims to eat. Strings allowed the dancers to manipulate the masks so that the beaks opened and snapped shut with spectacular effect. Isolated in museums as "art," the masks doubtless lose some of the shocking vivacity they have in performance; nevertheless their bold forms and color schemes retain power and meaning that can be activated by the viewer's imagination.

The Southwest

The Native American peoples of the southwestern United States include, among others, the Pueblo (sedentary village-dwelling groups) and the Navajo. The Pueblo groups are heirs of the Ancestral Puebloans (Anasazi) and Hohokam cultures, which developed a fully settled, agricultural way of life

around 700. Earlier societies had developed agriculture in the Southwest as early as 3500 BCE. The Ancestral Puebloans built apartmentlike villages and cliff dwellings whose ruins are found throughout the Four Corners region (New Mexico, Colorado, northern Arizona, and Utah) of the American Southwest. The Navajo, who arrived in the region sometime during the eleventh century or even later, developed a semi-sedentary way of life based on agriculture and (after the introduction of sheep by the Spanish) sheepherding. Being

26–16 | **CHILKAT BLANKET**
Tlingit people. Before 1928. Mountain-goat wool and shredded cedar bark, 55⅛ × 63¾" (140 × 162 cm). American Museum of Natural History, New York.

THE ⬤BJECT SPEAKS

HAMATSA MASKS

During the harsh winter season, when spirits are thought to be most powerful, many northern people seek spiritual renewal through their ancient rituals—including the potlatch, or ceremonial gift giving, and the initiation of new members into the prestigious Hamatsa Society. With snapping beaks and cries of "Hap! Hap! Hap!" ("Eat! Eat! Eat!"), Hamatsa, the people-eating spirit of the north, and his three assistants—horrible masked monster birds—begin their wild, ritual dance. The dancing birds threaten and even attack the Kwakwaka'wakw people who gather for the Winter Ceremony.

In the Winter Ceremony, youths are captured, taught the Hamatsa lore and rituals, and then in a spectacular theater-dance performance are "tamed" and brought back into civilized life. All the members of the community, including singers, gather in the main room of the great house, which is divided by a painted screen (SEE FIG. 26–15). The audience members fully participate in the performance; in early times, they brought containers of blood so that when the bird-dancers attacked them, they could appear to bleed and have flesh torn away.

Whistles from behind the screen announce the arrival of the Hamatsa (danced by an initiate), who enters through the central hole in the screen in a flesh-craving frenzy. Wearing hemlock, a symbol of the spirit world, he crouches and dances wildly with outstretched arms as attendants try to control him. He disappears but returns again, now wearing red cedar and dancing upright. Finally tamed, a full member of society, he even dances with the women.

Then the masked bird-dancers appear—first Raven-of-the-North-End-of-the-World, then Crooked-Beak-of-the-End-of-the-World, and finally the untranslatable Huxshukw, who cracks open skulls with his beak and eats the brains of his victims. Snapping their beaks, these masters of illusion enter the room backward, their masks pointed up as though the birds are looking skyward. They move slowly counterclockwise around the floor. At each change in the music they crouch, snap their beaks, and let out their wild cries of "Hap! Hap! Hap!" Essential to the ritual dances are the huge carved and painted wooden masks, articulated and operated by strings worked by the dancers. Among the finest masks are those by Willie Seaweed (1873–1967), a Kwakwaka'wakw chief, whose brilliant colors and exuberantly decorative carving style determined the direction of twentieth-century Kwakwaka'wakw sculpture.

The Canadian government, abetted by missionaries, outlawed the Winter Ceremony and potlatches in 1885, claiming the event was injurious to health, encouraged prostitution, endangered children's education, damaged the economy, and was cannibalistic. But the Kwakwaka'wakw refused to give up their "oldest and best" festival—one that spoke powerfully to them in many ways, establishing social rank and playing an important role in arranging marriages. By 1936, the government and the missionaries, who called the Kwakwaka'wakw "incorrigible," gave up. But not until 1951 could the Kwakwaka'wakw people gather openly for winter ceremonies, including the initiation rites of the Hamatsa Society.

Edward S. Curtis HAMATSA DANCERS, KWAKWAKA'WAKW
Canada. Photographed 1914. Smithsonian Institution Libraries, Washington, D.C.

The photographer Edward S. Curtis (1868–1952) devoted thirty years to documenting the lives of Native Americans. This photograph shows participants in a film he made about the Kwakwaka'wakw. For the film, his Native American assistant, Richard Hunt, borrowed family heirlooms and commissioned many new pieces from the finest Kwakwaka'wakw artists. Most of the pieces are now in museum collections. The photograph shows carved and painted posts, masked dancers (including those representing people-eating birds), a chief at the left (holding a speaker's staff and wearing a cedar neck ring), and spectators at the right.

Attributed to Willie Seaweed
KWAKWAKA'WAKW BIRD MASK
Alert Bay, Vancouver Island, Canada. Prior to 1951. Cedar wood, cedar bark, feathers, and fiber, 10 × 72 × 15" (25.4 × 183 × 38.1 cm). Collection of the Museum of Anthropology, Vancouver, Canada.
(A6120)

The name "Seaweed" is an anglicization of the Kwakwaka'wakw name *Siwid,* meaning "Paddling Canoe," "Recipient of Paddling," or "Paddled To"—referring to a great chief to whose potlatches guests paddled from afar. Willie Seaweed was not only the chief of his clan, but a great orator, singer, and tribal historian who kept the tradition of the potlatch alive during years of government repression.

26–17 | Laura Gilpin **TAOS PUEBLO**
Tewa. Taos, New Mexico. Photographed 1947. Amon Carter
Museum, Fort Worth, Texas.

© 1979 Laura Gilpin Collection (neg. # 2528.1)

Laura Gilpin, photographer of the landscape, architecture, and people of the American Southwest, began her series on the Pueblos and
Navajos in the 1930s. She published her work in four volumes of
photographs between 1941 and 1968.

among the very few Native American tribal groups whose
reservations are located on their actual ancestral homelands,
both groups have managed to maintain the continuity of
their traditions despite Euro-American pressure. Today, their
arts reflect the adaptation of traditional forms to new tech-
nologies, new mediums, and the influences of the dominant
American culture that surrounds them.

THE PUEBLOS. Some Pueblo villages, like those of their
ancient ancestors, consist of multistoried dwellings of considerable architectural interest to today's environmentalists. One
of these, **TAOS PUEBLO**, shown here in a photograph taken in
1947 by the American photographer of the Southwest, Laura
Gilpin (1891–1979), is located in north-central New Mexico
(**FIG. 26–17**). The northernmost of the surviving Pueblo
communities, Taos once served as a trading center between
Plains and Pueblo peoples. Taos burned in 1690 but was
rebuilt about 1700 and has often been modified since. "Great
Houses" (multifamily dwellings) stand on either side of Taos
Creek. Bordering on a plaza that opens toward the neighboring mountains, they rise in a stepped fashion to provide a
series of roof terraces that can serve as viewing platforms. The
plaza and roof terraces are centers of communal life and ceremony, as can be seen in Pablita Velarde's painting of the winter solstice celebrations (SEE FIG. 26–19).

CERAMICS. Pottery traditionally was a woman's art among
Pueblo peoples. Wares were made by coiling and other hand-
building techniques, and then fired at low temperature in
wood bonfires. The best-known twentieth-century Pueblo
potter was Maria Montoya Martinez (1887–1980) of San
Ildefonso Pueblo in New Mexico. Inspired by prehistoric
blackware pottery that was unearthed at nearby archaeological excavations, she and her husband, Julian Martinez
(1885–1943), developed a distinctive ceramics style decorated
with matte (dull, nongloss) black forms on a lustrous black
background (**FIG. 26–18**). Maria made pots covered with a
slip that was then burnished. Using additional slip, Julian

26–18 | Maria Montoya Martinez and
Julian Martinez **BLACKWARE STORAGE JAR**
San Ildefonso Pueblo, New Mexico. c. 1942.
Ceramic, height 18¾" (47.6 cm), diameter
22½" (57.1 cm). Museum of Indian Arts and
Culture/Laboratory of Anthropology,
Museum of New Mexico, Santa Fe.

Art and Its Context
NAVAJO NIGHT CHANT

This chant accompanies the creation of a sand painting during a Navajo curing ceremony. It is sung toward the end of the ceremony and indicates the restoration of inner harmony and balance.

> In beauty (happily) I walk.
> With beauty before me I walk.
> With beauty behind me I walk.
> With beauty below me I walk.
> With beauty above me I walk.
> With beauty all around me I walk.
> It is finished (again) in beauty.
> It is finished in beauty.

(Cited in Washington Mathews, *American Museum of Natural History Memoir, no. 6*. New York, 1902, page 145.)

painted the pots with designs that interpreted traditional Pueblo imagery in the then fashionable Art Deco style. After firing, the burnished ground became a lustrous black and the slip painting retained a matte surface. By the 1930s, production of blackware in San Ildefonso had become a communal enterprise. Family members and friends all worked making pots, and Maria signed all the pieces so that, in typical pueblo communal solidarity, everyone profited from the art market.

THE SANTA FE INDIAN SCHOOL. In the 1930s Anglo-American art teachers and dealers worked with Native Americans of the Southwest to create a distinctive, stereotypical "Indian" style in several mediums—including jewelry, pottery, weaving, and painting—to appeal to tourists and collectors. A leader in this effort was Dorothy Dunn (1903–91), who taught painting in the Santa Fe Indian School, an off-reservation government boarding school in New Mexico, from 1932 to 1937. Dunn inspired her students to create a painting style that combined the outline drawing and flat colors of folk art, the decorative qualities of Art Deco, and "Indian" subject matter. She and her students formed the Studio School. Restrictive as the school was, Dunn's success made painting a viable occupation for young Native American artists.

Pablita Velarde (1918–2006), from Santa Clara Pueblo in New Mexico and a 1936 graduate of Dorothy Dunn's school, was only a teenager when one of her paintings was selected for exhibition at the Chicago World's Fair in 1933. Thereafter, Velarde began to document Pueblo ways of life in a large series of murals for Bandelier National Monument. **KOSHARES OF TAOS** (FIG. 26–19) illustrates a moment during a ceremony celebrating the winter solstice when koshares, or clowns, take over the plaza from the Katsinas. Katsinas—the supernatural counterparts of animals, natural phenomena like clouds, and geological features like mountains—are central to traditional Pueblo religion. Katsinas manifest themselves in the human dancers who impersonate them during the winter

solstice ceremony, as well as in the small figures known as Katsina dolls that are given to children as educational aids in learning to identify the masks. Velarde's painting combines bold, flat colors and a simplified decorative line with European perspective. Her paintings, with their Art Deco abstraction, influenced the popular idea of the Indian style in art.

THE NAVAJOS. Navajo women are renowned for their skill as weavers. According to Navajo mythology, the universe itself is a weaving, its fibers spun by Spider Woman out of sacred cosmic materials. Spider Woman taught the art of weaving to Changing Woman (a Mother Earth figure who changes through the seasons), and she in turn taught it to Navajo women. The earliest Navajo blankets have simple horizontal stripes, like those of their Pueblo neighbors, and are limited to the white, black, and brown colors of natural sheep's wool. Over time, the weavers developed finer techniques and introduced more intricate patterns. In the mid-nineteenth century, they began unraveling the colored fibers from commercially manufactured and dyed blankets and reusing the yarn in their own work. By 1870–90 they were weaving spectacular blankets that were valued as prestige items among the Plains peoples as well as Euro-American collectors.

SAND PAINTING. Another traditional Navajo art, sand painting, is the exclusive province of men. Sand paintings are made to the accompaniment of chants by shaman-singers in the course of healing and blessing ceremonies, and they have great sacred significance (see "Navajo Night Chant," above). The paintings depict mythic heroes and events; and as ritual art, they follow prescribed rules and patterns that ensure their power. To make them, the singer dribbles pulverized colored stones, pollen, flowers, and other natural colors over a hide or sand ground. The rituals are intended to cure by restoring harmony to the world. The paintings are not meant to be seen by the public and certainly not to be displayed in

26–19 | Pablita Velarde **KOSHARES OF TAOS**
Santa Clara Pueblo, New Mexico. 1946–47. Watercolor on paper, 13⅞ × 22⅞" (35.3 × 56.9 cm). Philbrook
Museum of Art, Tulsa, Oklahoma.
Museum Purchase (1947.37)

museums. They are meant to be destroyed by nightfall of the day on which they are made.

In 1919 a respected shaman-singer named Hosteen Klah (1867–1937) began to incorporate sand-painting images into weaving, breaking with the traditional prohibitions. Many Navajos took offense at Klah both for recording the sacred images and for doing so in what was traditionally a woman's art form. Klah had learned to weave from his mother and sister. The Navajo traditionally recognize at least three genders and perhaps as many as five or more; Hosteen Klah was a *nadle*, or Navajo third-gender. Hence, he could learn both female and male arts; that is, he was trained both to weave and to heal. Hosteen Klah was not breaking artistic barriers in a conventional sense, but rather exemplifying the complexities of the traditional Navajo gender system. Klah's work was ultimately accepted because of his great skill and prestige.

The **WHIRLING LOG CEREMONY** sand painting, woven into tapestry (FIG. 26–20), depicts part of the Navajo creation myth. The Holy People create the Earth's Surface and divide it into four parts. They create humans, and bring forth corn, beans, squash, and tobacco—the four sacred plants. A male-female pair of humans and one of the sacred plants stands in each of the four quarters, defined by the central cross. The four Holy People (the tall sticklike figures) surround the

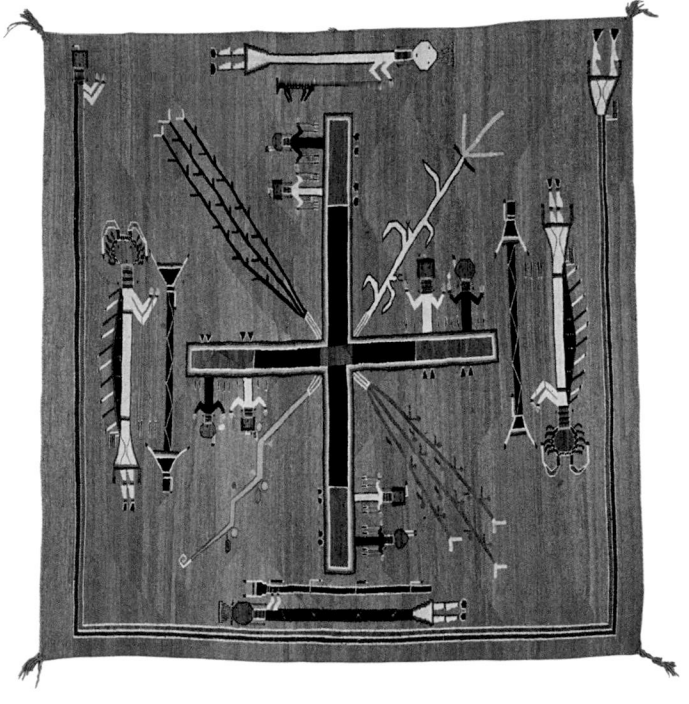

26–20 | Hosteen Klah **WHIRLING LOG CEREMONY**
Sand painting; tapestry by Mrs. Sam Manuelito. Navajo, c. 1925. Wool, 5'5" × 5'10" (1.69 × 1.82 m). Heard Museum, Phoenix, Arizona.

26–21 | Bill Reid **THE SPIRIT OF HAIDA GWAII**
Haida, 1991. Bronze, approx. 13 × 20′ (4 × 6 m). Canadian Embassy, Washington, D.C.

image, and the guardian figure of Rainbow Maiden frames the scene on three sides. Since the open side represents the east, her head is in the northeast corner and her feet are in the southeast. Like all Navajo artists, Hosteen Klah hoped that the excellence of the work would make it pleasing to the spirits. Recently shaman-singers have made permanent sand paintings on boards for sale, but they usually introduce slight errors in them to render the paintings ceremonially harmless.

A NEW BEGINNING

The Institute of American Indian Arts (IAIA), founded in 1962 in Santa Fe and attended by Native American students from all over North America, supports Native American aspirations in the arts today just as Dorothy Dunn's Studio School had in the 1930s. Staffed by major Native American artists, the school encourages the incorporation of indigenous ideals in the arts without creating an official "style." As alumni achieved distinction and the IAIA museum in Santa Fe established a reputation for excellence, the institute has led Native American art into the mainstream of contemporary art (see Chapter 31).

Other artists, such as the Canadian Haida artist Bill Reid (1920–98), have sought to sustain and revitalize traditional art in their work. For example, trained as a woodcarver, painter, and jeweler, Reid revived the art of carving totem poles and dugout canoes in the Haida homeland of Haida Gwaii—"Islands of the People"—known on maps today as the Queen Charlotte Islands. Late in life he began to create large-scale sculpture in bronze. With their black patina, these works recall traditional Haida carvings in shiny black argillite.

An imposing piece, Reid's **THE SPIRIT OF HAIDA GWAII** now stands outside the Canadian Embassy in Washington, D.C. (**FIG. 26–21**). This sculpture, which Reid viewed as a metaphor for modern Canada's multicultural society, depicts a boatload of figures from the natural and mythic worlds struggling to paddle forward.

The dominant figure is a shaman in a spruce-root basket hat and Chilkat blanket holding a speaker's pole. On the prow, the place reserved for the chief in a war canoe, sits the Bear. He faces backward rather than forward, and is bitten by an Eagle, with formline-patterned wings. The Eagle, in turn, is bitten by the Seawolf. The Eagle and the Seawolf, together with the man behind them, nevertheless continue paddling.

At the stern, steering the canoe, is the Raven, the trickster in Haida mythology. The Raven is assisted by Mousewoman, the traditional guide and escort of humans in the spirit realms. According to Reid, the work represents a "mythological and environmental lifeboat," where "the entire family of living things . . . whatever their differences, . . . are paddling together in one boat, headed in one direction."

THE NATIONAL MUSEUM OF THE AMERICAN INDIAN. In 1989 Congress established the National Museum of the American Indian within the Smithsonian Institution. After many years of discussion and negotiation, the art of indigenous peoples is finally achieving full recognition by the museum establishment. Championed by curator/collectors such as Ralph T. Coe, exhibitions of contemporary as well as traditional Native American arts are held in major American and European museums. In September of 2004, the **NATIONAL MUSEUM OF THE AMERICAN INDIAN** finally opened on the Mall in Washington, D.C., directly below Capitol Hill and across from the National Gallery of Art (FIG. 26–22).

Inspired by the colors, textures, and forms of the American Southwest, the museum building establishes a new presence of Native Americans on the Mall. Symbolizing the Native ethic of environmental concern, the National Museum of the American Indian is surrounded by boulders ("Grandfather Rocks"), water, and plantings that recall the varied landscapes of North America, including wetlands, meadows, forest, and traditional cropland with corn, squash, and tomatoes. These are not gardens; rather they are intended to evoke indigenous environments. The entrance to the museum on the east side faces the morning sun and recalls the orientation of prairie tepees. Inside the building a Sun Marker of stained glass in the south wall throws its dagger of light across the vast atrium as the day progresses. Once again the great spirits of Earth and sky take form in a creation of the art of the Americas.

IN PERSPECTIVE

After 1492, the arrival of Europeans completely altered the destiny of the Americas. In Mesoamerica and South America the break with the past was sudden and violent; in North America the change took place more gradually, but the outcome was much the same. In both North and South America, natives succumbed to European disease to which they had no immunity, especially smallpox, leading to massive population loss and social disruption. Many present-day Native American ethnic groups, however, were formed by combinations of various survivor groups.

In the south, the Spanish came as conquerors to exploit the wealth of the New World. Aztecs, Incas, and others, who were heirs to long-established building traditions, had built huge ceremonial complexes and housing for substantial

Defining Art
CRAFT OR ART?

In many world cultures, the distinction between "fine art" and "craft" does not exist. The traditional Western academic hierarchy of materials—in which marble, bronze, oil, and fresco are valued more than terra cotta and watercolor—and the equally artificial hierarchy of subjects—in which history painting, including religious history, stands supreme—are irrelevant to non-Western art.

The indigenous peoples of the Americas did not produce objects as works of art. In their eyes all pieces were utilitarian objects, adorned in ways necessary for their intended purposes. A work was valued for its effectiveness and for the role it played in society. Some, like a Sioux baby carrier (SEE FIG. 26–11), enrich mundane life with their aesthetic qualities. Others, such as Pomo baskets (see "Basketry," page 882), commemorate important events. The function of an Inca tunic may have been to identify or confer status on its owner or user through its material value or symbolic associations. And as with art in all cultures, many pieces have had great spiritual or magical power. Such works of art cannot be fully comprehended or appreciated when they are seen only on pedestals or encased in glass boxes in museums or galleries. They must be imagined, or better yet seen, as acting in their societies. How powerfully might our minds and emotions be engaged if we saw Kwakwaka'wakw (Kwakiutl) masks functioning in religious drama, changing not only the outward appearance, but also the very essence of the individual.

At the beginning of the twentieth century, European and American artists broke away from the academic bias that extolled the classical heritage of Greece and Rome. They found new inspiration in the art—or craft, if you will—of many different non-European cultures. Artists explored a new freedom to use absolutely any material or technique that effectively challenged outmoded assumptions and opened the way for a free and unfettered delight in, and understanding of, Native American art as well as the art of other non-Western cultures. The intellectual community as well as collectors, dealers, and critics have come to appreciate the non-Western aesthetics and to treasure forgotten and ignored arts on their own terms. And the more recent twentieth- and twenty-first-centuries conception of art as a multimedia adventure has helped validate works of art once seen only in ethnographic collections and in the homes of private collectors. Today objects once called "primitive" are recognized as great works of art and acknowledged to be an essential dimension of a twenty-first-century worldview. The line between "art" and "craft" seems more artificial and less relevant than ever before.

26–22 | **NATIONAL MUSEUM OF THE AMERICAN INDIAN**
The Smithsonian Institution, Washington, D.C. Opened September, 2004. Architectural design: GBQC in association with Douglas Cardinal (Blackfoot). Architectural consultants: Johnpaul Jones (Cherokee-Choctaw) and Ramona Sakiestewa (Hopi). Landscape consultant: Donna House (Navajo-Oneida), ethno-botanist.

populations in cities. They had also performed feats of engineering in road networks and in drainage and irrigation works. Their monumental sculpture in stone and ceramic survived the Spanish onslaught, as did some examples of their magnificent textiles, but their plentiful objects in silver and gold were almost all melted down and carted off. Some traditional arts, especially in weaving and pottery, continue to the present day.

In North America, the Europeans came not as military men seeking riches to plunder, but as families seeking land to farm. Unlike the Spaniards, they found no large cities with urban populations to resist them. However, although they imagined that the lands they settled were an untended wilderness, in fact nearly all of North America was populated and possessed by indigenous peoples. Over the next 400

years, by means of violence, bribery, and treaties, the English colonies and, in turn, the United States displaced nearly all Native Americans from their ancestral homelands. What indigenous art Euro-Americans encountered they viewed as a curiosity, not art.

During the past century, the indigenous arts of the Americas have undergone a reevaluation that has renewed the conception of what constitutes "American art," especially as diverse artists continue to revive indigenous traditions, revisit native outlooks, and restate ancient truths in new ways. After being pushed to the brink of extinction, Native American cultures are now experiencing a revival in both North and South America, as Native Americans assert themselves politically, and as Euro-Americans come to appreciate the connections between native history and the land.

AZTEC, A VIEW OF THE WORLD
PAGE FROM *CODEX FEJERVARY-MAYER*
c.1400–1519/21

**AZTEC, FEATHER HEADDRESS
OF MONTEZUMA**
BEFORE 1519

INCA, MACCHU-PICCHU
PERU
450–1530

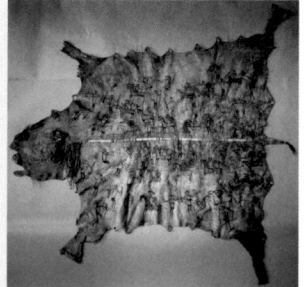

BATTLE-SCENE, HIDE PAINTING
MANDAN, NORTH DAKOTA
1797–1800

SHOULDER BAG
DELAWARE, KANSAS
c.1860

HAIDA, BILL REID
THE SPIRIT OF HAIDA GWAII
1991

ART OF THE
AMERICAS
AFTER 1300

1300

◄ **Eastern Woodlands Culture**
c. 1300

1400

◄ **Aztec Empire at Its Height**
c. 1400–1519/21

◄ **Inca Empire at Its Height**
c. 1438–1532

1500

◄ **Cortés Conquers Aztec Empire**
c. 1519–24

◄ **Pizarro Conquers Inca Empire**
c. 1532

1600

1700 ◄ **Plains Nomadic Culture** 1700–1870

1800

◄ **Louisiana Purchase** 1803

◄ **Transcontinental Railway Complete**
1869

◄ **Winter Ceremony Outlawed**
1885–1951

1900

2000

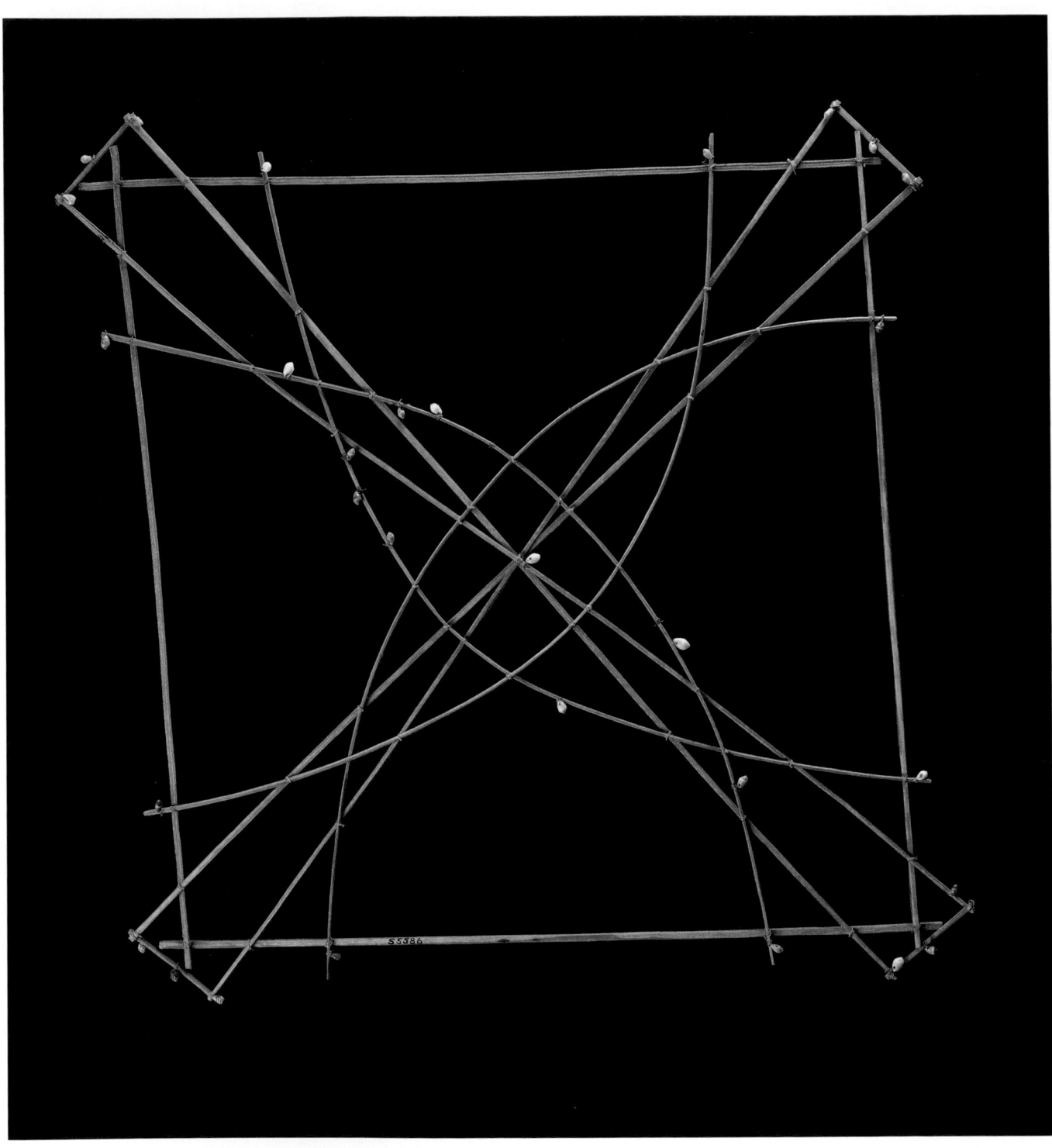

27–1 | *WAPEPE* **NAVIGATION CHART**   Marshall Islands, Micronesia. 19th century. Sticks, coconut fiber, shells. 29½ × 29½″ (75 × 75 cm).

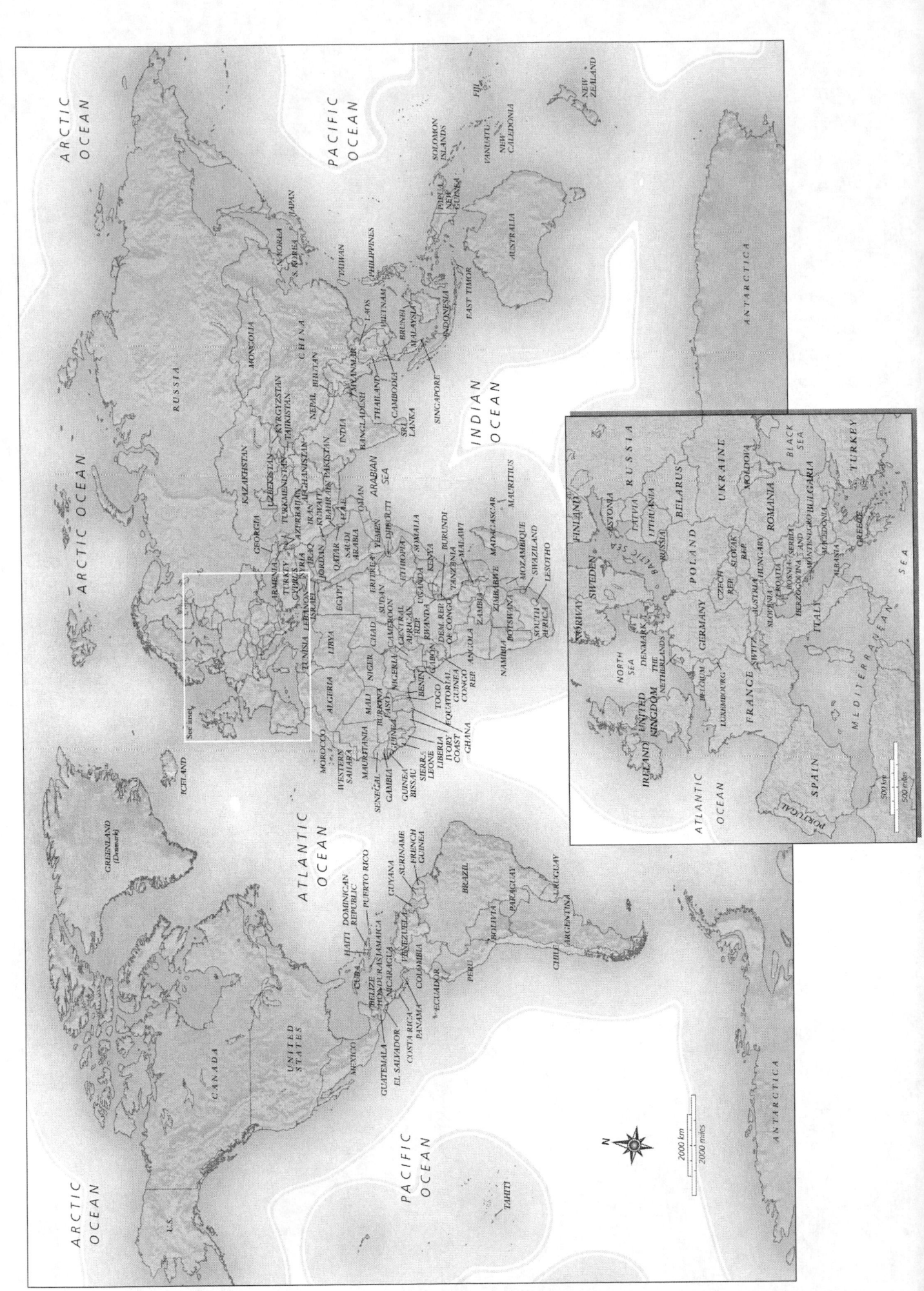

GLOSSARY

abacus The flat slab at the top of a **capital**, directly under the **entablature**.

absolute dating A method of assigning a precise historical date to periods and objects based on known and recorded events in the region as well as technically extracted physical evidence (such as carbon-14 disintegration). See also **radiometric dating, relative dating**.

abstract, abstraction Any art that does not represent observable aspects of nature or transforms visible forms into a stylized image. Also: the formal qualities of this process.

acropolis The **citadel** of an ancient Greek city, located at its highest point and housing temples, a treasury, and sometimes a royal palace. The most famous is the Acropolis in Athens.

acroterion (acroteria) An ornament at the corner or peak of a roof.

adobe Sun-baked blocks made of clay mixed with straw. Also: the buildings made with this material.

adyton The back room of a Greek temple. At Delphi, the place where the **oracles** were delivered. More generally, a very private space or room.

aedicula (aediculae) A decorative architectural frame, usually found around a niche, door, or window. An aedicula is made up of a **pediment** and **entablature** supported by **columns** or **pilasters**.

agora An open space in a Greek town used as a central gathering place or market. See also forum.

aisle Passage or open corridor of a church, hall, or other building that parallels the main space, usually on both sides, and is delineated by a row, or **arcade**, of **columns** or piers. Called side aisles when they flank the **nave** of a church.

album A book consisting of a series of paintings or prints (album leaves) mounted into book form.

all'antica Meaning, "in the ancient manner."

allegory In a work of art, an image (or images) that symbolically illustrates an idea, concept, or principle, often moral or religious.

alloy A mixture of metals; different metals melted together.

amalaka In Hindu architecture, the circular or square-shaped element on top of a spire (*shikhara*), often crowned with a **finial**, symbolizing the cosmos.

ambulatory The passage (walkway) around the **apse** in a basilican church or around the **central space in a central-plan building**.

amphiprostyle Term describing a building, usually a temple, with **porticoes** at each end but without **columns** along the other two sides.

amphora An ancient Greek jar for storing oil or wine, with an egg-shaped body and two curved handles.

aniconic A symbolic representation without images of human figures, very often found in Islamic art.

animal interlace Decoration made of interwoven animals or serpents, often found in Celtic and early medieval Northern European art.

ankh A looped cross signifying life, used by ancient Egyptians.

appropriation Term used to describe an artist's practice of borrowing from another source for a new work of art. While in previous centuries artists often copied one another's figures, motifs, or compositions, in modern times the sources for appropriation extend from material culture to works of art.

apse, apsidal A large semicircular or polygonal (and usually vaulted) niche protruding from the end wall of a building. In the Christian church, it contains the altar. Apsidal is an adjective describing the condition of having such a space.

arabesque A type of linear surface decoration based on foliage and **calligraphic** forms, usually characterized by flowing lines and swirling shapes.

arcade A series of **arches**, carried by **columns** or **piers** and supporting a common wall or lintel. In a blind arcade, the arches and supports are engaged (attached to the wall) and have a decorative function.

arch In architecture, a curved structural element that spans an open space. Built from wedge-shaped stone blocks called **voussoirs**, which, when placed together and held at the top by a trapezoidal **keystone**, form an effective space-spanning and weight-bearing unit. Requires buttresses at each side to contain the outward thrust caused by the weight of the structure. **Corbel** arch: arch or **vault** formed by **courses** of stones, each of which projects beyond the lower course until the space is enclosed; usually finished with a **capstone**. Horseshoe arch: an arch of more than a half-circle; typical of western Islamic architecture. Ogival arch: a pointed arch created by S curves. Relieving arch: an arch built into a heavy wall just above a post-and-lintel structure (such as a gate, door, or window) to help support the wall above by transferring the load to the side walls.

archaic smile The curved lips of an ancient Greek statue, usually interpreted as an attempt to animate the features.

architrave The bottom element in an **entablature**, beneath the **frieze** and the **cornice**.

art brut French for "raw art." Term introduced by Jean Dubuffet to denote the often vividly **expressionistic** art of children and the insane, which he considered uncontaminated by culture.

articulated Joined; divided into units; in architecture, divided into parts to make spatial organization intelligible.

ashlar A highly finished, precisely cut block of stone. When laid in even **courses**, ashlar masonry creates a uniform face with fine joints. Often used as a facing on the visible exterior of a building, especially as a veneer for the **façade**. Also called **dressed stone**.

assemblage Artwork created by gathering and manipulating two and/or three-dimensional found objects.

astragal A thin convex decorative **molding**, often found on classical **entablatures**, and usually decorated with a continuous row of beadlike circles.

atelier The studio or workshop of a master artist or craftsperson, often including junior associates and apprentices.

atmospheric perspective See **perspective**.

atrial cross The cross placed in the atrium of a church. In Colonial America, used to mark a gathering and teaching place.

atrium An unroofed interior courtyard or room in a Roman house, sometimes having a pool or garden, sometimes surrounded by columns. Also: the open courtyard in front of a Christian church; or an entrance area in modern architecture.

automatism A technique whereby the usual intellectual control of the artist over his or her brush or pencil is foregone. The artist's aim is to allow the subconscious to create the artwork without rational interference.

avant-garde Term derived from the French military word meaning "before the group," or "vanguard." Avant-garde denotes those artists or concepts of a strikingly new, experimental, or radical nature for the time.

axis mundi A concept of an "axis of the world," which marks sacred sites and denotes a link between the human and celestial realms. For example, in Buddhist art, the axis mundi can be marked by monumental freestanding decorative pillars.

baldachin A canopy (whether suspended from the ceiling, projecting from a wall, or supported by columns) placed over an honorific or sacred space such as a throne or church altar.

bargeboards Boards covering the rafters at the gable end of a building; bargeboards are often carved or painted.

barrel vault See **vault**.

bar tracery See **tracery**.

bas-de-page French: bottom of the page; a term used in manuscript studies to indicate pictures below the text, literally at the bottom of the page.

base Any support. Also: masonry supporting a statue or the **shaft** of a **column**.

basilica A large rectangular building. Often built with a **clerestory**, side **aisles** separated from the center **nave** by **colonnades**, and an **apse** at one or both ends. Roman centers for administration, later adapted to Christian church use. Constantine's architects added a transverse aisle at the end of the nave called a **transept**.

bay A unit of space defined by architectural elements such as **columns**, **piers**, and walls.

beehive tomb A **corbel-vaulted** tomb, conical in shape like a beehive, and covered by an earthen mound.

Benday dots In modern printing and typesetting, the individual dots that, together with many others, make up lettering and images. Often machine- or computer-generated, the dots are very small and closely spaced to give the effect of density and richness of tone.

bestiary A book describing characteristics, uses, and meaning illustrated by moralizing tales about real and imaginary animals, especially popular during the Middle Ages in western Europe.

bi A jade disk with a hole in the center.

biomorphic Adjective used to describe forms that resemble or suggest shapes found in nature.

black-figure A style or technique of ancient Greek pottery in which black figures are painted on a red clay ground. See also **red-figure**.

bodhisattva   In Buddhism, a being who has attained enlightenment but chooses to remain in this world in order to help others advance spiritually. Also defined as a potential Buddha.

boss   A decorative knoblike element. Bosses can be found in many places, such as at the intersection of a Gothic vault rib. Also buttonlike projections in decorations and metalwork.

bracket, bracketing   An architectural element that projects from a wall to support a horizontal part of a building, such as beams or the eaves of a roof.

brandea   An object, such as a linen strip, having contact with a relic and taking on the power of the relic.

buon fresco   *See* **fresco**.

cairn   A pile of stones or earth and stones that served both as a prehistoric burial site and as a marker of underground tombs.

calligraphy   Handwriting as an art form.

calyx krater   *See* **krater**.

came (cames)   A lead strip used in the making of leaded or **stained-glass** windows. Cames have an indented vertical groove on the sides into which the separate pieces of glass are fitted to hold the design together.

cameo   Gemstone, clay, glass, or shell having layers of color, carved in **low relief** to create an image and ground of different colors.

camera obscura   An early cameralike device used in the Renaissance and later for recording images of nature. Made from a dark box (or room) with a hole in one side (sometimes fitted with a lens), the camera obscura operates when bright light shines through the hole, casting an upside-down image of an object outside onto the inside wall of the box.

canon of proportions   A set of ideal mathematical ratios in art based on measurements of the human body.

capital   The sculpted block that tops a **column**. According to the conventions of the orders, capitals include different decorative elements. See **order**. Also: a historiated capital is one displaying a narrative.

capriccio   A painting or print of a fantastic, imaginary landscape, usually with architecture.

capstone   The final, topmost stone in a **corbel arch** or vault, which joins the sides and completes the structure.

cartoon   A full-scale drawing used to transfer the outline of a design onto a surface (such as a wall, canvas, panel, or tapestry) to be painted, carved, or woven.

cartouche   A frame for a **hieroglyphic** inscription formed by a rope design surrounding an oval space. Used to signify a sacred or honored name. Also: in architecture, a decorative device or plaque, usually with a plain center used for inscriptions or epitaphs.

caryatid   A sculpture of a draped female figure acting as a column supporting an **entablature**.

catacomb   A subterranean burial ground consisting of tunnels on different levels, having niches for urns and **sarcophagi** and often incorporating rooms (cubiculae).

celadon   A high-fired, transparent **glaze** of pale bluish-green hue whose principal coloring agent is an oxide of iron. In China and Korea, such glazes typically were applied over a pale gray **stoneware** body, though Chinese potters sometimes applied them over **porcelain** bodies during the Ming (1368-1644) and Qing (1644-1911) dynasties. Chinese potters invented celadon glazes and initiated the continuous production of celadon-glazed wares as early as the third century CE.

cella   The principal interior room at the center of a Greek or Roman temple within which the cult statue was usually housed. Also called the **naos**.

cenotaph   A funerary monument commemorating an individual or group buried elsewhere.

centering   A temporary structure that supports a masonry **arch** and **vault** or **dome** during construction until the mortar is fully dried and the masonry is self-sustaining.

centrally planned building   Any structure designed with a primary central space surrounded by symmetrical areas on each side. For example, **Greek-cross plan** (equal-armed cross).

ceramics   A general term covering all types of wares made from fired clay, including **porcelain** and **terra cotta**.

chaitya   A type of Buddhist temple found in India. Built in the form of a hall or **basilica**, a chaitya hall is highly decorated with sculpture and usually is carved from a cave or natural rock location. It houses a sacred shrine or stupa for worship.

chamfer   The slanted surface produced when an angle is trimmed or beveled, common in building and metalwork.

chasing   Ornamentation made on metal by incising or hammering the surface.

chattri (chattris)   A decorative pavilion with an umbrella-shaped **dome** in Indian architecture.

chevron   A decorative or heraldic motif of repeated Vs; a zigzag pattern.

chiaroscuro   An Italian word designating the contrast of dark and light in a painting, drawing, or print. Chiaroscuro creates spatial depth and volumetric forms through gradations in the intensity of light and shadow.

chiton   A thin sleeveless garment, fastened at waist and shoulders, worn by men and women in ancient Greece.

citadel   A fortress or defended city, if possible placed in a high, commanding location.

clapboard   Horizontal overlapping planks used as protective siding for buildings, particularly houses in North America.

clerestory   The topmost zone of a wall with windows in a **basilica** extending above the **aisle** roofs. Provides direct light into the central interior space (the **nave**).

cloisonné   An enamel technique in which metal wire or strips are affixed to the surface to form the design. The resulting areas (cloisons) are filled with enamel (colored glass).

cloister   An open space, part of a monastery, surrounded by an **arcaded** or **colonnaded** walkway, often having a fountain and garden, and dedicated to nonliturgical activities and the secular life of the religious. Members of a cloistered order do not leave the monastery or interact with outsiders.

codex (codices)   A book, or a group of **manuscript** pages (folios), held together by stitching or other binding on one side.

coffer   A recessed decorative panel that is used to reduce the weight of and to decorate ceilings or **vaults**. The use of coffers is called coffering.

colonnade   A row of **columns**, supporting a straight lintel (as in a **porch** or **portico**) or a series of arches (an **arcade**).

colophon   The data placed at the end of a book listing the book's author, publisher, illuminator, and other information related to its production. Also, in East Asian handscrolls, the inscriptions which follow the painting are called colophons.

column   An architectural element used for support and/or decoration. Consists of a rounded or polygonal vertical **shaft** placed on a **base** and topped by a decorative **capital**. In classical architecture, built in accordance with the rules of one of the architectural **orders**. Columns can be free-standing or attached to a background wall (**engaged**).

complementary color   The primary and secondary colors across from each other on the color wheel (red and green, blue and orange, yellow and purple). When juxtaposed, the intensity of both colors increases. When mixed together, they negate each other to make a neutral gray-brown.

Composite order   *See* **order**.

cong   A square or octagonal jade tube with a cylindrical hole in the center. A symbol of the earth, it was used for ritual worship and astronomical observations in ancient China.

connoisseurship   A term derived from the French word connoisseur, meaning "an expert," and signifying the study and evaluation of art based primarily on formal, visual, and stylistic analysis. A connoisseur studies the style and technique of an object to deduce its relative quality and possible maker. This is done through visual association with other, similar objects and styles. See also **contextualism**; **formalism**.

contextualism   An interpretive approach in art history that focuses on the culture surrounding an art object. Unlike **connoisseurship**, contextualism utilizes the literature, history, economics, and social developments (among other things) of a period, as well as the object itself, to explain the meaning of an artwork. See *also* **connoisseurship**.

contrapposto   An Italian term meaning "set against," used to describe the twisted pose resulting from parts of the body set in opposition to each other around a central axis.

corbel, corbeling   An early roofing and **arching** technique in which each course of stone projects slightly beyond the previous layer (a corbel) until the uppermost corbels meet. Results in a high, almost pointed **arch** or **vault**. A corbel table is a ledge supported by corbels.

corbeled vault   *See* **vault**.

Corinthian order   *See* **order**.

cornice   The uppermost section of a Classical **entablature**. More generally, a horizontally projecting element found at the top of a building wall or **pedestal**. A raking cornice is formed by the junction of two slanted cornices, most often found in **pediments**.

course   A horizontal layer of stone used in building.

crenellation   Alternating high and low sections of a wall, giving a notched appearance and creating permanent defensive shields in the walls of fortified buildings.

crockets   A stylized leaf used as decoration along the outer angle of spires, pinnacles, gables, and around **capitals** in Gothic architecture.

cuneiform An early form of writing with wedge-shaped marks impressed into wet clay with a stylus, primarily used by ancient Mesopotamians.

curtain wall A wall in a building that does not support any of the weight of the structure. Also: the freestanding outer wall of a castle, usually encircling the inner bailey (yard) and keep (primary defensive tower).

cyclopean construction or **masonry** A method of building using huge blocks of rough-hewn stone. Any large-scale, monumental building project that impresses by sheer size. Named after the Cyclopes (sing. Cyclops) one-eyed giants of legendary strength in Greek myths.

cylinder seal A small cylindrical stone decorated with incised patterns. When rolled across soft clay or wax, the resulting raised pattern or design (**relief**) served in Mesopotamian and Indus Valley cultures as an identifying signature.

dado (dadoes) The lower part of a wall, differentiated in some way (by a **molding** or different coloring or paneling) from the upper section.

daguerreotype An early photographic process that makes a positive print on a light-sensitized copperplate; invented and marketed in 1839 by Louis-Jacques-Mandé Daguerre.

demotic writing The simplified form of ancient Egyptian hieratic writing, used primarily for administrative and private texts.

dharmachakra Sanskrit for "wheel" (*chakra*) and "law" or "doctrine" (*dharma*); often used in Buddhist iconography to signify the "wheel of the law."

diptych Two panels of equal size (usually decorated with paintings or reliefs) hinged together.

dogu Small human figurines made in Japan during the Jomon period. Shaped from clay, the figures have exaggerated expressions and are in contorted poses. They were probably used in religious rituals.

dolmen A prehistoric structure made up of two or more large upright stones supporting a large, flat, horizontal slab or slabs.

dome A round **vault**, usually over a circular space. Consists of a curved masonry vault of shapes and cross sections that can vary from hemispherical to bulbous to ovoidal. May use a supporting vertical wall (**drum**), from which the vault springs, and may be crowned by an open space (**oculus**) and/or an exterior **lantern**. When a dome is built over a square space, an intermediate element is required to make the transition to a circular drum. There are two types: A dome on **pendentives** (spherical triangles) incorporates **arched**, sloping intermediate sections of wall that carry the weight and thrust of the dome to heavily buttressed supporting **piers**. A dome on **squinches** uses an arch built into the wall (**squinch**) in the upper corners of the space to carry the weight of the dome across the corners of the square space below. A half-dome or conch may cover a semicircular space.

domino construction System of building construction introduced by the architect Le Corbusier in which reinforced concrete floor slabs are floated on six freestanding posts placed as if at the positions of the six dots on a domino playing piece.

Doric order See **order**.

dressed stone See **ashlar**.

drum The wall that supports a **dome**. Also: a segment of the circular **shaft** of a **column**.

drypoint An **intaglio** printmaking process by which a metal (usually copper) plate is directly inscribed with a pointed instrument (**stylus**). The resulting design of scratched lines is inked, wiped, and printed. Also: the print made by this process.

earthenware A low-fired, opaque **ceramic** ware that is fired in the range of 800 to 900 degrees Celsius. Earthenware employs humble clays that are naturally heat resistant; the finished wares remain porous after firing unless **glazed**. Earthenware occurs in a range of earth-toned colors, from white and tan to gray and black, with tan predominating.

echinus A cushionlike circular element found below the **abacus** of a Doric **capital**. Also: a similarly shaped **molding** (usually with egg-and-dart motifs) underneath the **volutes** of an Ionic **capital**.

electron spin resonance techniques Method that uses magnetic field and microwave irradiation to date material such as tooth enamel and its surrounding soil.

emblema (emblemata) In a mosaic, the elaborate central motif on a floor, usually a self-contained unit done in a more refined manner, with smaller **tesserae** of both marble and semiprecious stones.

encaustic A painting technique using pigments mixed with hot wax as a medium.

engaged column A **column** attached to a wall. See also column.

engraving An intaglio printmaking process of inscribing an image, design, or letters onto a metal or wood surface from which a print is made. An engraving is usually drawn with a sharp implement (burin) directly onto the surface of the plate. Also: the print made from this process.

entablature In the **Classical orders**, the horizontal elements above the **columns** and **capitals**. The entablature consists of, from bottom to top, an **architrave**, a **frieze**, and a **cornice**.

entasis A slight swelling of the **shaft** of a Greek column. The optical illusion of entasis makes the column appear from afar to be straight.

exedra (exedrae) In architecture, a semicircular niche. On a small scale, often used as decoration, whereas larger exedrae can form interior spaces (such as an **apse**).

expressionism, expressionistic Terms describing a work of art in which forms are created primarily to evoke subjective emotions rather than to portray objective reality.

façade The face or front wall of a building.

faience Type of **ceramic** covered with colorful, opaque glazes that form a smooth, impermeable surface. First developed in ancient Egypt.

fang ding A square or rectangular bronze vessel with four legs. The fang ding was used for ritual offerings in ancient China during the Shang dynasty.

fête galante A subject in painting depicting well-dressed people at leisure in a park or country setting. It is most often associated with eighteenth-century French Rococo painting.

filigree Delicate, lacelike ornamental work.

fillet The flat ridge between the carved out flutes of a **column shaft**. See also **fluting**.

finial A knoblike architectural decoration usually found at the top point of a spire, pinnacle, canopy, or gable. Also found on furniture; also the ornamental top of a staff.

fluting In architecture, evenly spaced, rounded parallel vertical grooves **incised** on **shafts** of **columns** or columnar elements (such as **pilasters**).

foreshortening The illusion created on a flat surface in which figures and objects appear to recede or project sharply into space. Accomplished according to the rules of **perspective**.

formal analysis See **formalism**.

formalism, formalist An approach to the understanding, appreciation, and valuation of art based almost solely on considerations of form. This approach tends to regard an artwork as independent of its time and place of making. See also **connoisseurship**.

four-iwan mosque See **iwan** and **mosque**.

fresco A painting technique in which waterbased pigments are applied to a surface of wet plaster (called **buon fresco**). The color is absorbed by the plaster, becoming a permanent part of the wall. **Fresco secco** is created by painting on dried plaster, and the color may flake off. Murals made by both these techniques are called frescoes.

fresco secco See **fresco**.

frieze The middle element of an **entablature**, between the **architrave** and the **cornice**. Usually decorated with sculpture, painting, or **moldings**. Also: any continuous flat band with **relief sculpture** or painted decorations.

frottage A design produced by laying a piece of paper over a textured surface and rubbing with charcoal or other soft medium.

fusuma Sliding doors covered with paper, used in traditional Japanese construction. Fusuma are often highly decorated with paintings and colored backgrounds.

galleria See **gallery**.

gallery In church architecture, the story found above the side **aisles** of a church, usually open to and overlooking the nave. Also: in secular architecture, a long room, usually above the ground floor in a private house or a public building used for entertaining, exhibiting pictures, or promenading. *Also*: a building or hall in which art is displayed or sold. Also: *galleria*.

garbhagriha From the Sanskrit word meaning "womb chamber," a small room or shrine in a Hindu temple containing a holy image.

genre A type or category of artistic form, subject, technique, style, or medium. See also genre painting.

gesso A ground made from glue, gypsum, and/or chalk forming the ground of a wood panel or the priming layer of a canvas. Provides a smooth surface for painting.

gilding The application of paper-thin **gold leaf** or gold pigment to an object made from another medium (for example, a sculpture or painting). Usually used as a decorative finishing detail.

giornata (giornate) Adopted from the Italian term meaning "a day's work," a giornata is the section of a **fresco** plastered and painted in a single day.

glaze See **glazing**.

glazing An outermost layer of vitreous liquid (**glaze**) that, upon firing, renders **ceramics** waterproof and forms a decorative surface. In painting, a technique particularly used with oil mediums in which a transparent layer of paint (**glaze**) is laid over another, usually lighter, painted or glazed area.

gloss A type of clay **slip** used in **ceramics** by ancient Greeks and Romans that, when fired, imparts a colorful sheen to the surface.

golf foil A thin sheet of gold.

gold leaf Paper-thin sheets of hammered gold that are used in **gilding**. In some cases (such as Byzantine **icons**), also used as a ground for paintings.

gopura The towering gateway to an Indian Hindu temple complex. A temple complex can have several different gopuras.

Grand Manner An elevated style of painting popular in the eighteenth century in which the artist looked to the ancients and to the Renaissance for inspiration; for portraits as well as history painting, the artist would adopt the poses, compositions, and attitudes of Renaissance and antique models.

Grand Tour Popular during the eighteenth and nineteenth centuries, an extended tour of cultural sites in southern Europe intended to finish the education of a young upper-class person from Britain or North America.

grattage A pattern created by scraping off layers of paint from a canvas laid over a textured surface. See also *frottage*.

Greek-cross plan See **centrally planned building**.

Greek-key pattern A continuous rectangular scroll often used as a decorative border. Also called a **meander pattern**.

grid A system of regularly spaced horizontally and vertically crossed lines that gives regularity to an architectural plan. Also: in painting, a grid enables designs to be enlarged or transferred easily.

grisaille A style of monochromatic painting in shades of gray. Also: a painting made in this style.

groin vault See **vault**.

guild An association of craftspeople. The medieval guild had great economic power, as it set standards and controlled the selling and marketing of its members' products, and as it provided economic protection, group solidarity, and training in the craft to its members.

hall church A church with a **nave** and **aisles** of the same height, giving the impression of a large, open hall.

handscroll A long, narrow, horizontal painting or text (or combination thereof) common in Chinese and Japanese art and of a size intended for individual use. A handscroll is stored wrapped tightly around a wooden pin and is unrolled for viewing or reading.

hanging scroll In Chinese and Japanese art, a vertical painting or text mounted within sections of silk. At the top is a semicircular rod; at the bottom is a round dowel. Hanging scrolls are kept rolled and tied except for special occasions, when they are hung for display, contemplation, or commemoration.

haniwa Pottery forms, including cylinders, buildings, and human figures, that were placed on top of Japanese tombs or burial mounds.

hemicycle A semicircular interior space or structure.

henge A circular area enclosed by stones or wood posts set up by Neolithic peoples. It is usually bounded by a ditch and raised embankment.

hieratic In painting and sculpture, a formalized style for representing rulers or sacred or priestly figures.

hieratic scale The use of different sizes for significant or holy figures and those of the everyday world to indicate importance. The larger the figure, the greater the importance.

high relief Relief sculpture in which the image projects strongly from the background. See also **relief sculpture**.

himation In ancient Greece, a long loose outer garment.

historicism The strong consciousness of and attention to the institutions, themes, styles, and forms of the past, made accessible by historical research, textual study, and archaeology.

history painting Paintings based on historical, mythological, or biblical narratives. Once considered the noblest form of art, history paintings generally convey a high moral or intellectual idea and are often painted in a grand pictorial style.

hollow-casting See **lost-wax casting**.

hypostyle hall A large interior room characterized by many closely spaced **columns** that support its roof.

icon An image in any material representing a sacred figure or event in the Byzantine, and later in the Orthodox, Church. Icons were venerated by the faithful, who believed them to have miraculous powers to transmit messages to God.

iconoclasm The banning or destruction of images, especially icons and religious art. Iconoclasm in eighth- and ninth-century Byzantium and sixteenth- and seventeenth-century Protestant territories arose from differing beliefs about the power, meaning, function, and purpose of imagery in religion.

iconographic See **iconography**.

iconography The study of the significance and interpretation of the subject matter of art.

iconostasis The partition screen in a Byzantine or Orthodox church between the **sanctuary** (where the Mass is performed) and the body of the church (where the congregation assembles). The iconostasis displays **icons**.

idealism *See* idealization.

idealization A process in art through which artists strive to make their forms and figures attain perfection, based on pervading cultural values and/or their own mental image of beauty.

ideograph A written character or symbol representing an idea or object. Many Chinese characters are ideographs.

ignudi Heroic figures of nude young men.

illumination A painting on paper or **parchment** used as illustration and/or decoration for **manuscripts** or **albums**. Usually done in rich colors, often supplemented by gold and other precious materials. The illustrators are referred to as illuminators. Also: the technique of decorating manuscripts with such paintings.

impasto Thick applications of pigment that give a painting a palpable surface texture.

impost, impost block A block, serving to concentrate the weight above, imposed between the **capital** of a **column** and the springing of an arch above.

in antis Term used to describe the position of columns set between two walls, as in a **portico** or a **cella**.

incising A technique in which a design or inscription is cut into a hard surface with a sharp instrument. Such a surface is said to be incised.

ink painting A monochromatic style of painting developed in China using black ink with gray **washes**.

inlay To set pieces of a material or materials into a surface to form a design. *Also:* material used in or decoration formed by this technique.

installation art Artworks created for a specific site, especially a gallery or outdoor area, that create a total environment.

intaglio Term used for a technique in which the design is carved out of the surface of an object, such as an engraved seal stone. In the graphic arts, intaglio includes **engraving**, etching, and **drypoint**—all processes in which ink transfers to paper from incised, ink-filled lines cut into a metal plate.

intarsia Decoration formed through wood **inlay**.

intuitive perspective See **perspective**.

Ionic order See **order**.

iwan A large, **vaulted** chamber in a **mosque** with a monumental arched opening on one side.

jamb In architecture, the vertical element found on both sides of an opening in a wall, and supporting an **arch** or lintel.

japonisme A style in French and American nineteenth-century art that was highly influenced by Japanese art, especially prints.

jasperware A fine-grained, unglazed, white **ceramic** developed by Josiah Wedgwood, often colored by metallic oxides with the raised designs remaining white.

jataka **tales** In Buddhism, stories associated with the previous lives of Shakyamuni, the historical Buddha.

joined-wood sculpture A method of constructing large-scale wooden sculpture developed in Japan. The entire work is constructed from smaller hollow blocks, each individually carved, and assembled when complete. The joined-wood technique allowed the production of larger sculpture, as the multiple joints alleviate the problems of drying and cracking found with sculpture carved from a single block.

joggled voussoirs Interlocking voussoirs in an arch or lintel, often of contrasting materials for colorful effect.

kantharos A type of Greek vase or goblet with two large handles and a wide mouth.

key block A key block is the master block in the production of a colored **woodblock print**, which requires different blocks for each color. The key block is a flat piece of wood with the entire design carved or drawn on its surface. From this, other blocks with partial drawings are made for printing the areas of different colors.

keystone The topmost **voussoir** at the center of an **arch**, and the last block to be placed. The pressure of this block holds the arch together. Often of a larger size and/or decorated.

kiln An oven designed to produce enough heat for the baking, or firing, of clay.

kinetic art Artwork that contains parts that can be moved either by hand, air, or motor.

kondo The main hall inside a Japanese Buddhist temple where the images of Buddha are housed.

kore (korai) An Archaic Greek statue of a young woman.

kouros (kouroi) An Archaic Greek statue of a young man or boy.

krater An ancient Greek vessel for mixing wine and water, with many subtypes that each have a distinctive shape. **Calyx krater:** a bell-shaped vessel with handles near the base that resemble a flower calyx. Volute krater: a type of krater with handles shaped like scrolls.

kufic An ornamental, angular Arabic script.

kylix A shallow Greek vessel or cup, used for drinking, with a wide mouth and small handles near the rim.

lacquer A type of hard, glossy surface varnish used on objects in East Asian cultures, made from the sap of the Asian sumac or from shellac, a resinous secretion from the lac insect. Lacquer can be layered and manipulated or combined with pigments and other materials for various decorative effects.

lakshana Term used to designate the thirtytwo marks of the historical Buddha. The lakshana include, among others, the Buddha's golden body, his long arms, the wheel impressed on his palms and the soles of his feet, and his elongated earlobes.

lamassu Supernatural guardian-protector of ancient Near Eastern palaces and throne rooms, often represented sculpturally as a combination of the bearded head of a man, powerful body of a lion or bull, wings of an eagle, and the horned headdress of a god, and usually possessing five legs.

lancet A tall narrow window crowned by a sharply pointed **arch**, typically found in Gothic architecture.

lantern A turretlike structure situated on a roof, **vault**, or **dome**, with windows that allow light into the space below.

lekythos (lekythoi) A slim Greek oil vase with one handle and a narrow mouth.

limner An artist, particularly a portrait painter, in England during the sixteenth and seventeenth centuries and in New England during the seventeenth and eighteenth centuries.

lingam shrine A place of worship centered on an object or representation in the form of a phallus (the lingam), which symbolizes the power of the Hindu god Shiva.

literati The English word used for the Chinese *wenren* or the Japanese *bunjin*, referring to well-educated artists who enjoyed literature, **calligraphy**, and painting as a pastime. Their painting are termed **literati painting**.

literati painting A style of painting that reflects the taste of the educated class of East Asian intellectuals and scholars. Aspects include an appreciation for the antique, small scale, and an intimate connection between maker and audience.

lithograph See **lithography**.

lithography Process of making a print (**lithograph**) from a design drawn on a flat stone block with greasy crayon. Ink is applied to the wet stone and adheres only to the greasy areas of the design.

loggia Italian term for a covered open-air. **gallery**. Often used as a corridor between buildings or around a courtyard, loggias usually have **arcades** or **colonnades**.

lost-wax casting A method of casting metal, such as bronze, by a process in which a wax mold is covered with clay and plaster, then fired, melting the wax and leaving a hollow form. Molten metal is then poured into the hollow space and slowly cooled. When the hardened clay and plas-

ter exterior shell is removed, a solid metal form remains to be smoothed and polished.

low relief Relief sculpture whose figures project slightly from the background. See also **relief sculpture**.

lunette A semicircular wall area, framed by an arch over a door or window. Can be either plain or decorated.

lusterware Ceramic pottery decorated with metallic **glazes**.

madrasa An Islamic institution of higher learning, where teaching is focused on theology and law.

maenad In ancient Greece, a female devotee of the wine god Dionysos who participated in orgiastic rituals. She is often depicted with swirling drapery to indicate wild movement or dance. (Also called a Bacchante, after Bacchus, the Roman name of Dionysos.)

majolica Pottery painted with a tin glaze that, when fired, gives a lustrous and colorful surface.

mandala An image of the cosmos represented by an arrangement of circles or concentric geometric shapes containing diagrams or images. Used for meditation and contemplation by Buddhists.

mandapa In a Hindu temple, an open hall dedicated to ritual worship.

mandorla Light encircling, or emanating from, the entire figure of a sacred person.

manuscript A handwritten book or document.

maqsura An enclosure in a Muslim mosque, near the mihrab, designated for dignitaries.

martyrium (martyria) In Christian architecture, a church, chapel, or shrine built over the grave of a martyr or the site of a great miracle.

mastaba A flat-topped, one-story structure with slanted walls over an ancient Egyptian underground tomb.

matte Term describing a smooth surface that is without shine or luster.

mausoleum A monumental building used as a tomb. Named after the tomb of Mausolos erected at Halikarnassos around 350 BCE.

meander See **Greek-key pattern**.

medallion Any round ornament or decoration. Also: a large medal.

megalith A large stone used in prehistoric building. Megalithic architecture employs such stones.

megaron The main hall of a Mycenaean palace or grand house, having a columnar **porch** and a room with a central fireplace surrounded by four **columns**.

memento mori From Latin for "remember that you must die." An object, such as a skull or extinguished candle, typically found in a *vanitas* image, symbolizing the transience of life.

memory image An image that relies on the generic shapes and relationships that readily spring to mind at the mention of an object.

menorah A Jewish lamp-stand with seven or nine branches; the nine-branched menorah is used during the celebration of Hanukkah. Representations of the seven-branched menorah, once used in the Temple of Jerusalem, became a symbol of Judaism.

metope The carved or painted rectangular panel between the **triglyphs** of a **Doric frieze**.

mihrab A recess or niche that distinguishes the wall oriented toward Mecca (*qibla*) in a **mosque**.

minaret A tall slender tower on the exterior of a mosque from which believers are called to prayer.

minbar A high platform or pulpit in a **mosque**.

miniature Anything small. In painting, miniatures may be illustrations within **albums** or **manuscripts** or intimate portraits.

mirador In Spanish and Islamic palace architecture, a very large window or room with windows, and sometimes balconies, providing views to interior courtyards or the exterior landscape.

mithuna The amorous male and female couples in Buddhist sculpture, usually found at the entrance to a sacred building. The mithuna symbolize the harmony and fertility of life.

moat A large ditch or canal dug around a castle or fortress for military defense. When filled with water, the moat protects the walls of the building from direct attack.

mobile A sculpture made with parts suspended in such a way that they move in a current of air.

modeling In painting, the process of creating the illusion of three-dimensionality on a two-dimensional surface by use of light and shade. In sculpture, the process of molding a three-dimensional form out of a malleable substance.

module A segment or portion of a repeated design. Also: a basic building block.

molding A shaped or sculpted strip with varying contours and patterns. Used as decoration on architecture, furniture, frames, and other objects.

monolith A single stone, often very large.

mortise-and-tenon joint A method of joining two elements. A projecting pin (tenon) on one element fits snugly into a hole designed for it (mortise) on the other. Such joints are very strong and flexible.

mosaic Images formed by small colored stone or glass pieces (tesserae), affixed to a hard, stable surface.

mosque An edifice used for communal Muslim worship.

mudra A symbolic hand gesture in Buddhist art that denotes certain behaviors, actions, or feelings.

mullion A slender vertical element or **colonnette** that divides a window into subsidiary sections.

muqarnas Small nichelike components stacked in tiers to fill the transition between differing vertical and horizontal planes.

naos The principal room in a temple or church. In ancient architecture, the **cella**. In a Byzantine church, the **nave** and **sanctuary**.

narthex The vestibule or entrance porch of a church.

naturalism, naturalistic A style of depiction that seeks to imitate the appearance of nature. A naturalistic work appears to record the visible world.

nave The central space of a **basilica**, two or three stories high and usually flanked by **aisles**.

necking The molding at the top of the **shaft** of the **column**.

necropolis A large cemetery or burial area; literally a "city of the dead."

nemes headdress The royal headdress of Egypt.

niello A metal technique in which a black sulfur alloy is rubbed into fine lines engraved in a metal (usually gold or silver). When heated, the alloy becomes fused with the surrounding metal and provides contrasting detail.

nishiki-e A multicolored and ornate Japanese print.

nocturne A night scene in painting, usually lit by artificial illumination.

nonrepresentational art An **abstract** art that does not attempt to reproduce the appearance of objects, figures, or scenes in the natural world. Also called nonobjective art.

oculus (oculi) In architecture, a circular opening. Oculi are usually found either as windows or at the apex of a **dome**. When at the top of a dome, an oculus is either open to the sky or covered by a decorative exterior lantern.

ogee An S-shaped curve. See **arch**.

olpe Any Greek vase or jug without a spout.

one-point perspective See **perspective**.

opithodomos In greek temples, the entrance porch or room at the back.

oracle A person, usually a priest or priestess, who acts as a conduit for divine information. Also: the information itself or the place at which this information is communicated.

orant The representation of a standing figure praying with outstretched and upraised arms.

orchestra The circular performance area of an ancient Greek theater. In later architecture, the section of seats nearest the stage or the entire main floor of the theater.

order A system of proportions in Classical architecture that includes every aspect of the building's plan, elevation, and decorative system. Composite: a combination of the Ionic and the Corinthian orders. The **capital** combines acanthus leaves with **volute** scrolls. **Corinthian:** the most ornate of the orders, the Corinthian includes a **base**, a fluted **column shaft** with a capital elaborately decorated with acanthus leaf carvings. Its **entablature** consists of an **architrave** decorated with **moldings**, a **frieze** often containing **sculptured reliefs**, and a **cornice** with dentils. Doric: the column shaft of the Doric order can be fluted or smooth-surfaced and has no base. The Doric **capital** consists of an undecorated **echinus** and **abacus**. The Doric entablature has a plain architrave, a frieze with **metopes** and **triglyphs**, and a simple cornice. Ionic: the column of the Ionic order has a base, a fluted shaft, and a capital decorated with volutes. The Ionic entablature consists of an architrave of three panels and moldings, a frieze usually containing sculpted relief ornament, and a cornice with dentils. **Tuscan:** a variation of Doric characterized by a smooth-surfaced column shaft with a base, a plain architrave, and an undecorated frieze. A colossal order is any of the above built on a large scale, rising through several stories in height and often raised from the ground by a **pedestal**.

orthogonal Any line running back into the represented space of a picture perpendicular to the imagined picture plane. In linear perspective, all orthogonals converge at a single **vanishing point** in the picture and are the basis for a **grid** that maps out the internal space of the image. An orthogonal plan is any plan for a building or city that is based exclusively on right angles, such as the grid plan of many modern cities.

pagoda An East Asian **reliquary** tower built with successively smaller, repeated stories. Each story is usually marked by an elaborate projecting roof.

palace complex A group of buildings used for living and governing by a ruler and his or her supporters, usually fortified.

palmette A fan-shaped ornament with radiating leaves.

parapet A low wall at the edge of a balcony, bridge, roof, or other place from which there is a steep drop, built for safety. A parapet walk is the passageway, usually open, immediately behind the uppermost exterior wall or battlement of a fortified building.

parchment A writing surface made from treated skins of animals. Very fine parchment is known as **vellum**.

parterre An ornamental, highly regimented flowerbed. An element of the ornate gardens of seventeenth-century palaces and châteaux.

pastel Dry pigment, chalk, and gum in stick or crayon form. Also: a work of art made with pastels.

pedestal A platform or **base** supporting a sculpture or other monument. Also: the block found below the base of a Classical **column** (or **colonnade**), serving to raise the entire element off the ground.

pediment A triangular gable found over major architectural elements such as Classical Greek **porticoes**, windows, or doors. Formed by an **entablature** and the ends of a sloping roof or a raking **cornice**. A similar architectural element is often used decoratively above a door or window, sometimes with a curved upper **molding**. A broken pediment is a variation on the traditional pediment, with an open space at the center of the topmost angle and/or the horizontal cornice.

pendentive The concave triangular section of a **vault** that forms the transition between a square or polygonal space and the circular base of a **dome**.

peplos A loose outer garment worn by women of ancient Greece. A cloth rectangle fastened on the shoulders and belted below the bust or at the waist.

peripteral A term used to describe any building (or room) that is surrounded by a single row of columns. When such **columns** are engaged instead of freestanding, called pseudo-peripteral.

peristyle A surrounding **colonnade** in Greek architecture. A peristyle building is surrounded on the exterior by a colonnade. Also: a peristyle court is an open colonnaded courtyard, often having a pool and garden.

perspective A system for representing three-dimensional space on a two-dimensional surface. **Atmospheric** perspective: A method of rendering the effect of spatial distance by subtle variations in color and clarity of representation. **Intuitive perspective:** A method of giving the impression of recession by visual instinct, not by the use of an overall system or program. Oblique perspective: An intuitive spatial system in which a building or room is placed with one corner in the picture plane, and the other parts of the structure recede to an imaginary vanishing point on its other side. Oblique perspective is not a comprehensive, mathematical system. **One-point** and multiple-point **perspective** (also called linear, scientific or mathematical perspective): A method of creating the illusion of three-dimensional space on a two-dimensional surface by delineating a horizon line and multiple orthogonal lines. These recede to meet at one or more points on the horizon (called **vanishing** points), giving the appearance of spatial depth. Called scientific or mathematical because its use requires some

knowledge of geometry and mathematics, as well as optics. **Reverse perspective:** A Byzantine perspective theory in which the orthogonals or rays of sight do not converge on a vanishing point in the picture, but are thought to originate in the viewer's eye in front of the picture. Thus, in reverse perspective the image is constructed with orthogonals that diverge, giving a slightly tipped aspect to objects.

photomontage A photographic work created from many smaller photographs arranged (and often overlapping) in a composition.

picture plane The theoretical spatial plane corresponding with the actual surface of a painting.

picture stone A medieval northern European memorial stone covered with figural decoration. See also **rune stone**.

picturesque A term describing the taste for the familiar, the pleasant, and the pretty, popular in the eighteenth and nineteenth centuries in Europe. When contrasted with the sublime, the picturesque stood for all that was ordinary but pleasant.

piece-mold casting A casting technique in which the mold consists of several sections that are connected during the pouring of molten metal, usually bronze. After the cast form has hardened, the pieces of the mold are disassembled, leaving the completed object.

pier A masonry support made up of many stones, or rubble and concrete (in contrast to a **column shaft** which is formed from a single stone or a series of **drums**), often square or rectangular in plan, and capable of carrying very heavy architectural loads.

pietra dura Italian for "hard stone." Semi-precious stones selected for color variation and cut in shapes to form ornamental designs such as flowers or fruit.

pietra serena A gray Tuscan limestone used in Florence.

pilaster An **engaged** columnar element that is rectangular in format and used for decoration in architecture.

pillar In architecture, any large, freestanding vertical element. Usually functions as an important weight-bearing unit in buildings.

plate tracery See **tracery**.

plinth The slablike **base** or **pedestal** of a column, statue, wall, building, or piece of furniture.

pluralism A social structure or goal that allows members of diverse ethnic, racial, or other groups to exist peacefully within the society while continuing to practice the customs of their own divergent cultures. Also: an adjective describing the state of having many valid contemporary styles available at the same time to artists.

podium A raised platform that acts as the foundation for a building, or as a platform for a speaker.

polychrome See **polychromy**.

polychromy The multicolored painted decoration applied to any part of a building, sculpture, or piece of furniture.

polyptych An altarpiece constructed from multiple panels, sometimes with hinges to allow for movable wings.

porcelain A high-fired, vitrified, translucent, white **ceramic** ware that employs two specific clays—kaolin and petuntse—and that is fired in the range of 1,300 to 1,400 degrees Celsius. The relatively high proportion of silica in the body clays renders the finished porcelains translucent. Like **stonewares**, porcelains are glazed to enhance their aesthetic appeal and to aid in keeping them clean. By definition, porcelain is white, though it may be covered with a **glaze** of bright color or subtle hue. Chinese potters were the first in the world to produce porcelain, which they were able to make as early as the eighth century.

porch The covered entrance on the exterior of a building. With a row of **columns** or **colonnade**, also called a **portico**.

portal A grand entrance, door, or gate, usually to an important public building, and often decorated with sculpture.

portico In architecture, a projecting roof or porch supported by columns, often marking an entrance. See also porch.

post-and-lintel construction An architectural system of construction with two or more vertical elements (posts) supporting a horizontal element (lintel).

potassium-argon dating Technique used to measure the decay of a radioactive potassium isotope into a stable isotope of argon, an inert gas.

potsherd A broken piece of ceramic ware.

Praire Style A style of architecture initiated by the American Frank Lloyd Wright (1867-1959), in which he sought to integrate his structures in an "organic" way into the surrounding natural landscape, often having the lines of the building follow the horizontal contours of the land. Since Wright's early buildings were built in the Prairie States of the Midwest, this type of architecture became known as the Prairie Style.

primitivism The borrowing of subjects or forms usually from non-Western or prehistoric sources by Western artists. Originally practiced by Western artists as an attempt to infuse their work with the naturalistic and expressive qualities attributed to other cultures, especially colonized cultures, primitivism also borrowed from the art of children and the insane.

pronaos The enclosed vestibule of a Greek or Roman temple, found in front of the **cella** and marked by a row of **columns** at the entrance.

proscenium The stage of an ancient Greek or Roman theater. In modern theater, the area of the stage in front of the curtain. Also: the framing **arch** that separates a stage from the audience.

psalter In Jewish and Christian scripture, a book containing the psalms, or songs, attributed to King David.

punchwork Decorative designs that are stamped onto a surface, such as metal or leather, using a punch (a handheld metal implement).

putto (putti) A plump, naked little boy, often winged. In classical art, called a cupid; in Christian art, a cherub.

pylon A massive gateway formed by a pair of tapering walls of oblong shape. Erected by ancient Egyptians to mark the entrance to a temple complex.

qibla The mosque wall oriented toward Mecca indicated by the mihrab.

quatrefoil A four-lobed decorative pattern common in Gothic art and architecture.

quincunx A building in which five **domed** bays are arranged within a square, with a central unit and four corner units. (When the central

unit has similar units extending from each side, the form becomes a **Greek cross**.)

quoin A stone, often extra large or decorated for emphasis, forming the corner of two walls. A vertical row of such stones is called quoining.

radiometric dating A method of dating prehistoric works of art made from organic materials, based on the rate of degeneration of radiocarbons in these materials. *See also* **relative dating, absolute dating**.

raigo A painted image that depicts the Amida Buddha and other Buddhist deities welcoming the soul of a dying worshiper to paradise.

raku A type of **ceramic** pottery made by hand, coated with a thick, dark **glaze**, and fired at a low heat. The resulting vessels are irregularly shaped and glazed, and are highly prized for use in the Japanese tea ceremony.

readymade An object from popular or material culture presented without further manipulation as an artwork by the artist.

realism In art, a term first used in Europe around 1850 to designate a kind of **naturalism** with a social or political message, which soon lost its didactic import and became synonymous with naturalism.

red-figure A style and technique of ancient Greek vase painting characterized by red clay-colored figures on a black background. (The figures are reversed against a painted ground and details are drawn, not engraved, as in black-figure style.) See also **black-figure**.

register A device used in systems of spatial definition. In painting, a register indicates the use of differing **groundlines** to differentiate layers of space within an image. In sculpture, the placement of self-contained bands of **reliefs** in a vertical arrangement. In printmaking, the marks at the edges used to align the print correctly on the page, especially in multiple-block color printing.

registration marks In Japanese **woodblock** printing, these were two marks carved on the blocks to indicate proper alignment of the paper during the printing process. In multicolor printing, which used a separate block for each color, these marks were essential for achieving the proper position or registration of the colors.

relative dating See also **radiometric dating**.

relief sculpture A three-dimensional image or design whose flat background surface is carved away to a certain depth, setting off the figure. Called high or **low (bas) relief** depending upon the extent of projection of the image from the background. Called **sunken relief** when the image is carved below the original surface of the background, which is not cut away.

reliquary A container, often made of precious materials, used as a repository to protect and display sacred relics.

repoussé A technique of hammering metal from the back to create a protruding image. Elaborate reliefs are created with wooden armatures against which the metal sheets are pressed and hammered.

reverse perspective See **perspective**.

rhyton A vessel in the shape of a figure or an animal, used for drinking or pouring liquids on special occasions.

rib vault See **vault**.

ridgepole A longitudinal timber at the apex of a roof that supports the upper ends of the rafters.

rosette A round or oval ornament resembling a rose.

rotunda Any building (or part thereof) constructed in a circular (or sometimes polygonal) shape, usually producing a large open space crowned by a **dome**.

round arch See **arch**.

roundel Any element with a circular format, often placed as a decoration on the exterior of architecture.

rune stone A stone used in early medieval northern Europe as a commemorative monument, which is carved or inscribed with runes, a writing system used by early Germanic peoples.

running spirals A decorative motif based on the shape formed by a line making a continuous spiral.

rustication In building, the rough, irregular, and unfinished effect deliberately given to the exterior facing of a stone edifice. Rusticated stones are often large and used for decorative emphasis around doors or windows, or across the entire lower floors of a building. Also, masonry construction with conspicuous, often beveled joints.

salon A large room for entertaining guests; a periodic social or intellectual gathering, often of prominent people; a hall or **gallery** for exhibiting works of art.

sanctuary A sacred or holy enclosure used for worship. In ancient Greece and Rome, consisted of one or more temples and an altar. In Christian architecture, the space around the altar in a church called the chancel or presbytery.

sarcophagus (sarcophagi) A stone coffin. Often rectangular and decorated with **relief sculpture**.

scarab In Egypt, a stylized dung beetle associated with the sun and the god Amun.

school of artists An art historical term describing a group of artists, usually working at the same time and sharing similar styles, influences, and ideals. The artists in a particular school may not necessarily be directly associated with one another, unlike those in a workshop or **atelier**.

scribe A writer; a person who copies texts.

scriptorium (scriptoria) A room in a monastery for writing or copying manuscripts.

scroll painting A painting executed on a rolled support. Rollers at each end permit the horizontal scroll to be unrolled as it is studied or the vertical scroll to be hung for contemplation or decoration.

seals Personal emblems usually carved of stone in **intaglio** or **relief** and used to stamp a name or legend onto paper or silk. They traditionally employ the archaic characters appropriately known as "seal script," of the Zhou or Qin. Cut in stone, a seal may state a formal given name, or it may state any of the numerous personal names that China's painters and writers adopted throughout their lives. A treasured work of art often bears not only the seal of its maker but also those of collectors and admirers through the centuries. In the Chinese view, these do not disfigure the work but add another layer of interest.

scarification Ornamental decoration applied to the surface of the body by cutting the skin for cultural and/or aesthetic reasons.

seraph (seraphim) An angel of the highest rank in the Christian hierarchy.

serdab In Egyptian tombs, the small room in which the ka statue was placed.

sfumato Italian term meaning "smoky," soft, and mellow. In painting, the effect of haze in an image. Resembling the color of the atmosphere at dusk, sfumato gives a smoky effect.

sgraffito Decoration made by incising or cutting away a surface layer of material to reveal a different color beneath.

shaft The main vertical section of a column between the capital and the base, usually circular in cross section.

shaftgrave A deep pit used for burial.

shikhara In the architecture of northern India, a conical (or pyramidal) spire found atop a Hindu temple and often crowned with an *amalaka*.

shoji A standing Japanese screen covered in translucent rice paper and used in interiors.

sinopia The preparatory design or underdrawing of a **fresco**. Also: a reddish chalklike earth pigment.

site-specific sculpture A sculpture commissioned and/or designed for a particular spot.

slip A mixture of clay and water applied to a **ceramic** object as a final decorative coat. Also: a solution that binds different parts of a vessel together, such as the handle and the main body.

spandrel The area of wall adjoining the exterior curve of an arch between its **springing** and the **keystone**, or the area between two arches, as in an **arcade**.

springing The point at which the curve of an arch or vault meets with and rises from its support.

squinch An **arch** or lintel built across the upper corners of a square space, allowing a circular or polygonal **dome** to be more securely set above the walls.

stained glass Molten glass is given a color that becomes intrinsic to the material. Additional colors may be fused to the surface (flashing). Stained glass is most often used in windows, for which small pieces of differently colored glass are precisely cut and assembled into a design, held together by **cames**. Additional painted details may be added to create images.

stele (stelae) A stone slab placed vertically and decorated with inscriptions or reliefs. Used as a grave marker or memorial.

stereobate A foundation upon which a Classical temple stands.

still life A type of painting that has as its subject inanimate objects (such as food, dishes, fruit, or flowers).

stoa In Greek architecture, a long roofed walkway, usually having columns on one long side and a wall on the other.

stoneware A high-fired, vitrified, but opaque **ceramic** ware that is fired in the range of 1,100 to 1,200 degrees Celsius. At that temperature, particles of silica in the clay bodies fuse together so that the finished vessels are impervious to liquids, even without **glaze**. Stoneware pieces are glazed to enhance their aesthetic appeal and to aid in keeping them clean (since unglazed ceramics are easily soiled). Stoneware occurs in a range of earth-toned colors, from white and tan to gray and black, with light gray predominating. Chinese potters were the first in the world to produce stoneware, which they were able to make as early as the Shang dynasty.

stucco A mixture of lime, sand, and other ingredients into a material that can be easily molded or modeled. When dry, produces a very durable surface used for covering walls or for architectural sculpture and decoration.

stupa In Buddhist architecture, a bell-shaped or pyramidal religious monument, made of piled earth or stone, and containing sacred relics.

stylobate In Classical architecture, the stone foundation on which a temple **colonnade** stands.

stylus An instrument with a pointed end (used for writing and printmaking), which makes a delicate line or scratch. Also: a special writing tool for **cuneiform** writing with one pointed end and one triangular wedge end.

sublime Adjective describing a concept, thing, or state of high spiritual, moral, or intellectual value; or something awe-inspiring. The sublime was a goal to which many nineteenth-century artists aspired in their artworks.

sunken relief See **relief sculpture**.

syncretism In religion or philosophy, the union of different ideas or principles.

taotie A mask with a dragon or animal-like face common as a decorative motif in Chinese art.

tapestry Multicolored pictorial or decorative weaving meant to be hung on a wall or placed on furniture.

tatami Mats of woven straw used in Japanese houses as a floor covering.

tempera A painting medium made by blending egg yolks with water, pigments, and occasionally other materials, such as glue.

tenebrism The use of strong **chiaroscuro** and artificially illuminated areas to create a dramatic contrast of light and dark in a painting.

terra cotta A medium made from clay fired over a low heat and sometimes left unglazed. Also: the orange-brown color typical of this medium.

tessera (tesserae) The small piece of stone, glass, or other object that is pieced together with many others to create a mosaic.

tetrarchy Four-man rule, as in the late Roman Empire, when four emperors shared power.

thatch A roof made of plant materials.

thermo-luminescence dating A technique that measures the irradiation of the crystal structure of material such as flint or pottery and the soil in which it is found, determined by luminescence produced when a sample is heated.

tholos A small, round building. Sometimes built underground, as in a Mycenaean tomb.

thrust The outward pressure caused by the weight of a vault and supported by buttressing. See **arch**.

tierceron In **vault** construction, a secondary rib that arcs from a **springing** point to the rib that runs lengthwise through the vault, called the ridge rib.

tokonoma A niche for the display of an art object (such as a screen, scroll, or flower arrangement) in a Japanese hall or tearoom.

tondo A painting or **relief sculpture** of circular shape.

torana In Indian architecture, an ornamented gateway arch in a temple, usually leading to the stupa.

toron In West African **mosque** architecture, the wooden beams that project from the walls. Torons are used as support for the scaffolding erected annually for the replastering of the building.

tracery Stonework or woodwork applied to wall surfaces or filling the open space of windows. In **plate tracery**, opening are cut through the wall. In **bar tracery**, **mullions** divide the space into vertical segments and form decorative patterns at the top of the opening or panel.

transept The arm of a cruciform church, perpendicular to the **nave**. The point where the nave and transept cross is called the crossing. Beyond the crossing lies the **sanctuary**, whether **apse**, choir, or chevet.

travertine A mineral building material similar to limestone, typically found in central Italy.

trefoil An ornamental design made up of three rounded lobes placed adjacent to one another.

triglyph Rectangular block between the **metopes** of a **Doric frieze**. Identified by the three carved vertical grooves, which approximate the appearance of the end of a wooden beam.

triptych An artwork made up of three panels. The panels may be hinged together so the side segments (**wings**) fold over the central area.

trompe l'oeil A manner of representation in which the appearance of natural space and objects is re-created with the express intention of fooling the eye of the viewer, who may be convinced that the subject actually exists as three-dimensional reality.

trumeau A column, pier, or post found at the center of a large portal or doorway, supporting the lintel.

tugra A calligraphic imperial monogram used in Ottoman courts.

Tuscan order *See* **order**.

twisted perspective A convention in art in which every aspect of a body or object is represented from its most characteristic viewpoint.

ukiyo-e A Japanese term for a type of popular art that was favored from the sixteenth century, particularly in the form of color **woodblock prints**. Ukiyo-e prints often depicted the world of the common people in Japan, such as courtesans and actors, as well as landscapes and myths.

urna In Buddhist art, the curl of hair on the forehead that is a characteristic mark of a buddha. The urna is a symbol of divine wisdom.

ushnisha In Asian art, a bulge on the top of the head which symbolizes the Buddha's enlightenment.

vanishing point In a **perspective** system, the point on the horizon line at which **orthogonals** meet. A complex system can have multiple vanishing points.

vanitas An image, especially popular in Europe during the seventeenth century, in which all the objects symbolize the transience of life. Vanitas paintings are usually of **still lifes** or genre subjects.

vault An **arched** masonry structure that spans an interior space. Barrel or tunnel vault: an elongated or continuous semicircular vault, shaped like a half-cylinder. **Corbeled** vault: a vault made by projecting courses of stone. **Groin** or cross vault: a vault created by the intersection of two barrel vaults of equal size which creates four side compartments of identical size and shape. Quadrant or half-barrel vault: as the name suggests, a half-barrel vault. Rib vault: ribs (extra masonry) demarcate the junctions of a groin vault. Ribs may function to reinforce the groins or may be purely decorative. See also **corbeling**.

veduta (vedute) Italian for "vista" or "view."

Paintings, drawings, or prints often of expansive city scenes or of harbors.

vellum   A fine animal skin prepared for writing and painting. See also parchment.

veneer   In architecture, the exterior facing of a building, often in decorative patterns of fine stone or brick. In decorative arts, a thin exterior layer of finer material (such as rare wood, ivory, metal, and semiprecious stones) laid over the form.

verism   A style in which artists concern themselves with capturing the exterior likeness of an object or person, usually by rendering its visible details in a finely executed, meticulous manner.

vihara   From the Sanskrit term meaning "for wanderers." A vihara is, in general, a Buddhist monastery in India. It also signifies monks' cells and gathering places in such a monastery.

vimana   The main element of a Southern Indian Hindu temple, usually in the shape of a pyramidal or tapering tower raised on a **plinth**.

volute   A spiral scroll, as seen on an Ionic **capital**.

votive figure   An image created as a devotional offering to a god or other deity.

voussoirs   The oblong, wedge-shaped stone blocks used to build an **arch**. The topmost voussoir is called a **keystone**.

warp   The vertical threads in a weaver's loom. Warp threads make up a fixed framework that provides the structure for the entire piece of cloth, and are thus often thicker than **weft** threads. See also **weft**.

wash   A diluted watercolor or ink. Often washes are applied to drawings or prints to add tone or touches of color.

wattle and daub   A wall construction method combining upright branches, woven with twigs (wattles) and plastered or filled with clay or mud (daub).

weft   The horizontal threads in a woven piece of cloth. Weft threads are woven at right angles to and through the **warp** threads to make up the bulk of the decorative pattern. In carpets, the weft is often completely covered or formed by the rows of trimmed knots that form the carpet's soft surface. See also **warp**.

white-ground   A type of ancient Greek pottery in which the background color of the object is painted with a slip that turns white in the firing process. Figures and details were added by painting on or **incising** into this **slip**. White-ground wares were popular in the Classical period as funerary objects.

wing   A side panel of a **triptych** or **polyptych** (usually found in pairs), which was hinged to fold over the central panel. Wings often held the depiction of the donors and/or subsidiary scenes relating to the central image.

woodblock print   A print made from one or more carved wooden blocks. In Japan, woodblock prints were made using multiple blocks carved in relief, usually with a block for each color in the finished print. See also **woodcut**.

woodcut   A type of print made by carving a design into a wooden block. The ink is applied to the block with a roller. As the ink remains only on the raised areas between the carved-away lines, these carved-away areas and lines provide the white areas of the print. Also: the process by which the woodcut is made.

x-ray style   In Aboriginal art, a manner of representation in which the artist depicts a figure or animal by illustrating its outline as well as essential internal organs and bones.

yaksha, yakshi   The male (yaksha) and female (yakshi) nature spirits that act as agents of the Hindu gods. Their sculpted images are often found on Hindu temples and other sacred places, particularly at the entrances.

ziggurat   In Mesopotamia, a tall stepped tower of earthen materials, often supporting a shrine.

BIBLIOGRAPHY

Susan V. Craig

This bibliography is composed of books in English that are appropriate "further reading" titles. Most items on this list are available in good libraries, whether college, university, or public institutions. I have emphasized recently published works so that the research information would be current. There are three classifications of listings: general surveys and art history reference tools, including journals and Internet directories; surveys of large periods that encompass multiple chapters (ancient art in the Western tradition, European medieval art, European Renaissance through eighteenth-century art, modern art in the West, Asian art, and African and Oceanic art and art of the Americas); and books for individual chapters 1 through 32.

General Art History Surveys and Reference Tools

Adams, Laurie Schneider. *Art across Time.* 2nd ed. New York: McGraw-Hill, 2002.

Barnet, Sylvan. *A Short Guide to Writing about Art.* 8th ed. New York: Pearson/Longman, 2005.

Boström, Antonia. *Encyclopedia of Sculpture.* 3 vols. New York: FitzroyDearborn, 2004.

Broude, Norma, and Garrard, Mary D., eds. *Feminism and Art History: Questioning the Litany.* Icon Editions. New York: Harper & Row, 1982.

Chadwick, Whitney. *Women, Art, and Society.* 3rd ed. New York: Thames and Hudson, 2002.

Chilvers, Ian, ed. *The Oxford Dictionary of Art.* 3rd ed. New York: Oxford Univ. Press, 2004.

Curl, James Stevens. *A Dictionary of Architecture and Landscape Architecture.* 2nd ed. Oxford: Oxford Univ. Press, 2006.

Davies, Penelope J.E., et al. *Janson's History of Art: The Western Tradition.* 7th ed. Upper Saddle River, NJ: Prentice Hall, 2006.

Dictionary of Art, The. 34 vols. New York: Grove's Dictionaries, 1996.

Encyclopedia of World Art. 16 vols. New York: McGraw-Hill, 1972–83.

Frank, Patrick, Duane Preble, and Sarah Preble. *Preble's Artforms.* 8th ed. Upper Saddle River, NJ: Prentice Hall, 2006.

Gardner, Helen. *Gardner's Art through the Ages.* 12th ed. Ed. Fred S. Kleiner & Christin J. Mamiya. Belmont, CA: Thomson/Wadsworth, 2005.

Gaze, Delia, ed. *Dictionary of Women Artists.* 2 vols. London: Fitzroy Dearborn Publishers, 1997.

Griffiths, Antony. *Prints and Printmaking: An Introduction to the History and Techniques.* 2nd ed. London: British Museum Press, 1996.

Hadden, Peggy. *The Quotable Artist.* New York: Allworth Press, 2002.

Hall, James. *Illustrated Dictionary of Symbols in Eastern and Western Art.* New York: Icon Editions, 1994.

Holt, Elizabeth Gilmore, ed. *A Documentary History of Art.* 3 vols. New Haven: Yale Univ. Press, 1986.

Honour, Hugh, and John Fleming. *The Visual Arts: A History.* 7th ed. Upper Saddle River, NJ: Prentice Hall, 2005.

Hults, Linda C. *The Print in the Western World: An Introductory History.* Madison: Univ. of Wisconsin Press, 1996.

Johnson, Paul. *Art: A New History.* New York: Harper-Collins, 2003.

Kaltenbach. G. E. *Pronunciation Dictionary of Artists' Names.* 3rd ed. Rev. Debra Edelstein. Boston: Little, Brown, and Co., 1993.

Kemp, Martin. *The Oxford History of Western Art.* Oxford: Oxford Univ. Press, 2000.

Kostof, Spiro. *A History of Architecture: Settings and Rituals.* 2nd ed. Rev. Greg Castillo. New York: Oxford Univ. Press, 1995.

Mackenzie, Lynn. *Non-Western Art: A Brief Guide.* 2nd ed. Upper Saddle River, NJ: Prentice Hall, 2001.

Marmor, Max, and Alex Ross, eds. *Guide to the Literature of Art History 2.* Chicago: American Library Association, 2005.

Onians, John, ed. *Atlas of World Art.* New York: Oxford Univ. Press, 2004.

Roberts, Helene, ed. *Encyclopedia of Comparative Iconography: Themes Depicted in Works of Art.* 2 vols. Chicago: Fitzroy Dearborn, 1998.

Rogers, Elizabeth Barlow. *Landscape Design: A Cultural and Architectural History.* New York: Harry N. Abrams, 2001.

Sayre, Henry M. *Writing about Art.* 5th ed. Upper Saddle River, NJ: Pearson/Prentice Hall, 2006.

Sed-Rajna, Gabrielle. *Jewish Art.* Trans. Sara Friedman and Mira Reich. New York: Abrams, 1997.

Slatkin, Wendy. *Women Artists in History: From Antiquity to the Present.* 4th ed. Upper Saddle River, NJ: Prentice Hall, 2000.

Sutton, Ian. *Western Architecture: From Ancient Greece to the Present.* World of Art. New York: Thames and Hudson, 1999.

Trachtenberg, Marvin, and Isabelle Hyman. *Architecture: From Prehistory to Postmodernity.* 2nd ed. Upper Saddle River, NJ: Prentice Hall, 2001.

Tufts, Eleanor. *Our Hidden Heritage: Five Centuries of Women Artists.* New York: Paddington Press, 1974.

West, Shearer. *Portraiture.* Oxford History of Art. Oxford: Oxford Univ. Press, 2004.

Wilkins, David G., Bernard Schultz, and Katheryn M. Linduff. *Art Past, Art Present.* 5th ed. Upper Saddle River, NJ: Prentice Hall, 2005.

Watkin, David. *A History of Western Architecture.* 4th ed. New York: Watson-Guptill Publications, 2005.

Art History Journals: A Select List of Current Titles

African Arts. Quarterly. Los Angeles: Univ. of California at Los Angeles, James S. Coleman African Studies Center, 1967-

American Art: The Journal of the Smithsonian American Art Museum. 3/year. Chicago: Univ. of Chicago Press, 1987-

American Indian Art Magazine. Quarterly. Scottsdale, AZ: American Indian Art Inc, 1975-

American Journal of Archaeology. Quarterly. Boston: Archaeological Institute of America, 1885-

Antiquity: A Periodical of Archaeology. Quarterly. Cambridge, UK: Antiquity Publications Ltd, 1927-

Apollo: The International Magazine of the Arts. Monthly. London: Apollo Magazine Ltd, 1925-

Architectural History. Annually. Farnham, UK: Society of Architectural Historians of Great Britain, 1958-

Archives of American Art Journal. Quarterly. Washington, D.C.: Archives of American Art, Smithsonian Institution, 1960-

Archives of Asian Art. Annually. New York: Asia Society, 1945-

Ars Orientalis: The Arts of Asia, Southeast Asia, and Islam. Annually. Ann Arbor: Univ. of Michigan Dept. of Art History, 1954-

Art Bulletin. Quarterly. New York: College Art Association, 1913-

Art History: Journal of the Association of Art Historians. 5/year. Oxford: Blackwell Publishing Ltd, 1978-

Art in America. Monthly. New York: Brant Publications Inc, 1913-

Art Journal. Quarterly. New York: College Art Association, 1960-

Art Nexus. Quarterly. Bogata, Colombia: Arte en Colombia Ltda, 1976-

Art Papers Magazine. Bi-monthly. Atlanta: Atlanta Art Papers Inc, 1976-

Artforum International. 10/year. New York: Artforum International Magazine Inc, 1962-

Artnews. 11/year. New York: Artnews LLC, 1902-

Bulletin of the Metropolitan Museum of Art. Quarterly. New York: Metropolitan Museum of Art, 1905-

Burlington Magazine. Monthly. London: Burlington Magazine Publications Ltd, 1903-

Dumbarton Oaks Papers. Annually. Locust Valley, NY: J. J. Augustin Inc, 1940-

Flash Art International. Bimonthly. Trevi, Italy: Giancarlo Politi Editore, 1980-

Gesta. Semiannually. New York: International Center of Medieval Art, 1963-

History of Photography. Quarterly. Abingdon, UK: Taylor & Francis Ltd, 1976-

International Review of African American Art. Quarterly. Hampton, VA: International Review of African American Art, 1976-

Journal of Design History. Quarterly. Oxford: Oxford Univ. Press, 1988-

Journal of Egyptian Archaeology. Annually. London: Egypt Exploration Society, 1914-

Journal of Hellenic Studies. Annually. London: Society for the Promotion of Hellenic Studies, 1880-

Journal of Roman Archaeology. Annually. Portsmouth, RI: Journal of Roman Archaeology LLC, 1988-

Journal of the Society of Architectural Historians. Quarterly. Chicago: Society of Architectural Historians, 1940-

Journal of the Warburg and Courtauld Institutes. Annually. London: Warburg Institute, 1937-

Leonardo: Art, Science and Technology. 6/year. Cambridge, MA: MIT Press, 1968-

Marg. Quarterly. Mumbai, India: Scientific Publishers, 1946-

Master Drawings. Quarterly. New York: Master Drawings Association, 1963-

October. Cambridge, MA: MIT Press, 1976-

Oxford Art Journal. 3/year. Oxford: Oxford Univ. Press, 1978-

Parkett. 3/year. Züürich, Switzerland: Parkett Verlag AG, 1984-

Print Quarterly. Quarterly. London: Print Quarterly Publications, 1984-

Similous: Netherlands Quarterly for the History of Art. Quarterly. Apeldoorn, Netherlands: Stichting voor Nederlandse Kunsthistorische Publicaties, 1966-

Woman's Art Journal. Semiannually. Philadelphia: Old City Publishing Inc, 1980-

Internet Directories for Art History Information

ARCHITECTURE AND BUILDING
http://library.nevada.edu/arch/rsrce/websrce/contents.html

A directory of architecture websites collected by Jeanne Brown at the Univ. of Nevada at Las Vegas. Topical lists include architecture, building and construction, design, history, housing, planning, preservation, and landscape architecture. Most entries include a brief annotation and the last date the link was accessed by the compiler.

ART HISTORY RESOURCES ON THE WEB
http://witcombe.sbc.edu/ARTHLinks.html

Authored by Christopher L. C. E. Witcombe of Sweet Briar College in Virginia since 1995, the site includes an impressive number of links for various art historical eras as well as links to research resources, museums, and galleries. The content is frequently updated.

ART IN FLUX. A DIRECTORY OF RESOURCES FOR RESEARCH IN CONTEMPORARY ART
http://www.boisestate.edu/art/artinflux/intro.html

Cheryl K. Shutleff of Boise State Univ. in Idaho has authored this directory, which includes sites selected according to their relevance to the study of national or international contemporary art and artists. The subsections include artists, museums, theory, reference, and links.

ARTCYCLOPEDIA: THE FINE ARTS SEARCH ENGINE

With over 2,100 art sites and 75,000 links, this is one of the most comprehensive web directories for artists and art topics.
The primary searching is by artist's name but access is also available by artistic movement, nation, timeline and medium.

MOTHER OF ALL ART HISTORY LINKS PAGES
http://www.art-design.umich.edu/mother/

Maintained by the Dept. of the History of Art at the Univ. of Michigan, this directory covers art history departments, art museums, fine arts schools and departments as well as links to research resources. Each entry includes annotations.

VOICE OF THE SHUTTLE
http://vos.ucsb.edu

Sponsored by Univ. of California, Santa Barbara, this directory includes over 70 pages of links to humanities and humanities-related resources on the Internet. The structured guide includes specific sub-sections on architecture, on art (modern & contemporary), and on art history. Links usually include a one sentence explanation and the resource is frequently updated with new information.

YAHOO! ARTS>ART HISTORY
http://dir.yahoo.com/Arts/Art_History/
Another extensive directory of art links organized into subdivisions with one of the most extensive being "Periods and Movements." Links include the name of the site as well as a few words of explanation.

Ancient Art in the Western Tradition, General

Amiet, Pierre. *Art in the Ancient World: A Handbook of Styles and Forms.* New York: Rizzoli, 1981.
Beard, Mary, and John Henderson. *Classical Art: From Greece to Rome.* Oxford History of Art. Oxford: Oxford Univ. Press, 2001.
Boardman, John. *Oxford History of Classical Art.* New York: Oxford Univ. Press, 2001.
Chitham, Robert. *The Classical Orders of Architecture.* 2nd ed. Boston: Elsevier/Architectural Press, 2005.
Ehrich, Robert W., ed. *Chronologies in Old World Archaeology.* 3rd ed. 2 vols. Chicago: Univ. of Chicago Press, 1992.
Gerster, Georg. *The Past from Above: Aerial Photographs of Archaeological Sites.* Ed. Charlotte Trüümpler. Trans. Stewart Spencer. Los Angeles: The J. Paul Getty Museum, 2005.
Groenewegen-Frankfort, H. A., and Bernard Ashmole. *Art of the Ancient World: Painting, Pottery, Sculpture, Architecture from Egypt, Mesopotamia, Crete, Greece, and Rome.* Library of Art History. Upper Saddle River, NJ: Prentice Hall, 1972.
Haywood, John. *The Penguin Historical Atlas of Ancient Civilizations.* New York: Penguin, 2005.
Lloyd, Seton, and Hans Wolfgang Muller. *Ancient Architecture.* New York: Rizzoli, 1986.
Milleker, Elizabeth J., ed. *The Year One: Art of the Ancient World East and West.* New York: Metropolitan Museum of Art, 2000.
Nagle, D. Brendan. *The Ancient World: A Social and Cultural History.* 6th ed. Upper Saddle River, NJ: Pearson Prentice Hall, 2006.
Romer, John, and Elizabeth Romer. *The Seven Wonders of the World: A History of the Modern Imagination.* New York: Henry Holt, 1995.
Saggs, H. W. F. *Civilization before Greece and Rome.* New Haven: Yale Univ. Press, 1989.
Smith, William Stevenson. *Interconnections in the Ancient Near East: A Study of the Relationships between the Arts of Egypt, the Aegean, and Western Asia.* New Haven: Yale Univ. Press, 1965.
Tadgell, Christopher. Imperial Form: *From Achaemenid Iran to Augustan Rome.* New York: Whitney Library of Design, 1998.
——. *Origins: Egypt, West Asia and the Aegean.* New York: Whitney Library of Design, 1998.
Trigger, Bruce G. *Understanding Early Civilizations: A Comparative Study.* New York: Cambridge Univ. Press, 2003.
Winckelmann, Johann Joachim. *History of the Art of Antiquity. Trans.* Harry Francis Mallgrave. Texts & Documents. Los Angeles: Getty Research Institute, 2006.
Woodford, Susan. *The Art of Greece and Rome.* 2nd ed. New York: Cambridge Univ. Press, 2004.

European Medieval Art, General

Backman, Clifford R. *The Worlds of Medieval Europe.* New York: Oxford Univ. Press, 2003.
Bennett, Adelaide Louise, et al. *Medieval Mastery: Book Illumination from Charlemagne to Charles the Bold: 800–1475.* Trans. Lee Preedy and Greta Arblaster-Holmer. Turnhout: Brepols, 2002.
Benton, Janetta Rebold. *Art of the Middle Ages. World of Art.* New York: Thames & Hudson, 2002.
Binski, Paul. *Painters.* Medieval Craftsmen. London: British Museum Press, 1992.
Brown, Sarah, and David O'Connor. *Glass-painters.* Medieval Craftsmen. London: British Museum Press, 1992.
Calkins, Robert C. *Medieval Architecture in Western Europe: From A.D. 300 to 1500.* 1v. CD-ROM. New York: Oxford Univ. Press, 1998.
Cherry, John F. *Goldsmiths.* Medieval Craftsmen. London: British Museum Press, 1992.
Clark, William W., *Medieval Cathedrals.* Greenwood Guides to Historic Events of the Medieval World. Westport, CT: Greenwood Press, 2006.
Coldstream, Nicola. *Masons and Sculptors. Medieval Craftsmen.* London: British Museum Press, 1991.
———. *Medieval Architecture.* Oxford History of Art. Oxford: Oxford Univ. Press, 2002.
De Hamel, Christopher. *Scribes and Illuminators.* Medieval Craftsmen. London: British Museum Press, 1992.
Duby, Georges. *Art and Society in the Middle Ages.* Trans. Jean Birrell. Malden, MA: Blackwell Publishers, 2000.
——. *Sculpture: The Great Art of the Middle Ages from the Fifth to the Fifteenth Century.* New York: Skira/Rizzoli, 1990.
Eames, Elizabeth S. *English Tilers.* Medieval Craftsmen. London: British Museum Press, 1992.
Fossier, Robert, ed. *The Cambridge Illustrated History of the Middle Ages.* Trans. Janet Sondheimer & Sarah Hanbury Tenison. 3 vols. Cambridge, U.K.: Cambridge Univ. Press, 1986–97.
Hurlimann, Martin, and Jean Bony. *French Cathedrals.* Rev. & enlg. London: Thames and Hudson, 1967
Jotischky, Andrew, and Caroline Susan Hull. *The Penguin Historical Atlas of the Medieval World.* New York: Penguin, 2005.
Kenyon, John. *Medieval Fortifications.* Leicester: Leicester Univ. Press, 1990.
Labarge, Margaret Wade. *A Small Sound of the Trumpet: Women in Medieval Life.* London: Hamilton, 1990.
Pfaffenbichler, Matthias. *Armourers.* Medieval Craftsmen. London: British Museum Press, 1992.
Rebold Benton, Janetta. *Art of the Middle Ages.* World of Art. New York: Thames & Hudson, 2002.
Sekules, Veronica. *Medieval Art.* Oxford History of Art. New York: Oxford Univ. Press, 2001.
Snyder, James, Henry Luttikhuizen, and Dorothy Verkerk. *Art of the Middle Ages.* 2nd ed. Upper Saddle River, NJ: Prentice Hall, 2006.
Staniland, Kay. *Embroiderers.* Medieval Craftsmen. London: British Museum Press, 1991.
Stokstad, Marilyn. *Medieval Art.* 2nd ed. New York: Westview, 2004.
———. *Medieval Castles.* Greenwood Guides to Historic Events of the Medieval World. Westport, CT: Greenwood Press, 2005.
Wixom, William D., ed. *Mirror of the Medieval World.* New York: Metropolitan Museum of Art, 1999.

European Renaissance through Eighteenth-Century Art, General

Black, C. F., et al. *Cultural Atlas of the Renaissance.* New York: Prentice Hall General Reference, 1993.
Blunt, Anthony. *Art and Architecture in France, 1500–1700.* 5th ed. Rev. Richard Beresford. Pelican History of Art. New Haven: Yale Univ. Press, 1999.
Brown, Jonathan. *Painting in Spain: 1500–1700.* Pelican History of Art. New Haven: Yale Univ. Press, 1998.
Cole, Bruce. *Italian Art, 1250–1550: The Relation of Renaissance Art to Life and Society.* New York: Harper & Row, 1987.
Graham-Dixon, Andrew. *Renaissance.* Berkeley: Univ. of California Press, 1999.
Harbison, Craig. *The Mirror of the Artist: Northern Renaissance Art in Its Historical Context.* Perspectives. New York: Abrams, 1995.
Harris, Ann Sutherland. *Seventeenth-Century Art & Architecture.* Upper Saddle River, NJ: Pearson Prentice Hall, 2005
Harrison, Charles, Paul Wood, and Jason Gaiger. *Art in Theory 1648–1815: An Anthology of Changing Ideas.* Oxford: Blackwell, 2000.
Hartt, Frederick, and David G. Wilkins. *History of Italian Renaissance Art: Painting, Sculpture, Architecture.* 6th ed. Upper Saddle River, NJ: Prentice Hall, 2007
Jestaz, Bertrand. *The Art of the Renaissance.* Trans. I. Mark Paris. New York: Abrams, 1995.
Levenson, Jay A., ed. Circa 1492: *Art in the Age of Exploration.* Washington: National Gallery of Art, 1991.
McCorquodale, Charles. *The Renaissance: European Painting, 1400–1600.* London: Studio Editions, 1994.
Minor, Vernon Hyde. *Baroque & Rococo: Art & Culture.* New York: Abrams, 1999.
Murray, Peter. *Renaissance Architecture.* History of World Architecture. Milan: Electa, 1985.
Paoletti, John T., and Gary M. Radke. *Art in Renaissance Italy.* 3rd ed. Upper Saddle River, NJ: Prentice Hall, 2006.
Ripa, Cesare. *Baroque and Rococo Pictorial Imagery: The 1758-60 Hertel Edition of Ripa's 'Iconologia.'* Introd., transl., & commentaries Edward A. Maser. The Dover Pictorial Archives Series. New York: Dover Publications, 1991
Smith, Jeffrey Chipps. *The Northern Renaissance.* Art & Ideas. New York: Phaidon Press, 2004.
Stechow, Wolfgang. *Northern Renaissance, 1400–1600: Sources and Documents.* Upper Saddle River, NJ: Prentice Hall, 1966.
Summerson, John. *Architecture in Britain, 1530–1830.* 9th ed. Yale Univ. Press Pelican History of Art. New Haven: Yale Univ. Press, 1993.
Waterhouse, Ellis K. *Painting in Britain, 1530 to 1790.* 5th ed. Yale Univ. Press Pelican History of Art. New Haven: Yale Univ. Press, 1994.
Whinney, Margaret Dickens. *Sculpture in Britain: 1530–1830.* 2nd ed. Rev. John Physick. Pelican History of Art. London: Penguin, 1988.

Modern Art in the West, General

Arnason, H. Harvard. *History of Modern Art: Painting, Sculpture, Architecture, Photography.* 5th ed. Rev. Peter Kalb. Upper Saddle River, NJ: Prentice Hall, 2004.
Ballantyne, Andrew, ed. *Architectures: Modernism and After.* New Interventions in Art History, 3. Malden, MA: Blackwell, 2004.
Barnitz, Jacqueline. *Twentieth- Century Art of Latin America.* Austin: Univ. of Texas Press, 2001.
Bjelajac, David. *American Art: A Cultural History.* Rev. & exp. ed. Upper Saddle River, NJ: Prentice Hall, 2005.
Bowness, Alan. *Modern European Art.* World of Art. New York: Thames and Hudson, 1995.
Brettell, Richard R. *Modern Art, 1851–1929: Capitalism and Representation.* Oxford History of Art. Oxford: Oxford Univ. Press, 1999.
Chipp, Herschel Browning. *Theories of Modern Art: A Source Book by Artists and Critics.* California Studies in the History of Art. Berkeley: Univ. of California Press, 1984.
Clarke, Graham. *The Photograph.* Oxford History of Art. Oxford: Oxford Univ. Press, 1997
Craven, David. *Art and Revolution in Latin America, 1910–1990.* New Haven: Yale Univ. Press, 2002.
Craven, Wayne. *American Art: History and Culture.* Rev. ed. Boston: McGraw-Hill, 2003.
Doordan, Dennis P. *Twentieth-Century Architecture.* New York: Abrams, 2002.
Doss, Erika. *Twentieth-Century American Art.* Oxford: Oxford Univ. Press, 2002.
Edwards, Steve, and Paul Wood, eds. *Art of the Avant-Gardes.* Art of the 20th Century. New Haven: Yale Univ. Press in assoc. with the Open Univ., 2004.
Foster, Hal, et al. *Art Since 1900: Modernism, Antimodernism, Postmodernism.* New York: Thames & Hudson, 2004.
Gaiger, Jason, ed. *Frameworks for Modern Art. Art of the 20th Century.* New Haven: Yale Univ Press in assoc. with the Open Univ., 2003.
———, and Paul Wood, eds. *Art of the Twentieth Century: A Reader.* New Haven: Yale Univ. Press, 2003
Hamilton, George Heard. *Painting and Sculpture in Europe, 1880–1940.* 6th ed. Pelican History of Art. New Haven: Yale Univ. Press, 1993.
Hammacher, A. M. *Modern Sculpture: Tradition and Innovation.* Enlg. ed. New York: Abrams, 1988.
Harrison, Charles, and Paul Wood, eds. *Art in Theory: 1900–2000: An Anthology of Changing Ideas.* 2nd ed. Oxford: Blackwell, 2002.
Hunter, Sam, John Jacobus, and Daniel Wheeler. *Modern Art: Painting, Sculpture, Architecture, Photography.* 3rd rev. & exp. ed. Upper Saddle River, NJ: Prentice Hall, 2004.
Krauss, Rosalinde. *Passages in Modern Sculpture.* Cambridge, MA: MIT Press, 1977.
Mancini, JoAnne Marie. *Pre-Modernism: Art-World Change and American Culture from the Civil War to the Armory Show.* Princeton: Princeton Univ. Press, 2005.
Marien, Mary Warner. *Photography: A Cultural History.* New York: Harry N. Abrams, 2002.
Meecham, Pam, and Julie Sheldon. *Modern Art: A Critical Introduction.* 2nd ed. New York: Routledge, 2005.
Newlands, Anne. *Canadian Art: From Its Beginnings to 2000.* Willowdale, Ont.. Firefly Books, 2000.
Harris, Ann Sutherland, and Linda Nochlin. *Women Artists: 1550–1950.* Los Angeles: Los Angeles County Museum of Art, 1976.
The Phaidon Atlas of Contemporary World Architecture. London: Phaidon, 2004.
Powell, Richard J. *Black Art: A Cultural History.* 2nd ed. World of Art. New York: Thames and Hudson, 2002.
Rosenblum, Naomi. A World History of Photography. 3rd ed. New York: Abbeville, 1997

Ruhrberg, Karl. *Art of the 20th Century*. Ed. Ingo F. Walther. 2 vols. New York: Taschen, 1998

Scully, Vincent Joseph. *Modern Architecture and Other Essays*. Princeton: Princeton Univ. Press, 2003

Stiles, Kristine, and Peter Howard Selz. *Theories and Documents of Contemporary Art: A Sourcebook of Artists' Writings*. California Studies in the History of Art, 35. Berkeley: Univ. of California Press, 1996.

Tafuri, Manfredo. *Modern Architecture*. History of World Architecture. 2 vols. New York: Electa/Rizzoli, 1986.

Traba, Marta. *Art of Latin America, 1900-1980*. Washington, D.C.. Inter-American Development Bank, 1994.

Upton, Dell. *Architecture in the United States*. Oxford History of Art. Oxford: Oxford Univ. Press, 1998.

Wood, Paul, ed. *Varieties of Modernism*. Art of the 20th Century. New Haven: Yale Univ. Press in assoc. with the Open Univ., 2004.

Woodham, Jonathan M. *Twentieth Century Design*. Oxford History of Art. Oxford: Oxford Univ. Press, 1997

Asian Art, General

Addiss, Stephen, Gerald Groemer, and J. Thomas Rimer, eds. *Traditional Japanese Arts and Culture: An Illustrated Sourcebook*. Honolulu: Univ. of Hawai'i Press, 2006.

Barnhart, Richard M. Three *Thousand Years of Chinese Painting*. New Haven: Yale Univ. Press, 1997

Blunden, Caroline, and Mark Elvin. *Cultural Atlas of China*. 2nd ed. New York: Checkmark Books, 1998.

Brown, Kerry, ed. *Sikh Art and Literature*. New York: Routledge in collaboration with the Sikh Foundation, 1999.

Bussagli, Mario. *Oriental Architecture*. History of World Architecture. 2 vols. New York: Electa/Rizzoli, 1989.

Chang, Leon Long-Yien, and Peter Miller. *Four Thousand Years of Chinese Calligraphy*. Chicago: Univ. of Chicago Press, 1990.

Chung, Yang-mo. *Arts of Korea*. Ed. Judith G. Smith. New York: Metropolitan Museum of Art, 1998.

Clark, John. *Modern Asian Art*. Honolulu: Univ. of Hawaii Press, 1998.

Clunas, Craig. *Art in China*. Oxford History of Art. Oxford: Oxford Univ. Press, 1997

Collcutt, Martin, Marius Jansen, and Isao Kumakura. *Cultural Atlas of Japan*. New York: Facts on File, 1988.

Craven, Roy C. *Indian Art: A Concise History*. Rev. ed. World of Art. New York: Thames and Hudson, 1997.

Dehejia, Vidya. *Indian Art*. Art & Ideas. London: Phaidon Press, 1997

Fisher, Robert E. *Buddhist Art and Architecture*. World of Art. New York: Thames and Hudson, 1993.

Fu, Xinian. *Chinese Architecture*. Ed. & exp. Nancy S. Steinhardt. The Culture & Civilization of China. New Haven: Yale Univ. Press, 2002.

Hearn, Maxwell K., and Judith G. Smith, eds. *Arts of the Sung and Yüan: Papers Prepared for an International Symposium*. New York: Dept. of Asian Art, Metropolitan Museum of Art, 1996.

Heibonsha Survey of Japanese Art. 31 vols. New York: Weatherhill, 1972–80.

Hertz, Betti-Sue. *Past in Reverse: Contemporary Art of East Asia*. San Diego: San Diego Museum of Art, 2004.

Japanese Arts Library. 15 vols. New York: Kodansha International, 1977–87

Kerlogue, Fiona. *Arts of Southeast Asia*. World of Art. New York: Thames & Hudson, 2004.

Khanna, Balraj, and George Michell. *Human and Divine: 2000 Years of Indian Sculpture*. London: Hayward Gallery Pub., 2000.

Lee, Sherman E. *A History of Far Eastern Art*. 5th ed. Ed. Naomi Noble Richards. New York: Abrams, 1994.

—— *China, 5000 Years: Innovation and Transformation in the Arts*. New York: Solomon R. Guggenheim Museum, 1998.

Liu, Cary Y., and Dora C.Y. Ching, eds. *Arts of the Sung and Yüan: Ritual, Ethnicity, and Style in Painting*. Princeton: Art Museum, Princeton Univ., 1999.

McArthur, Meher. *The Arts of Asia: Materials, Techniques, Styles*. New York: Thames & Hudson, 2005.

———. *Reading Buddhist Art: An Illustrated Guide to Buddhist Signs and Symbols*. New York: Thames & Hudson, 2002.

Mason, Penelope. *History of Japanese Art*. 2nd ed. Upper Saddle River, NJ: Pearson Prentice Hall, 2005.

Michell, George. *Hindu Art and Architecture*. World of Art. London: Thames & Hudson, 2000.

——— *The Penguin Guide to the Monuments of India*. 2 vols. New York: Viking, 1989.

Mitter, Partha. *Indian Art*. Oxford History of Art. Oxford: Oxford Univ. Press, 2001.

Nickel, Lukas, ed. *Return of the Buddha: The Qingzhou Discoveries*. London: Royal Academy of Arts, 2002.

Pak, Youngsook, and Roderick Whitfield. *Buddhist Sculpture*. Handbook of Korean Art. London: Laurence King, 2003.

Stanley-Baker, Joan. *Japanese Art*. Rev. & exp. ed. World of Art. New York: Thames and Hudson, 2000.

Sullivan, Michael. *The Arts of China*. 4th ed., Exp. & rev. Berkeley: Univ. of California Press, 1999.

Thorp, Robert L., and Richard Ellis Vinograd. *Chinese Art & Culture*. New York: Abrams, 2001.

Topsfield, Andrew, ed. *In the Realm of Gods and Kings: Arts of India*. London: Philip Wilson, 2004.

Tucker, Jonathan. *The Silk Road: Art and History*. Chicago: Art Media Resources, 2003.

Tregear, Mary. *Chinese Art*. Rev. ed. World of Art. New York: Thames and Hudson, 1997

Vainker S. J. *Chinese Pottery and Porcelain: From Prehistory to the Present*. London: British Museum, 1991.

Varley, H. Paul *Japanese Culture*. 4th ed., Updated & exp. Honolulu: Univ. of Hawaii Press, 2000.

African and Oceanic Art and Art of the Americas, General

Anderson, Richard L., and Karen L Field, eds. *Art in Small-Scale Societies: Contemporary Readings*. Englewood Cliffs, NJ: Prentice-Hall, 1993.

Bacquart, Jean-Baptiste. *The Tribal Arts of Africa*. New York: Thames and Hudson, 1998.

Bassani, Ezio, ed. *Arts of Africa: 7000 Years of African Art*. Milan: Skira, 2005.

Benson, Elizabeth P. *Retratos: 2,000 Years of Latin American Portraits*. San Antonio: San Antonio Museum of Art, 2004.

Berlo, Janet Catherine, and Lee Ann Wilson. *Arts of Africa, Oceania, and the Americas: Selected Readings*. Upper Saddle River, NJ: Prentice Hall, 1993.

Calloway, Colin G.. *First Peoples: A Documentary Survey of American Indian History*. Boston and New York: Bedford/St. Martin's, 2004.

Coote, Jeremy, and Anthony Shelton, eds. *Anthropology, Art, and Aesthetics*. New York: Oxford Univ. Press, 1992.

D'Azevedao, Warren L. *The Traditional Artist in African Societies*. Bloomington: Indiana Univ. Press, 1989.

Drewal, Henry, and John Pemberton III. *Yoruba: Nine Centuries of African Art and Thought*. New York: Center for African Art, 1989.

Evans, Susan Toby. *Ancient Mexico & Central America: Archaeology and Culture History*. New York: Thames & Hudson, 2004.

———, and David L. Webster, eds. *Archaeology of Ancient Mexico and Central America : An Encyclopedia*. New York: Garland Pub., 2001.

———, and Joanne Pillsbury, eds. *Palaces of the Ancient New World: A Symposium at Dumbarton Oaks, 10th and 11th October, 1998*. Washington, D.C.. Dumbarton Oaks Research Library and Collection, 2004.

Geoffroy-Schneiter, Bééréénice. *Tribal Arts*. New York: Vendome Press, 2000.

Guidoni, Enrico. *Primitive Architecture*. Trans. Robert Eric Wolf. History of World Architecture. New York: Rizzoli, 1987

Hiller, Susan, ed. & comp. *The Myth of Primitivism: Perspectives on Art*. London: Routledge, 1991.

Mack, John, ed. *Africa, Arts and Cultures*. London: British Museum, 2000.

Mexico: Splendors of Thirty Centuries. New York: Metropolitan Museum of Art, 1990.

Murray, Jocelyn, ed. *Cultural Atlas of Africa*. Rev. ed. New York: Facts on File, 1998.

Nunley, John W., and Cara McCarty. *Masks: Faces of Culture*. New York: Abrams in assoc. with the Saint Louis Art Museum, 1999.

Perani, Judith, and Fred T. Smith. *The Visual Arts of Africa: Gender, Power, and Life Cycle Rituals*. Upper Saddle River, NJ: Prentice Hall, 1998.

Phillips, Tom. *Africa: The Art of a Continent*. London: Prestel, 1996.

Price, Sally. *Primitive Art in Civilized Places*. Chicago: Univ. of Chicago Press, 1989.

Rabineau, Phyllis. *Feather Arts: Beauty, Wealth, and Spirit from Five Continents*. Chicago: Field Museum of Natural History, 1979.

Schuster, Carl, and Edmund Carpenter. *Patterns that Connect: Social Symbolism in Ancient & Tribal Art*. New York: Abrams, 1996.

Scott, John F. *Latin American Art: Ancient to Modern*. Gainesville: Univ. Press of Florida, 1999.

Stepan, Peter. *Africa*. Trans. John Gabriel & Elizabeth Schwaiger. World of Art. London: Prestel, 2001.

Visonàà, Monica Blackmun, et al. *A History of Art in Africa*. Upper Saddle River, NJ: Prentice Hall, 2000.

Chapter 1
Prehistoric Art in Europe

Aujoulat, Norbert. *Lascaux: Movement, Space, and Time*. New York: H. N. Abrams, 2005.

Bahn Paul G. *The Cambridge Illustrated History of Prehistoric Art*. Cambridge Illustrated History. Cambridge, U.K.: Cambridge Univ. Press, 1998.

Bataille, Georges. *The Cradle of Humanity: Prehistoric Art and Culture*. Ed. and intro. Stuart Kendall. Trans. Michelle Kendall & Stuart Kendall. New York: Zone Books, 2005.

Berghaus, Gunter. *New Perspectives on Prehistoric Art*. Westport, CT: Praeger, 2004

Chippindale, Christopher. *Stonehenge Complete*. 3rd ed. New York: Thames and Hudson, 2004.

Clottes, Jean. *Chauvet Cave: The Art of Earliest Times*. Salt Lake City: Univ. of Utah Press, 2003.

———. *World Rock Art*. Trans. Guy Bennett. Los Angeles: Getty Conservation Institute, 2002.

———, and J. David Lewis-Williams. *The Shamans of Prehistory: Trance and Magic in the Painted Caves*. Trans. Sophie Hawkes. New York: Harry N. Abrams, 1998.

Cunliffe, Barry W., ed. *The Oxford Illustrated History of Prehistoric Europe*. New York: Oxford Univ. Press, 2001.

Forte, Maurizio, and Alberto Siliotti. *Virtual Archaeology: Re-Creating Ancient Worlds*. New York: Abrams, 1997.

Freeman, Leslie G. *Altamira Revisited and Other Essays on Early Art*. Chicago: Institute for Prehistoric Investigation, 1987

Gowlett, John A. J. *Ascent to Civilization: The Archaeology of Early Humans*. 2nd ed. New York: McGraw-Hill, 1993.

Guthrie, R. Dale. *The Nature of Paleolithic Art*. Chicago: Univ. of Chicago Press, 2005.

Jope, E. M. *Early Celtic art in the British Isles*. 2 vols. New York: Oxford Univ. Press, 2000.

Leakey, Richard E. and Roger Lewin. *Origins Reconsidered: In Search of What Makes Us Human*. New York: Doubleday, 1992.

Leroi-Gourhan, Andréé. *The Dawn of European Art: An Introduction to Paleolithic Cave Painting*. Trans. Sara Champion. Cambridge, U.K.: Cambridge Univ. Press, 1982.

Lewis-Williams, J. David. *The Mind in the Cave: Consciousness and the Origins of Art*. New York: Thames & Hudson, 2002.

Marshack, Alexander. *The Roots of Civilization: The Cognitive Beginnings of Man's First Art, Symbol, and Notation*. New York: McGraw-Hill, 1972.

Megaw, Ruth, and Vincent Megaw. *Celtic Art: From Its Beginnings to the Book of Kells*. Rev. and exp. ed. New York: Thames and Hudson, 2001.

O'Kelly, Michael J. *Newgrange: Archaeology, Art, and Legend. New Aspects of Antiquity*. London: Thames and Hudson, 1982.

Price, T. Douglas, and Gray M. Feinman. *Images of the Past*. 3rd ed. Mountain View, CA: Mayfield, 2000.

Renfrew, Colin, ed. *The Megalithic Monuments of Western Europe*. London: Thames and Hudson, 1983.

Ruspoli, Mario. *The Cave of Lascaux: The Final Photographs*. New York: Abrams, 1987.

Sandars, N. K. *Prehistoric Art in Europe*. 2nd ed. Pelican History of Art. New Haven: Yale Univ. Press, 1992.

Sura Ramos, Pedro A. *The Cave of Altamira*. Gen. Ed. Antonio Beltran. New York: Abrams, 1999.

Sieveking, Ann. *The Cave Artists*. Ancient People and Places, vol. 93. London: Thames and Hudson, 1979.

White, Randall. *Prehistoric Art: The Symbolic Journey of Humankind*. New York: Harry N. Abrams, 2003.

Chapter 2
Art of the Ancient Near East

Akurgal, Ekrem. *Ancient Civilizations and Ruins of Turkey: From Prehistoric Times until the End of the Roman Empire*. 5th ed. London: Kegan Paul, 2002.

Aruz, Joan, ed. *Art of the First Cities: The Third Millennium B.C. from the Mediterranean to the Indus*. New York: Metropolitan Museum of Art, 2003.

Bahrani, Zainab. *The Graven Image: Representation in Babylonia and Assyria*. Archaeology, Culture, and Society Series. Philadelphia: Univ. of Pennsylvania Press, 2003.

Boardman, John. *Persia and the West: An Archaeological Investigation of the Genesis of Achaemenid Art*. New York: Thames & Hudson, 2000.

Bottero, Jean. *Everyday Life in Ancient Mesopotamia*. Trans. Antonia Nevill. Baltimore, MD.: Johns Hopkins Univ. Press, 2001.

Charvat, Petr. *Mesopotamia before History*. Rev. & updated ed. New York: Routledge, 2002.

Collon, Dominique. *Ancient Near Eastern Art*. Berkeley: Univ. of California Press, 1995.

Crawford, Harriet. *Sumer and the Sumerians*. 2nd ed. New York: Cambridge Univ. Press, 2004.

Curtis, J.E., and J. E. Reade, eds. *Art and Empire: Treasures from Assyria in the British Museum*. New York: Metropolitan Museum of Art, 1995.

Curtis, John, and Nigel Tallis, eds. *Forgotten Empire: The World of Ancient Persia*. Berkeley: Univ. of California Press, 2005.

Downey, Susan B. *Mesopotamian Religious Architecture: Alexander through the Parthians*. Princeton: Princeton Univ. Press, 1988. Ferrier, R. W., ed. Arts of Persia. New Haven: Yale Univ. Press, 1989.

Frankfort, Henri. *The Art and Architecture of the Ancient Orient*. 5th ed. Pelican History of Art. New Haven: Yale Univ. Press, 1996.

Haywood, John. *Ancient Civilizations of the Near East and Mediterranean*. London: Cassell, 1997

Lloyd, Seton. *Ancient Turkey: A Traveller's History of Anatolia*. Berkeley: Univ. of California Press, 1989.

Meyers, Eric M., ed. *The Oxford Encyclopedia of Archaeology in the Near East*. 5 vols. New York: Oxford Univ. Press, 1997.

Moorey, P. R. S. *Idols of the People: Miniature Images of Clay in the Ancient Near East*. The Schweich Lectures of the British Academy; 2001. New York: Oxford Univ. Press, 2003.

Polk, Milbry, and Angela M. H. Schuster. *The Looting of the Iraq Museum, Baghdad: The Lost Legacy of Ancient Mesopotamia*. New York: Harry N. Abrams, 2005.

Reade, Julian. *Assyrian Sculpture*. Cambridge, MA: Harvard Univ. Press, 1999.

Roaf, Michael. *Cultural Atlas of Mesopotamia and the Ancient Near East*. New York: Facts on File, 1990.

Roux, Georges. *Ancient Iraq*. 3rd ed. London: Penguin, 1992.

Zettler, Richard L., and Lee Horne, ed. *Treasures from the Royal Tombs of Ur*. Philadelphia: Univ. of Pennsylvania, Museum of Archaeology and Anthropology, 1998.

CHAPTER 3
Art of Ancient Egypt

Arnold, Dieter. *Temples of the Last Pharaohs*. New York: Oxford Univ. Press, 1999.

Arnold, Dorothea. *When the Pyramids Were Built: Egyptian Art of the Old Kingdom*. New York: Metropolitan Museum of Art, 1999.

Baines, John, and Jaromír Málek. *Cultural Atlas of Ancient Egypt*. Rev. ed. New York: Facts on File, 2000.

Brier, Bob. *Egyptian Mummies; Unraveling the Secrets of an Ancient Art*. New York: Morrow, 1994.

Casson, Lionel. *Everyday Life in Ancient Egypt*. Rev. & exp. ed. Baltimore, Md.. Johns Hopkins Univ. Press, 2001.

Egyptian Art in the Age of the Pyramids. New York: Metropolitan Museum of Art, 1999.

The Egyptian Book of the Dead: The Book of Going Forth by Day: Being the Papyrus of Ani (Royal Scribe of the Divine Offerings). Trans. Raymond O. Faulkner. 2nd rev. ed. San Francisco: Chronicle, 1998.

Freed, Rita E. Sue D'Auria, and Yvonne J Markowitz. *Pharaohs of the Sun: Akhenaten, Nefertiti, Tutankhamen*. Boston: Museum of Fine Arts in assoc. with Bulfinch Press/Little, Brown and Co., 1999.

Hawass, Zahi A. *Tutankhamun and the Golden Age of the Pharaohs*. Washington, D.C.. National Geographic, 2005.

Johnson, Paul. *The Civilization of Ancient Egypt*. Updated ed. New York: HarperCollins, 1999.

Kozloff, Arielle P., and Betsy M. Bryan. *Egypt's Dazzling Sun: Amenhotep III and His World*. Cleveland: Cleveland Museum of Art, 1992.

Lehner, Mark. *The Complete Pyramids: Solving the Ancient Mysteries*. New York: Thames and Hudson, 1997.

Málek, Jaromir. *Egypt: 4000 Years of Art*. London: Phaidon, 2003.

Pemberton, Delia. *Ancient Egypt*. Architectural Guides for Travelers. San Francisco: Chronicle, 1992.

Robins, Gay. *The Art of Ancient Egypt*. Cambridge, MA: Harvard Univ. Press, 1997.

Roehrig, Catharine H., Renee Dreyfus, and Cathleen A. Keller. *Hatshepsut, from Queen to Pharaoh*. New York: The Metropolitan Museum of Art, 2005.

Russmann, Edna R. *Egyptian Sculpture: Cairo and Luxor*. Austin: Univ. of Texas Press, 1989.

Smith, Craig B. *How the Great Pyramid Was Built*. Washington, D.C.. Smithsonian Books, 2004.

Smith, W. Stevenson. *The Art and Architecture of Ancient Egypt*. 3rd ed. Rev. William Kelly Simpson. Pelican History of Art. New Haven: Yale Univ. Press, 1999.

Strudwick, Nigel, and Helen Studwick. *Thebes in Egypt: A Guide to the Tombs and Temples of Ancient Luxor*. Ithaca, NY: Cornell Univ. Press, 1999.

Thomas, Thelma K. *Late Antique Egyptian Funerary Sculpture: Images for this World and for the Next*. Princeton: Princeton Univ. Press, 2000.

Tiradritti, Francesco. *Ancient Egypt: Art, Architecture and History*. Trans. Phil Goddard. London: British Museum, 2002.

The Treasures of Ancient Egypt: From the Egyptian Museum in Cairo. New York: Rizzoli, 2003.

Wilkinson, Richard H. *The Complete Temples of Ancient Egypt*. New York: Thames & Hudson, 2000.

———. *Reading Egyptian Art: A Hieroglyphic Guide to Ancient Egyptian Painting and Sculpture*. London: Thames and Hudson, 1992.

Ziegler, Cristiane, ed. *The Pharaohs*. New York: Rizzoli, 2002.

Zivie-Coche, Christiane. *Sphinx: History of a Monument*. Trans. David Lorton. Ithaca, NY: Cornell Univ. Press, 2002.

CHAPTER 4
Aegean Art

Barber, R. L. N. *The Cyclades in the Bronze Age*. Iowa City: Univ. of Iowa Press, 1987

Castleden, Rodney. *The Knossos Labyrinth: A New View of the "Palace of Minos" at Knossos*. London: Routledge, 1990.

———. *Mycenaeans*. New York: Routledge, 2005.

Demargne, Pierre. *The Birth of Greek Art*. Trans. Stuart Gilbert & James Emmons. Arts of Mankind. New York: Golden, 1964.

Dickinson. Oliver. *The Aegean Bronze Age*. Cambridge World Archaeology. Cambridge, U.K.: Cambridge Univ. Press, 1994.

Doumas, Christos. *The Wall-Paintings of Thera*. 2nd ed. Trans. Alex Doumas. Athens: Kapon Editions, 1999.

Fitton, J. Lesley. *Cycladic Art*. 2nd ed. London: British Museum, 1999.

Getz-Gentle, Pat. *Personal Styles in Early Cycladic Sculpture*. Madison: Univ. of Wisconsin Press, 2001.

Hamilakis, Yannis. ed. *Labyrinth Revisited: Rethinking 'Minoan' Archaeology*. Oxford: Oxbow, 2002.

Higgins, Reynold. *Minoan and Mycenean Art*. Rev. ed. World of Art. New York: Thames and Hudson, 1997.

Hitchcock, Louise. *Minoan architecture: A Contextual Analysis*. Studies in Mediterranean Archaeology and Literature, Pocket-Book, 155. Jonsered: P. Åströöms Förlag, 2000.

Immerwahr, Sara Anderson. *Aegean Painting in the Bronze Age*. University Park: Pennsylvania State Univ. Press, 1990.

Preziosi, Donald, and Louise Hitchcock. *Aegean Art and Architecture*. Oxford History of Art. Oxford: Oxford Univ. Press, 1999.

CHAPTER 5
Art of Ancient Greece

Barletta, Barbara A. *The Origins of the Greek Architectural Orders*. New York: Cambridge Univ. Press, 2001.

Beard, Mary. *The Parthenon*. Cambridge, MA: Harvard Univ. Press, 2003.

Belozerskaya, Marina, and Kenneth Lapatin. *Ancient Greece: Art, Architecture, and History*. Los Angeles: J. Paul Getty Museum, 2004.

Boardman, John. *Early Greek Vase Painting: 11th–6th Centuries B.C.. A Handbook*. World of Art. London: Thames and Hudson, 1998.

———. *Greek Sculpture: The Archaic Period: A Handbook*. World of Art. New York: Thames and Hudson, 1991.

———. *Greek Sculpture: The Classical Period: A Handbook*. London: Thames and Hudson, 1985.

———. *Greek Sculpture: The Late Classical Period and Sculpture in Colonies and Overseas*. World of Art. New York: Thames and Hudson, 1995.

——— *The History of Greek Vases: Potters, Painters, and Pictures*. New York: Thames & Hudson, 2001.

Burn, Lucilla. *Hellenistic Art: From Alexander the Great to Augustus*. London: British Museum Press, 2004.

Camp, John M. *The Athenian Agora: Excavations in the Heart of Classical Athens*. New York: Thames and Hudson, 1986.

Carpenter, Thomas H. *Art and Myth in Ancient Greece: A Handbook*. World of Art. London: Thames and Hudson, 1991.

Clark, Andrew J., Mava Elston, Mary Louise Hart. *Understanding Greek Vases: A Guide to Terms, Styles, and Techniques*. Los Angeles: J. Paul Getty Museum, 2002.

De Grummond, Nancy T. and Brunilde S. Ridgway. *From Pergamon to Sperlonga: Sculpture in Context*. Berkeley: Univ. of California Press, 2000.

Donohue, A. A. *Greek Sculpture and the Problem of Description*. New York: Cambridge Univ. Press, 2005.

Fullerton, Mark D. *Greek Art*. Cambridge, U.K.: Cambridge Univ. Press, 2000.

Hurwit, Jeffrey M. *The Art and Culture of Early Greece 1100–480 B.C.* Ithaca, NY: Cornell Univ. Press, 1985.

———, and Adam D. Newton. *The Acropolis in the Age of Pericles*. 1 v. & CD-ROM. New York: Cambridge Univ. Press, 2004.

Karakasi, Katerina. *Archaic Korai*. Los Angeles: The J. Paul Getty Museum, 2003.

Lagerlof, Margaretha Rossholm. *The Sculptures of the Parthenon: Aesthetics and Interpretation*. New Haven: Yale Univ. Press, 2000.

Lawrence, A. W. *Greek Architecture*. 5th ed. Rev. R. A. Tomlinson. Pelican History of Art. New Haven: Yale Univ. Press, 1996.

Martin, Roland. *Greek Architecture: Architecture of Crete, Greece, and the Greek World*. History of World Architecture. New York: Electa/Rizzoli, 1988.

Osborne, Robin. *Archaic and Classical Greek Art*. Oxford History of Art. Oxford: Oxford Univ. Press, 1998.

Palagia, Olga. ed. *Greek Sculpture: Function, Materials, and Techniques in the Archaic and Classical Periods*. New York: Cambridge Univ. Press, 2006.

———, and J.J. Pollitt., eds. *Personal Styles in Greek Sculpture*. Yale Classical Studies, v. 30. New York: Cambridge Univ. Press, 1996.

Pedley, John Griffiths. *Greek Art and Archaeology*. 3rd ed. Upper Saddle River: Prentice-Hall, 2002.

Pollitt, J. J. *The Art of Ancient Greece: Sources and Documents*. 2nd ed. Cambridge, U.K.: Cambridge Univ. Press, 1990.

Ridgway, Brunilde Sismondo. *The Archaic Style in Greek Sculpture*. 2nd ed. Chicago: Ares, 1993.

——. *Fifth Century Styles in Greek Sculpture*. Princeton: Princeton Univ. Press, 1981.

——. *Fourth Century Styles in Greek Sculpture*. Wisconsin Studies in Classics. Madison: Univ. of Wisconsin Press, 1997

——. *Hellenistic Sculpture 1: The Styles of ca. 331–200 B.C.* Wisconsin Studies in Classics. Madison: Univ. of Wisconsin Press, 1990.

Stafford, Emma J. *Life, Myth, and Art in Ancient Greece*. Los Angeles. J. Paul Getty Museum, 2004.

Stewart, Andrew F. *Greek Sculpture: An Exploration*. 2 vols. New Haven: Yale Univ. Press, 1990.

Whitley, James. *The Archaeology of Ancient Greece*. New York: Cambridge Univ. Press, 2001.

CHAPTER 6
Etruscan and Roman Art

Bianchi Bandinelli, Ranuccio. Rome: *The Centre of Power: Roman Art to A.D. 200*. Trans. Peter Green. Arts of Mankind. London: Thames and Hudson, 1970.

——. Rome: *The Late Empire: Roman Art A.D. 200–400*. Trans. Peter Green. Arts of Mankind. New York: Braziller, 1971.

Borrelli, Federica. *The Etruscans: Art, Architecture, and History*. Ed. Stefano Peccatori & Stefano Zuffi. Trans. Thomas Michael Hartmann. Los Angeles: J. Paul Getty Museum, 2004.

Breeze, David John. *Hadrian's Wall*. 4th ed. London: Penguin, 2000.

Brendel, Otto J. *Etruscan Art*. 2nd ed. Yale Univ. Press Pelican History Series. New Haven: Yale Univ. Press, 1995.

Ciarallo, Annamaria, and Ernesto De Carolis, eds. *Pompeii: Life in a Roman Town*. Milan: Electa, 1999.

Conlin, Diane Atnally. *The Artists of the Ara Pacis: The Process of Hellenization in Roman Relief Sculpture*. Studies in the History of Greece & Rome. Chapel Hill: Univ. of North Carolina Press, 1997

Cornell, Tim, and John Matthews. *Atlas of the Roman World*. New York: Facts on File, 1982.

D'Ambra, Eve. *Roman Art*. Cambridge, U.K.: Cambridge Univ. Press, 1998.

Elsner, Ja. *Imperial Rome and Christian Triumph: The Art of the Roman Empire A.D. 100–450*. Oxford History of Art. Oxford: Oxford Univ. Press, 1998.

Gabucci, Ada. *Ancient Rome: Art, Architecture, and History*. Eds. Stefano Peccatori & Stephano Zuffi. Trans. T. M. Hartman. Los Angeles, CA: J. Paul Getty Museum, 2002.
——. ed. *The Colosseum*. Los Angeles, CA: J. Paul Getty Museum, 2002.
Grant, Michael. *Art in the Roman Empire*. London: Routledge, 1995.
Guillaud, Jacqueline, and Maurice Guillaud. *Frescoes in the Time of Pompeii*. New York: Potter, 1990.
Haynes, Sybille. *Etruscan Civilization: A Cultural History*. Los Angeles: J. Paul Getty Museum, 2000.
Holloway, R. Ross. *Constantine & Rome*. New Haven: Yale Univ. Press, 2004.
L'Orange, Hans Peter. *The Roman Empire: Art Forms and Civic Life*. New York: Rizzoli, 1985.
MacDonald, William L. *The Architecture of the Roman Empire: An Introductory Study*. Rev. ed. Yale Publications in the History of Art. New Haven: Yale Univ. Press, 1982.
——. *The Pantheon: Design, Meaning, and Progeny*. Cambridge, MA: Harvard Univ. Press, 1976.
——, and John A. Pinto. *Hadrian's Villa and Its Legacy*. New Haven: Yale Univ. Press, 1995.
Mazzoleni, Donatella. *Domus: Wall Painting in the Roman House*. Los Angeles: J. Paul Getty Museum, 2004.
Packer, James E., and Kevin Lee Sarring. *The Forum of Trajan in Rome: A Study of the Monuments. California Studies in the History of Art, 31*. 2 vols., portfolio and microfiche. Berkeley: Univ. of California Press, 1997.
Pollitt, J. J. *The Art of Rome, c. 753 B.C.–337 A.D.. Sources and Documents*. Upper Saddle River, NJ: Prentice Hall, 1966.
Ramage, Nancy H., and Andrew Ramage. *Roman Art: Romulus to Constantine*. 4th ed. Upper Saddle River, NJ: Prentice Hall, 2004.
Spivey, Nigel. *Etruscan Art*. World of Art. New York: Thames and Hudson, 1997.
Stamper, John W. *The Architecture of Roman Temples: The Republic to the Middle Empire*. New York: Cambridge Univ. Press, 2005.
Stewart, Peter. *Roman Art*. New York: Oxford Univ. Press, 2004.
——— *Statues in Roman Society: Representation and Response*. Oxford Studies in Ancient Culture and Representation. New York: Oxford Univ., 2003.
Strong, Donald. *Roman Art*. 2nd ed. rev. & annotated. Ed. Roger Ling. Pelican History of Art. New Haven: Yale Univ. Press, 1995.
Ward-Perkins, J. B. *Roman Architecture*. History of World Architecture. New York: Electa/Rizzoli, 1988.
——. *Roman Imperial Architecture*. Pelican History of Art. New Haven: Yale Univ. Press, 1981.
Wilson Jones, Mark. *Principles of Roman Architecture*. New Haven: Yale Univ. Press, 2000.

CHAPTER 7
Jewish, Early Christian, and Byzantine Art

Age of Spirituality: Late Antique and Early Christian Art, Third to Seventh Century. New York: Metropolitan Museum of Art, 1979.
Beckwith, John. *The Art of Constantinople: An Introduction to Byzantine Art 330–1453*. 2nd ed. London: Phaidon, 1968.
——. *Early Christian and Byzantine Art*. 2nd ed. Pelican History of Art. Harmondsworth, UK: Penguin, 1979.
Carr, Annemarie Weyl. *Byzantine Illumination, 1150–1250: The Study of a Provincial Tradition*. Chicago: Univ. of Chicago Press, 1987.
Cioffarelli, Ada. *Guide to the Catacombs of Rome and Its Surroundings*. Rome: Bonsignori, 2000.
Cormack, Robin. *Byzantine Art*. Oxford History of Art. Oxford: Oxford Univ. Press, 2000.
Cutler, Anthony. *The Hand of the Master: Craftsmanship, Ivory, and Society in Byzantium (9th–11th Centuries)*. Princeton: Princeton Univ. Press, 1994.
Demus, Otto. *The Mosaic Decoration of San Marco, Venice*. Ed. Herbert L. Kessler. Chicago: Univ. of Chicago Press, 1988.
Durand, Jannic. *Byzantine Art*. Paris: Terrail, 1999.
Eastmond, Antony, and Liz James, ed. *Icon and Word The Power of Images in Byzantium: Studies Presented to Robin Cormack*. Burlington, VT: Ashgate, 2003.
Evans, Helen C., ed. *Byzantium: Faith and Power (1261-1557)*. New York: Metropolitan Museum of Art, 2004.
———, and William D. Wixom, eds. *The Glory of Byzantium: Art and Culture of the Middle Byzantine era, A.D. 843-1261*. New York: Abrams, 1997.
Fine, Steven. *Art and Judaism in the Greco-Roman World: Toward a New Jewish Archaeology*. New York: Cambridge Univ. Press, 2005.
Gerstel, Sharon E. J. *Beholding the Sacred Mysteries: Programs of the Byzantine Sanctuary*. Monograph on the Fine Arts, 56. Seattle: Published by College Art Association in assoc. with Univ. of Washington Press, 1999.
Grabar, Andréé. *Byzantine Painting: Historical and Critical Study*. Trans. Stuart Gilbert. New York: Rizzoli, 1979.
Jensen, Robin Margaret. *Understanding Early Christian Art*. New York: Routledge, 2000.
Kitzinger, Ernst. *Byzantine Art in the Making: Main Lines of Stylistic Development in Mediterranean Art, 3rd–7th Century*. Cambridge, MA: Harvard Univ. Press, 1977.
Krautheimer, Richard, and Slobodan Curcic. *Early Christian and Byzantine Architecture*. 4th ed. Pelican History of Art. New Haven: Yale Univ. Press, 1992.
Levine, Lee I. and Zeev Weiss, eds. *From Dura to Sepphoris: Studies in Jewish Art and Society in Late Antiquity*. Journal of Roman Archaeology: Supplementary Series, no. 40. Portsmouth, R.I.: Journal of Roman Archaeology, 2000.
Lowden, John. *Early Christian and Byzantine Art*. Art & Ideas. London: Phaidon, 1997
Maguire, Henry. *The Icons of Their Bodies: Saints and their Images in Byzantium*. Princeton: Princeton Univ. Press, 1996.
Mainstone, R. J. *Hagia Sophia: Architecture, Structure and Liturgy of Justinian's Great Church*. London: Thames and Hudson, 1988.
Mango, Cyril. *Art of the Byzantine Empire, 312–1453: Sources and Documents*. Upper Saddle River, NJ: Prentice Hall, 1972.
Mathew, Gervase. *Byzantine Aesthetics*. London: J. Murray, 1963.
Mathews, Thomas P. *Byzantium: From Antiquity to the Renaissance. Perspectives*. New York: Abrams, 1998.
———. *The Clash of Gods: A Reinterpretation of Early Christian Art*. Rev. & exp. ed. Princeton: Princeton Univ. Press, 1999.
Milburn, R. L. P. *Early Christian Art and Architecture*. Berkeley: Univ. of California Press, 1988.
Olin, Margaret. *The Nation without Art: Examining Modern Discourses on Jewish Art*. Lincoln: Univ. of Nebraska Press, 2001.
Olsson, Birger and Magnus Zetterholm, eds. *The Ancient Synagogue from Its Origins until 200 C.E.. Papers Presented at an International Conference at Lund University, October 14-17, 2001*. Coniectanea Biblica: New Testament Series, 39. Stockholm: Almqvist & Wiksell International, 2003.
Ousterhout, Robert. *Master Builders of Byzantium*. Princeton: Princeton Univ. Press, 1999.
Rodley, Lyn. *Byzantine Art and Architecture: An Introduction*. Cambridge, U.K.: Cambridge Univ. Press, 1994.
Rutgers, Leonard Victor. *Subterranean Rome: In Search of the Roots of Christianity in the Catacombs of the Eternal City*. Leuven: Peeters, 2000.
Tadgell, Christopher. *Imperial Space: Rome, Constantinople and the Early Church*. New York: Whitney Library of Design, 1998.
Teteriatnikov, Natalia. *Mosaics of Hagia Sophia, Istanbul: The Fossati Restoration and the Work of the Byzantine Institute*. Washington, D.C.. Dumbarton Oaks Research Library and Collection, 1998.
Tronzo, William. *The Cultures of his Kingdom: Roger II and the Cappella Palatina in Palermo*. Princeton: Princeton Univ. Press, 1997.
Vio, Ettore. *St. Mark's: The Art and Architecture of Church and State in Venice*. New York: Riverside Book Co., 2003.
Webb, Matilda. *The Churches and Catacombs of Early Christian Rome: A Comprehensive Guide*. Brighton, UK: Sussex Academic Press, 2001.
Weitzmann, Kurt. *Late Antique and Early Christian Book Illumination*. New York: Braziller, 1977
——. *Place of Book Illumination in Byzantine Art*. Princeton: Art Museum, Princeton Univ., 1975.
Wharton, Annabel Jane. *Refiguring the Post ClassicalCity: Dura Europe, Jerash, Jerusalem and Ravenna*. New York: Cambridge Univ. Press, 1995.
White, L. Michael. *The Social Origins of Christian Architecture*. 2 vols. Baltimore: Johns Hopkins Univ. Press, 1990.

CHAPTER 8
Islamic Art

Al-Faruqi, Ismail R, and Lois Lamya'al Faruqi. *Cultural Atlas of Islam*. New York: Macmillan, 1986.
Atasoy, Nurhan. *Splendors of the Ottoman Sultans*. Ed. and Trans. Tulay Artan. Memphis, TN: Lithograph, 1992.
Atil, Esin. *The Age of Sultan Suleyman the Magnificent*. Washington, D.C.: National Gallery of Art, 1987.
Baer, Eva. *Islamic Ornament*. New York: New York Univ. Press, 1998.
Baker, Patricia L. *Islam and the Religious Arts*. New York: Continuum, 2004.
Barry, Michael. *Figurative Art in Medieval Islam and the Riddle of Bihzâåd of Herâåt (1465-1535)*. Paris: Flammarion, 2004.
Blair, Sheila S., and Jonathan Bloom. *The Art and Architecture of Islam 1250–1800. Pelican History of Art*. New Haven: Yale Univ. Press, 1994.
Carboni, Stefano, and David Whitehouse. *Glass of the Sultans*. New York: Metropolitan Museum of Art, 2001.
Denny, Walter B. *Iznik: The Artistry of Ottoman Ceramics*. New York: Thames & Hudson, 2004.
Dodds, Jerrilynn D., ed. al-Andalus: The Art of Islamic Spain. New York: Metropolitan Museum of Art, 1992.
Ecker, Heather. *Caliphs and Kings: The Art and Influence of Islamic Spain*. Washington, D.C.: Arthur M. Sackler Gallery, Smithsonian Institution, 2004.
Ettinghausen, Richard, Oleg Grabar, and Marilyn Jenkins-Madina. *Islamic Art and Architecture, 650–1250*. 2nd ed. Yale Univ. Press Pelican History of Art. New Haven: Yale Univ. Press, 2001. Reissue ed. 2003.
Frishman, Martin, and Hasan-Uddin Khan. *The Mosque: History, Architectural Development and Regional Diversity*. London: Thames and Hudson, 1994.
Grabar, Oleg. *The Formation of Islamic Art*. Rev. ed. New Haven: Yale Univ. Press, 1987
—— *The Great Mosque of Isfahan*. New York: New York Univ. Press, 1990.
——. *Mostly Miniatures: An Introduction to Persian Painting*. Princeton: Princeton Univ. Press, 2000.
——, Mohammad al-Asad, Abeer Audeh, and Said Nuseibeh. *The Shape of the Holy; Early Islamic Jerusalem*. Princeton: Princeton Univ. Press, 1996.
Hillenbrand, Robert. *Islamic Art and Architecture*. World of Art. London: Thames and Hudson, 1999.
Irwin, Robert. *The Alhambra*. Cambridge, MA: Harvard Univ. Press, 2004.
Khatibi, Abdelkebir, and Mohammed Sijelmassi. *The Splendour of Islamic Calligraphy*. Rev. & exp. ed. New York: Thames and Hudson, 1996.
Komaroff, Linda, and Stefano Carboni, eds. *The Legacy of Genghis Khan: Courtly Art and Culture in Western Asia, 1256- 1353*. New York: Metropolitan Museum of Art, 2002.
Lentz, Thomas W., and Glenn D. Lowry. *Timur and the Princely Vision: Persian Art and Culture in the Fifteenth Century*. Los Angeles: Los Angeles County Museum of Art, 1989.
Necipo lu, Güülru. *The Age of Sinan: Architectural Culture in the Ottoman Empire*. Princeton: Princeton Univ. Press, 2005.
Petruccioli, Attilio, and Khalil K. Pirani, eds. *Understanding Islamic Architecture*. New York: Routledge Curzon, 2002.
Roxburgh, David J., ed. *Turks: A Journey of a Thousand Years, 600-1600*. London: Royal Academy of Arts, 2005.
Sims, Eleanor, Boris I. Marshak, and Ernest J. Grube. *Peerless Images: Persian Painting and Its Sources*. New Haven: Yale Univ. Press, 2002.
Stanley, Tim, Mariam Rosser-Owen, and Stephen Vernoit. *Palace and Mosque: Islamic Art from the Middle East*. London: V & A Publications, 2004.
Steele, James. *An Architecture for People: The Complete Works of Hassan Fathy*. New York: Whitney Library of Design, 1997.
Stierlin, Henri. *Islamic Art and Architecture: From Isfahan to the Taj Mahal*. New York: Thames & Hudson, 2002.
Suhrawardy, Shahid. *The Art of the Mussulmans in Spain*. New York: Oxford Univ. Press, 2005.
Tadgell, Christopher. *Four Caliphates: The Formation and Development of the Islamic Tradition*. London: Ellipsis, 1998.
Ward, R. M. *Islamic Metalwork*. New York: Thames and Hudson, 1993.
Watson, Oliver. *Ceramics from Islamic Lands*. New York: Thames & Hudson in assoc. with the al-Sabah Collection, Dar al-Athar al-Islamiyyah, Kuwait National Museum, 2004.

CHAPTER 9
Art of South and Southeast Asia before 1200

Atherton, Cynthia Packert. *The Sculpture of Early Medieval Rajasthan*. Studies in Asian Art and Archaeology, v. 21. New York: Brill, 1997.
Behl, Benoy K. *The Ajanta Caves: Artistic Wonder of Ancient Buddhist India*. New York: Abrams, 1998.
Behrendt, Kurt A. *The Buddhist Architecture of Gandhara*. Handbook of Oriental Studies: Section Two: India, v. 17. Boston: Brill, 2004.

Berkson, Carmel. *Elephanta: The Cave of Shiva*. Princeton: Princeton Univ. Press, 1983.
Chakrabarti, Dilip K. *India, an Archaeological History: Palaeolithic Beginnings to Early Historic Foundations*. New York: Oxford Univ. Press, 1999.
Chandra, Pramod. *The Sculpture of India, 3000 B.C.–1300 A.D.* Washington, D.C.: National Gallery of Art, 1985.
Craven, Roy C. *Indian Art: A Concise History*. Rev. ed. World of Art. New York: Thames and Hudson, 1997
Czuma, Stanislaw J. *Kushan Sculpture: Images from Early India*. Cleveland: Cleveland Museum of Art, 1985.
Dehejia, Vidya. *Art of the Imperial Cholas*. New York: Columbia Univ. Press, 1990.
——— *The Sensuous and the Sacred: Chola Bronzes from South India*. New York: American Federation of Arts, 2002.
Dessai, Vishakha N., and Darielle Mason, eds. *Gods, Guardians, and Lovers: Temple Sculptures from North India, A.D. 700–1200*. New York: Asia Society Galleries, 1993.
Dhavalikar, Madhukar Keshav. *Ellora*. New York: Oxford Univ. Press, 2003.
Girard-Geslan, Maud. *Art of Southeast Asia*. Trans. J.A. Underwood. New York: Harry N. Abrams, Inc., 1998.
Huntington, Susan L. *The Art of Ancient India: Buddhist, Hindu, Jain*. New York: Weatherhill, 1985.
——. *Leaves from the Bodhi Tree: The Art of Pala India (8th–12th Centuries) and Its International Legacy*. Dayton, OH: Dayton Art Institute, 1990.
Hutt, Michael. *Nepal: A Guide to the Art and Architecture of the Kathmandu Valley*. Boston: Shambala, 1995.
Knox, Robert. *Amaravati: Buddhist Sculpture from the Great Stupa*. London: British Museum, 1992.
Khanna, Sucharita. *Dancing Divinities in Indian Art: 8th-12th Century A.D.* Delhi: Sharada Pub. House, 1999.
Kramrisch, Stella. *The Art of Nepal*. New York: Abrams, 1964.
——. *Presence of Siva*. Princeton: Princeton Univ. Press, 1981.
Meister, Michael, ed. *Encyclopedia of Indian Temple Architecture*. 2 vols. in 7. Philadelphia: Univ. of Pennsylvania Press, 1983.
Michell, George. *Hindu Art and Architecture*. World of Art. London: Thames & Hudson, 2000.
Mitter, Partha. *Indian Art*. Oxford History of Art. Oxford: Oxford Univ. Press, 2001.
Neumayer, Erwin. *Lines on Stone: The Prehistoric Rock Art of India*. New Delhi: Manohar, 1993.
Pal, Pratapaditya, ed. *The Ideal Image: The Gupta Sculptural Tradition and Its Influence*. New York: Asia Society, 1978.
Poster, Amy G. *From Indian Earth: 4,000 Years of Terracotta Art*. Brooklyn: Brooklyn Museum, 1986.
Skelton, Robert, and Mark Francis. *Arts of Bengal: The Heritage of Bangladesh and Eastern India*. London: Whitechapel Gallery, 1979.
Stierlin, Henri. *Hindu India: From Khajuraho to the Temple City of Madurai*. New York: Taschen, 1998.
Tadgell, Christopher. *India and South-East Asia: The Buddhist and Hindu Tradition*. New York: Whitney Library of Design, 1998.
Williams, Joanna G. *Art of Gupta India, Empire and Province*. Princeton: Princeton Univ. Press, 1982.

CHAPTER 10
Chinese and Korean Art before 1279

Ciarla, Roberto, ed. *The Eternal Army: The Terracotta Soldiers of the First Chinese Emperor*. Vercelli: White Star, 2005.
Fong, Wen, ed. *Beyond Representation: Chinese Painting and Calligraphy, 8th–14th Century*. Princeton Monographs in Art and Archaeology. New York: Metropolitan Museum of Art, 1992.
Fraser, Sarah Elizabeth. *Performing the Visual: The Practice of Buddhist Wall Painting in China and Central Asia, 618-960*. Stanford, CA: Stanford Univ. Press, 2004.
James, Jean M. *A Guide to the Tomb and Shrine Art of the Han Dynasty 206 B.C.–A.D. 220*. Chinese Studies, 2. Lewiston, NY: Edwin Mellen Press, 1996.
Karetzky, Patricia Eichenbaum. *Court Art of the Tang*. Lanham, MD: Univ. Press of America, 1996.
Kim, Kumja Paik. *Goryeo Dynasty: Korea's Age of Enlightenment, 918-1392*. San Francisco: Asian Art Museum—Chong-Moon Lee Center for Asian Art and Culture in cooperation with the National Museum of Korea and the Nara National Museum, 2003.
Li, Jian, ed. *The Glory of the Silk Road: Art from Ancient China*. Dayton, OH: Dayton Art Institute, 2003.
Little, Stephen, and Shawn Eichman. *Taoism and the Arts of China*. Chicago: Art Institute of Chicago, 2000.
Liu, Cary Y., Dora C.Y. Ching, and Judith G. Smith. *Character & Context in Chinese Calligraphy*. Princeton: Art Museum, Princeton Univ., 1999.
Luo, Zhewen. *Ancient Pagodas in China*. Beijing, China: Foreign Languages Press, 1994.
Ma, Ch'eng-yuan. *Ancient Chinese Bronzes*. Ed. Hsio-Yen Shih. Hong Kong: Oxford Univ. Press, 1986.
Murck, Alfreda. *Poetry and Painting in Song China: The Subtle Art of Dissent*. Harvard-Yenching Institute Monograph Series, 50. Cambridge, MA: Harvard Univ. Asia Center for the Harvard-Yenching Institute, 2000.
Ortiz, Valéérie Malenfer. *Dreaming the Southern Song Landscape: The Power of Illusion in Chinese Painting. Studies in Asian Art and Archaeology, v. 22*. Boston: Brill, 1999.
Paludan, Ann. *Chinese Tomb Figurines*. Hong Kong: Oxford Univ. Press, 1994.
Portal, Jane. *Korea: Art and Archaeology*. New York: Thames & Hudson, 2000.
Rawson, Jessica. *Mysteries of Ancient China: New Discoveries from the Early Dynasties*. London: British Museum Press, 1996.
Rhie, Marylin M. *Early Buddhist Art of China and Central Asia*. 2 vols in 3. Handbuch der Orientalistik. Vierte Abteilung; China, 12. Leiden: Brill, 1999.
Scarpari, Maurizio. *Splendours of Ancient China*. London: Thames & Hudson, 2000.
So, Jenny F. ed. *Noble Riders from Pines and Deserts: The Artistic Legacy of the Qidan*. Hong Kong: Art Museum, the Chinese Univ. of Hong Kong, 2004.
Sturman, Peter Charles. *Mi Fu: Style and the Art of Calligraphy in Northern Song*. New Haven: Yale Univ. Press, 1997.
Wang, Eugene Y. *Shaping the Lotus Sutra: Buddhist Visual Culture in Medieval China*. Seattle: Univ. of Washington Press, 2005.
Watson, William. *The Arts of China to AD 900*. Pelican History of Art. New Haven: Yale Univ. Press, 1995.
——— *The Arts of China 900-1620*. Yale Univ. Press Pelican History of Art. New Haven: Yale Univ. Press, 2000. Reissue ed. 2003.
Watt, James C.Y. *China: Dawn of a Golden Age, 200-750 AD*. New York: Metropolitan Museum of Art, 2004.
Whitfield, Susan, and Ursula Sims-Williams, eds. *The Silk Road: Trade, Travel, War and Faith*. Chicago: Serindia Publications, 2004.
Wu Hung. *Monumentality in Early Chinese Art and Architecture*. Stanford: Stanford Univ. Press, 1995.
Yang, Xiaoneng, ed. *The Golden Age of Chinese Archaeology: Celebrated Discoveries from the People's Republic of China*. Washington D.C.: National Gallery of Art, 1999.

CHAPTER 11
Japanese Art before 1392

Cunningham, Michael R. *Buddhist Treasures from Nara*. Cleveland: Cleveland Museum of Art, 1998.
Fowler, Sherry D. *Muroji: Rearranging Art and History at the Japanese Buddhist Temple*. Honolulu: Univ. of Hawaii Press, 2005.
Harris, Victor, ed. *Shinto: The Sacred Art of Ancient Japan*. London: British Museum, 2001.
Izutsu, Shinry, and Shory œmori. *Sacred Treasures of Mount Kÿ_ya: The Art of Japanese Shingon Buddhism*. Honolulu: Koyasan Reihokan Museum, 2002.
Kenrick, Douglas Moore. *Jomon of Japan: The World's Oldest Pottery*. New York: Kegan Paul International, 1995.
Kurata, Bunsaku. *Horyu-ji, Temple of the Exalted Law: Early Buddhist Art from Japan*. New York: Japan Society, 1981.
LaMarre, Thomas. *Uncovering Heian Japan: An Archaeology of Sensation and Inscription*. Asia-Pacific. Durham, NC. Duke Univ. Press, 2000.
Miki, Fumio. *Haniwa*. Trans. and adapted by Gino Lee Barnes. Arts of Japan, 8. New York: Weatherhill, 1974.
Mino, Yutaka. *The Great Eastern Temple: Treasures of Japanese Buddhist Art from Todai-ji*. Chicago: Art Institute of Chicago, 1986.
Mizoguchi, Koji. *An Archaeological History of Japan: 30,000 B.C. to A.D. 700*. Philadelphia: Univ. of Pennsylvania Press, 2002.
Nishiwara, Kyotaro, and Emily J. Sano. *The Great Age of Japanese Buddhist Sculpture, A.D. 60–1300*. Fort Worth, TX: Kimbell Art Museum, 1982.
Pearson, Richard J. *Ancient Japan*. Washington, D.C.: Sackler Gallery, 1992.
Rosenfield, John M. *Japanese Arts of the Heian Period: 794–1185*. New York: Asia Society, 1967.
Soper, Alexander Coburn. *Evolution of Buddhist Architecture in Japan*. Princeton Monographs in Art and Archaeology, no. 22. New York: Hacker Art, 1978.
The Tale of Genji: Legends and Paintings. Intro. Miyeko Murase. New York: G. Braziller, 2001.
Washizuka, Hiromitsu, et al. *Transmitting the Forms of Divinity: Early Buddhist Art from Korea and Japan*. Ed. Naomi Noble Richard. New York: Japan Society, 2003.
Yiengpruksawan, Mimi Hall. *Hiraizumi: Buddhist Art and Regional Politics in Twelfth-Century Japan*. Harvard East Asian Monographs, 171. Cambridge, MA: Harvard Univ. Asia Center, 1998

CHAPTER 12
Art of the Americas before 1300

Baudez, Claude F., and Sydney Picasso. *Lost cities of the Maya. Trans. Caroline Palmer*. Discoveries. New York: Harry N. Abrams, 1992.
Benson, Elizabeth P., and Beatriz de la Fuente. *Olmec Art of Ancient Mexico*. Washington, D.C.. National Gallery of Art, 1996.
Berrin, Kathleen, ed. *Feathered Serpents and Flowering Trees: Reconstructing the Murals of Teotihuacan*. San Francisco: Fine Arts Museums of San Francisco, 1988.
Brody, J. J. *Anasazi and Pueblo Painting*. Albuquerque: Univ. of New Mexico Press, 1991.
———, Catherine J. Scott, and Steven A. LeBlanc. *Mimbres Pottery: Ancient Art of the American Southwest: Essays*. New York: Hudson Hills Press in assoc. with The American Federation of Arts, 1983.
Clark, John E., and Mary E. Pye, eds. *Olmec Art and Archaeology in Mesoamerica*. Studies in the History of Art, 58: Symposium Papers, 35. Washington, D.C.: National Gallery of Art, 2000.
Clayton, Lawrence A., editor. *The De Soto Chronicles: The Expedition of Hernando de Soto to North America, 1539-`1543*. Tuscaloosa: University of Alabama Press, 1995.
Coe, Michael D., and Rex Koontz. *Mexico: From the Olmecs to the Aztecs*. 5th ed. rev. & exp. New York: Thames & Hudson, 2002.
Fagan, Brian M. *Chaco Canyon: Archeologists Explore the Lives of an Ancient Society*. New York: Oxford Univ. Press, 2005.
Hall, Robert L. *An Archaeology of the Soul: North American Indian Belief and Ritual*. Urbana: Univ. of Illinois Press, 1997
Herring, Adam. *Art and Writing in the Maya Cities, A.D. 600-800: A Poetics of Line*. Cambridge, U.K.: Cambridge Univ. Press, 2005.
Heyden, Doris, and Paul Gendrop. *Pre-Columbian Architecture of Mesoamerica*. Trans. Judith Stanton. History of World Architecture. New York: Electa/Rizzoli, 1988
Korp, Maureen. *The Sacred Geography of the American Mound Builders*. Native American Studies. Lewiston, NY: Edwin Mellen, 1990.
Kubler, George. *The Art and Architecture of Ancient America: The Mexican, Maya, and Andean Peoples*. 3rd ed. Pelican History of Art. New Haven: Yale Univ. Press, 1990.
Labbéé, Armand J. *Shamans, Gods, and Mythic Beasts: Colombian Gold and Ceramics in Antiquity*. New York: American Federation of Arts, 1998.
Loendorf, Lawrence L., Christopher Chippindale, and David S. Whitley, eds. *Discovering North American Rock Art*. Tucson: Univ. of Arizona Press, 2005.
Martin, Simon, and Nikolai Grube. *Chronicle of the Maya Kings and Queens: Deciphering theDynasties of the Ancient Maya*. New York: Thames & Hudson, 2000.
Miller, Mary Ellen. *The Art of Mesoamerica: from Olmec to Aztec*. 3rd ed. World of Art. London: Thames and Hudson, 2001.
——. *Maya Art and Architecture*. World of Art. London: Thames and Hudson, 1999.
Miller, Mary Ellen, and Simon Martin. *Courtly Art of the Ancient Maya*. San Francisco: Fine Arts Museums of San Francisco, 2004.
Milner, George R. *The Moundbuilders: Ancient Peoples of Eastern North America*. Ancient Peoples and Places. London: Thames & Hudson, 2004.
Noble, David Grant. *In Search of Chaco: New Approaches to an Archaeological Enigma*. Santa Fe, NM: School of American Research Press, 2004.
O'Connor, Mallory McCane. *Lost Cities of the Ancient Southeast*. Gainesville: Univ. Press of Florida, 1995.
Pasztory, Esther. *Pre-Columbian Art*. Cambridge, U.K.: Cambridge Univ. Press. 1998.
———. Teotihuacan: An Experiment in Living. Norman: Univ. of Oklahoma Press, 1997.

Pillsbury, Joanne, ed. *Moche Art and Archaeology in Ancient Peru*. Studies in the History of Art: Center for Advanced Study in the Visual Arts, 63: Symposium Papers, 40. Washington, D.C.: National Gallery of Art, 2001.

Power, Susan C. *Early Art of the Southeastern Indians: Feathered Serpents & Winged Beings*. Athens: Univ. of Georgia Press, 2004.

Rohn, Arthur H., and William M. Ferguson. *Puebloan Ruins of the Southwest*. Albuquerque: Univ. of New Mexico Press, 2006.

Schobinger, Juan. *The Ancient Americans: A Reference Guide to the Art, Culture, and History of Pre-Columbian North and South America*. Trans. Carys Evans Corrales. 2 vols. Armonk, NY: Sharp Reference, 2001.

Sharer, Robert J. and Loa P. Traxler. *The Ancient Maya*. 6th ed. Stanford, CA: Stanford Univ. Press, 2006.

Stierlin, Henri, and Anne Stierlin, *The Maya: Palaces and Pyramids of the Rainforest*. London: Taschen, 2001.

Stone-Miller, Rebecca. *Art of the Andes: From Chavin to Inca*. 2nd ed. World of Art. New York: Thames and Hudson, 2002.

Townsend, Richard F. and Robert V. Sharp, eds. *Hero, Hawk, and Open Hand: American Indian Art of the Ancient Midwest and South*. Chicago: Art Institute of Chicago, 2004.

Von Hagen, Adriana, and Craig Morris. *The Cities of the Ancient Andes*. New York: Thames and Hudson, 1998.

Chapter 13
Art of Ancient Africa

Ben-Amos, Paula. *The Art of Benin*. Rev. ed. Washington, D.C.. Smithsonian Institution Press, 1995.

Blier, Suzanne Preston. *The Royal Arts of Africa: The Majesty of Form*. New York: H.N. Abrams, 1998.

Cole, Herbert M. *Igbo Arts: Community and Cosmos*. Los Angeles: Fowler Museum of Cultural History, Univ. of California, 1984.

Connah, Graham. *African Civilizations: An Archaeological Perspective*. 2nd ed. Cambridge, U.K.: Cambridge Univ. Press, 2001.

———. *Forgotten Africa: An Introduction to Its Archaeology*. New York: Routledge, 2004.

Coulson, David, and Alec Campbell. *African Rock Art: Paintings and Engravings on Stone*. New York: Harry N. Abrams, Inc., 2001.

Darish, Patricia J. "Memorial Head of an Oba: Ancestral Time in Benin Culture," in *Tempus Fugit, Time Flies*. Ed. Jan Schall. Kansas City: The Nelson Atkins Museum of Art, 2000. Pgs. 290-97

Eyo, Ekpo, and Frank Willett. *Treasures of Ancient Nigeria*. Ed. Rollyn O. Kirchbaum. New York: Knopf, 1980.

Ezra, Kate. *Royal Art of Benin: The Perls Collection in the Metropolitan Museum of Art*. New York: Metropolitan Museum of Art, 1992.

Garlake, Peter S. *Early Art and Architecture of Africa*. Oxford History of Art. Oxford: Oxford Univ. Press, 2002.

——— *The Hunter's Vision: The Prehistoric Art of Zimbabwe*. Seattle: Univ. of Washington Press, 1995.

Grunne, Bernard de. *The Birth of Art in Africa: Nok Statuary in Nigeria*. Paris: A. Biro, 1998.

Huffman, Thomas N. *Symbols in Stone: Unravelling the Mystery of Great Zimbabwe*. Johannesburg: Witwatersrand Univ. Press, 1987

LaViolette, Adria Jean. *Ethno-Archaeology in Jennée, Mali: Craft and Status among Smiths, Potters, and Masons*. Oxford: Archaeopress, 2000.

Le Quellec, Jean-Loïc. *Rock Art in Africa: Mythology and Legend*. Trans. Paul Bahn. Paris: Flammarion, 2004.

M'Bow, Babacar, and Osemwegie Ebohon. *Benin, a Kingdom in Bronze: The Royal Court Art*. Ft. Lauderdale, FL: African American Research Library and Cultural Center, Broward County Library, 2005.

Phillipson, D. W. *African Archaeology*. 3rd ed. New York: Cambridge Univ. Press, 2005.

Schädler, Karl-Ferdinand. *Earth and Ore: 2500 Years of African Art in Terra-Cotta and Metal*. Trans. Geoffrey P. Burwell. Müünchen: Panterra, 1997

Chapter 14
Early Medieval Art in Europe

Alexander, J. J. G. *Medieval Illuminators and Their Methods of Work*. New Haven: Yale Univ. Press, 1992.

The Art of Medieval Spain, A.D. 500–1200. New York: Metropolitan Museum of Art, 1993.

Backhouse, Janet, D. H. Turner, and Leslie Webster. *The Golden Age of Anglo-Saxon Art, 966–1066*. Bloomington: Indiana Univ. Press, 1984.

Bandman, Gunter. Early Medieval Architecture as Bearer

of Meaning. New York: Columbia Univ. Press, 2005.

Beckwith, John. *Early Medieval Art: Carolingian, Ottonian, Romanesque*. World of Art. New York: Oxford Univ. Press, 1974.

Calkins, Robert G. *Illuminated Books of the Medieval Ages*. Ithaca, NY: Cornell Univ. Press, 1983.

Carver, Martin. *Sutton Hoo: A Seventh-Century Princely Burial Ground and Its Context*. London: British Museum Press, 2005.

Davis-Weyer, Caecilia. *Early Medieval Art, 300–1150: Sources and Documents*. Upper Saddle River, NJ: Prentice Hall, 1971.

Diebold, William J. *Word and Image: An Introduction to Early Medieval Art*. Boulder, CO: Westview Press, 2000.

Dodwell, C. R. *Pictorial Arts of the West 800–1200*. Yale Univ. Press Pelican History of Art. New Haven: Yale Univ. Press, 1993.

Farr, Carol. *The Book of Kells: Its Function and Audience*. London: British Library, 1997.

Fernie, E. C. *The Architecture of the Anglo-Saxons*. London: Batsford, 1983.

Fitzhugh, William W., and Elisabeth I. Ward, eds. *Vikings: The North Atlantic Saga*. Washington, D.C.: Smithsonian Institution Press, 2000.

Harbison, Peter. *The Golden Age of Irish Art: The Medieval Achievement, 600–1200*. London: Thames and Hudson, 1998.

Henderson, George. *From Durrow to Kells: The Insular Gospel-Books, 650–800*. London: Thames and Hudson, 1987

Horn, Walter W., and Ernest Born. *Plan of Saint Gall: A Study of the Architecture and Economy of and Life in a Paradigmatic Carolingian Monastery*. California Studies in the History of Art, 19. 3 vols. Berkeley: Univ. of California Press, 1979.

Lasko, Peter. *Ars Sacra, 800–1200*. 2nd ed. Pelican History of Art. New Haven: Yale Univ. Press, 1994.

McClendon, Charles B. *The Origins of Medieval Architecture: Building in Europe, A.D 600-900*. New Haven: Yale Univ. Press, 2005.

Mayr-Harting, Henry. *Ottonian Book Illumination: An Historical Study*. 2nd rev. ed. 2 vols. London: Harvey Miller, 1999.

Mentréé, Mireille. *Illuminated Manuscripts of Medieval Spain*. New York: Thames and Hudson, 1996.

Nees, Lawrence. *Early Medieval Art*. Oxford History of Art. Oxford: Oxford Univ. Press, 2002.

Nordenfalk, Carl Adam Johan. *Early Medieval Book Illumination*. New York: Rizzoli, 1988.

Richardson, Hilary, and John Scarry. *An Introduction to Irish High Crosses*. Dublin: Mercier, 1990.

Stalley, R. A. *Early Medieval Architecture*. Oxford History of Art. Oxford: Oxford Univ. Press, 1999.

Wickham, Chris. *Framing the Early Middle Ages: Europe and the Mediterranean 400-800*. New York: Oxford Univ. Press, 2005.

Williams, John, ed. *Imaging the Early Medieval Bible*. The Penn State Series in the History of the Book. University Park: Pennsylvania State Univ. Press, 1999.

Wilson, David M. *Anglo-Saxon Art: From the Seventh Century to the Norman Conquest*. London: Thames and Hudson, 1984.

———, and Ole Klindt-Jensen. *Viking Art*. 2nd ed. Minneapolis: Univ. of Minnesota Press, 1980.

Chapter 15
Romanesque Art

Armi, C. Edson. *Design and Construction in Romanesque Architecture: First Romanesque Architecture and the Pointed Arch in Burgundy and Northern Italy*. New York: Cambridge Univ. Press, 2004.

Barral i Altet, Xavier. *The Romanesque: Towns, Cathedrals and Monasteries*. Taschen's World Architecture. New York: Taschen, 1998.

Cahn, Walter. *Romanesque Manuscripts: The Twelfth Century*. A Survey of Manuscripts Illuminated in France. 2 vols. London: H. Miller, 1996.

"Cloister Symposium, 1972" in *Gesta*, v.12 #1/2, 1973, pgs. v-132.

Davis-Weyer, Caecilia. *Early Medieval Art, 300–1150*. Sources and Documents. Upper Saddle River, NJ: Prentice Hall, 1971.

Dimier, Anselme. *Stones Laid before the Lord: A History of Monastic Architecture*. Trans. Gilchrist Lavigne. Cistercian Studies Series, no. 152. Kalamazoo, MI: Cistercian Publications, 1999.

Evans, Joan. *Cluniac Art of the Romanesque Period*. Cambridge, U.K.: Cambridge Univ. Press, 1950.

Fergusson, Peter. *Architecture of Solitude: Cistercian Abbeys in Twelfth-Century England*. Princeton: Princeton Univ. Press, 1984.

Forsyth, Ilene H. *The Throne of Wisdom: Wood Sculptures of the Madonna in Romanesque France*. Princeton: Princeton Univ. Press, 1972.

Gaud, Henri, and Jean-Franççois Leroux-Dhuys. *Cistercian Abbeys: History and Architecture*. Kööln: Köönnemann, 1998

Hawthorne, John G. and Cyril S. Smith, eds. *On Divers Arts: The Treatise of Theophilus*. New York: Dover Press, 1979.

Hearn, M. F. *Romanesque Sculpture: The Revival of Monumental Stone Sculptures in the Eleventh and Twelfth Centuries*. Ithaca, NY: Cornell Univ. Press, 1981.

Hicks, Carola. *The Bayeux Tapestry: The Life Story of a Masterpiece*. London: Chatto & Windus, 2006

Kubach, Hans Erich. *Romanesque Architecture*. History of World Architecture. New York: Electa/Rizzoli, 1988.

Mââle, Emile. *Religious Art in France, the Twelfth Century: A Study of the Origins of Medieval Iconography*. Bollingen Series. Princeton: Princeton Univ. Press, 1978.

Minne-Sèève, Viviane, and Hervéé Kergall. *Romanesque and Gothic France: Architecture and Sculpture*. Trans. Jack Hawkes & Lory Frankel. New York: Harry N. Abrams, 2000.

O'Neill, John Philip, ed. *Enamels of Limoges: 1100-1350*. Trans. Sophie Hawkes, Joachim Neugroschel, & Patricia Stirneman. New York: Metropolitan Museum of Art, 1996.

Petzold, Andreas, *Romanesque Art*. Perspectives. New York: Abrams, 1995.

Radding, Charles M., and William W. Clark. *Medieval Architecture, Medieval Learning: Builders and Masters in the Age of Romanesque and Gothic*. New Haven: Yale Univ. Press, 1992.

Schapiro, Meyer. *The Romanesque Sculpture of Moissac*. New York: Braziller, 1985.

Seidel, Linda. *Legends in Limestone: Lazarus, Gislebertus, and the Cathedral of Autun*. Chicago: Univ. of Chicago Press, 1999.

Stones, Alison, Jeanne Krochalis, Paula Gerson, and Annie Shaver-Crandell. *The Pilgrim's Guide: A Critical Edition*. 2 vols. London: Harvey Miller, 1998.

Swanson, R. N. *The Twelfth-Century Renaissance*. Manchester: Manchester Univ. Press, 1999.

Toman, Rolf, ed. *Romanesque: Architecture, Sculpture, Painting*. Trans. Fiona Hulse & Ian Macmillan. Kööln: Köönnemann, 1997.

The Year 1200. 2 vols. New York: Metropolitan Museum of Art, 1970

Zarnecki, George, Janet Holt, and Tristam Holland, eds. *English Romanesque Art, 1066–1200*. London: Weidenfeld and Nicolson, 1984.

Chapter 16
Gothic Art of the Twelfth and Thirteenth Centuries

Armi, C. Edson. *The "Headmaster" of Chartres and the Origins of "Gothic" Sculpture*. University Park: Pennsylvania State Univ. Press, 1994.

Binding, Güünther. *High Gothic: The Age of the Great Cathedrals*. Taschen's World Architecture. London: Taschen, 1999.

Binski, Paul. *Becket's Crown: Art and Imagination in Gothic England, 1170-1350*. New Haven: Yale Univ. Press, 2004.

Bony, Jean. *French Gothic Architecture of the 12th and 13th Centuries*. California Studies in the History of Art. Berkeley: Univ. of California Press, 1983.

Camille, Michael. *Gothic Art: Glorious Visions*. Perspectives. New York: Abrams, 1996.

Cennini, Cennino. *The Craftsman's Handbook (Il libro dell'arte)*. Trans. D.V. Thompson. New York: Dover, 1954.

Crosby, Sumner McKnight. *The Royal Abbey of Saint-Denis from Its Beginnings to the Death of Suger, 475–1151*. Yale Publications in the History of Art. New Haven: Yale Univ. Press, 1987.

Erlande-Brandenburg, Alain. *Gothic Art*. Trans. I. Mark Paris. New York: Abrams, 1989.

———. *Notre-Dame de Paris*. New York: Abrams, 1998.

Favier, Jean. *The World of Chartres*. Trans. Francisca Garvie. New York: Abrams, 1990.

Frankl, Paul. *Gothic Architecture*. Rev. Paul Crossley. Yale Univ. Press Pelican History of Art. New Haven: Yale Univ. Press, 2000.

Frisch, Teresa G. *Gothic Art, 1140–c.1450: Sources and Documents*. Upper Saddle River, NJ: Prentice Hall, 1971.

Grodecki, Louis, and Catherine Brisac. *Gothic Stained Glass, 1200–1300.* Ithaca, NY: Cornell Univ. Press, 1985.

Kren, Thomas, and Mark Evans, eds. *A Masterpiece Reconstructed: The Hours of Louis XII.* Los Angeles: The J. Paul Getty Museum, 2005.

Moskowitz, Anita Fiderer. *Nicola & Giovanni Pisano: The Pulpits: Pious Devotion, Pious Diversion.* London: Harvey Miller Publishers, 2005.

Murray, Stephen. *Notre-Dame, Cathedral of Amiens: The Power of Change in Gothic.* New York: Cambridge Univ. Press, 1996.

Nussbaum, Norbert. *German Gothic Church Architecture.* Trans. Scott Kleager. New Haven: Yale Univ. Press, 2000.

Panofsky, Erwin. *Abbot Suger on the Abbey Church of St.-Denis and Its Art Treasures.* 2nd ed. Ed. Gerda Panofsky-Soergel. Princeton: Princeton Univ. Press, 1979.

——. *Gothic Architecture and Scholasticism.* Latrobe, PA: Archabbey 1951.

Parry, Stan. *Great Gothic Cathedrals of France.* New York: Viking Studio, 2001.

Sauerlander, Willibald. *Gothic Sculpture in France, 1140–1270.* Trans. Janet Sandheimer. London: Thames and Hudson, 1972.

Scott, Robert A. *The Gothic Enterprise: A Guide to Understanding the Medieval Cathedral.* Berkeley: Univ. of California Press, 2003.

Simsom Otto Georg von. *The Gothic Cathedral: Origins of Gothic Architecture and the Medieval Concept of Order.* 3rd ed. Bollingen Series. Princeton: Princeton Univ. Press, 1988.

Smart, Alastair. *The Dawn of Italian Painting, 1250–1400.* Ithaca, NY: Cornell Univ. Press, 1978.

Suckale, Robert, and Matthias Weniger. *Painting of the Gothic Era.* Ed. Ingo F. Walther. New York: Taschen, 1999.

Villard, de Honnecourt. *The Sketchbook of Villard de Honnecourt.* Ed. Theodore Bowie. Bloomington: Indiana Univ., 1960.

Wieck, Roger S. *Time Sanctified: The Book of Hours in Medieval Art and Life.* New York: Braziller, 1988.

Williamson, Paul. *Gothic Sculpture 1140–1300.* Pelican History of Art. New Haven: Yale Univ. Press, 1995.

Chapter 17
Fourteenth Century Art in Europe

Alexander, Jonathan, and Paul Binski, eds. *Age of Chivalry: Art in Plantagenet England, 1200–1400.* London: Royal Academy of Arts, 1987.

Art from the Court of Burgundy: The Patronage of Philip the Bold and John the Fearless 1364-1419. Cleveland: The Cleveland Museum of Art, 2004.

Backhouse, Janet. *Illumination from Books of Hours.* London: British Library, 2004.

Boehm, Barbara Drake, and Jiřií Fajt, eds. *Prague: The Crown of Bohemia, 1347-1437.* New York: Metropolitan Museum of Art, 2005.

Bony, Jean. *The English Decorated Style: Gothic Architecture Transformed, 1250-1350.* The Wrightsman Lecture, 10th. Oxford: Phaidon Press Limited, 1979.

Borsook, Eve. *The Mural Painters of Tuscany: From Cimabue to Andrea del Sarto.* 2nd ed. rev. & enlg. Oxford Studies in the History of Art and Architecture. Oxford: Clarendon Press 1980.

Branner, Robert. *St. Louis and the Court Style in Gothic Architecture.* Studies in Architecture, v. 7. London, A. Zwemmer, 1965.

Bruzelius, Caroline Astrid. *The 13th-Century Church at St-Denis. Yale Publications in the History of Art, 33.* New Haven: Yale University Press, 1985.

Fajt, Jiřií, ed. *Magister Theodoricus, Court Painter to Emperor Charles IV: The Pictorial Decoration of the Shrines at Karlstejn Castle.* Prague : National Gallery, 1998.

Ladis, Andrew. ed, *The Arena Chapel and the Genius of Giotto: Padua.* Giotto and the World of Early Italian Art, 2. New York: Garland Pub., 1998.

Moskowitz, Anita Fiderer. *Italian Gothic Sculpture: c. 1250-c. 1400.* New York: Cambridge Univ. Press, 2001.

Norman, Diana, ed. Siena, *Florence, and Padua: Art, Society, and Religion 1280-1400.* 2 vols. New Haven: Yale Univ. Press in assoc. with the Open Univ., 1995.

Paolucci, Antonio. *The Origins of Renaissance Art: The Baptistry Doors, Florence.* Trans. Françcoise Pouncey Chiarini. New York: George Braziller, 1996.

Poeschke, Joachim. *Italian Frescoes, the Age of Giotto, 1280-1400.* New York: Abbeville Press, 2005.

Welch, Evelyn S. *Art in Renaissance Italy, 1350-1500.* New Ed. Oxford: Oxford Univ. Press, 2000.

White, John. *Art and Architecture in Italy, 1250 to 1400.* 3rd ed. Pelican History of Art. Harmondsworth, UK: Penguin, 1993.

Wieck, Roger S. *Painted Prayers: The Book of Hours in Medieval and Renaissance Art.* New York: George Braziller in assoc. with the Pierpont Morgan Library, 1997.

Chapter 18
Fifteenth-Century Art in Northern Europe and the Iberian Peninsula

Baxandall, Michael. *The Limewood Sculptors of Renaissance Germany.* New Haven Yale Univ. Press, 1980.

Blum, Shirley. *Early Netherlandish Triptychs: A Study in Patronage. California Studies in the History of Art.* Berkeley: Univ. of California Press, 1969.

Borchert, Till-Holger. *Age of Van Eyck: The Mediterranean World and Early Netherlandish Painting, 1430-1530.* New York: Thames & Hudson, 2002.

Cavallo, Adolph S. *The Unicorn Tapestries at the Metropolitan Museum of Art.* New York: The Museum, 1998.

Chastel, Andrèè. *French Art: The Renaissance, 1430–1620.* Paris: Flammarion, 1995.

Dhanens, Elisabeth. Van Eyck: The Ghent Altarpiece. New York: Viking Press, 1973.

Flanders in the Fifteenth Century: Art and Civilization. Detroit: Detroit Institute of Arts, 1960.

Füüssel, Stephan. *Gutenberg and the Impact of Printing.* Trans. Douglas Martin. Burlington, VT: Ashgate Pub., 2005.

Kuskin, William, ed. *Caxton's Trace: Studies in the History of English Printing.* Notre Dame, IN: Univ. of Notre Dame Press, 2006.

Lane, Barbara G. *The Altar and the Altarpiece: Sacramental Themes in Early Netherlandish Painting.* New York: Harper & Row, 1984.

Marks, Richard, and Paul Williamson, eds. *Gothic: Art for England 1400-1547.* London: V & A, 2003.

Meiss, Millard. *French Painting in the Time of Jean de Berry: The Limbourgs and their Contemporaries.* 2 vols. New York: G. Braziller, 1974

Müüller, Theodor. *Sculpture in the Netherlands, Germany, France, and Spain: 1400–1500.* Trans. Elaine & William Robson Scott. Pelican History of Art. Harmondsworth, Eng.: Penguin, 1966.

Päächt, Otto. *Early Netherlandish Painting: From Rogier van der Weyden to Gerard David.* Ed. Monika Rosenauer. Trans. David Britt. London: Harvey Miller, 1997

Panofsky, Erwin. *Early Netherlandish Painting.* Its Origins and Character. 2 vols. Cambridge, MA: Harvard Univ. Press, 1966.

Parshall, Peter W. and Rainer Schoch. *Origins of European Printmaking: Fifteenth-Century Woodcuts and their Public.* Washington, D.C.: National Gallery of Art, 2005.

Plummer, John. *The Last Flowering: French Painting in Manuscripts, 1420–1530, from American Collections.* New York: Pierpont Morgan Library, 1982.

Scott, Kathleen L. *Later Gothic Manuscripts, 1390–1490.* A Survey of Manuscripts Illuminated in the British Isles, 6. 2 vols. London: H. Miller, 1996.

Snyder, James. *Northern Renaissance Art: Painting, Sculpture, the Graphic Arts from 1350 to 1575.* 2nd.ed Rev. Larry Silver and Henry Luttikhuizen. Upper Saddle River, NJ: Prentice Hall, 2005.

Vos, Dirk de. *The Flemish Primitives: The Masterpieces.* Princeton: Princeton Univ. Press, 2002.

Zuffi, Stefano. *European Art of the Fifteenth Century.* Trans. Brian D. Phillips. Art through the Centuries. Los Angeles: J. Paul Getty Museum, 2005.

Chapter 19
Renaissance Art in Fifteenth-Century Italy

Adams, Laurie Schneider. *Italian Renaissance Art.* Boulder, CO: Westview Press, 2001.

Ahl, Diane Cole, ed. *The Cambridge Companion to Masaccio.* New York: Cambridge Univ. Press, 2002.

Alexander, J.J.G. *The Painted Page: Italian Renaissance Book Illumination, 1450–1550.* Munich: Prestel, 1994.

Ames-Lewis, Francis. *Drawing in Early Renaissance Italy.* 2nd ed. New Haven: Yale Univ. Press, 2000.

——. *The Intellectual Life of the Early Renaissance Artist.* New Haven: Yale Univ. Press, 2000.

Baxandall, Michael. *Painting and Experience in Fifteenth-Century Italy: A Primer in the Social History of Pictorial style.* Oxford: Clarendon, 1972.

Boskovits, Miklóós. *Italian Paintings of the Fifteenth Century.* The Collections of the National Gallery of Art. Washington, D.C.: National Gallery of Art, 2003.

Botticelli and Filippino: Passion and Grace in Fifteenth-Century Florentine Painting. Milano: Skira, 2004.

Brown, Patricia Fortini. *Art and Life in Renaissance Venice. Perspectives.* New York: Harry N. Abrams, 1997 Reissued. Upper Saddle River, NJ: Prentice Hall, 2006.

Christianity and the Renaissance: Image and Religious Imagination in the Quattrocento. Syracuse, NY: Syracuse Univ. Press, 1990.

Christiansen, Keith, Laurence B. Kanter, and Carl Brandon Strehlke. *Painting in Renaissance Siena, 1420–1500.* New York: Metropolitan Museum of Art, 1988.

Christine, de Pisan. *The Book of the City of Ladies.* Trans. Rosalind Brown-Grant. London: Penguin Books, 1999.

Gilbert, Creighton, ed. *Italian Art, 1400–1500: Sources and Documents.* Evanston: Northwestern Univ. Press, 1992.

Heydenreich, Ludwig Heinrich. *Architecture in Italy, 1400–1500.* Rev. Paul Davies. Pelican History of Art. New Haven: Yale Univ. Press, 1996.

Hind, Arthur M. *An Introduction to a History of Woodcut.* New York: Dover, 1963.

Huizinga, Johan. *The Autumn of the Middle Ages.* Trans. Rodney J. Payton & Ulrich Mammitzsch. Chicago: Univ. of Chicago Press, 1996.

Hyman, Timothy. *Sienese Painting: The Art of a City-Republic (1278-1477).* World of Art. New York: Thames & Hudson, 2003.

King, Ross. *Brunelleschi's Dome: How a Renaissance Genius Reinvented Architecture.* New York: Walker & Co., 2000.

Lavin, Marilyn Aronberg, ed. *Piero della Francesca and his Legacy.* Studies in the History of Art, 48: Symposium Papers, 28. Washington, D.C.: National Gallery of Art, 1995.

Levey, Michael. *Early Renaissance.* Harmondsworth, UK. Penguin, 1967.

Päächt, Otto. *Venetian Painting in the 15th Century: Jacopo, Gentile and Giovanni Bellini and Andrea Mantegna.* Ed. Margareta Vyoral-Tschapka & Michael Päächt. Trans. Fiona Elliott. London: Harvey Miller Pub., 2003.

Partridge, Loren W. *The Art of Renaissance Rome, 1400-1600.* Perspectives. New York: Harry N. Abrams, 1996. Reissue Ed. Upper Saddle River, NJ: Prentice Hall, 2006.

Poeschke, Joachim. *Donatello and his World: Sculpture of the Italian Renaissance.* Trans. Russell Stockman. New York: H. N. Abrams, 1993.

Randolph, Adrian W. B., *Engaging Symbols: Gender, Politics, and Public Art in Fifteenth-Century Florence.* New Haven: Yale Univ. Press, 2002.

Seymour, Charles. *Sculpture in Italy 1400–1500.* Pelican History of Art. Harmondsworth, UK. Penguin, 1966.

Troncelliti, Latifah. The Two Parallel Realities of Alberti and Cennini: The Power of Writing and the Visual Arts in the Italian Quattrocento. Studies in Italian Literature, v. 14. Lewiston, N.Y: Edwin Mellen Press, 2004.

Turner, Richard. *Renaissance Florence: The Invention of a New Art. Perspectives.* New York: Abrams, 1997. Reissue ed. Upper Saddle River, NJ: Prentice Hall, 2006.

Walker, Paul Robert. *The Feud that Sparked the Renaissance: How Brunelleschi and Ghiberti Changed the Art World.* New York: William Morrow, 2002.

Welch, Evelyn S. *Art and Society in Italy, 1350–1500.* Oxford History of Art. Oxford: Oxford Univ. Press, 1997.

Chapter 20
Sixteenth-Century Art in Italy

Acidini Luchinat, Cristina, et al. *The Medici, Michelangelo, & the Art of Late Renaissance Florence.* New Haven: Yale Univ. Press, 2002.

Andrews, Lew. *Story and Space in Renaissance Art: The Rebirth of Continuous Narrative.* New York: Cambridge Univ. Press, 1995.

Bambach, Carmen. *Drawing and Painting in The Italian Renaissance Workshop: Theory and Practice, 1330–1600.* Cambridge, U.K.: Cambridge Univ. Press, 1999.

Barriault, Anne B., ed. *Reading Vasari.* London: Philip Wilson in assoc. with the Georgia Museum of Art, 2005.

Brown, Patricia Fortini. *Art and Life in Renaissance Venice.* Perspectives. New York: Abrams, 1997.

Burroughs, Charles. *The Italian Renaissance Palace Facade: Structures of Authority, Surfaces of Sense.* Cambridge, U.K.: Cambridge Univ. Press, 2002.

Cellini, Benvenuto. *My Life.* Trans. & notes Julia Conaway Bondanella & Peter Bondanella. Oxford World's Classics. New York: Oxford Univ. Press, 2002.

Chastel, Andréé. *The Age of Humanism: Europe, 1480–1530.* Trans. Katherine M. Delavenay & E. M. Gwyer. London: Thames and Hudson, 1963.
Chelazzi Dini, Giulietta, Alessandro Angelini, and Bernardina Sani. *Sienese Painting: From Duccio to the Birth of the Baroque.* New York: Abrams, 1998.
Cole, Alison. *Virtue and Magnificence: Art of the Italian Renaissance Courts.* Perspectives. New York: Abrams, 1995. Reissue ed. Art of the Italian Courts. Prespectives. Upper Saddle River, NJ: Prentice Hall, 2006.
Dixon, Annette, ed. *Women Who Ruled: Queens, Goddesses, Amazons in Renaissance and Baroque Art.* Ann Arbor: Univ. of Michigan Museum of Art, 2002.
Franklin, David, ed. *Leonardo da Vinci, Michelangelo, and the Renaissance in Florence.* Ottawa: National Gallery of Canada in assoc. with Yale Univ. Press, 2005.
Freedberg, S. J. *Painting in Italy, 1500 to 1600.* 3rd ed. Pelican History of Art. New Haven: Yale Univ. Press, 1993.
Goffen, Rona. *Renaissance Rivals: Michelangelo, Leonardo, Raphael, Titian.* New Haven: Yale Univ. Press, 2002.
Gröössinger, Christa. *Picturing Women in Late Medieval and Renaissance Art.* New York: St. Martin's Press, 1997
Hall, Marcia B. *After Raphael: Painting in Central Italy in the Sixteenth Century.* New York: Cambridge Univ. Press, 1999.
———., ed. *The Cambridge Companion to Raphael.* New York: Cambridge Univ. Press, 2005.
Hollingsworth, Mary. *Patronage in Sixteenth Century Italy.* London: Murray, 1996.
Hopkins, Andrew. *Italian Architecture: From Michelangelo to Borromini.* World of Art. New York: Thames & Hudson, 2002.
Hughes, Anthony. *Michelangelo.* London: Phaidon, 1997.
Huse, Norbert, and Wolfgang Wolters. *Art of Renaissance Venice: Architecture, Sculpture and Painting, 1460–1590.* Trans. Edmund Jephcott. Chicago: Univ. of Chicago Press, 1990.
Jacobs, Fredrika Herman. *Defining the Renaissance Virtuosa: Women Artists and the Language of Art History and Criticism.* Cambridge, U.K.: Cambridge Univ. Press, 1997.
Joannides, Paul. *Titian to 1518: The Assumption of Genius.* New Haven: Yale Univ. Press, 2001.
King, Ross. *Michelangelo & the Pope's Ceiling.* New York: Walker & Company, 2003.
Klein, Robert, and Henri Zerner. *Italian Art, 1500–1600: Sources and Documents.* Upper Saddle River, NJ: Prentice Hall, 1966.
Kliemann, Julian-Matthias, and Michael Rohlmann, *Italian Frescoes: High Renaissance and Mannerism, 1510-1600.* Trans. Steven Lindberg. New York: Abbeville Press, 2004.
Landau, David, and Peter Parshall. *The Renaissance Print: 1470–1550.* New Haven: Yale Univ. Press, 1994.
Lieberman, Ralph. *Renaissance Architecture in Venice, 1450–1540.* New York: Abbeville, 1982.
Lotz, Wolfgang. *Architecture in Italy, 1500–1600.* Rev. Deborah Howard. Pelican History of Art. New Haven: Yale Univ. Press, 1995.
Manca, Joseph. *Moral Essays on the High Renaissance: Art in Italy in the Age of Michelangelo.* Lanham, MD: Univ. Press of America, 2001.
Mann, Nicholas, and Luke Syson, eds. *The Image of the Individual: Portraits in the Renaissance.* London: British Museum Press, 1998.
Meilman, Patricia, ed. *The Cambridge Companion to Titian.* New York: Cambridge Univ. Press, 2004
Mitrovic, Branko. *Learning from Palladio.* New York: W. W. Norton, 2004.
Murray Linda. The High Renaissance and Mannerism: Italy, the North and Spain, 1500–1600. World of Art. London: Thames and Hudson, 1995.
Olson, Roberta J. M. Italian Renaissance Sculpture. World of Art. New York: Thames and Hudson, 1992.
Partridge, Loren W. The Art of Renaissance Rome, 1400–1600. New York: Abrams, 1996.
Pietrangeli, Carlo, et al. The Sistine Chapel: The Art, the History, and the Restoration. New York: Harmony, 1986.
Pilliod, Elizabeth. *Pontormo, Bronzino, Allori: A Genealogy of Florentine Art.* New Haven: Yale Univ. Press, 2001.
Poeschke, Joachim. *Michelangelo and his World: Sculpture of the Italian Renaissance.* Trans. Russell Stockman. New York: Harry N. Abrams, 1996.
Pope-Hennessy, Sir John. *Italian High Renaissance and Baroque Sculpture.* 3rd ed. Oxford: Phaidon, 1986.
——. *Italian Renaissance Sculpture.* 3rd ed. Oxford: Phaidon, 1986.
Rosand, David. *Painting in Cinquecento Venice: Titian, Veronese, Tintoretto.* Rev. ed. Cambridge, U.K.: Cambridge Univ. Press, 1997
Rowe, Colin, and Leon Satkowski. *Italian Architecture of the 16th Century.* New York: Princeton Architectural Press, 2002.
Rowland, Ingrid D. *The Culture of the High Renaissance: Ancients and Moderns in Sixteenth Century Rome.* Cambridge, U.K.: Cambridge Univ. Press, 1998.
Shearman, John. *Mannerism.* Harmondsworth, UK. Penguin, 1967. Reissue ed. New York: Penguin Books, 1990.
Vasari, Giorgio. *The Lives of the Artists.* Trans. Julia Conaway Bondanella & Peter Bondanella. New York: Oxford Univ. Press, 1991.
Verheyen, Egon. *The Paintings in the Studiolo of Isabella d'Este at Mantua.* Monographs on Archaeology and Fine Arts. New York: New York Univ. Press, 1971.
Williams, Robert. *Art, Theory, and Culture in Sixteenth-Century Italy: From Techne to Metateche.* Cambridge, U.K.: Cambridge Univ. Press, 1997

Chapter 21
Sixteenth-Century Art in Northern Europe and the Iberian Peninsula

Bartrum, Giulia. *Albrecht Düürer and his Legacy: The Graphic Work of a Renaissance Artist.* London: British Museum Press, 2002.
Bartrum, Giulia. *German Renaissance Prints 1490-1550.* London: British Museum Press, 1995.
Buck, Stephanie, and Jochen Sander. *Hans Holbein the Younger: Painter at the Court of Henry VIII.* Trans. Rachel Esner & Beverley Jackson. New York: Thames & Hudson, 2004.
Chapuis, Julien. *Tilman Riemenschneider: Master Sculptor of the Late Middle Ages.* Washington, D.C.. National Gallery of Art, 1999.
Cloulas, Ivan, and Michèèle Bimbenet-Privat. *Treasures of the French Renaissance.* Trans. John Goodman. New York: Harry N. Abrams, 1998.
Davies, David, and John H. Elliott. *El Greco.* London: National Gallery, 2003.
Dixon, Laurinda. *Bosch.* Art & Ideas. New York: Phaidon, 2003.
Foister, Susan. *Holbein and England.* New Haven: Published for Paul Mellon Centre for Studies in British Art by Yale Univ. Press, 2004.
Hayum, Andréé. *The Isenheim Altarpiece: God's Medicine and the Painter's Vision.* Princeton Essays on the Arts. Princeton: Princeton Univ. Press, 1989.
Hearn, Karen, ed. *Dynasties: Painting in Tudor and Jacobean England, 1530-1630.* New York: Rizzoli, 1996.
Koerner, Joseph Leo. *The Reformation of the Image.* Chicago: Univ. of Chicago Press, 2004.
Kubler, George. *Building the Escorial.* Princeton: Princeton Univ. Press, 1982.
Osten, Gert von der, and Horst Vey. *Painting and Sculpture in Germany and the Netherlands, 1500–1600.* Pelican History of Art. Harmondsworth, UK: Penguin, 1969.
Price, David Hotchkiss. *Albrecht Düürer's Renaissance: Humanism, Reformation, and the Art of Faith.* Studies in Medieval and Early Modern Civilization. Ann Arbor: Univ. of Michigan Press, 2003.
Roberts-Jones, Philippe, and Francoise Roberts-Jones. *Pieter Bruegel.* New York: Harry N. Abrams, 2002.
Smith, Jeffrey Chipps. *Nuremberg, a Renaissance City, 1500–1618.* Austin: Huntington Art Gallery, Univ. of Texas, 1983.
Strong, Roy C. *Artists of the Tudor Court: The Portrait Miniature Rediscovered, 1520–1620.* London: Victoria and Albert Museum, 1983.
The Word Made Image: Religion, Art, and Architecture in Spain and Spanish America, 1500-1600. Fenway Court, 28. Boston: Published by the Trustees of the Isabella Stewart Gardner Museum, 1998.
Wheeler, Daniel. *The Chateaux of France.* New York: Vendome Press, 1979.
Zerner, Henri. *Renaissance Art in France: The Invention of Classicism.* Paris: Flammarion, 2003.
Zorach, Rebecca. *Blood, Milk, Ink, Gold: Abundance and Excess in the French Renaissance.* Chicago: Univ. of Chicago Press, 2005.

Chapter 22
Baroque Art

Adams, Laurie Schneider. *Key Monuments of the Baroque.* Boulder, CO: Westview Press, 2000.
The Age of Caravaggio. New York: Metropolitan Museum of Art, 1985.
Allen, Christopher. *French Painting in the Golden Age.* World of Art. New York: Thames & Hudson, 2003.
Alpers, Svetlana. *The Making of Rubens.* New Haven: Yale Univ. Press, 1995.
Barberini, Maria Giulia, et al. *Life and the Arts in the Baroque Palaces of Rome: Ambiente Barocco.* Eds. Stefanie Walker and Frederick Hammond. New Haven: Published for the Bard Graduate Center for Studies in the Decorative Arts, New York by Yale Univ. Press, 1999.
Blankert, Albert. *Rembrandt: A Genius and his Impact.* Melbourne: National Gallery of Victoria, 1997
Boucher, Bruce. *Italian Baroque Sculpture.* World of Art. New York: Thames and Hudson, 1998.
Brown, Beverly Louise, ed. *The Genius of Rome, 1592-1623.* London: Royal Academy of Arts, 2001.
Careri, Giovanni. *Baroques.* Tran. Alexandra Bonfante-Warren. Princeton: Princeton Univ. Press, 2003.
Chong, Alan, and Wouter Kloek. *Still-Life Paintings from the Netherlands, 1550-1720.* Zwolle: Waanders Publishers, 1999.
Franits, Wayne E. *Dutch Seventeenth-Century Genre Painting: Its Stylistic and Thematic Evolution.* New Haven: Yale Univ. Press, 2004.
Harbison, Robert. *Reflections on Baroque.* Chicago: Univ. of Chicago Press, 2000.
Kiers, Judikje, and Fieke Tissink. *Golden Age of Dutch Art: Painting, Sculpture, Decorative Art.* London: Thames and Hudson, 2000.
Lagerlof, Margaretha Rossholm. *Ideal Landscape: Annibale Caracci, Nicolas Poussin, and Claude Lorrain.* New Haven: Yale Univ. Press, 1990.
McPhee, Sarah. *Bernini and the Bell Towers: Architecture and Politics at the Vatican.* New Haven: Yale Univ. Press, 2002.
Millon, Henry A., ed. *The Triumph of the Baroque: Architecture in Europe, 1600-1750.* New York: Rizzoli, 1999.
Morrissey, Jake. *The Genius in the Design: Bernini, Borromini, and the Rivalry that Transformed Rome.* New York: William Morrow, 2005.
Slive, Seymour. *Dutch Painting 1600–1800. Pelican History of Art.* New Haven: Yale Univ. Press, 1995.
Stratton, Suzanne L., ed. *The Cambridge Companion to Veláázquez.* New York: Cambridge Univ. Press, 2002.
Summerson, John. *Inigo Jones.* New Haven: Published for the Paul Mellon Centre for Studies in British Art by Yale Univ. Press, 2000.
Vlieghe, Hans. *Flemish Art and Architecture, 1585–1700.* Pelican History of Art. New Haven: Yale Univ. Press, 1998. Reissue ed. 2004.
Wheelock Jr., Arthur K. *Flemish Paintings of the Seventeenth Century.* Washington, D.C.: National Gallery of Art, 2005.
Wittkower, Rudolf. *Art and Architecture in Italy, 1600 to 1750.* 3 vols. 4th ed. Rev. Joseph Connors & Jennifer Montague. Pelican History of Art. New Haven: Yale Univ. Press, 1999.
Zega, Andrew, and Bernd H. Dams. *Palaces of the Sun King: Versailles, Trianon, Marly: The Chââteaux of Louis XIV.* New York: Rizzoli, 2002.

Chapter 23
Art of India after 1200

Asher, Catherine B. *Architecture of Mughal India.* New York: Cambridge Univ. Press, 1992.
Beach, Milo Cleveland. *Mughal and Rajput Painting.* New York: Cambridge Univ. Press, 1992.
Guy, John, and Deborah Swallow, eds. *Arts of India, 1550–1900.* London: Victoria and Albert Museum, 1990.
Khanna, Balraj, and Aziz Kurtha. *Art of Modern India.* London: Thames and Hudson, 1998.
Koch, Ebba. *Mughal Art and Imperial Ideology: Collected Essays.* New Delhi: Oxford Univ. Press, 2001.
Michell, George. *Hindu Art and Architecture.* World of Art. London: Thames & Hudson, 2000.
Moynihan, Elizabeth B., ed. *The Moonlight Garden: New Discoveries at the Taj Mahal.* Asian Art & Culture. Washington, D.C.: Arthur M. Sackler Gallery, Smithsonian Institution, 2000.
Nou, Jean-Louis. *Taj Mahal.* Text by Amina Okada & M. C. Joshi. New York: Abbeville, 1993.
Pal, Pratapaditya. *Court Paintings of India, 16th-19th Centuries.* New York: Navin Kumar, 1983.
———. *The Peaceful Liberators: Jain Art from India.* New York: Thames and Hudson, 1994.
Rossi, Barbara. *From the Ocean of Painting: India's Popular Paintings, 1589 to the Present.* New York: Oxford Univ. Press, 1998.
Schimmel, Annemarie. *The Empire of the Great Mughals: History, Art and Culture.* Ed. Burzine K. Waghmar. Trans.

Corinne Attwood. London: Reaktion Books, 2004.

Stronge, Susan. *Painting for the Mughal Emperor: The Art of the Book, 1560-1660*. London: V&A, 2002.

Tillotson, G. H. R. *Mughal India*. Architectural Guides for Travelers. San Francisco: Chronicle, 1990.

———, *The Rajput Palaces: The Development of an Architectural Style, 1450–1750*. New York: Oxford Univ. Press, 1999.

———. *The Tradition of Indian Architecture: Continuity, Controversy and Change since 1850*. New Haven: Yale Univ. Press, 1989.

Verma, Som Prakash. *Painting the Mughal Experience*. New York: Oxford Univ. Press, 2005.

Welch, Stuart Cary. *The Emperors' Album: Images of Mughal India*. New York: Metropolitan Museum of Art, 1987.

———. *India: Art and Culture 1300–1900*. New York: Metropolitan Museum of Art, 1985.

CHAPTER 24
Chinese and Korean Art after 1279

Andrews, Julia Frances, and Kuiyi Shen. *A Century in Crisis: Modernity and Tradition in the Art of Twentieth-Century China*. New York: Guggenheim Museum, 1998.

Barnhart, Richard M. *Painters of the Great Ming: The Imperial Court and the Zhe School*. Dallas: Dallas Museum of Art, 1993.

Barrass, Gordon S. *The Art of Calligraphy in Modern China*. London: British Museum, 2002.

Berger, Patricia Ann. *Empire of Emptiness: Buddhist Art and Political Authority in Qing China*. Honolulu: Univ. of Hawaii Press, 2003.

Bickford, Maggie. *Ink Plum: The Making of a Chinese Scholar-Painting*. New York: Cambridge Univ. Press, 1996.

Billeter, Jean Franççois. *The Chinese Art of Writing*. New York: Skira/Rizzoli, 1990.

Bush, Susan, and Hsui-yen Shih, eds. *Early Chinese Texts on Painting*. Cambridge, MA: Harvard Univ. Press, 1985.

Cahill, James. *The Distant Mountains: Chinese Painting in the Late Ming Dynasty, 1580–1644*. New York: Weatherhill, 1982.

———. *Hills beyond a River: Chinese Painting of the Y'uan Dynasty, 1279–1368*. New York: Weatherhill, 1976.

———. *Parting at the Shore: Chinese Painting of the Early and Middle Ming Dynasty 1368–1580*. New York: Weatherhill, 1978.

Chung, Anita. *Drawing Boundaries: Architectural Images in Qing China*. Honolulu: Univ. of Hawaii Press, 2004.

Clunas, Craig. *Pictures and Visualities in Early Modern China*. Princeton: Princeton Univ. Press, 1997.

Fang, Jing Pei. *Treasures of the Chinese Scholar: Form, Function and Symbolism*. Ed. J. May Lee Barrett. New York: Weatherhill, 1997.

Fong Wen C,. and James C. Y. Watt. *Possessing the Past: Treasures from the National Palace Museum, Taipei*. New York: Metropolitan Museum of Art, 1996.

Fong, Wen C. *Between Two Cultures: Late-Nineteenth- and Twentieth-Century Chinese Paintings from the Robert H. Ellsworth Collection in the Metropolitan Museum of Art*. New York: Metropolitan Museum of Art, 2001.

Hearn, Maxwell K. and Judith G. Smith, eds. *Chinese Art: Modern Expressions*. New York: Dept. of Asian Art, the Metropolitan Museum of Art, 2001.

Ho, Chuimei, and Bennet Bronson. *Splendors of China's Forbidden City: The Glorious Reign of Emperor Qianlong*. Chicago: Field Museum, 2004.

Ho, Wai-kam. *The Century of Tung Ch`i-ch`ang*. 2 vols. Kansas City: Nelson-Atkins Museum of Art, 1992

Kim, Hongnam. *The Life of a Patron: Zhou Lianggong (1612-1672) and the Painters of Seventeenth-Century China*. New York: China Institute in America, 1996.

Knapp, Ronald G. *China's Vernacular Architecture: House Form and Culture*. Honolulu: Univ. of Hawaii Press, 1989.

Lee, Sherman, and Wai-Kam Ho. *Chinese Art under the Mongols: The Y'uan Dynasty, 1279–1368*. Cleveland: Cleveland Museum of Art, 1968.

Lim, Lucy. ed. *Wu Guanzhong: A Contemporary Chinese Artist*. San Francisco: Chinese Culture Foundation, 1989.

Liu, Laurence G. *Chinese Architecture*. New York: Rizzoli, 1989.

Moss, Paul. *Escape from the Dusty World: Chinese Paintings and Literati Works of Art*. London: Sydney L. Moss Ltd., 1999.

Ng, So Kam. *Brushstrokes: Styles and Techniques of Chinese Painting*. San Francisco: Asian Art Museum of San Francisco, 1993.

The Poetry [of] Ink: The Korean Literati Tradition, 1392-1910. Paris: Rééunion des Muséées Nationaux: Muséée National des Arts Asiatiques Guimet, 2005.

Smith, Karen. *Nine Lives: The Birth of Avant-Garde Art in New China*. Zurich: Scalo, 2006.

Till, Barry. *The Manchu Era (1644-1912), Arts of China's Last Imperial Dynasty*. Victoria, B.C. Art Gallery of Greater Victoria, 2004.

Vainker, S. J. *Chinese Pottery and Porcelain: From Prehistory to the Present*. London: British Museum, 1991.

Watson, William. *The Arts of China 900–1620*. Pelican History of Art. New Haven: Yale Univ. Press, 2000.

Weidner, Marsha Smith, *Views from Jade Terrace: Chinese Women Artists, 1300–1912*. Indianapolis, IN: Indianapolis Museum of Art, 1988.

CHAPTER 25
Japanese Art after 1392

Addiss, Stephen. *The Art of Zen: Painting and Calligraphy by Japanese Monks, 1600–1925*. New York: Abrams, 1989.

Berthier, Franççois. *Reading Zen in the Rocks: The Japanese Dry Landscape Garden*. Trans. & essay Graham Parkes. Chicago: Univ. of Chicago Press, 2000.

Brinker, Helmut, and Hiroshi Kanazawa. *Zen, Masters of Meditation in Images and Writings*. Trans. Andreas Leisinger. Artibus Asiae: Supplementum, 40. Züürich: Artibus Asiae, 1996.

Calza, Gian Carlo. *Ukiyo-e*. New York: Phaidon, 2005.

Carpenter, John T. ed. *Hokusai and his Age: Ukiyo-e Painting, Printmaking and Book Illustration in Late Edo Japan*. Amsterdam: Hotei, 2005.

Clark, Timothy, et al. *The Dawn of the Floating World, 1650-1765: Early Ukiyo-e Treasures from the Museum of Fine Arts, Boston*. London: Royal Academy of Arts, 2001.

Guth, Christine. *Art of Edo Japan: The Artist and the City 1615–1868*. Perspectives. New York: Abrams, 1996.

Hickman, Money L. *Japan's Golden Age: Momoyama*. New Haven: Yale Univ. Press, 1996.

Jordan, Brenda G. and Victoria Weston, eds. *Copying the Master and Stealing his Secrets: Talent and Training in Japanese Painting*. Honolulu: Univ. of Hawaii Press, 2003.

Levine, Gregory P. A. *Daitokuji: The Visual Cultures of a Zen Monastery*. Seattle: Univ. of Washington Press, 2005.

McKelway, Matthew P. *Traditions Unbound: Groundbreaking Painters of Eighteenth-Century Kyoto*. San Francisco: Asian Art Museum—Chong-Moon Lee Center, 2005.

Miyajima, Shin´ichi, and Sato Yasuhiro. *Japanese Ink Painting*. Ed. George Kuwayama. Los Angeles: Los Angeles County Museum of Art, 1985.

Munroe, Alexandra. *Japanese Art after 1945: Scream Against the Sky*. New York: Abrams, 1994.

Murase, Miyeko, ed. *Turning Point: Oribe and the Arts of Sixteenth-Century Japan*. New York: Metropolitan Museum of Art, 2003.

Newland, Amy Reigle, ed. *The Hotei Encyclopedia of Japanese Woodblock Prints*. 2 vols. Amsterdam: Hotei Publishing, 2005.

Parker, Joseph D. *Zen Buddhist Landscape Arts of Early Muromachi Japan (1336-1573)*. SUNY Series in Buddhist Studies. Albany: State Univ. of New York Press, 1999.

Phillips, Quitman E. *The Practices of Painting in Japan, 1475-1500*. Stanford, CA: Stanford Univ. Press, 2000.

Plutschow, Herbert E. Rediscovering Rikyu and the Beginnings of the Japanese Tea Ceremony. Folkestone: Global Oriental, 2003.

Seo, Aubrey Yoshiko. *The Art of Twentieth-Century Zen: Paintings and Calligraphy by Japanese Masters*. Boston: Shambala, 1998.

Singer, Robert T., and John T. Carpenter. *Edo, Art in Japan 1615–1868*. Washington, D.C.. National Gallery of Art, 1998.

Till, Barry. *The Arts of Meiji Japan, 1868–1912: Changing Aesthetics*. Victoria, BC. Art Gallery of Victoria, 1995.

CHAPTER 26
Art of the Americas after 1300

Bauer, Brian S. *Ancient Cuzco: Heartland of the Inca*. Joe R. and Teresa Lozano Long Series in Latin American and Latino Art and Culture. Austin: Univ. of Texas Press, 2004.

Burger, Richard L. and Lucy C., eds. *Machu Picchu: Unveiling the Mystery of the Incas*. New Haven: Yale Univ. Press, 2004.

Berlo, Janet Catherine, and Ruth B. Phillips. *Native North American Art*. Oxford History of Art. Oxford: Oxford Univ. Pres, 1998.

Bingham, Hiram. *Lost City of the Incas: The Story of Machu Picchu and Its Builders*. London: Weidenfeld & Nicolson, 2002.

Boone, Elizabeth Hill. *The Aztec World. Exploring the Ancient World*. Washington, D.C.: Smithsonian Books, 1994.

Broder, Patricia Janis. *American Indian Painting and Sculpture*. New York: Abbeville, 1981.

———. *Earth Songs, Moon Dreams: Paintings by American Indian Women*. New York: St. Martin's Press, 1999.

Brown, Steven C. *Native Visions: Evolution in Northwest Coast Art from the Eighteenth through the Twentieth Century*. Seattle: Seattle Art Museum in assoc. with the Univ. of Washington Press, 1998.

Diaz del Castillo, Bernal. *Discovery and Conquest of Mexico, 1517-1521*. Ed. Genaro Garcíía. Trans. & notes A. P. Maudslay. New intro. Hugh Thomas. Originally published: New York: Farrar, Straus, and Cudahy, 1956. New York: DeCapo Press, 1996.

Duffek, Karen, and Charlotte Townsend-Gault, eds. *Bill Reid and Beyond: Expanding on Modern Native Art*. Vancouver: Douglas & McIntyre, 2004.

Feest, Christian F. *Native Arts of North America*. Updated ed. World of Art. New York: Thames and Hudson, 1992.

Fields, Virginia M., and Victor Zamudio-Taylor. *The Road to Aztlan: Art from a Mythic Homeland*. Los Angeles: Los Angeles County Museum of Art, 2001.

Griffin-Pierce, Trudy. *Earth is my Mother, Sky is my Father: Space, Time, and Astronomy in Navajo Sandpainting*. Albuquerque: Univ. of New Mexico Press, 1992.

Holm, Bill. *Northwest Coast Indian Art; An Analysis of Form*. Thomas Burke Memorial Washington State Museum Monograph, 1. Seattle, Univ. of Washington Press, 1965.

Hughes, Paul. *Time Warps: Ancient Andean Textiles*. London: Fine Textile Art, 1995.

Kaufman, Alice, and Christopher Selser. *The Navajo Weaving Tradition: 1650 to the Present*. New York: Dutton, 1985.

Macnair, Peter L., Robert Joseph, and Bruce Grenville. *Down from the Shimmering Sky: Masks of the Northwest Coast*. Vancouver: Douglas & McIntyre, 1998.

Matos Moctezuma, Eduardo, and Felix R. Solíís Olguíín. *Aztecs*. London: Royal Academy of Arts, 2002.

Moseley, Michael. *The Incas and Their Ancestors: The Archaeology of Peru*. London: Thames and Hudson, 1992.

Nabokov, Peter, and Robert Easton. *Native American Architecture*. New York: Oxford Univ. Press, 1989

Rushing III, W. Jackson, ed. *Native American Art in the Twentieth Century: Makers, Meanings, Histories*. New York: Routledge, 1999

Shaw, George Everett. *Art of the Ancestors: Antique North American Indian Art*. Aspen, CO: Aspen Art Museum, 2004.

Solíís, Felipe R. *The Aztec Empire*. New York: Guggenheim Museum Publications, 2004.

Taylor, Colin F. *Buckskin & Buffalo: The Artistry of the Plains Indians*. New York: Rizzoli, 1998.

Townsend, Richard, ed. *The Aztecs*. 2nd rev. ed. Ancient Peoples and Places. London: Thames and Hudson, 2000.

Trimble, Stephen. *Talking with the Clay: The Art of Pueblo Pottery*. Santa Fe: School of American Research Press, 1987

Wood, Nancy C. *Taos Pueblo*. New York: Knopf, 1989.

CHAPTER 27
Art of Pacific Cultures

Brandon, Reiko Mochinaga, and Loretta G. H. Woodard. *Hawaiian Quilts: Tradition and Transition*. Honolulu: Honolulu Academy of Arts, 2004.

Caruana, Wally. *Aboriginal Art*. World of Art. New York: Thames and Hudson, 1996.

D'Alleva, Anne. *Arts of the Pacific Islands*. Perspectives. New York: Abrams, 1998.

Herle, Anita, ed. *Pacific Art: Persistence, Change, and Meaning*. Honolulu: Univ. of Hawai'i Press, 2002.

Kaeppler, Adrienne Lois, Christian Kaufmann, and Douglas Newton. *Oceanic Art*. Trans. Nora Scott & Sabine Bouladon. New York: Abrams, 1997.

Kirch, Patrick Vinton. *The Lapita Peoples: Ancestors of the Oceanic World*. The Peoples of South-East Asia and the Pacific. Cambridge, MA: Blackwell, 1997.

Kjellgren, Eric. *Splendid Isolation: Art of Easter Island.* New York: Metropolitan Museum of Art, 2001.
Küüchler, Susanne, and Graeme Were. *Pacific Pattern.* London: Thames & Hudson, 2005.
Lilley, Ian, ed. *Archaeology of Oceania: Australia and the Pacific Islands.* Malden, MA: Blackwell, 2006.
McCulloch, Susan. *Contemporary Aboriginal Art: A Guide to the Rebirth of an Ancient Culture.* Honolulu: Univ. of Hawaii Press, 1999.
Moore, Albert C. *Arts in the Religions of the Pacific: Symbols of Life.* Religion and the Arts Series. New York: Pinter Publishers, 1995.
Morwood, M. J. *Visions from the Past: The Archaeology of Australian Aboriginal Art.* Washington, D.C.. Smithsonian Institution Press, 2002.
Neich, Roger, and Mick Pendergrast. *Traditional Tapa Textiles of the Pacific.* London: Thames and Hudson, 1997
Newton, Douglas, ed. *Arts of the South Seas: Island Southeast Asia, Melanesia, Polynesia, Micronesia; The Collections of the Muséée Barbier-Mueller.* Trans. David Radzinowicz Howell. New York: Prestel, 1999.
Rainbird, Paul. *The Archaeology of Micronesia.* Cambridge World Archaeology. New York: Cambridge Univ. Press, 2004.
Smidt, Dirk, ed. *Asmat Art: Woodcarvings of Southwest New Guinea.* New York: George Braziller in assoc. with Rijksmuseum voor Volkenkunde, Leiden, 1993.
Starzecka, D. C., ed. *Maori Art and Culture.* London: British Museum Press, 1996.
Taylor, Luke. *Seeing the Inside: Bark Painting in Western Arnhem Land.* Oxford Studies in Social and Cultural Anthropology. New York: Oxford Univ. Press, 1996.
Thomas, Nicholas. *Oceanic Art.* World of Art. New York: Thames and Hudson, 1995.
———, Anna Cole and Bronwen Douglas, eds. *Tattoo: Bodies, Art, and Exchange in the Pacific and the West.* Durham: Duke Univ. Press, 2005.

Chapter 28
Art of Africa in the Modern Era

Anatsui, El. *El Anatsui Gawu.* Llandudno, Wales, U.K.. Oriel Mostyn Gallery, 2003.
Astonishment and Power. Washington, D.C.: National Museum of African Art, Smithsonian Institution, 1993.
Beckwith, Carol, and Angela Fisher. *African Ceremonies.* 2 vols. New York: Harry N. Abrams, 1999.
Binkley, David A. "Avatar of Power: Southern Kuba Masquerade Figures in a Funerary Context" in *Africa-Journal of the International African Institute*, v.57· 1, 1987. Pgs. 75-97.
Cameron, Elisabeth L. *Art of the Lega.* Los Angeles: UCLA Fowler Museum of Cultural History, 2001.
Cole, Herbert M., ed. *I Am Not Myself: The Art of African Masquerade.* Los Angeles: Fowler Museum of Cultural History, Univ. of California, 1985.
——. *Icons: Ideals and Power in the Art of Africa.* Washington, D.C.. National Museum of African Art, Smithsonian Institution, 1989.
A Fiction of Authenticity: Contemporary Africa Abroad. St. Louis: Contemporary Art Museum St. Louis, 2003.
Fogle, Douglas, and Olukemi Ilesanmi. *Julie Mehretu: Drawing into Painting.* Minneapolis, MN: Walker Art Center, 2003.
Gillow, John. *African Textiles.* San Francisco: Chronicle Books, 2003.
Graham, Gilbert. *Dogon Sculpture: Symbols of a Mythical Universe.* Brookville, NY: Hillwood Art Museum, Long Island Univ., C.W. Post Campus, 1997.
Hess, Janet Berry. *Art and Architecture in Postcolonial Africa.* Jefferson, NC. McFarland & Co., 2006.
Jordáán, Manuel, ed. Chokwe! *Art and Initiation Among the Chokwe and Related Peoples.* Munich: Prestel-Verlag., 1998
Kasfir, Sidney Littlefield. *Contemporary African Art.* World of Art. London: Thames and Hudson, 2000.
Morris, James, and Suzanne Preston Blier. *Butabu: Adobe Architecture of West Africa.* New York: Princeton Architectural Press, 2004.
Oguibe, Ole, and Okwui Enwezor. *Reading the Contemporary: African Art from Theory to the Marketplace.* Cambridge, MA: MIT Press, 1999.
Pemberton III, John, ed. *Insight and Artistry in African Divination.* Washington, D.C.: Smithsonian Institution Press, 2000.
Perrois, Louis, and Marta Sierra Delage. *The Art of Equatorial Guinea: The Fang Tribes.* New York: Rizzoli, 1990.
Picton, John, et al. *El Anatsui: A Sculpted History of Africa.* London: Saffron Books in conjunction with the October Gallery, 1998.
Roberts, Mary Nooter, and Allen F. Roberts, eds. *Memory: Luba Art and the Making of History.* New York: Museum for African Art, 1996.
Roy, Christopher D. *Art of the Upper Volta Rivers.* Meudon, France: Chaffin, 1987.
Schildkrout, Enid, and Curtis A. Keim. *African Reflections: Art from Northeastern Zaire.* Seattle: Univ. of Washington Press, 1990.
Sieber, Roy, and Roslyn Adele Walker. *African Art in the Cycle of Life.* Washington, D.C.. National Museum of African Art, Smithsonian Institution, 1987
Stepan, Peter, and Iris Hahner-Herzog. *Spirits Speak: A Celebration of African Masks.* Munich. Prestel, 2005.
Van Damme, Annemieke. *Spectacular Display: The Art of Nkanu Initiation Rituals.* Washington, D.C.. Smithsonian National Museum of African Art, 2001.
Vogel, Susan Mullin. *Baule . African Art, Western Eyes.* New Haven: Yale Univ. Press, 1997.
Walker, Roslyn Adele. *O?_lo?_?_we?_?_ of Ise?_?_: A Yoruba Sculptor to Kings.* Washington, D.C.. National Museum of African Art, Smithsonian Institution, 1998.

Chapter 29
Eighteenth-Century Art in Europe and the Americas

Bailey, Colin B., Philip Conisbee, and Thomas W. Gaehtgens. *The Age of Watteau, Chardin, and Fragonard: Masterpieces of French Genre Painting.* New Haven: Yale Univ. Press in assoc. with the National Gallery of Canada, Ottawa, 2003.
Boime, Albert. *Art in an Age of Revolution, 1750–1800.* Chicago: Univ. of Chicago Press, 1987.
Bowron, Edgar Peters, and Joseph J. Rishel, eds. *Art in Rome in the Eighteenth Century.* London· Merrell, 2000.
Craske, Matthew. *Art in Europe, 1700–1830: A History of the Visual Arts in an Era of Unprecedented Urban Economic Growth.* Oxford History of Art. Oxford: Oxford Univ. Press, 1997.
Goodman, Elise, ed. *Art and Culture in the Eighteenth Century: New Dimensions and Multiple Perspectives.* Studies in Eighteenth-Century Art and Culture. Newark: Univ. of Delaware Press, 2001 Irwin, David G. Neoclassicism. Art & Ideas. London: Phaidon, 1997
Jarrasséé, Dominique. *18th-Century French Painting.* Trans. Murray Wyllie. Paris: Terrail, 1999.
Kalnein, Wend von. *Architecture in France in the Eighteenth Century.* Trans. David Britt. Pelican History of Art. New Haven: Yale Univ. Press, 1995.
Levey, Michael. *Painting in Eighteenth-Century Venice.* 3rd ed. New Haven: Yale Univ. Press, 1994.
Lewis, Michael J. *The Gothic Revival.* World of Art. New York: Thames & Hudson, 2002.
Lovell, Margaretta M. *Art in a Season of Revolution: Painters, Artisans, and Patrons in Early America.* Early American Studies. Philadelphia: Univ. of Pennsylvania Press, 2005.
Monneret, Sophie. *David and Neo-Classicism.* Trans. Chris Miller & Peter Snowdon. Paris: Terrail, 1999.
Montgomery, Charles F., and Patrick E. Kane, eds. *American Art, 1750–1800: Towards Independence.* Boston: New York Graphic Society, 1976.
Poulet, Anne L. *Jean-Antoine Houdon: Sculptor of the Enlightenment.* Washington, D.C.. National Gallery of Art, 2003.
Summerson, John. *Architecture of the Eighteenth Century. World of Art.* New York: Thames and Hudson, 1986.
Wilton, Andrew, and Ilaria Bignamini, eds. *Grand Tour: The Lure of Italy in the Eighteenth Century.* London: Tate Gallery, 1996.
Young, Hilary, ed. *The Genius of Wedgwood.* London: Victoria & Albert Museum, 1995.

Chapter 30
Nineteenth-Century Art in Europe and the United States

Adams, Steven. *The Barbizon School and the Origins of Impressionism.* London: Phaidon, 1994.
Bajac, Quentin. The Invention of Photography. Discoveries. New York: Harry N. Abrams, 2002.
Barger, M. Susan, and William B. White. *The Daguerreotype: Nineteenth-Century Technology and Modern Science.* Washington, D.C.. Smithsonian Institution, 1991.
Benjamin, Roger. *Orientalist Aesthetics: Art, Colonialism, and French North Africa, 1880-1930.* Berkeley: Univ. of California Press, 2003.
Bergdoll, Barry. *European Architecture, 1750-1890.* Oxford History of Art. New York: Oxford Univ. Press, 2000.
Blakesley, Rosalind P. *Russian Genre Painting in the Nineteenth Century.* Oxford Historical Monographs. New York: Oxford Univ. Press, 2000.
Blüühm, Andreas, and Louise Lippincott. *Light!: The Industrial Age 1750-1900: Art & Science, Technology & Society.* New York: Thames & Hudson, 2001.
Boime, Albert. *Art in an Age of Bonapartism, 1800–1815.* Chicago: Univ. of Chicago Press, 1990.
Boime, Albert. Art in an Age of Counterrevolution, 1815-1848. Chicago: Univ. of Chicago Press, 2004.
Butler, Ruth, and Suzanne G. Lindsay. *European Sculpture of the Nineteenth Century.* The Collections of the National Gallery of Art Systematic Catalogue. Washington, D.C.: National Gallery of Art, 2000.
Callen, Anthea. *The Art of Impressionism: Painting Technique & the Making of Modernity.* New Haven: Yale Univ. Press, 2000.
Chu, Petra ten-Doesschate. *Nineteenth Century European Art.* New York: Abrams, 2003.
Denis, Rafael Cardoso, and Colin Trodd. *Art and the Academy in the Nineteenth Century.* New Brunswick, NJ: Rutgers Univ. Press, 2000.
Eisenman, Stephen. *Nineteenth Century Art: A Critical History.* 2nd ed. New York: Thames and Hudson, 2002.
Eitner, Lorenz. *Nineteenth Century European Painting: David to Cezanne.* Rev. ed. Boulder: Westview Press, 2002.
Frazier, Nancy. *Louis Sullivan and the Chicago School.* New York: Knickerbocker Press, 1998.
Fried, Michael. *Manet's Modernism, or, The Face of Painting in the 1860s.* Chicago: Univ. of Chicago Press, 1996.
Gerdts, William H. *American Impressionism.* 2nd ed. New York: Abbeville, 2001.
Greenhalgh, Paul, ed. *Art nouveau, 1890-1914.* London: V&A Publications, 2000.
Grigsby, Darcy Grimaldo. *Extremities: Painting Empire in Post-Revolutionary France.* New Haven: Yale Univ. Press, 2002.
Groseclose, Barbara. *Nineteenth-Century American Art.* Oxford History of Art. Oxford: Oxford Univ. Press, 2000.
Harrison, Charles, Paul Wood, and Jason Gaiger. *Art in Theory 1815–1900: An Anthology of Changing Ideas.* Oxford: Blackwell, 1998.
Herrmann, Luke. *Nineteenth Century British Painting.* London: Giles de la Mare, 2000.
Hirsh, Sharon L. *Symbolism and Modern Urban Society.* New York: Cambridge Univ. Press, 2004.
Holt, Elizabeth Gilmore, ed. *The Expanding World of Art, 1874–1902.* New Haven: Yale Univ. Press, 1988.
Kaplan, Wendy. *The Arts & Crafts Movement in Europe & America: Design for the Modern World.* New York: Thames & Hudson in assoc. with the Los Angeles County Museum of Art, 2004.
Kapos, Martha, ed. *The Post-Impressionists: A Retrospective.* New York: Hugh Lauter Levin Associates, 1993.
Kendall, Richard. *Degas: Beyond Impressionism.* London: National Gallery Publications, 1996.
Lambourne, Lionel. *Japonisme: Cultural Crossings between Japan and the West.* New York: Phaidon, 2005.
Lemoine, Bertrand. *Architecture in France, 1800–1900.* Trans. Alexandra Bonfante-Warren. New York: Harry N. Abrams, 1998.
Lochnan, Katharine Jordan. *Turner Whistler Monet.* London: Tate Publishing in assoc. with the Art Gallery of Ontario, 2004.
Noon, Patrick J. *Crossing the Channel: British and French Painting in the age of Romanticism.* London: Tate Pub., 2003.
Pissarro, Joachim. *Pioneering Modern Painting: Céézanne & Pissarro 1865-1885.* New York: Museum of Modern Art, 2005
Rodner, William S. *J.M.W. Turner: Romantic Painter of the Industrial Revolution.* Berkeley: Univ. of California Press, 1997.
Rosenblum, Robert, and H. W. Janson. *19th Century Art.* Rev. & updated ed. Upper Saddle River, NJ: Pearson Prentice Hall, 2005.
Rubin, James H. *Impressionism.* Art & Ideas. London: Phaidon, 1999.
Rybczynski, Witold. *A Clearing in the Distance: Frederick Law Olmsted and America in the Nineteenth Century.* New York: Scribner, 1999.
Smith, Paul. *Seurat and the Avant-Garde.* New Haven: Yale Univ. Press, 1997
Thomson, Belinda. *Impressionism: Origins, Practice, Reception.* Thames & Hudson World of Art. New York: Thames & Hudson, 2000.
Twyman, Michael. *Breaking the Mould: The First Hundred Years of Lithography.* The Panizzi Lectures, 2000. London: British Library, 2001.

Vaughan, William, and Francoise Cachin. *Arts of the 19th Century.* 2 vols. New York: Abrams, 1998.

Werner, Marcia. *Pre-Raphaelite Painting and Nineteenth-Century Realism.* New York: Cambridge Univ. Press, 2005.

Zemel, Carol M. *Van Gogh's Progress: Utopia, Modernity, and Late-Nineteenth-Century Art.* California Studies in the History of Art, 36. Berkeley: Univ. of California Press, 1997.

CHAPTER 31
Modern Art In Europe And The Americas

Ades, Dawn, comp. *Art and Power: Europe under the Dictators, 1930-45.* Stuttgart, Germany: Oktagon in assoc with Hayward Gallery, 1995.

Antliff, Mark, and Patricia Leighten. *Cubism and Culture.* World of Art. London: Thames & Hudson, 2001.

Bailey, David A. *Rhapsodies in Black: Art of the Harlem Renaissance.* London: Hayward Gallery, 1997.

Balken, Debra Bricker. *Debating American Modernism: Stieglitz, Duchamp, and the New York Avant-Garde.* New York: American Federation of Arts, 2003.

Barron, Stephanie, ed. *Degenerate Art: The Fate of the Avant-Garde in Nazi Germany.* Los Angeles: Los Angeles County Museum of Art, 1991.

Barron, Stephanie, and Wolf-Dieter Dube, eds. *German Expressionism: Art and Society.* New York: Rizzoli, 1997

Bochner, Jay. *An American Lens: Scenes from Alfred Stieglitz's New York Secession.* Cambridge, MA: MIT Press, 2005.

Bohn, Willard. *The Rise of Surrealism: Cubism, Dada, and the Pursuit of the Marvelous.* Albany: State Univ. of New York Press, 2002.

Bowlt, John E., and Evgeniia Petrova, eds. *Painting Revolution: Kandinsky, Malevich and the Russian Avant-Garde.* Bethesda, MD: Foundation for International Arts and Education, 2000.

Bown, Matthew Cullerne. *Socialist Realist Painting.* New Haven: Yale Univ. Press, 1998.

Brown, Milton. *Story of the Armory Show: The 1913 Exhibition That Changed American Art.* 2nd ed. New York: Abbeville, 1988.

Chassey, Eric de, ed. *American art: 1908-1947, from Winslow Homer to Jackson Pollock.* Trans. Jane McDonald. Paris: Reunion des Musees Nationaux, 2001.

Corn, Wanda M. *The Great American Thing: Modern Art and National Identity, 1915–1935.* Berkeley: Univ. of California Press, 1999.

Curtis, Penelope. *Sculpture 1900–1945: After Rodin.* Oxford History of Art. Oxford: Oxford Univ. Press, 1999.

Elger, Dietmar. *Expressionism: A Revolution in German Art.* Ed. Ingo F. Walther. Trans. Hugh Bever. New York: Taschen, 1998.

Fer, Briony. *On Abstract Art.* New Haven: Yale Univ., 1997

Fletcher, Valerie J. *Crosscurrents of Modernism: Four Latin American Pioneers: Diego Rivera, Joaquín Torres-García, Wifredo Lam, Matta.* Washington, D.C.: Hirshhorn Museum and Sculpture Garden in assoc. with the Smithsonian Institution Press, 1992.

Folgarait, Leonard. *Mural Painting and Social Revolution in Mexico, 1920-1940: Art of the New Order.* New York: Cambridge Univ. Press, 1998.

Forgáács, Eva. *The Bauhaus Idea and Bauhaus Politics.* Trans. John Báátki. New York: Central European Univ. Press, 1995.

Frank, Patrick. *Los Artistas del Pueblo: Prints and Workers' Culture in Buenos Aires, 1917-1935.* Albuquerque: Univ. of New Mexico Press, 2006.

Grant, Kim. *Surrealism and the Visual Arts: Theory and Reception.* New York: Cambridge Univ. Press, 2005.

Green, Christopher. *Art in France: 1900–1940.* Pelican History of Art. New Haven: Yale Univ. Press, 2000. Reissue ed. 2003.

Haiko, Peter, ed. *Architecture of the Early XX Century.* Trans. Gordon Clough. New York: Rizzoli, 1989.

Harris, Jonathan. *Federal Art and National Culture: The Politics of Identity in New Deal America.* Cambridge Studies in American Visual Culture. New York: Cambridge Univ. Press, 1995.

Harrison, Charles, Francis Frascina, and Gill Perry. *Primitivism, Cubism, Abstraction: The Early Twentieth Century.* New Haven: Yale Univ. Press, 1993.

Haskell, Barbara. *The American Century: Art & Culture, 1900–1950.* New York: Whitney Museum of American Art, 1999.

Herbert, James D. *Fauve Painting: The Making of Cultural Politics.* New Haven: Yale Univ. Press, 1992.

Hill, Charles C. *The Group of Seven: Art for a Nation.* Toronto: National Gallery of Canada, 1995.

Karmel, Pepe. *Picasso and the Invention of Cubism.* New Haven: Yale Univ. Press, 2003.

Lista, Giovanni. *Futurism.* Trans. Susan Wise. Paris: Terrail, 2001.

McCarter, Robert, ed. *On and by Frank Lloyd Wright: A Primer of Architectural Principles.* New York: Phaidon Press, 2005.

Moudry, Roberta, ed. *The American Skyscraper: Cultural Histories.* New York: Cambridge Univ. Press, 2005

Rickey, George. *Constructivism: Origins and Evolution.* Rev. ed. New York: G. Braziller, 1995.

Taylor, Brandon. *Collage: The Making of Modern Art.* London: Thames & Hudson, 2004.

Weston, Richard. *Modernism.* London: Phaidon, 1996.

White, Michael. *De Stijl and Dutch Modernism.* Critical Perspectives in Art History. New York: Manchester Univ. Press, 2003.

Whitfield, Sarah. *Fauvism.* World of Art. New York: Thames and Hudson, 1996.

Whitford, Frank. *Bauhaus.* World of Art. London: Thames and Hudson, 1984.

Zurier, Rebecca, Robert W. Snyder, and Virginia M. Mecklenburg. *Metropolitan Lives: The Ashcan Artists and Their New York.* Washington, D.C.: National Museum of American Art, 1995.

Chapter 32
The International Scene Since 1945

Alberro, Alexander, and Blake Stimson, eds. *Conceptual Art: A Critical Anthology.* Cambridge, MA: MIT Press, 1999.

Archer, Michael. *Art Since 1960.* 2nd ed. World of Art. New York: Thames and Hudson, 2002.

Atkins, Robert. *Artspeak: A Guide to Contemporary Ideas, Movements, and Buzzwords.* 2nd ed. New York: Abbeville, 1997.

Ault, Julie. *Art Matters: How the Culture Wars Changed America.* Ed. Brian Wallis, Marianne Weems, & Philip Yenawine. New York: New York Univ. Press, 1999.

Battcock, Gregory. *Minimal Art: A Critical Anthology.* Berkeley: Univ. of California Press, 1995.

Beardsley, John. *Earthworks and Beyond: Contemporary Art in the Landscape.* 3rd ed. New York: Abbeville, 1998.

Bird, Jon, and Michael Newman, eds. *Rewriting Conceptual Art.* Critical Views. London: Reaktion, 1999.

Bishop, Claire. *Installation Art: A Critical History.* New York: Routledge, 2005.

Blais, Joline, and Jon Ippolito. *At the Edge of Art.* London: Thames & Hudson, 2006.

Buchloh, Benjamin H. D. *Neo-Avantgarde and Culture Industry: Essays on European and American Art from 1955 to 1975.* Cambridge, MA: MIT Press, 2000.

Carlebach, Michael L. *American Photojournalism Comes of Age.* Washington, D.C.: Smithsonian Institution Press, 1997

Causey, Andrew. *Sculpture since 1945.* Oxford History of Art. Oxford: Oxford Univ. Press, 1998.

Corris, Michael, ed. *Conceptual Art: Theory, Myth, and Practice.* New York: Cambridge Univ. Press, 2004.

Craven, David. *Abstract Expressionism as Cultural Critique: Dissent during the McCarthy Period.* Cambridge Studies in American Visual Culture. New York: Cambridge Univ. Press, 1999.

Day, Holliday T. *Crossroads of American Sculpture: David Smith, George Rickey, John Chamberlain, Robert Indiana, William T. Wiley, Bruce Nauman.* Indianapolis, IN: Indianapolis Museum of Art, 2000.

De Oliveira, Nicolas, Nicola Oxley, and Michael Petry. *Installation Art in the New Millennium: The Empire of the Senses.* New York: Thames & Hudson, 2003.

De Salvo, Donna M., ed. *Open Systems: Rethinking Art c. 1970.* London: Tate, 2005.

Fabozzi, Paul F. *Artists, Critics, Context: Readings In and Around American Art Since 1945.* Upper Saddle River, NJ: Prentice Hall, 2002.

Fineberg, Jonathan David. *Art Since 1940: Strategies of Being.* 2nd ed. New York: Abrams, 2000.

Flood, Richard, and Frances Morris. *Zero to Infinity: Arte Povera, 1962-1972.* Minneapolis, MN: Walker Art Center, 2001.

Follin, Frances. *Embodied Visions: Bridget Riley, Op Art and the Sixties.* London: Thames & Hudson, 2004.

Ghirardo, Diane. *Architecture after Modernism.* World of Art. New York: Thames and Hudson, 1996.

Goldberg, Roselee. *Performance Art: From Futurism to the Present.* Rev. ed. World of Art. London: Thames and Hudson, 2001.

Goldstein, Ann. *A Minimal Future?: Art as Object 1958-1968.* Los Angeles: Museum of Contemporary Art, 2004.

Grande, John K. *Art Nature Dialogues: Interviews with Environmental Artists.* Albany: State Univ. of New York Press, 2004.

Grosenick, Uta, and Burkhard Riemschneider, eds. *Art at the Turn of the Millennium.* New York: Taschen, 1999.

Grunenberg, Christoph, ed. *Summer of Love: Art of the Psychedelic Era.* London: Tate, 2005.

Herskovic, Marika, ed. *American Abstract Expressionism of the 1950s: An Illustrated Survey: With Artists' Statements, Artwork and Biographies.* New York: New York School Press, 2003.

Hitchcock, Henry Russell, and Philip Johnson. *The International Style.* New York: W. W. Norton, 1995.

Hopkins, David. *After Modern Art: 1945–2000.* Oxford History of Art. Oxford: Oxford Univ. Press, 2000.

Jencks, Charles. *The New Paradigm in Architecture: The Language of Post-Modernism.* New Haven: Yale Univ. Press, 2002.

Jodidio, Philip. *New Forms: Architecture in the 1990s.* New York: Taschen, 2001.

Johnson, Deborah, and Wendy Oliver, eds. *Women Making Art: Women in the Visual, Literary, and Performing Arts Since 1960.* Eruptions, vol. 7. New York: Peter Lang, 2001.

Jones, Caroline A. *Machine in the Studio: Constructing the Postwar American Artist.* Chicago: Univ. of Chicago Press, 1996.

Joselit, David. *American Art Since 1945.* World of Art. London: Thames and Hudson, 2003.

Katzenstein, Inées, ed. *Listen, Here, Now!: Argentine art of the 1960s: Writings of the Avant-Garde.* New York: Museum of Modern Art, 2004.

Legault, Rééjean, and Sarah Williams Goldhagen, eds. *Anxious Modernisms: Experimentation in Postwar Architectural Culture.* Montrééal: Canadian Centre for Architecture, 2000.

Lucie-Smith, Edward. *Movements in Art since 1945.* World of Art. London: Thames and Hudson, 2001.

Madoff, Steven Henry, ed. *Pop Art: A Critical History.* The Documents of Twentieth Century Art. Berkeley: Univ. of California Press, 1997

Moos, David, ed. *The Shape of Colour: Excursions in Colour Field Art, 1950-2005.* Toronto: Art Gallery of Ontario, 2005.

Paul, Christiane. *Digital Art.* World of Art. London: Thames and Hudson, 2003.

Phillips, Lisa. *The American Century: Art and Culture, 1950–2000.* New York: Whitney Museum of American Art, 1999.

Ratcliff, Carter. *The Fate of a Gesture: Jackson Pollock and Postwar American Art.* New York: Farrar, Straus, Giroux, 1996.

Reckitt, Helena, ed. *Art and Feminism.* Themes and Movements. London: Phaidon, 2001.

Risatti, Howard, ed. *Postmodern Perspectives: Issues in Contemporary Art.* 2nd ed. Upper Saddle River, NJ: Prentice Hall, 1998.

Robertson, Jean, and Craig McDaniel. *Themes of Contemporary Art: Visual Art after 1980.* New York: Oxford Univ. Press, 2005.

Robinson, Hilary, ed. *Feminism-Art-Theory: An Anthology, 1968-2000.* Malden, MA: Blackwell Publishers, 2001.

Rorimer, Anne. *New Art in the 60s and 70s: Redefining Reality.* New York: Thames & Hudson, 2001.

Rush, Michael. *New Media in Late 20th-Century Art.* World of Art. London: Thames and Hudson, 1999.
——— *Video Art.* New York: Thames & Hudson, 2003.

Sandler, Irving. *Art of the Postmodern Era: From the Late 1960s to the Early 1990s.* New York: Icon Editions, 1996.

Shohat, Ella. *Talking Visions: Multicultural Feminism in a Transnational Age.* Documentary Sources in Contemporary Art, 5. New York: New Museum of Contemporary Art, 1998.

Sylvester, David. *About Modern Art.* 2nd ed. New Haven: Yale Univ. Press, 2001.

Waldman, Diane. *Collage, Assemblage, and the Found Object.* New York: Abrams, 1992.

Weintraub, Linda, Arthur Danto, and Thomas McEvilley. *Art on the Edge and Over: Searching for Art's Meaning in Contemporary Society, 1970s–1990s.* Litchfield, CT: Art Insights, 1996.

CREDITS

Columbia Museum of Anthropology; BOX. The Philbrook Museum of Art.

Chapter 27

27-1 Jeffrey Dykes / Peabody Essex Museum; 27-2 Australian Tourist Commission; 27-3 E. Brandl / Courtesy AIATSIS Pictorial Collection; 27-4 Kluge-Ruhe / Aboriginal Art Collection / University ofVirginia Library; 27-5 Marilyn Stokstad / Photo Courtesy Anthony Forge; 27-6 Photograph © 2007 The Metropolitan Museum of Art, NY; 27-7 R. Berle Clay; 27-8 Federated States of Micronesia; 27-9 James Balog / Black Star; 27-10 Peabody Essex Museum; 27-11 By permission of The British Library; 27-12 Robert Newcombe / The Nelson-Atkins Museum of Art; 27-13 Museum of New Zealand Te Papa Tongarewa; 27-14 Bishop Museum; 27-15 Dr. Joyce D. Hammond; 27-16 Art Gallery of South Australia; BOX. Bishop Museum MAP: Prehistoric Architecture in Micronesia, William N. Morgan , p. 60, ©1988. BOX: Otago Museum, Dunedin.

Chapter 28

28-1 Sarah DaVanzo Collection; 28-2 Margaret Courtney-Clarke / Corbis / Bettmann; 28-03 Igor Delmas; 28-4 University of Iowa Museum of Art; 28-5, 28-11 Margaret Thompson Drewal / Eliot Elisofon Photographic Archives / National Museum of African Art / Smithsonian Institution; 28-6 Charles & Josette Lenars / Corbis-NY; 28-7 Frederick John Lamp; 28-8 Photo by Don Cole; 28-9 The Field Museum; 28-10 University of Pennsylvania Museum of Archaeology and Anthropology, Philadelphia; 28-12, 28-20, BOXES: Franko Khoury /National Museum of African Art / Smithsonian Institution; 28-13 © Angelo Turconi; 28-14, 28-17 Eliot Elisofon / Eliot Elisofon Photographic Archives / National Museum of African Art / Smithsonian Institution; 28-15 Royal Anthropological Institute of Great Britain and Ireland; 28-16 Detroit Institute of Arts; 28-18 © David A. Binkley / Patricia Darish; 28-19 Hughes Dubois / Musee Dapper; 28-21 Photograph Courtesy October Gallery, London; 28-22 Courtesy The Project, New York.

Chapter 29

29-1 Photograph © 2007 Museum of Fine Arts, Boston; 29-2 Wim Swaan / The Getty Research; 29-3 Martin von Wagner Museum der Universitat Wurzburg / Antikensammlung; 29-4, 29-5, 29-18 © Achim Bednorz, Koln; 29-7 Picture Press Bild - und Textagentur GmbH, Munich, Germany; 29-8 Gerard Blott / Reunion des Musees Nationaux / Art Resource, NY; 29-9 Erich Lessing / Art Resource, NY; 29-10 National Museum of Stockholm; 29-11 Frick Art Reference Library; 29-12 Photograph © 1990 The Metropolitan Museum of Art; 29-13 John Hammond / National Trust Photographic Library, England; 29-14 The Royal Collection © 2008, Her Majesty Queen Elizabeth II; 29-15 Fine Arts Museums of San Francisco; 29-16 IKONA; 29-17 C. Jean / Art Resource, NY; 29-20 Palazzo Barberini, Galleria Nazionale d' Arte Antica / Canali Photobank; 29-21 English Heritage / National Monuments Record / (c) Crown copyright; 29-22 A.F. Kersting; 29-23 Richard Bryant / Arcaid; 29-24, 29-25 Courtesy Wedgwood Museum Trust Limited, Barlaston, Staffordshire; 29-26, 29-29 © National Gallery, London; 29-27 Photograph © 2007, The Art Institute of Chicago. All Rights Reserved; 29-28 Photograph © Board of Trustees, National Gallery of Art, Washington, D.C.

29-30 Katherine Wetzel / Virginia Museum of Fine Arts, Richmond; 29-31, 29-36 National Gallery of Canada, Ottawa; 29-32 The Detroit Institute of Arts; 29-33 Tate; 29-34 French Government Tourist Office; 29-37 Portland Art Museum; 29-38 Caisse Nationale des Monuments Historique et des Sites, Paris; 29-39 Photograph © 1980 The Metropolitan Museum of Art; 29-40 © Reunion des Musees Nationaux, Paris, France / Art Resource, NY; 29-41 Cussac / Musees Royaux des Beaux-Arts de Belgique; 29-42 Musee National du Chateau de Versailles / Art Resource / Reunion des Musees Nationaux; 29-43 The Library ofVirginia; 29-45 Denver Art Museum; 29-47 © David R. Frazier Photolibrary, Inc. / Alamy Images; 29-48 Photograph © 2006 Board of Trustees, National Gallery of Art, Washington, D.C., BOX. National Museum of Women in the Arts, Washington, DC, BOX: Courtesy of Philip Pocock; BOX. The Royal Collection © 2006, Her Majesty Queen Elizabeth II; BOX: British Embassy.

Chapter 30

30-1 Lauros-Giraudon / Art Resource, NY; 30-2, 30-3, 30-4, 30-8 RMN Reunion des Musees Nationaux / Art Resource, NY; 30-5 The Cleveland Museum of Art; 30-6 Yale University Art Gallery; 30-7 Getty Images – Stockbyte; 30-9 © Bernard Boutrit / Woodfin Camp and Associates, Inc; 30-10 Gregory; 30-11 Courtesy of the Hispanic Society of America; 30-12 © Museo Nacional Del Prado / Erich Lessing / Art Resource, NY; 30-13 Oronoz / © Museo Nacional Del Prado; 30-14 Osterreichische Galerie im Belvedere, Vienna; 30-15 Tate Gallery / Art Resource, NY; 30-16 Photo by Graydon Wood, 1988; 30-17 Frick Art Reference Library; 30-18, 30-32, 30-35, 30-52 Erich Lessing / Art Resource, NY; 30-19 Photograph © 1995 The Metropolitan Museum of Art; 30-20 © The Royal Academy of Arts; 30-21 Photograph © 1997 The Metropolitan Museum of Art, NY; 30-22, 30-24 The New York Public Library / Art Resource, NY; 30-26 © Leo Sorel; 30-27 Societe Francaise de Photographie; 30-28, 30-82 George Eastman House; 30-29 Science & Society Picture Library; 30-30 Caisse Nationale des Monuments Historique et des Sites, Paris; 30-31 V & A Images / Victoria and Albert Museum; 30-33 Roger-Viollet Agence Photographique, 30-34 Giraudon / Art Resource, NY; 30-36 © 2006 Dahesh Museum of Art, NY. All Rights Reserved; 30-37 Bridgeman Art Library; 30-38, 30-39, 30-49, 30-55, 30-73, BOXES: RMN Reunion des Musees Nationaux / Art Resource, NY; 30-40 The Carnegie Museum of Art, Pittsburgh; 30-41 Gerard Blot / Art Resource / Musee d'Orsay; 30-42 © 1922 The Metropolitan Museum of Art, NY; 30-43 © State Russian Museum / CORBIS. All Rights Reserved; 30-44 Thomas Jefferson University; 30-44 The Bridgeman Art Library; 30-45 Philadelphia Museum of Art; 30-46 Manchester City Art Galleries; 30-47 William Morris Gallery; 30-48 Photograph © 1988 The Detroit Institute of Arts; 30-50 RMN Reunion des Musees Nationaux/Art Resource, NY / © 2007 Edouard Manet/ARS,NY; 30-51 Photography © The Art Institute of Chicago; 30-53 Photograph © 2007 The Metropolitan Museum of Art; 30-53 Photograph © 1996 The Metropolitan Museum of Art; 30-54 The Nelson-Atkins Museum of Art; 30-56 © 1980 The Metropolitan Museum of Art; 30-57 Photography © The Art Institute of Chicago; 30-58 Philadelphia Museum of Art; 30-59 Dean Beasom / Photograph © Board of Trustees, National Gallery of Art, Washington, D.C., 30-60 © National Gallery, London; 30-61 John Webb / Courtauld Institute of Art; 30-62 The Samuel Courtauld Trust / Courtauld Institute of Art Gallery; 30-63 Photograph © 2007, The Art Institute of Chicago. All Rights Reserved; 30-64 Philadelphia Museum of Art; 30-65 Photograph © 2006, The Art Institute of Chicago. All Rights Reserved. 30-66 Photograph © 2000 The Museum of Modern Art, New York / Art Resource, NY; 30-67 Photograph © 2007, The Art Institute of Chicago. All Rights Reserved; 30-68 J. G. Berizzi / Art Resource / RMN Reunion des Musees Nationaux, France; 30-69 The Museum of Modern Art / Licensed by Scala Art Resource, NY; 30-70 Koninklijk Museum voor Schone Kunsten, Antwerp / © 2007 ARS, NY / SABAM, Brussels; 30-71 J. Lathion / © Nasjonal galleriet / © 2007 ARS,NY / ADAGP, Paris; 30-72 Art Resource, NY / Smithsonian American Art Museum; 30-74 Hirshhorn / Smithsonian; 30-75 Bayerische Staatsgemaldesammlungen, Neue Pinakothek, Munich; 30-76 Ch. Bastin & J. Evrard / © ARS,NY / SOFAM, Brussels; 30-77 Fine Arts Museums of San Francisco; 30-78 Corbis/Bettmann; 30-79 Bildarchiv der Osterreichische Nationalbibliothek; 30-80 Digital image © The Museum of Modern Art / Licensed by SCALA Art Resource, NY; 30-81 San Diego Museum of Art; 30-83 Museum of the City of NY; 30-84 © Corbis. All Rights Reserved; 30-85 Library of Congress. 30-86 © Art on file / Louis H. Sullivan / Corbis-NY; BOX. Musee Fabre; BOX: City of NY, Department of Parks; BOX. Tate Gallery / Art Resource, New York; BOX: The Brooklyn Museum of Art / Central Photo Archive; BOX:Van Gogh Museum Enterprises.

Chapter 31

31-1 New York Public Library / Art Resource, NY; 31-2 Photograph © Board of Trustees, National Gallery of Art, Washington, D.C., 31-3 San Francisco Museum of Modern Art / © Succession H. Matisse, Paris /ARS,NY / Photo: Ben Blackwell; 31-4 © 1995 the Barnes Foundation / 2008 Succession H. Matisse, Paris / ARS,NY; 31-5 Staatliche Museen zu Berlin, Preussischer Kulturbesitz, Nationalgalerie / Art Resource, NY; 31-6 Photograph by Jamison Miller; 31-8 Digital Image © The Museum of Modern Art / Licensed by SCALA Art Resource, NY; 31-9 © 2007 ARS, NY / Art Resource / Bildarchiv Preussischer Kulturbesiz; 31-10 Martin Buhler / Kunstmuseum; 31-11 Photograph © 2007 The Metropolitan Museum of Art, NY; 31-12 Walker Art Center, Minneapolis; 31-13 The Solomon R. Guggenheim Museum, NY / © 2008 ARS, NY; 31-14 The Solomon R. Guggenheim Museum, NY / © 2008 ARS, NY; 31-15 Photograph © The Metropolitan Museum of Art / © ARS, NY / VG Bild-Kunst, Bonn; 31-16 RMN Reunion des Musees Nationaux / Art Resource, NY / © 2008 Estate of Pablo Picasso / © ARS, NY; 31-17 Photograph © Board of Trustees, National Gallery of Art, Washington, D.C.; 31-18 Museum of Modern Art / Licensed by SCALA Art Resource, NY / © 2007 Estate of Pablo Picasso / © ARS, NY; 31-19 Peter Lauri / Kunstmuseum Bern; 31-20 The Solomon R. Guggenheim Museum / George Braque © 2002 ARS, NY / ADAGP, Paris; 31-21 Art Resource, NY / © 2007 Estate of Pablo Picasso / ARS, NY; 31-22 © 2007 Estate of Pablo Picasso / ARS, NY; 31-23 RMN Reunion des Musees Nationaux / Art Resource, NY / © 2008 Estate of Pablo Picasso / ARS, NY; 31-24, 31-25 Emanuel Hoffman Foundation. Kunstsammlung Basel, Switzerland / © L & M Services, B.V. Amsterdam, 20031010; 31-26 Museum of Modern Art / Licensed by SCALA Art Resource, NY; 31-27 Digital Image © The Museum of Modern Art / Licensed by Scala / Art Resource, NY; 31-28 Art Resource, NY; 31-29 Stedelijk Museum Amsterdam; 31-30 © Estate ofVladimir Tatlin / RAO Moscow / Licensed by VAGA, NY; 31-30 Annely Juda Fine Art; 31-31 Photograph ©2006 Museum Associates / LACMA; 31-35 © Philadelphia Museum of Art: The Louise and Walter Arensberg Collection, 1950. 1998-74-1 / © 2007 ARS, NY / ADAGP, Paris / Succession Marcel Duchamp; 31-36 Lynn Rosenthal, 1998 / Philadelphia Museum of Art / © 2006 ARS, NY; 31-37 Solomon R. Guggenheim Museum, NY / © 2008 ARS, NY; 31-39 Photo by James Via; 31-40 Photograph © 2000 The Metropolitan Museum of Art, NY; 31-41 Photography © The Art Institute of Chicago; 31-42 The Minneapolis Institute of Arts / © 2008 The Georgia O'Keeffe Foundation / ARS, NY; 31-43 Guilherme Augusto do Amaral / Malba-Coleccion Costantini, Buenos Aires; 31-44 The Museum of Fine Arts, Houston; 31-45 Art Museum of the Americas; 31-46 Bob Schalkwijk / © 2001 Banco de Mexico Diego Rivera & Frida Kahlo Museums Trust. Av. Cinco de Mayo No. 2, Col. Centro, Del. Cuauhtemoc 06059, Mexico, D.F. Reproduction authorized by the Instituto Nacional de Bellas Artes y Literatura / Art Resource, NY; 31-47 National Gallery of Canada; 31-48 Trevor Mills / Vancouver Art Gallery; 31-49 Gerald Zugmann Fotographie KEG, 31-50 Vanni / Art Resource, NY; 31-51 Anthony Scibilia / Art Resource, NY / © 2001 ARS, NY / ADAGP, Paris / FLC, 31-52 Heidrich Blessing / Chicago Historical Society; 31-53 David R. Phillips / Chicago Architecture Foundation; 31-54 Fallingwater; 31-55 Sante Fe Railroad; 31-56 Cass Gilbert / The New-York Historical Society; 31-57 © Estate of Aleksandr Rodchenko / RAO Moscow Licensed by VAGA, NY; 31-58 Van Abbemuseum; 31-59 Estate ofVera Mukhina; 31-60 Hickey-Robertson / The Menil Collection, Houston. © 2008 Mondrian / Holtzman Trust c/o HCR International, Warrenton, VA; 31-61 Florian Monheim / Artur Architekturbilder Agentur GmbH; 31-62 Jannes Linders Photography; 31-63 Fred Kraus / Bauhausarchiv-Museum fur Gestaltung; 31-64 Michael Nedzweski / The Busch-Reisinger Museum / © President and Fellows of Harvard College, Massachusetts; 31-65 The Museum of Modern Art/Licensed by SCALA Art Resource, NY; 31-66 © Banco de Mexico Trust / Reproduction authorized by the Instituto Nacional de Bellas Artes y Literatura. Palacio de Bellas Artes, Mexico City; 31-67 Schomburg Center for Research in Black Culture, New York Public Library / Art Resource, NY; 31-68 Howard University Libraries; 31-69 © 2007 ARS, NY; 31-70 Tate Gallery, London / Art Resource, NY; 31-71 The Henry Moore Foundation / Tate Picture Gallery; 31-72 The Museum of Modern Art / Licensed by SCALA Art Resource, NY / © 2007 ARS, NY; 31-73 Stedelijk Museum, Amsterdam; 31-74 The Solomon R. Guggenheim Foundation, NY / © 2008 ARS, NY; 31-75 The Museum of Modern Art / Licensed by SCALA Art Resource, NY / © 2006 ARS,NY; 31-76

Chapter 32

INDEX